EMPIRICAL FOUNDATIONS OF INFORMATION AND SOFTWARE SCIENCE V

EMPIRICAL FOUNDATIONS OF INFORMATION AND SOFTWARE SCIENCE V

Edited by
Pranas Zunde
School of Information and Computer Science
Georgia Institute of Technology
Atlanta, Georgia

and
Dan Hocking
U.S. Army Institute for Research in Management
  Information, Communications, and Computer Science
Atlanta, Georgia

PLENUM PRESS • NEW YORK AND LONDON

Library of Congress Cataloging-in-Publication Data

Symposium on Empirical Foundations of Information and Software Science
(6th : 1988 : Atlanta, Ga.)
    Empirical foundations of information and software science V /
edited by Pranas Zunde and Dan Hocking.
        p.   cm.
    "Proceedings of the Sixth Symposium on Empirical Foundations of
Information and Software Science, held October 19-21, 1988, in
Atlanta, Georgia"--T.p. verso.
    Includes bibliographical references and index.
    ISBN-13: 978-1-4684-5864-0   e-ISBN-13: 978-1-4684-5862-6
    DOI: 10.1007/978-1-4684-5862-6
    1. Computer science--Congresses. 2. Computer software-
-Congresses.   I. Zunde, Pranas, 1923-   . II. Hocking, Dan.
III. Title.
QA75.5.S956   1988
004--dc20   90-7948
                                                           CIP

Proceedings of the Sixth Symposium on Empirical Foundations
of Information and Software Science,
held October 19-21, 1988, in Atlanta, Georgia

© 1990 Plenum Press, New York
Softcover reprint of the hardcover 1st edition 1990
A Division of Plenum Publishing Corporation
233 Spring Street, New York, N.Y. 10013

SYMPOSIUM ADVISORY COMMITTEE

Dr. William Curtis, Microelectronics and Computer Technology Corporation; Dr. Sushil Jajodia, National Science Foundation; John R. Mitchell, U.S. Army Institute for Research in Management Information, Communications, and Computer Sciences (AIRMICS); Dr. John J. O'Hare, Office of Naval Research; Dr. Michael G. Shafto, National Aeronautics and Space Administration.

SYMPOSIUM ORGANIZATION COMMITTEE

Dan Hocking, AIRMICS, Atlanta, Georgia; Annelise Mark Pejtersen, Riso National Laboratory, Roskilde, Denmark; Dr. Edward Omiecinski, Dr. Vladimir Slamecka and Dr. Pranas Zunde (chairman), all of Georgia Institute of Technology, Atlanta, Georgia.

The organizers gratefully acknowledge partial funding of the symposium by the U.S. Army Institute for Research in Management Information, Communications, and Computer Sciences, Atlanta, Georgia.

PREFACE

This is the proceedings of the Sixth Symposium on Empirical Foundations of Information and Software Sciences (EFISS), which was held in Atlanta, Georgia, on October 19-21, 1988. The purpose of the symposia is to explore subjects and methods of scientific inquiry which are of common interest to information and software sciences, and to identify directions of research that would benefit from the mutual interaction of these two disciplines.

The main theme of the sixth symposium was modeling in information and software engineering, with emphasis on methods and tools of modeling. The symposium covered topics such as models of individual and organizational users of information systems, methods of selecting appropriate types of models for a given type of users and a given type of tasks, deriving models from records of system usage, modeling system evolution, constructing user and task models for adaptive systems, and models of system architectures.

This symposium was sponsored by the School of Information and Computer Science of the Georgia Institute of Technology and by the U.S. Army Institute for Research in Management Information, Communications, and Computer Sciences (AIRMICS).

The Editors

CONTENTS

I. KEYNOTE ADDRESS

SOFTWARE FOR HUMAN HARDWARE?

Melvin Kranzberg

School of Social Sciences
Georgia Institute of Technology
Atlanta, Georgia 30332-0345
(404) 894-6835

Abstract: Because we live in a "Scientific and Technical Age", we like to think that our decisions and actions are based on scientific findings and technological rationality. But the human mind does not always obey the dictates of science and reason; instead, "human hardware" -- engrained emotions, likes and dislikes, fears and hopes -- sometimes lead people to disregard the scientific evidence, thereby creating difficulties.

Problems arising from disregard of the human element in the man-machine relationship can be found in the organization of work as the Industrial Revolution advanced. Near the beginning of this century, Henry Ford's moving assembly-line decreased costs, and Frederick W. Taylor's "Scientific Management" gave rise to the field of Industrial Engineering by breaking down each operation to its simplest form, so that the worker could perform his task speedily and without great skill. In brief, it treated the worker as a machine. However, Elton Mayo's experiments showed that production would increase if management treated the works as human beings, giving consideration to their thoughts and feelings.

While automation has great potential for improving quality and productivity in both manufacturing and service trades, robotic machines do not eliminate skilled workers. Indeed, to enable the robots to work most efficiently, highly-trained technical personnel are needed to oversee and back up the machines. Only if information and software systems take into consideration human feelings and capabilities -- the "human hardware" -- can they capitalize fully on the computer's growing informational and analytical capacity.

When an American warship patrolling the Persian Gulf shot down a civilian Iranian airliner in July 1988, several commissions were appointed to look into the cause of this tragedy. One committee's report concluded that the radar and computing equipment abroad the *U.S.S. Vincennes* functioned perfectly, indicating that the airplane was not heading toward the ship nor diving to drop a bomb. But the *Vincennes* officers and crewmen had allowed their prepossession with notions of Iranian duplicity--as well as fears evoked by memories of the *Stark* incident in May 1987, when an American frigate was hit by two missiles launched in error by an Iraqi plane--to ignore the computerized evidence, to misinterpret the course and mission of the Iranian passenger plane, and shoot it down. In brief, the human mind, which we usually regard as "software," had become hardened to accept only its fright, not its sight.

Similar evidence of the hardening of the "software-ish" human mind is presented by an informal poll which I had conducted after the presidential debates of 1988 -- and which professional poll takers affirmed in their more scientific surveys. After each presidential debate I asked a group of colleagues just who they thought had won. Not surprisingly, all the Republicans said Bush, while the Democrats declared Dukakis the victor. Obviously the human mind is not always a pliable device following the dictates of reason based upon what some would term incontrovertible evidence; instead, the human mind can also be a device of hardened attitudes, hearing only what it wants to hear and not entirely open to new evidence or to rational discourse.

Empirical Foundations of Information and Software Science V
Edited by P. Zunde and D. Hocking, Plenum Press, New York, 1990

Because I am a historian of technology, the *Vincennes* incident and the partisan reactions to the presidential debates made me think about the mind-computer interface in the historical context of the man-machine interface--and I start with the Industrial Revolution.

Most people regard James Watt's invention of the steam engine as the start of the Industrial Revolution. Actually, a series of landmark inventions in the British textile industry in the 18th century introduced power-driven machines and the factory system -- two hallmarks of the Industrial Revolution -- long before Watt came on the scene with his steam engine.

The introduction of heavy machinery powered by waterwheels led to large-scale factory production and compelled a rational organization of job functions -- a division of labor -- quite different from the old handicraft tradition. In his famous *Wealth of Nations*, published in 1776, Adam Smith (1937) gave the classical example of this new production system in a pin factory, where "the important business of making a pin" was divided into about eighteen distinct operations. According to Smith, a single worker without machinery "could scarce, perhaps with his utmost industry, make one pin in a day, and certainly could not make twenty." But with the introduction of machinery and the division of labor, a single worker could make as many as 4,800 pins a day. Productivity greatly increased, depending far more on machines and on the rational organization of processes than on the worker's individual skill. The rational organization of work plus mechanization led to mass production. The material basis for mass production rested on precision machine-tools that could produce large numbers of identical parts at relatively low cost and with a greatly reduced work force.

The production of many identical parts -- interchangeable parts -- and their assembly into finished products came to be called the "American System of Manufactures" because it achieved its fullest development in our country. Although Eli Whitney has been given credit for interchangeable parts, his ideas had appeared earlier in Sweden, France, and Britain, and were already pioneered in arms factories in America, and they received their fullest application in the United States. By the third quarter of the 19th century, the American system was employed in making small arms, clocks, textile machinery, sewing machines, and a host of other products.

The pioneering work on the American System was done in government armories. Why? Because mass production requires mass consumption, and until relatively recent times, the only large-scale demand for standardized, uniform goods came from the military.

Only when the American System proved successful in making small arms was it applied to industrial products meant for the civilian market. But it was the military impetus which then, as still today, provided the stimulus for much technological innovation.

With the development of machine tools and interchangeable parts, the stage was set for the moving assembly line and further innovations in the management of production.

Though prototypes of the moving assembly line can be traced back to antiquity, the true ancestor of this industrial technique was the 19th-century meat-packing industry in Cincinnati and Chicago, where overhead trolleys were employed to convey carcasses from worker to worker, each of whom cut off a piece of the carcass as it passed. In other words, this was a moving "disassembly line."

Drawing upon observations of the meat-packing industry, Henry Ford designed an assembly line in 1913 to assemble magneto flywheels, where it cut down the manufacturing time from 20 minutes to only 5 minutes. When he applied the technique to assembling the automobile chassis, he eventually cut down the time from 12-1/2 man-hours for each chassis to 93 man-minutes. By the end of April 1914 Ford had drastically reduced the price of an automobile, changing it from a luxury and bringing it within the reach of the common man.

The assembly line spread throughout U.S. industry, bringing dramatic gains in productivity, and the replacement of skilled workers with low-cost relatively unskilled labor performing minutely subdivided tasks. Such low--cost production created a huge market, and a hierarchy of supervisors and managers became necessary to control the many elements and people involved in large-scale production.

Almost contemporaneous with Ford's moving assembly line was Scientific Management, which refined and sophisticated mass production techniques. The originator of Scientific Management was a mechanical engineer, Frederick W. Taylor, and from his work, an entirely new discipline -- Industrial Engineering -- emerged.

In Taylor's thinking, the role of factory management was to determine the best way for the worker to do his job, to provide him with proper tools, to train him to follow precise instructions, and to provide incentives for good performance. To accomplish this, Taylor concentrated on job analysis and time-motion studies; that is, he broke each job down into its constituent motions, analyzed these to determine which were essential, and timed the workmen with a stopwatch. With superfluous motion eliminated, the worker, following almost a machine-like routine, greatly increased his productivity. Furthermore, in order to avoid "down time," Taylor delegated some tasks, such as sharpening tools and keeping machines in order, to specialists whose sole function that was. Industrial engineering ultimately came to include all elements of factory operation within its compass -- the layout of the factory, materials handling, and product design, as well as the actual labor operations on the product itself.

Taylor and his disciples thought that Scientific Management would be a blessing to the workers, enabling them to do their work with a minimum of effort and receiving more money for it. But, some employers used time and motion studies to set very high norms of production and speed up the production line while still keeping wages down.

Taylor's movement was called Scientific Management because he thought it applied scientific principles to the actual work process itself. Previous advances in manufacturing had come through applying scientific principles to the machines, making them more efficient: Taylor attempted to apply the same scientific principles to the work process itself. That seems logical, but in the process he neglected the human element, and the complaint was that instead of regarding the work process as a man-machine interface, he was making the worker into a machine; so it was basically a machine-machine interface, with one of the machines being a human being.

As a result, when Scientific Management was first applied in widespread fashion in the decade after 1910, fierce opposition arose, especially from the unions. They detested the speed-up and particularly complained that Taylorism deprived working men of a voice in the conditions and functions of their work.

To enable the combination of human labor and machine technology to achieve its fullest potential, industrial engineers called upon the social sciences. In the process, another set of new disciplines emerged: Industrial Psychology and Industrial Sociology.

The key discovery which showed the importance of the social context to mass production technology resulted from experiments made by Elton Mayo, a social psychologist, at Western Electric's Hawthorne Plant, between 1924 and 1932. Mayo had earlier studied problems of physical fatigue among textile workers, and he was called to the Hawthorne works when the industrial engineers were considering the possible effect on productivity of changes in illumination. The question was simple: What intensity of light would enable the worker to produce more?

Choosing two groups of employees working under similar conditions to produce the same part, the investigators told them that they would be experimenting on the effects of lighting on their work. The investigators then varied the intensity of the light for the test group but kept it constant for the control group. But to Mayo's surprise, the output of both groups rose. Even when the researchers told the girls in one group that the light was going to be changed and then did not change it, the girls expressed satisfaction, saying that they liked the "increased" illumination -- and productivity continued to rise. Mayo realized that the significant variable was not the
physiological one of eyesight related to illumination, but rather the psychological one of the workers' perception of their jobs.

In a second series of experiments, test and control groups were subjected to changes in wages, rest periods, work weeks, temperature, humidity, and other factors. But no matter how physical conditions were varied, the output continued to increase; indeed, even when conditions were returned to what they had been before the experiment, productivity still remained 25% above the original amount. Mayo concluded that the reason was the attitudes of the workers toward their jobs and toward the company. Merely by asking their cooperation, the investigators had stimulated a new attitude among the employees, who now felt themselves part of an important group whose help and advice were being sought by their employers.

As an aside, it should be noted that the "quality control" groups in Japanese factories nowadays, to which American production experts have been paying lots of attention, are really nothing more than outgrowths of Mayo's findings. What happened is that the Japanese took very seriously the results and recommendations of American Management consultants, such as W. Edwards Deming. As a result, using ideas originally formulated by Americans, but which American management had come to neglect, the Japanese have forged ahead of us in productivity and workers' devotion to duty and company.

Mayo's studies had suggested that consultation, usually in the form of interviews between labor and management, gave workmen a sense of belonging to a team. Industrial engineers and industrial sociologists since then have suggested additional approaches toward improving motivation and productivity. These include job alternation to relieve boredom on the job; job enlargement, or having the workman perform several tasks of his project rather than performing a single operation all the time; and job enrichment, redesigning the job to make it more challenging and interesting to the worker.

Another outgrowth of scientific management was the development of human-factors engineering, designing the machine to fit man's physiological makeup. In a sense, by applying scientific principles, sometimes known as ergonomics, human factors engineers reverse Taylor, who sought to accommodate the human element in the work process to the machine; human factor engineers attempt to accommodate the machine to the human mind and body.

Now the logical conclusion to this evolution of mass-production is automation and automatic control. Even though automation might be regarded as just another step in the mechanization trend that began early in the Industrial Revolution, it is truly revolutionary in its means and results. For, in an automated factory, the tasks formerly performed by machine operators on a production line are performed by robots, which are self-controlled electronically by means of feedback mechanisms.

Automation evolved from three interrelated technological trends: first, the development of powered machinery for production operations, starting with the Industrial Revolution; second, the introduction of materials-handling equipment during the manufacturing process, which evolved in the last part of the 19th century; and third, the perfecting of control systems through the development of the computer.

The computer has advanced spectacularly in the past four decades. When the first electronic computer, the ENIAC, was introduced, it weighed 30 tons, filled an entire room with 17,000 vacuum tubes, 1,500 relays, 70,000 resistors, 10,000 capacitors, 6,000 switches, required a 10-ton air conditioner to keep it cool enough to operate, and cost almost half a million dollars in 1940s bucks.

Then in the early 1970s came the microprocessor, the computer on a chip. Today, a tiny silicon chip about the size of a fingernail contains the equivalent of about 450,000 vacuum tubes, and is embodied in a computing device costing less than a thousand dollars. As late as 1950, it took a computer 16 minutes to execute a million instructions; today it is done in less than a second.

As Tom Forester has put it, "If the automobile and airplane business had developed like the computer business, a Rolls-Royce would cost $2.75 cents and would run for three million miles on one gallon of gas. And a Boeing 767 would cost just $500 and would circle the globe in 20 minutes on five gallons of gas."

The microchip computer employed in a feedback system enabled a robotic machine to adjust itself to unpredictably varying conditions. Such automatic controls make possible automation. One obvious effect of automation is to increase productivity and reduce costs. Other benefits include product reliability through quality control, reduction of waste, and improved safety by having robots perform dangerous tasks such as welding and painting.

Automatic controls transform the nature of human work. The classical Industrial Revolution took the burdens off the backs of men and changed the handicraft worker to a machine operator. The skill was built into the machine, and a semi-skilled worker could operate it. But with automatic control, the production worker is no longer a machine operator but a machine supervisor. He sits in front of a control panel looking at dials, while the computer within the robotic machine actually operates it. The worker thus becomes a machine overseer rather than a machine operator, for his responsibility is to monitor complex and expensive computerized equipment.

When automatic control technology was still relatively young, the first generation of industrial robots could perform only simple tasks, like welding. Even today the robot's senses of touch and sight are still quite primitive by human standards; so when a robot puts together widgets, all the widgets have to be just so, for the robot gets confused by slight irregularities and differences.

To overcome this difficulty, here at Georgia Tech we are developing robots that have better vision and can feel more sensitively, thereby enlarging their capacities. But even so, we still have not reached the stage of robots completely replacing human beings in the workplace -- and we might never do so. While robots can perform repetitive tasks faster than human beings, and without getting bored, distracted, or preoccupied, they sometimes break down. So we need workers to back up the robots and maintain their productivity.

In a sense, this represents a turnabout of Henry Ford's and Scientific Management's fragmentation of jobs so that the worker required little skill or intelligence, with the planning and mental functions carried on by engineering specialists separated from the physical work. That approach was based upon the notion that the workers are stupid.

But robotic machines can be termed "stupid" in another sense. While perfect for specific tasks, they are not easily adaptable to other production operations. Hence the most recent development is a reorientation of the assembly lines to accommodate a combination of the automatically-controlled robot and the worker. If automated production is to be successful, we must employ the worker's training and intelligence, his mind as well as his hand, in order to handle the more complicated operations of the new manufacturing processes.

For example, up until a short time ago, American workers were not permitted to stop the moving assembly line in order to make sure that quality was being maintained. But now, copying the Japanese, who learned it from us while we forgot it, workers can stop the line when something is amiss.

One way to improve quality is by what is called "Group Assembly," which actually started in the automobile factories in Sweden. It means that a group of workers is responsible for the entire product, rather than individual workers just doing one little task each. If something is wrong, the workers can push a button and hold things in place while they fix it. It this works out well -- and it has in Sweden and Japan -- it will mean that smaller numbers of more highly-skilled workers, working with sophisticated, computer-controlled equipment, will replace the unskilled thousands of workers in most of today's assembly-line

In brief, American industry is learning that the highly-skilled worker, who had supposedly gone the way of the dinosaur, is indispensable. There are now serious shortages of craftsmen skilled in the mechanical trades and of knowledgeable workers for the new automated devices. So, although automatic control systems may eliminate unskilled jobs, they increase the demand for highly skilled operators.

In her recent book, *In the Age of the Smart Machine*, Shoshana Zuboff (1988) goes even further. Her message -- oversimplified somewhat -- is that "a smart machine" requires a smart worker.

The introduction of computers and control mechanisms also affects the organization of work in the information sector of the economy; in other words, it brings automation into the office, further mechanizing a process which began with the typewriter and the adding machine back in the previous century. It can provide exact control of inventory, raw materials, parts, and finished goods, and reduce accounting costs in the billing process.

If the old Industrial Revolution took the burdens off men's backs, it can be said that the computer revolution takes the burdens off men's minds, freeing them from routine and repetitive tasks which have long stultified the human imagination.

But while automation in the production line and the office promises to eliminate both physical and mental drudgery while lowering costs and improving quality, it is not quite the paradise that some of our futurists would have us believe.

Since automation allows fewer people to produce more goods, and since much production has shifted abroad because of internationalization through lower costs, the result has been the diminution of employment in traditional American industries.

Yet, more people are at work now in the United States than ever before. Most are in the service sector, which involves a wide number of occupations. Automation in the office is proceeding apace, and the futurist Alvin Toffler points out that computerized information and communication devices will enable office employees to work at home. Yes, computerized information and communication devices do make it possible for more people to work at home at their own pace rather than going to an office at set times, but the fact is that, with very few exceptions, such as writing and editing, the piece-rate processing of insurance forms, and the like, it is not happening on the widespread scale that Toffler predicted. The reason is simple: As the ancient philosophers pointed out, man is a political and social animal. People like to get together; they derive intellectual stimulus and social satisfaction from personal contacts. For the workplace is more than a place to make a living; it is also the locale of the social interchange which is a hallmark of our human species.

It is not my intention to downgrade automation either on the production line or in the office. If robotics can free production workers from back-breaking and dangerous tasks, it is obviously of service to mankind; if automation in the office frees clerks and secretaries from routine and repetitive tasks, that too represents a human gain.

But there are also problems involved. One is how to provide employment for those thrown out of work by automated mechanisms either in factory or office. Another is to improve the educational level so that we will have workers who can perform their tasks in a more highly technical and computerized society.

In a 1986 book entitled *The Control Revolution*, James R. Beniger (1986), a sociologist, argued that today's Information Society is an outgrowth of the Industrial Revolution. By bringing about a dramatic rise in the speed, amount, and complexity of industrial processes in order to produce more goods, the Industrial Revolution necessitated a "Control Revolution," which in turn relies upon the collection, processing, and transmission of information in new and dramatic ways in order to cope with unprecedented problems of distribution, production, and marketing.

The Control Revolution marked a dramatic leap in the ability to exploit information. Large managerial hierarchies for new means of distributing mass-produced goods were introduced: department stores, chain stores, mail order houses. And the need to have a large and predictable demand for products led to mass communication through advertising and market-feedback technologies.

But bureaucratic control of consumption by national advertisers does not always work in accordance with Beniger's dicta. For example, a few years ago, Coca-Cola sought to control the soft-drink market by introducing "New Coke." But despite market surveys and enormous advertising expenditures, consumption habits were not ready for the change -- and Classic Coke has retained the allegiance of Americans. The point is that Beniger's attempt to interpret all history by linking together technical advancements with increasing social control does not necessarily correspond to the historical facts.

Nor do modern computers always bring about effective control. You will recall that in George Orwell's *1984*, Big Brother controlled all society through his control of information. When electronic computers were first introduced, their huge size and great expense threatened to make information a monopoly. But then came the transistor and compact computers. Indeed, as the hackers from Cal Tech showed when they seized control of the scoreboard at the Rose Bowl a few years ago, "Little Brother" can mess up Big Brother's control of information!

I bring this up to show that "control" systems, no matter their complexity and technological virtuosity, do not always succeed in controlling what they are supposed to control. Indeed, Leroy Emkin, of our Software Engineering Research Center at Georgia Tech, has warned of the dangers posed by over-reliance on computerized controls in everyday life. Computer errors, he says, "can lead to loss of life and liberty."

But the errors, as shown by the *Vincennes* incident, are not necessarily in the computers or in their software. Indeed, the information can be correct, but human beings can misinterpret it. So we must constantly remind ourselves that computing devices and the software that directs them are very much human products -- designed, made, and utilized by and for human beings, and hence subject to human shortcomings as well as to human ingenuity, human logic, human thought, and human imagination.

Hence the challenge is to create information and software systems that capitalize on the computer's growing informational and analytical capabilities while at the same time taking into consideration human frailties and shortcomings. So, to conclude, let me turnabout the metaphor which is embodied in the title of this paper, and refer to hardware and software in their commonly-used meanings.

Nowadays I use my students' preoccupation with computers as a metaphor to make them aware of the interaction of human and social elements with purely technical elements in the history of technology. In order to make the computer a usable device, I point out that we need both "hardware" and "software." The hardware, the computing device itself, is of no use without the "software," which provides it with the data, the programming instructions, the methodologies and the questions as well as the logic to answer the questions. But the software is no use without the hardware and is subject to its capabilities and limitations. We need both, the technical and human elements, in order to make both our technology and our society work better.

In my talks with some of my anti-technological humanistic colleagues, I relate an anecdote told about Fritz Kreisler, the great violinist. A woman came up to him after a concert and gushed, "Oh, Maestro, your violin makes such beautiful music." Kreisler picked up his violin (a Stradivarius, no less), held it to his ear, and said, "I don't hear any music coming out of it."

You see, the beautiful music coming out of the violin did not come from the instrument, the hardware, alone; it depended upon the human element, the software. And all technology represents this combination of human ingenuity expressed in the machine, with human needs and purposes in utilizing it. If the machine is imperfect or if the software is faulty, the music which emerges will be discordant. But when man and machine work together for human purposes, they can make some very beautiful music. And that mission provides empirical foundations for information and software scientists. We are delighted that you have gathered here at Georgia Tech to join the chorus making that beautiful music come to life.

REFERENCES

Beniger, J. R., 1986, *The Control Revolution*, Harvard University Press, Cambridge, Mass.
Smith, A., 1937, *The Wealth of Nations*, Random House (reprint), New York.
Zuboff, S., 1988, *In the Age of the Smart Machine: The Future of Work and Power*, Basic Books, New York.

II. INVITED PAPERS

SOFTWARE PROCESS MODELING: THE TRIAD APPROACH

Gregory A. Hansen and Marc I. Kellner

Software Engineering Institute
Carnegie Mellon University
Pittsburgh, Pennsylvania 15213-3890

Abstract: The Software Engineering Institute (SEI) has undertaken a project that will attempt to capture, through models, the software engineering process as currently practiced in some organizations. This paper will present the *Triad Approach* to process model development - a philosophical perspective on modeling. We are convinced that for models of organizational processes to be most useful, it is necessary to go beyond simply describing a process. In particular, we believe that process models should support the engineering of processes, i.e., should facilitate (1) predictions of the impacts on manpower requirements, time-to-completion, and other measures, resulting from proposed changes to the process, and (2) analyses of the process, using the model, for completeness, correctness, and consistency. The *Triad Approach* provides a framework for characterization of processes and for their testing and validation. This paper presents the modeling philosophy being developed on the SEI project and discusses the need for automated tools to support modeling.

1.   INTRODUCTION

The Software Engineering Institute (SEI) has undertaken a project that will attempt to capture through models the software engineering process as currently practiced in some organizations. The ultimate goal of this effort is to facilitate the ongoing improvement of software engineering processes. This paper presents the *Triad Approach* to modeling software engineering processes. The Triad approach is based on the premise that for a description of a process to be considered a model, it must be executable, or capable of running in a simulation mode. It must also be amenable to automated analysis for issues such as completeness, correctness, and consistency.

2.   PROCESS VIEWS

Considerable attention has been devoted to software process modeling (or process programming) during the past few years (*Fourth International Software Process Workshop: Representing and Enacting the Software Process*, 1988; Humphrey, 1988; Kellner, 1988; Kellner and Hansen, 1988; Kellner and Hansen, 1989; Lehman, 1987; Osterweil, 1987; Phillips, 1988; Phillips, 1989; Rombach and Mark, 1989; Williams, 1988(a),1988(b)). The goal of our work is to develop predictive models of the software engineering processes that will support reasoning about the process, including the ability to reason about the impact of changes to the process. In order to construct such a model, we have previously identified (Kellner, 1988; Kellner and Hansen, 1988; Kellner and Hansen, 1989) four necessary perspectives of a process description:

- a functional perspective that describes what activities are performed;

- a behavioral perspective that describes when activities are performed, how they are accomplished, and why activities begin and end;

- an implementational perspective that describes who and where activities are performed; and

- a data perspective that describes the products of activities and attributes of the process itself.

These perspectives are somewhat abstract. In order to operationalize them, it is necessary to be more concrete about the modeling constructs to be utilized in addressing the four perspectives. In addition, it is important to recognize that the various perspectives must be interrelated and mesh properly, in order to fully describe a process.

The Triad modeling approach is built upon the recognition that a process must be modeled using different constructs. We have identified three relatively concrete constructs from which we can derive models, and provide sufficient information to develop executable models. They are: states, activities, and objects; thus, the term *Triad*. Moreover, these three constructs are related, so we have defined relations interconnecting and interpenetrating the three constructs. States, activities, objects, and relations are explained in more detail below:

- An activity is a collection of operations. An activity may or may not produce an output; however, we typically expect an operation to have inputs and outputs (operands). Activities also have attributes, such as the organization performing the activity, the amount of time required to perform it, the amount of resources required to perform the activity, etc.

- An object is a participant in an activity. It may be an operator (agent) or an operand, and has attributes defined via relations. Objects are classified according to types, and object types may include people, data, various software products, and so on. Objects are said to have "attributes", which describe their properties at some moment in time. Attributes can be any description of an object, either exact or relative. For example, a software module may be described as "large" or "consisting of 1000 lines of code". The exact nature of object attributes used in modeling depends upon information the attribute is intended to provide.

- A state is a mapping of an object to a "position" in a process at any given moment of time. Objects are said to migrate through states, and relations are used to determine how and under what circumstances an object migrates through a process.

- A relation is a mapping instruction. Relations serve many purposes, including: mapping attributes to objects and activities; defining the trigger conditions for state transitions; and relating states and sub-states, activities and subactivities, and object type hierarchies.

States, relations, and attributes are time-varying information, and thus vary with the current situation. On the other hand, activities and objects are time-invariant blueprints or patterns. Figure 1 illustrates the Triad model.

The Triad approach offers a more concrete set of constructs that respond to our previous list of required modeling perspectives. The functional perspective is addressed primarily through activities, augmented by the flow of objects through those activities. The behavioral perspective is addressed primarily through states, taking an object orientation. The implementational perspective is covered primarily through objects and certain attributes. Of course, the data perspective is also covered by objects and attributes. Finally, relations interconnect these constructs, ensuring that they mesh together properly.

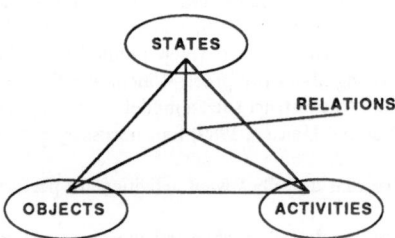

Figure 1. The Triad Modeling Approach.

Following a brief discussion of current process modeling techniques, the remainder of this paper explores the Triad modeling approach in more detail. It is worth noting that although the focus of this work is on modeling software processes, our techniques and approach are applicable to a wide variety of organizational processes.

3. CURRENT PROCESS MODELING TECHNIQUES

In 1987 and 1988, the SEI conducted a pilot study that sought to apply technology to an information management process (Hansen, Kellner, Over, and Przybylinski, 1988). To better understand the process, we decided to model it using currently available techniques. We examined task oriented modeling, which is popular in Department of Defense regulations, and decided not to use this technique. We examined data-flow oriented modeling and decided that this technique would allow us to quickly communicate to our client and ourselves basic information about the process. Recognizing the limitations of data-flow oriented models, we also used a state transition modeling technique to develop a more informative model of the process. The following paragraphs discuss the capabilities and limitations of each of these modeling techniques.

3.1 Task Oriented Models

A task oriented model is one that focuses on the tasks performed in a process. These types of models usually resemble flow charts used to document software systems. In the software development process, this includes activities such as "design a module", "code a module", "review a module", and so on. The task oriented view of the process is often used, for example, to develop work breakdown structure reports, in which the activities of project personnel are predicted and tracked.

One problem with task models is that they imply an exact and usually sequential order to the activities in the process. The "waterfall" model, for example, can either imply that requirements analysis for a module must be completed before design for that module is begun, or that all requirements must be completed before any design can begin. In practice, the former scenario is true, while the latter is not. Thus, some modules can be in design while other requirements are still being specified. In addition, design may lead to a reexamination and even change to the requirements. Usually, task oriented models do not adequately show such parallelism or feedback.

Figure 2 is an example of a flow chart that was developed describing the process used to maintain certain documentation (called Technical Orders) at a government facility. Technical Orders (TOs) are basically user documentation that describe the operation of an airplane, and are updated every time the

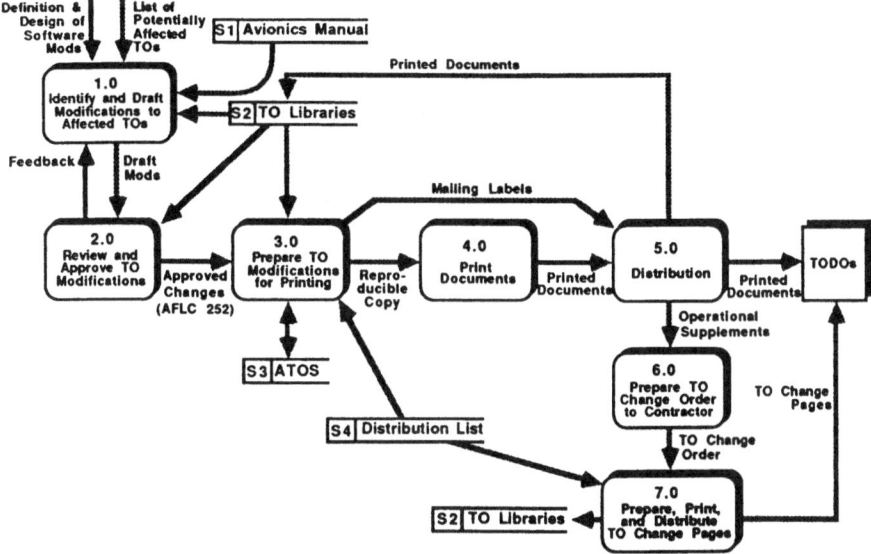

Figure 2. Flowchart of TO Modification Process.

avionics software for the airplane is updated. Notice that this diagram presents tasks only, and that:

- There is no representation of data flowing between tasks, nor are process step inputs and outputs presented.

- There is no information about events, such as task activation and termination. It can be assumed that either the process is continuous, with processing being performed constantly, or that it is discrete, with tasks executing until they finish and data passed in packages.

- There is no sense of the deadlines for steps or the duration of tasks, even though there are regulations that mandate completion of tasks in prescribed amounts of time.

Nonetheless, this model is superior to a purely textual description of the process, and at least communicates to a process participant some sense of the relationships among the tasks in the process.

3.2 Data-flow Oriented Models

This type of model was originally developed to show the flow of data or information between activities and data stores. Data-flow diagramming continues to be a popular means of performing systems analysis. Data-flow models, however, are not adequate for process modeling, although there have been attempts to utilize them to model software development activities.

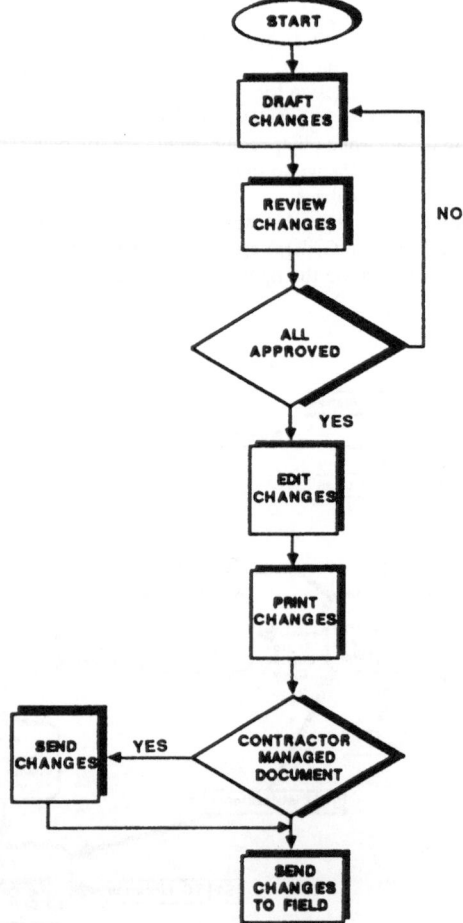

Figure 3. Data-flow Diagram of the TO Modification Process.

Data-flow oriented models, in contrast to task oriented models, focus on the flow of information and products through a process. The main difference between the two models is that a data-flow oriented model will reflect the fact that classes of objects exist, and these objects are utilized during the process. The output of process steps is made explicit, rather than implicit as in task oriented models.

Figure 3 is a data-flow model of the TO modification process. This model is more informative than the task oriented model in that it shows the inputs to and outputs from each process step. It also illustrate the existence of data "stores" or repositories. This model was developed by SEI personnel to enhance our own, as well as the process participants', knowledge of the process, and to that degree, was successful.

However, our goal was to decrease delays in the process, applying technology to the TO modification process where necessary.   This model provides no information about task timing or duration,   nor information about task termination and activation. Moreover, even though data was shown to flow between tasks, there is no information about how the data is transmitted or about the physical medium used to transmit the data. When considering technology insertion into a process, this information is important. Ultimately, we obtained this information, but continued to search for a modeling tool that would provide more capabilities.

4.   THE TRIAD MODELING APPROACH

We have found that at least three types of models must be developed to correctly communicate an overall sense of a process. Two of these are state models and activity models. In addition, we are finding that object models are necessary to determine the attributes of objects in a process. By investigating these three models, we can determine the relations that must be developed to interrelate them and create an executable model.

4.1   State Models

In state oriented models, a process undergoes an evolution in which states are entered and exited. Relations are established for triggering the transition between states, so that a sense of timing and causality is created. States may contain substates with entrance and exit criteria.

Figure 4 is a state oriented model of the Technical Order modification process. Although it shows the same activities taking place as in the data-flow diagram, it demonstrates that at least some of those activities can occur in parallel.   For example, the state in the lower left of the diagram, called PREPARE_PRINT, contains two orthogonal components (DOC_PREP and PRINT) separated by a dashed line.   This notation indicates parallelism (concurrency) between these two components. Since many documents are worked on simultaneously, some may still be in the preparation stage while others have progressed to being printed. Only when all have been printed, does the process leave PREPARE_PRINT. It does not show the flow of data, however, so this model alone is not sufficient to completely describe a process.

In the triad approach to modeling, state modeling is used to represent an object oriented view of a process. We must define objects of interest at some atomic level, and trace these objects through a process. Our use of states, therefore, is to describe the operations in which an entity participates in a process. As an object migrates through a process, it will develop changing properties, which we refer to as *attributes*. For example, if we were to model a software maintenance process, we might want to trace the operations upon a software "problem". This problem, initially a conceptual object, will undergo changes in properties, ultimately being instantiated as a code module. An attribute of a problem, then, would be the form in which it exists at any time.

State transitions define the circumstances under which an object will migrate between states. In the Triad modeling approach, we call those circumstances triggers. A trigger is a combination of events and conditions that causes the exit from a state and the entrance into another state, and, therefore, triggers are the logical relations between states. Triggers can express quite complex logic for state transitions.

State models are also used to provide information about parallelism in a process, and the timing associates with steps in a process. The Triad approach also relates time to state transitions, in that we may occasionally give an activity a minimum or maximum existence time, and force transitions. States, then, provide behavioral information about a process. Relations are used to determine transitions between states and also the amount of time that is or can be spent in a state. This satisfies the "why and when" aspects of modeling.

4.2   Activity Models

In the Triad approach, activity models are basically data-flow models, and we use them to represent

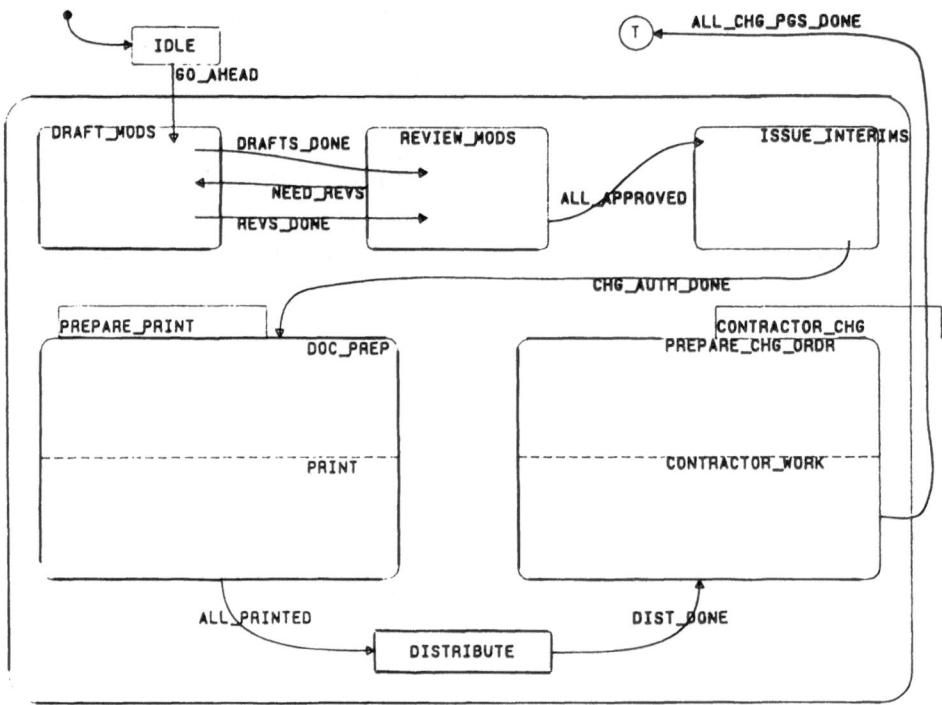

Figure 4. State Diagram of the TO Modification Process

a functional view of a process by decomposing it into activities corresponding to major tasks. Each activity can be further decomposed in a hierarchical fashion representing its constituent subtasks. Each activity must relate to some state(s) in the state models. Activity models are important, then, to represent the relations among all the different subtasks that comprise a process, and also to represent the flow of information between activities.

The Triad modeling approach uses states in an interesting manner. Our concept of modeling relegates decisions about process paths to state models rather than activity models. Most modeling techniques use decision points to determine the next action in a sequence of actions. Our approach is to determine the possible states through which an object may migrate, and to determine the circumstances under which migrations will take place. Thus, decision points as such do not exist, but multiple state transition possibilities exist. This concept has been used successfully in "meta-programming" experiments (Przybylinski, 1986). The difference in techniques is subtle and admittedly philosophical.

Activity modeling, therefore, describes the "what" of processes, and, again, relations are necessary to provide complete information. States are used to determine decision paths, the timing of activities, and the values of certain attributes. Attributes can also be used to provide partial information about the "who and where" of modeling. For example, one attribute of a process may be the location in which that process is performed.

4.3   Object Models

Objects are the operands or operators of some action. In the Triad modeling approach, an object is the atomic element associated with a state model, or the input to or output from an activity. The inputs to and outputs from activities represent high levels of abstraction of the atomic elements of state models.

To create executable models with inferencing capabilities, we will develop conceptual "object models" using knowledge engineering techniques to capture information about objects, or object attributes. Knowledge engineering will also be used to determine attributes of activities; therefore, in an object-oriented sense, activities will be treated as "objects".

Object attributes may refer to any aspect of an object that seems important. For example, to predict the resources required to develop a set of software modules, we may create a set of 50 "complex" modules and 50 "simple" modules and trace them through a software development process. Assuming that the terms "complex" and "simple" relate to an amount of time required to perform some tasks, we can predict the total amount of time to develop the 100 modules. In this case, we have created attributes that describe individual modules, and have related these attributes to activity attributes.

We can define attributes for individuals participating in a process and for organizations participating in the process. If person A is a faster worker than person B, we can perform some analysis to determine where in the process each worker should be utilized. The point is that some attributes of objects are not easily established, and that we must then rely on some technique to augment our own intuition about objects.

4.4   Relations

Relations define the circumstances under which objects enter and exit states, activities begin and end, and how attributes (both for objects and activities) are related to state. As previously stated, the Triad approach uses state models to capture decisions instead of activity models. Our philosophy is to simplify activity charts as much as possible, to show all *possible* activities, and to utilize state transition relations to determine what activities occur depending upon certain circumstances.

In addition to well-defined, direct relations with which we are all familiar, one also encounters more fuzzy sorts of relations which must be considered.

4.4.1 Causal Relations. State transitions are triggered by circumstances. Triggers, then, can be thought of as IF...THEN relations, or *causal relations*. Often, one of several possible transitions may be triggered by a set of circumstances, thus, causal relations can be described as follows: If (circumstance A) then (consequence B with some probability). These relations are important for analyzing the effectiveness of alternative procedures in processes.

For example, an organization may mandate that no coding begin until design has been written, reviewed, approved and incorporated into a document. As time proceeds, that organization may concede that, under certain conditions, coding of a module may begin prior to a formal design review. Such an organization may wish to determine the impact on cost and schedule created by using this option, particularly if rework is required for non-formally approved modules. The triad approach to models will show both possible paths and assign some probability that alternate paths will be taken. These probabilities can either be determined through empirical studies or intuition. In addition, we will predict extra resources required for rework of modules that have failed with errors that might have been uncovered in a review. This is the type of information an organization needs to perform risk analysis of process changes, and causality provides a mechanism for that analysis.

4.4.2 Influences on a Process. In decision theory, a decision basis is a collection of components that represent the alternatives, states, preferences, and relations in a decision situation (Henrion Breese, 1988). When enough information is known about possible alternate paths, the decision basis can be captured in relations. However, there are occurrences outside of the process being modeled that indirectly affect the process. We call these occurrences *influences*. An influence is a condition that causes a process to change in some way, even though the condition is not identifiably related to any activity in the process.

For example, politics influences many of the decisions that affect our lives, but it is almost impossible to predict when politics will be an influence, and what effect that influence will have. Peer pressure is another example of an influence. "Quality" is an influence (sometimes referred to as an indicator) that has an effect on software development. An organization's "commitment to quality" is an influence, but is difficult to measure.

A good example of an influence can be drawn from a study conducted by the SEI. The SEI analyzed a process used by a software development organization to change documentation to reflect software changes. We discovered that the process involved seven organizations and seven distinct steps. The output of the process was change pages that were incorporated into notebooks by users in the field. The SEI view of the process was one of information management, the output of which happened to be change pages. The view of the management of the software development organization was that the process was one of creating change pages.

Prior to the SEI study, the management of the organization decided to invest a large sum of money inserting technology into the page preparation (typesetting, drafting, composition, layout, etc.) portion of the process. This has an unusual influence on the other participants in the process: because so much attention was given to this technology insertion, and so much money was spent, they believed that they were in the *page changing* business, when in reality, they were in the *information management* business. Because of this, other attempts to improve the overall process were systematically rejected. It was not until the SEI developed a model of the process that the resistance to change began to dissipate.

In process modeling, influences should be considered and captured as causal relations when enough data exist to support the relations.

5. SUMMARY OF THE TRIAD APPROACH TO PROCESS MODELING

The following summarizes the use of the process modeling constructs described thus far:

- State models communicate behavior of the process, to determine the events and conditions that drive the process, and to provide timing information. The state models also provide valuable and necessary information about parallelism in the process and the timing of events. Relations, of course, will force state transitions to happen within given time constraints. State models are atomic in nature and apply to an object.

- Activity models provide a global view of a process, and to determine the flow of information between tasks. Activity models provide information about all the different processes which form a larger process, and, therefore, provide information about the state models which must be developed.

- Object models determine object attributes, which provide information which is used by the other models to determine the behavior of the system.

- Relations define the attributes of objects and activities depending upon existing conditions, and to provide behavioral information about state models. Relations may be embedded in object and activity definitions.

6. FUTURE DIRECTIONS

We have determined the characteristics of a modeling environment for the development of executable models. Such an environment should:

1. Utilize a highly visual approach.

2. Provide comprehensive descriptions of model components.

3. Support multiple, complementary views.

4. Support multiple levels of abstraction.

5. Use formally defined syntax and semantics.

6. Provide a simulation capability.

7. Support "what if" analysis.

For our work in process modeling, we are seeking an object-oriented visual language with automated inferencing capabilities. Unfortunately, we have been unable to find such an environment. Instead, we expect to integrate heterogeneous tools to create an environment, or extract information from several tools, and incorporate that information into yet another tool.

We have had success building state and activity models with the tool STATEMATE, offered by i-Logix of Burlington, Massachusetts. The statechart of the Technical Order process contained in this document was developed using STATEMATE. We are also exploring the use of Ptech, a process engineering environment offered by Associative Design Technologies, Grafton, Massachusetts.

Ultimately, we expect to integrate tools using an expert system. Expert system shells are convenient for capturing relations in terms of rules, and for storing object and activity attributes as frames.

The results of these efforts will be documented in a future paper.

ACKNOWLEDGEMENTS

This work was sponsored by the Department of Defense. The views and conclusions are those of the authors and should not be interpreted as representing official policies, either expressed or implied, of the Software Engineering Institute, Carnegie Mellon University, the Department of Defense, or the U.S. Government.

REFERENCES

Fourth International Software Process Workshop: Representing and Enacting the Software Process, May 11-13, 1988. Held at Moretonhampstead, Devon, UK.

Hansen, Greg, Kellner, Marc, Over, Jim, and Przybylinski, Stan, 1988, *The Analysis of the Technique Order Production Process at Ogden Air Logistics Center and the Recommendations for the Improvement of the Process,* Technical Report CMU/SEI-87-TR-12, Software Engineering Institute, Carnegie Mellon University, January.

Henrion Breese, Horvitz, 1988, *Decision Theory in Expert Systems and Artificial Intelligence,* June 1988.

Humphrey, Watts S., 1988, The Software Engineering Process: Definition and Scope, *Proceedings of the 4th International Software Process Workshop: Representing and Enacting the Software Process,* ACM, pp. 34-35.

Kellner, Marc I., 1988, Representation Formalisms for Software Process Modeling, *Proceedings of the 4th International Software Process Workshop: Representing and Enacting the Software Process,* ACM, pp. 43-46.

Kellner, Marc I., and Hansen, Gregory A., 1988, *Software Process Modeling,* Technical Report CMU/SEI-88-TR-9, Software Engineering Institute, Carnegie Mellon University, May 1988.

Kellner, Marc I., and Hansen, Gregory A., 1989, Software Process Modeling: A Case Study, *Proceedings of the 22nd Hawaii International Conference on Systems Science,* IEEE, 1989.

Lehman, M. M., 1987, Process Models, Process Programs, Programming Support, *Proceedings of the 9th International Conference on Software Engineering,* IEEE, pp. 14-16.

Osterweil, Leon, 1987, Software Processes are Software Too, *Proceedings of the 9th International Conference on Software Engineering,* IEEE, pp. 2-12.

Phillips, Richard W., 1988, State Change Architecture: A Protocol for Executable Process Models, *Proceedings of the 4th International Software Process Workshop: Representing and Enacting the Software Process,* ACM, pp. 74-76.

Phillips, Richard W., 1989, State Change Architecture: A Protocol for Executable Process Models, *Proceedings of the 22nd Hawaii International Conference on Systems Science,* IEEE.

Przybylinski, Stan, 1986, DARTS: A Knowledge Based Reuse Paradigm, *Army Research Office Workshop on Future Directions in Computer Architecture and Software.*

Rombach, H. Dieter, and Mark, Leo, 1989, Software Process & Product Specifications: A Basis for Generating Customized Software Engineering Information Bases, *Proceedings of the 22nd Hawaii International Conference on Systems Science,* IEEE.

Williams, Lloyd G., 1988(a), Software Process Modeling: A Behavioral Approach, *Proceedings of the 10th International Conference on Software Engineering,* IEEE, pp. 174-186.

Williams, Lloyd G., 1988(b), A Behavioral Approach to Software Process Modeling, *Proceedings of the 4th International Software Process Workshop: Representing and Enacting the Software Process,* ACM, pp. 108-111.

MODELING THE SOFTWARE DESIGN PROCESS

Bill Curtis and Neil Iscoe

MCC Software Technology Program
P. O. Box 200195
Austin, Texas 78720

Abstract: There are many levels at which the software development process can be modeled. MCC-STP's Empirical Studies Team has developed a layered behavioral model to guide our analyses of these processes. We have performed empirical studies of processes at each of these levels. At the level of individual cognitive problem-solving processes, we conducted a thinking aloud protocol study wherein software professionals were given a specification for an elevator system (a lift) and instructed to design a control system for it to the level of detail that they would hand over to a competent programmer for implementation. In this Lift Experiment we were seeking to determine the primary breakdowns experienced during design to determine the functionality that should be explored in developing prototypes of design tools. At the team and project levels, we videotaped three months worth of requirements and design meetings of a project team designing an object server. We analyzed these tapes to determine how group dynamics altered the processes we observed during individual design problem-solving, and what types of design technology should be provided in the group meeting environment. Finally, at the organizational and business milieu levels we conducted on-site interviews with personnel from 17 large software development projects to gather case study information on actual design processes. Transcripts of these interviews were analyzed to model factors affecting the processes of making design decisions and communicating them across the project. In this paper models of the software process developed at each of the levels are described and the aggregation of their effects across levels are discussed.

ARE WE MODELING THE RIGHT SOFTWARE PROCESSES?

Software Productivity and Quality Factors

Although the primary focus for increasing software productivity and quality has been on improved methods, tools, and environments, their impact in empirical studies of software productivity and quality on large projects from several industrial environments has been disappointing compared to the impact of other factors.

- In IBM Federal Division, Walston and Felix (1977) found that the complexity of the customer interface, the users' involvement with requirements definition, and the experience of the project team had more productivity impact than the use of software methods and tools.

- In the Defense and Space Group at TRW, Boehm (1981) found that the capability of the team assigned to the project had twice the productivity impact of the complexity of the product, and four times the impact of software tools and practices.

- In NASA's Software Engineering Laboratory, McGarry (1982) reported that the single largest factor affecting productivity and quality was differences among programmers.

Empirical Foundations of Information and Software Science V
Edited by P. Zunde and D. Hocking, Plenum Press, New York, 1990

21

- In identifying a broad set of factors that accounted for two-thirds of the variation in software productivity, Vosburgh, Curtis, Wolverton, Albert, Malec, Hoben, and Liu (1984) argued that half of this variation was affected by factors over which project management had little control (factors other than the use of software engineering practices and tools).

In these studies human and organizational factors presented boundary conditions that limited the situations in which methods, tools, and environments could increase software productivity and quality. To improve project outcomes, we must understand how these human and organizational factors affect the execution of software development tasks (Weinberg, 1971; Curtis, 1985; Boehm, 1987; DeMarco & Lister, 1987).

This paper reports a field study we conducted to obtain data that would support modeling the important, and often elusive, process components underlying the requirements and design of large, complex systems. We wanted to synthesize process models from empirical evidence collected from actual development projects, rather than from textbook descriptions of the process.

The Focus of Software Process Models

The focus of most software process models, most notably the waterfall model (Royce, 1970), has been on the management aspects of development: what artifacts should become available and what order of tasks should be executed to produce them. This focus assumes that great leverage can be exercised over productivity by coordinating who should do what by when. Most textbook models assume that software development tasks can be executed by any competent software engineer with little variation in performance and that software requirements and specifications are fairly stable.

The studies cited earlier are disturbing in their implications about the variability among software engineers and project teams in performing their development tasks and the impact this variability has on project outcomes. Substantial variability in performance (Curtis, 1981) or changes in requirements hamper project coordination, and make planning, tracking, and explaining project outcomes extremely difficult. Predictability weakens when the processes modeled are controlled by highly variable factors that are not modeled.

Many of the technologies purported to improve software productivity and quality only affect a few of the factors that exert the most influence over outcomes on large projects (Brooks, 1987). As the size of the system increases, the social organization required to produce it grows in complexity and the factors controlling productivity and quality may change in their relative impact. Technologies that enhance productivity on medium-sized systems may have less influence on large projects where factors that, while benign on medium size systems, ravage project performance when unleashed by a gargantuan system that may involve the coordination of many companies. A great danger on large projects is that management will be deceived by the simplicity of the prescribed processes and will not understand what pitfalls are likely to await them (Fox, 1982). Our objective has been to describe a few of these problems in greater detail.

Overview of the Field Study

This field study consisted of interviews with personnel on 17 large system development projects. The interviews revealed each project's design activities from the perspectives of those whose actions constituted the process. In a similar field study, Zelkowitz, Yeh, Hamlet, Gannon, and Basili (1984) identified discrepancies between the state of the art and the state of practice in using software engineering tools and methods. Our interviews provided detailed descriptions of development problems to help identify high-leverage factors for improving such processes as problem formulation, requirements definition, and analysis, and software architectural design. We focused on how requirements and design decisions were made, represented, communicated, changed, as well as how these decisions impacted subsequent development processes.

Projects were interviewed from nine companies in such businesses as computer manufacturing, telecommunications, consumer electronics, and aerospace. We sought to study projects that involved at least 10 people, were past the design phase, and involved real-time, distributed, or embedded applications. We conducted hour-long structured interviews on-site with systems engineers, senior software designers, and the project manager. On one-third or less of the projects, we were able to interview the division general manager, customer representatives, and the testing/QA team leader. Participants were guaranteed anonymity, and the information reported was "sanitized" so that no individual person, project, or company could be identified.

Analysis of the interview transcripts revealed the processes underlying a number of classic software development problems. The three most salient problems, in terms of the additional effort or mistakes attributed to them, were: 1) the thin spread of application domain knowledge, 2) fluctuating and conflicting requirements, and 3) communication and coordination breakdowns. We distinguished among these three problems because they operated through different mechanisms and may require different solutions. In the next section we will summarize our observations about these problems and their processes.

PROBLEMS ON LARGE SOFTWARE DEVELOPMENT PROJECTS

The Thin Spread of Application Domain Knowledge

The deep application-specific knowledge required to successfully build most large, complex systems was thinly spread through most software development staffs. This problem was especially characteristic of projects where software was embedded in a larger system (e.g., avionics or telephony), or where the software implemented a specific application function (e.g., transaction processing). These systems contrast with applications currently taught in computer science departments, like single processor operating systems and compilers. Although most software developers were knowledgeable in the computational structures and techniques of computer science, many began their career as novices in the application domains that constituted their company's business. As a result, software development required a substantial time commitment to learning the application domain.

Specification mistakes often occurred when designers did not have sufficient application knowledge to interpret the customer's intentions from the requirements statement. Customer representatives and system engineers complained that implementation had to be changed because development teams had misconceptions of the application domain. Even when a project had experts in each of its functional domains, they were often unable to model the effect of component integration on processing or storage constraints.

Many forms of information had to be integrated to understand an application domain. For instance, project members had to learn how the system would behave under extreme conditions such as a jet fighter entering battle at night during bad weather, a telephone switch undergoing peak load on Mother's Day, or an automated factory with machines running at different speeds. Software developers had to learn and integrate knowledge about diverse areas such as the capabilities of the total system, the architecture of a special-purpose embedded computer (often a microprocessor), application-specific algorithms, the structure of the data to be processed and how it reflected the structure of objects and processes in the application domain, and occasionally even more esoteric bodies of knowledge about how different users performed specific tasks.

The need to integrate knowledge from many domains underlay the phenomenon of the "project guru", an exceptional designer who could map deep application knowledge into a computational architecture. Exceptional designers were adept at identifying unstated requirements, constraints, or exception conditions. They often exerted extraordinary influence over the direction of the design team, and worked hard at coordinating a common understanding among the staff of the application domain and the system's intended behavior.

The large cost of learning an application area was a significant corporate expense. The time estimated for a new project assignee to become productive ranged from 6 months to a year. Major changes in the business application or in the underlying technology required additional learning. However, as the technical staff's application knowledge matured, the organization's cost and schedule for developing systems was reduced, while its productivity and quality were increased. Managing learning, especially of the application domain, was a major factor in a software business's productivity, quality, and costs.

The time devoted to learning and coordinating application-specific information was buried within the design phase and could not be accounted for separately. Learning costs were paid for in several ways: in planned training, in exposure to customers, in prototypes and simulations, in defects, in budget or schedule overruns, and in canceled projects. Customers were usually unwilling to pay for training, since they believed the contractor should already have the required knowledge. Thus, the time required for design was often seriously underestimated, since these estimates were usually based only on the time actually spent designing. The time spent educating project personnel about the application domain and coordinating their understanding of the system was omitted.

Fluctuating and Conflicting Requirements

Fluctuation or conflict among system requirements caused problems on every large project we interviewed. On one project we were told that hardware changes could cause a redesign of the software every six months. Fluctuation and conflict among requirements resulted from factors in the business market such as differing needs among customers, the changing needs of a single customer, changes in underlying technologies or in competitors' products, regulatory constraints, and, as discussed earlier, from misunderstanding the application domain. However, internal company factors such as corporate politics, marketing plans, research results, product line consistencies, and financial conditions also had significant effects.

Product requirements fluctuated most frequently when different customers had separate needs or when the needs of a single customer changed over time. Analyzing requirements for commercial products was difficult without an explicit statement of at least one customer's needs. The requirements were often defined for the first customer to place an order, even though project personnel knew that other customers would state different requirements. During development, designers tried to raise the product specification from the specific (driven by a single customer) to the general (driven by a market of customers), although it often continued to evolve from the specific to the specific.

Even when a customized system was developed for one client, the requirements often provided a moving target for designers. During system development, the customer, as well as the developer, learned about the application domain. The dialectic through which the developer generated the requirements revealed new possibilities to the customer (Gould and Lewis, 1985). As customers learned more about the systems' capability and understood their application better, they envisioned many features they wished they had included in the requirements.

Many customers misunderstood the tradeoffs between requested functions, the capability of existing technology, the delivery schedule, and the cost. They learned of these tradeoffs through an iterative negotiation with the system design team, as the requirements were translated into a design and costs could be estimated. Each cycle was driven by trying to balance and integrate technical and non-technical constraints into the product requirements. Customers rarely understood the complexity of the development process, and underestimated the effort required to re-engineer the software, especially when the system involved tight timing or storage constraints. As a result, they could not understand why changes to the requirements were so costly.

Internal company groups, such as marketing, often acted as a customer. They could add noise to requirements definition, since their requirements occasionally differed from those of potential customers. A common tension occurred, for instance, when marketing wanted to redesign a system to take advantage of new technology, while existing customers did not want to lose their investment in software that ran on the current system. On several projects, the requirements - and even the understanding of the product - varied among strategic planning, marketing, and product planning groups. The design team had to reduce the conflict between these contending forces in their design. This conflict varied with how deeply groups like marketing understood the customer's application and the limits of existing technology. Marketing groups understood why customers (who weren't necessarily users) would buy the system, but this often differed from the application-specific information about product use that was needed for design.

Resolving conflicts among system requirements generated both inside the company and in the marketplace, created a feedback cycle in which many groups provided inputs or constraints that had to be negotiated into a design. When presented with the requirements statement, the design team negotiated to reduce conflicts and limit requirements to those that could be implemented within schedule, budget, and technical constraints. Some of the toughest decisions involved tradeoffs between system features and windows of opportunity in the market. Technical requirements were traded off against business decisions involving delivery dates and other marketing and sales issues.

Resolving some conflicts required knowledge of actual user behavior that was scarce on many design teams. One solution was to design a flexible system that could be easily modified to accommodate future changes and technologies. Yet, to satisfy schedule and hardware constraints a smorgasbord of features was eliminated to make way for the expanded flexible implementations of those that remained. However, it was difficult to enforce agreements across teams, and programmers often created a hidden source of requirements fluctuation as they added unrequired enhancements.

There was a natural tension between getting requirements right and getting them stable. Although this tradeoff appeared to be a management decision, it was just as often determined by system engineers. Many designers believed that requirements should act as a point of departure for clarifying poorly understood functions interactively with the customer. They argued that specifications should not be hardened while still learning about the application domain or the capabilities of the proposed architecture. That is, specifications should be formalized at the rate that uncertainty about technical decision is reduced. The communication and coordination processes within a project became crucial to coping with the incessant fluctuation and conflict among requirements.

Communication and Coordination Breakdown

A large number of groups had to coordinate their activities, or at least share information, during software development. Organizational boundaries to communication among groups both within companies and in the business milieu inhibited the integration of application with computation knowledge. These communication barriers were often unappreciated since the artifacts produced by one group (e.g., marketing) were assumed to convey all the information needed by the next group (e.g., system design). However, designers complained that constant verbal communication was needed between customer, requirements, and engineering groups. Organizational structures separating engineering groups (hardware, software, and systems) often inhibited timely communication about application functionality in one direction, and feedback about implementation problems that resulted from system design in the other direction.

A software engineer normally communicated most frequently with team members, slightly less frequently with other teams on the project, much less often with corporate groups, and except for rare cases, very infrequently with external groups. Communication at each of these levels involved different content. For example, communication at the team level mostly concerned system design, implementation, or personal issues. At the project level, proportionately more of the communication was related to coordinating technical activities and discussing constraints on the system. Communication at the company level generally concerned product attributes, progress, schedules, or resources. Communication with external organizations involved user requirements, contractual issues, operational performance, delivery planning, and future business. Thus, communication to each higher level involved a change in the content of the message, a different context for interpreting the message, and a more restricted channel for transmission (e.g., the more removed the level, the less the opportunity for face-to-face transmission). Communication difficulties were often due to the geographic separation, to cultural differences, and to environmental factors.

Some communication breakdowns between project teams were avoided when one or more project members spanned team or organizational boundaries (Adams, 1976). One type of *boundary-spanner* was the chief system engineer, who translated customer needs into terms understood by software developers. Boundary-spanners translated information from a form used by one team into a form that could be used by other teams. Boundary-spanners had good communication skills and a willingness to engage in constant face-to-face interaction; they often became hubs for the information networks that assisted a project's technical integration. In addition, they were often crucial in keeping communication channels open between rival groups.

Project managers often found it difficult to establish communication between project teams unless communication channels opened naturally. Since documentation did not provide sufficient communication, reviews were often the most effective channels. In fact, communication was often cited as a greater benefit of formal reviews than was their "official" purpose of finding defects. At other times, communication among teams was thwarted by managers for a variety of reasons.

The social structure of the project was occasionally factored into architectural decisions. The system partitioning that reduced connectivity among components also affected communication among project personnel. Higher connectivity among components required more communication among developers to maintain agreed interface definitions. Occasionally the partitioning was based not only on the logical connectivity among components, but also on the social or communications connectivity among the staff.

On most large projects, the customer interface was an *organizational communications* issue and this interface too often restricted opportunities for developers to talk with end users. For instance, the formal chain of communication between the developer and the end user was often made more remote by having to traverse two nodes involving the developer's marketing group and the end user's manager. At the same time this interface was often cluttered with communications from non-user components of the customer's organization, each with its particular concerns. Typically, development organizations said they would like to have, but could not get, a single point of customer contact for defining system requirements. None of the large projects we interviewed had a lone point of customer contact for defining requirements.

One of the most significant challenges to government or commercial development teams was to coordinate communications from different customer sources to develop a consistent understanding of the customer's requirements. When several customer sources gave inconsistent input, project personnel had to negotiate among them to clarify requirements. Conversely, different project members needed to provide consistent answers to the customer, and establishing a single point of contact for coordinating these communications was difficult.

IMPLICATIONS FOR SOFTWARE PROCESS MODELS

Processes Absent in Current Software Process Models

The descriptions provided in our interviews indicated how productivity and quality factors influenced project performance. The most frequent statement we heard from participants was of the form, "You've got to understand, this isn't the way we develop software here". This type of comment suggested that these developers held a model of how software development should occur, and they were frustrated that the conditions surrounding their project would not let them work from the model. This comment's frequency also suggested that the model most developers envisioned accounted poorly for the environmental conditions and organizational context of software development. The participants we interviewed were uniformly motivated to do a good job, but they had to mold their development process to navigate a maze of contingencies.

Our interviews indicated that developing large software systems must be treated, at least in part, as a learning, negotiation, and communication process. These processes are poorly described in software process models that focus instead on how a software product evolves through a series of artifacts such as requirements, functional specifications, code, and so on. Much early activity on a project involved learning not only about the application and its environment, but also about new hardware, new development tools and languages, and other changeable technologies. Software developers had to integrate substantial knowledge from several domains before they could learn about design and implementation decisions being made on other parts of the system in order to ensure the integration of their components. Characteristically, customers also underwent a learning process as the project team explained the implications of their requirements. This learning process was a major source of requirements volatility.

Although far from the only issues participants described, requirements issues were a recurring theme in our interviews. The three problems we described provide, among other things, three views of the requirements problem: how system requirements were understood, how their instability affected design, and how they were communicated throughout a project. Although a circumscribed requirements phase can be identified in most software process models, requirement processes occur throughout the development cycle.

To manage uncertainty about requirements and design decisions more effectively, process models need to include components for exposure to and modeling of the application and its environment by more than an initial team of system engineers. Important design decisions made late in the design process need information about the application's behavior and environment that was frequently not anticipated early in the specification process. Prototyping is one approach to this problem, but an approach that varies in importance with the amount of information that designers and implementors share about the application domain. Design is in part an educational process, and trial and error learning (prototyping) is only one approach to education, albeit a powerful one. Most process models do not account for education on the application or new system technologies.

The desire to have a process model that provides management accountability inhibits designing a process that most managers will admit is the way development really happens. Although it is popular to say that you want to build an initial version to throw away (Brooks, 1975), few projects accommodate this approach. Prototyping and other development alternatives attempt to provide a way of managing the technical uncertainties of a project. The hallmark of management accountability is to present a set of milestones that indicate a clear understanding of how project objectives will be reached. The inclusion of an unplanned prototype or a redesign in the process is an admission that there is a learning component involved. However, few process models provide for the level of uncertainty and change experienced on most projects.

Few process models account for the perturbations that result from changes in the strategic objectives of the company or from changing conditions in the customer's environment. Process models should include recommendations concerning how organizational designs should be tailored to expedite development processes best suited for different types of large system projects. In particular, most process models do not provide guidelines for handling the often Byzantine customer interface experienced on many large projects. Some customer interfaces are so complex that the process of managing them is one of leading negotiations among the various factions within the customer environment. Few process models elaborate the negotiation process that not only precedes specification, but attends any torrent of requests for changes.

Improving Software Productivity and Quality

Many of the technologies purported to improve software productivity and quality only affect a few of the factors that exert the most influence over outcomes on large projects. When asked what kind of tools would help them most, most participants had difficulty identifying a tool, other than an occasional request for performance analysis or cross-referencing tools. They did not see their problems being solved by the current generation of software development tools. As the size of the system increases, the social organization required to produce it grows in complexity and the factors controlling productivity and quality change in their relative impact. Technologies that enhance productivity on small or medium-sized systems have less influence on large projects where factors that were irrelevant in developing small systems, ravage project performance when unleashed by a gargantuan system that may involved the coordination of many companies. These are the problems that the next generation of software development tools must address.

Three issues, in particular, must be addressed if software productivity and quality are to be improved. The first is to increase the amount of application domain knowledge across the entire software development staff. Designers of software development environments should discover ways in which these environments can creatively facilitate the staff-wide sharing and integration of knowledge. Second, software development tools and methods must accommodate change as an ordinary process and support the representation of uncertain design decisions. For instance, the essence of simulation and prototyping is a process of exploration, discovery, and change. Whether design decisions are delayed, or whether new requirements are negotiated among several customer components, change management and propagation is crucial throughout the design and development process. Finally, any software development environment must become a medium of communication to integrate people, tools, and information. If information created outside of the software tools environment must be manually entered, developers will find ways around using the tools, and information will be lost. Losing information and poor communication supports makes the coordination task more difficult. Thus, three capabilities that we believe must be supported in a software development environment are knowledge sharing and integration, change facilitation, and broad communications and coordination.

Existing software process models do not provide enough insight into actual development processes to guide research on new software development technologies. Models that only prescribe a series of development tasks provide no tools for analyzing how much new information must be learned by a project staff, how discrepant requirements should be negotiated, how design teams resolved architectural conflicts, and how these and similar factors contribute to a project's inherent uncertainty and risk. Boehm's (1988) spiral model is a promising attempt to manage these issues at a macro level. In order to improve research on software development environments, we believe that software process models must be expanded to account for the processes that software developers report causing the most difficulty. Elsewhere, we have proposed how to account for some of these processes in a layered behavioral model that can be superimposed on existing software development process models (Curtis, Krasner, and Iscoe, 1988).

REFERENCES

Adams, J. S., 1976, *The Structure and Dynamics of Behavior in Organizational Boundary Roles, Handbook of Industrial and Organization Psychology*, Dunnette, M. D., ed., Rand-McNally, Chicago, pp. 1175-1199.

Boehm, B. W., 1981, *Software Engineering Economics*, Prentice-Hall, Englewood Cliffs, NJ.

Boehm, B. W., 1987, *Improving Software Productivity*, IEEE Computer, Vol. 20, No. 9, pp. 43-57.

Boehm, B. W., 1988, A Spiral Model of Software Development and Maintenance, *IEEE Computer*, Vol. 21, No. 5, pp. 61-72.

Brooks, F. P., 1975, *The Mythical Man-Month*, Addison-Wesley, Reading, MA.

Brooks, F. P., 1987, No Silver Bullet, *IEEE Computer*, Vol. 20, No. 4, pp. 10-19.

Curtis, B., 1981, Substantiating Programmer Variability, *Proceedings of the IEEE*, Vol. 69, No. 7, p. 846.

Curtis, B., ed., 1985, *Human Factors in Software Development* (2nd ed.), IEEE Computer Society, Washington, D.C.

Curtis, B., Krasner, H., and Iscoe, N., 1988, A Field Study of the Software Design Process for Large Systems, *Communications of the ACM*, Vol. 31, No. 11, pp. 1268-1287.

DeMarco, T., and Lister, T. A., 1987, *Peopleware*, Dorset, New York.

Fox, J. M., 1982, *Software and Its Development*, Prentice-Hall, Englewood Cliffs, NJ.

Gould, J. D., and Lewis, C., 1985, Designing for Usability: Key Principles and What Designers Think, *Communications of the ACM*, Vol. 28, No. 3, pp. 300-311.

McGarry, F. E., 1982, What Have We Learned in the Last Six Years?, *Proceedings of the Seventh Annual Software Engineering Workshop (SEL-82-007)*, NASA-GSFC, Greenbelt, MD.

Royce, W. W., 1970, Managing the Development of Large Software Systems, *Proceedings of IEEE WESCON*, IEEE Computer Society, D.C., pp. 1-9.

Vosburgh, J., Curtis, B., Wolverton, R., Albert, B., Malec, H., Hoben, S., and Liu, Y., 1984, Productivity Factors and Programming Environments, *Proceedings of the Seventh International Conference on Software Engineering*, IEEE Computer Society, Washington, D.C., pp. 143-152.

Walston, C. E., and Felix, C. P., 1977, A Method of Programming Measurement and Estimation, *IBM Systems Journal*, Vol. 16, No. 1, pp. 54-73.

Weinberg, G. M., 1971, *The Psychology of Computer Programming*, Van Nostrand Reinhold, New York.

Zelkowitz, M., Yeh, R., Hamlet, R., Gannon, J., and Basili, V., 1984, Software Engineering Practices in the U.S. and Japan, *IEEE Computer*, Vol. 17, No. 6, pp. 57-66.

METHODOLOGICAL PRINCIPLES OF UNCERTAINTY IN INFORMATION

SYSTEMS MODELING

George J. Klir

Department of Systems Science
Thomas J. Watson School
State University of New York, Binghamton
New York 13903

Abstract: System modeling permeates all disciplines of science, both natural and artificial. The general concepts of system modeling are presented in summary fashion. The key role of uncertainty in system modeling is discussed including the principles of maximum and minimum uncertainty. Recent results regarding conceptualization of uncertainty, which demonstrate that uncertainty is a multidimensional concept, are overviewed, and the implications for modeling in information and software engineering are discussed.

INTRODUCTION

It is argued that systems modeling permeates in a very fundamental way all disciplines of science, be they oriented to the natural or to the artificial. General methodological issues associated with systems modeling are overviewed. The key role of uncertainty in system modeling is discussed, particularly the principles of maximum and minimum uncertainty. Recent results regarding conceptualization of uncertainty, which demonstrate that uncertainty is a multidimensional concept, are overviewed and their implications for modeling in information and software engineering are discussed.

1.   SYSTEMS MODELING

Perhaps the most fundamental classification of sciences is into the *sciences of the natural* and the *sciences of the artificial* (Simon, 1969). The two classes of sciences involve, respectively, the following two types of problem-solving activities:

(a)   *systems inquiry* -- the full scope of activities by which we attempt to construct systems that are adequate models of some aspect of reality;

(b)   *systems design* -- the full scope of activities by which we attempt to construct systems that are adequate models of desirable man-made objects.

We can see that a common feature of all disciplines of science, be they oriented to the natural or to the artificial, is *systems modeling*: the construction of systems that adequately model some aspect of natural or man-made reality. It is important at this point that the concept of a system not be confused with a part of reality (an object of the real world). A *system* is (in my terminology) always an abstraction that characterizes an appropriate type of relationship among some abstract entities. To qualify as a *model* of some aspect of reality, a system must be supplemented with appropriate mappings from relevant entities of the real world into the abstract entities of the system, and these mappings must be *homomorphic* with respect to the relationship involved. In many instances, these mappings cannot be defined mathematically but only in terms of appropriate physical devices (measuring instruments) and their homomorphism can be established only on pragmatic grounds (relevant reality behaves according to the model).

It follows from the foregoing that every model must invariably contain three principal components: a set of abstract entities, a relationship among these entities, and a set of homomorphic mappings that gives the abstract entities a realworld interpretation. In systems inquiries, a model is developed for the purpose of understanding some phenomenon of reality, be it natural or man-made, making adequate predictions or retrodictions, learning how to control the phenomenon in any desirable way, and utilizing all these capabilities for various ends. In systems design, a model is developed for the purpose of prescribing operations by which a conceived artificial object can be constructed in such a way that desirable objective criteria are satisfied within given constraints.

Every prescriptive model (as a result of systems design) is based upon some technological primitives. These are explanatory models, each resulting from some systems inquiry, that are accepted as valid. Hence, appropriate systems inquiries are always a prerequisite for every systems design.

2. CONCEPTUAL FRAMEWORKS FOR SYSTEMS MODELING

Systems modeling is an activity that requires a conceptual framework within which one operates. Each framework determines the scope of systems that can be described within it and leads to some specific taxonomy of these systems. Several conceptual frameworks have been proposed that attempt to capture the full scope of systems we are currently able to envision (Klir, 1985(a); Mesarovic and Takahara, 1975; Wymore, 1969; Zeigler, 1976). The differences in terminology and mathematical formulation among them are considerable. Little work has been done to rigorously compare the categories of systems that emerge from these seemingly different frameworks. We can only speculate, based on a rather limited evidence (Islam, 1974), that the differences in systems categories emerging from these broad frameworks are relatively minor and can be reconciled.

One of the broad conceptual frameworks, which is a result of my own work, is known in the literature as the *General Systems Problem Solver (GSPS)* (Klir, 1985(a)). The kernel of the GSPS is a *hierarchy of epistemological types of systems*, which represents the most rudimental taxonomy of systems. To see a brief outline of the basic levels in this hierarchy see (Klir, 1985(a)).

At the lowest level of the epistemological hierarchy, we define an *experimental frame* in terms of appropriate variables, their state sets (value sets), and an interpretation of these as real world attributes. In addition, some supporting medium (such as time, space, or a population) within which the variables change their states must also be specified. Furthermore, variables may be classified as input and output variables.

An *experimental frame* (also called a *source system*) may be viewed as a *data description language*. When actual data described in this language become available, we move to the next level in the hierarchy; systems on this level are called *data systems*.

When the variables of the experimental frame are characterized by a relationship among them, we move to a level that is still higher in the hierarchy. It is assumed on this level that the relationship among the variables is invariant with respect to the supporting medium involved. That is, it is time-invariant, space-invariant, space-time-invariant, population-invariant, etc. Systems on this level are called *behavior systems*.

Climbing further up the hierarchy involves two principles of integrating systems as components in larger systems. According to the first principle, several behavior systems (or sometimes lower level systems) that may share some variables or interact in some other way are viewed as subsystems integrated into one overall system. Overall systems of this sort are called *structure systems*. The subsystems forming a structure system are often called its elements.

When elements of a structure system are themselves structure systems, we call the overall system a *second order structure system*. *Higher order structure systems* are defined recursively in the same way.

According to the second integrating principle, an overall system is viewed as varying (in time, space, etc.) within a class of systems of any of the other types. The change from one system to another in the delimited class is described by a replacement procedure that is invariant with respect to the supporting medium involved (time, space, etc.). Overall systems of this type are called *metasystems*.

In principle, the replacement procedure of a metasystem may also change. Then, an invariant (changeless) higher level procedure is needed to describe the change. Systems of this sort, with two levels of replacement procedures, are called *metasystems of second order*. *Higher order metasystems* are then defined recursively in the same way.

Structure systems whose elements are metasystems are also allowed by the framework, similarly as metasystems defined in terms of structure systems.

The key feature of the epistemological hierarchy is that every system defined on some level in the hierarchy entails knowledge associated with all corresponding systems on lower levels and, at the same time, contains some knowledge that is not available in any of these lower level systems.

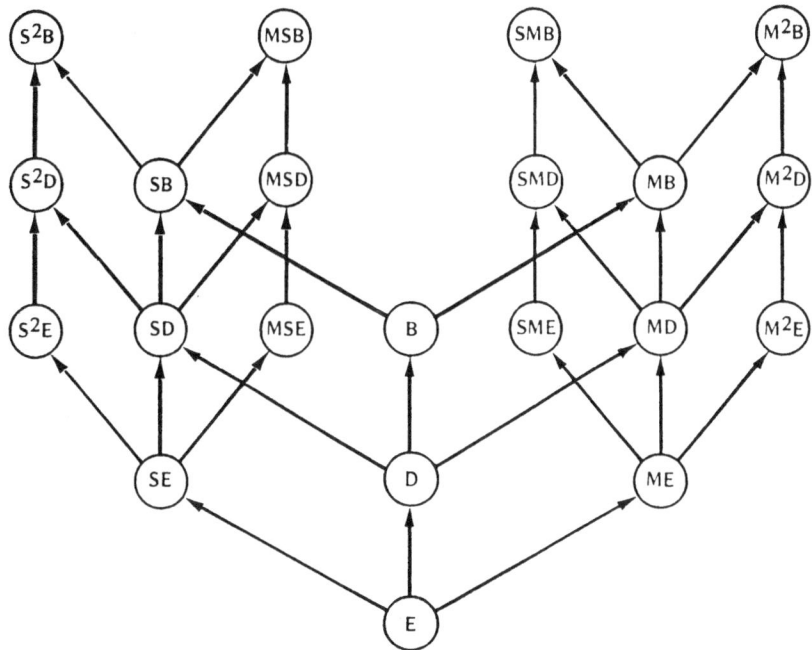

Figure 1. Epistemological Hierarchy of Systems Categories. (Notation: E-experimental or source system; D-data system; B-behavior system; SE, SD, SB-structure systems based on source data, and behavior systems, respectively; S^2E, S^2D, S^2B-second order structure systems of the three types; ME, MD, MB-meta-systems, based on source, data, and behavior systems, respectively; M^2E, M^2D, M^2B-second order metasystems of the three types; SME, SMD, SMB-structure systems based on metasystems of the three types; MSE, MSD, MSB-metasystems based on structure systems of the three types.

The number of levels in the epistemological hierarchy is potentially infinite. For each particular number of levels,' the hierarchy is a semi-lattice. In praxis, however, only a part of the lattice for a small number of levels is usually considered. For five levels, for example, a part of the semilattice (which is also a semilattice) is expressed by the Hasse diagram in Figure 1. The circle represent the various epistemological categories of systems, the arrows indicate the ordering from lower to higher categories. Symbols E, D, B denote experimental frames (source systems), data systems, and behavior systems, respectively. Symbol S, used as a prefix stands for structure systems. For example, SB denotes structure systems whose elements are behavior systems, and SD denotes structure systems whose elements are data systems. Symbol S^2 denotes structure systems of second order. For example, S^2B denotes structure systems of structure systems whose elements are behavior systems. Symbols M and M^2 denote metasystems and meta-metasystems, respectively. Combinations SM and MS denote structure systems whose elements are metasystems and metasystems whose elements are structure systems, respectively. The diagram in Figure 1 describes only a part of the epistemologicals hierarchy; it can be extended in an obvious way to combinations such as S^3B, S^2MB, SMSB, M^2SB, S^2MB, etc.

3.   UNCERTAINTY, COMPLEXITY, AND INFORMATION

When constructing systems of certain category as models in a systems inquiry or design, we apply various *preference orderings* defined on the category involved. The most fundamental preference ordering is always based upon the degree of conformity of the model to the relevant data or design specifications. Ideally, we should require that the model conform to the data or design specifications perfectly. That is, we should require that the model be based on a deterministic system capable of reproducing the data or satisfying the specifications exactly. However, such a requirement is often too strong and unrealistic since it would result in excessively complex systems. When we relax this requirement, allowing nondeterministic systems, we inevitably introduce some sort of *uncertainty* (descriptive, predictive, retrodictive, prescriptive) in the model. This uncertainty can be utilized for reducing *complexity* of the resulting model. The more uncertainty we allow, the simpler model can be obtained.

Complexity and uncertainty are always key criteria for comparing models. When operationally defined, they induce two preference orderings on the relevant category of systems. In general, we try to minimize both complexity and uncertainty in systems modeling. Unfortunately, the two criteria conflict with each other. When we reduce complexity, uncertainty increases or, at best, remains the same.

Although systems complexity can be defined in many different ways (Klir, 1985(b)), the common denominator of the various complexity measures is that they are somehow expressed in terms of the shortest descriptions of systems in a given language. In order to be able to compare systems by complexity, we must describe them in the same language. The concept of complexity is closely connected with the concept of information, usually referred to as *descriptive information* (Lofgren, 1977).

The concept of uncertainty is also closely connected with the concept of information. When our uncertainty in some situation is reduced by an action (such as observation, performing an experiment, or receiving a message), the action may be viewed as a source of information pertaining to the situation under consideration. The amount of information obtained by the action may be measured by the reduction in uncertainty due to the action. This alternative type of information may be well described by the term *"uncertainty-based information"*.

The two types of information, the descriptive information and the uncertainty-based information, do not involve any semantic or pragmatic aspects. Consequently, they do not fully capture the concept of information, as we understand it in the context of human communication. This is no shortcoming when the concepts are applied within given semantic and pragmatic frameworks, as typical in systems modeling.

4.   METHODOLOGICAL PRINCIPLES OF UNCERTAINTY

The capability of measuring information in terms of uncertainty is essential for dealing with two broad classes of problems that are fundamental to systems modeling:

(a)   problems involving reasoning in which conclusions are not entailed in the given premises, referred to in this paper as *ampliative reasoning*;

(b)   problems of *systems simplification*.

Ampliative reasoning is indispensable for systems modeling in a variety of ways. For example, whenever we make inferences from a system based on aggregated variables about a comparable system based on disaggregated variables or from subsystems into the corresponding overall system, we use ampliative reasoning. Systems simplification is opposite, at least to some extent, to ampliative reasoning in the context of system modeling. It involves problems such as the various ways of aggregating variables, excluding variables, or breaking overall systems into subsystems. We simplify systems models either to make them more manageable and understandable or to increase their credibility. On intuitive grounds, we can easily see that the following general principles are fundamental for dealing with these classes of problems.

A general *principle of ampliative reasoning* may be expressed by the following requirement: in any ampliative inference, use all but no more information than available. This principle requires that conclusions resulting from ampliative inferences maximize the relevant uncertainty within the constraints representing the premises. This principle, which may appropriately be called the *principle of maximum uncertainty*, guarantees that our ignorance be fully recognized when we try to enlarge our claims beyond the given premises and, at the same time, that all information contained in the premises be fully utilized. That is, our conclusions are maximally noncommittal with regard to missing information in the premises. When uncertainty is conceptualized in terms of probability theory, this principle becomes the well established *principle of maximum entropy*; its author is Jaynes, who proposed it initially in the context of statistical mechanics (Jaynes, 1983).

A general principle of *systems simplification* may be expressed as follows: a sound simplification or a system should minimize the loss of relevant information (or increase of relevant uncertainty) while achieving the required reduction of complexity. That is, we should accept only such simplifications at any desirable level of complexity for which the loss of relevant information (or increase of relevant uncertainty) is minimal. This principle, which may be called the *principle of minimum uncertainty*, guarantees that no information is wasted in the process of simplification. For probabilistic systems, this principle becomes the *principle of minimum entropy*.

When combined, the principles of maximum and minimum entropy have proven to form a powerful

Table 1

Measures of Uncertainty: A Summary

Name	Formula	Meaning of Symbols
Hartley measure	$I(A) = \log_2 |A|$	A: a subset of X $|A|$: cardinality of A
Shannon entropy	$H(p) = -\sum_{i=1}^{n} p_i \log_2 p_i$	p: probability distribution $p = (p_1, p_2, \ldots, p_n)$
U-uncertainty	$U(r) = \sum_{i=1}^{n} (r_i - r_{i+1}) \log_2 i$	r: possibility distribution $r = (r_1, r_2, \ldots, r_n), r_{n+1} = 0,$ $r_i \geq r_{i+1}$
Dissonance	$E(m) = -\sum_{A \subseteq X} m(A) \log_2 Pl(A)$	m: basic assignment Pl: plausibility function $Pl(A) = \sum m(B)$, where $B \cap A \neq \emptyset$
Confusion	$C(m) = \sum_{A \subseteq X} m(A) \log_2 Bel(A)$	m: basic assignment Bel: belief function $Bel(A) = \sum m(B)$, where $B \subseteq A$
Nonspecificity	$V(m) = \sum_{A \subseteq X} m(A) \log_2 |A|$	m: basic assignment $|A|$: cardinality of A
Fuzziness	$f_c(A) = |X| - \sum_{x \in X} |\mu_A(x)$ $- c(\mu_A(x))|$	μ_A: membership function of fuzzy set A c: fuzzy complement $|X|$: cardinality of X

methodological tool. Great skill and success in using this tool for developing predictive models in many application areas has been demonstrated by Christensen (1980-1981; 1983; 1986).

5.　　BROADER VIEWS OF UNCERTAINTY AND UNCERTAINTY-BASED INFORMATION

Notwithstanding the great significance and practical success of classical information theory, particularly the principles of maximum and minimum entropy, it has increasingly been recognized that probability theory captures only one type of uncertainty. During the last few years, significant progress has been made in understanding the concept of uncertainty in fuzzy set theory (Yager et al., 1987), possibility theory (Dubois and Prade, 1988), and the Dempster-Shafer evidence theory (Shafer, 1976). Several different types of uncertainty are now recognized within these mathematical theories, and this broader perspective helps us also to understand better the meaning of the classical Shannon entropy. Well justified measures of these various un-certainty types are specified in Table 1, where X denotes a universal set (assumed here to be finite). A self-contained summary of these uncertainty measures is contained in one of my recent papers (Klir, 1987); a thorough coverage can be found in a graduate text I co-authored with Tina Folger (Klir and Folger, 1988). Using Table 1 as a guide, let me overview these measures. I assume here that the reader is familiar with basic notions of probability, possibility, evidence, and fuzzy set theories (also covered in Klir and Folger (1988)).

The *Hartley measure* is, along with the Shannon entropy, one of the classical measures of uncertainty. It was introduced by Hartley in 1928 (Hartley, 1928) in the context of classical set theory. It measures the information necessary for the characterization of one particular element of a set containing N elements or, alternatively, the uncertainty associated with a choice among N possible alternatives. This measure, which is totally independent of any probabilistic assumptions (Rényi, 1970), has often been dismissed as a special case of the Shannon entropy. This view is ill-conceived since the two measures represent totally different types of uncertainty. The Hartley formula is a simple measure of *nonspecificity*. When it is generalized to possibility theory, we obtain the U-uncertainty. When it is further generalized to evidence theory, we obtain the general measure of nonspecificity V. The *Shannon entropy*, on the other hand, measures a degree of conflict associated with a situation under uncertainty. When generalized to evidence theory, it bifurcates into two measures, referred to as *dissonance* and *confusion*. In fuzzy set theory and possibility theory, we can also define a measure of *fuzziness*, which is still another type of uncertainty.

The U-uncertainty was initially formulated in terms of fuzzy set theory interpretation of possibility theory (Dubois and Prade, 1988) by Higashi and Klir (1983). In this interpretation, it has the form

$$U(r) = \int_0^1 \log_2 |A_\alpha| d\alpha,$$ (1)

where $|A_\alpha|$ denotes the cardinality of the $\propto$-cut A_α. An alternative, more convenient formulation of the U-uncertainty is given in Table 1, where it is assumed that the possibility distribution is ordered. The uniqueness of the U-uncertainty as a possibilistic measure of uncertainty was proven by Klir and Mariano (1987); Ramer proved the uniqueness of its generalized form in evidence theory, given by function V in Table 1 (Ramer, 1987).

The dissonance and confusion measures, which are generalizations of the Shannon entropy in evidence theory, were derived by Yager (1983) and Höhle (1982), respectively. They are often referred to as *entropy-like measures*. The uniqueness of these measures has not been established as yet.

The measure of fuzziness defined in Table 1 is based on the idea proposed by Yager (1979) that the degree of fuzziness of a fuzzy set can be measured by the lack of distinction between the set and its complement. This idea was further developed by Higashi and Klir (1982).

Except for the classical set theory and probability theory, where uncertainty of only one type is applicable (nonspecificity in set theory and dissonance in probability theory), uncertainty is basically a multi-dimensional entity. The following are the types of uncertainty applicable in the various mathematical theories of current interest:

(1)   *possibility theory* -- nonspecificity and fuzziness;

(2)   *fuzzy set theory* -- nonspecificity and fuzziness;

(3)   *evidence theory* -- nonspecificity, dissonance, and confusion;

(4)   *fuzzified evidence theory* (Yager, 1986) -- non-specificity, dissonance, confusion, and fuzziness.

This means that the classical one-dimensional information theory will have to be extended into a multidimensional information theory. Such a research program involves many challenging philosophical, mathematical, and computational issues. For example, the maximum and minimum uncertainty principles will lead either to various multiple objective criteria optimization problems or to single objective criteria optimization problems in which the objective functions would represent the relevant total uncertainties. Considering evidence theory as an example, the total uncertainty may be expressed as the sum of the three types of uncertainties, $V(m) + E(m) + C(m)$. The principle of maximum uncertainty for a problem defined within a universal set X would then be formulated as follows: determine a basic assignment $m(A)$, for all $A \subset X$, that maximizes the function

$$T(m) = \sum_{A \subset X} m(A) \log_2 \frac{|A|}{Bel(A) \cdot Pl(A)}$$ (2)

subject to given constraints $c_1, c_2, ...$, which represent the available information relevant to the matter of concern, as well as the general constraints of evidence theory.

6.   IMPLICATIONS FOR INFORMATION SYSTEMS MODELING

The maximum and minimum entropy principles have already proved very useful in information and software sciences, but their potential in these areas has not been fully realized as yet. Let me mention a few relevant examples.

Ferdinand (1974) introduced the concept of a defect entropy in a system and employed the maximum entropy principle to the investigation of the effect of modularity in a system on the number of expected defects in the system. He then applied his general results to software engineering (Ferdinand, 1972), where for each size of a computer program he determined the optimal size of modules to implement the program for which the number of expected defects is minimized. This is clearly an important result pertaining to quality control in software engineering. Bard (1980(a);1980(b)) employed the maximum entropy principle in the area of computer systems modeling and performance analysis. In particular, he used the principle for estimating state probabilities of a computer system when the probabilities of certain aggregate states are known. Other successful applications of the maximum and minimum entropy principles have been demonstrated in the areas of probabilistic data bases (Cavallo and Pittarelli, 1987; Lee, 1987; Malvestuto, 1986), image processing (Skilling, 1986), and expert systems (Kanal and Lemmer, 1986).

In spite of these successful applications of the principles of maximum and minimum entropy, it is now established that these principles involve only one of several possible types of uncertainty. This is a consequence of mathematical properties of probability theory, which do not allow any imprecision in characterizing situations under uncertainty, be it imprecision in the form of nonspecificity or vagueness. The only type of uncertainty that can be conceptualized in terms of probability theory is conflict among degrees of belief allocated to mutually exclusive alternatives. This severely limits the utilization of uncertainty as a commodity that can be traded for a reduction of complexity or increase of credibility of models in the modeling business. It is undeniable that major research must yet be undertaken not only to develop sound multidimensional principles of uncertainty in the novel mathematical theories (such as fuzzy set theory, possibility theory, or the Dempster-Shafer theory), but also to learn how to use these theories in various application areas.

Some of the novel mathematical theories capable of conceptualizing uncertainty have already been shown essential in certain areas of information systems, particularly those oriented to the storage and manipulation of knowledge in a manner compatible with human thinking. This includes the design of database and information storage and retrieval systems, as well as the design of computerized expert systems.

The need to handle information that is less than perfect in the sense of being incomplete, fragmentary, vague, contradictory, or nonspecific is the primary motivation for applying fuzzy set theory and the other novel formalisms to the design of databases and information storage and retrieval systems. The database that can accommodate imperfect information is capable of storing and manipulating not only precise facts, but also subjective experts opinions, judgments, and values that are specified in linguistic terms. Several models for databases and information retrieval systems that employ fuzzy set theory or possibility theory have been proposed during the last few years. Some examples: Buckles and Petry (1983), developed a fuzzy relational database that contains the classical (crisp) relational database as a special case; Umano (1984), Ruspini (1982), and Zemankova and Kandel (1985) described the use of possibility theory in database design; Prade (1984) discussed the applicability of possibility theory in the handling of incomplete information; the justification and advantages of applying fuzzy set theory to information retrieval system design were discussed by Radecki (1983) and this type of application was further developed by Buell (1982).

The literature describing the use of different methods of approximate reasoning is extensive. A book on the applications of fuzzy set theory in expert systems was published a few years ago (Negoita, 1985); it contains extensive notes annotating additional selected readings in the area. Another, more recent book regarding the design of fuzzy expert systems was co-authored by Hall and Kandel (1986). A large number of papers dealing with applications of fuzzy logic and the Dempster-Shafer theory to expert systems were collected by Gupta et al. (Gupta et al., 1985); this collection contains papers discussing theoretical issues in approximate reasoning, their application to expert systems design, and some actual expert systems that have been implemented using these methods of managing uncertainty.

7.   CONCLUSIONS

The relationship among complexity, credibility, and uncertainty of systems models, which is of utmost importance to systems modeling, is not well understood as yet. We only know that uncertainty is a valuable commodity, which can be traded for a reduction of complexity or increase of credibility of models. We also know that this trading should be handled by sound principles of maximum and minimum uncertainty and that these principles should involve all types of uncertainty we currently recognize. Since well-justified measures of the various types of uncertainty are now available for several mathematical frameworks in which uncertainty can be conceptualized, these principles can be made operational at a scale previously unsuspected. It is undeniable that major mathematical research must yet be undertaken to actually make these principles operational in the novel mathematical frameworks, where uncertainties of several types co-exist. However, the issues to be researched are fairly well determined since the foundations of uncertainty have been laid out in all these frameworks.

A turning point in our understanding of the concept of uncertainty was reached when it became clear that more than one type of uncertainty must be recognized within the Dempster-
-Shafer theory, and even within the restricted domain of possibility theory. This new insight into the concept of uncertainty was obtained by examining uncertainty within mathematical frameworks more

general than the two classical theories employed for characterizing uncertainty (classical set theory and probability theory).

The emergence of generalizations of existing mathematical theories is a significant current trend in mathematics, as exemplified by the change in emphasis from quantitative to qualitative from functions to relations, from graphs to hypergraphs, from ordinary geometry (Euclidean as well as non-Euclidean) to fractal geometry, from ordinary automata to dynamic cellular automata, from classical analysis to a study of singularities (catastrophe theory), from ordinary artificial languages to developmental languages, from precise analysis to interval analysis, from classical logic to logic of inconsistency, from two-valued logic to multiple-valued logics, from single objective into multiple objective criteria optimization, and, as most relevant to the subject of this paper, from probability measures to fuzzy measures and from classical set theory to fuzzy set theory. These generalizations, stimulated primarily by advances in computer technology and modern systems thinking, have enriched not only our insights but also our capabilities for modeling the intricacies of the real world.

As indicated in Section 6, the broader mathematical theories conceptualizing uncertainty have already been proven essential in the area of information systems modeling. The next step should be to replace the current ad hoc procedures for dealing with uncertainty of the various types with multi-dimensional principles of maximum and minimum uncertainty, principles that must yet be properly developed. This is my message to this conference.

REFERENCES

Bard, Y., 1980(a), Estimation of State Probabilities Using the Maximum Entropy Principle, *IBM Journal of Research and Development*, Vol. 24, No. 5, pp. 563-569.

Bard, Y., 1980(b), A Model of Shared DASD and Multipathing, *ACM Communications*, Vol. 23, No. 10, pp. 564-572.

Buckles, B. P., and Petry, F. E., 1983, Information-Theoretical Characterization of Fuzzy Relational Databases, *IEEE Trans. on Systems, Man, and Cybernetics*, Vol. SMC-13, No. 1, pp. 74-77.

Buell, D. A., 1982, An Analysis of Some Fuzzy Subset Applications to Information Retrieval Systems, *Fuzzy Sets and Systems*, Vol. 7, pp. 35-42.

Cavallo, R., and Pittarelli, M., 1987, The Theory of Probabilistic Databases, *Proc. 13th Very Large Scale Databases Conf.*, Brighton, pp. 71-81.

Christensen, R., 1980-1981, *Entropy Minimax Sourcebook (4 volumes)*, Entropy Limited, Lincoln, Mass.

Christensen, R., 1983, *Multivariate Statistical Modeling*, Entropy, Lincoln, Mass.

Christensen, R., 1986, Entropy Minimax Multivariate Statistical Modeling, *Intern. J. of General Systems*, Vol. 11, No. 3, pp. 231-277, (I. Theory); Vol. 12, No. 3, 1986, pp. 227-305 (II. Applications).

Dubois, D., and Prade, H., 1988, *Possibility Theory*, Plenum Press, New York.

Ferdinand, A. E., 1972, *Quality in Programming*, IBM Technical Report 21, 485, Kingston, NY, June 1972.

Ferdinand, A. E., 1974, A Theory of System Complexity, *Intern. J. of General Systems*, Vol. 1, No. 1, pp. 19-33.

Gupta, M. M., Kandel, A., Bandler, W., and Kiszka, J. B., (eds.), 1985, *Approximate Reasoning in Expert Systems*, North-Holland, New York.

Hall, L., and Kandel, A., 1986, *Designing Fuzzy Expert Systems*, TÜV Rheinland, Köln.

Hartley, R.V.L., 1928, Transmission of Information, *The Bell Systems Technical J.*, Vol. 7, pp. 535-563.

Higashi, M., and Klir, G. J., 1982, On Measures of Fuzziness and Fuzzy Complements, *Intern. J. of General Systems*, Vol. 8, No. 3, pp. 169-180.

Higashi, M., and Klir, G. J., 1983, Measures of Uncertainty and Information Based on Possibility Distributions, *Intern. J. of General Systems*, Vol. 9, No. 1, pp. 43-58.

Höhle, U., 1982, Entropy with Respect to Plausibility Measures, *Proc. 12th IEEE Intern. Symp. on Multiple Valued Logic*, Paris, pp. 167-169.

Islam, S., 1974, Toward Integration of Two System Theories by Mesarovic and Wymore, *Intern. J. of General Systems*, Vol. 1, No. 1, pp. 35-40.

Jaynes, E. T., 1983, *Papers on Probability, Statistics and Statistical Physics*, Rosenkrantz, R. D., ed., Reidel, Boston.

Kanal, L. N., and Lemmer, J. F., (eds.), 1986, *Uncertainty in Artificial Intelligence*, North-Holland, New York.

Klir, G. J., 1985(a), *Architecture of Systems Problem Solving*, Plenum Press, New York.

Klir, G. J., 1985(b), The Many Faces of Complexity, *The Science and Praxis of Complexity*, The United Nations University, Tokyo, pp. 81-98.

Klir, G. J., 1987, When Do We Stand on Measures of Uncertainty, Ambiguity, Fuzziness, and the Like?, *Fuzzy Sets and Systems*, Vol. 24, No. 2, pp. 141-160.

Klir, G. J., and Folger, T. A., 1988, *Fuzzy Sets, Uncertainty and Information*, Prentice Hall, Englewood Cliffs, NJ.

Klir, G. J., and Mariano, M., 1987, On the Uniqueness of Possibilistic Measure of Uncertainty and Information, *Fuzzy Sets and Systems*, Vol. 24, No. 2, 197-219.

Lee, T. T., 1987, An Information-Theoretic Analysis of Relational Databases, *IEEE Trans. on Software Engineering*, Vol. SE-13, No. 10, pp. 1049-1072.

Lofgren, L. 1977, Complexity of Descriptions of Systems: A Foundational Study, *Intern. J. of General Systems*, Vol. 3, pp. 197-214.

Malvestuto, F. M., 1986, Statistical Treatment of the Information Content of a Database, *Information Systems*, Vol. 11, No. 3, pp. 211-223.

Mesarovic, M. D., and Takahara, Y., 1975, *General Systems Theory: Mathematical Foundations*, Academic Press, New York.

Negoita, C. V., 1985, *Expert Systems and Fuzzy Systems*, Benjamin/Cummings, Menlo Park, CA.

Prade, H., 1984, Lipski's Approach to Incomplete Information, Data Bases Restated and Generalized in the Setting of Zadeh's Possibility Theory, *Information System*, Vol. 9, No. 1, pp. 27-42.

Radecki, T., 1983, A Theoretical Background for Applying Fuzzy Set Theory in Information Retrieval, *Fuzzy Sets and Systems*, Vol. 10, pp. 169-183.

Ramer, A., 1987, Uniqueness of Information Measure in the Theory of Evidence, *Fuzzy Sets and Systems*, Vol. 24, No. 2, pp. 183-196.

Rényi, A., 1970, *Probability Theory*, North-Holland, Amsterdam, (Chapter IX, *Introduction to Information Theory*, pp. 540-616).

Ruspini, E. H., 1982, Possibility Theory Approaches for Advanced Information Systems, *Computer*, Sept. 1982, pp. 83-91.

Shafer, G., 1976, *A Mathematical Theory of Evidence*, Princeton University Press, Princeton.

Simon, H. A., 1969, *The Sciences of the Artificial*, MIT Press, Cambridge, Mass.

Skilling, J., 1986, Theory of Maximum Entropy Image Reconstruction, *Maximum Entropy and Bayesian Methods in Applied Statistics*, Justice, J. H., ed., Cambridge University Press, Cambridge.

Umano, M., 1984, Retrieval from Fuzzy Database by Fuzzy Relational Algebra, *Fuzzy Information Knowledge Representation and Decision Analysis*, Sanchez, E., (ed.), Pergamon Press, Oxford, pp. 1-6.

Wymore, A. W., 1969, *A Mathematical Theory of Systems Engineering: The Elements*, John Wiley, New York.

Yager, R. R., 1979, On the Measure of Fuzziness and Negation. Part I: Membership in the Unit Interval, *Intern. J. of General Systems*, Vol. 5, No. 4, pp. 221-229.

Yager, R. R., 1983, Entropy and Specificity in a Mathematical Theory of Evidence, *Intern. J. of General Systems*, Vol. 9, No. 4, pp. 249-260.

Yager, R. R., 1986, Toward General Theory of Reasoning with Uncertainty: Nonspecificity and Fuzziness, *Intern. J. of Intelligent Systems*, Vol. 1, No. 1, pp. 45-67.

Yager, R. R. et al. (eds.), 1987, *Fuzzy Sets and Applications: Selected Papers by L.A. Zadeh*, Wiley-Interscience, New York.

Zeigler, B. P., 1976, *Theory of Modelling and Simulation*, John Wiley, New York.

Zemankova, M., and Kandel, A., 1985, Implementing Imprecision in Information Systems, *Information Sciences*, Vol. 37, pp. 107141.

CAST - MODELLING APPROACHES IN SOFTWARE DESIGN

Franz Pichler

Institute of Systems Science
Department of Systems Theory and Information Engineering
Johannes Kepler University Linz
A-4040 Linz - Austria

Abstract: Production of software for complex scientific and engineering computing requires high quality design. This paper explores application of system theory instrumented modelling and simulation with automated support to the design of software. The paper discusses the Development of Computer Aided Systems Theory (CAST) method banks as a research program at Johannes Kepler University of Linz/Austria.

1. INTRODUCTION

A fundamental requirement for the production of software for application in the field of complex scientific and engineering computing is high quality of design. This paper is devoted to software design of that type as seen from the viewpoint of systems theory. The use of systems theory allows modelling in a top-down fashion, so that an initial given specification of requirements is realized by a goal specification which is well suited for programming. For that task we consequently pursue a systems theory instrumented modelling and simulation philosophy. It is evident that modelling in that sense requires computer support. Therefore, in order to design models for simulation - and problem-solving software, we suggest the development of CAST-method banks. CAST stands for "Computer *A*ided *S*ystems *T*heory", a research program at the Johannes Kepler University of Linz/Austria.

The application of CAST tools for the design of software allows optimal representation and structuring such that an effective implementation on any hardware is possible. Furthermore, CAST instrumented design of software allows the consideration of important features in an early stage of the design process, e.g., "design for testability" or "design for portability".

2. CAST METHOD BANK CONCEPT

Systems theory has found important applications in engineering, especially in electrical engineering and in control engineering. "Linear Systems Theory" for example, offers important concepts and methods for modelling and simulation tasks, when ordinary linear differential - or difference equations are the dominant mathematical objects. This is for example the case for electrical networks of the lumped RLC kind. Due to the progress in analog circuit chip technology this field of application is today becoming increasingly more important.

Systems theory supports the functional (behavioral) part of the design process. It enables the "top down" refinement of models such that a proper level of description for interfacing with subsequent engineering design and assembling techniques is attainable. A CAST method bank is defined as an interactive method bank for systems theory, which supports the application of systems theory in such design tasks. As for any method bank, we can assume that a CAST method bank is described in a 3-level model as shown in Figure 1.

Empirical Foundations of Information and Software Science V
Edited by P. Zunde and D. Hocking, Plenum Press, New York, 1990

39

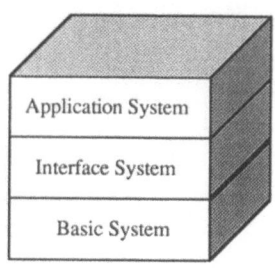

Figure 1. 3-Level Model of a CAST Method Bank.

The basic system is established by the programming environment (which is offered on a certain workstation). The application system, in which we are here primarily interested, realizes the CAST specific functions. To be more specific, the application system has to provide the means for storing and recalling the different systems objects needed in CAST. Furthermore, it has to offer to the user the CAST specific transformations for the manipulation of such systems object enabling the attainment of a proper refinement of models as well as of related problem-solution methods.

The interface system realizes in a user friendly fashion the functions needed by the application systems. As a framework for the realization of the application system of a CAST-method bank Pichler (1988) suggests the use of the so called STIPS-machine STIPS.M. We will here briefly describe the construction of STIPS.M and, subsequently, extend this concept by introducing a more structured Turing-machine-like framework in the form of the STIX-machine STIX.M.

STIX.M is best described as a kind of state machine for symbolic processing of (formal) systems specifications. The "state set" X is given by mathematical objects, which are either interpreted as formal models (in the case of a synthesis task) or as intermediate results (in the case of an analysis task). The transformations T which relate the states of STIPS.M to each other are assumed to be of one of the following kinds:

(1) a transformation T uniquely relates a system specification S to another system specification S'; S' = T(S).

(2) a transformation T uniquely relates a set (S_i) of systems specifications to another systems specification S'; S'=T((S_i)).

It is convenient to define the (partial) state machine STIPS.M by the tripel STIPS.M = (X,T,Δ), where T denotes a set of all transformations **T** and Δ is a set of productions of the kind S, T→S' and S_1,

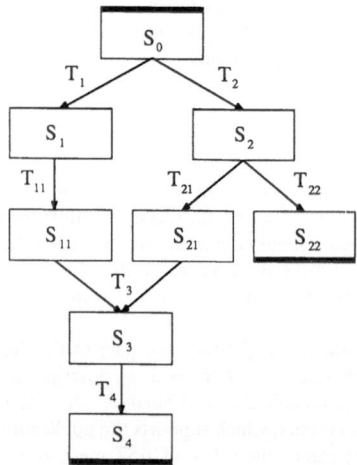

Figure 2. State-trajectory of a STIPS-machine.

$S_2,...,S_k,T \rightarrow S'$) which define for STIPS.M the state transition. For the operation of STIPS.M the selection of the transformation which should be applied is done by the user.

Figure 2 shows a state-trajectory of an hypothetical STIPS.machine.

For the proper and sequential selection of state transitions in STIPS.M we add a control part CONTR.M = (N,M) consisting of a petri-net N = (P,T,n) together with an associated set M of markings. Here P denotes the set of places, T is the set of transformations of STIPS.M and n is a function $n:T \rightarrow P(P) \times P(P)$ which assigns to each transformation T a pair n(t) = (U,V), where U are the pre-places of T and V are the post-places of T.

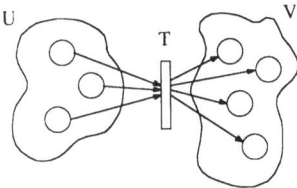

The initialization of the petri-net N is determined by the selection of an initial marking $m_0:P \rightarrow N_0$ from M. A transformation T of STIPS.M may be selected for application if the existing making m of CONTR.M allows the firing of T in N.

We demonstrate the working of CONTR.M for STIPS.M using the example in Figure 2. A possible control-machine for this example of a STIPS-machine is shown in Figure 3. It is initialized by a marking m_0.

The state graph of the initialized control machine is shown in the diagram for Figure 4.

The specific individual markings of the state diagram of Figure 4 are given in Table 1.

Our example of CONTR.M for STIPS.M shows that the following input-words w navigate STIPS.M from the initial systems specifications S_0 to the final systems specification $\{S_4,S_{22}\}$

$$w_1 = T_1 T_2 T_{22} T_{21} T_3 T_4$$
$$w_2 = T_1 T_2 T_{21} T_{22} T_3 T_4$$
$$w_3 = T_1 T_2 T_{21} T_3 T_{22} T_4$$
$$w_4 = T_1 T_2 T_{21} T_3 T_4 T_{22}$$

In order to make STIPS.M a Turing-like machine for symbol information processing we have to equip STIPS.M (in addition to CONTR.M) with I/O channels which interface with the user-environment.

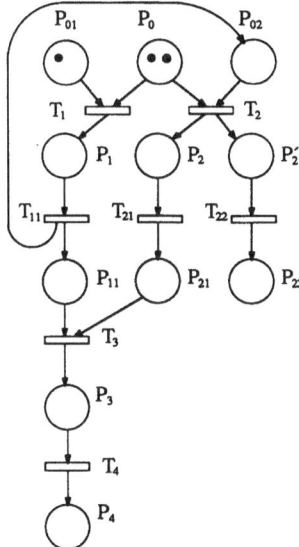

Figure 3. A Control-Machine CONTR.M for the trajectory in Figure 2.

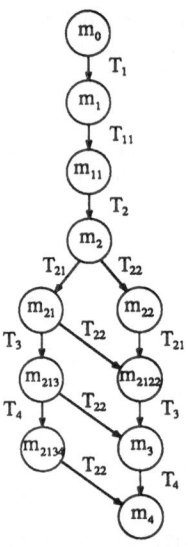

Figure 4. State Diagram of the Control Machine of Figure 3.

The input-channel is provided by an input-coding α A→ P(X)xM which maps a given problem definition A from **A** into a pair $\alpha(A)$ = $((S_i),m_0)$ consisting of an initial systems object (S_i) of STIPS.M together with an initial marking m_0 for **N**.

The output-channel is realized by an output-coding β:P(X) →**B** which maps a systems   object (S_i')

Table 1

Markings $m_0,...,m_4$ From the State Diagram of Figure 4

1 2 0 0 0 0 0 0 0 0 0 m_0	0 1 0 1 0 0 0 0 0 0 0 m_1	0 1 1 0 0 0 1 0 0 0 0 m_{11}	0 0 0 0 1 1 1 0 0 0 0 m_2
0 0 0 0 1 1 1 0 0 0 m_{21}	0 0 0 0 1 0 1 0 1 0 0 m_{221}	0 0 0 0 0 1 0 0 0 1 0 m_{213}	0 0 0 0 0 0 1 1 1 0 0 m_{2122}
0 0 0 0 0 1 0 0 0 0 1 m_{2134}	0 0 0 0 0 0 0 0 1 0 1 m_3	0 0 0 0 0 0 0 0 1 0 1 m_4	$P_{01}P_0P_{02}$ $P_1\ P_2\ P_2'$ $P_{11}P_{21}P_{22}$ P_3 P_4 m

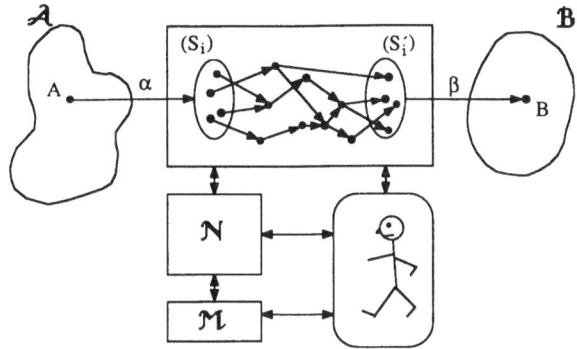

Figure 5. STIX.M Schematic Block Diagram.

which is finally reached by STIPS.M into a proper goal specification which is to be accepted by the users of CAST results.

We have now finished the imbedding of STIPS.M into a more structured framework which also takes full care of control and of I/O functions. We call the structure consisting of STIPS.M together with CONTR.M and α and β a STIX-machine STIX.M = (STIPS.M, CONTR.M,A,B,α,β).

In Figure 5 we show a schematic block-diagram of STIX.M.

The construction of the STIX-machine STIX.M is similar to the concept of the X-machine as introduced by Eilenberg (1974). The motivation to enrich the function of STIPS.M in that fashion came from reading the papers of Holcombe (1987; 1988), in which the X-machine is applied to similar problems of systems specifications, especially to the problem of specifying a user-interface.

3. CAST.FSM, A CAST METHOD BANK FOR FINITE STATE MACHINES

In this section, we want to report on an application of the concept of the STIX-machine for the implementation of an interactive method bank to be applied to the design of Finite State Machines. The intended use of such a CAST.method bank is in the field of VLSI-design, where a scientific support design approach is badly needed. It will help us cope with the complexity of and the increasing number of requirements placed on the design of such circuitry (e.g, "design for testability").

In the following, we will give a short description of this method bank, which we have designated as CAST.FSM. The reader interested in more details is advised to consult Pichler and Prähofer (1988), Mittelmann (1988), and Pichler and Schwärtzel (1988).

Figure 6 shows a 3-level model of CAST.FSM.

For the basic system of CAST.FSM an Interlisp-D/Loops programming environment is used; it is run on a Xerox "dandelion" workstation 1108 (or equivalently Siemens workstation 5815). The features of this programming environment (object oriented programming, window-techniques, mouse) allow a convenient implementation of the application system STIX.FSM.

Now we will give a short description of STIX.FSM. We would like to begin by discussing STIPS.FSM, the state machine for symbolic transformation of FSM-specific systems objects. The following FSM systems specifications considered in STIPS.M are typically:

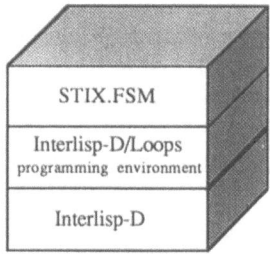

Figure 6. 3-Level Model of CAST.FSM.

(a)

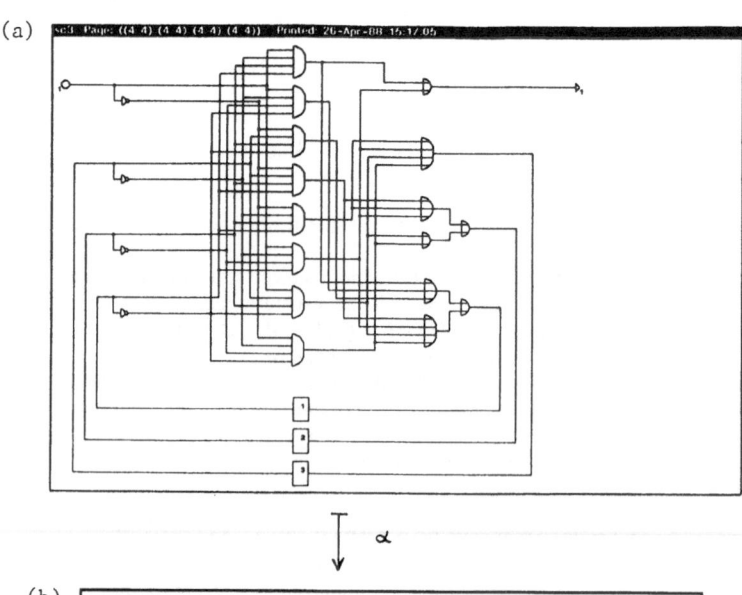

α

(b)

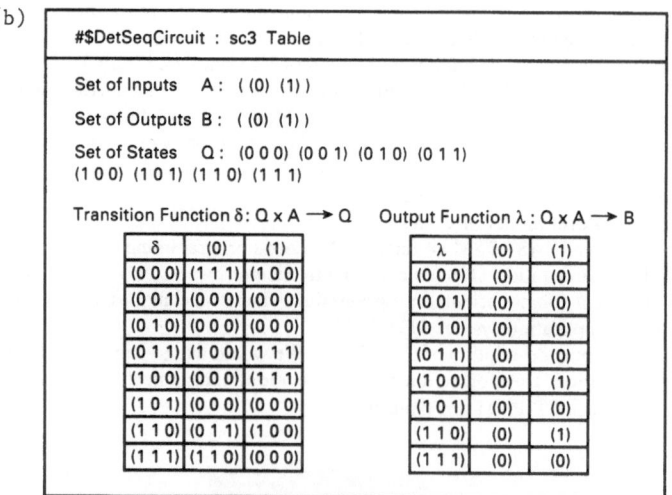

#$DetSeqCircuit : sc3 Table

Set of Inputs   A: ((0) (1))

Set of Outputs B: ((0) (1))

Set of States   Q: (0 0 0) (0 0 1) (0 1 0) (0 1 1) (1 0 0) (1 0 1) (1 1 0) (1 1 1)

Transition Function δ: Q x A → Q   Output Function λ: Q x A → B

δ	(0)	(1)
(0 0 0)	(1 1 1)	(1 0 0)
(0 0 1)	(0 0 0)	(0 0 0)
(0 1 0)	(0 0 0)	(0 0 0)
(0 1 1)	(1 0 0)	(1 1 1)
(1 0 0)	(0 0 0)	(1 1 1)
(1 0 1)	(0 0 0)	(0 0 0)
(1 1 0)	(0 1 1)	(1 0 0)
(1 1 1)	(1 1 0)	(0 0 0)

λ	(0)	(1)
(0 0 0)	(0)	(0)
(0 0 1)	(0)	(0)
(0 1 0)	(0)	(0)
(0 1 1)	(0)	(0)
(1 0 0)	(0)	(1)
(1 0 1)	(0)	(0)
(1 1 0)	(0)	(1)
(1 1 1)	(0)	(0)

Figure 7.   (a) Boolean Logic Diagram BLD of a sequential switching circuit.
(b) FSM = α(BLD) in table form.

- Finite State Machines (FSM) given by the δ/λ table
- Linear Finite State Machines (FSM) given by the associated matrices
- Finite sequences (works) over an arbitrary alphabet
- Register Flow Machines (RFM)(= Turing-machine model of an FSM)
- Networks of FSM's
- Lattices of FSM's
- Partitions of the FSM-state set

These objects may appear as part of the initial systems specification (S_i) or as objects which are reached by intermediate states of symbolic processing. They form a part of the database X of STIX.FSM.

From the set **T** of transformations of STIX.FSM which are implemented in CAST.FSM we will here mention the following examples:

- computation of the quotient FSM/δ of FSM

- computation of the lattice L(FSM) of FSM

- computation of a linear realization of FSM

- computation of a realization of FSM by binary shift registers.

(a)

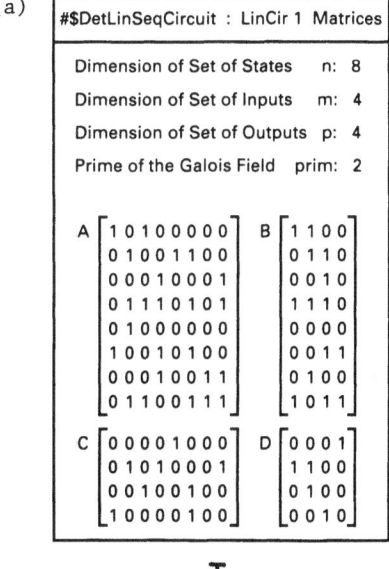

(b)

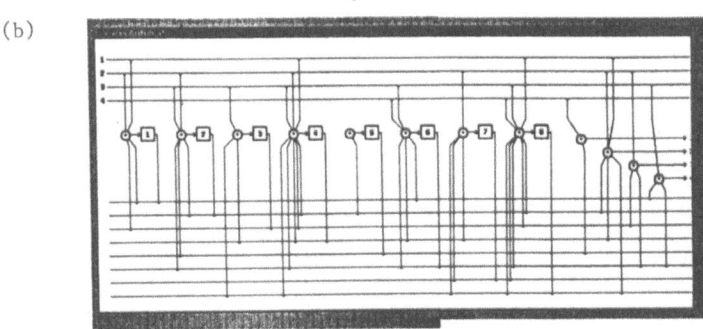

Figure 8. (a) LFSM in matrix form.
(b) Information Flow Diagram IFD = β(LFSM).

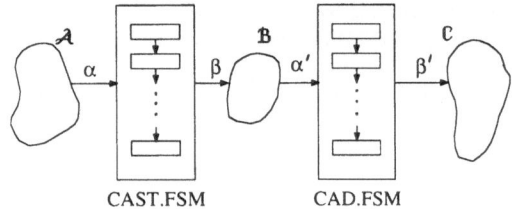

CAST.FSM   CAD.FSM

Figure 9. Connection of CAST.FSM to CAD tools for FSM hardware design.

computation of a binary linear shift register of minimal length which generates a given periodic binary sequence.

At the current stage of the development of CAST.FSM we have omitted to implement the control machine CONTR.M. However, a later version of CAST.FSM will have the full features of STIX.M.

Concerning input-coding and output-coding, these functions are only partly realized in CAST.FSM. Figure 7 shows an example of input coding, which is defined for a Boolean Logic Diagram BLD of a sequential switching circuit. The BLD can be edited by CAST.FSM and mapped into a corresponding finite state machine; FSM $= \alpha$(BLD).

For certain systems objects the current version of CAST.FSM also makes possible the application of the output coding β during symbolic processing. Generally, β has in CAST.FSM the task of transforming computed results into a CAD-acceptable form. Figure 8 shows an example of such a transformation in CAST.FSM, where a linear finite state machine LFSM is represented by β as an information flow diagram IFD $= \beta$(LFSM).

Figure 9 shows how CAST.FSM is connected with the CAD tools which might be available for FSM hardware design.

4.   CAST TOOLS FOR SOFTWARE DESIGN

Just as in the case of hardware, one could imagine that CAST methods might also be applied to the functional portion of software design. Certainly, for special areas of software design such tools already exist (even when they are not identified as "CAST methods"). This is especially true for application software in communication engineering and digital signal processing and also in the field of control engineering (Jamshidi and Herget, 1985). However, there are also some elaborated parts of systems theory, which, when implemented on a CAST method bank, could give strong support to software design in a wide area of applications. As examples we point to the work of Klir (1985), Zeigler (1984), Rozenblit (1988), and Wymore (1976, 1980). However, we want to mention the fact, that for the general applicability of CAST methods in software design, it will also be necessary to develop new avenues in systems theory which take into account the special properties of software design. It will be especially important to develop systems types which are close enough to the data-and control-structures used in programming. However, the driving force for such an "updating" of systems theory has to come from computer science itself. One can ask oneself at this point why such a contribution has not yet been developed. Theoretical computer science has so far largely concentrated its efforts upon the development of the theory of algorithms (complexity of algorithms, theory of computability), the theory of automata (in the sense of the Chomsky-hierarchy) and the related theory of formal languages and other special problem areas. These subjects were of considerable practical interest in the sixties, when the need for new programming languages and effective compilers for it, was urgent. It seems that until today theoretical computer science is still evolved in the same type of research. The "software crisis" of which the computer science community became aware in the mid sixties gave birth to the field of software engineering (Bauer, 1973). However, it seems to me, that theoretical computer science did not devote sufficient attention to this field. The contributions which have come from programming usually apply only to lower levels and usually emphasize the structural part of software design, in which programming languages dominantly influence the design activities. For the higher levels of software design these results are of less importance. A similar situation can be seen in hardware design, where physical and electrical aspects of transistor logic are of minor importance above the register transfer level.

The foregoing arguments, although they might seem provoking to most of the readers, will, hopefully, serve to stimulate a renewed theoretical investigation of software design for early phases of the design cycle.

Furthermore, it could encourage the implementation of the results in the form of tools for method banks.

In such activities, in which modelling and simulation techniques obviously play an important role, there is also a chance for systems theory and for "CAST" to make substantial contributions.

5. FIRST STEPS TOWARD A CAST METHOD BANK FOR SOFTWARE DESIGN

In the following we will try to apply the concept if the STIX-machine STIX.M, which was introduced in Chapter 2, to the construction of the application system of a CAST-method bank for software design. However, it should be mentioned, that our investigation only has exploratory character and will have to be corrected on the basis of practical experience after implementation and application.

As defined in Chapter 2, a STIX-machine STIX.M can be defined by the list $STIX.M = (STIPS.M, CONTR.M, A, \alpha, B, \beta)$.

To facilitate comprehension, we want to repeat the significance of the individual components of STIX.M.

(STIPS.M)   The state machine STIPS.M, which is the "CPU" for STIX.M consists of a tripel $STIPS.M = (X, T, \Delta)$ where X is the set of systems specifications, T is the set of systems transformations and Δ denotes the state transition relation which is usually defined by means of production rules of the kind, $S, T \rightarrow S'$ and $(S_i), T \rightarrow S'$, respectively, where $s, s' \in X$, $(S_i) \in P(X)$ and $T \in T$.

(CONTR.M)   The control-machine $CONTR.M = (N, M)$ consists of the petri-net $N = (P, T, n)$ together with the set M of markings of the kind $m : P \rightarrow N_0$ for N.

(A, α) α is a map $\alpha : A \rightarrow P(X) \times M$ which maps a given problem definition A into an initial systems problems $\alpha(A) = ((S_i) m_0)$ of STIX.M.

(B, β) β is a map $\beta : P(X) \rightarrow$ which translates a result (S_i') which is attained by STIX.M into a goal-specific form $\beta((S_i'))$, that can be accepted by the subsequent CAD tool.

To apply STIX.M to software design we have to identify the meaning of the different components in respect to that special domain. The goal is to get a specific STIX-machine STIX.SOF which can serve for the implementation of an application system CAST.SOF of a CAST method bank for software design.

The set A of STIX.SOF has to be defined according to the usual requirements which are valid in software design. We will not explore here the different techniques which are currently being used. Certainly the best techniques for the construction of A of STIX.SOF would be ones, which facilitate the implementation of input coding α.

The image $\alpha(A)$ of a problem definition A by α is generally given by $\alpha(A) = (S_i), m_0)$. In STIX.SOF (S_i) has to consist of a set of systems specifications which are relevant to software design. The marking m_0 "points" to a subset of systems specifications of (S_i) at which transformations (which are also determined by m_0) can be initially applied. At this point we must decide, whether a modeling task (synthesis problem) or a problem solving task (analysis problem) is to be done by STIX.SOF.

In the case of a modeling task, the set (S_i) very often consists of relations (or functions) which describe the behavior of the system. In this case, the marking m_0 often fulfills the purpose of putting constraints on the initial relations and on the systems specifications computed therewith. In the second case, the case in which STIX.SOF is being applied to the solution of an analysis problem, a requirement is that $\alpha(A) = ((S_i), m_0)$ describes a well-defined system theoretical problem. This must be addressed to (S_i). Here the marking $m_0 : P \rightarrow N_0$ plays an important role in the definition of this system-problem and also in the definition of the constraints on the problem-solving process. In solving analysis problems all known systems-types may be used for the definition of (S_i) in STIX.M.

Next, we want to investigate some questions which are related to the STIPS-machine STIPS.SOF of STIX.SOF. Here again, we should distinguish between synthesis and analysis. In the case of synthesis our problem is to transform (S_i) by a sequence of well-selected transformations T into a data-structure well-suited for subsequent programming.

There are a number of methods known from software engineering which can help us to find a proper systems theoretical interpretation for the kind of symbolic processing of systems specifications required by STIPS.SOF. As early contributions to this theme we refer to Zurcher and Randell (1968) and Bauer (1973). Both deal with "top-down" design techniques in the general sense of "structured programming". Their counterparts in systems theory are the methods for top-down design of multi-strata systems (Mesarovic, Macko, and Takahara, 1970). Again, the same philosophy has been applied to the development of the existing software design techniques, such as for example the Jackson-method.

Finally, we want to mention a few ideas for the construction of the output coding β of STIX.SOF. Any goal-specification (S$_i$') which is reached by STIX.SOF should be acceptable for the programming task which has to follow.

The currently available user interface techniques (window, mouse, and menu techniques) allow the construction of β such that these requirements are optimally fulfilled.

6. CONCLUSION

In this paper we have tried to show what role systems theory can play in software design. One central aspect is the provision of CAST method banks, which are interactive method banks, for the enhancement of the skills of the software designer. As a basic framework for the construction of the application system of such a method bank we have introduced the concept of the STIX-machine STIX.M.

To give a concrete example of a CAST method bank we discussed in Section 3 CAST.FSM, an interactive method bank for finite state machine design. CAST.FSM is implemented in INTERLISP-D/LOOPS on a XEROX dandelion workstation 1108.

Section 4 dealt with basic questions concerning the applicability of systems theory to software design.

Section 5 discussed some ideas for the construction of STIX.SOF, a STIX-machine for software design.

Since the author is by no means a specialist in practical aspects of software design, it is all too clear that many arguments, which were presented here, will not be generally acceptable to software design specialists.

However, I hope, that the content of this paper will stimulate discussion concerning software design tools which allow the application of systems theory.

7. ACKNOWLEDGEMENTS

I should like to thank Herbert Prähofer and Hermann Hellwagner their helpful and stimulating comments.

8. REFERENCES

Bauer, F. L., ed., 1973, Advanced Course on Software Engineering, *Lecture Notes in Economics and Mathematical Systems*.

Eilenberg, S., 1974, *Automata, Languages and Machines*, Vol. A, Academic Press.

Holcombe, M., 1987, Goal Directed Task Analysis and Formal Interface Specifications, *International Command & Control, Communications & Information Systems*, Vol. 1, No. 4, pp. 14-22.

Holcombe, M., 1988, X-Machines as a Basis for Dynamic Systems Specification, *Software Engineering Journal*, March 1988 pp. 69-88.

Jamshidi, M., and Herget, C. J., 1985, *Computer-Aided Control Systems Engineering*, Series 1, North Holland, Amsterdam, Springer Verlag, Berlin.

Klir, G. J., 1985, *The Architecture of Problem Solving*, Plenum Publishing Corporation, New York.

Mesarovic, M. D., Macko, D., and Takahara, Y., 1970, *Theory of Hierarchical, Multi-level Systems*, Academic Press, New York.

Mittelmann, R., 1988, Object Oriented Implementation of Petri Nets Concepts, *Cybernetics and Systems '88*, Trappl, R., ed., Kluwer Academic Publishers, Dordrecht, pp. 759-766.

Pichler, F., 1988, CAST-Computer Aided Systems Theory: A Framework for Interactive Method Banks, *Cybernetics and Systems '88*, Trappl, R., ed., Kluwer Academic Publishers, Dordrecht, pp. 731-736.

Pichler, F., and Prähofer, H., 1988, CAST.FSM Computer Aided Systems Theory: Finite State Machines, *Cybernetics and Systems '88*, Trappl, R., ed., Kluwer Academic Publishers, Dordrecht, pp. 737-742.

Pichler, F., and Schwärtzel, H., 1989, CAST: Computerunterstützte Systemtheorie Konstruktion interaktiver Methodenbanken, book manuscript 1988 (intended for publication at Springer Verlag Berlin 1989).

Rozenblit, J., 1988, Systems Theory Instrumented Simulation Modeling, *Proceedings of the 1988 Winter Simulation Conference*, San Diego, California, December 1988 (to appear).

Wymore, A. W., 1976, *Systems Engineering Methodology for Interdisciplinary Teams*, John Wiley & Sons, New York.

Wymore, A. W., 1980, *A Mathematical Theory of System Design*, Engineering Experiment Station, College of Engineering, The University of Arizona, Tucson.

Zeigler, B. P., 1984, *Multifaceted Modelling and Discrete Event Simulation*, Academic Press, London.

Zurcher, F. W., and Randell, B, 1968, Interactive Multi-Level Modelling, *IFIP Congress Proceedings*, Amsterdam, North Holland, 1968, pp. D138-D142.

ORGANIZATIONAL INTEGRATION:

MODELING TECHNOLOGY AND MANAGEMENT

Brian R. Gaines

Knowledge Science Institute
University of Calgary
Calgary, Alberta
CANADA T2N 1N4
gaines@calgary.cdn

Abstract: In many major areas of activity, the factory, the office, the hospital, there is a move towards computer integrated systems involving the total functioning of the organization. MAP, TOP, and MIB are not just network specifications, application-oriented expansions of the ISO-OSI parameters. They each involve new conceptual frameworks for the role of computers within their areas of application. They each entail major changes in the way their user organizations operate. This paper presents a model of the information technologies underlying computer-integrated systems, their relation to the structure and culture of the organization, the state of the art in those technologies at research, innovation and product line levels, and the potential and problems in their integration.

INTRODUCTION

In many major areas of activity - factories, offices, banks, hospitals - there is a move towards computer integrated systems involving the total functioning of the organization. Integrated heterogeneous network architectures such as MAP, TOP and MIB are not just network specifications, application-oriented expansions of the ISO-OSI parameters. They each involve new conceptual frameworks for the role of computers within their areas of application. They each entail major changes in the way their user organizations operate. We have entered an era of *system integration* where the dominant theme in information systems development is the integration of diverse technologies into unified systems.

In the late 1960s suppliers of computer-based information systems found it necessary to form separate system integration divisions to cope with the complexities of hard- ware and software interaction and integration. The ad hoc activities of such divisions have grown to become major cost centers, and it is no longer possible to treat system integration as a fairly informal customization stage in system pro- duction. This has focused developmental effort on system integration as a major technology in its own right.

In the 1980s integration is the primary developmental thrust in all areas, and at all levels, of information systems:

- For personal computer applications it is the integration of spread-sheets, word processors, databases and telecommunications in packages such as *Symphony* and *Framework*, or through environments such as that of the MacIntosh and *Windows* (Gordon, 1984);

- For data processing it is the integration of all records within an organization into a uniformly structured database at the core of all applications (Nolan, 1983);

- For network technology it is the integration of diverse services on a broad-band carrier, such as a fibre-optic link, to provide integrated service digital networks (Bartee, 1986);

Empirical Foundations of Information and Software Science V
Edited by P. Zunde and D. Hocking, Plenum Press, New York, 1990

51

- For network applications it is the integration of diverse multiple sub-systems within a single networking framework through protocols such as MAP (General Motors, 1984), TOP (Boeing, 1986) and MIB (Leopold, 1986);

- For frontiers computer research it is the integration of the fourth generation technologies of databases, distributed systems and supercomputers, together with the fifth generation technologies of pattern recognition, artificial intelligence and expert systems, to provide a new generation of knowledge-based systems (Moto-oka, 1982; Gaines, 1984);

- For frontiers information science research it is the integration of the multiple disciplines of knowledge processing - philosophy, neurology, psychology, linguistics, anthropology and sociology - to provide new foundations for knowledge science (STA, 1985; Gaines, 1986(b)).

As usual in the development of new technologies, however, the thrust towards integrated systems, while solving old problems also creates new ones:

- First, the overall complexity of the total system after integration can be very high. This is, of course, the object - to design, develop, and implement complex systems by integrating a number of simpler ones. Success in such an approach to system design is critically dependent on decoupling the system layers - only the functionality of the lower levels must be relevant to the upper levels -consideration of their implementation and operation should be irrelevant to the system design. How- ever, this decoupling is not easily achieved - it becomes the major, and most problematic, design objective.

- Second, the problems of designing complex systems are exacerbated if the components include not only hardware and software, but also people. The livewire component may be designed in part by selection and training, but there remains a massive residual uncertainty about its functionality and performance that conventionally requires human "management". The integration of people and the associated management processes into large-scale integrated systems presents major new problems. In particular, the management structures already in place are unlikely to be appropriate to the overall integrated system. Major changes in organizational structure and corporate culture will generally be necessary to the effective implementation and operation of large-scale integrated systems.

- Third, the classic approach to the design of complex systems is based on homogeneous system concepts - that the overall system is designed as a set of related components developed with mutual interaction in mind. Heterogeneity may be introduced in the design of such systems, but its introduction is a design decision made in the light of overall system functioning, not as a result of the fairly anarchical evolution of systems not originally intended to be integrated. However, we have to face the problem in large-scale heterogeneous systems that they have not been 'designed', and that large part of the systems created by our attempts at integration are anarchical. We cannot 'homogenize' such systems but we still need some overall conceptual model that is sufficiently homogeneous, at least in the facilities the model offers us, for us to manage them.

Fortunately, the advances in technology that have created these problems also bring with them the means of solution (Gaines, 1988(a)). Knowledge-based systems provide a technology suited to modeling the diversity and complexity of integrated heterogeneous systems. The model can encompass as much detail as required to capture the important features of the system. The operational form of the model makes it possible to simulate system behavior at various levels of detail. The high-level representation makes it possible to use the model to aid designers and advise users. There are major problems in keeping the model up-to-date which place important constraints on the implementation and application of such knowledge-based systems. However, these constraints are intrinsic to the operation of heterogeneous systems, and the modeling approach throws light on the fundamental problems.

The research described in this paper is targeted on the development of knowledge-based network support systems in which an object-oriented knowledge base is used to model a heterogeneous system. The support system is designed to be effective with a minimal knowledge base of: the processors and peripherals on the network; software packages and where they can be run; users and their normal activities; and active processes and current loading. The object structure allows this knowledge to be expanded to greater levels of detail in particular areas as required. The system supports users of varying levels of skill and requirements to make more effective use of the network computing resources by advising them on

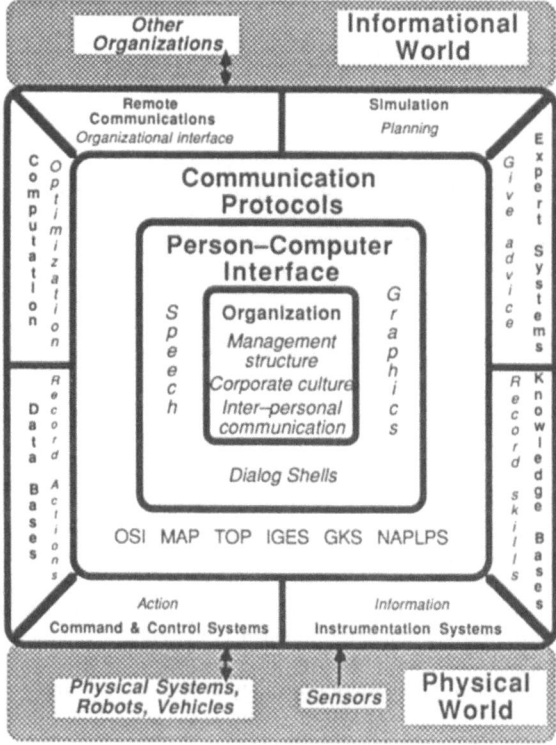

Figure 1. Structure of an Integrated Heterogeneous System.

software, processor and processing availability. It also supports network managers in resource planning, security violation detection and load balancing.

The concepts underlying the intelligent network support system design are that: much can be achieved through the availability of small amount of processible knowledge *about* the network; it is better to keep a small knowledge base correct than to provide a large knowledge base that is out of date; and there will be a heterogeneity of knowledge requirements and the capabilities to keep the knowledge base up-to-date. The initial implementation is in Smalltalk on a network of some 30 workstations under NCS, including Sun, Apollo, Macintosh, Iris, and Symbolics, and access to Vax, Butterfly, Multics and Cyber 205 mainframes. The overall design is targeted on communities without specialist computing knowledge using heterogeneous networks for purposes such as computer-integrated manufacturing, dispersed process instrumentation and control, and collaborative research.

INTEGRATED HETEROGENEOUS SYSTEMS

Figure 1 shows the information systems in a typical integrated heterogeneous system, such as a banking system using ATMs or a modern production unit using computer integrated manufacturing techniques. The outer ring comprises eight basic information technologies that together support the organization and its interface to the physical and organizational worlds. The center shows the organization itself with its corporate structure, and the rings surrounding it show the human interfaces and communication protocols necessary for the systems' management and integrated operation. The figure has been simplified to the minimum structure necessary to support an effective integrated system, and the residual complexity shows the need to consider the total context of the information technology involved. Such a system will not necessarily succeed if any one component, or even several, are advanced state-of-the-art technologies. However, it will probably fail if one component is inadequate or the total system is not well-integrated.

The Organization

The central core is the people that manage and operate the system, their organization and value systems. The overt operation of the system is part of the *technical culture* of the organization in Hall's (1959) terms. It can be communicated, documented, and partially programmed. It can also be changed fairly readily in response to new requirements and technologies. The management structure of the organization is part of its *formal culture*. Only part of it is overt and documented, and it is resistant to change. What has come to be called the "corporate culture" (Deal and Kennedy, 1982) is in Hall's terms the *informal culture* of the organization. It pervades the organization, is communicated by example, undocumented, and changes only slowly or under pressures of survival. The managerial structures and social processes of the organization are not normally treated as part of its information technology. However, to be successful the technical systems must be consistent with the organizational structures and processes. This applies particularly to inter-personal communications where computer networks will not be used if they violate the managerial and social norms of the organization, and to command and control paths which have to conform to existing authority and procedures that may not be those of the organization chart.

Person-Computer Interface

Recognition that the managerial structure of the organization dominates its style of operation draws attention to person-computer interaction as a critical technology. Advances in graphics, voice input/output, and intelligent terminals has improved the technical repertoire for interaction. Widespread contact with low-cost personal computers has increased computer literacy and user acceptance of the technology. However, much remains to be done to bring the human engineering of computer-based systems to the same level of professionalism as hardware and software engineering (Gaines and Shaw, 1986(a),; Gaines and Shaw, 1986(b)). For command and control systems involving expert systems and simulation, information presentation and ease of communication are of prime importance. A technically powerful system will be wasted unless it is comprehensible and accessible to its users, and gives them confidence in the basis of its operations.

Communication Protocols

The days of single-vendor, special-purpose systems designed against a static, well-defined specification are long gone. Integrated systems involve all aspects of the operation of an organization. Equipment from many vendors, purchased at different times, for different purposes, by different parts of the organization, has to operate together. In this lies the major practical obstacles to the creation of effective integrated systems at the present. The technical problems are beginning to be resolved at the lower levels by the adoption of industry standards in communication protocols such as the open systems interconnection (OSI) standard (Day and Zimmerman, 1983), the provision in data-processing and database packages for the import and export of data from "foreign" systems,and the provision of data-communications for parameter-setting and data-collection in control and instrumentation systems. These alone are necessary, but not sufficient to allow the widespread creation of integrated systems. They provide a syntactic framework for system integration, but no coherent semantics in which to express it.

The Applications Ring: Basic Technologies

The outer ring in Figure 1 shows the main information technologies in integrated systems and their typical applications. Moving counter-clockwise around the ring:

Remote Communications are necessary to interface the organization with the organizational world in which it operations. A particular organization is part of an infrastructure each part of which is trying to optimize its own operations.

Communication Systems perform the classical number-crunching tasks under the control of algorithms that with modern software engineering have a high degree of accuracy, conformity to specification, and reliability.

Database Systems have become the classic core of an organization's information system, recording all its activities in a coordinated fashion and making the information available on a controlled basis to those systems and people with a legitimate need to know.

Control Systems are now increasingly integrated with information systems so that decisions can be implemented directly in the physical world.

Instrumentation Systems are also increasingly integrated to provide timely information on the state of the physical world and the effectiveness of operations.

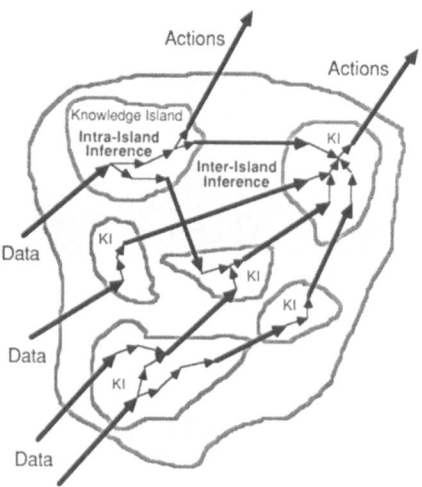

Figure 2. Modeling Through Heterogeneous Knowledge Islands.

The Applications Ring: Decision Technologies

Three technologies in the outer ring of Figure 1 are particularly relevant to decision aids in integrated systems.

Knowledge Bases are distinguished from databases by containing inference rules rather than facts. The rules may necessarily be heuristic in nature, generating plausible advice rather than hard facts. Whereas databases record an organization;s activities, knowledge bases record its skills.

Expert Systems are the means to apply a knowledge base to the solution of a particular problem. They stand in relation to the knowledge base as does conventional computation to the data base. They differ in that their role as advisors and dependence on heuristics makes *accountability* and *comprehensibility* of major importance. An expert system has to be able to justify and explain the basis of its advice.

Simulation has been separated from other forms of computation because it is based on a model of some other system and it is the relation of the simulated model to that of the system modeled that is of paramount importance. The models used in simulation to infer the behavior of a system are generally deeper than the models used in expert systems to infer the proper advice about a system, even though both may be concerned with the same system (Gaines, 1986(a)).

HETEROGENEITY AND KNOWLEDGE-BASED SYSTEMS

What is it about knowledge-based systems technology that makes it better fitted to support the management of a heterogeneous system? The answer is best seen through contrast. A conventional corporate database might contain information relevant to most of the areas shown in Figure 1. It might contain powerful programs relating to each area. However, each of the programs and associated datasets would serve a specialist function within the corporation. There would be very little direct connection between them. They would be used in a connected fashion by the corporation, but the connections would be created by the human management of their application, not through information processing within the database itself. Information technology has provided us with a collection of powerful, but disconnected, specialist tools. Knowledge-based systems provide the means of integrating these tools into a coherent *knowledge support system* aiding the management of complex systems. Human knowledge is based on *heterogeneous integration* - on the pooling of diverse sources of information and diverse resources to achieve desired objectives. Knowledge-based systems can model such heterogeneous integration using information-processing facilities, and, hence, can support human objectives through those facilities.

The essential features of a knowledge-based system are shown in Figure 2. Each specialist area of knowledge is represented as a *knowledge island* that has within it the datasets and procedures specific to that knowledge. Data from external sources triggers off processing within an island that eventually results in processed data being passed from one island to another. This in turn triggers further data processing in the other knowledge island which eventually propagates to other islands. Some islands have external

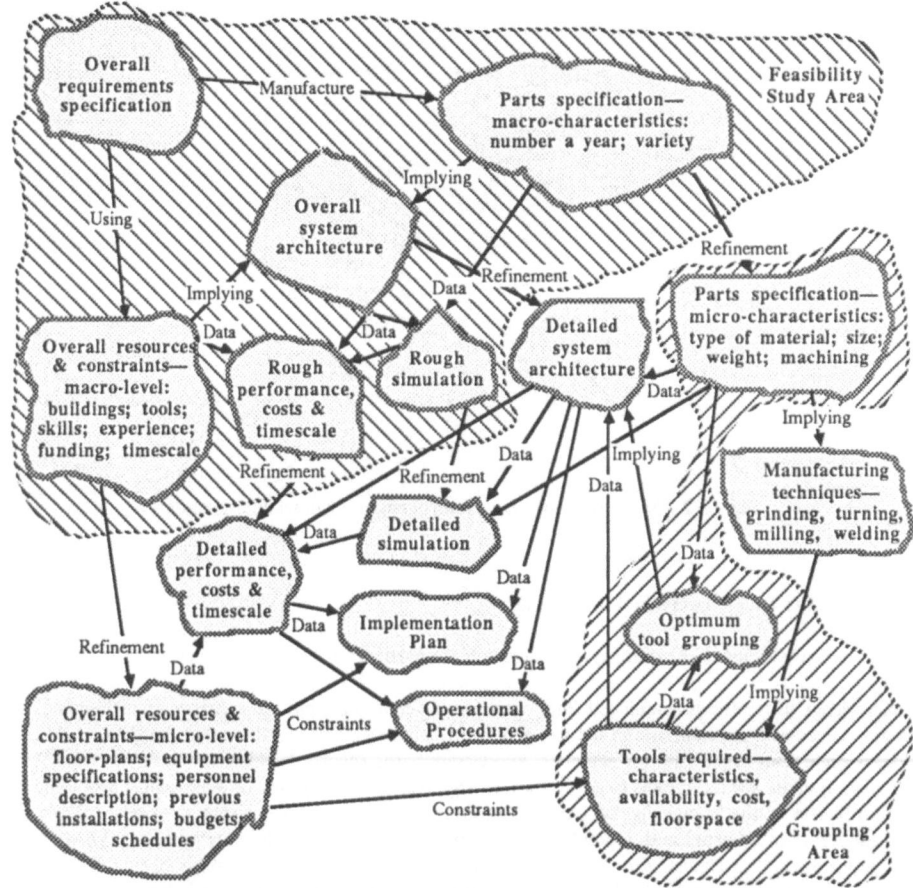

Figure 3. Knowledge Islands in Computer-Integrated Manufacturing.

connections that pass conclusions, recommendations for action, out to the external world. Islands are distinguished by the relative homogeneity of the data and processing within them. Connections between them represent data which is relevant to more than one island, but probably relevant in very different ways. The structure is fully recursive in that islands generally have sub-islands within them and group naturally into areas.

To make the abstract model of Figure 2 more concrete, Figure 3 shows an analysis of planning for flexible manufacturing in terms of the knowledge islands involved derived from interactive knowledge acquisition (Gaines, 1986(c)). At the top left, the *overall requirements specification* is the starting point of any feasibility study of FMS. They key constructs here were found to be the obvious pair: *low-volume - high-volume* and *low-variety - high-variety*, but other significant constructs were also elicited that affect the feasibility of FMS implementation such as *FMS-already-in-use - FMS-not-in-use* and *commitment-to-existing-machines - new-plant*. The experience dimension and the difference between restructuring and green-field situations are obviously relevant to the decision-making, but could be missed in an analysis that concentrated only on quantitative parameters.

The experience/resources dimension refines naturally to the knowledge island concerned with *overall resources and constraints*. The volume/variety dimension refines to a quantitative description of the *parts specification* in parts per year and the number of different parts. Consideration of the resources and parts islands can give enough information to prime the *overall system architecture* island. This in its turn can lead to *rough performance* estimates which can provide sufficient data for *rough simulation* using the fuzzy linguistic model approach (Wenstop, 1981; Gaines and Shaw, 1985. The performance estimates and simulation presentation form a basis for conclusions about the feasibility of an FMS for a particular requirement and the six knowledge islands involved may be grouped together as a *feasibility study area*. This sub-system is already a useful tool for the preliminary stages of FMS planning.

The knowledge islands described may be refined to a further level of detail on two main paths. The macro description of resources and constraints may be refined to a micro description that lists floor-plans, personnel, machines and so on. Much of this will be available in existing corporate administrative databases, but some information will probably be missing. The macro description of parts may be refined to a micro description that completely characterizes each part and its manufacturing process. Much of this will be available in existing corporate engineering and production databases, but, again, some will be missing. The *parts specification* leads naturally to a *manufacturing techniques* knowledge island which itself leads to that for *tools required*. The parts and tools islands form another useful sub-system, the *grouping area*, where the *optimum tool grouping* knowledge island takes the detailed specification of parts and their machine utilization requirements and uses these to derive nearly optimal groupings of machinery.

The central region of detailed architecture, performance and simulation is complicated more by the data requirements than by the complexity of computation required. It is unlikely to be cost-effective for any organization to gather the detail required on a wide range of machines and field-experience (although if widespread use of MAP develops much more data is potentially available at low cost). The knowledge islands in this area will evolve through successive refinements of those already described in a way determined by mainstream industry trends and cost-effectiveness. The tendency for leading suppliers tend to be used again, because there is more knowledge of their products is one phenomenon of this region.

The importance of Figure 3 as an illustration of knowledge-based systems lies in the heterogeneity of the knowledge involved. The domain analyzed, FMS implementation, is relatively coherent, yet involves considering a diversity of requirements and constraints with little direct relationship between them. The whole of Figure 3 would itself be only one knowledge island in an overall manufacturing plan, which itself would be only one knowledge island in a corporate plan.

KNOWLEDGE STRUCTURES FOR HETEROGENEOUS SYSTEMS

What are the natural knowledge islands for integrated heterogeneous systems? Figure 1 captures the key problem areas for such systems and these should form the top level knowledge islands, but what about the relations between them? How do the corporate culture, person-computer interface, network protocols, information technologies, physical and informational worlds relate, and how does this affect operations? The only strongly formalized and standardized structures within Figure 1 are the network protocols, and it is useful to examine these in more detail because they involve concepts that are useful in formalizing more of topics encompassed in Figure 1.

The most important concept underlying the OSI Reference Model is that of *virtual circuits*. Designers of a particular level are concerned primarily with its relation with the equivalent level in the system with which it is communicating. They need have little concern with the levels above or below it. Hence, they think in terms of messages passing directly between equivalent levels, through a "virtual circuit", rather than through the multiple levels of the actual system. The top level above the OSI defined layers is the "user level virtual circuit", representing the interactions between user program through the communications network, and, hence, the interactions between users themselves, and their activities, if the programs are interactive.

This concept of virtual circuits between users, and user activities, is very powerful in enabling Figure 1 to be restructured to provide a more integrated framework for the other sections not directly included in the communications protocol. It can be redrawn in such a way that the relation of managerial and operations considerations to higher-level protocols in the network is apparent. Figure 4 shows the same conceptual blocks as those in Figure 1, but now in hierarchical form with the person-computer interface, information systems, organizational structure and external worlds shown as higher level "layers" above the network layer. In OSI terms these upper layers may be seen as subsuming and extending the presentation and application layers of the protocol, and give substance to the user level virtual circuit.

The virtual circuits between the human-computer interface layer and the information systems layer in Figure 4 are easy to understand. Users of a computer terminal do not think of themselves as communicating through a network, but rather as directly interacting with some data-processing sub-system. This layer goes beyond the OSI specification, but it forms a natural extension of it, encompassing the technical aspects of the interaction between people and computing systems.

The virtual circuits at the level above, between the organizational layer and the external world layer, extend the OSI concept a step further. The sales manager does not see himself as interacting with a complex administrative and productive system, but rather as communicating directly with a customer organization by supplying it with goods. The chief executive does not see himself as concerned with that level of communication, but rather as communicating directly with the board and shareholders through a flow of profits and dividends. The main problem in extending the model to management level is that people are necessarily involved, and they have different dynamics from technical systems. However, this is also true for the level below where human-computer interaction is involved, and models have been developed at this level that integrate the human and technical components within a hierarchical layered communication model (Gaines, 1988(d)).

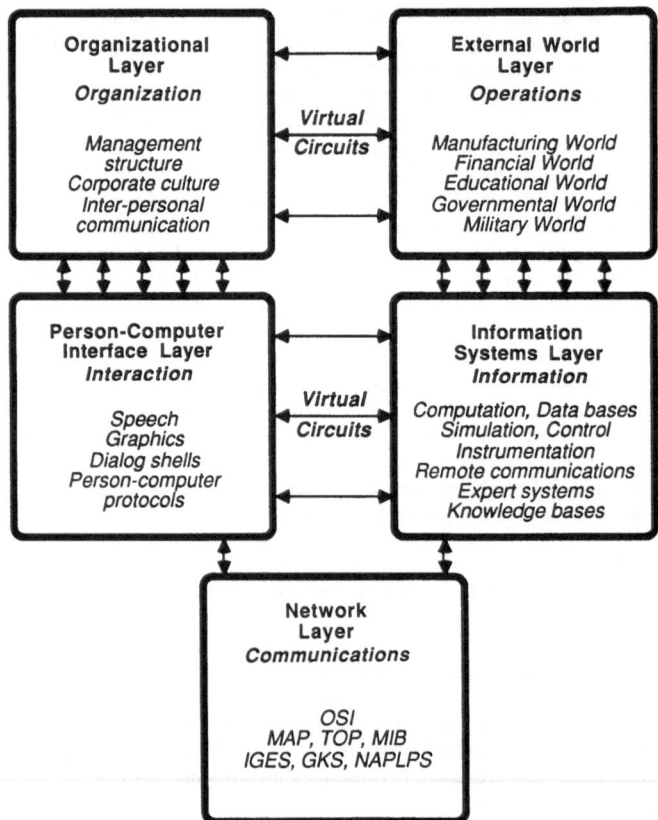

Figure 4. Knowledge Structures for Heterogeneous Systems
as a Hierarchical Protocol.

KNOWLEDGE-BASED MODELING OF HETEROGENEOUS NETWORKS

Figure 4 is a major step towards modeling an integrated heterogeneous network as a structure of knowledge islands of the form in Figure 2. Each of the boxes represents a major conceptual structure in information and management science. The vertical links between boxes represent a change in levels of abstraction. The horizontal links between boxes represent conceptual information flows, or virtual circuits. The overall framework of Figure 4 partitions a heterogeneous system into relatively well-known domains, and the links between them represent relatively well-defined flows.

Note that the partitioning is functional rather than geographic. It is based on the type of activities being undertaken rather than their location in the network or organization.

Note that the functionality is abstract rather than specific. It is based on the basic nature of the activities rather than their specific technical or organizational roles. These other dimensions, of the physical and logical organization of the network, and of its domain-specific functionality, are additional to those analyzed through Figure 4.

Note also that Figure 4, although well-structured, encompasses highly heterogeneous systems - it conceptually packages functionality and flows, but presupposes nothing about how they are implemented.

Figure 4 is the basis of our generic intelligent network support system. Each box represents an island of knowledge about the system: the communications; the information systems, hardware and software; the user interfaces; the users and their organization; and the world in which they are operating. Within each box there is knowledge about the items and issues relating to its operation. Between boxes there is knowledge about inter-relations, basically the answer to why? and how? questions. The following discussion outlines some of the issues we are addressing.

Network Layer

The network layer in practical systems is heterogeneous and fallible. There are gateways and bridges that attempt to be transparent to the user, and succeed for many transactions, but fail in others through delays, unreliability, address conflicts, lack of reciprocity, and so on. The network model needs to have a minimal, coarse-grained representation of connectivity, data-rates, protocols, and traffic. For critical activities the model may need to be more detailed, but this need should be minimized since there is no point in developing a uniform network substratum using the OSI model and then attempting to continually double-guess it.

The network layer is also significant for instrumentation. It is relatively easy to pull out information about traffic at a level sufficient to indicate the nature of the underlying activity. In theory, it is best to instrument the higher level virtual circuits, but in practice the upper levels of the network layer are more accessible. The actual traffic flows may be used as a basis for updating the dynamic model of the network.

Our overall model in Figure 4 may be seen as an extension of the network layer to include higher-level virtual circuits. This is both a useful technical concept with connotations of standardization, modularization, information flow analysis, and so on, and also a useful system metaphor for user understanding of the system - what levels am I specifying? - what virtual circuits am I using?

Information Systems Layer

The information systems layer encompasses the processes that may be run on the system and thus, incidentally, the hardware and software supporting them. This process-oriented framework is important because to the rest of the system it does not matter, in theory, on what platform or with which package a process is executed. In practice, it may matter in terms of cost, execution time, reliability, and so on, but these can be accounted as process parameters. In practice also, what this viewpoint brings to light, is that many process specifications are currently only available in behavioral terms - that this package should be executed on this platform. There is no difficulty in modeling this form of behavioral specification, but its restrictions in terms of system robustness, flexibility, and adaptation are apparent in the model. There are often equivalences between process specifications that hold over a limited range of conditions - that this package on this platform is equivalent to that package on that platform for these specific purposes. This type of information is well-suited to a knowledge-based model.

Chalfan (1986) has shown how the use of a knowledge-based system encompassing input-output parameters and range of performance can make obsolescent software both reusable and also usable for new purposes. Her approach can be generalized to all software on a heterogeneous network. The main problem is keeping the knowledge-base up-to-date. We are cautious about depending on system administrators or developers to maintain the knowledge-base even when prompted by versioning tools. This voluntary updating needs to be automatically monitored by the system so that all changes are noted and traceable even when no explicit reasons are documented. Provision also needs to be made for documenting user experience through annotation, particularly when new software is mounted. In general, the problem is one of providing easy and natural channels for knowledge flows from users, developers, and administrators to the knowledge-base. Artificial intelligence can only supplement, not replace, the massive knowledge acquisition and processing system which is the user community.

The problems of modeling the information systems layer should not be overstated, however. A knowledge-base which maintains only a fairly coarse record of the software is able to provide users with on-line advice, the means to trace problem dependencies on software changes, and the means to track their sources and possibly rectify them through backtracking to previous versions. This is a natural extension of the use of CASE tools in supporting software in the developmental phase to the use of similar tools in supporting system evolution (Gaines, 1988(c)).

Person-Computer Interface Layer

The separation of user interfaces to processes from the processes themselves is essential to effective system modeling. To treat person-computer interaction as another process misses essential distinctions between computer-based and human-based activities. Computers are deterministic machines following strict causal dynamics - they are best modeled as state-determined systems. People are teleological entities having choice in their actions following goal-directed dynamics - they are best modeled as intention-directed systems. At the interface the anticipatory, intentional system that is the person manipulates the state-determined, causal system that is the computer. We have to model both sides of this interaction and the conformity between them, that is, does the action achieve the goal?

In their interactions with others, people establish conventions which in many respects operate like the causal dynamics of physical systems. In particular, they are used to building models of the conventions being followed in a novel interaction. Much of human interface design consists of establishing and following conventions which are simple and natural to the user. However, there is a high degree of arbitrariness about these conventions and different systems may operate very effectively within their own domains with widely varying conventions. This is a major source of heterogeneity at the person-computer interface as these systems are integrated in a networked environment. The term 'user model' is generally used to refer to the knowledge of the family of conventions expected by a particular user.

The person-computer interface layer model has to make provisions for information about interface conventions used by particular packages, the conventions expected by particular users, and the intentions of particular users, either expressed or inferred. This model can be used to manage the interface to convert between conventions if possible, to warn the user of unexpected conventions, to diagnose inconsistencies between user intentions and actions, and to advise the user about actions which may fulfil intentions.

Organizational Layer

A surprising number of phenomena in the organizational layer may be modeled using existing techniques and knowledge. For example, the concept of 'power' has a precise operational definition in terms of the potential to change the behavior of some other entity (Miles, 1980). It is possible to use a model of the capabilities available to a user of the system to determine how much power that user has over any aspect of the behavior of the system. To exercise that power, a user must have the knowledge to carry out the required actions, and determining whether the power is exercisable is far more difficult because the users' states of knowledge will generally be unknown. It is possible to infer some aspects of users' knowledge from their activities in carrying out their intentions if their intentions are known, and it is often possible to infer intentions from the outcomes of the activities.

This definition of power may also be used to analyze the changes in the power structure of an organization brought about by the introduction of new technologies. To be the sole source of information is to have the power to make someone communicate with you to obtain that information, and, hence, to monitor their activity leading to their need to know. If computer access to the information offers an alternative source then this power is lost together with its use to maintain awareness of others' activities. If this awareness is necessary to the performance of some task then it may be necessary to support it by some other means.

It is possible currently to model very complex organizational dynamics and behavior through message passing in object-oriented systems. A person may be modeled as having intentions, capabilities for action, and knowledge about these capabilities, the intentions of others and their capabilities. Some actions may be on the physical world whereas others may be on the social world, such as passing intentions or knowledge to others, and accepting or refusing intentions. Such models can reproduce complex social behavior involving group coordination in carrying out tasks. We are incorporating an organizational model of this type in the intelligent network support system to investigate its utility in modeling the organizational layer of Figure 4. It could be thought of as a dynamic implementation of a 'Procedure Manual' for a corporation.

External World Layer

The external world layer of Figure 4 encapsulates most of the domain-specific aspects of the system operation - what is its overall role? - what are the values by which its performance is measured? - what is the terminology for the various system functions and activities? The model at this level needs to make provision for these to be 'plugged-in' and kept up-to-date. We have developed knowledge acquisition tools that elicit these domain-specific conceptual structures and terminology (Shaw and Gaines, 1988). We are investigating the use of these as a front-end to a general, but coarsely structured, socio-economic model as a basis for modelling the external world layer.

ABSTRACTIONS: AGENCY, ACCOUNTABILITY AND IMPACT

One important feature of a knowledge-based modeling approach is that it allows levels of abstraction to be introduced that relate phenomena of the system shown in Figure 1, through the knowledge structure shown in Figure 4, back to fundamental systemic concepts. For example, the essential difference between the people and the technological components of the system noted above, is a distinction between *agency* and *actuality*, between teleological and causal systems. The importance of this difference, and the system dynamics it generates, show up very clearly in the systemic analysis of the causes and responsibility for

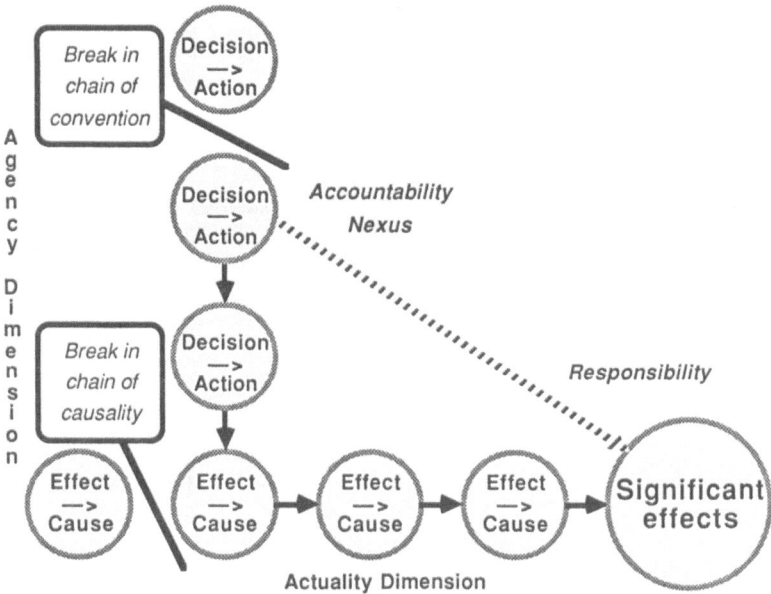

Figure 5. Abstract Knowledge Structures for Accountability Analysis.

significant effects, such as a security violation. Figure 5 shows a 'significant effect' on the far right with the chain of physical causation leading up to it on the left. The critical point in this physical analysis is precisely that at which the chain of causation breaks - that is, where human intervention is indicated because a choice was made. A second chain can then be responsible for that choice. The critical point in this social analysis is again precisely at that point where the chain breaks - this time, where human choice was made without adequate authority or justification. This defines the *accountability nexus*, the link from an agent to the responsibility for the significant effect.

Real-life situations involved many interlinked chains of the form shown in Figure 5, and the 'breaks' are rarely clear-cut. A combination of interdependent causes and interdependent accountabilities are generally involved and both the apportionment of responsibility and the generation, or prevention, of similar situations are complex problems. However, this is not to say that the situation is so vague as to be unanalyzable. Quite the contrary, careful tracing of the chains of causality and accountability is just what is needed to maximize the chance of success or control the possibility of disaster. This application of abstract systemic notions to the modeling of concrete system activities is at the heart of a knowledge-based modeling approach - in particular, it is the basis of audit and security trails in our system.

This example may also be used to illustrate the application of knowledge-based modeling to the planning functions within an organization. At the top level of intentionality within an organization, the chains of reasoning may be seen as concerned with the potential impact of the choices available in any decision to be made. Figure 6 shows the logic of Figure 5 extended to show the dimensions of *impact analysis* of any human choice or decision. There are three basic logics underlying Figure 6:

- first, a system of *values* whereby certain consequences of the decision are regarded as desirable and others as undesirable;

- second, a system of *knowledge* whereby certain consequences of the decision are known in advance and others are not; and

- third, a logic of *impact* in which certain consequences of the decision are in some regions of impact and others are in different regions.

These regions are, in general, temporal, spatial, social, cultural, economic, anywhere where boundaries may be drawn. Figure 6 shows the temporal dimension divided into short, medium, long, and indefinite term effects:

- The short term is one of initiating entrepreneurial activity to implement the decision;

61

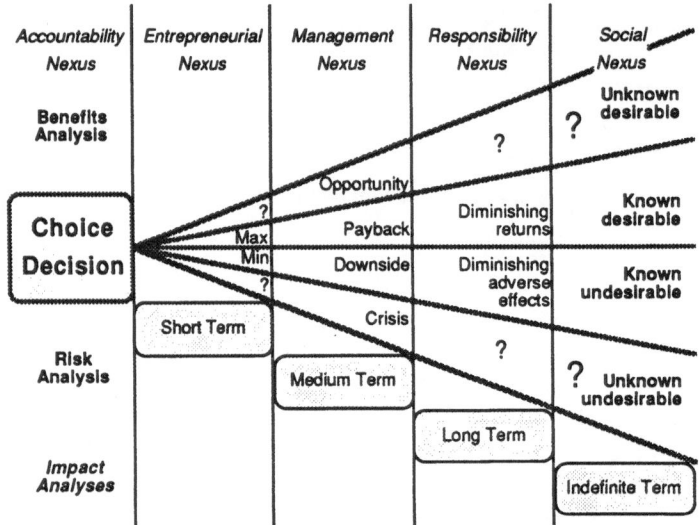

Figure 6. Knowledge Structures Underlying Impact Analysis.

- the medium term is one of management activity to follow through the consequences of the decision activation, maximizing the desired effects and containing the undesired effects; and

- the indefinite term is one of society picking up the unexpected consequences of the decision beyond any reasonable responsibility horizons.

Thus, the distinctions and models discussed may be used as a basis for a detailed analysis of organizational phenomena involving a mix of physical and human processes. There are strong analogies between the actuality and agency dimensions. However, there are also fundamental differences between backward-looking causal processes and forward-looking intentional processes. Operations research has been primarily concerned with the mathematical foundations of causal processes in the past, and this is still an essential component in the analysis of manufacturing systems. We have to extend the models to incorporate the intentional processes of people. The relevant foundations are being generated currently by work on knowledge acquisition for expert systems where a new paradigm is being used in information systems design - modeling expert activity in decision and control rather than the dynamics of the system about which decisions are being made (Gaines, 1988(b)). The switch from a physical paradigm, not to a psychological paradigm, but rather to a balanced paradigm that incorporates models of both physical and human systems, is precisely that required for organizational integration.

CONCLUSIONS

This paper has presented a model of the information technologies underlying computer-integrated systems, their relation to the structure and culture of the organization, the state of the art in those technologies, and the potential and problems in their integration. Our research is targeted on operational-izing this model and using it on-line in large-scale heterogeneous networks with the model parameters continuously updated from empirical data. Intelligent network support systems modeling a heterogeneous system to provide administrative and user support are feasible at the current state of the art in object-oriented systems. They require the development of overall organizational models that encompass corporate goals and management systems as well as the technological infrastructure supporting these.

This paper has developed such an organizational model and discussed its application to the development of an intelligent network support system for integrated heterogeneous systems. Hopefully, the concepts discussed in this paper will be useful to some of the many research and development groups now grappling with the opportunities and problems of large-scale networked systems. We welcome criticism, suggestions, and collaboration in our own research. The developments reported here are part of a program of research in 'knowledge science' in which we are attempting to give a formal structure to knowledge-based systems, knowledge processing and acquisition, and to investigate the role and application of knowledge-based systems to major problem domains in science, engineering, and organizational effectiveness.

ACKNOWLEDGEMENTS

Financial assistance for this work has been made available by the Natural Sciences and Engineering Research Council of Canada.

REFERENCES

Bartee, T. C., ed., 1986, *Digital Communications*, Sams, Indianapolis.

Boeing, 1985, *TOP: Technical and Office Protocols*, Boeing Computer Services, Seattle, WA.

Chalfan, K., 1986, An Expert System for Design Analysis, *Coupling Symbolic and Numerical Computing in Expert Systems*, Kowalik, J. S., ed., North-Holland, Amsterdam, pp. 179-190.

Day, J. D., and Zimmerman, H., 1983, The OSI Reference Model, *Proceedings IEEE*, Vol. 71, No. 12, December, pp. 1334-1340.

Deal, T. E., and Kennedy, A. A., 1982, *Corporate Cultures: The Rites and Rituals of Corporate Life*, Addison-Wesley, Reading, Massachusetts.

Gaines, B. R., 1984, Perspectives on Fifth Generation Computing, *Oxford Surveys in Information Technology*, Vol. 1, pp. 1-53.

Gaines, B. R., 1986(a), Expert Systems and Simulation in Industrial Applications, *Intelligent Simulation Environments*, Luker, P. A., and Adelsberger, H. H., eds., Vol. 17, No. 1, (January), Society for Computer Simulation, LaJolla, California, pp. 144-149.

Gaines, B. R., 1986(b), Sixth Generation Computing: A Conspectus of the Japanese Proposals, *ACM SIGART Newsletter*, (95), January, pp. 39-44.

Gaines, B. R., 1986(c), *Expert Systems and Simulation in the Design of an FMS Advisory System, Simulation in Manufacturing*, Hurrion, R. D., ed., pp. 311-324, IFS Conferences, Bedford, UK.

Gaines, B. R., 1988(a), Structure, Development and Applications of Expert Systems in Integrated Manufacturing, *Artificial Intelligence Implications for CIM*, Kusiak, A., ed., IFS Conferences, Bedford, UK, pp. 117-161.

Gaines, B. R., 1988(b), *Knowledge Acquisition: Developments and Advances, Expert Systems and Intelligent Manufacturing: Proceedings of the Second International Conference and the Leading Edge in Production Planning and Control*, Oliff, M. D., ed., pp. 410-434, North-Holland, New York.

Gaines, B. R., 1988(c), Software Engineering for Knowledge-based Systems, *Proceedings of CASE'88, Second International Workshop on Computer-Aided Software Engineering*, 14-1-14-7.

Gaines, B. R., 1988(d), A Conceptual Framework for Person-Computer Interaction in Distributed Systems, *IEEE Transactions on Systems, Man & Cybernetics*, to appear.

Gaines, B. R., and Shaw, M. L. G., 1985, From Fuzzy Sets to Expert Systems, *Information Science*, Vol. 36, No. 1-2, July, pp. 5-16.

Gaines, B. R., and Shaw, M. L. G., 1986(a), From Timesharing to the Sixth Generation: The Development of Human-Computer Interaction Part I, *International Journal of Man-Machine Studies*, Vol. 1, No. 1, January, pp. 1-27.

Gaines, B. R., and Shaw, M. L. G., 1986(b), Foundations of Dialog Engineering: The Development of Human-Computer Interaction Part II, *International Journal of Man-Machine Studies*, Vol. 1, No. 2, February, pp. 101-123.

General Motors, 1984, *General Motors Manufacturing Automation Protocol*, General Motors Corporation, Warren, Michigan.

Gordon, P. 1984, What is Integrated Software?, *PC World*, Vol. 2, No. 11, October, pp. 72-77.

Hall, E. T., 1959, *The Silent Language*, Doubleday, New York.

Leopold, G., 1986, Bus Standard for Hospitals is Next, *Electronics*, Vol. 59, No. 11, pp. 17-18, March.

Miles, R. H., 1980, *Macro Organizational Behavior*, Scott Foresman, Glenview, Illinois.

Moto-oka, T., ed., 1982, *Fifth Generation Computing Systems*, North-Holland, Amsterdam.

Nolan, R. L., 1983, Computer Data Bases: The Future is Now, *Catching Up With the Computer Revolution*, Salerno, L. M., ed., Wiley, New York, pp. 225-248.

Shaw, M. L. G., and Gaines, B. R., 1988, A Methodology for Recognizing Consensus, Correspondence, Conflict and Contrast in a Knowledge Acquisition System, *Proceedings of the Third AAAI Knowledge Acquisition for Knowledge-Based Systems Workshop*, Banff, November.

STA, 1985, *Promotion of R&D on Electronics and Information Systems That May Complement or Substitute for Human Intelligence*, Science and Technology Agency, Tokyo.

Wenstop, F., 1981, Deductive Verbal Models of Organizations, *Fuzzy Reasoning and its Applications*, Mamdani, E. H., and Gaines, B. R., eds., pp. 149-167, Academic Press, London.

PARALLEL MODELS IN SOFTWARE LIFE CYCLE

Aditya P. Mathur

Software Engineering Research Center
Department of Computer Science
Purdue University
W. Lafayette, IN 47907

Abstract: Demand for high quality software has led to the infusion of several innovative techniques for use in different phases of the software life cycle. The knowledge based techniques proposed by Yau and Liu (1986), Yau and Tsai (1987) and high quality testing proposed by DeMillo (Acree, DeMillo, Budd, and Sayward, 1979) are just two examples of such innovation. One of the major impediments to the use of these techniques is their high computational requirements. A trivial solution to this problem is the use of parallel computers. However, arbitrary use of parallel computers may lead to poor utilization efficiency of the machine.

In this paper we proposed and analyze parallel models for implementation of the two techniques cited above. These models are algorithm guided and, therefore, could be ported to any of the several architectures. For mutation based testing, we have presented three models that differ from each other in their complexity and potential for providing speedups on MIMD architectures. For knowledge based maintenance, we present one model that can be implemented on an MIMD machine.

1.   INTRODUCTION

Software life cycle consists of several phases. According to one classification (Sommerville, 1985), the five phases of the life cycle are: requirements analysis and design, system and software design, implementation and unit testing, system testing, and operation and maintenance. There have been several estimates of the relative cost of each of these phases. According to Sommerville (1985), testing may consume anywhere from 28% to 50% of the entire software development cost. According to Beizer (1984) and Boehm (1987), testing and maintenance can together contribute over 80% of the total life cycle cost. The importance of testing and maintenance is further enhanced when we consider the development of life-critical software such as that found in military equipment, the space shuttle, and several other systems.

The goal of the testing and maintenance phases are the same: to produce high reliability software. However, the methodology differs. Over the past several years, the demand for highly reliable software has led researchers to propose several innovative techniques for use in testing and maintenance phases. Mutation based testing (Acree, DeMillo, Budd, and Sayward, 1979) and knowledge based maintenance (Yau and Tsai, 1987), are two such techniques. A common disconcerting attribute of both these techniques has been their high computational requirement. Mutation based testing can potentially generate a large number of mutants[1] that need to be executed before the program under test can be shown to be highly reliable. Knowledge based maintenance uses logical reasoning to generate answers to queries based on a collection of rules and a large fact, or knowledge base. Execution of a large number of mutants and reasoning on a large knowledge base could be time consuming operations on traditional sequential machines. This computational requirement is considered to be one of the key impediments to the

---

[1]Section 2 provides the definition of a mutant and other related terms.

Empirical Foundations of Information and Software Science V
Edited by P. Zunde and D. Hocking, Plenum Press, New York, 1990

65

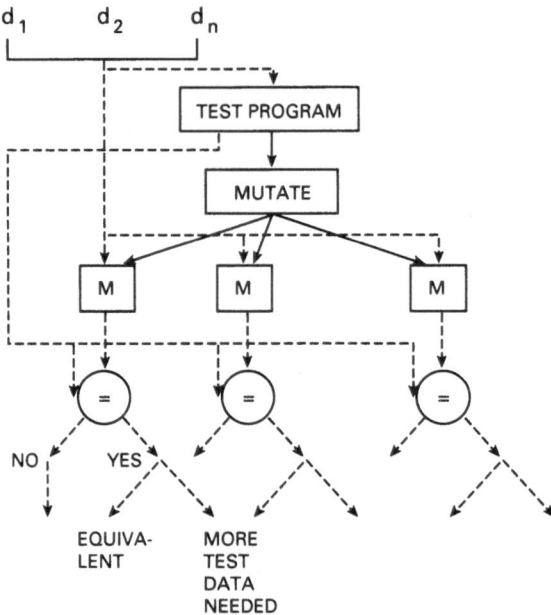

Figure 1. Relation of Operations in Mutation Analysis.

widespread use of tools based on these techniques.

With the parallel computers fast becoming commonplace, it is natural to consider their application in tackling the computational requirements of the two techniques mentioned above. Past work (Mathur and Galiano, 1987; Mathur and Krauser, 1986) has revealed that such an application certainly has the potential of reducing computing times. However, care needs to be exercised in scheduling computations in order to achieve high processor utilization.

In this paper we propose formal models of mutation based software testing and knowledge based software maintenance. Our models can be used to guide the implementation of tools based on these techniques on a variety of parallel architectures. We also introduce a mathematical notation to describe these models. Such a notation has the advantages of unambiguous specification and ease of automated manipulation.

The remainder of this paper is organized in two parts. In the first part we present three parallel models of mutation based software testing. In the second part we present one parallel model of the knowledge based maintenance approach. In section 2 we provide a brief introduction to mutation based testing. Section 3 introduces definitions of concepts and operators that we need to specify our models. Section 4 presents the parallel models for mutation based testing. Section 6 is an introduction to knowledge based maintenance. Section 7 presents a parallel model of knowledge based maintenance. We conclude in section 8.

2.   MUTATION BASED SOFTWARE TESTING

Let P denote the program under test. We are assuming that P is written in any of the well known programming languages like C, Fortran 77, or Ada. Let $S_1', S_2', ..., S_n'$ denote the executable statement sequence in P.

Mutation analysis implies the existence of a set O of *mutant operators*, referred to simply as *operators*. These operators define the generation of mutant programs for the test program P. Let $\#O$ denote the number of operators for a language L. Note that mutant operators are language dependent (Acree, DeMillo, Budd, and Sayward, 1979).

The application of each operator on a statement S_j' causes the generation of zero or more mutant programs (Bowser and Budinger; DeMillo, Guindi, King, and McCracken, 1987). These programs, also known as *mutants*, are syntactically correct transformations of P. The transformed programs are called *mutants*. We denote by $M_{i,j}^x$. The ith mutant produced by an operator $x \in O$ when applied on statement S_j'. Each $M_{i,j}^x$ differs from P in exactly one statement, namely the statement corresponding to S_j'. We shall

66

denote the number of mutants produced by applying operator x on statement S_j by k_j^x. Thus, the total number of mutants generated, denoted by $\#M$, can be computed by the formula:

$$M = \sum_{x \in O} \sum_{j=1}^{n} k_j^x \tag{1}$$

Let D denote the set of test cases used for testing P. The elements of D, the individual test cases, will be denoted by d or d_i, $1 \leq i \leq n$, as required, n is the total number of test cases.

Testing P involves executing P on D. For each element d_i of D, this execution produces a result set denoted by Rp_i. Next, all mutants must be executed on each $d \in D$. The result set obtained by executing $M_{i,j}^x$ on test case d_i is denoted by $Rm_{i,j,l}^x$.

Figure 1 depicts how mutation based testing can be organized. The test program P is mutated by applying mutant operators. Each mutant so generated, denoted by M in the figure, is executed against all the test cases. The result set produced for a mutant-test case pair, $Rm_{i,j,l}^x$, is compared with the result set Rp_l generated by executing P on the corresponding test case. If the two sets are the same, the mutant is considered *killed*. If none of the test cases in D can kill a mutant, then either one of these conditions is true: (i) the mutant is equivalent to P or (ii) more test data is needed to kill it. The existence of *live* mutants demands further testing on the part of the software engineer. The ratio of the number of killed mutants and total mutants generated provides an estimate of program reliability. The higher the ratio, the more reliable is the program.

3. DEFINITIONS

In this section, we introduce some useful terminology and operators used in our parallel models. To begin with, we define k_j, M_j^x, and M_j as:

$$k_j = \sum_{x \in O} k_j^x \tag{2}$$

$$M_j^x = \bigcup_{i=1}^{k_j^x} M_{i,j}^x \tag{3}$$

$$M_j = \bigcup_{x \in O} M_j^x \tag{4}$$

Thus, k_j denotes the total number of mutants generated from statement S_j, M_j^x is the set of all mutants generated by applying mutant operator x on statement Sj, and M_j is the set of all mutants generated from statement S_j. We shall use $\iota(M_{i,j}^x$ to denote the index of mutant $M_{i,j}^x$. The index uniquely identifies a mutant. For any program P, $P(d)$ denotes the output obtained by executing P on test case d.

Execution Sequence: Let $\Psi_d(z)$ denote the execution sequence of a program z on test case $d \in D$, where z can be P or any of the mutants. Note that $\Psi_d(z)$ is finite if z terminates. We shall represent $\Psi_d(z)$, for all $d \in D$ and all mutants z, by a sequence of integers, each integer in the sequence being drawn from the integer sequence $[1 \dots n]$. For example, if P consists of four statements ($n = 4$), then $\Psi_d(P)$ could be $[1,2,1,2,3,4]$. Let $\nu_d(z)$ denote the length of $\Psi_d(z)$.

With each element of the execution sequence, we associate a *position*. Thus, the position of the first element is 1, that of the second element is 2 and so on.

Split Point: For a mutant $M_{i,j}^x$, we define $\Lambda(j,d)$ to be a position in $\Psi_d(P)$ that corresponds to the *first* execution of the mutated statement S_j^x in P. ($\Lambda(j,d)$-1) is defined as the split point of M. Note that all mutants in M_j share the same split point with respect to a given case.

Mutant Preamble: Let $p_d(z,r,s)$, $1 \leq r$, $s \leq n$, and $r \leq s$, denote the subsequence of $\Psi_d(z)$ starting at position r and ending at position s. We shall refer to $p_d(z,1,s)$ to be the *preamble* for mutant z executing on a test case d.

With any execution sequence, or subsequence, w, we associate a *cost* denoted by $\Gamma(w)$. This cost would depend on, among other factors, the time to execute the sequence.

The eval Operator: For a given mutant m, test case $d \in D$, and test program P, *eval* is defined as:

$$eval(m, d) = \begin{cases} \phi & \text{if } m(d) \neq P(d) \\ \{\iota(M_{i,j}^x)\} & \text{otherwise} \end{cases} \tag{5}$$

eval takes a mutant and a test case as its arguments and generates a set. The generated set could be empty or contain an index corresponding to the mutant that is its argument. Note that *eval* generating an empty set implies that the mutant supplied as its argument is killed.

The **ceval** operator: For a given mutant m, test case $d \in D$, and test program P, *ceval* is defined as:

$$ceval(m, d) = \begin{cases} \phi & \text{if } m(d_s), \text{ for any } 1 \leq s \leq n \\ \{ \iota (M_{i,j}^x) \} & \text{otherwise} \end{cases} \tag{6}$$

ceval is similar to *eval* except that it generates ϕ if $m(d')$ is different from $P(d')$ for any test case $d' \in D$. An instance of *eval* (*ceval*) is an application of the operator on a given mutant-test case pair. When we are not concerned about any specific mutant or test case, we shall denote instances of *eval* (*ceval*) by $e_1, e_2, ... (ce_1, ce_2, ...)$.

Both *eval* and *ceval* are abstract operators. The *execution* of an instance of *eval*, or *ceval*, is the execution of the operator on a real machine.[2]

Parallel Evaluator: Given e_1 and e_2, $e_1 \parallel e_2$ denotes concurrent application of e_1 and e_2. This definition is valid if we replace e_1 by ce_1 and e_2 by ce_2. The parallel evaluator operator has side effect as indicated by the following relation:

$$e_1 \parallel e2 = e_1 \bigcup e_2$$

Once again, the above relation is also valid for instances of *ceval*.

The following are two simple properties of $\parallel$:

$$e_1 \parallel e_2 = e_2 \parallel e_1 \tag{7}$$

$$e_1 \parallel (e_2 \parallel e_3) = (e_1 \parallel e_2) \parallel e_3 \tag{8}$$

We use the abbreviation $\parallel_{1 \leq i \leq l}(e_i)$ for the concurrent evaluation of l instances of *eval* (*ceval*).

Note that the $\parallel$ operator has been used by other researchers also in defining parallel models (Chandy and Misra, 1988; Hoare, 1985). However we have extended the definition found in the literature to meet the special requirements of mutation.

Delayed Parallel Evaluator: Let e_1 be an instance of *eval*. $P \rightarrow |^c e_1$ implies the following:

1. Evaluation of P on a test case d begins before any instances of *eval* are executed.

2. Immediately after condition c is satisfied, the state of e_1 is initialized to that of P and execution of e_1 proceeds concurrently with that of P. By the *state* of P we refer to the entire set of values of program variables of P and the program counter.

The above definition is also valid for the *ceval* operator. $\rightarrow |^c$ denotes the delayed parallel evaluator. Note that once condition c is satisfied, and the state of P is transferred, the delayed parallel evaluator behaves exactly like the parallel evaluator. The execution of P and e_1 may terminate in any sequence.

We now extend the definition of the delayed parallel evaluator to include multiple instances of *eval(ceval)*. Given l instances of *eval(ceval)*, the delayed parallel operator can be used to specify the concurrent execution of each of these instances as:

$$P \rightarrow |_D^{C_1} e_1 \rightarrow |_D^{C_2} e_2 ... \rightarrow |_D^{C_1} e_l \tag{9}$$

The semantics of the above expression can be described as follows:

1. Start the execution of P.

2. The execution of an instance of *eval* (*ceval*) can be initiated immediately after the corresponding condition is satisfied. Prior to initiating the execution, the state of the instance of *eval* (*ceval*) to be executed is initialized to that of the current state of P.

---

[2]In a mutation based testing tool, the **eval** (**ceval**) operator may correspond to the execution of a mutant m on test case d and the comparison of its output with $P(d)$ to generate the status of the mutant.

We shall abbreviate the expression in (9) as:

$$P \to \|_{1 \leq j \leq l}^{C_j} \ e_j \tag{10}$$

The following property holds for the $\to\|$ operator:

$$P \to \|^{c_1} \ e_1 \to \|^{c_2} \ e_2 = P \to \|^{c_2} \ e_2 \to \|^{c_1} \ e_1 \tag{11}$$

Index set of a test: Given a program P under test, a test set D, and the set of mutants of P, the *index set* of P, with respect to D, is the set of all indices $_i(M_{i,j}^x)$ such that $M_{i,j}^x$ is not killed by any test case in D.[3] We shall denote such an index set by $I(P,D)$. In a software testing experiment, size of the index set provides a measure of how good is D. An empty index set implies that all mutants were killed when executed against one or more test cases of D. This implies a good test set.

Mutation based testing essentially produces the index set of the program under test with respect to the test cases supplied by the user.[4] An empty index set implies a good test set and also indicates that P is highly reliable.

A model of mutation based software testing is a formal definition of the index set in terms of the *eval* or *ceval* operators. In our case, such a definition is functional, and, therefore, usable to guide the implementation of a mutation based software testing tool. Our models are parallel because they specify the concurrency that can be achieved for the execution of different instances of *eval* (*ceval*).

4.   PARALLEL MODELS OF MUTATION BASED SOFTWARE TESTING

In this section, we present and analyze three different parallel models of mutation based testing. We name these models as:

1.   *Model I*: MIMD model with no inter-mutant communication.

2.   *Model II*: MIMD model with inter-mutant communication.

3.   *Model III*: MIMD model using split-execution.

We first describe each of these three models and then provide a comparative analysis. We refer to all our models as MIMD models because of two reasons:

●   The execution of different instances of *eval(ceval)* may execute independently by the interpretation of independent instruction streams.

●   The models are suitable for implementation on an MIMD machine such as, for example, Intel's iPSC or Ncube's/10.

4.1 MIMD Model With No Inter-Mutant Communication

Using the terminology introduced earlier, an MIMD model with no communication between mutants, is specified as follows:

$$I(P,D) = \|_{1 \leq i \leq l} \ (e_i), \ where \ l = n \times \sum_{j=1}^{n} M_j \tag{12}$$

In (12) there are as many instances of *eval* as there are mutant-test case pairs.

---

[3]Until a mutant is killed, it is said to be *live*.

[4]The test cases could also be generated automatically by a test case generator such as the one reported in DeMillo and Offutt (1988).

4.2 MIMD Model With Inter-Mutant Communication

By definition it is sufficient for a mutant to be killed by one test case so that it is not in the index set being computed. This observation leads us to the following model:

$$I(P,D) = |_{1 \le i \le l} (ce_i), \text{ where } l = n \times \sum_{j=1}^{n} M_j \qquad (13)$$

Note that in (13) we have used instances of *ceval* instead of using instances of *eval*. As shown later by our analysis, this model is superior to (12).

4.3 MIMD Model Using Split Execution

This is the most complex of the three models presented in this paper. Before we formally specify this model, we explain the underlying approach.

From our earlier description of mutation analysis we know that mutants generated by mutating a given statement of P, differ from P by exactly that statement. Thus, all the statements in a mutant are identical to that in P except for the one that was mutated. This fact is exploited in the model based on split execution.

If P and one of its mutants are executed on a given test case, it is evident that they will go through an identical state sequence during the entire preamble of the mutant. Once the execution sequence of P has gone past the preamble of the mutant, the states of P and its mutant may differ. We exploit this fact by initiating the *eval(ceval)* on a mutant only after P has executed past its preamble.

To be able to formally specify our model, we need to formalize the notion of *the execution of P passing the preamble of a mutant.* We denote the rth element in $\Psi_d(P)$ by $e_d(r) = 1 \le r'\langle v_d(P)$. Next, we define a *split condition*, denoted by c_j for all mutants obtained by mutating statement S_j^i in P, as:

$$c_j: e_d(r') \ne j, e_d(r) = j \quad 1 \le r' < r \le v_d(P),$$
$$\text{and for } r' < r, \ e_d(r') \ne j \qquad (14)$$

Thus, condition c_j, for example, would be true, just before S_j^i is to be executed for the first time during the execution of P.[5]

We can now define our model based on split execution. It is specified as follows:

$$I(P,D) = P \to |_{\substack{1 \le j \le n \\ 1 \le i \le k_j^x \\ \forall x \in O \\ \forall d \in D}}^{c_j} ceval(M_{i,j}^x, d) \qquad (15)$$

In model (15) we have intentionally used *ceval* as it leads to a model that has the advantage of inter-mutant communication. Replacing *ceval* by *eval* in model (15) provides a variant of (15).

5.   ANALYSIS OF PARALLEL MODELS

The parallel models described above can be implemented in several different ways on a parallel machine. Thus, the speedup that can be achieved with each model depends on the nature of the implementation and the architecture of the underlying machine. Further, a detailed and complete analysis is significantly complex and requires several assumptions such as the structure of the program under test and the *goodness* of the test set D. In this section, we shall make more simplifying assumptions to keep the analysis simple, though realistic. Our assumptions lead to the conservative estimates of speedups.

Let the machine on which our parallel models are to be implemented consist of N identical processors. These processors are interconnected by a suitable interconnection network (Hwang and Briggs, 1984). We assume an MIMD architecture with each processor having its own local memory.

Let $t(z)$ denote the time taken to execute a program z. We make the following assumptions about P, its mutants, and the test cases:

---

[5]Note that one may also interpret (14) as being true immediately after the first execution of S_j^i. This interpretation is incorrect due to the fact that the sate of P needs to be transferred to the **eval** operator whose execution will be initiated when the split condition is true.

1.   The mutant execution time is constant. We shall denote this time by t_m. Thus, $t(z) = t_m$, for all

$$z \in \bigcup_{j=1}^{n} (M_j) .$$

2. p denotes the probability of a test case in D killing a mutant. p depends on the nature of the mutant and the test case on which the mutant executes.

3. α is the fraction of the total time a mutant takes to execute before it is killed.[6] Thus, if a mutant is not killed, it executes for t_m time limits, otherwise it executes for $(\alpha \times t_m)$ time units.

4. $\eta = N$. This assumption simplifies mutant scheduling as described below.

We now define the *speedup* obtained by using a model Z, denoted by γz, as:

$$\gamma z = \frac{\texttt{time to execute all instances of eval (ceval) on 1 processor}}{\texttt{time to execute all instances of eval (ceval) on N processors}} \tag{16}$$

In the above definition, whether the *eval* or the *ceval* operator is used, depends on the model Z. For example, model I uses the *eval* operator. In the analysis given below, we will derive a formula that can be used for computing γ for each of the three models presented earlier.

5.1 Computing The Speedup For Model I

Model I implies the execution of a total of $(\#M \times \eta)$ *eval* operators. In accordance with our assumption above, we have a total of $N(= \eta)$ processors. Thus, all the *eval* operators can be executed in a total of $\#M$ scheduling *passes*. In each pass, a total of η instances of *eval* are scheduled for concurrent execution on the N processors. There are several possible execution orderings. However, model I does not imply any specific ordering.

With our multiple pass scheme, it is easy to compute the speedup as:

$$\gamma I = \frac{\#M \times \eta}{\left(\dfrac{\#M \times \eta}{N}\right)} = N \tag{17}$$

5.2 Computing The Speedup For Model II

An implementation based on model II can be done in multiple scheduling passes as described above. The passes will now satisfy the following properties:

1. *PR 1*: Each pass may be terminated prematurely, i.e., before the execution of all currently executing *ceval* operators is complete.

2. *PR 2*: In one pass, all instances of *ceval* corresponding to the *same* mutant are scheduled for execution.

The first of the two properties is a consequence of the definition of *ceval*. The second property stems from the architecture of the underlying machine and the definition of *ceval*. (6) implies that if a mutant gets killed, all other executing *ceval's* will terminate. However, to implement this feature of our model, the processor that is executing the *ceval* corresponding to the killed mutant m needs to communicate this fact (that a mutant has been killed) to all other processors executing *ceval*. If these *other ceval* executing processors correspond to a mutant different from m, then such a communication is of no use. Instead, the fact that a mutant has been killed has to be saved, perhaps, by the host processor, and ensure that the same mutant is not scheduled later. This would imply a different *overhead* term in equation (18).

---

[6]This assumption is valid if *weak mutation* as defined in Girgis and Woodward (1985), and in Howden (1982) is being used.

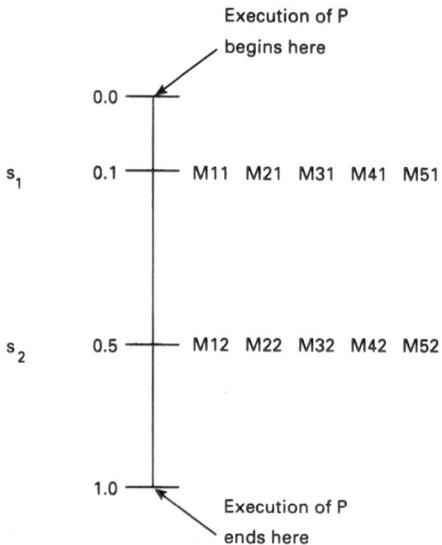

Figure 2. Split Points in a Test Program P.

We denote by $\delta(N)$ the overhead incurred in informing the remaining processors that the mutant has been killed. This overhead depends on the number of processors executing *ceval*, and the topology in which they are arranged (Hwang and Briggs, 1984). For example, if the processors are arranged linearly, then $\delta(N) = O(\log N)$.

With the above properties holding for each scheduling pass, we can compute the speedup that can beobtained when using Model II as follows:

$$\gamma II = \frac{(\alpha + p \times \eta - 1) \times t_m \times \#M}{((1-p) \times t_m + p \times \alpha \times (t_m + \delta)) \times \#M} \tag{18}$$

5.3 Computing The Speedup for Model III

The scheduling strategy based on Model III is significantly more complex than the ones described above. To describe this strategy, we refer to Figure 2. This figure shows the test program and n possible split points denoted by $s_1, s_2, ..., s_n$. Note that if *all* mutant operators have been applied, then n is the maximum split points in the test program. In our analysis, we shall use this upper bound on the split points to derive the most conservative speedup estimate for our scheduling strategy.

Recall that a split point is defined using the execution sequence of P. Thus, a split point s_i will correspond to statement S_j', $1 \le i, j \le n$. As each split point corresponds to a unique statement in P, we can define a mapping function f as:

$$f : \{s_1, s_2, ..., s_n\} \rightarrow \{1, 2, ..., n\}$$

For example, if P has four statements denoted by S_1', S_2', S_3', and S_4', then f could be $f(s_1) = 2, f(s_2) = 1, f(s_3) = 3$, and $f(s_4) = 4$.

As stated earlier in section 3, the split condition, $c_i, 1 \le i \le n$, is true immediately after execution reaches the split point. Model III implies that all *ceval* operators on mutants corresponding to a split point are ready for scheduling when that split point is reached. However, there may not be sufficient processors to schedule all *ceval*'s that become available.

A *split phase* is a sequence of scheduling passes that are initiated when the execution of P reaches a split point. Within each split phase, each *ceval*, operating on a live mutant obtained by mutating the corresponding program statement, is available for execution.

We further assume that the execution of P proceeds on the host processor. As the host is a sequential machine, P is executed only on one test case at a time. Thus, the scheduling passes we use cannot satisfy properties *PR 1* and *PR 2* described while discussing Model II. To ensure the correct implementation of *ceval*, we need to save the status of each *ceval* operator for use during subsequent phases. A split phase, or any of its passes, cannot terminate prematurely.

Let us now obtain the most conservative estimate of the speedup that can be obtained when *split phase* scheduling is used. We know that there can be at most n split phases for each test case. Thus, the maximum number of split phases is $n \times \eta$. We shall denote by $S_{i,j}$ the ith split phase corresponding to the jth test case.

Split phase $S_{i,j}$ can have at most k_{f_i} mutants, which implies at most $k_{f(i)}$ instances of *ceval*. However, as some of these mutants may have been killed by earlier test cases, we can expect a total of $(p^{j-1} \times k_{f(i)})$ instances of *ceval* to be executed in $S_{i,j}$.

To compute the time required for each split phase, we note that the split phase scheduling is carried out according to the algorithm described below.

Algorithm [Split phase scheduling]

1. $\forall d \in D$ *do* {loop 1}

    2. start execution of P on d.
    3. *for* $i = 1$ *to* n *do* {loop 2}

        4. Suspend execution of P when it reaches split point i.
        5. *while ceval's* from previous split point are still executing *do* ;
        6. Initiate execution of *ceval's* corresponding to $S_{i,d}$.
        7. Resume execution of P from split point i.

{end of loop 2}

{end of loop 1}

To compute the speedup, we need to find the time taken to execute the above algorithm. Let $\gamma^j_{i,i+1}, 1 \le i \le n$ denote the time to execute P from split point s_{i-1} to s_i for the $j^{th}, 1 \le j \le \eta$ test case. Thus, for example, $\gamma^j_{0,1}$ is the time to move from step 2 to step 4 in the above algorithm for the jth test case. For convenience, we have assumed a fictitious split point s_0 immediately preceding the first statement of P. s_0 does not generate any mutants $(k_0 = 0)$.

Step 6 in the above algorithm consists of four sub-steps: (a) initialize the nodes with *ceval* code, (b) broadcast the current status of P to each node, (c) save status of each *ceval* once it completes execution, and (d) initiate execution of each *ceval*. The time required for sub-steps (a), (b), and (c) is denoted by $\rho^j_i, 1 \le i \le \eta$. ρ is the *overhead* incurred for one split phase.

The time to complete sub-step (d) for $S_{i,j}$ can be computed as:

$$\left\lceil \frac{p^{(j-1)} \times k_{f(i)}}{N} \right\rceil \times t_m \tag{19}$$

Step 5 in the above algorithm may imply waiting on the part of the host processor. Among other factors, this wait time depends on the time to complete the previous split phase. If the nodes have not completed the previous phase, then the host waits for the nodes to complete the execution of *ceval's*. If the nodes have completed the previous split phase, then the host can immediately proceed to step 7.

The duration between the resumption of execution of P at split point i and the resumption of execution of P at split point $i+1$, for the jth execution of loop 2 in Algorithm 1, can be computed as:

$$p^j_{i+1} + \max\left(r^j_{i+1,i}, \left\lceil \frac{p^{(j-1)} \times k_{f(i)}}{N} \right\rceil \times t_m \right) \tag{20}$$

Using (20) we can now compute the time for all split phases against all test cases as:

$$\sum_{j=1}^{n} \left(r^j_{1,0} + \sum_{i=1}^{n} \left(p^j_i + \max\left(r^j_{i,i-1}, \left\lceil \frac{p^{(j-1)} \times k_{f(i-1)}}{N} \right\rceil \times t_m \right) \right) \right) \tag{21}$$

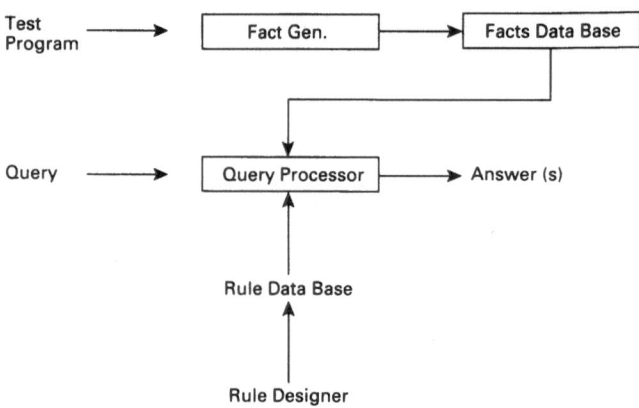

Figure 3. Components of a Knowledge Based Maintenance System.

Using (21), we now obtain the formula for estimating the speedup that can be achieved by using Model III.

$$\gamma III = \frac{(\alpha + p \times \eta - 1) \times \#M}{\sum_{j=1}^{n} \left(r_{1,0}^{j} + \sum_{i=1}^{n} \left(p_{i}^{j} + \max \left(r_{i,i-1}^{j}, \left\lceil \frac{p^{(j-1)} \times k_{f(i-1)}}{N} \right\rceil \times t_{m} \right) \right) \right)} \tag{22}$$

5.4 Summary of Analysis of Parallel Models

We have derived formulae to compute the speedup that can be obtained when using any of the three models for scheduling mutants. It is important to note that the speedup formulae derived above are valid for the implementation described. There are several other ways for implementing each model that we leave for the interested reader to work out.

One of the key problems in the use of the speedup formulae derived above is posed by the need for an accurate estimate of the probability p and the overheads denoted by ρ and δ. A high value of p implies a good test set D. This in turn implies higher speedups for both Model II and III. The overhead can be estimated by some sample executions of P on test cases in D. Both the overheads depend on the underlying machine architecture too. Hence, any reasonable estimate will be machine specific.

6.   KNOWLEDGE BASED SOFTWARE MAINTENANCE

Maintenance is another important phase in the software life cycle. Maintenance phase may, in general, require testing. Thus, the models described earlier could be useful during the maintenance phase too. However, there are several other problems that may need to be tackled during this phase. For example, if a new feature is to be added in the program, the maintenance engineer might like to know what variables are affected when changes are made in the program to implement this feature.

A knowledge based technique for use during the maintenance phase was proposed by Yau and others in Yau and Liu (1986), and Yau and Tsai (1987). A system based on this technique is structured as shown in Figure 3.

The *facts generator* inputs the program under maintenance and generates a set of relations that represent facts about this program. These relations form the *facts data base* also known as the *extensional data base (EDB)* in the logic programming literature. For example, the relation *assign* may contain facts about all the assignments in the program. This table can be referenced when facts about any assignment statement are needed to answer a query from the maintenance engineer. The relational tables are language dependent. The contents of the relational tables, facts, are program dependent.

The system provides several *maintenance tools*, each corresponding to a set of *rules*. The set of all rules is the rule data base also known as the *intentional data base (IDB)*. Examples of maintenance tools include data flow analyzers, data flow anomaly detector, and logical ripple effect analyzer.

To use the system, the maintenance engineer inputs a query about the program under maintenance. The system then *compiles* (Henschen and Naqvi, 1984) this query into one consisting of only literals corresponding to names of relations (facts) in the EDB. The compiled query is then evaluated and all possible answers presented to the engineer.

A key problem in the system described above is its performance. For large programs, the EDB and the relations it contains could be large. The evaluation of the compiled query may require taking the join of these relations, thereby generating large intermediate relations. This process could be both time and space intensive. In the next section we describe a parallel model for query evaluation.

7. PARALLEL MODELS OF KNOWLEDGE BASED SOFTWARE MAINTENANCE

7.1 Definitions and Terminology

Relations and facts: We use the term *n-ary relation* as in data base terminology. The term *n-ary predicate* is used as in logic programming terminology. A relation is a set of tuples with a fixed arity. In our case, a tuple is also a *fact* in the extensional database. For the purpose of illustration, we shall use the following relations introduced in Yau and Liu (1986):

1. *ident*: A 3-ary relation on *tuple-id, identifier,* and *syntax-class.* For example, *ident*(4, a variable) is a tuple representing the following fact about the program: "a is an identifier belonging to the syntactic class variable". This fact is tuple number 4. Tuples are numbered for convenience of manipulation.

2. *statement*: A 4-ary relation on *statement-id, label-id, syntax-class,* and *syntax-class-id.* For example, *statement*(4, 0, assign, 2) represents the following fact about a program: "statement 4 is an unlabeled assignment statement with syntax class identifier being 2". The syntax-class-id can be used as the tuple-id to get further *facts,* about the current fact, in the relation corresponding to syntax-class *assign.*

3. *assignment*: A 4-ary relation on *tuple-id, left-class, left-class-id,* and *expression-id.* For example, the fact *assignment*(1,*variable*,1,1) represents the following: "the first assignment statement in the program assigns to a variable more about which can be found in tuple 1 of the relation representing *variable*". More about the expression on the right side of this assignment can be found in tuple 1 of the relation representing *expression*".

4. *variable*: A 3-ary relation on *variable-id, syntax-class,* and *identifier-id.* For example, the fact *variable*(1,*identifier*,4f) corresponds to: "more on variable identified as 1 can be found in tuple 4 of the relation representing identifiers".

Term: A *term* is defined as: (a) a constant is a term, (b) a variable is a term, (c) if f is a function name and $t_1, t_2 ..., t_n$ are terms, then $f(t_1, t_2 ..., tn)$ is a term, and (d) nothing else is a term.

Literal: If R denotes a k-ary predicate and $t_1, t_2 ..., t_n$ are terms, then $R(t_1, t_2 ..., t_k)$ is a positive literal. In our case, all relation names will also be used as predicate names. Thus, for example, *ident*(4,a,var) is a literal with terms *4, a,* and *var.* This is also an example of an *instantiated* literal as it does not contain any variable terms. As another example, *ident*(X,Y,var) is a literal with variable terms X and Y, and constant term *var.*

We use $R_1, R_2, ...$ to denote relations. Terms corresponding to R_i will be denoted by $t_{i,1}, t_{i,2}, ... t_{i,k_i}$, where k_i is the arity of R_i. We shall use upper case letters or $X_1, X_2, ...$ to denote variable terms, and lower case letters or $a_1, a_2, ...$ to denote constant terms.

Instantiation: For a literal $R_i(t_{i,1}, t_{i,2}, ... t_{i,k_i})$ and a tuple $\alpha = [a_1, a_2, ..., a_{k_i}]$ in relation R_i, an *instantiation* can be defined if and only if for each constant term $t_{i,j}$, we have $t_{i,j} = a_j, 1 \le j \le k_i$. The instantiated literal can be written as $R_i(a_1, a_2, ..., a_{k_i})$ and α is said to have instantiated the literal $R_i(t_{i,1}, t_{i,2}, ... t_{i,k_i})$.

Query: A query is a conjunction and/or disjunction of literals. For example, if R_1 and R_2 denote two predicates, then $R_1(t_{1,1}, t_{1,2}, ..., t_{1,k_1})$ & $R_2(t_{2,1}, t_{2,2}, ..., t_{2,k_2})$ & ..., $R_N(t_{N,1}, t_{N,2}, ..., t_{N,k_N})$ is a query consisting of N predicates. The symbol & denotes conjunction. We shall denote a query with N literals by q_N.

In terms of the relations described above, the following is a valid query:

statement(X1, X2, assign, X3) & assignment(X3, var, X4, X5)

It can be stated informally as *which statements in the program are assignment statements?* Here variable *X1* corresponds to the statement-id, *X3* is the tuple-id corresponding to syntax-class *assign, assign* and *var* are constants. We deal with only *safe* queries, i.e., ones that yield finite answers.

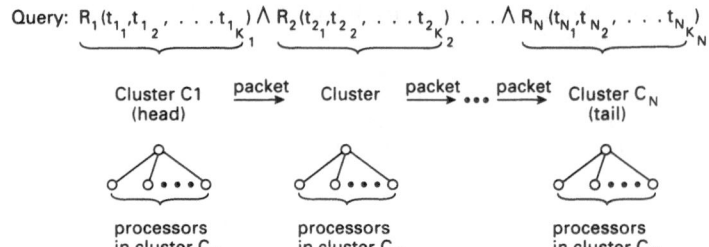

Query: $R_1(t_{1_1}, t_{1_2}, \ldots, t_{1_{K_1}}) \wedge R_2(t_{2_1}, t_{2_2}, \ldots, t_{2_{K_2}}) \ldots \wedge R_N(t_{N_1}, t_{N_2}, \ldots, t_{N_{K_N}})$

Figure 4. A Pipeline of Clusters of Processors.

7.2 A Clustered Pipeline Model

In this section we present one model for parallel evaluation of conjunctive queries. Recall that we are assuming that the queries have been compiled and, hence, can be evaluated against the data base. For several other parallel models, see DeGroot (1984) and Wolfson and Silberschatz (1987).

First, we provide an informal description of our model. We assume that to evaluate a query q_N, we have N clusters of processors. The clusters are arranged in a pipeline. We denote the clusters by $C_1, C_2, \ldots, C_N$. Thus, the pipeline consists of cluster C_i connected to cluster C_{i+1} with C_1 being the *head* and C_N the *tail* of the pipeline. We shall refer to the remaining clusters as the *body* of the pipeline. Figure 4 shows such a pipeline. Cluster C_i attempts to satisfy the ith literal in the query.

The evaluation of q_N begins at the head. Tuples, representing facts, from relation R_1 are *matched* against terms $t_{1,1}, t_{1,2}, \ldots, t_{1,k_1}$. Any matching tuple is assembled into a *packet* and transmitted to the next cluster in the pipeline. Note that there is one packet generated for each matching tuple.

Within the body, each cluster receives packets from its left neighbor. Cluster $i, i > 1$, then attempts to find the tuples from R_i that match the incoming packet and terms $t_{i,1}, t_{i,2}, \ldots, t_{i,k_i}$. Any matching tuple is again passed on to the right neighbor after assembling it into a packet.

The above process continues till C_1 has no more packets to transmit. C_1 then transmits a special *terminating* packet, recognized by all clusters, to C_2. After C_2 has completed processing the previous packet, it transmits the terminating packet to C_3 and terminates query evaluation. The terminating packet is thus transmitted to all the clusters. The *answer(s)* to the query lie in the packets generated by the tail. We are not concerned with exactly how these answers are extracted from the packet and then presented to the user. We shall now present a more precise description of the cluster pipeline model.

7.3 Formal Specification of the Cluster Pipeline Model

A packet is a sequence of zero or more tuples. Let $\pi_i, 1 \le i \le N$ denote the packet generated by cluster C_i. π_i is recursively defined as follows:

$$\pi_0 = []$$

$$\pi_1 = \alpha, \ \alpha \text{ is a tuple in relation } R_1 \text{ and can instantiate } R_1(t_{1,1}, t_{1,2}, \ldots, t_{1,k_1}).$$

$$\pi_i = \pi_{i-1} \circ \alpha, \ i > 1, \text{ where } \alpha \text{ is tuple in } R_i, \tag{23}$$
it can instantiate $R_i(t_{i,1}, t_{i,2}, \ldots, t_{i,k_i})$, and for each $t_{i,j}$
that is also a term in $R_{i-1}(t_{i-1,1}, t_{i-1,2}, \ldots, t_{i-1,k_{i-1}})$
$t_{i,j} = t_{i-1,j}$, for $1 \le j \le k_{i-1}$

$\circ$ in the above definition denotes the tuple catenation operator. As an example, consider the query:

$$R_1(X, Y, c) \ \& \ R_2(Z, X, e) \tag{24}$$

Let a tuple $\alpha = [a, b, c]$ instantiate the first literal in the above query. Then $\pi_1 = [a, b, c]$. If $\beta = [d, b, e]$ is a tuple that can instantiate the second literal in the above query, then $\pi_2 = \alpha \circ \beta = [a, b, c, d, b, e]$. Note that according to the definition of a packet, the largest packet generated while evaluating query q_N can be of $\sum_{j=1}^{N}(k_j)$ elements, an element being a constant term.

We now introduce a process named *gen-packet*(i, π_{i-1}, π_i) that executes in cluster C_i. It receives a sequence of packets, each denoted by π_{i-1} from cluster $C_{i-1}, 1 \langle i \leq N$, and generates a sequence of packets each denoted by π_i. Each packet generated is transmitted to cluster $(i + 1), 1 \leq i \leq (N - 1)$. The *gen-packet* process terminates when it can generate no more packets.

Using the *gen-packet* process, we can now formally specify our cluster pipeline model of knowledge based software maintenance:

$$\|_{1 \leq i \leq N} (gen\text{-}packet(1, \pi_{i-1}, \pi_i)) \tag{25}$$

Note that $\|$ is the parallel operator defined earlier. The *gen-packet* process is defined below.

Algorithm: Definition of *gen-packet*(i, π_{i-1}, π_i).

Inputs:
   1. A packet from cluster $(i-1)$.
   2. Tuples corresponding to relation R_i.

Output:
   1. Packet π_i transmitted to cluster $(i+1), 1 \leq i \leq N$.

Method:

begin
/* Receive a packet π_{i-1} from cluster C_{i-1} if $i \rangle 1$.*/

do *forever*

   if$(i > 1)$ *then*
      get-packet$(i-1, \pi_{i-1})$

   if π_{i-1} is not a terminating packet then
      begin

        /*Instantiate the corresponding literal against each tuple α in R_i */

          while *there-remains-a-tuple-to-be-considered-in-R_i* do
            begin

              get-next-tuple α;
              if α can instantiate $R_i(t_{i,1}, t_{i,2}, ..., t_{i,ki})$ then
                begin

                  instantiate $R_i(t_{i,1}, t_{i,2}, ..., t_{i,ki})$;
                  compute π_i using α and π_{i-1};
                  if $i \langle N$ *then* send π_i to C_{i+1}

              end ;

          end ; /* of packet generation using packet π_{i-1}.*/

   if $(i = 1)$ *then* send terminating packet to C_{i+1} ;

   else /* if π_{i-1} is a terminating packet */
      if $(i \langle N)$ *then* send π_{i-1} to C_{i+1} and terminate;

end /* end of algorithm */.

The model specified by (25) can be implemented in several ways on a parallel machine. Regardless of the method of implementation, two related problems need to be tackled:

     1.   Idle time of a cluster while waiting for packets to arrive from the neighboring cluster.

2. Assigning processors to clusters.

Depending on the nature of the query, a cluster will generate packets only at a certain rate. A cluster needs to suspend generating packets when (a) the neighboring cluster is not ready to receive the packet that has been just computed and (b) there is no packet to process. This idle time can be reduced by assigning the largest number of instantiations. Within a cluster, different processors can be assigned to process different subsets of tuples of a relation. For example, if a cluster has only two processors, one of them can process all odd numbered tuples and the other can process all even numbered tuples (Wolfson and Silberschatz, 1987). The processors within a cluster can be structured as a two level tree as shown in Figure 4. The root processors in each cluster can be responsible for handling the inter- and intra-cluster traffic consisting of packets and tuples.

8. CONCLUSIONS AND FUTURE WORK

In this paper, we have presented parallel models for two important phases of the software life cycle, namely the testing and maintenance functions. Our models are general for the testing and maintenance techniques considered. They are amenable to a variety of implementations on different parallel architectures. We have presented the performance analysis of one implementation based on our models for testing.

Further research is needed to (a) generate benchmarks when the implementations described above are applied on large programs and (b) obtain a dynamic load balancing algorithm to improve the performance of the cluster pipeline model.

It is our contention that in all phases of the software life cycle, performance bottlenecks are likely to arise when knowledge based or other novel approaches, such as mutation analysis, are used. These bottlenecks can be overcome by either the efficient use of existing parallel architectures or by designing architectures suited specially to the algorithms used in a life cycle phase. An example of such an architecture can be found in Krauser and Mathur, 1986). We believe that the models like the ones presented in this paper can be used as the basis for further research in developing and evaluating new architectures suitable for use in the entire software life cycle.

REFERENCES

Acree, A. T., DeMillo, R. A., Budd, T. A., and Sayward, F. G., 1979, *Mutation Analysis*, Technical Report, GIT-ICS-79/08, Georgia Institute of Technology, Atlanta, GA.

Beizer, Boris, 1984, *Software System Testing and Quality Assurance*, van Nostrand Reinhold Company, New York.

Boehm, Barry, 1987, Industrial Software Metrics Top 10 List, *IEEE Software*, September 1987, pp. 84-85.

Bowser, John H., and Budinger, Carolyn A., *Procedures Used in the Testing of Mothra*, Available from Software Engineering Research Center, Georgia Institute of Technology, Atlanta, GA.

Chandy, K. Mani, and Misra, Jayadev, 1988, *Parallel Program Design*, Addison-Wesley.

DeGroot, Doug, 1984, Restricted AND-Parallelism, *Proceedings of the International Conference on Fifth Generation Computer Systems*, edited by ICOT, pp. 471-478.

DeMillo, R. A., Guindi, D. S., King, K. N., and McCracken , W. M., 1987, *An Overview of the Mothra Testing Environment*, Technical Report, SERC-TR-3-P, Software Engineering Research Center, Purdue University, W. Lafayette, IN.

DeMillo, R. A., Hocking, D. E., and Merrit, M. J., 1981, *A Comparison of Some Reliable Test Data Generation Procedures*, Technical Report, GIT-ICS-81/08, Georgia Institute of Technology, Atlanta, GA 30332.

DeMillo, Richard A., McCracken, W. Michael, Martin, R. J., and Passafume, John F., 1987, *Software Testing and Evaluation*, The Benjamin/Cummings Publishing Company Inc., Menlo Park, CA.

DeMillo, R. A., and Offutt, A. J., 1988, Experimental Results of Automatically Generated Adequate Test Cases, *Proceedings of the Second Workshop on Software Testing, Verification, and Analysis*, July 19-21, 1988, Banff, Canada.

Girgis, M. R., and Woodward, M. R., 1985, *An Integrated System for Program Testing Using Weak Mutation and Data Flow Analysis*, Technical Report, 85/1, Department of Computer Science, Liverpool, January 1985.

Henschen, L. J., and Naqvi, S. A., 1984, On compiling Queries in Recursive First-Order
  Databases, *Journal of ACM*, Vol. 31, (1), January 1984, pp. 47-85.

Hoare, C. A. R., 1985, *Communicating Sequential Processes*, Prentice-Hall Internation
  UK, Ltd.

Hwang, Kai and Briggs, Faye   ' A., 1984, *Computer Architecture and Parallel Processing*,
  McGraw Hill Book Company, New York.

Howden, William E., 1982, Weak Mutation Testing and Completeness of Test Sets,
  IEEE Trans. on Software Eng., Vol. SE-8, (4), July 1982, pp. 371-379.

Krauser, E. W., and Mathur, Aditya P., 1986, Program Testing on a Massively Parallel
  Transputer Based System, *Proceedings of the ISMM International Symposium on Mini and Micro-
  Computers and Their Applications*, Austin, Texas, Nov. 10-12, 1986, pp. 67-71.

Mathur, Aditya P., and Galiano, E., 1987, *Inducing Vectorization: A Formal Analysis*,
  Technical Report, Software Engineering Research Center, Department of Computer Science,
  Purdue University, W. Lafayette, IN.

Mathur, Aditya P., and Krauser, E. W., 1986, *Modeling Mutation on a Vector
  Processor*, Technical Report, GIT-SERC-87/07, Software Engineering Research Center, Georgia
  Institute of Technology, Atlanta, GA.

Rego, Vernon, and Mathur, Aditya P., 1988, *Stochastic Models of A Program
  Unification Technique for Concurrency Enhancement*, Technical Report, Dept. of Computer
  Sciences, Purdue University, W. Lafayette, IN 47907.

Sommerville, I., 1985, *Software Engineering*, Addison-Wesley Publishing Company,
  Second Edition.

Wolfson, Ouri, and Silberschatz, Avi, 1987, *Distributed Processing of Logic Programs*,
  Technical Report #466, October 1987, TECHNION - Israel Institute of Technology, Computer
  Science Department.

Yau, S. S., and Liu, Sying-Syang, 1986, A Knowledge Based Software Maintenance
  Environment, *Proceedings of COMPSAC-86*, October 8-10, 1986.

Yau, S. S., and Tsai, J. J., 1987, Knowledge Representation of Software Component
  Interconnection Information for Large Scale Software Modifications, *IEEE Trans. Software Eng.*,
  Vol. SE-13, (3), pp. 355-361, March 1987.

III. MODELING METHODOLOGIES

A METHODOLOGY FOR ELICITING USERS COGNITIVE MODELS

OF COMPUTER-BASED SYSTEMS

Sven A Carlsson

Dept. of Information & Computer Science
University of Lund
Sölvegatan 14 A
S-223 62 Lund, Sweden
BITNET: ADBSC@SELDC52

Abstract: Over the past couple of years there has been a growing attention to mental models of artifacts like computer-based systems. It is assumed that research on mental models can enhance our understanding of computer-based systems uses; an understanding which can influence how we design and assess computer-based systems.

This paper presents an approach to mental modelling which is based on Kelly's (1955) personal construct psychology. The primary purpose of this paper is to present and apply a version of the Role Construct Repertoire Interview, a methodology used to elicit a person's mental model of a domain.

A study conducted in a natural setting of three spreadsheet program users are used to exemplify the applicability of the methodology. The more general use of the methodology in the information systems area is also discussed.

1. INTRODUCTION

Over the last couple of years there has been a growing interest in different forms of mental models of artifacts like computer-based systems. There is a growing amount of effort going into this area of research. It is suggested that mental models can enhance our understanding of computer-based systems uses, an understanding which can influence how we design and assess computer-based systems. So far, research on human-computer interaction and mental models has mainly focused on tasks requiring routine cognitive skill: "Such behavior occurs in situations that are familiar and repetitive, and which people master with practice and training, but where the variability in the task, plus the induced variability arising from error, keeps the task from becoming completely routine and requires cognitive involvement" (Card, Moran, and Newell, 1980, p 33). An example of these type of tasks is text editing. In the example we will use later, spreadsheet program model building and use, the editing of a spreadsheet model by entering previous month's figures in the model can be regarded as a task requiring routine cognitive skill. This type of task can be contrasted with tasks that require more than routine cognitive skill like manuscript composition or spreadsheet model building. The above mental models and type of tasks used in experiments and used as examples mean that focus has been on time to perform a specific task, errors made during the accomplishment of a task, and so on. Or in other words, the focus has mainly been on mechanics of system use.

This paper presents an approach to mental modelling which is based on Kelly's (1955) personal construct psychology. Kelly viewed each man as a "...personal scientist, classifying, categorizing and theorizing about his world, anticipating on the basis of his theories and acting on the basis of his anticipation" (Shaw, 1980, p 7). The primary purpose of this paper is to present and apply a version of the Role Construct Repertoire Interview (RCRI), a methodology used to examine and bring into awareness

Empirical Foundations of Information and Software Science V
Edited by P. Zunde and D. Hocking, Plenum Press, New York, 1990

83

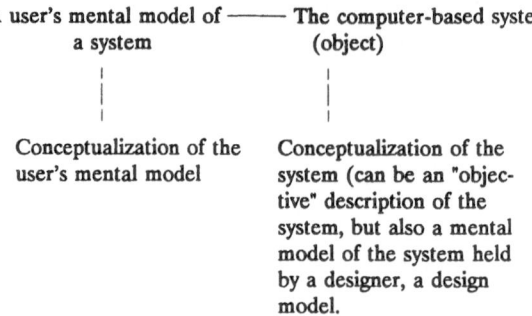

Figure 1. Different mental models in human-computer interaction.

the conceptual system, mental model, held by a person. Here the methodology is used for eliciting a person's mental model of a computer-based system.[1]

The remainder of the paper is organized as follows. In the next section we discuss the use of mental models in human-computer interaction. This is by no means an exhaustive portrayal of work on mental models and human-computer interaction, but it does illustrate the type of work conducted in this area. Section 3 gives a brief presentation of Kelly's personal construct theory. This is followed by a presentation of the Role Construct Repertoire Interview, and how collected data can be analyzed. Section 5 presents an application of the methodology: a study of three spreadsheet users in a natural setting. In the final section we discuss the applicability of the methodology in the information systems area.

2. MENTAL MODELS AND HUMAN-COMPUTER INTERACTION

Gardner (1985) in his extensive and comprehensive review of the history of cognitive science and related fields like Artificial Intelligence and psychology, points out that mental models and mental representations can play an important role in enhancing our understanding of cognitive processes. According to Gardner, a mental model/representation is a "set of constructs that can be invoked for the explanation of cognitive phenomena, ranging from visual perception to story comprehension" (ibid, p 383). This is a general definition that holds for most research on mental models, but as pointed out by Johnson-Laird (1983) mental models can take many forms and serve many purposes.

Mental models have in the last couple of years got more attention in studies of human-computer interaction. These studies are part of general studies of human-artifact interaction, where artifacts can be things like hand calculators (Young, 1983), control panel devices, and computer-based systems, like text editors (Card, Moran, and Newell, 1983).

As pointed out by several researchers, the notions and concepts of "mental models", "user models", "users conceptual models", and so on, are not very clear. Within research on human-computer interaction there is a widespread use of these terms. There exist several definitions with different focus, different purposes of the mental models, and different representations of mental models (see, for example, Young (1983) for discussions on definitions and roles of mental models). However, the lowest common denominator seems to be that a person has a representation or metaphor to guide his actions with a computer-based system, which also makes it possible for a person to interpret events.

We will discuss below how the notion of a mental model is used here (Our "definition" is in line with those used in Norman & Draper (1986), and by Young (1983)). A user's mental model of a computer-based system is the internal representation that person forms of the system (Figure 1). This is

---

[1]The methodology has within the IS-field been used for eliciting the information sources used, or desired to be used, by decision makers (see for example, Stabell (1974, 1978), Mancuso and Shaw (1988), Fuglseth and Stabell (1985), Grudnitski (1981, 1984), and Carlsson (1988)).

Some researchers are advocating the use of personal construct psychology and RCRI in the area of expert systems, especially for one of the harder problems, namely knowledge acquisition (Shaw and Gaines, 1987; Boose, 1986). Both Shaw (1980) and Monk (1985), suggest that RCRI can be used to explore users' attitudes to and perception of a computer-based system.

a type of model which we are not yet able to fully capture and represent (it is doubtful if we ever will be able to capture a person's mental model completely). The conceptualization of a user's mental model is an externalized model of a user's mental model. An externalized model is captured and represented by some available methodology, for example, captured by "verbal protocols" and represented in the form of production rules.

Unless otherwise stated, when we talk about mental models we are referring to the conceptualizations of peoples' mental models.

There also exist other types of user/mental models, for example:

- A model an "intelligent" system or program constructs of its users, that is, the system's model of the people who interact with the system (Rich, 1983, Fjeldstad & Konsynski, 1987)

- A mental model a system designer develops to help him in the design of a system. This is, in most cases, a more or less generalized model of a typical user.

One major approach to mental modelling is based on information-processing psychology with its roots in the seminal work of Newell and Simon (1972). In this approach, a user's knowledge of how to perform a computer-based task can be represented as a collection of production rules. These types of models are useful in predicting and explaining time to learn a system's time to perform a task, errors made during performance, and so on. So far the approach has, in human-computer interaction, mainly been applied for tasks requiring routine cognitive skill, like text editing. For different examples of this approach see Card, Moran, and Newell (1983), Kieras & Polson (1985), Polson & Kieras (1985), Polson (1987), Carlsson & Stabell (1986), and Lerch (1986).

The above types of models are not very useful in capturing and representing a person's perception of a computer-based system that is not directly linked to how to perform specific tasks using the system. There are at least three causes for this:

- Although the models can capture some of the processes that occur in human-computer interaction, they can not capture more overlapping processes that link activities, that is, they can not "see" aspects of the interaction/ use process that extend over activities separated in time. For example, a person might perceive two commands in a system as rather identical. This might be based on other things than the specific functions of the commands. It might be based on the person considering these commands as not very useful, hard to use, and hard to correct errors once the commands are completed, and so on. This perception, which will have an impact on how a person uses a system, can not be captured and represented in the above types of mental models.

- The models are low-level and assume a one-to-one relationship between a user's mental model and task execution (Carlsson and Stabell, 1986). This means that the models are mainly useful for analysis of the mechanics of system use.[2] The models can be useful in evaluating different systems of the same type, for example, different spreadsheet programs or text editors (for text editor examples see Card, Moran, and Newell (1983). In the case of spreadsheet programs, the models can also be useful in factoring out mechanics of spreadsheet program (SP) use, which means that the other time of spreadsheet program use might be linked to substantive aspects of SP use.

- As noted above the models have mainly been used for tasks requiring routine cognitive skill like text editing. For tasks requiring more than routine cognitive skills, like manuscript composition or spreadsheet model building, these models are less relevant.

We want to point out that the approach we will discuss below can not supersede the above mental modelling approaches. Instead the approach should be seen as a complement and supplement to these other approaches.

---

[2]It should be noted that there are models of different grains. Card, Moran, and Newell (1983) GOMS models ranged from a model at the unit task level to keystroke-level models (The acronym GOMS stands for Goals, Operators, Methods, and Selection rules). The models we are discussing here are the models at the keystroke-level, since it seems to us that they are the models that have had most impact on human-computer interaction research.

3. PERSONAL CONSTRUCT PSYCHOLOGY

The methodology of mental modelling we present and discuss has its roots in Kelly's (1955) personal construct psychology, which is a theory that is established in practice.[3] It is beyond the scope of this paper to give more than a glimpse of Kelly's fascinating theory (for an introduction to the theory the reader is referred to Bannister and Fransella (1980) and Shaw (1981)). Fortunately, the basic ideas of personal construct psychology are comprehensible on an intuitive basis. These basic ideas are presented briefly to give an understanding of the RCRI methodology which will be presented in the next section.

Kelly presented his theory in the form of a fundamental postulate, which he then elaborated by means of eleven corollaries. The fundamental postulate states that "A person's processes are psychologically channelized by the ways in which he anticipates events." (Kelly, 1955, p 46). As pointed out above, Kelly viewed man as a personal scientist, man-the-scientist. Kelly expressed his view in the following way: "Now what would happen if we were to reopen the question of human motivation and use our long-range view of man to infer just what it is that sets the course of his endeavor?...Might not the individual man, each in his own personal way, assume more of the stature of a scientist, ever seeking to predict and control the course of events with which he is involved? Would he not have his theories, test his hypotheses, and weigh his experimental evidence? And, if so, might not the differences between the personal viewpoints of different men correspond to the differences between the theoretical points of view of different scientists?" (ibid, p 5).

According to Kelly, a person interprets and makes sense of events and things he perceives by use of his personal construct system, which is a system a person develops. This system is composed of both related and unrelated hierarchies of constructs (constructs are categories having special characteristics; the notion of constructs will be clearer when we, in the next section, present the RCRI). A person also tries to anticipate the likely outcome of future events based on his personal construct system. When this does not work, he modifies his construct system.

Although Kelly developed his theory in the area of clinical psychology, his methodology has been applied in other areas and domains, for example to elicit perceptions of portfolios, managerial problems, information sources, political parties, and consumer products. Here the focus will be on users perceptions of a spreadsheet program, that is, users beliefs about and attitudes towards the SP.

Contrasting the models, in the human-computer interaction context, discussed in Section 2, to the type of mental model elicited by RCRI, the later type of model does not capture the mechanics of system use. Instead, it is more related to the substantive aspect of use. It is a type of model that a person develops and changes depending on system use and the person's reflections on system use.

4. ROLE CONSTRUCT REPERTORY INTERVIEW

The Role Construct Repertoire Interview methodology was developed by Kelly to sample interpersonal perceptions. At a more general level, it is used to elicit persons' perceptions of different domains. Specific interviews may be conducted in various ways, however, the fundamental principle is similar. In this section we present and discuss how to conduct RCRI interviews and how data can be analyzed. We are using data from our study of spreadsheet programmers to exemplify (The setting of the study is presented in Section 5.1).

4.1 Design of Role Construct Repertory Interviews

For the interviewer's part, RCRI consists of four steps (for more thorough presentations see Kelly (1955) and EasterbySmith (1981)):

1. Generation of a role list and a sort list (a pre-interview activity);
2. Generation of objects;
3. Generation of constructs; and
4. Rating of objects on constructs.

Generation of a Role List and Objects. Before an interview, the interviewer has to work out a list of roles. A role is a short sentence (role) that should help the subject generate a specific object that he is familiar with and that comes from the domain of interest. The subject should write on a card, with a

---

[3]See, for example, Shaw (1981), Mancuso and Shaw (1988), and the *International Journal of Personal Construct Psychology*.

Table 1

SP-Commands and Their Functions *

OBJECT	EXPLANATION
1. PF1 D	DELETE, a row or column
2. PF1 B	BLANK, erase the content of a cell
3. PF1 S	SPLIT, the screen in windows
4. PF1 Q	DISC, loading, saving, quit
5. PF1 G	GENERAL, editing and other jobs for the whole worksheet
6. PF1 I	INSERT, a row or column
7. PF1 C	COPY, formulas and so on to other columns and/or rows
8. PF1 L	LOCK, headings so they do not scroll
9. PF1 E	EDIT, one or several cells
10. PF1 P	PRINT, the result or the model
11. PF1 T	EMPTY, the whole model or part of it
12. PF1 V	VERSION, shows the version number of the program
13. PF1 ?	STATUS, shows the status of the program, for example, column width, memory left
14. &TEXT(Argument)	prespecified FUNCTIONS, for example, &SUM(B1:B10)
15. TEXT	Letters and characters
16. NUMBERS	Numerals
17. OPERATORS	+, -, /, *, **

*The letters D, B, S, and so on are the first letter in the name of the command.
PF 1 is function-key one.

number equal to the role number, the identifier of an object that fits the role. The objects can also be given by the interviewer.

In this study RCRI was used to capture a person's perceptions of a spreadsheet program used by him. All objects in this study were pre-specified, that is generated by the interviewer. They were the commands of the highest menu-level in the SP pre-specified functions, numbers, operators, and text (see Table 1).

Generation of Constructs. The classical approach to generate constructs, which are bipolar attributes, is to elicit them from triads according to a sort list generated before the interview. The subject is presented three objects at a time and asked to say in what way two of the objects are alike and different from the third. The person is then asked to say what is the opposite of the way the first two objects were alike.

For example, when presented the triad DISC (PF1 Q), STATUS (PF1 ?), and COPY (PF1 C) a person said "DELETE and DISC are useful". He was then asked, "What is, in this context, the opposite of useful?". To this question the person answered "not useful". The construct would then be "useful not useful".

It is also possible to provide the constructs. The advantage of having a subject generate the constructs is that they are his own constructs, he is using his own words/sentences.[4] In our study we used 13 sortings to generate the constructs. This number of sortings is in line with what can be found in other RCRI-interviews.

Rating of Objects on Constructs. In the final step, the subject rates the objects on the constructs. The most common method is to use a 5- or 7-point Likert scale, for example:

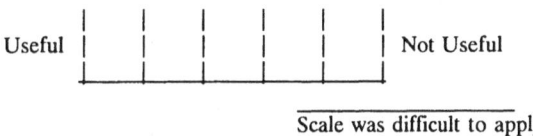

Scale was difficult to apply

---

[4]Providing constructs would be like the semantic differential technique (Osgood, Suci, and Tannenbaum, 1957), since the subject is not asked to contribute his own constructs, that is, his own descriptions of objects.

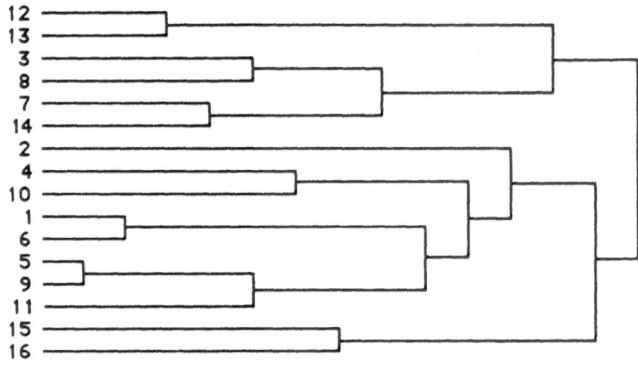

Constructs

No.	Constructs Description
1.	Steers the program (input-output, etc.) *vs* Program-processing
2.	Used *vs* Not used
3.	Verbal *vs* Numerical
4.	Changes the material *vs* Does not change the material
5.	Processes the material *vs* Sorts the material
6.	Memory commands *vs* Content of memory
7.	Delete *vs* Insert
8.	Manipulating, operational *vs* Descriptive
9.	Not useful *vs* Useful
10.	Complicated function/command *vs* Simple function
11.	Easy to use *vs* Hard to use
12.	Execute *vs* Prepare
13.	Expands the program *vs* Reduces the program
14.	Input/output function *vs* Editing function
15.	Often used *vs* Not used often
16.	Changes the form of the model *vs* Changes the content of the model

Figure 2. Hierarchical Cluster Diagram of Constructs Using Data From One SP RCRI.

It is also possible to use ranking or dichotimizing (a 2-point scale) for rating of objects on constructs. In our study we conducted ten SP RCRI with each subject (for one subject, it was eleven SP RCRI). The interviews were conducted every fourth to fifth week.

4.2 Analysis and Interpretation of RCRI Data

There exist several different methods to analyze collected RCRI data, for example factor analysis, multidimensional scaling, cluster analysis and principal component analysis.

We will discuss and exemplify some of these methods and also present a way to link the data to a theory of human-information processing, namely complexity theories.

Hierarchical Cluster Analysis. The output of an RCRI can be represented as a matrix, in our case as a matrix of ratings of SP-commands along constructs. One type of analysis that can be done on the data is hierarchical cluster analysis. The purpose of cluster analysis is to cluster objects in a meaningful and important way (Johnson, 1967; Anderberg, 1973; Romesburg, 1984). Hierarchical cluster analysis generates a hierarchy of clusterings having the characteristic that a new cluster is a merging of two or more previous clusters. At any stage in the clustering process, the next cluster is made up of the most similar clusters. The output of the process shows the sequences of mergings.

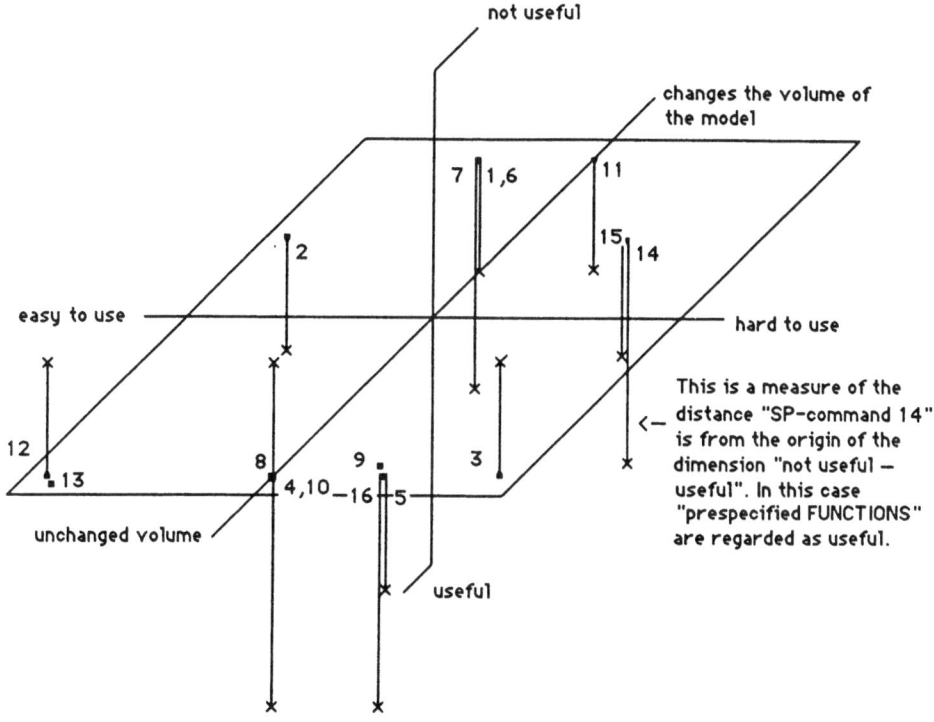

Figure 3. A Three-Dimensional Map of SP-commands. (For descriptions of the
the SP-commands see Table 1.) In this figure object numbers 15 and
16 are "Logical operators" respectively "Operators".

For an example of one of the study's subject, see Figure 2.[5] The focus here is on the constructs. It is
also possible to do an analysis with focus on SP-commands. The output of such an analysis would show
the clusterings of the different SP-commands.

The raw data matrix (not shown) and the cluster diagram suggest that this person perceives the
"processing" SP-commands to be most "useful" commands although these commands are on the "hard to
use" side (the cluster comprising constructs 5, 9, and 11). Furthermore, the analysis indicates, that "often
used" is linked to commands that "changes the content of the model" (the cluster comprising constructs 15
and 16).

Multidimensional Scaling. Another analytic technique is multidimensional scaling (Carroll and Arabie,
1980). The purpose of multidimensional scaling (MDS) is to locate the objects in a geometric space based
on the construct ratings of the objects.

Figure 3 shows a three-dimensional map of the SP-commands for one person.

Looking at Figure 3, we see that map contains three dimensions:

- Useful - Not useful

- Easy to use - Hard to use

- Changes the volume of the model - Unchanged volume

It is clear from the figure that this person perceives some of the SP-commands as useful and some as
not useful and also that some SP-commands are easy to use while others are hard to use. The two

---

[5]The hierarchical clustering was generated using Johnson's (1967) "diameter" rule for choice of clusters.
We will return to hierarchical cluster analysis in Section 4.2.3.

evaluative dimensions show that this user perceives SPLIT (PF1 S) as not very useful and also as hard to use. This can be contrasted with "pre-specified FUNCTIONS" which are considered to be equally hard to use but are considered very useful. Other useful functions/commands are OPERATORS, DISC, PRINT, and COPY. The later three are also considered to be more easy to use.

The third dimension, which is a descriptive dimension, shows how the person perceives the activeness of a command in changing the volume of an SP model.

Complexity Theories. It is also possible to link RCRI-data to a theory of information-processing and measure different aspects of a person's construct system. Here a measure of integrative complexity is used. The measure is rooted in the complexity theories (Schroder, Driver, and Streufert, 1967; Streufert & Streufert, 1978; and Streufert and Swezey, 1986).

Complexity theories are individual information processing theories; they focus on the *how* of information processing. Or in other words they are *structural* approaches to individual information processing. Integrative complexity is a central concept in cognitive complexity theories. It reflects an individual's *differentiation* and *integration* of his cognitive structure of a domain. Differentiation concerns how an individual uses constructs to discriminate between objects in a domain. Integration concerns how an individual interrelates his constructs.

It should be noted that cognitive complexity is a style that might change over time due to training, education, practice, reflection, and other factors. It is also possible that an individual might be more cognitively complex in one domain than in another.

Integrative Complexity, IC. Stabell developed a measure of integrative complexity, IC, in response to methodological problems with previous measures.[6] The output from an RCRI interview is a N *K matrix (that is, a person's rating of N objects on K constructs). IC is calculated from this matrix by a series of transformations.

To quote Stabell: "The Goodman and Kruskal (1954) lambda measure of association for symmetric, nominal scales was used to compute a measure of construct similarity for each and all pairs of constructs. The result is a K by K matrix of construct similarity measures. The construct similarity matrix is transformed into two different hierarchical clusters by applying Johnson's (1967) hierarchical clustering scheme and, respectively, the "diameter" rule and the "connectedness" rule for choice of clusters. The measure of integrative complexity is the difference between the two hierarchical clusters obtained which is computed using a metric proposed by Boorman and Oliver (1973) to compare valued trees.

$$IC = (1/[K(K-1)]) \sum_{j=1}^{K-1} \sum_{i=j+1}^{K} |c_{ij}|$$

where, IC = integrative complexity; K = number of constructs, c_{ij} = value of the lowest node in common between construct i and construct j in the hierarchical cluster obtained using the "connectedness rule"; and d_{ij} = value of the lowest node in common between construct i and construct j in the hierarchical cluster obtained using the "diameter rule" (Johnson, 1967).

Low scores on IC correspond to a situation where "...constructs are used in a balanced fashion to discriminate between" objects "... and a situation where constructs are equally interrelated, a situation that corresponds to a conceptual system with high integrative complexity" (Stabell, 1978, pp. 126-127).

High integrative complexity, low scores on IC, is not good per se. Cognitive complexity has to be related to a subject's environment. The complexity theories suggest that there should be a fit between a person's cognitive structure and environmental complexity.

In Section 5 we will return to integrative complexity when presenting the study of the three SP users.

Content Analysis. The above ways to analyze the data are structural approaches. It is also possible to analyze the words and sentences used by a person, that is, to analyze the generated constructs. Content Analysis discusses the specific words and concepts that are used, for example, "useful vs not useful" (evaluative constructs) and "changes the volume of the model vs unchanged volume" (descriptive constructs), and whether concrete or abstract concepts are used. These type of analyses can be linked to theories of "changes in concepts". It is beyond the scope of this paper to present and discuss the different theories concerned with development and changes in a person's concepts, but, for example, there are theories suggesting that more use of descriptive and abstract constructs indicates a more developed mental model.

---

[6]For a thorough discussion of different measures of cognitive structure, see Streufert and Streufert (1978), and Streufert and Swezey (1986). For a discussion of IC and its relationships to other measures of integrative complexity and measures of cognitive structure, see Stabell (1974, 1978).

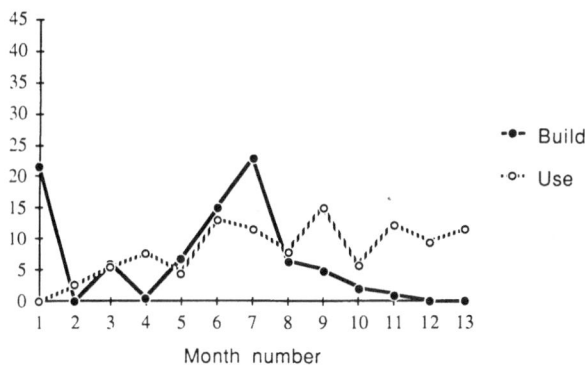

Figure 4. Spreadsheet Program Use for Person A.

4.3 Computer-Based Support

The RCRI methodology seems to be tedious, and it is if one is doing more advanced analyses without any computer-based support. But there exist on the market today several computer packages that can be used in the process (see for example, Mancuso & Shaw (1988), Shaw and Gaines (1988), and Shaw (1988)). It is possible to have computer-support for all the steps of RCRI and for analyses of collected data. For example, the RepGrid system described by Shaw (1988) can be used to generate objects, generate constructs, distribute constructs for ratings, and analyses and feedback. The system is implemented on Apple Macintosh and the personal computers can be linked in a local net.

5. AN APPLICATION OF THE METHODOLOGY: A STUDY OF SPREADSHEET PROGRAM USERS

In this section a description of the procedures followed and the results obtained from an application of the methodology in a natural setting is presented. First, we present the setting for the study and how the SP was used by the three persons. We then turn to the mental models of the three SP users.

5.1 The Setting

To study SP use in a natural setting, a longitudinal study was set up. The study was conducted in several departments in a city administration, over a time period of 15 months. Fourteen subjects participated voluntarily in the study. They all took a two-day course on the actual SP at the beginning of the study. The course was held during working hours, and the participants had all applied for the course voluntarily. The course was regarded as a job-related course by the participants' superiors.

Before the SP-course, the subjects were, according to Rockart & Flannery's classification of end users, nonprogramming end users "whose only access to computer-stored data is through software provided by others ... Access to computerized data is through a limited, menu-driven environment or a strictly followed set of procedures" (1983, p 778). Of the fourteen course participants only three actually become SP users.[7] The SP-course instructors did not try to have the participants learn any specific model of the SP.[8] The course was keystroke-oriented, trying to teach the participants the mechanics of SP use.

---

[7]The results of other parts of the study are found in Carlsson (1988a, in preparation). The non-use phenomena is explored in Carlsson (1988b, in preparation).

[8]An important distinction is between artificial and natural mental models (Johnson-Laird, 1983). Artificial models are acquired through cultural training and education, for example, models governing domains of pure mathematics. Natural mental models are acquired without explicit training and education. In the case of computer-based systems, explicit models of a system can be taught and such a model can have an impact on how a person perceives a system. The development of an artificial mental model can also be supported by manuals. A natural model can develop and evolve by experiential learning, a cyclic process of (1) concrete experience which is followed by (2) observation and reflection, which leads to (3) the formation of generalizations and abstract concepts, which then leads to (4) "hypotheses" to be tested

Table 2

Some Descriptive Statistics of SP Use

	Person A	Person B	Person C
Number of SP sessions/month	10.7	10.3	11.2
Number of SP model use sessions/month	7.4	7.5	8.2
Number of SP build sessions/month	3.3	2.9	2.9
Estimated SP sessions per week, from a pre-course interview	1	1-3	2-3
No. of models built	7	8	11
"Institutional" models, for repetitive use	6	7	8-9

Data was collected for three spreadsheet program users for a period of 13 months. To collect data on SP use, a simple blank form that a user filled out every time he used the SP was used. The blank form took only a couple of minutes to fill out.

The collected data shows SP uses in terms of:

1. Overall number of SP sessions and time spent in these sessions (SP use). This includes use of previously built SP models and building and re-building (changing) SP models.

2. Number of build/change sessions and time spent in these sessions, that is, sessions where a new model was built or an old one was changed (formulas and structure of a model were changed).

3. Number of sessions where a previously built model was used, without changing the model's structure and formulas, and time spent in these sessions (SP model use).

Table 2 shows the SP use for the three SP users.[9] Looking at the table we see that overall use for the three does not differ very much. Figures 4-6 show that over the 13 months there were fluctuations in model use and model building, especially in model building.

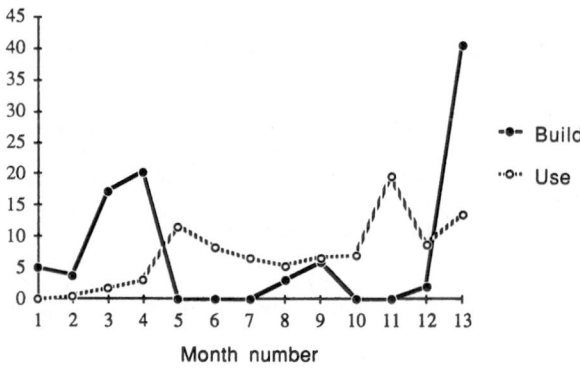

Figure 5. Spreadsheet Program Use for Person B.

in future situations, which in turn lead to new concrete experiences (Kolb, 1984). In our study, we assume that the SP-users develop models that can be considered as more natural than artificial.

[9]Comparing this study's SP use with data from other studies, we conclude that after a couple of months our subjects become average SP users in terms of number of SP sessions and time spent in these sessions (see Lee (1986), Mittman and Moore (1984), Pyburn (1986-87), and Quillard et al (1983)).

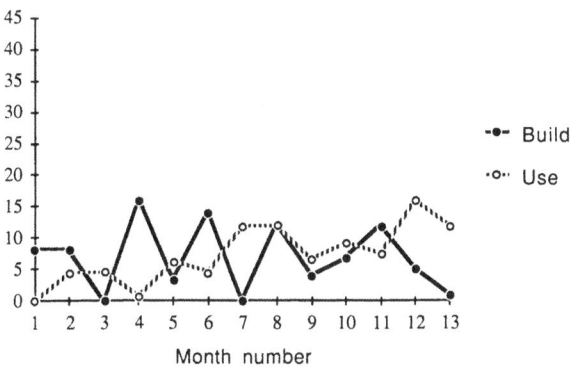

Figure 6. Spreadsheet Program Use for Person C.

5.2 Mental Models of the Spreadsheet Program

Compared to many other things and events in a person's environment, an SP can not be regarded as a complex domain. An SP is also a domain that is stable in that an SP does not change over time. On the other hand, an SP is used to build and use different SP models.

If it is true that an SP is a less complex domain, then we can hypothesize that a person will develop a mental model of the SP that is rather stable over time and that this model would be developed rather

quickly (in a couple of days of SP use). We can also hypothesize that a person's IC value would be rather high since an SP is not a complex domain, that is, a less complex mental model will work.

Figure 7 shows IC values for the three persons for the SP RCRI. The figure shows that:

- The IC values were not stable over time. We also see differences between the three. A's and B's IC values were more stable than C's, with a slow decrease over the months.

- The IC values were rather high (compared to what has been found in other studies on information sources; Stabell (1974), Fuglseth and Stabell (1985), and Carlsson (1988a)).

As we hypothesized, the IC values were rather high, which means low integrative complexity. A situation with low integrative complexity is a situation where there are fewer constructs that are used (differentiation) and also that there are fewer interrelationships between the constructs (integration). Lower integrative complexity also means that it is easier to change a construct system (the mental model). This partly explains why the IC values were rather unstable. But it is not likely that low integrative complexity leads to changes in the conceptual structure. There must be a reason for changing the conceptual structure. Kelly's theory proposes that a person changes and modifies his construct system if it is not "adequate" to him.

Other studies in different domains have shown that people develop construct systems that they think

Table 3

Correlation Between Integrative Complexity (IC) and Spreadsheet Program (SP) use. For A, n = 10 for B, n = 10; and for C, n = 11

	Build Time	Model Use Time
IC, A	-.265	-.525
IC, B	-.135	-.670**
IC, C	.591*	-.045

* p < .05
** p < .025

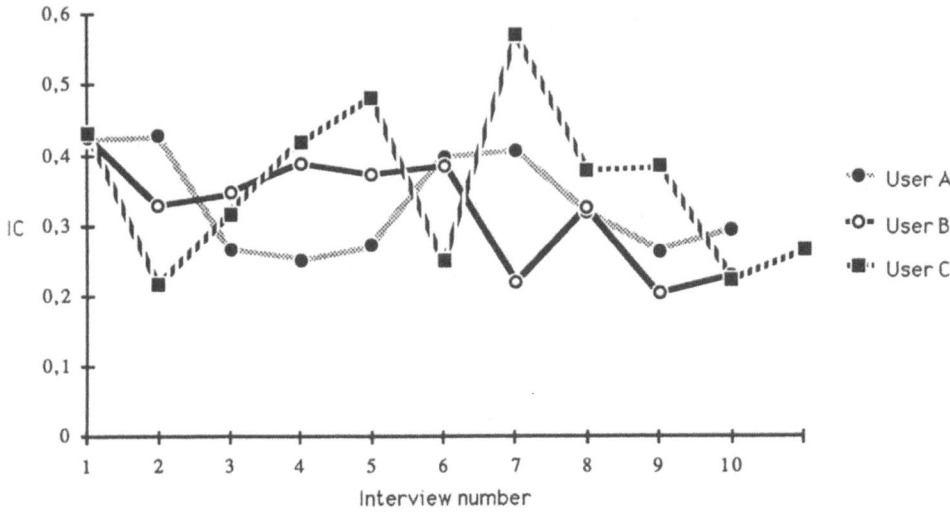

Figure 7. Integrative Complexity (IC) for Users A, B, and C.

are "adequate". When they encounter problems in using their mental models, they modify their models. For example, studies of students learning a subject have shown this process. This suggests that a user modifies his model so that the model becomes more adequate. The study also suggests that developing a stable mental model of this type is a process that takes a lot of time.

A correlation analysis was also done to see the relationships between IC and SP use. Table 3 shows the correlations between IC and two different SP use measures, model building time and model use time. Of the six relationships, two are statistically significant. It is interesting to note that A and B have negative relationships between SP use and IC. This suggests, in their case, that more model building and model use leads to the development of more complex cognitive structures.

6. SUMMARY AND FURTHER RESEARCH

We have in this paper presented and applied a methodology for eliciting users cognitive models (mental models) of an SP. We have also presented different methods to analyze data collected by RCRI.

The methodology can be applied to other types of computer-based systems, and it can be used in different stages in development and use of computer-based systems. A few examples will indicate the applicability of the methodology:

- For communication. One can have people do ratings on each others constructs. A designer of a computer-based system can rate the objects on a user's constructs the way he thinks the user would do such a rating. This would indicate how the designer thinks the user perceives the system. This can be compared to the user's ratings. Different users can also do ratings on each other's constructs. The overall purpose is to enhance the communication of how one perceives a system and to gain an understanding of how another perceives the same system. This is an important aspect in design and assessment of computer-based systems.

- Feedback. Several researchers have suggested adaptive design to computer-based systems, especially DSS. Critical in adaptive design is feedback from the users. The RCRI methodology can be used as a tool in such a feedback process. Cluster analysis and MDC as discussed in sections 4.2.1-4.2.2 can be used by a designer in assessing the need for changes or to assess the impact of a change in a system.

The study also indicates that we need further research in mental modelling. We have previously been working with a keystroke-level model of WP use (Carlsson and Stabell (1986), which is a model in line with the models discussed in Section 2. Work is in progress on mental models of other types, for example, models that focus on overall structural properties of spreadsheet use. Compared to the keystroke-level models, these models focus less on spreadsheet program use, and more on design and use of spreadsheet models.

94

We have also developed a composite metric for spreadsheet models which consists of (Carlsson and Konsynski, 1987):

- Volume, represented by effort, which reflects the cognitive effort in building and interpreting an SP model. It is related to an SP model in terms of operators and operands.

- Data flow, which reflects the communications of data in an SP model. It also considers the combinatorial aspects of data flows.

- Spatial layout of models, which reflects the spatial properties of an SP model.

In future research we will try to integrate the work into mental models, spreadsheet model complexity metrics and task complexity.[10]

ACKNOWLEDGEMENTS

Thanks and acknowledgements are extended to the author's mentor and advisor, Charles Stabell. He also thanks Benn Konsynski for providing a stimulating environment while he was a visiting scholar at the University of Arizona.

REFERENCES

Anderberg, M. R., 1973, *Cluster Analysis for Applications*, Academic Press, New York, NY.

Bannister, J., and Fransella, F., 1980, *Inquiring Man: The Psychology of Personal Constructs*, 2nd ed., Penguin, Harmondsworth, England.

Boorman, S. A., and D. C. Oliver, 1973, Metrics on Spaces of Finite Trees, *Journal of Mathematical Psychology*, Vol. 10, pp. 26-59.

Boose, J. H., 1986, *Expertise Transfer for Expert Systems Design*, Elsevier, New York, NY.

Campbell, D. J., 1988, Task Complexity: A Review and Analysis, *Academy of Management Review*, Vol. 13, No. 1, pp. 40-52.

Card, S. K., Moran, T. P., and Newell, A., 1980, Computer Text-Editing: An Information-Processing Analysis of a Routine Cognitive Skill, *Cognitive Psychology*, Vol. 12, pp. 32-74.

Card, S. K., Moran, T. P., and Newell, A., 1983, *The Psychology of Human-Computer Interaction*, Lawrence Erlbaum, Hillsdale, N.Y.

Carlsson, S. A., 1988a, A Longitudinal Study of Spreadsheet Program Use, *Journal of Management Information Systems*, Vol. 5, No. 1, pp. 82-100.

Carlsson, S. A., 1988b, Why Johnny Can't or Won't Spreadsheet, *The 11th Information Systems Research Seminar in Scandinavia*, Roros, Norway, August 10-12.

Carlsson, S. A., (in preparation), *User Model and Use of Decision Support Systems: A Cognitive Learning Perspective*, Ph.D. thesis in preparation, Dept. of Information and Computer Science, University of Lund, Lund, Sweden.

Carlsson, S. A., and Konsynski, B. R., 1987, *A Complexity Metric for Spreadsheet Models*, Unpublished working papers.

Carlsson, S. A., and Stabell, C. B., 1986, Spreadsheet Programs and Decision Support: A Keystroke-level Model of System User, *Decision Support Systems: A Decade in Perspective*, E. McLean and H. Sol, eds., North-Holland, Amsterdam, pp. 113-128.

Carroll, J. D., and Arabie, P., 1980, Multidimensional Scaling, *Annual Review of Psychology*, Vol. 31, pp. 607-649.

Easterby-Smith, M., 1981, The Design, Analysis, and Interpretation of Repertory Grids, *Recent Advances in Personal Construct Technology*, Shaw, M., ed., Academic Press, London, pp. 9-30.

Fjeldstad, O. D., and Konsynski, B. R., 1987, Knowledge-Based Support of the User-DSS Interaction, *Proceedings of the Twentieth Hawaii International Conference on Systems Sciences*, pp. 581-589.

Fuglseth, A. M., and Stabell, C. B., 1985, Capture, Representation, and Diagnosis of User Information Perception, *Knowledge Representation for Decision Support Systems*, Methlie, L. B., and Sprague, R. H., eds., North-Holland, Amsterdam, pp. 191-210.

---

[10]For discussions of different approaches to task complexity, see Campbell (1988) and Wood (1986). In future work we will apply some of these approaches to measure/assess complexity of tasks/activities supported by computer-based systems.

Gardner, H., 1985, *The Minds New Science: A History of the Cognitive Revolution*, Basic Books, New York, NY.

Grudnitski, G., 1981, A Methodology for Eliciting Information Relevant to Decision Makers, *Proceedings of the Second International Conference on Information Systems*, Cambridge, MA, pp. 105-120.

Grudnitski, G., 1984, Eliciting Decision-Makers' Information Requirements: Application of the Rep Test Methodology, *Journal of the Management Information Systems*, Vol. 1, No. 1, pp. 11-32.

Johnson, S. C., 1967, Hierarchical Clustering Schemes, *Psychometrika*, Vol. 32, No. 3, pp. 241-254.

Johnson-Laird, P. N., 1983, *Mental Models: Towards a Cognitive Science of Language, Inference, and Consciousness*, Harvard University Press, Cambridge, MA.

Kelly, G. A., 1955, *The Psychology of Personal Constructs*, W W Norton & Company, New York, NY.

Kieras, D. E., and Polson, P. G., 1985, An Approach to the Formal Analysis of User Complexity, *International Journal of Man-Machine Studies*, Vol. 22, pp. 365-394.

Kolb, D. A., 1984, *Experiential Learning: Experience as The Source of Learning and Development*, Prentice-Hall, Englewood Cliffs, NJ.

Lee, D. M. S., 1986, Usage Pattern and Sources of Assistance for Personal Computer Users, *MIS Quarterly*, Vol. 10, No. 4, pp. 313-325.

Lerch, F. J., 1986, *Computerized Financial Planning: Discovering Cognitive Difficulties in Model Building*, Ph.D. Dissertation, University of Michigan.

Mancuso, J. C., and Shaw, M. L. G., eds., 1988, *Cognition and Personal Structure: Computer Access and Analysis*, Praeger, New York, NY.

Mittman, B. S., and Moore, J. H., 1984, Senior Management Computer Use: Implications for DSS Designs and Goals, *Transactions of the Fourth International Conference on Decision Support Systems*, DSS-84, Dallas, TX, pp. 42-49.

Monk, A., 1985, *How and When to Collect Behavioral Data, Fundamentals of Human-Computer Interaction*, A. Monk, ed., Academic Press, London, pp. 69-79.

Moran, T. P., 1983, Getting Into a System: External-Internal Task Mapping Analysis, *Proceedings of the CHI '83 Conference on Human Factors in Computing Systems, December 12-15*, Boston, Association for Computing Machinery, New York, pp. 45-49.

Newell, A., and Simon, H., 1972, *Human Problem Solving*, Prentice-Hall, Englewood Cliffs, NJ.

Norman, D. A., Draper, S. W., eds., 1986, *User Centered System Design: New Perspectives on Human-Computer Interaction*, Lawrence Erlbaum, Hillsdale, NJ.

Osgood, C. E., Suci, G. J., and Tannenbaum, P. H., 1957, *The Measurement of Meaning*, University of Illinois Press, Urbana, IL.

Polson, P. G., 1987, A Quantitative Theory of Human-Computer Interaction, *Interfacing Thought: Cognitive Aspects of Human-Computer Interaction*, J. M. Carroll, ed., MIT Press, Cambridge, MA, 184-235.

Polson, P. G., and Kieras, D. E., 1985, A Quantitative Model of the Learning and Performance of Text Editing Knowledge, *Proceedings CHI '85 Human Factors in Computing Systems, April 14-18*, San Francisco, Association for Computing Machinery, New York, 213-220.

Pyburn, P. J., 1986-87, Managing Personal Computer Use: The Role of Corporate Management Information Systems, *Journal of Management Information Systems*, Vol. 3, No. 3, pp. 49-70.

Quillard, J. A., Rockart, J. F., Wilde, E., Vernon, M., and Mock., G., 1983, *A Study of the Corporate Use of Personal Computers*, CISR Working Paper No. 109, Sloan School of Management, Massachusetts Institute of Technology, Cambridge, MA.

Rich, E., 1983, Users are Individuals: Individualizing User Models, *International Journal of Man-Machine Studies*, Vol. 18, No. 3, pp. 199-214.

Rockart, J. F., and Flannery, L. S., 1983, The Management of End User Computing, *Communications of the ACM*, Vol. 26, No. 10, pp. 776-784.

Romesburg, C., 1984, *Cluster Analysis for Researchers*, Lifetime Learning, Belmont, CA.

Schroder, H. M., Driver, M. J., and Streufert, S., 1967, *Human Information Processing*, Holt, Rinehart & Winston, New York.

Shaw, M. L. G., 1980, *On Becoming a Personal Scientist: Interactive Computer Elicitation of Personal Models of the World*, Academic Press, London.

Shaw, M. L. G., ed., 1981, *Recent Advances in Personal Construct Technology*, Academic Press, New York, NY.

Shaw, M. L. G., 1988, Interactive Elicitation and Exchange of Knowledge, to appear in the *International Journal of Personal Construct Psychology*.

Shaw, M. L. G., and Gaines, B. R., 1988, An Interactive Knowledge Elicitation Technique Using Personal Construct Technology, *Knowledge Acquisition for Expert Systems: A Practical Handbook*, A Kidd, ed.,Plenum Press, New York, NY.

Stabell, C. B., 1974, *Individual Differences in Managerial Decision Making Processes: A Study of*

Conversational Computer System Usage, Unpublished Ph.D. Dissertation, Massachusetts Institute of Technology, Cambridge, MA.

Stabell, C. B., 1978, Integrative Complexity of Information Environment Perception and Information Use, *Organizational Behavior and Human Performance*, Vol. 22, No. 1, pp. 116-124.

Streufert, S., and Streufert, S. C., 1978, *Behavior in the Complex Environment*, V.H. Winston & Sons, Washington, D.C.

Streufert, S., and Swezey, R. W., 1986, *Complexity, Managers, and Organizations*, Academic Press, New York, NY.

Wood, R. E., 1986, Task Complexity: Definition of the Construct, *Organizational Behavior and Human Decision Processes*, Vol. 37, No. 1, pp. 60-82.

Young, R. M., 1983, Surrogates and Mappings: Two Kinds of Conceptual Models of Interactive Devices, *Mental Models*, D. Gentner and A. L. Stevens, eds., Lawrence Erlbaum Associates, Hillsdale, NJ, pp. 35-52.

USE OF A BLACKBOARD FRAMEWORK TO MODEL SOFTWARE DESIGN

J. I. A. Siddiqi*, J. H. Sumiga**,
and   B. Khazaei**

*Dept. of Computer Studies
Sheffield City Polytechnic
Pond Street
Sheffield, U.K.
**School of Computing
The Polytechnic
Wolverhampton
West Midlands, U.K.

Abstract: The paper proposes a model of program designer behavior, based on the blackboard architecture, that has the capability of describing multi-directional decision-making by means of hierarchical (i.e., 'top-down' and 'bottom-up'), heterarchical, sequential and incremental planning strategies for the design process. It is expressed in terms of cognitive processes that operate on, and communicate via, information posted on a specific blackboard structure. These processes, or specialists, are an extension of the set proposed by Hayes-Roth and Hayes-Roth (1979) for opportunistic planning. Additional specialists in our characterization are divided into those that correspond to general problem-solving methods and those relating specifically to the program design task. These include specialists that note features of the problem, those that analogize and make assessments about sub-problems and those that modify policies. Details of an experimental study involving the collection of verbal and video protocols are also reported. The proposed model is used as an explanatory framework for the results obtained. These are also discussed in relation to other cognitive models of the program design process.

1. INTRODUCTION

Empirical investigation of the software development process has been recognized, in the past decade, as an important area of research. The results of such research could yield guidelines for software construction and the functional capabilities of knowledge-based support tools.

The early work of Shneiderman (1979) proposed a syntactic and semantic model of programmers. Sheppard et al. (1979) attempted to identify the multiplicity of factors which characterize programmers abilities. Soloway and Ehrlich (1984) have shown the importance of plans in the programming task.

Our own work has advanced a cognitive model of designer behavior. It is based on the empirically supported view that program design is a problem-solving task involving repeated application of decomposition and elaboration (Siddiqi, 1984). The former activity is viewed as goal generation. The latter is considered to consist of the allocation of known 'clusters' or plans to the existing decomposition structure (Siddiqi, 1985, 1987). The results also indicate that general problem-solving strategies of a heterarchical nature are employed opportunistically, in problem decomposition (i.e., in a 'do what you can' and 'fit the rest around it' manner) (Ratcliff and Siddiqi, 1985).

Some of these findings are in accordance with results recently published by Guindon et al. (1987), Kant (1985), Khazaei (1987) and Rist (1987).

The model presented here is a refinement of our previous work (Siddiqi, 1984, 1987). It reinforces the principle that programming and, in particular, program design can be viewed as a planning activity.

Empirical Foundations of Information and Software Science V
Edited by P. Zunde and D. Hocking, Plenum Press, New York, 1990

99

Many accord with this view; indeed as has been pointed out by Jefferies et al. (1981):

"The task of design involves a complex set of processes. Starting from a global statement of the problem a designer must develop a precise plan for a solution that will be realized in some concrete way..."

The refinement, which produces a richer theory of program design with an emphasis on problem decomposition, is based on a blackboard architecture (Hayes-Roth and Hayes-Roth, 1979). It incorporates specific forms of sequential planning and island-driving (Siddiqi and Sumiga, 1987).

Section 2 details the proposed model and our choice of specialists, characterizing multi-directional decision-making and incremental planning strategies. Section 3 provides specific details of an observational study and the application of the model to explain subject's behavior, as recorded in the form of verbal and video protocols. Section 4 discusses the results of the experimental study, in the context of the program design process. In the concluding section, brief consideration is given to issues relating to the sufficiency of the model.

2. THE MODEL

In our model, the planning process is simulated using many distinct cognitive specialists whose actions result in decisions being recorded on a blackboard structure. This structure enables specialists to interact and communicate by allowing them access to previously made decisions, irrespective of which specialist made them.

The function of specialists is to make tentative decisions to be incorporated into a proposed plan. Different specialists influence different aspects of a plan, ranging from high-level issues such as the approach taken, to detailed ordering of specific operations. Specialists consist of two components: the condition component and the action component. The former determines the circumstances under which it can be activated, while the latter describes the effect it has on the blackboard.

The blackboard structure, as suggested by Hayes-Roth and Hayes-Roth, consists of five planes reflecting different conceptual categories of decisions. In addition, each plan is partitioned into hierarchically organized 'levels of abstraction', such that decisions recorded at each level are potential refinements of those recorded on the level above.

In order to model the program design process, we propose the characterization shown in Figure 1.

The *executive plane* consists of a two level hierarchy. The first level (priorities) is where specialists record decisions about the priorities associated with the allocation of resources.

The *meta-design plane* consists of four levels: problem definition, design approach, policies and evaluation criteria. These are not hierarchical but reflect different aspects of the designer's approach. The first two levels respectively contain decisions about understanding the problem specification and how to generate solutions. For instance, should the designer rigidly follow a specific methodology, e.g., structured programming, then the decision recorded would be to use step-wise refinement, whereas if no particular discipline is followed then ad-hoc and intuitively based approaches would be chosen. The policy level indicates the global aims, constraints and desirable features of an acceptable solution. These can often reflect the designer's intentions, for example 'Do the bits I can do and then worry about the rest'. The final level, corresponds to decisions made about how a potential design is to be judged.

The *design abstraction plane* and the *design plane* each contain four hierarchically organized levels. There is a strong interaction between corresponding levels on these two planes, such that decisions recorded on a level of the former plane usually characterize types of decisions to be incorporated on the corresponding level of the latter plane. On the design abstraction plane, the four levels are: intentions, schemes, strategies and tactics. The corresponding levels on the design plane are: outcomes, algorithms, procedures, and operations.

The intentions level is where specialists record decisions about low-level aims such as satisfying problem requirements. A decision made at this level could result in a corresponding decision on the outcomes level, refining the recorded intention(s), for example, naming the particular problem requirements to be satisfied. The schemes level contains decisions as to how the intentions and outcomes are to be achieved and the algorithms level records decisions about the specific way the scheme is to be implemented. The strategies level is where specialists record decisions which refine those made at the schemes and the algorithms levels, these being made more specific at the procedures level. A similar relationship exists between the tactics and operations levels.

The *observations plane* can be seen as a series of slots containing observations, perceived by the designer to be pertinent to the solution of the problem. Among the slots we have found most relevant to the design process are: observations about structures (e.g., problems, data or processes); similarities (e.g.,

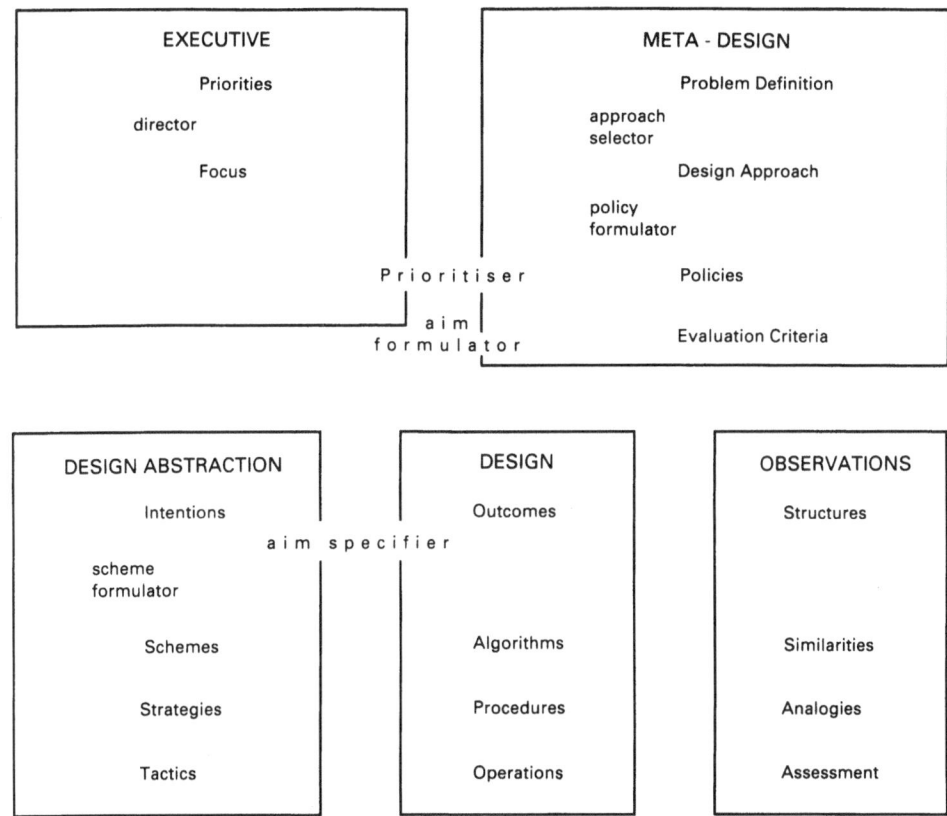

Figure 1. The Blackboard Planes and Some Example Specialists.

structural similarities); analogies (e.g., similar problems previously solved); and assessment (e.g., perceived difficulty of individual tasks).

Our choice of specialists for program design, from those identified by Hayes-Roth and Hayes-Roth for the planning process, are shown in Figure 1. This set of specialists, whose names are intended to suggest their function, constitute a framework for high-level decision-making. Each specialists is shown as linking the level from which it is triggered, to where its decision is recorded. Some specialists are triggered immediately by a decision being posted, while others may require the presence of additional configurations of prior decisions. For example, the recording of a decision on the policies level will, in general, initiate a chain of decisions involving the prioritizer and director specialists, thereby forming the necessary configuration for triggering the aim formulator.

The additional specialists required for our characterization can be divided into those that correspond to general problem-solving methods and those relating specifically to the program design task. The former set include:

- A *features noter*, which records relevant features of the problem specification on the observations plane.

- A *comparator* that notes similarities in problem features, recording these on the similarities level.

- An *analogizer*, which identifies previously attempted sub-problems in the problem being solved, and records its decision on the analogies level.

- An *assessor*, which notes the perceived level of difficulty of sub-problems, on the assessment level.

A *policy modifier*, which alters the policy and is triggered by specific configurations of decisions on the lower-level planes. This specialist is largely responsible for producing decision flows in a 'bottom-up' direction.

The domain-dependent specialists include *algorithm*, *procedure* and *operations retrievers*, which perform low-level retrieval from long-term memory and find a data structure analyzer, which records observations about structural properties of the data.

In the next section, this model is used to explain subject behavior in an observational study, the model being used as a framework for interpreting the sequence of decisions made during the design process.

3. EXPERIMENTAL REPORT

We follow the traditional approach, as used by Hayes-Roth and Hayes-Roth, that of demonstrating sufficiency by interpreting subjects' protocols. The empirical evidence to be presented in this section originates from an observational study involving six subjects, all of whom were second year Computer Science undergraduates (Khazaei, 1987). Each subject was asked to produce a program for the signal problem (see Appendix 1 for problem specification and two possible decompositions). The subjects were asked to verbalize as they were attempting to solve the problem. Their verbal and written reports were recorded. In addition, reports were taken after they had completed the problem. The usual methods for protocol collection and analysis were adopted. For a more detailed discussion, see Siddiqi and Khazaei (1987).

Figure 2. Stage 1.

NOTE: In the text, vehicle count, survey length, wait period and longest wait period are denoted by VC, SL, WP, and LWP, respectively.

3.1 Interpretation of Protocols

The following is a major portion of one subject's protocol, in the sequence in which it occurred. The format used is to first present a section of the subject's protocol, then a narrative description of the subject's behavior followed by a characterization of this in terms of the proposed model.

Our starting point is when the problem specification is presented to the subject.

The subject read aloud the statement of the problem, which is interpreted as the recording of decision 1 on the problem definition level, as shown in Figure 2.

The subject then carried out a selective re-read of the problem specification:

"A clock is started at the beginning of the survey and at one second intervals thereafter, it transmit a two(pause) transfer a zero."

This is interpreted as the invocation of the features noter specialist, which records the Observation that the specification contains a data stream (decision 2).

The subject then drew a pictorial representation of a detector, clearly indicating input of signals 0, 1, and 2. This behavior is explained as the subject noting the presence of a data stream and viewing its structure as a sequence of signals.

In terms of the model, this corresponds to the triggering of the approach selector, policy formulator, prioritizer, director, and data structure analyzer which record decisions 3 - 7.

From the video protocol there was evidence of a considerable amount of cognitive processing being carried out. The subject started to draw a flowchart, i.e., wrote 'Start', 'Get Input', and continued to complete the major portion of it by distinguishing between signal types and incrementing counters for vehicle count (VC) and survey length (SL). At this point, he said:

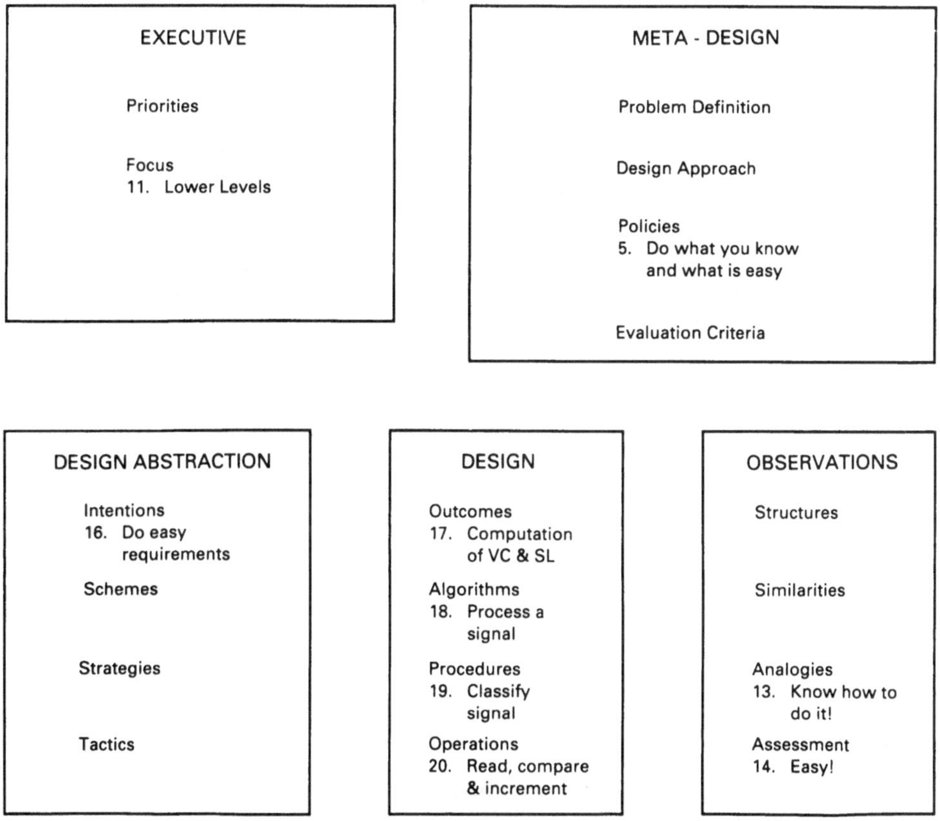

EXECUTIVE

Priorities

Focus
11. Lower Levels

META - DESIGN

Problem Definition

Design Approach

Policies
5. Do what you know
    and what is easy

Evaluation Criteria

DESIGN ABSTRACTION

Intentions
16. Do easy
     requirements

Schemes

Strategies

Tactics

DESIGN

Outcomes
17. Computation
     of VC & SL

Algorithms
18. Process a
     signal

Procedures
19. Classify
     signal

Operations
20. Read, compare
     & increment

OBSERVATIONS

Structures

Similarities

Analogies
13. Know how to
     do it!

Assessment
14. Easy!

Figure 3. Stage 2.

"This sort of gives me an indication of what kind of questions have to be asked when the data comes in (pauses and re-explains) processing the data as it comes in..."

Simplistically this behavior corresponds to the subject solving most of the problem by deciding to process the data stream a signal at a time and then concentrating on the easier 6 tasks, namely the computation of VC and SL.

In terms of our model, a richer explanation is as follows. Decision 8, which changes the focus, arises because the first part of the priority, to find the structure of the data, has been completed. The intention to satisfy the requirements of computing VC, SL, etc., results from the invocation of the aim formulator and the aim specifier, recording decisions 9 and 10. This in turn results in a focusing on lower levels of the design abstraction and design planes (decision 11). The scheme formulator, because the data stream is perceived as a sequence of signals, records decision 12, i.e., to process the data stream. A significant portion of the high-level decision-making has been carried out by this stage.

Our conjecture that the subject initially concentrates on the easier parts of the problem is supported by the following protocol obtained through retrospective, rather than concurrent, probing.

"As you can see, I tend to write blocks in no apparent order. I tend to do it in easiness order.... I tend to do the easy parts first, and leave the nasty little bits until either my confidence is built-up or alternatively, I can't escape from doing them anymore."

In terms of our model, the subject making the crucial observations that the computation of VC and SL are familiar and easy tasks, is characterized by the firing of the analyzer and assessor specialists which record decisions 13 and 14 - see Figure 3).

These opportunistic realizations produce a change in policy, to 'Do what you know and what is easy' through the invocation of the policy modifier, recorded as decision 15. The policy change initiates the invocation of the aim formulator and the aim specifier, which record decisions 16 and 17. Since the tasks of computing VC and SL were both familiar and considered to be easy, they form an achievable 'island of certainty'. Consequently, the algorithm, procedure and operations retrievers are successively fired (decision 18 - 20). At this point of development, the subject had drawn the following structure:

```
Start
   |
Get input
   |
Is input 1? -----car = car + 1
   |
Is input 2? -----time = time + 1
   |
```

The subject continued to complete the flowchart by adding a termination condition and a loop. We characterize this by the recording of decisions 21 - 24 by the scheme formulator, algorithm, procedures and operations retrievers, respectively. For the sake of brevity, these decisions have been omitted from the diagrams.

At this point, the subject said:

"This won't have the interval timer on it here because at the moment it is only counting the total amount of time and the total number of cars.... ... We've got no indication of the period of time between adjacent cars.... ... Somewhere here (refers to the flowchart) there's got to be a second timer...."

This corresponds to the start of the next stage of development. The subject has realized that there is more to be done, i.e., the interval between cars needs to be computed. He has also adopted a policy of 'Fitting the rest around what has been done', i.e., the addition of components to compute the waiting period (WP) and, eventually, the longest waiting period (LWP).

In our model (see Figure 4), this is represented by a change in policy, to one of 'doing the next bit', recorded as decision 25. This then results in some high-level decision-making shown as the cycle of decisions 26 - 29, in order to formulate a potentially achievable goal, namely finding WP (see decision 30). Our conjecture that this is also a known and not too difficult task is supported by the following protocol:

"At the moment, I'm thinking basically about the structure, about putting in the car timer. Now I am fairly certain that the way to do it is..."

The essential part of this stage is the subject's observations, via the analogizer and assessor, that finding WP is a known and not too difficult task (decisions 31 and 32)... The result of this is another invocation of the policy modifier, which changes the policy to one of attempting to fit the remaining part of the design around the structure already produced (decision 33).

There is a considerable amount of further protocol recording the subject's attempts to complete and elaborate his solution. Although not presented, this has also been characterized by our model. Briefly, this concerns the subject adding in the detail of components to compute WP and LWP, in that order. It was also observed that he separately developed the components necessary to fulfil these sub-tasks and then added them to his outline solution.

4. DISCUSSION OF RESULTS

The previous section presented an interpretation of one subject's protocol, both in behavioral terms and in terms of our proposed model. In the observational study carried out, the model was applied to the protocols of several subjects solving the signal problem. This study identified certain general behavioral characteristics in the program design process, on which the discussion now focuses.

Although programming is not purely a 'top-down' activity, nevertheless, there is the presence of some high-level decision-making with a 'top-down' hierarchical flow. Observations, as exemplified by the sequence of decisions 1 to 7, shown in Figure 2, confirm this.

A commonly reported behavioral trait is goal generation, i.e., searching for potentially achievable goals. This, in our model, is characterized by a decision cycle involving changes in the focus of attention from the higher-level to the lower-level planes. Illustrative examples of this cycle are decisions 8 to 11 (see Figure

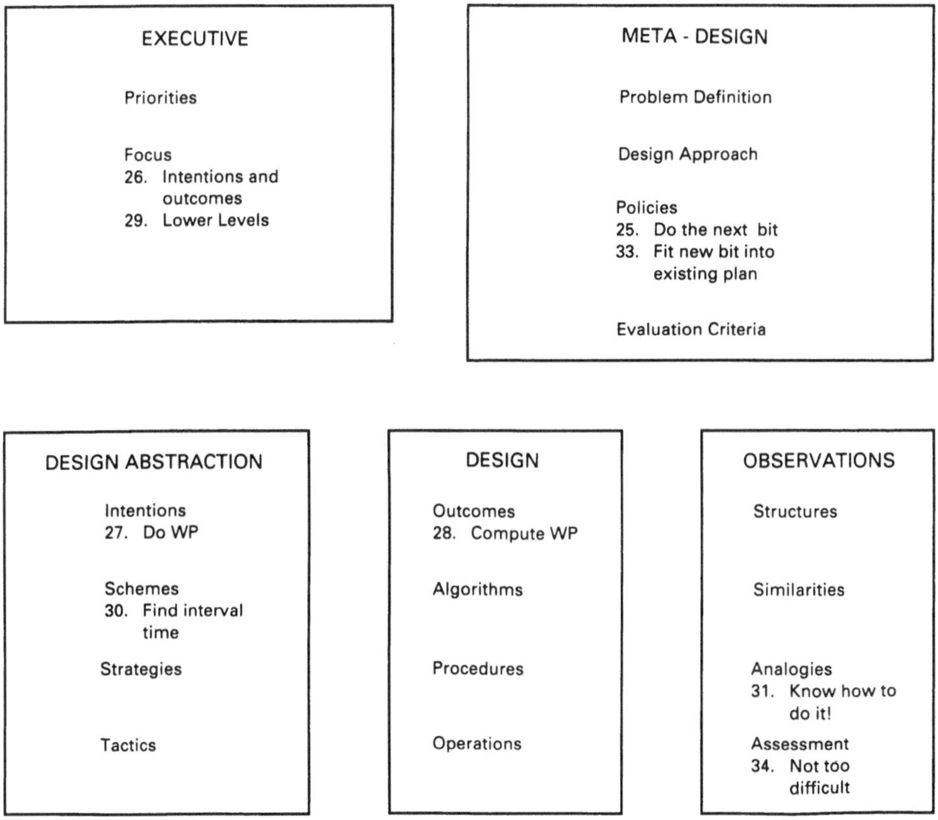

Figure 4. Stage 3.

2), and decisions 26 to 29 (see Figure 3). These occur at different stages of development, the former occurring in the first stage, the latter occurring in the third stage. Both, however, result in the formulation of new schemes which are potentially achievable goals.

Following the conception of a potentially achievable goal, it is necessary to adopt a suitable policy to formulate an island. In our model, this policy modification corresponds to the invocation of the analogizer, assessor, and policy modifier specialists. The study revealed that most subjects tended to modify their policy to one of doing things in 'easiness' order. This is most likely to be a result of their lack of experience. Examples of this behavior are decisions 13 to 15 (Figure 3) and decisions 31 to 33 (Figure 4). This process of 'island formulation' represents the development of an 'island of certainty', i.e., a solvable sub-goal of the problem. This is equivalent to Rist's (1987) notion of a 'focal idea' and building a plan around it, and Kant's (1985) concept of a 'kernel structure'.

In the study, it was observed that when subjects had formulated 'islands of certainty', they were immediately able to elaborate them. In our model, this goal elaboration is characterized by the invocation of the algorithm procedure and operations retrieval specialists. In Figure 3, decisions 18 to 20 exemplify this behavior. Soloway and Ehrlich's (1984) characterize this behavior as the retrieval of known plans.

The model provides a plausible description of decisions generally made during program design. It also captures most of the behavioral characteristics observed in other empirical studies of program design. The reason it can do both of these is that it has the capability of characterizing multi-directional planning. For instance, when the designer proceeded cautiously, i.e., used 'least commitment' and/or 'divide and conquer' approaches, the flow of decision-making was seen to be from the meta-design plane to the design abstraction and design planes. In program design terms this is known as 'top-down' decomposition of step-wise refinement. In cases where the designer used synthetic techniques or 'most commitment' approaches, the decision-making proceeded in a reverse direction. For instance, a decision made on the design plane caused a change in the policy level of the meta-design plane, which corresponds to 'bottom-up' design.

5. CONCLUSION

The primary aim of this work, of which the initial part is reported here, is to develop an operational model which synthesizes the behavioral characteristics identified in existing empirical studies of the software development process. A major goal of this paper has been an attempt to demonstrate the sufficiency of the model. While an informal demonstration of this has been provided, there still remains much to be explained about program designer behavior. In particular, several subjects exhibited types of behavior loosely corresponding to conceptual modelling and mental execution (Siddiqi, 1984; Hoc, 1977) and Hayes-Roth and Hayes-Roth, 1979). The model is currently being extended by the addition of further specialists and work on a prototype is currently in progress.

REFERENCES

Guindon, R., Krasner, H., and Curtis, B., 1987, Cognitive Processes in Software Design: Activities in Early, Upstream Design, *Proceedings of Human-Computer Interaction-INTERACT '87*, Stuttgart.
Hayes-Roth, B., and Hayes-Roth, F., 1979, A Cognitive Model of Planning, *Cognitive Science*, Vol. 3, pp. 275-310.
Hoc, J. M., 1977, Role of Mental Representation in Learning a Programming Language, *International Journal of Man-Machine Studies*, Vol. 9, pp. 87-105.
Jefferies, R., Turner, A. A., Polson, P. G., and Atwood, M. E., 1979, The Processes Involved in Designing Software, *Cognitive Skills and Their Acquisition*, Chapter 8, Anderson, J., ed., Lawrence Erlbaum, Hillsdale, NJ.
Kant, E., 1985, Understanding and Automating Algorithm Design, *IEEE Trans. on Software Engineering*, Vol. SE-11, No. 11.
Khazaei, B., 1987, *Determinants of Program Designer Behavior: An Empirical Investigation*, Internal Report, SCIT, The Polytechnic, Wolverhampton.
Ratcliff, B., and Siddiqi, J. I. A., 1985, An Empirical Investigation Into Problem Decomposition Strategies Used in Program Design, *International Journal of Man-Machine Studies*, Vol. 22, pp. 77-90.
Rist, R., 1987, *Schema Creation in Programming*, Working Paper, Cognitive Science Program, Dept. of Psychology, Yale University.
Sheppard, S. B., Curtis, B., Milliman, P., and Love, L. T., 1979, Modern Coding Practices and Programmer Performance, *Computer*, 12, pp. 41-49.
Shneiderman, B., and McKay, D., 1979, Syntactic/Semantic Interactions in Programmer Behavior: A Model and Experimental Results, *Int. J. Computer and Information Sciences*, Vol. 8, pp. 219-238.

Siddiqi, J. I. A., 1984, *An Empirical Investigation Into Problem Decomposition Strategies Used in Program Design*, Ph.D. Thesis, University of Aston in Birmingham.

Siddiqi, J. I. A., 1985, A Model of Program Designer Behavior, *Proceedings of the Conference of the British Computer Society Human Computer Interaction Specialist Group: People and Computers; Design in the Interface*, Johnson, P., and Cook, S., eds.

Siddiqi, J. I. A., 1987, How do Software Practitioners Write Programs? An Empirical Study, *Empirical Foundations of Information and Software Sciences IV*, Zunde, P., and Agrawal, J. C., eds., Plenum Press, New York, NY, pp. 325-332.

Siddiqi, J. I. A., and Ratcliff, B., 1988, The Influence of Specification on Problem Decomposition in Program Design, to appear in *International Journal of Man-Machine Studies*.

Siddiqi, J. I. A., and Khazaei, 1987, To Intervene, or Not to Intervene..., *The Fifth Symposium on Empirical Foundations of Information and Software Sciences*, Roskilde, Denmark.

Siddiqi, J. I. A., and Sumiga, J. H., 1987, Empirical Evaluation of a Proposed Model of the Program Design Process, *Empirical Foundations of Information and Software Sciences IV*, Zunde, P., and Agrawal, J. C., eds., Plenum Press, New York, NY, pp. 333-345.

Soloway, E., and Ehrlich, K., 1984, Empirical Studies of Programming Knowledge, *IEEE Trans. Software Engineering*, Vol. 10, No. 5, pp. 595-609.

APPENDIX

Problem Specification

A traffic survey is conducted automatically by placing a detector at the roadside, connected by data-links to a computer. Whenever a vehicle passes the detector, it transmit a signal consisting of the number 1. A clock in the detector is started at the beginning of the survey and at one second intervals thereafter it transmit a signal consisting of the number 2. At the end of the survey, the detector transmit a 0. Each signal is received by the computer as a single number (i.e., it is impossible for two signals to arrive at the same time). Design a program which reads such a set of signals and outputs the following:

(a) the length of the survey period;

(b) the number of vehicles recorded;

(c) the length of the longest waiting period without a vehicle.

THE ENTITY-RELATIONSHIP DATA MODEL CONSIDERED HARMFUL

G. M. Nijssen, D. J. Duke, and S. M. Twine

Department of Computer Science
University of Queensland
St. Lucia, 4067
AUSTRALIA

Abstract: In the world of Information Systems, the Entity-Relationship model (first defined by Chen in 1976) is widely taught and also widely used in practice. Despite the fact that the ER model is commonly considered a conceptual data model, it violates the Conceptualisation Principle as defined in the International Standards Organization report of 1982. In this paper, we will show that the ER model contains too many different ways to represent (or encode) the same proposition (or fact). Indeed, it is possible to claim that the ER model is essentially a reincarnation of the CODASYL DDL/DML model (as defined in the CODASYL DBTG report of 1971).

As the number of fact-encoding mechanisms increases, so must the complexity of any design procedure. This means that it is very difficult to provide the ER designer with effective prescriptive guidance on how to perform the design task.

The ER graphical notation is often claimed to be a good medium for communication between the users and the EDP professionals. We will show that this graphical notation does not support effective validation procedures that involve the user (the only person who truly knows the semantics of the application).

1. INTRODUCTION

The ER data model is widely taught as a conceptual data model in universities, and used as such in practice. We claim that the ER data model is harmful because its use *necessarily introduces conceptually irrelevant detail* into the resulting conceptual schema. Specifically:

- It has too many fact encoding constructs.

- It has too few declarative constraints.

- It has a graphical representation which is inadequate as a good basis for effective user validation of the conceptual schema (difficult to populate and difficult to express essential declarative constraints).

- As a consequence of these three factors, it is difficult to provide prescriptive guidance for the ER schema designer, even in principle.

2. IS THE ER DATA MODEL A CONCEPTUAL DATA MODEL?

Before we concern ourselves with whether or not the ER model is a conceptual data model, it would be prudent to answer the following 2 questions:

Empirical Foundations of Information and Software Science V
Edited by P. Zunde and D. Hocking, Plenum Press, New York, 1990

109

(1) What is a data model?

(2) What does it mean for a data model to be conceptual?

A data model is a set of concepts which can be used to describe the possible (permitted) propositions recorded about a Universe of Discourse. More specifically, a data model provides:

A set of data structure types, or *fact encoding constructs*

A set of operators for use in populating or depopulating these fact encoding constructs (creating and destroying instances of these data structure types)

A set of constraints that are used to prescribe the permitted population states of the fact encoding constructs.

Examples of data models include: relational (Codd, 1970), network (*CODASYL: Database Task Group Report*, ACM, 1971), and hierarchical (Tsichritzis and Lochovsky, 1976) data models, ER (Chen, 1976), NIAM (Nijssen, 1986; Falkenberg, 1982; Meersman, 1988; Kent, 1986).

The ANSI/SPARC (Dogac and Chen, 1983) Report defined three levels of data description: conceptual (which is concerned with the semantics of the information to be recorded), internal (which is concerned with the physical implementation of the information to be recorded), and external (which is concerned with the presentation to the user of the information to be recorded).

It is commonly accepted that the data should first be described on the conceptual level, where its semantics are made explicit, before it is described on the internal and external levels. This allows the designer to consider the problems of representing the structure and semantics of the information separately from the problems of how to physically store that information and perform certain processes on that stored information with an acceptable efficiency, or present the information in a special way to a user or group of users.

The representation of the formal semantics of the information about some Universe of Discourse, at the conceptual level, is called a conceptual schema. In order to achieve this separation of conceptual, internal, and external levels, the Conceptualisation Principle (stated below) defines which aspects are relevant to the conceptual schema.

Conceptualisation Principle (van Griethuysen, 1982)

"A conceptual schema should only include conceptually relevant aspects, both static and dynamic, of the universe of discourse, thus excluding all aspects of (external or internal) data representation, physical data organization and access as well as all aspects of particular external user representation such as message formats, data structures, etc."

Structurally, a conceptual data model (or conceptual schema language) must include at least one data structure type capable of encoding propositions (or instantiated predicates) about the Universe of Discourse.

2.1 The ER Data Model

Although the ER model has evolved since its introduction by Chen in 1976, the core concepts of the model has remained essentially unchanged (a recent description can be found in Parent and Spaccapietra (1985).
The informal axiom of the ER model is that:

"the real world consists of entities and relationships" (Chen, 1976)

An entity is defined to be

"a thing" which can be distinctly identified", (Chen, 1976)

while a relationship is

"an association amongst entities" (Chen, 1976)

Relationships are simply propositions, with each place in the proposition holding a term which may either be another proposition or a value. These terms are called entities in the ER model.

However, the ER model also permits entities and relationships to possess properties, called *attributes*, whose values belong to *value sets*. Attributes which are used in the identification of an entity are commonly called *identifiers* of that entity (for example, in Teorey, Ynag, and Fry, 1986); non-identifying attributes are usually called *descriptors*.

Attributes are also classified on the basis of whether they can have more than one value at any point in time. Those attributes which are restricted to at most one value at any instant are called *mono-valued* (or single-valued). The other class of attribute is said to be *multi-valued*.

Since the conceptual schema must deal with the invariants of the information to be recorded, entities can be classified into entity sets and relationships can be classified into relationship sets.

Entities that have common properties are grouped into "entity sets". Entities (and, therefore, entity sets) can be partitioned into two classes: strong entity (sets) and weak entity (sets). *Strong* entities are identified solely on the basis of their own attributes, while *weak* entities are identified using a combination of their own attributes, and the attributes of other entities involved in a relationship with the first.

Each relationship is a member of one membership set. A relationship set is formally defined as:

$$\{[e_1, e_2, ..., e_n] \mid e_1 \in E_1, e_2 \in E_2, e_n \in E_n\}$$

where $E_1 ... E_n$ are entity sets.

Note that the entity sets above need not be distinct (i.e., a relationship may involved more than one entity from an entity set). Following this definition, a relationship is a tuple of the form $[e_1, e_2, ..., e_n]$ where $e_i \in E_i$.

The abstraction from entities and relationships to entity sets and relationship sets can easily be represented as a set of logical propositions. Formally, each set (whether consisting of entities or relationships) corresponds to a unary proposition which states that an entity or relationship is a member of a particular entity or relationship set. Even better, a sorted predicate logic distinguishes this type of information on a syntactic level, rather than just treating the information as another set of propositions about the Universe of Discourse.

A formal definition of attributes requires more care, as there are two attribute classes to consider.

Single valued attributes are easily defined as functions from entity or relationship sets to value sets, thus:

$$f: E_i \text{ or } R_i \rightarrow V_i$$

There is a problem in defining multi-valued attributes, however. That is, are multi-valued attribute sets or multi-sets (collections in which an element can be repeated)? Since the answer will not affect the arguments in this paper, we will assume, for simplicity, that multi-valued attributes are sets. Following this assumption, such an attribute can be formally defined as a function from an entity set or relationship to a *set* of values drawn from a value set:

$$f: E_i \text{ or } R_i \rightarrow PV_i \quad (PV \text{ is the power set of } V)$$

Various extensions to the ER model have been proposed, such as compound attributes Parent and Spaccapietra (1985), generalization hierarchies and subtypes (Teorey, Yang, and Fry, 1986). These extended ER models still contain the basic ER model at their hearts, so they must also include the non-conceptual distinctions made in that core model.

2.2 A Small Example

To illustrate how an ER schema can be used to represent information about a Universe of Discourse, we will develop a simple example based around a small information system that records subject and time-tabling information for a university or college. Additionally, this information system will record a few details of persons involved in studying of teaching within the University. (We will assume that a person within this restricted UoD is uniquely identified by their family name.)

We begin by informally describing the universe of discourse by means of examples of input forms and output reports that the system described above might be expected to provide, together with a brief explanation of the information contained in these forms and reports.

Figure 1 contains populated examples of an input form that might be provided for the entry of details about persons studying or teaching (or both) at the University.

The information contained on these forms can be interpreted as follows:

University of Eastern Australia	University of Eastern Australia
Person Details	**Person Details**
Family Name : Smith Date of Birth : 10/07/1967 Vehicles :	Family Name : Stuy Date of Birth : 01/11/1968 Vehicles :

University of Eastern Australia	University of Eastern Australia
Person Details	**Person Details**
Family Name : Longlan Date of Birth : 12/12/1952 Vehicles : WHE 209	Family Name : Wilson Date of Birth : 05/09/1953 Vehicles : PED 342, GHE 912

Figure 1. Data Entry Forms for Person Details.

Smith was born on 10/07/1967.

Wilson was born on 5/9/1953 and may park the following vehicles on campus: 'PED 342', and 'GHE 912'

Longlan was born on 12/12/1952 and may park the following vehicles on campus: 'WHE 209'

People may enroll in subjects, and are awarded grades for enrollments. Figure 2 illustrates the record of one person's enrollments.
An informal interpretation of this information would be:

In 1987, Stuy studied 'CS 114' and 'CS 108' (which are offered by the CS department), 'MA 101' (which is offered by the MATH department), and 'PH 112' (which is offered by the PHYSICS department).

Of course subjects have to be taught, and this activity is one of the reasons for having a university in the first place. Figure 3 is an example of an output report showing teaching responsibilities, and the computer facilities that each department will make use of.
This example represents the following information:

The CS department uses the 'IBM 3083', 'VAX 1100', and 'Macintosh' computer facilities.
Wilson teaches CS 108 in 1988.
Suen-Tan teaches MA 101 in 1988.

Finally, since students are not overly enthusiastic about taking lessons on wet lawns, we need to schedule class times and rooms. An example of a timetable is illustrated in Figure 4.

University of Eastern Australia		
Student Record for: Stuy		
Year	**Subject**	**Grade**
1987	CS 114	6
	CS 108	7
	MA 101	2
	PH 112	5
1988	CS 202	
	CS 219	
	MA 101	

Figure 2. Output Report on Enrollments.

| University of Eastern Australia | | | |

Departmental Teaching Duties and Facilities (1988)

Department	Facilities	Subject-Nr	Lecturer
CS	IBM 3083 VAX 1100 Macintosh	108 114 202 219 300	Wilson Parker Wilson McGilbert Armstrong
MA	VAX 1100	101 102 219	Suen-Tan Whitworth McGilbert
PH	IBM 3083 CRAY 11-80 VAX 1100	112 150	Wilson Howarth

Figure 3. Departmental Facilities and Teaching Duties.

This timetable records the following information:

CS 108 is held in room 21 at Mon 0900.
CS 219 is held in room 63 at Mon 0900.
MA 219 is held in room 23 at Mon 0900.

Scheduling also requires knowledge of room capacity. This information can be found in Figure 5. This example data is interpreted as:

Room 10 has a capacity of 250 people.
Room 15 has a capacity of 20 people.

The significant set of examples illustrated above constitutes a valid set of propositions about the University UoD. One possible ER schema that permits these propositions to be recorded is shown in Figure 6. We make no claims that this schema is necessarily the *best* schema for describing the given UoD; however, it is certainly a syntactically correct ER, and in the following discussion we will mention several of the decisions taken in producing this schema.

Having specified some propositions about a Universe of Discourse, and produced an ER schema that represents this UoD, we can now examine *how* these propositions are encoded in the ER schema.

The structural components (or proposition-encoding constructs) of the ER data model are relationships and attributes which can, in turn, be subdivided into mono-valued and multi-valued attributes). Taking each construct in turn, we examine which propositions about the UoD are represented using the construct, with examples.

University of Eastern Australia	TIMETABLE				
	Mon	Tues	Wed	Thurs	Fri
9.00	cs 108 21 cs 219 63 ma 219 23	cs 114 21	ma 102 21 ph 150 23	ph 112 63	
10.00	cs 219 63	ma 101 21 ma 102 63	cs 300 63 ph 112 61	cs 202 23	
11.00		cs 114 21	ma 101 63	cs 202 23	cs 108 21

Figure 4. Timetable.

University of Eastern Australia	
Room Capacities.	
Room	Capcity
10	250
15	20
21	270
23	100
61	70
63	120

Figure 5. Room Capacities.

Construct 1: Relationship Set Involving Entity Sets.

Person studies Subject.

Person Stuy *studies* Subject CS202
Person Smith *studies* Subject MA101

Person teaches Subject.

Person Wilson *teaches* Subject MA300
Person Longlan *teaches* Subject CS300

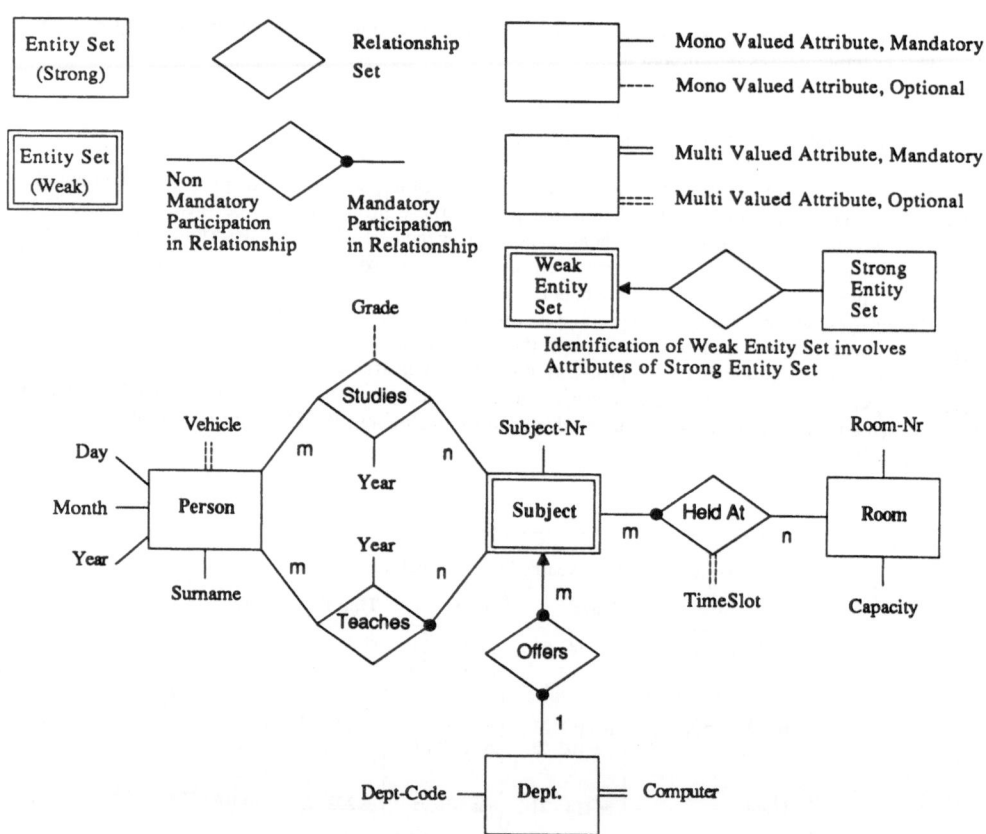

Figure 6. ER Schema for University UoD.

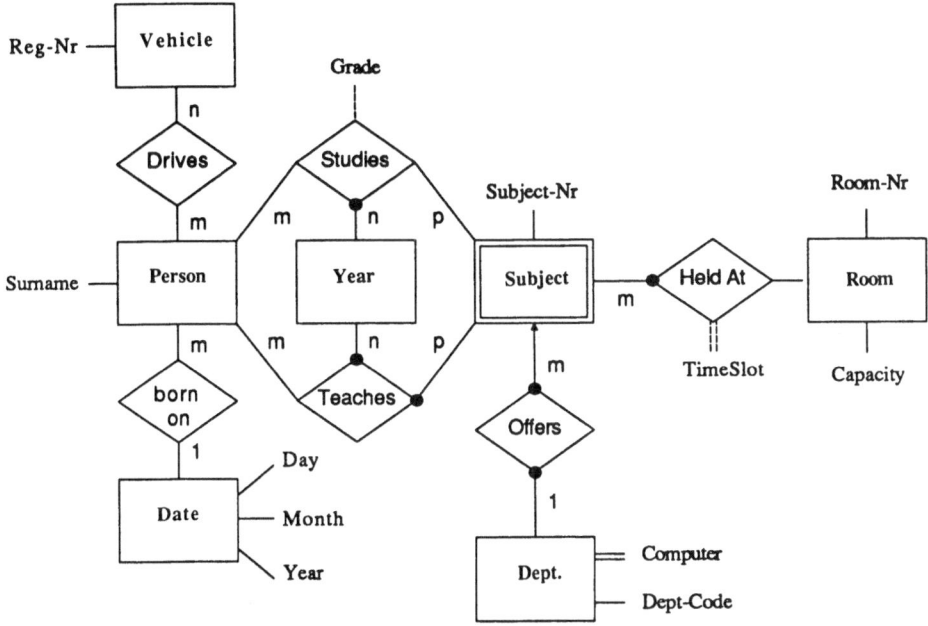

Figure 7. An Alternative Representation of the University UoD.

Subject held at Time-Slot in Room.

>   Subject CS108 *held at* Time-Slot Mon, 0900 *in* Room 21
>   Subject MA219 *held at* Time-Slot Mon, 0900 *in* Room 23

Construct 2: Mono-valued Attribute.

Following a definition given earlier, a mono-valued attribute is simply a property of an entity or relationship that can have at most one value at a given point in time. The following facts about the UoD are represented as mono-valued attributes:

Surname, Birth-Day, Birth-Month, and Birth-Year of Person.

- Example: The Person whose Surname is 'Smith', was born on Day 10, Month 07, Year 1967.

Grade attribute of 'Studies' relationship.

- Example: Person Stuy was awarded a grade of 7 for Subject CS108 in Year 1987.

Subject NR of Subject.

- Example: There exists a Subject with the number 114

Dept-Code of Dept.

- Example: There exists a Department called CS

Day and Time of Time-Slot.

- Example: There exists a Time-Slot at Mon 1000

Room-Nr of Room.

- Example: There exists a Room numbered 110

Construct 3: Multi-valued Attribute.

A multi-valued attribute is similar to a mono-valued attribute, with the distinction that at any point in time the attribute may contain more than one value. The multi-valued attributes from the College example are:

Vehicle of Person.

- Example: Person Smith can park the Vehicles PED342 and GHE912 on the campus

Computer of Department

- Example: Department PH uses Computer VAX 1100

Of course there are other possible ER representations, such as that shown in Figure 7 for the Universe of Discourse described above.

Note that Subject is an example of a *weak* entity set, since a particular subject is identified by the combination of Subject NR (an attribute of Subject), and Dept-Code (an attribute of Department).

We will have more to say about this apparent freedom of expression in the major section. For the remainder of this paper, we will refer to the initial ER model of our UoD, as illustrated in Figure 6.

2.3 Analysis of the ER Constructs

In the example above, we have illustrated the three proposition (or fact) encoding mechanisms provided by the ER data model:

- entity set + mono-valued attribute + value set
- entity set + multi-valued attribute + value set
- relationship set + entity sets

The first point that we should check is that these are indeed *distinct* fact encoding constructs. For example, is it possible to claim that a mono-valued attribute is just a special case of a multi-valued attribute?

If it were indeed the case that mono- and multi-valued attributes were examples of the one fact encoding construct (just 'attributes'), then the same set of *operators* used to modify the population of this construct should be applicable in both the mono- and multi-valued cases.

Now consider the operator that adds a new value to an attribute (we will certainly need such an operator if attributes are to ever have a non-null population).

(1) In the case of a mono-valued attribute, the operator must check whether the attribute *has any* value associated with it. If the attribute has already been assigned a value the operation may either be rejected, or the old value must be replaced by the new value depending on the semantics assigned to the (ADD mono-valued attribute) operator.

(2) However, if an attribute is multi-valued, the add operator need only check that the value to be inserted has not already been assigned to the attribute assuming multi-valued attributes are to be treated as sets).

Conclusion: mono-valued and multi-valued attributes are distinct fact encoding constructs.

Are relationships and attributes distinct fact encoding constructs? The trivial solution is to say 'yes', since they are defined as distinct concepts.

Intuitively, they are different because relationships can be used to represent n-ary propositions, while attributes can only be used to represent binary propositions.

We can be more formal in our assertion. Certainly, relationship sets and mono-valued attributes are distinct fact encoding concepts by way of the same argument used to distinguish between mono- and multi-valued attributes. However, we have already said that a multi-valued attribute has associated with it at any point in time a set of values, and by definition a relationship set is a time varying set of relationships. Is it possible to claim that multi-valued attributes and relationship sets are subtypes of a 'set' fact encoding construct?

Again, let us consider the 'ADD item' operator for such a construct.

(1) In the case of a multi-valued attribute, the item to be added is simply a value, and the operator need only check that the value is not already in the set before adding it.

(2) In the case of relationships, the item is a tuple of entities specified by way of the identifier attributes for each entity involved.

What happens if we add to a relationship set a relationship containing an entity about which nothing is currently known?

One possibility is that the new entity should be created, implying that the *add relationship* operator must make use of the *add attribute* operator (either mono- or multi-valued) to create the new entity and its identifying attributes.

The other possibility is that the *add relationship* request is rejected on the grounds that a component entity of the relationship does not exist.

Irrespective of the action taken, it is still necessary for the *add relationship* operator to check each component entity of a relationship. No such check need be, or can be, performed for adding a value to a multi-valued attribute.

Conclusion: Relationships and Multi-Valued attributes are distinct fact encoding constructs.

Conclusion: Logical propositions can be represented in three ways in the ER model:

- relationship set + entity sets
- entity set + mono-valued attribute + value set
- entity set + multi-valued attribute + value set

Is this specialization of constructs necessary? The answer is no. We can define a type of constraint, called a *uniqueness* constraint, over the places of a logical predicate. A uniqueness constraint requires that any combination of terms of the predicate places involved in the constraint operation at most one proposition (in the set of propositions with that predicate). As an aside: the order of places in a predicate is not strictly a conceptual distinction and can be eliminated (as it is in Falkenberg's object-role model (Falkenberg, 1982)).

(1) An ER relationship involving n roles will be equivalent to a predicate with n places, with corresponding roles in the ER relationship and places in the predicate being filled by entities from corresponding entity sets. Uniqueness constraints on the predicate places are determined by the cardinality constraint on the ER relationship.

(2) A mono-valued attribute of an entity set is equivalent to a binary predicate; one place is filled by the entity set, the other is filled by the value set of the attribute.

There is a uniqueness constraint covering the predicate place which is played by the entity set.

(3) A multi-valued attribute of an entity set is treated similarly to the mono-valued case, except that the uniqueness constraint covers both places of the binary predicate.

Conclusion: The distinction between relationships, mono-valued attributes, and multi-valued attributes is not a necessary one.

In the ER data model, propositions are (un!)necessarily partitioned into three classes.

We also stated that entity sets could be accommodated within the minimal framework by having unary propositions, which state that a particular entity or relationship is a member of a certain entity or relationship set.

However, due to ER's specialization of relationships, the latter class of propositions must also be partitioned, into propositions that define entity set membership, and those that define value set membership.

This further specialization is necessary since an entity cannot be the attribute of another entity, and a value cannot play a role in a relationship.

2.4 ER and CODASYL: A Family Resemblance?

Recall that the ER model offers three ways to encode a fact:

- relationship set + entity sets
- entity set + mono-valued attribute + value set
- entity set + multi-valued attribute + value set

This tripartite specialization is reminiscent of that found in another, earlier, data model. This is the network data model as defined by the CODASYL report of 1971. This model has three fact encoding constructs:

- CODASYL SET (or Coset) + records (as members and owners).
- record + data item + value
- record + repeating group + value

Figure 8 shows the equivalent CODASYL schema for the ER schema in Figure 6.
How was this mapping achieved?

(1) An ER entity set or non-functional relationship corresponds to a CODASYL record.

(2) An ER mono-valued attribute of an entity set corresponds to a data item in the corresponding CODASYL record.

(3) An ER multi-valued attribute of an entity set corresponds to a repeating group in the corresponding CODASYL record.

(4) An ER attribute (either mono- or multi-valued) of a relationship corresponds to a CODASYL record containing either a single data item (for mono-valued attributes) or a single repeating group (for multi-valued attributes).

(5) A functional ER relationship set corresponds to a CODASYL set.

As you can see, this is almost a one-to-one mapping of fact-encoding constructs between the outdated CODASYL DDL and the ER semantic data model.

2.6 ER Constraints - What Can Be Represented

If the structural components of a data model define the syntax of the facts to be stored within an information system, then it is the constraints provided by the data model that describe the semantics of that information, by prescribing the permitted population of each occurrence of a fact encoding construct on the schema.

While the ER data model provides several (in fact, too many!) constructs for describing the syntax or structure of the information to be stored in a database, the opposite is true when it comes to specifying the constraints that exist on the populations of the fact encoding constructs.

Before defining the ER constraints, we say that something is *known* about an entity if either:

A mono-valued attribute of the entity has been assigned a value.
A multi-valued attribute of the entity is non-empty.
The entity plays a role in the relationship.

The ER data model provides three explicit constraints:

Mandatory Attribute. An attribute of an entity set is mandatory if whenever anything is known about an entity, then that attribute must contain a value. Clearly, all identifier attributes of an entity set must be mandatory.

118

```
RECORD IS PERSON                              RECORD IS STUDIES
    SURNAME             CHAR 20                   PERSON          CHAR 20
    DAY                 DEC 2,0                    SUBJECT-CODE    CHAR 7
    MONTH               DEC 2,0                    GRADE           DEC 1,0
    YEAR                DEC 4,0                    YEAR            DEC 4,0
    NR-OF-VEHICLES      DEC 2,0
    VEHICLE             CHAR 6,                RECORD IS TEACHES
        OCCURS NR-OF-VEHICLES TIMES               PERSON          CHAR 20
                                                   SUBJECT-CODE    CHAR 7
                                                   YEAR            DEC 4,0

RECORD IS SUBJECT                             RECORD IS DEPT
    SUBJECT-NR          DEC 3,0                    DEPT-CODE       CHAR 4
    DEPT-CODE           CHAR 4                     NR-OF-COMPUTER  DEC 3,0
                                                   COMPUTER        CHAR 10,
RECORD IS ROOM                                        OCCURS NR-OF-COMPUTER TIMES
    ROOM-NR             DEC 2,0
    CAPACITY            DEC 3,0

RECORD IS TIME-SLOT                           RECORD IS HELD-AT
    DAY-NAME            CHAR 5                     SUBJECT-NR      DEC 3,0
    TIME               CHAR 5                      DEPT-NR         CHAR 4
                                                   ROOM-NR         DEC 2,0
                                                   DAY-NAME        CHAR 5
                                                   TIME            CHAR 5


SET IS PERSON-STUDIES                         SET IS SUBJECT-STUDIED
OWNER IS    PERSON                            OWNER IS    SUBJECT
MEMBER IS   STUDIES                           MEMBER IS STUDIES
    INSERTION IS AUTOMATIC                        INSERTION IS AUTOMATIC
    RETENTION IS MANDATORY                        RETENTION IS MANDATORY

SET IS OFFERED                                SET IS SUBJECT-HELD
OWNER IS    DEPARTMENT                        OWNER IS    SUBJECT
MEMBER IS   SUBJECT                           MEMBER IS   HELD-AT
    INSERTION IS AUTOMATIC                        INSERTION IS AUTOMATIC
    RETENTION IS MANDATORY                        RETENTION IS MANDATORY

SET IS ROOM-HELD                              SET IS TIME-HELD
OWNER IS    ROOM                              OWNER IS    TIME-SLOT
MEMBER IS   HELD-AT                           MEMBER IS HELD-AT
    INSERTION IS AUTOMATIC                        INSERTION IS AUTOMATIC
    RETENTION IS MANDATORY                        RETENTION IS MANDATORY
```

Figure 8. A CODASYL Schema for the University UoD.

Mandatory Participation. The participation of an entity set in a relationship set is mandatory if, whenever anything is known an entity from the entity set that plays the role, then that entity must participate in a relationship from that set.

Relationship Cardinality. This constraint is used to indicate the number of times that an entity (or, implicitly, a combination of entities if the relationship st is n-ary and $n > 2$) may play a particular role in a relationship set. Generally, only the values 1 or m, n, p, etc. (any number of times) are used.

Of course, any additional constraints can be formally expressed in a more general notation, for example, predicate logic. However, saying that this is a reasonable excuse for omitting certain constraints from the data model itself is like saying that a programming language is adequate because it forces you to call assembly language routines to implement all those things you can't express in the language itself!

2.6 ER Constraints - What Can't Be Represented

The Cardinality Constraint Problem. One problem with the ER schema shown in Figure 6 is that the

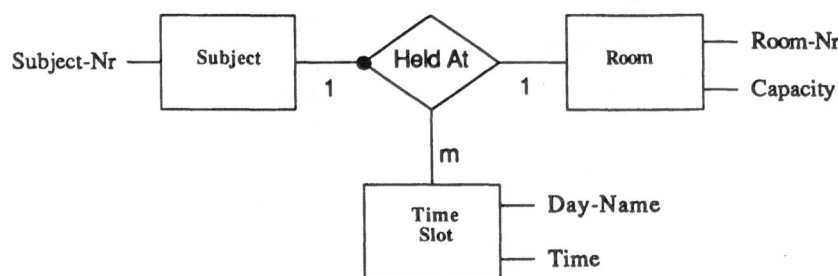

Figure 9. Partial ER Schema of Figure 5 with Time-Slot as an Entity Set.

'held-at' relationship set (involving Subjects and Rooms), and associated with a multi-valued attribute called 'time-slot' does not convey the full semantics of a timetable as shown in Figure 4.

Informally, the constraints that we would like to represent are:

(1) Any combination of a subject and time-slot must only occur in one relationship in the relationship set (you can only be in one place at any time)

(2) Any combination of a time-slot and a room must only occur in one relationship in the relationship set (no double bookings)

Unfortunately, subjects and rooms are represented as instances of entity sets in this relationship, but time-slots are represented as values of an attribute on that relationship. There are no ER constraints that can include both an entity set and an attribute, but both of the informal constraints involve a (multi-valued) attribute (time-slot) and an entity set (either room or subject).

Either we must omit this important constraint from the ER schema (thus allowing database pollution), or we must modify the ER schema to represent time-slots by instances of an entity set. The modification to the ER schema is shown in Figure 9.

Conclusion: The small set of constraints defined by the ER data model may force the transformation of an attribute to an entity set in order to formally represent a particular constraint.

The Multiple Identifiers Problem. Within the ER data model, attributes serve to identify entities; for example, in our UoD, a Person is identified by the value of their family-name attribute. To clearly indicate which are the identifier attributes for an entity, some offsprings of the original ER model (e.g., EER (Teorey, Yang, and Fry, 1986) use a different graphical notation for attributes. An example of this notation for one of the entity sets from our example is shown in Figure 10.

Now suppose that we extend the information recorded about people within our UoD to encompass a social security number. Such a number uniquely identifies a Person. We might be tempted to represent this section of the modified UoD as shown in Figure 11.

Now we have a problem. Does the presence of two identifier attributes for a person indicate that:

(1) A person is uniquely identified by the combination of family-name and social security number, or

(2) A person is uniquely identified EITHER by their family name OR by their social security number.

Following the current ER model, option (1) is correct (which is not what we wanted to represent). It is not possible, therefore, to represent multiple identification schemes for entities.

It can be argued that this problem has more to do with the chosen graphical conventions for present ER schemas than with the ER data model per se. However, in the initial discussion on data models we mentioned that a data model should provide a set of constraints. The ER data model clearly provides for cardinality constraints, mandatory role and attribute constraints, and the *identification* of identifier attributes. The model as such does *not* provide for the grouping of identifier attributes into identification schemes.

The problem becomes compounded once we widen identification to cover that of weak entity sets (where identification of a member entity involves the attribute of an entity from another entity set).   In

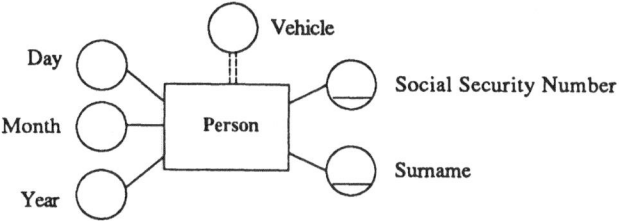

Figure 10. Alternative Representation for Attributes.

addition to forming groups of attributes for identification, there is also a need to form groups of attributes and relationship sets to define an identification scheme.

A Problem with Mandatory Participation Constraints. Examining the ER schema in Figure 6 reveals that a Person may study a subject in a year, and may teach a subject in a year. What we would like to say is that a Person must do one or the other (or possibly both).

Unfortunately, the mandatory role constraint provided by the ER data model applies to occurrences of an entity in *one* relationship, rather than occurrences of an entity in a *combination* of relationships.

Of course, we might also want to say that a combination of attributes are mandatory, or that the combination of a relationship and attribute is mandatory....

The General Constraint Problem. Having highlighted difficulties in representing certain constraints using the ER data model, it is time to try and generalize the problems encountered.

(1) ER constraints are defined on individual fact encoding constructs (or parts of such constructs), rather than on combinations of such constructs.

   Case: an entity identification scheme must include *all* identifier attributes of an entity set, since there is no way to define a *combination* of such attributes.

   Case: mandatory participation constraints or mandatory attribute constraints are defined on a *single* role or attribute, rather than a *combination* of roles or attributes. Further, it should be possible to define a constraint on a combination that involves both roles and attributes.

(2) The only constraints that the ER model defines on a role is a mandatory participation constraint (and that can only be defined on a single role).

The ER data model does not support the equivalent of a referential integrity constraint (or, in general, the definition of set theoretic relationships between the populations of proposition types). Such constraints, which (in ER) would restrict the population of a set of roles occur frequently in practice. Indeed, the relationship cardinality constraint could be seen as a trivial example of such constraints.

Case: People may study subjects and teach subjects. If we don't want the academic credibility of our

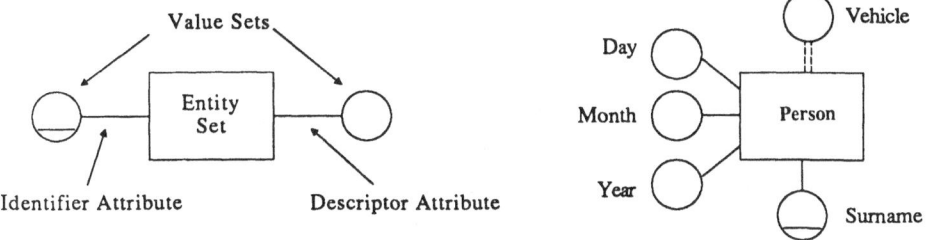

Figure 11. UoD with Two Ways of Identifying People.

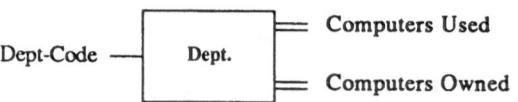

Figure 12. Departments Own and Use Computers.

university to suffer, then a person should not be permitted to study a subject that they teach in the same year.

Thus, we would like to say that if there is a 'teaches' relationship between a combination of Person, Year, and Subject (e.g., 'Smith' teaches 'MA 100' in '1988'), then that same combination may not occur in the 'studies' relationship (and vice versa).

Of course, there is no reason why such constraints should be confined to entities. Suppose that, in addition to recording which departments use which computers, we were to record which departments own which computers. The modification to the ER schema is shown in Figure 12.

We might want to specify a constraint that any department that owns a computer must use that computer, or more formally:

> The set of computers involved in the 'owns computer' attribute of a department must be a subset of the set of computers involved in the 'uses computer' attribute for that department.

The problem with this is that attributes are not built from roles! If they were, then we could even define such referential constraints that involved a combination of attributes, and roles from relationships. For example, the fact that a Subject is uniquely identified by its Subject-Nr and the Code of the Dept that offers it could be expressed by saying that:

> The combination of values for the roles played by the value set of the Subject-Nr attribute of a Subject, and the role played by Dept in the 'offers' relationship involving that subject must be unique.

Summary, so far. We have examined how the ER data model can be used to represent a Universe of Discourse, and have examined the fact encoding constructs involved in such a representation.

The ER model contains three distinct fact encoding constructs:

- entity set + mono-valued attribute + value set
- entity set + multi-valued attribute + value set
- relationship set + entity sets

Further, this distinction is not a necessary one, because they represent syntactic specializations of the same semantic construct.

The distinction between relationships and attributes requires a distinction between constraints defined for relationships, and those defined for attributes (e.g., mandatory role and mandatory attribute). This syntactic difference makes it difficult to define constraints over propositions encoded in different ways.

3. THE CONSEQUENCES FOR THE DESIGN PROCEDURE

In the previous section, we have examined the conceptual foundations of the ER data model. In this

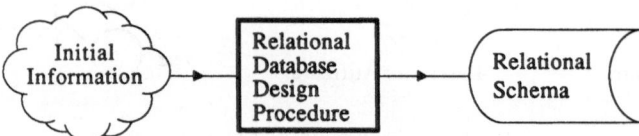

Figure 13. The Relational Database Design Procedure (RDDP).

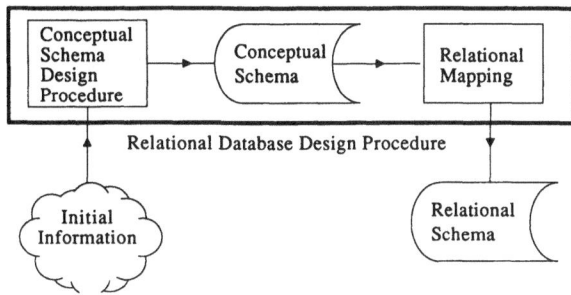

Figure 14. The RDDP, Version 2.

section, we will address the effect that these non-conceptual distinctions have on the process of designing an ER schema (and, hence, on the task of designing a good quality relational schema).

The task of designing a relational database is, in general, a complex one; it first involves the analysis of an unsuitably structured, and often incomplete, statement of the Universe of Discourse (UoD) and then the definition of columns and tables to record the information of interest about that UoD, together with the formal constraints on which propositions may be recorded. Figure 13 shows this process.

At almost every step along the path from initial information to relational database schema, there are many possible choices and only rarely are there any signposts to indicate which path to take. Inevitably, then, most relational database designers find themselves faced with an amorphous mass of information and very little guidance on how to formalize it. Too often, this forces the designer to adopt an intuitive, informal approach to the design task. We can only describe this as the "divine inspiration" design procedure: close your eyes and wait for inspiration to strike. Alas, it all too rarely does. In the Artificial Intelligence research world, this problem (as it applies to knowledge engineering) is particularly crippling and has long been identified as the "Feigenbaum Bottleneck" (Michie, 1983).

Clearly, the professional EDP community, together with some of the user community, needs good advice on how to perform this complex, but critical, design task. This advice is typically called a methodology. The term methodology literally means "a study of methods", but consistent misuse within the information systems literature has established it as a *de facto* synonym for "method". An alternative term (which we prefer) is *design procedure*.

Our guiding hypothesis is that the quality of the end product is highly dependent upon the quality of the initial information and the quality of the design procedure (and not least, the quality of the designer).

Of course, a design procedure is not going to magically solve all of the database designer's problems. *No* design procedure can *guarantee* a high quality result; but a good design procedure can substantially increase the possibilities of achieving a high quality result.

The "divine inspiration" design procedure proved to be an unacceptable solution for practical design problems. In an attempt to replace intuition with mathematics, it was proposed to base the relational database design procedure on normalization theory (Date, 1986; Kent, 1983). From a set of dependencies and a set of attribute names (the so-called Universal Relation for the UoD), the designer was supposed to generate a high quality database design.

Normalization provides a formal rule for detecting the *absence* of certain update anomalies, together with technical design procedures (such as decomposition of relations, or generation of minimal functional-dependency covers) for eliminating these anomalies. Unfortunately, the instructions that were to help the designer make the leap across the chasm from the Causal Relation to a fully normalized relational database were too complex for many designers to apply productively.

After the publication of the landmark ISO report, *Concepts and Terminology for the Conceptual Schema and the Information Base*, (van Griethuysen, 1982), it became clear to many researchers that this grand leap would be a lot easier if there was an intermediate platform (hopefully with solid foundations) to stop at. In this way, the grand, but unmanageable leap, would be reduced to two smaller, but theoretically manageable, leaps. This platform is, of course, the conceptual schema for the UoD being described (shown in Figure 14).

This means that the design procedure which takes the informal specification and generates a high-quality relational database can be split into two separate design procedures: one which generates a conceptual schema from the initial informal specification, and a second which transforms the conceptual schema into a (representationally equivalent) relational schema without redundancy or other update anomalies (Figure 15). Controlled redundancy can be re-introduced, on a principled basis, if it is necessary

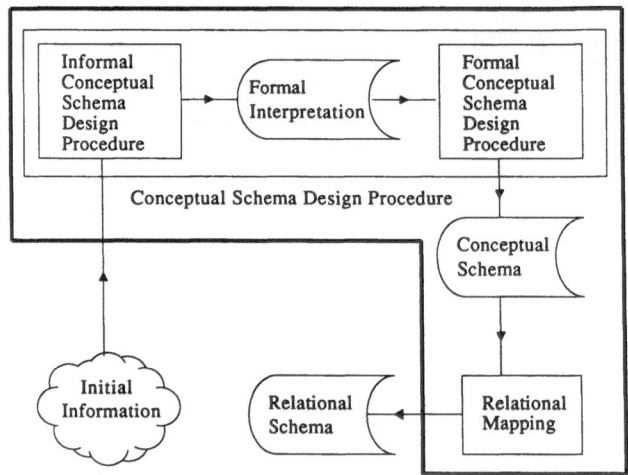

Figure 15. The RDDP, Version 3.

to satisfy performance requirements.

A relational schema and a conceptual schema are said to be representationally equivalent if every fact population that is permitted by the conceptual schema can be recorded as values in rows of the tables in the relational schema. However, such a relational schema will not be semantically equivalent to the conceptual schema, because it may permit facts to be recorded in tables that are not part of a valid population of the conceptual schema. This can happen because the relational model does not support the same range of constraints as most conceptual schema languages.

The goal is to have a *prescriptive* design procedure for designing a conceptual schema, and then an algorithmic procedure for synthesizing the resulting relational schema.

Sowa (1988) attributes to Perlis the remark that it is "not possible to map informal specifications into formal specifications by any formal algorithms". This is true, simply because informal specifications leave most of the interpretation conventions implicit. However, it is possible to provide informal, or heuristic, guidance to map an informal specification into a formal specification. These informal rules must help the user and the designer explicitly identify the relevant assumptions.

Clearly the informal part of the design task should have a starting point which is *familiar* to the users (who have to provide this initial information!). It has been our observation (Nijssen, 1986) that:

> most users are able to reason very well with examples of the information that they use in their everyday work, but are much less able to reason with abstractions of that information.

However, the example data is not sufficient by itself because it may contain ambiguity or other conceptually irrelevant material. We also need the *user's interpretation* of the example data. This is unavoidable, because the database design must support the activities of these users, and, therefore, must reflect *the way these users perceive their shared world*.

For example, there are a number of informal, but accepted, assumptions associated with the Person Details form for "Smith" in the previous section: that the birth date is set out in the European format, which is month, day, year (it could just as easily have been the USA format, which is month, day, year - but what a difference in the meaning of those data values!) and that the recorded vehicles are not those owned by the person, or those driven by the person, but those which will be left parked on the campus site by that person. Similarly, in the Student Record form, there is an important convention that the first part of the subject code (e.g., CS, MATH, or PHYS) identifies the department offering the subject and the second part (e.g., 114, 108) uniquely identifies a subject within a department's offerings. These data values can be used to identify the entities involved but these unwritten interpretation conventions must often supply the predicates (or verbs).

Clearly the user must have a very good understanding of these *interpretation conventions* in order to work with the data in question, even if she has difficulty in stating them explicitly in all cases.

The informal part of the design procedure must result in a formal specification of the user's *semantic interpretation* of the data in the UoD.

The important question, then, is on the division of labor between the formal and informal parts of the design task. It is desirable to make the informal part as small as possible, because it is not possible, even in principle, to give strong guidance on how to perform this task. Conversely, it is desirable to place the largest possible part of the design task in the formal part, because this activity can be strongly guided (and in some cases, may even be deterministic).

The decision of where to draw the dividing line between formal and informal parts will depend, primarily, on the content of the formal interpretation (which is essentially a preliminary version of the formal specification). This formal interpretation must contain, explicitly or implicitly, all of the information that is to be present in the conceptual schema.

In the case of an entity-relationship conceptual schema, this means the entities, attributes, relationships, and values. Each of the constraints that is to be formally represented in the conceptual schema must be stated here, either explicitly or implicitly (by means of a significant set of examples from which they may be inductively derived). In general, we can never ensure that a set of examples is significant with respect to any proposed constraint so, we must provide an *effective validation procedure*, which relies on *the user* to confirm or deny proposed constraints (Twine, 1988(a)).

Our experience suggests that as the number of proposition-encoding mechanisms increases, so does the proportion of the design task that must remain informal. Let's examine this claim.

There is an argument that supports the dichotomy between attributes and relationships (and thus between entities and values): the division is *natural*, and, therefore, users find it easy to specify which propositions are attributes and which propositions are relationships.

Carlo Batini's position paper (1987) from the 6th Entity Relationship conference eloquently states this case:

> This rich variety of [aggregation] mechanisms is important in the design activity, since the designer can choose among different structures to capture a variety of semantic relations among objects of the real world.

The aggregation mechanisms that Batini refers to are: the entity as an aggregation of attributes, and the relationship as an aggregation of entities. So, Batini is suggesting that the dichotomy is justified because attributes and relationships are used to model two different kinds of semantic relations. The claim is that this makes the task of modelling easier because it reflects some sort of natural division within the Universe of Discourse being modelled.

Section 2 demonstrated that attributes and relationships do not model different kinds of semantic relations. Instead, they represent different *syntactic* constructs for modelling (different subsets of) one and the same set of semantic relations.

Furthermore, experience with the ER model has shown that the process which divides proposition types into attributes and relationships is unguided and iterative: as attributes are associated with the different entity sets, it may be necessary to *reclassify* some entity sets as attributes and *vice versa*.

For example, assume we have an entity type PERSON, with an attribute DEPARTMENT. We can record the proposition, "Bob works for the Sales department" by placing the value SALES in the DEPARTMENT attribute for the entity BOB (which is a member of the entity set PERSON).

If we later discover that we need to record propositions like "The sales department has a 250,000 dollar budget" then we are in trouble, because it is not possible to represent a proposition involving two objects, which have both been encoded as values. To solve this, we must change the DEPARTMENT attribute into an entity set and create a relationship type EMPLOYS, which links members of the PERSON entity set with members of the new DEPARTMENT entity set. Now, the proposition "BOB works for the Sales department" is recorded by placing a 'conceptual link' between the entity BOB (in the entity set PERSON) and the entity SALES (in the entity set DEPARTMENT).

Finally, we may discover that there are no other propositions about employees to be recorded, other than which department they work for. In this case, the entity set PERSON could be regarded as unnecessary, and replaced by a (multi-valued) EMPLOYEES attribute of the DEPARTMENT entity type. In this case, the previous proposition would be recorded by giving that attribute the value BOB.

This attribute-entity type migration introduces an unnecessary *instability* into the modeling process. This is just a high-level version of the reprogramming that had to be performed whenever an equivalent change was made in a CODASYL DDL schema (Nijssen, 1975). Worst of all, no researcher seems to be able to find a general rule (either formal or heuristic) to indicate when this iteration is to stop, and the classification of entity sets and attributes can be considered complete.

There is *no* evidence to suggest that it is easy or natural to select, *a priori*, the entities, attributes and relationships for an ER conceptual schema. On the contrary, the opposite seems to be true: the task is commonly regarded as subjective, difficult, and iterative. Very few ER design procedures even include weak heuristic guidance for this step. Put simply, there appears to be no evidence to suggest that users find it easy to distinguish between the relationships and the attributes in their Universe of Discourse.

An alternative suggestion (by the relational theorists) was to start with a set of named attributes, together with all the functional dependencies, multi-valued dependencies and join dependencies between those attributes. The formal part of the design procedure can use the dependencies to cluster these attributes, forming entities and relationships. This work provides formal guidance for the task of clustering the attributes to construct a redundancy-free ER schema, but it relies on the users being able to provide abstract technical information (the set of dependencies). Our experience, and that of many others, is that users find it very difficult to reason at such an abstract level. So this is also essentially unsuitable for widespread application.

A viable alternative is if the initial formal specification consists of propositions about the Universe of Discourse. This means that the informal part of the design procedure is kept quite simple: it only requires the user to identify the relevant propositions in the example data. The formal part of the methodology can extract the type/subtype structure of these propositions, detect various constraints, and finally transform the conceptual schema into a representationally equivalent relational schema. NIAM (Nijssen, 1986; Nijssen and Halpin, 1989) is an example of such a methodology (which does not include the attribute/ relationship dichotomy). If required, this formal part of the methodology could select an encoding mechanism for each proposition type based on the knowledge of which other proposition types were to be recorded, and which semantic constraints exist over those proposition types.

The multiplicity of fact-encoding mechanisms in the ER model makes it harder to give formal support for the design procedure. The task of detecting constraints, or of transforming the schema between semantically equivalent representations, is complicated by the syntactic distinction between attributes and relationships. Rosenthal and Reiner (1987) observe that "the large number of constructs [in the ER model] is burdensome [for the task of schema transformations]". This is because a semantic constraint can be encoded in more than one syntactic form, depending on which way the underlying proposition type(s) have been encoded.

Similarly, the formal part of the methodology must now contain two methods for detecting and specifying uniqueness constraints: one for uniqueness constraints over propositions which are encoded using relationship instances (which are represented as relationship keys) and one for uniqueness constraints over propositions which are encoded using attributes and values (which can only be implicitly represented by making the attribute a single-valued attribute). Furthermore, in order to represent some constraints, it may be necessary to alter the classification of objects into attributes and entity sets (refer to the example in the subsection 2.6).

It is important to remember that the result of applying this methodology must be *validated* by the user to ensure that it models the correct UoD (as opposed to modelling the incorrect UoD in a consistent manner!).

There are essentially two alternatives: continuous validation after each derivation ("at each step along the production line") or validation after the last derivation. The former allows each derivation to be confirmed as valid or invalid, without permitting the validity/invalidity of other derivations to influence the validation. For example, if a later derivation is based on a previous (invalid) derivation, then it is automatically invalid, but the cause of the invalidity may be difficult to determine. This is often the case when prototyping is used as a validation mechanism: it is difficult to distinguish between conceptual errors and errors in implementing the prototype. Figure 16 illustrates the role of validation in a methodology.

For conceptual validation to be effective, it must be in the user's natural language. After all, the object of validation is to ensure that the conceptual schema reflects the user's interpretation of the UoD.

One effective strategy for validation, which has been tested extensively as part of the NIAM design procedure, is presenting the user with a *population* of each proposition type (regardless of which way it is encoded) which violates a proposed constraint, and asking whether or not this population is a permitted one (Twine, 1988(b)). In this way, the user can see whether the constraints are too restrictive (strong) or permissive (weak) without being forced to reason abstractly about possible populations and constraint definitions.

However, for this to work effectively, the conceptual data model requires a graphical notation in which the instances of a construct (the propositions encoded by a given syntactic mechanism) can be shown alongside the type specification of that construct. In the ER case, it must be possible to show entity instances next to their entity sets, values of attributes next to those attributes, and instances of relationships next to the specification of these relationships. Using the conventional ER notation, it is difficult to show the populations of several attribute (especially multi-valued attributes) without losing the "semantic connection" between the attribute values associated with the same entity instance. Similarly, it is difficult to show several instances of a relationship without becoming confused as to which entity instances are involved in which relationship instance.

Of course, because the distinction between attributes and relationships does not exist as such in the UoD (rather, it is imposed by the database designer) so it is a potential source of confusion for the user during any validation exercise.

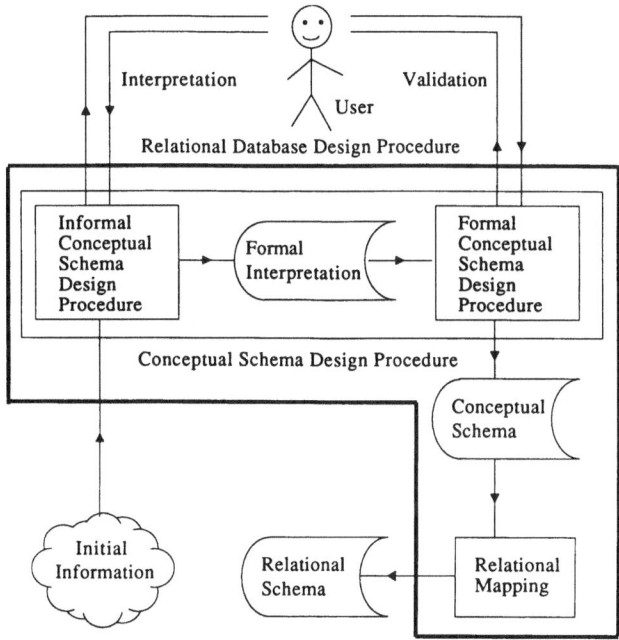

Figure 16. The RDDP Including Validation.

As a matter of sound graphical language design, it would be better to choose symbols which have a stronger resemblance to table headings, and which can be more easily populated. A populated NIAM schema which describes the UoD of the second section of this paper is presented in Figures 17 and 18.

The circles represent entity types. The boxes represent roles (equivalent to a place in a logical predicate or proposition). A series of connected roles represents a proposition type (or predicate). There is no distinction between attributes and relationships, nor between mono-valued and multi-valued attributes.

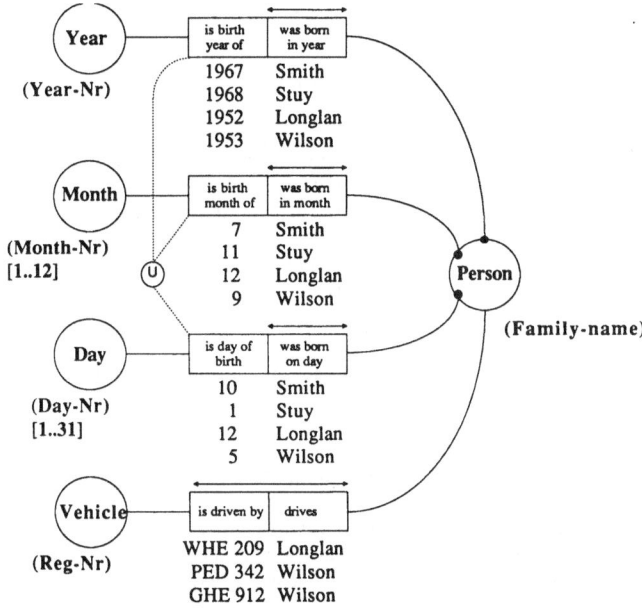

Figure 17. A NIAM Schema for the University UoD, Part 1.

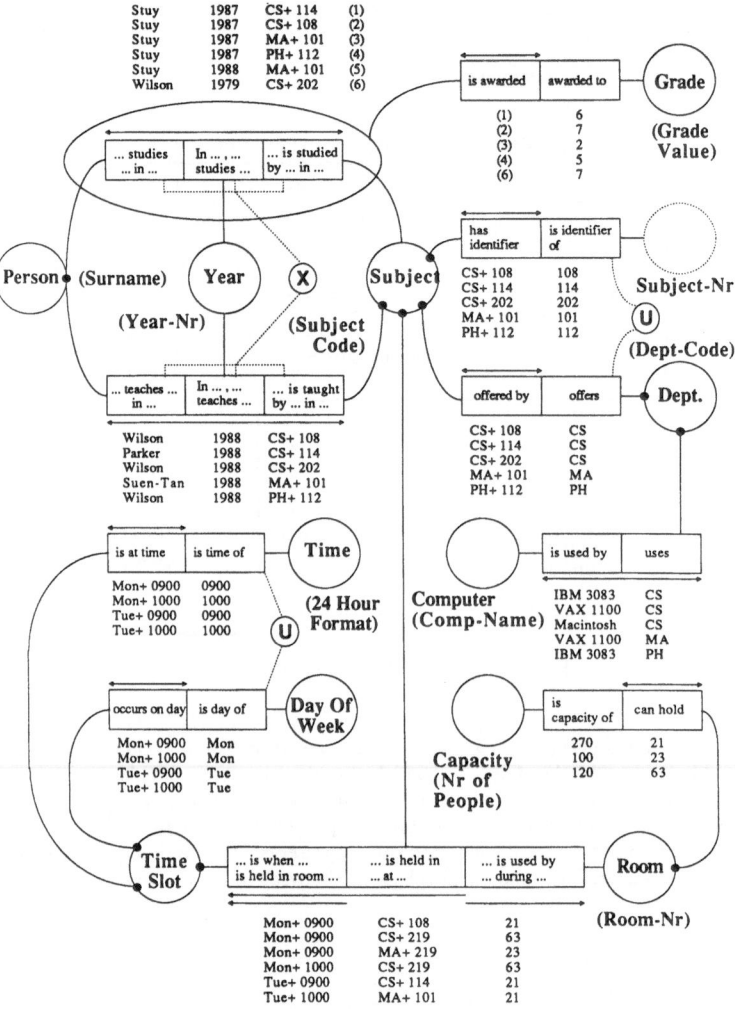

Figure 18. A NIAM Schema for the University UoD, Part 2.

NIAM makes a distinction between non-lexical entities (things, such as a person) and lexical entities (symbols, such as a person's name). Non-lexical entities cannot be directly represented (you can't write down a person), but they can be represented by a naming convention composed of directly representable lexical entities (you can write down a person's name). Simple naming conventions (where a single symbol serves to uniquely identify each entity of an entity type) are indicated by placing the name of the label type within parentheses, next to the name of the entity type. The population for a proposition type is shown directly beneath the boxes that represent the places of that proposition type.

Summary, So Far: The distinction between attributes and relationships has the following effects on a design procedure:

- if they are to be specified *a priori*, then they increase the informal portion of the design task (because they must be specified before the formal task can begin)

- if the encoding mechanism for a proposition is to be selected by the formal part of the design procedure, then these rules require, in general, the knowledge of certain constraints that hold over the propositions and, in any event, represent a purely syntactic (and semantically unnecessary distinctions)

- it forces the duplication of the methods required to identify and declare each type of constraint (because they must recognize the constraint in several syntactic variations). Because certain combinations of constraint and proposition-encoding mechanism cannot exist, the schema may need to be transformed in order to represent a constraint. Finally, it may be necessary to declare a constraint that involves (mono-valued or multi-valued) attributes and relationships which will require entity-attribute migration (if the constraint can be represented at all)

- it makes schema transformations more complex

- it makes validation more difficult because it requires users to deal with distinctions that do not exist in their Universe of Discourse.

4. CONCLUSIONS

The example ER schemas in the 2.4 and 2.5 subsections include certain 'solutions' which a good database designer would avoid intuitively. However, there is nothing in the ER model to exclude these solutions, and there is no formal design procedure to guide the designer away from these solutions.
The conclusion of this paper is simple:

The ER data model includes distinctions which are not relevant at the conceptual level. This has two significant effects: it weakens its representational power at the conceptual level, and it makes it extremely difficult to specify prescriptive design rules for the task of designing an ER conceptual schema.

The solution is equally simple. Eliminate the non-conceptual distinction between attributes and relationships. This will have the following consequences:

(1) it will eliminate the distinction between entity sets and value sets.

(2) constraints can then be specified using a single notation for each class of semantic constraint (rather than the current set of syntactic variations on a single semantic theme).

(3) the task of designing a good design procedure will be made much simpler (and therefore, research into this critical area can proceed much faster).

REFERENCES

Batini, C., 1987, Position Statement: E-R Modelling Versus Binary Modelling, *Proceedings of the 6th Conference on the Entity-Relationship Approach*.

Chen, P. P., 1976, The Entity-Relationship Model - Toward a Unified View of Data, *ACM Transactions on Database Systems*, Vol. 1, No. 1, March 1976, pp. 9-36.

CODASYL: Database Task Group Report, 1971, ACM, New York.

Codd, E. F., 1970, A Relational Model of Data for Large Shared Data Banks, *Communications of the ACM*, Vol. 13, No. 6, June 1970.

Date, C. J., 1986, *An Introduction to Database Systems (Volume 1, 4th Edition)*, Addison-Wesley.

Dogac, A., and Chen, P. P., 1983, Entity-Relationship Model in the ANSI/SPARC Framework, *Entity-Relationship Approach to Information Modelling and Analysis*, Chen, P. P., ed., North-Holland, pp. 357-374.

Falkenberg, E., 1982, Foundations of the Conceptual Schema Approach to Information Systems, *Lecture Notes of the NATO Advanced Study Institute on Database Management and Applications*, June 1-13, 1981, Portugal, North-Holland.

Kent, W., 1983, A Simple Guide to Five Normal Forms in Relational Database Theory, *Communications of the ACM*, Vol. 26, No. 2, February 1983.

Kent, W., 1986, The Realities of Data: Basic Properties of Data Reconsidered, *Proceedings of IFIP Conference on Data Semantics (DS-1)*, Steel, T. B., Jr., and Meersman, R., eds., Elsevier, North-Holland, pp. 175-188.

Meersman, R., 1988, Towards Models for Practical Reasoning about Conceptual Database Design, *Database Semantics (DS-2)*, Meersman, R., and Sernadas, A., eds., NorthHolland.

Michie, D., 1983, Inductive Rule Generation in the Context of the Fifth Generation, *Proceedings of the International Machine Learning Workshop*, pp. 65-70.

Nijssen, G. M., 1975, Two Major Flaws in the CODASYL DDL 1973 and Proposed Corrections,

Information Systems 1, Pergamon, pp. 114-132.

Nijssen, G. M., 1986, On Experience with Large-Scale Teaching and Use of Fact-based Conceptual Schemas in Industry and University, *Proceedings of IFIP Conference on Data Semantics (DS-1)*, Meersman, R., and Steel, T. B., Jr., eds., Elsevier North-Holland.

Nijssen, G. M., and Halpin, T. A., 1989, *Conceptual Schema and Relational Database Design: A Fact-Based Approach*, Prentice-Hall.

Parent, C., and Spaccapietra, S., 1985, Enhancing the Operational Semantics of the Entity-Relationship Model, *Database Semantics DS-1*, Steel, T. B., jr., and Meersman, R., eds., Elsevier North-Holland.

Rosenthal, A., and Reiner, D., 1987, Theoretically Sound Transformations for Practical Database Design, *Proceedings 6th Conference on the Entity-Relationship Approach*.

Sowa, J. F., 1988, Knowledge Representation in Databases, Expert Systems, and Natural Language, *Proceedings IFIP WG2.6/WG8.1 Conference on the Role of Artificial Intelligence in Databases and Expert Systems*, Guangzhou, China, July 1988.

Teorey, R. J., Yang, D., and Fry, J. P., 1986, A Logical Design Methodology for Relational Databases Using the Extended Entity-Relationship Model, *Computing Surveys*, Vol. 18, No. 2, June 1986, pp. 197-222.

Tsichritzis, D. C., and Lochovsky, F. H., 1976, Hierarchical Database Management: A Survey, *ACM Computing Surveys*, Vol. 8, No. 1, March 1976.

Twine, S., 1988(a), Towards a Knowledge Engineering Procedure, *Proceedings Expert Systems '88*, Brighton, UK, December 1988.

Twine, S., 1988(b), From Information Analysis Towards Knowledge Analysis, *Proceedings 2nd European Workshop on Knowledge Acquisition for Knowledge-Based Systems*, Bonn, Federal Republic of Germany, June 1988.

van Griethuysen, J. J., ed., 1982, *Concepts and Terminology for the Conceptual Schema and the Information Base*, Report of ISO TC97/SC5/WG5.

AUTOMATIC GENERATION OF CONCEPTUAL DATABASE DESIGN TOOLS

Fred Maryanski and Shuguang Hong

Computer Science and Engineering Department
University of Connecticut
Storrs, CT 06268

Abstract: The development of a database design tool for an object-oriented data model is a formidable task. In an attempt to reduce the implementation effort of this task, a software system, called *Seaweed*, is proposed to automatically generate database design tools from data model specifications. Three phases of design tool generation are defined in SeaWeed: data model specification in terms of the primitives of SeaWeed's meta-data model, implementation scheme formation based on an extended state transition diagram model, and database design tool generation by customizing reusable software components. SeaWeed combines techniques for meta-data modeling, software reusability, and artificial intelligence into a methodology for the automatic generation of database design tools.

1. INTRODUCTION

Research on object-oriented data models has made significant progress in enriching the semantics and extending the expressive power of conceptual models, but the development of complete, semantically rich database systems has provided a formidable implementation challenge. An approach that designs specific database system software for individual data models introduces severe limitations: redundant effort, expensive maintenance, and difficulty in meeting the requirements of new applications. To overcome those limitations, the Data Model Compiler (DMC) project (Maryanski et al., 1986) presents an alternative approach in which database system software is automatically generated from data model specifications, i.e., the input to the DMC is specific data models and the output from the DMC is the database system software corresponding to the input data models. The results of the initial research of the DMC project have been reported (Bedell and Maryanski, 1987; Hoelscher and Maryanski, 1987; Maryanski, Francis, Hong, and Peckham, to be published; Maryanski and Hong, 1985; Maryanski and Stock, 1987).

SeaWeed is an initial component of the second research phase of the project which aims at the automatic generation of database software. SeaWeed consists of a meta-data model, a reusable software component library, and a database design tool software generator. An object-oriented data model is first represented in terms of the primitives of SeaWeed's meta-data model. The data model specification is then processed by the software generator, and, finally, a conceptual database design tool software is automatically generated from reusable software components.

Unlike database design tools such as DDEW (Reiner et al., 1984), Sedaco (Farmer et al., 1985), ISIS (Goldman et al., 1985), Gambit (Braegger et al., 1985), and SECSI (Bouzeghoub and Gardarin, 1984; Bouzeghoub, Gardarin, and Metais, 1985), whose implementations are based on fixed data models, SeaWeed's meta-data model can be used to capture the semantics of a class of data models. Hence, SeaWeed can produce design tools for a class of data models.

Since it does not operate with a fixed data model, SeaWeed pursues the same direction as other extensible database projects such as Starburst (Schwarz et al., 1985), EXODUS (Carey et al., 1986; Richardson and Carey, 1987), and GENESIS (Batory, Leung, and Wise, to be published). Starburst aims at building an extensible relational database system to provide the flexibility for handling the requirements of new applications, but it assumed a fixed DBMS architecture. EXODUS allows the user to program the

Empirical Foundations of Information and Software Science V
Edited by P. Zunde and D. Hocking, Plenum Press, New York, 1990

131

application requirements and generates application specific database systems. GENESIS permits the implementations of DBMSs expressed as equations, and synthesizes DBMSs from reusable software modules. SeaWeed follows the compiler/generator direction by providing a data model specification language, which can be used to express the semantics of a particular data model, and a reusable software component library from which suitable software components can be selected to compose the conceptual database design tool. However, SeaWeed distinguishes itself from EXODUS, GENESIS, and others in its capability of expressing the semantics of data models, while others aim at the improvement of physical implementation.

The automatic generation of conceptual database design tool software from data model specifications is discussed in this paper. Section 2 briefly discusses SeaWeed's meta-data model and data model specification methodology. The software generation approach is presented in Section 3. Finally, the conclusion and ongoing research are presented in Section 4.

2. SPECIFICATION OF DATA MODEL

SeaWeed's meta-data model expresses the semantics of specific object-oriented data models. Due to the space limitations, this meta-data model is presented here through simple examples. A more detailed discussion of the meta-data model can be found in Hong and Maryanski (to be published).

2.1 Abstraction of Data Modeling

Data modeling is abstracted into three levels, physical database, conceptual data model, and meta-data model. At the *physical database* level, objects are modeled in terms of entities and relationships. For example, employee *John Smith* works on project *Engine Design*.

At the *conceptual data model* level, objects in a physical database are classified into object types, i.e., *entity types* and *relationship types*. For instance, all employees are classified into an entity type EMPLOYEE to which John Smith belongs, and the relationship that links employees to assigned projects belong to a relationship type WORK_FOR. The definition of a set of entity types and relationship types results in a *conceptual data model*, or data model for short.

At the *meta-data model* level, the object types of a data model are grouped into meta-object types in which they share the same data modeling capabilities. For example, there are two variants of the IS-A relationship, or the specialization/generalization relationship. One is restricted IS-A in which the properties of a super-type entity is inherited to its subtype entities without any change, and another is relaxed IS-A in which the properties inherited from super-type entity can be over-ridden in the subtype entities. Those variants of IS-A relationships can be specified as different meta-object types. In other words, the meta-object types defining a specific conceptual data model can be thought of as the meta-knowledge about that model.

2.2 Data Model Specification

SeaWeed's meta-data model captures the semantics of particular data models at the meta-data model level. This meta-data model consists of a set of meta-object types that may be classified into meta-entity types and meta-relationship types defined formally as follows.

> *meta-entity type* = (A,O,C,G)
> where
> > A: types of attributes,
> > O: types of data operations,
> > C: types of data constraints,
> > G: graphical representations

> *meta-relationship type* = (M-A,M-O,M-C,G)
> where
> > M-A: A ∪ {participants, concepts},
> > M-O: O ∪ {model operations},
> > M-C: C ∪ {model constraints},
> > G: graphical representations

2.2.1 Meta-Entity Types. A meta-entity type describes a class of entity types in terms of the types of attributes, data operations, and data constraints. Figure 1 shows the definition of a meta-entity type

META-ENTITY TYPE: ENTITY;

    – Here we define a general entity type which
    – could represent any object of interest

ATTRIBUTE

    key required;
    primitive attribute type;
    reference attribute type;
    set-of attribute type;
    derived attribute type;

END ATTRIBUTE

OPERATION

    insertion;
    deletion;
    modification;
    user-defined operation;

END OPERATION

CONSTRAINT

    insertion is nullified;
    deletion is restricted;
    modification is cascaded;
    user-defined constraint;

END CONSTRAINT

GRAPHICAL REPRESENTATION

    – see diagram in figure 3

END GRAPHICAL REPRESENTATION

Figure 1. META-Entity Type ENTITY.

ENTITY. In this example, five attribute types are selected; key attribute is required; all primitive attribute types (e.g., integer, real, character, etc.) are chosen; attributes can be references to other objects; attributes can be set-values; and attributes can be derived or inherited from other objects. The data operation types specify the operators that can be performed on any instance object of ENTITY, i.e., insertion, deletion, modification, and any user-defined operations. The data constraint types indicate the methods to enforce the constraints on those data operations which are very similar to the referential integrity constraints in the relational data model (Date, 1986).

    2.2.2 Meta-Relationship Types. The definition of a meta-relationship type is similar to that of meta-entity type, but has three additional properties, i.e., participant and concept definitions, model operations, and model constraints. Figure 2 shows an example of a relaxed version of IS-A relationship. The participant clause indicates which entity types can participate in a relationship type, while the concept clause specifies the conceptual roles played by those participants in that relationship type. In this example, any instance of object type of ENTITY can participate in the PARTIAL_ISA relationship. Two roles may be played by a participant, SUPERTYPE and SUBTYPE, depending on the context of connection to other object type, i.e., being the source or target of the connection.

    The model operations describe methods by which the properties of the participants are inherited. In this example, the inheritance from any SUPERTYPE to SUBTYPE is performed by executing the model operation PARTIAL_INHERITANCE which specifies that any property marked by "Y" is inherited. Inheritance occurs when any SUPERTYPE and SUBTYPE pair is created. On the type definition level, the inherited type definition can not be changed, and the user should resolve any naming conflict between the inherited properties and the properties of subtypes their own.

META-RELATIONSHIP TYPE: PARTIAL_ISA

    – Here we define a set of relationship called partial-isa

    – which allows partial inheritance between subtypes and supertypes

ATTRIBUTE

    PARTICIPANT (ENTITY);

    CONCEPT {

        (source - SUPERTYPE : ENTITY,

         target - SUBTYPE : ENTITY

)

    }

    key required;

END ATTRIBUTE

OPERATION

    PARTIAL_INHERITANCE on (SUPERTYPE, SUBTYPE)

    begin

        SUBTYPE < – SUPERTYPE marked by "Y";

        activate time = at (creating);

        level = type;

        protection = type;

        name conflict = user determines;

    end

END OPERATION

CONSTRAINT

    cardinality of (SUPERTYPE, SUBTYPE) is many-to-many;

    connection SUPERTYPE to SUBTYPE transitively;

    deletion of SUPERTYPE implies deletion of SUBTYPE;

    SUPERTYPE is created before SUBTYPE;

    insertion of SUBTYPE implies insertion of SUPERTYPE;

    modification of SUPERTYPE is propagated to SUBTYPE;

END CONSTRAINT

GRAPHICAL REPRESENTATION

    – seen figure 3

END GRAPHICAL REPRESENTATION

Figure 2. META-Relationship Type PARTIAL_ISA.

    The model constraints define the integrity rules and structural constraints of a relationship type. In this example, the model constraint states that the link between any SUPERTYPE and SUBTYPE is a transitively many-to-many relationship from SUPERTYPE to SUBTYPE. No cycle is allowed. If a SUPERTYPE is deleted, all its SUBTYPE's are also deleted. SUPERTYPE must be created before any of its SUBTYPE's. Any change made on the property of a SUPERTYPE is always propagated to its SUBTYPE's.

    In summary, the semantics of a data model are characterized by a set of meta-object types that are composed of unique types of attributes, data and model operations, and data and model constraints as shown by the above two examples.

    2.2.3 Graphical Representation. SeaWeed assumes that at the user interface of a generated database design tool, diagrams and forms are used as the metaphor for defining a conceptual database schema. The last step in the data model specification is to select or design the desired iconic representations for the meta-object types. Figure 3 gives the graphical representations for the meta-entity type ENTITY and PARTIAL_ISA. In that figure, the details of an object of type ENTITY are entered into a form and the PARTIAL_IS a relationship is depicted by a diagram in which participants, SUPERTYPE and SUBTYPE, are represented by rectangles, and the relationship between them by an arc.

    SeaWeed's user interface for data model specification consists of a language specific editor (Beshers, 1986) for meta-object type definition and graphical icon design interface as shown in Figure 3.

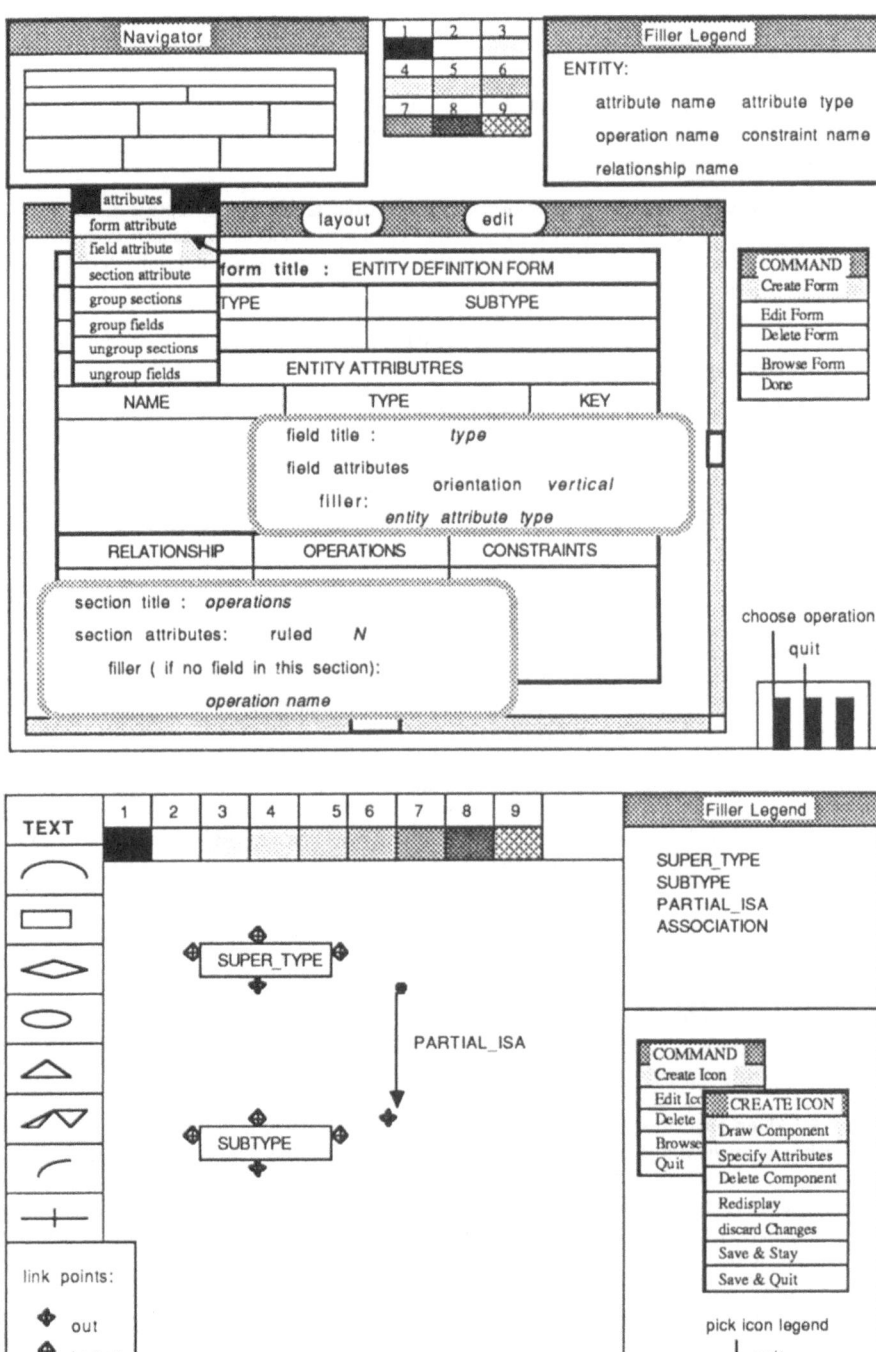

Figure 3. Graphical Representation for ENTITY and PARTIAL_ISA.

135

3. GENERATION OF DATABASE DESIGN TOOL

3.1 Structure of the Database Design Tool

The structure of the generated software is based on the framework of an existing database design tool, DBDT (Maryanski and Hong, 1985), which consists of three major components: form and diagram editors, error checking, and schema translation.

- *Form and Diagram Editors.* As mentioned in the previous section, a conceptual database schema is defined by filling forms and drawing diagrams. The functionality of the editors is to monitor the form completion and diagram development through a menu-driven graphical interface. It also automatically handles the data flow between diagrams and forms to avoid repetitious typing.

- *Error Checking.* Error checking is performed to ensure that the definition of a conceptual database schema corresponds exactly to the data model specification.

  Among the checks performed are the validity of attribute types and relationships definitions, and consistency and completeness of schema definitions.

- *Schema Translation.* The module translates an error-free conceptual database schema into the internal representation. In the current implementation, a conceptual database schema is translated into relationship representation.

More details about the structure of the generated tool can be found in Maryanski and Hong (1985).

3.2 Software Generation Approach

Software generation is performed in three steps: implementation scheme formation, software component generation, and system integration.

3.2.1 Implementation Scheme Formation. An implementation scheme contains the design requirements of the software to be generated. The software design is based on a state transition diagram model which is an extension of the models proposed by Olsen (1984) and Wasserman (1985). This model consists of states, called *tasks*, and transitions between states as defined in the following.

$(Q, \Sigma, \delta, \beta, F)$
where
     Q - the set of unique tasks,
     Σ - the set of transition conditions
     δ - the set of transitions,
     β - the initial task,
     F - the set of final tasks.

Tasks - A task encapsulates the data items and operations that manipulate the data items in a logical unit. A task can be *primitive* or *complex*. In a primitive task, the activities are executed without intervention by the user. Conversely, a complex task is composed of other tasks, called subtasks, which may be primitive and/or complex tasks, and interactions with the user, i.e., transitions between the subtasks. The relationship between a task and its subtasks is the *is-part-of* relationship, which forms a task hierarchy in which a complete task can be decomposed until all subtasks are primitive tasks.

Transition Conditions - Transition conditions describe the interaction between the system and the user, and the decisions made at the current task. A transition condition is associated with a data type which may be a conventional data type such as integer, character string, etc., or input/output devices such as cursor, mouse buttons, etc. System operations are defined for each data type to handle the input-output of the variable of that type. For example, if POSITION is defined on data type CURSOR, then the input operation is sampling the current cursor position on the screen (e.g., (x,y) in two dimensional screen), and the output operation is moving the cursor to the indicated position on the screen.

State Transitions - State transitions indicate the data and control flow among tasks. If the transition condition is matched, the control is passed to the next task. If no transition condition is matched, the default transition is taken.

The extended state transition diagram has four purposes. First, it models the interaction between the user and the system. Second, it decomposes the software design process into task hierarchies to modularize

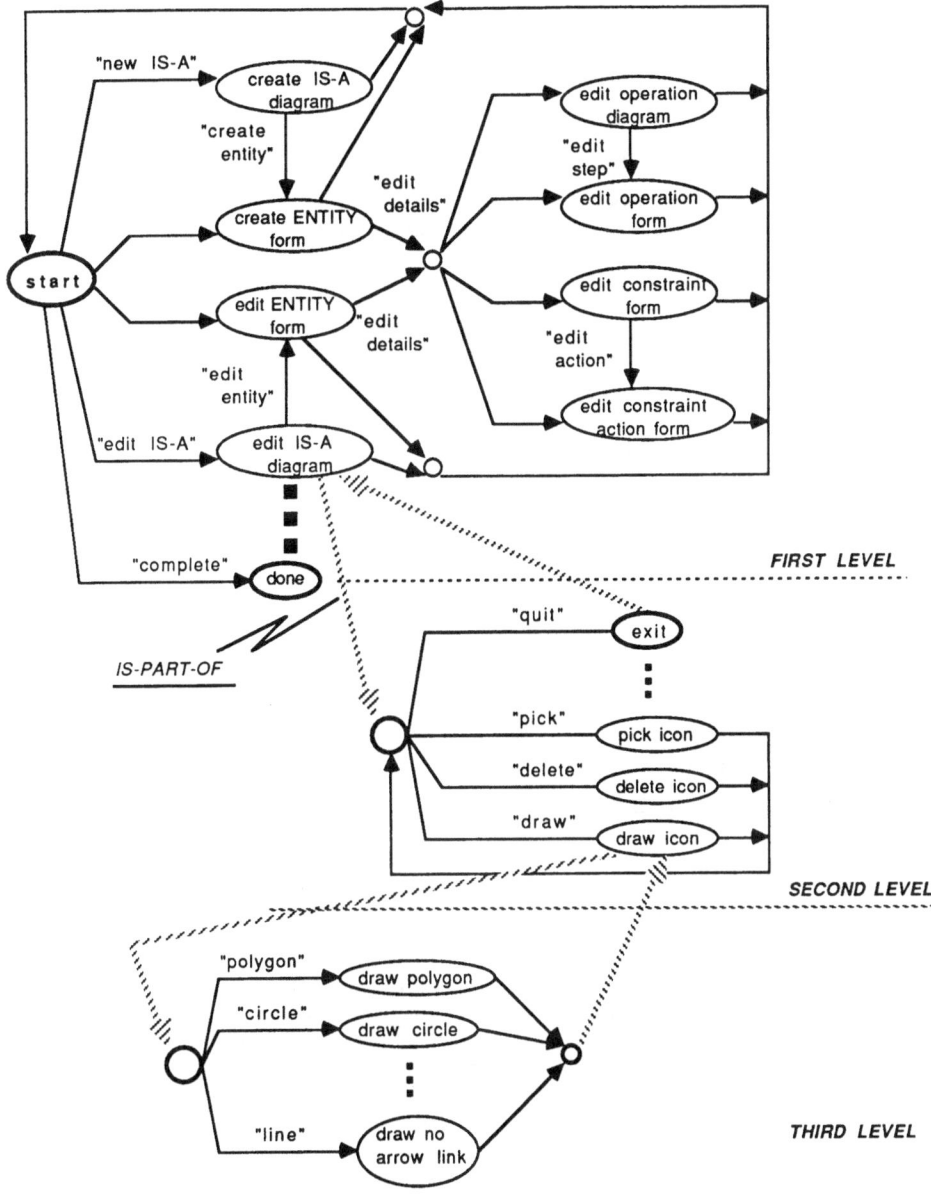

Figure 4. Task Hierarchies.

the state transition diagram and to provide a means for guiding the software design process. At the highest level, the software design can be decomposed into major tasks ignoring the details until later when subtasks are introduced in the hierarchy. Figure 4 shows an example of an incomplete task hierarchy. In that figure, task EDIT PARTIAL_ISA DIAGRAM is decomposed into subtasks at the second level at which one of subtasks, DRAW ICON, is in turn decomposed into subtasks at the third level. Unlike the stepwise refinement hierarchy in which only the design at the lowest level composes the final software system, the design at each level in a task hierarchy is a part of the final software system.

Third, this model identifies the functionality of each task so that it paves the way for the reuse of software components as discussed later. Fourth, it can be used as the composition model to integrate the final software system. Thus, a state transition diagram is an implementation model of the design tool software.

– This task edit a diagram for partial IS-A relationship
– in which rectangle is used to represent the participants
– and arc is used to represent relationship

FUNCTIONALITY: edit a diagram;

SUBTASKS:
diagram_init, pick_icon, draw_icon, ..., quit

DATA ITEMS:
command_menu – *list of menu entries*
node_type – *rectangle for entity ENTITY*
link_type – *arc for PARTIAL_ISA*
color – *YELLOW*
GLOBAL diagram : assoc_diagram of type DIAGRAM
command : type of COMMAND MENU ENTRY

OPERATIONS:
```
diagram_init();
loop
        command = menu_selection(command_menu);
        if ( command = PICK_ICON)
            then pick_icon(icon_legend);
        else
        if (command = DRAW_ICON)
            then draw_icon(icon_legend, assoc_diagram);
        else
            ...
```

END TASK

Figure 5. Definition of an Implementation Scheme.

For a new design tool, there is a corresponding task hierarchy. The generation of the task hierarchy is derived from the data model specification. Each meta-object type forms a task at the top level in that hierarchy. By assuming that the diagram is drawn first and the details are provided by forms, transitions are created between diagram tasks to form tasks. Example in Figure 4 actually represents the task hierarchy for the sample data model discussed in Section 1, i.e., meta-entity type ENTITY is represented by form, and meta-relationship PARTIAL_ISA is represented by diagrams. The tasks at the lower level are generated based on the structure of DBDT, i.e., reuse of the design of DBDT. At the second level, for example, the editing PARTIAL_ISA diagram consists of PICK_ICON, DRAW_ICON, etc. tasks and transitions among them, which are derived from the design of the DBDT.

An implementation scheme for a particular data model is the textual description of a task hierarchy and the detailed definition of each task in that hierarchy. Figure 5 shows the simplified implementation scheme for task EDIT PARTIAL IS-A DIAGRAM, which contains four components: task functionality, the data items, subtasks, and the data/control flows among them. The functionality of a task describes the purpose of that task. For instance, the functionality of that task is EDIT A DIAGRAM. In the data item segment, requirements of command menu, graphical representation of nodes and links, color, and data structure for storing the information of the diagram are specified. These data are obtained from the graphical representation of the given data model specification. In the operational portion, the data flow in terms of parameters of the subtasks and the control flow are indicated. Figure 5 is presented in textual form for purposes of illustration. Since those descriptions are internal to the system, they are written in a form that is very close to the syntax of programming language C.

3.2.2 Software Component Generation. A task is implemented by customizing the corresponding reusable software component according to the requirement of that task as discussed below.

Reusable Software Component Library. A reusable software component library serves as a depository of database design tool software. A reusable software component is modeled as an object that consists of four parts: the functionality, relationship with other components, data requirements, and subroutines. Those components are organized according to the IS-A and IS-PART-OF relationships so that the library

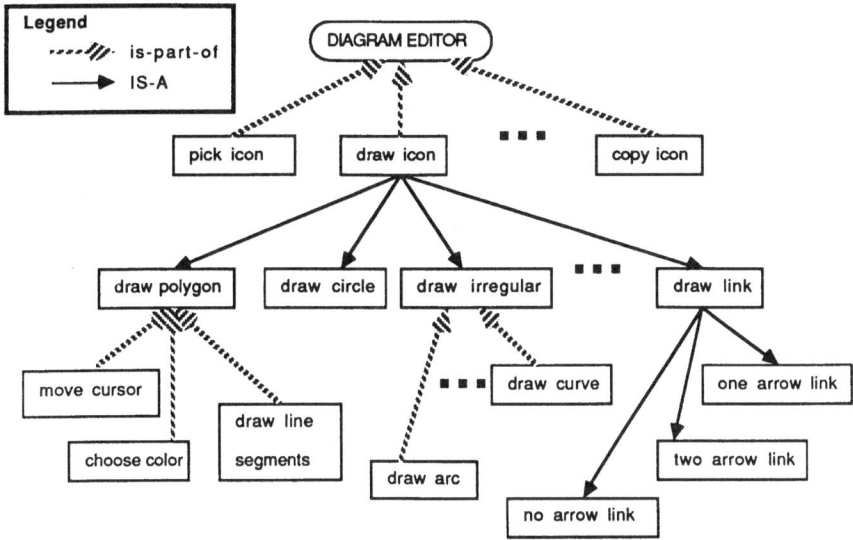

Figure 6. Reusable Software Component Library.

can be thought of as a very generic conceptual database design tool. Figure 6 shows the part of the library for editing diagrams. In that figure, the *is-a* relationship is depicted as a solid arc pointing from the supertype component to the subtype component, while the *is-part-of* relationship is shown as a dotted arc pointing from the subpart of the superpart.

Implementation of Tasks. The implementation of a task involves locating the desired reusable software component and binding the data model specific requirements with the component to create a customized version of that component. The present SeaWeed prototype assumes that for a given task, there exists exactly one reusable component in the library.[1] Hence, the finding of a reusable component for a given task is a straightforward process that matches the functionality of the task with that of a component.

The central issue of customizing the located reusable component is the binding of the data model specific requirements into the component. Fortunately, the approach of reuse of the design of DBDT has made this technical problem easier. The data model specific requirements, as discussed in the beginning of this section, are handled in the following ways:

- A generic data structure is defined for diagrams and forms. Looking at the implementation level, for instance, a diagram is composed of nodes and links which consist of points, lines, and associated text. Thus, a generic data structure for diagrams is feasible regardless of the differences in appearance among diagrams. A set of subroutines can then be coded to manipulate the diagram or form represented by the generic data structure.

- The menus, command menu or icon legend menu, can be treated in the same way as the above. That is, generic data structures are defined for size and content varying menus.

- A set of error checking subroutines are prepared for all possible checks. Error checks can be classified into two kinds, syntactic and semantic error checks. Syntactical error checking identifies errors such as typographical errors or omitted definitions. On the other hand, semantic error checking corrects errors such as improper attribute type illegal relationship connection, etc., which are specified as constraints in the data model definition. Thus, syntactic error checks are independent of any data model, but semantic error checks are data model specific. However, a set of semantic error checking functions can be prepared based on the classification of the data model constraints (see Hong and Maryanski (to be published) for the details of constraint classification).

Figure 7 shows a simplified reusable software component for editing a diagram. In that figure, data

---

[1]As discussed in the summary, an on-going project will remove this limitation.

component: *EDIT_DIAGRAM*

/* This component edits a generic diagram which is composed of */
/* generic nodes and links between them */

functionality: edit a diagram
data requirement:
    edit_menu : $ command_menu $
               – the menu data structure definition
    node   : $ node_type $
               – generic node data structure definition
    link   : $ link_type $
               – generic link data structure definition
    color   : COLOR = $ color $
    diagram : $ diagram $ DIAGRAM

local variable:
          menu_entry : $ command $ MENE_ENTRY;
          – other local variable declarations

subroutines:

    – subroutines that perform the operations for
    – drawing a diagram

end component

Figure 7. Reusable Component Definition.

items enclosed by "$" are the patterns to be used to match the data item requirement in the task definition. If that component is to be customized for task scheme EDIT PARTIAL IS-A DIAGRAM in Figure 5, for example, the EDIT_MENU data item would match the COMMAND_MENU entry in that scheme so that the EDIT_MENU contains only those menu entries listed in that task. Note that the library organization details, i.e., is-a and is-part-of relationships with other components, are omitted in Figure 7.

The customization involves some degree of reasoning and pattern matching. To provide more flexibility, a set of production rules is formed that guide the customization process. The discussion of those rules are beyond the scope of this paper.

3.2.3 Software System Integration. The integration of the new design tool is processed bottom-up. When all the tasks that compose a higher level task are implemented by customizing the reusable components, the higher level task is then assembled from those tasks by automatically generating code to glue those subtasks together in a manner that corresponds to the data and control flows among the subtasks. Since the data/control flows have been sketched in the task definition (e.g., see Figure 5), the code generation is rather a straightforward process. When the assembling process reaches the highest task level, the entire software system has been generated.

4. CONCLUSION

The automatic generation of conceptual database design tools from data model specifications has been discussed in this paper. Key research contributions of SeaWeed are its meta-data model and the unique paradigm of software generation. The combination of techniques for meta-data modeling, software reusability, and artificial intelligence can reduce the complexity and implementation effort in database design tool development.

However, several issues have not been addressed in SeaWeed's research such as the validation and testing of the software generated, automatic documentation generation, and evolution and maintenance of the reusable component library. Also, SeaWeed assumes there exists an exact reusable component for each implementation task. This assumption should be removed in order to extend its power. This issue is addressed by Mackellar and Maryanski (1988).

ACKNOWLEDGEMENT

The work of both authors was partially supported by grants ECS-8401487 and IRI-8704042 from the National Science Foundation.

REFERENCES

Batory, D. S., Leung, T. Y., and Wise, T. E., Implementation Concepts for an Extensible Data Model and Data Language, *ACM Transactions on Database Systems*, accepted for publication.

Beshers, G. M., 1986, *Regular Right Part Grammars and Maintained And Constructor Attributes in Language Based Editors*, Ph.D. Dissertation, Computer Science Department, University of Illinois at Urbana-Champaign.

Braegger, R. P., et al., 1985, Gambit: An Interactive Database Design Tool for Data Structures, Integrity Constraints, and Transactions, *IEEE Trans on Software Engineering*, Vol. SE-11, No. 7, July 1985, pp. 574-583.

Bouzeghoub, M., and Gardarin, G., 1984, The Design of an Expert System for Database Design, *New Applications of Data Bases*, Gardarin, G., and Gelenbe, E., eds., Academic Press, pp. 203-223.

Bouzeghoub, M., Gardarin, G., and Metais, E., 1985, Database Design Tools: An Expert System Approach, *Proc of 11th International Conference on VLDB*, August 1985, pp. 82-95.

Bedell, J., and Maryanski, F., 1987, Semantic Data Modeling Support for CAD, *Fall Joint Computer Conference*, October 1987, pp. 498-504.

Carey, M. J., et al., 1986, The Architecture of the EXODUS Extensible DBMS, *Proc of International Workshop on Object-Oriented Database Systems*, September 1985, pp. 52-65.

Date, C. J., 1986, *An Introduction to Database Systems*, Chapter 12, Vol. 1, 4th Edition, Addison-Wesley Publishing Company.

Farmer, D., et al., 1985, The Semantic Database Constructor, *IEEE Trans on Software Engineering*, Vol. SE-11, No. 7, July 1985, pp. 583-591.

Goldman, K. J., et al., 1985, ISIS: Interface for a Semantic Information System, *Proc of ACM-SIGMOD*, May 1985, pp. 328-342.

Hong, S., and Maryanski, F., A Meta-Data Model for Object-Oriented Data Models, *Information Sciences*, accepted for publication.

Hoelscher, S. M., and Maryanski, F., 1987, COMPASS: Computerized Office Management Package and Semantic System, *Conference on Human Computer Interaction*, August 1987, pp. 382.

Mackellar, B., and Maryanski, F., 1988, Reasoning By Analogy in Knowledge Base Systems, *4th International Conference on Data Engineering*, February 1988.

Maryanski, F., et al., 1986, The Data Model Compiler: A Tool for Generating Object-Oriented Database Systems, *International Workshop on Object-Oriented Database Systems (OODBS)*, September 1986, pp. 73-84.

Maryanski, F., Francis, S., Hong, S., and Peckham, J., Generation of Conceptual Data Models, *Data and Knowledge Engineering*, accepted for publication.

Maryanski, F., and Hong, S., 1985, A Tool for Generating Semantic Database Applications, *Proc of The IEEE Ninth International Computer Software & Applications Conference*, October 1985, pp. 368-375.

Maryanski, F., and Stock, D., 1987, SURF: A Semantic Update and Retrieval Facility, *National Computer Conference*, June 1987.

Olsen, D. R., 1984, Pushdown Automata for User Interface Management, *ACM Trans on Graphics*, Vol. 3, No. 3, July 1984, pp. 177-203.

Reiner, D., et al., 1984, The Database Design and Evaluation Workbench (DDEW) Project at CCA, *IEEE Database Engineering*, Vol. 7, No. 4, pp. 10-15.

Richardson, J. E., and Carey, M. J., 1987, Programming Constructs for EXODUS, *Proc of ACM SIGMOD Annual Conference*, May 1987, pp. 208-219.

Schwarz, P., et al., 1986, Extensibility in the Starburst Database System, *International Workshop on Object-Oriented Database Systems*, September 1986, pp. 85-92.

Wasserman, A. I., 1985, Extending State Transition Diagram for the Specification of Human-Computer Interaction, *IEEE Trans on Software Engineering*, Vol. SE-11, No. 8, August 1985.

IV. MODELING INFORMATION SYSTEMS

MODELING AND EVALUATION OF INFORMATION SYSTEMS

Oscar Barros

Departamento de Ingenieria Industrial
Universidad de Chile
Santiago, CHILE

Abstract: A general graphical model for organizational information Systems (IS) is proposed. This model is based on systems theory and general patterns of organizational processes regulation derived from empirical observation and experience. It includes generalized decision making and data manipulation functions to regulate generalized organizational processes through flows of information. The general IS model is shown to serve as a basic pattern to approach the design of any IS. In particular, it is shown that alternative IS structures or designs can be derived from it. Structures not only include information that will be computerized, but also the prescription of the decision making behavior of the information users. This problem of jointly studying alternative behavior-sets of information or structures can be related to and supported by organizational design theory. The existence of alternatives leads to a problem of evaluation for which a quantitative modeling approach is proposed. Connection with organization theory allows base modeling on the measuring of organizational effectiveness of each alternative.

INTRODUCTION

Several approaches to modeling Information Systems (IS) have been proposed. A few of the most popular ones are: Structured Analysis for the graphical modeling of data flows (Ross, 1977; De Marco, 1978), Entity Relationship Approach (Chen, 1976), Information Engineering (Martin and Finkelstein, 1981) for data modeling, and Structured Design for software modeling (Yourdon and Constantine, 1979).

Some of the modeling approaches have dealt with the problem of Information Systems requirements. Among these we find, on the one hand, formal methods primarily oriented to requirements specification such as SREM (Alford, 1985), MSG.84 (Berzins and Gray, 1985), HOS (Hamilton and Zelding, 1976) and PAISLey (Zave, 1982), of which SREM and HOS also attempt code generation. On the other hand, we have approaches which aim at determining or ascertaining requirements. E.g., Structured Analysis can be used to model an existing IS by means of data flow diagrams and by anchoring and adjustment derive the requirements for a proposed IS.[1]

A few of the methods for requirement determination have been characterized by Davis (1982) as normative for they prescribe a set of requirements based on the fundamental similarity of classes of object systems or information utilizing systems. I.e., normative approaches imply discovering general patterns that provide structure to requirement determination or, in other words, to develop general models of object systems and, hence, of IS. Most notable among these methods, BIAIT has provided empirical general characterizations of IS by establishing patterns of organizational purpose, functions, and data (Carlson, 1979; Kerner, 1979).

Our work aims at extending the class of normative approaches to requirement determination by:

---

[1]For a review of approaches to IS requirements determination, some of which use modeling, see Davis (1982).

Empirical Foundations of Information and Software Science V
Edited by P. Zunde and D. Hocking, Plenum Press, New York, 1990

145

i)   Developing a general graphic model for organizational Information Systems which explicitly includes the object or utilizing system. The model is based on systems theory and general patterns of organizational Process regulation derived from empirical observation and experience. These Processes are related to product/resource life cycle stages defined in other methodologies (Zachman, 1979; Ives and Dearmonth, 1984).

ii)   Using the general IS model to derive requirements. Here we extend the concept of requirements to include not only what will be computerized, but, also the prescription of the behavior of the users of information by means of policies, rules, procedures and the like. Since there are always alternative behaviors and, consequently, alternative sets of information requirements to support such behaviors, we are really talking about design. We chose to call this External Design (Barros, 1975) as opposed to internal or computer subsystem design. This problem of jointly studying alternative behaviors-sets of information requirements or External Designs can be related to and supported by Organization Design Theory (Gailbraith, 1977; Malone, 1987; Melcher, 1976). In fact we will show that these designs correspond to IS structures that are similar to organizational coordination structures as defined by Malone (1987) and others (Emery, 1969; Simon, 1970).

iii)   Developing a quantitative modeling approach to be able to evaluate alternatives or structures derived in (ii) and to select the best one. Connection with Organization theory allows base modeling on the measuring of organizational effectiveness of each alternative. Concepts and tools for modeling alternatives are related to Marschack's value of information ideas (Marschack, 1954, 1968), modeling of computer processes (Horning and Randell, 1973), Operations Research and Management Science (OR/MS) modeling and the software packages available to implement models in practice (Reiman and Waren, 1985).

The main thrust of this paper is integration and operationalization of ideas. Thus many diverse concepts coming from fields such as systems theory, Organization theory, information value theory, OR/MS modeling and modeling packages are put to work together in an operational methodology for the determination and evaluation of alternative structures. The methodology is purposely practical for we have based its development on hundred of real cases from which ideas have been derived and to which the methodology has been successfully applied.

AN INFORMATION SYSTEM MODEL

A Systemic Model

We start by recognizing that an Information System is embedded within the management system of an Organization. Now the purpose of the management system and, hence, of the IS, is to regulate the behavior of the Organization under the perturbations generated by a changing and non-controllable environment (Beer, 1972; Emery, 1969). Thus a relevant systemic theory to better understand Information Systems is regulation theory as developed by Ashby (1970). He proposed a general model for any regulation system, shown in Figure 1, that has the following components:

i)   T, a Machine defined by a transformation, i.e., for given disturbances and responses it produces well defined outcomes.

ii)   D, a producer of disturbances that affect the Machine and Regulator's behavior, usually called Environment.

iii)   R, a Regulator that produces well defined responses for given disturbances and known outcomes, also specified by a transformation.

iv)   C, a Controller that guides the behavior of R by means of strategies.

This regulation model includes, but is not the same as, the classical automatic feedback model (Beer, 1972; Forrester, 1970). Such model assumes that all regulation is made by error correction, i.e., comparing current state (outcome) of the machine, known by feedback, with desired state and making corrections accordingly. The regulation model also allows for anticipation (e.g., planning) whereby means

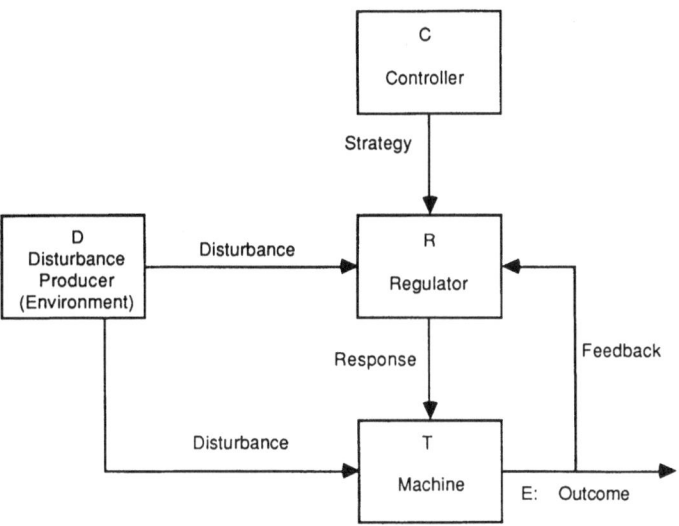

Figure 1. Model of a Regulator.

of the flow from D to R a disturbance (e.g., future sales for a manufacturing company) may be predicted in advance and regulation action or response (e.g., production plan in anticipation to sales) taken to manage the disturbance.

This simple, yet powerful, model, suitably adapted and detailed, will allow us to represent the problem of regulation in any Organization and to clarify the role of an IS in such regulation.

An Organizational Model

Starting with the general regulation model we try to map its components into Organization's elements and activities.

We begin by identifying the entities that are regulated and make up the Machine in any Organization. These are Organization Resources, i.e., materials, including products in which they are used, money, capital goods (assets) and human Resources. These entities have been identified in other works. Particularly Forrester (1961) found that in dynamic systems these entities originate flows and levels that define system's state. Control (regulation) is then exercised (by the Regulator) over the flow of these entities determining the system's behavior. Also, the BIAIT methodology has identified the same entities as "Unique Inventory Resources" (Carlson, 1979; Kerner, 1979). In the BIAIT terminology, these resources are managed by the equivalent of our Regulator.

A fifth entity appears in some cases, that is data. For example in a telephone network the regulated entity (Machine) is messages and we make decisions about its flows (e.g., routing), determining system's state (e.g., congestion). However, in general, in most systems of interest, data and information are means for regulation as we will see later, but in a few cases we may find regulated data and data about data for regulation purposes.[2] This brings out the dual nature of other Resources which can also be regulated and, at the same time, Regulator. This is the case of human Resources which when executing tasks are regulated (Machine) and when issuing orders are Regulators.

Resources do not always belong to the Organization. In many cases Resources are borrowed from the environment as it is the case, for example, of patients (human Resource) in a hospital.

We will treat regulated entities as the primitives of our Organization model and assume they are sufficient, in the sense that no other entities are needed to describe the regulated Machine in any real situation.

Now, in the act of regulation, entities (Resources) flow from the Environment into the Organization, are operated upon within the Organization and exit, not necessarily with the same identity, to the

---

[2]This subject can be further extended by thinking of data bases as resources and defining their management as a regulation problem (information resource management). This problem is a meta problem to us and we will not pursue this idea any further here.

Table 1

Examples of Organization Processes

REGULATED ENTITY (RESOURCE)	PROCESSES
Materials	inspect, transport, transform, machine, assemble, dispose, dispatch, etc.
Money	borrow, collect, invest, apply, pay, distribute, etc.
Capital Assets	install, use dispose, etc.
Human Resources	hire, train, develop, promote, assign, motivate, fire, etc.

Environment. The operations performed over the entities are the means for implementing the regulation. We will call these operations Processes.[3] Examples of these processes are shown in Table 1.

Processes can be classified into the generalized types shown in Figure 2, where the typical flows of resources that may exist are also displayed. Examples of instances of these generalized Processes for each regulated entity (Resources) are shown in Table 2. The generalized types and instances are based on the experience derived from hundreds of real cases known to the author (See Appendix 1).

Although independently developed, our concept of Processes is similar to the concept of a process proposed in the Jackson System Development (JSD) methodology (Cameron, 1986). JSD defines a process as a sequence of actions performed over a real life object (our Resources). For instance, in Cameron (1986), the process Book is defined as composed of the actions: acquire, classify, loan part and end part. It is obvious that these actions are, respectively, equivalent to our Processes: acquire, store, apply and transfer. The difference is that our Processes are generalized and valid for any IS and a JSD process is particular of an application. Furthermore, the use given to the idea of a process diverges in JSD and our model. JSD goes on to convert the set of actions that make up a process into a computing process that mimic the real life object (Cameron, 1986). We will use the Processes to derive the regulation (and information) needs an IS should satisfy as shown next.

The idea of Processes is also related to what other authors call object system (Davis, 1982; Verrijn-Stuart, 1986), which can be defined in brief as to what gives raise to the need of an IS. We think that Processes give a generalized operational description of such an object system.

Based on what we have seen so far we can state that the regulation problem in an Organization is to decide what Processes to perform over Resources at any given time, based on the knowledge of the state of such Processes previous to the decision and, possibly, a prediction about the future state of the Environment. Regulation as defined here is related to Malone's (1987) idea of coordination which he considers to be associated with the assignment of tasks to processors (our Processes).

We now identify the decision and other types of functions necessary to perform regulation in the sense we have defined. These functions make up what is the Regulator and Controller in the general regulation model. In identifying regulation functions we associate to each generalized Process, decision and data manipulation activities that may be necessary for its occurrence. The derived functions are listed in Table 3 and are shown in Figure 3, together with their relationships to Processes by means of information flows. Of course the flows are given just as examples since, as we will discuss later, they are at the heart of the IS design problem.

An example of the Processes, functions and flows for a simplified real situation is shown in Figure 4.

---

[3]This definition of Processes is consistent with the concept of "process" used to model the behavior of digital computer systems (Horning and Randell, 1973).

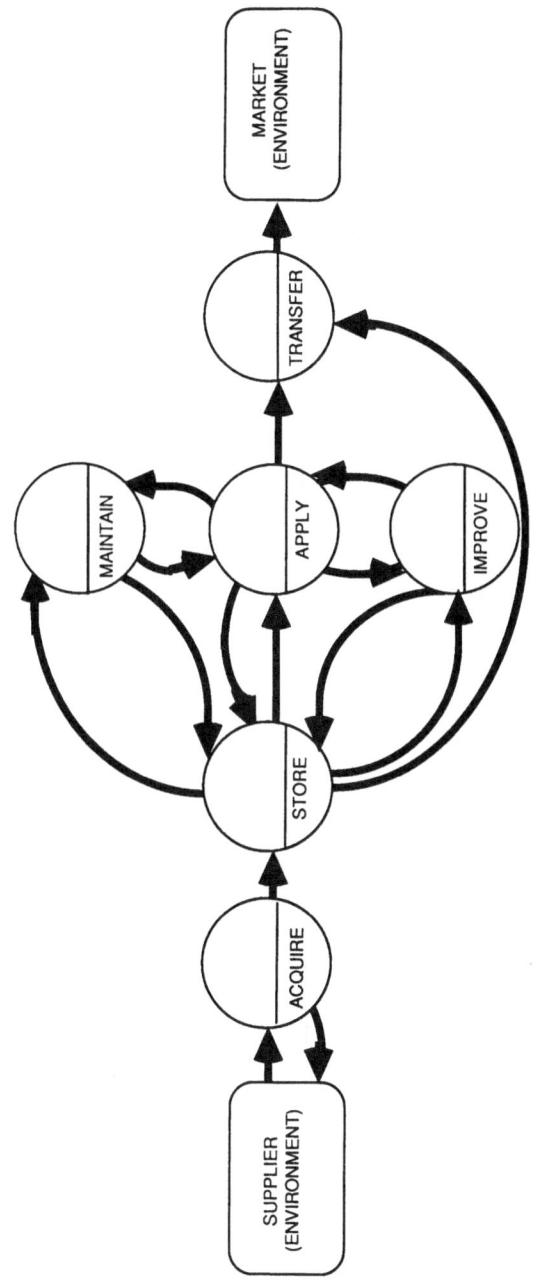

Figure 2. Generalized Organization Processes and Resource Flow.

149

Table 2

Instances of Generalized Processes for Resources

REGULATED ENTITY	GENERALIZED PROCESSES					
	ACQUIRE	STORE	APPLY	IMPROVE	MAINTAIN	TRANSFER
Materials	transport, inspect	move, inventory, distribute	use, handle, machine, transform, assemble	treat, correct	fix, clean	dispatch, dispose
Money	borrow, collect, inspect	move, distribute	use	invest	—	pay
Capital Assets	transport, test	move, inventory, distribute, install	assign, use, operate	modify, rebuild	fix, repair, prevent, overhaul	dispose
Human Resources	recruit, select, hire	pool	assign, instruct, give task	train, develop, promote	motivate, reward, check-up	fire, retire

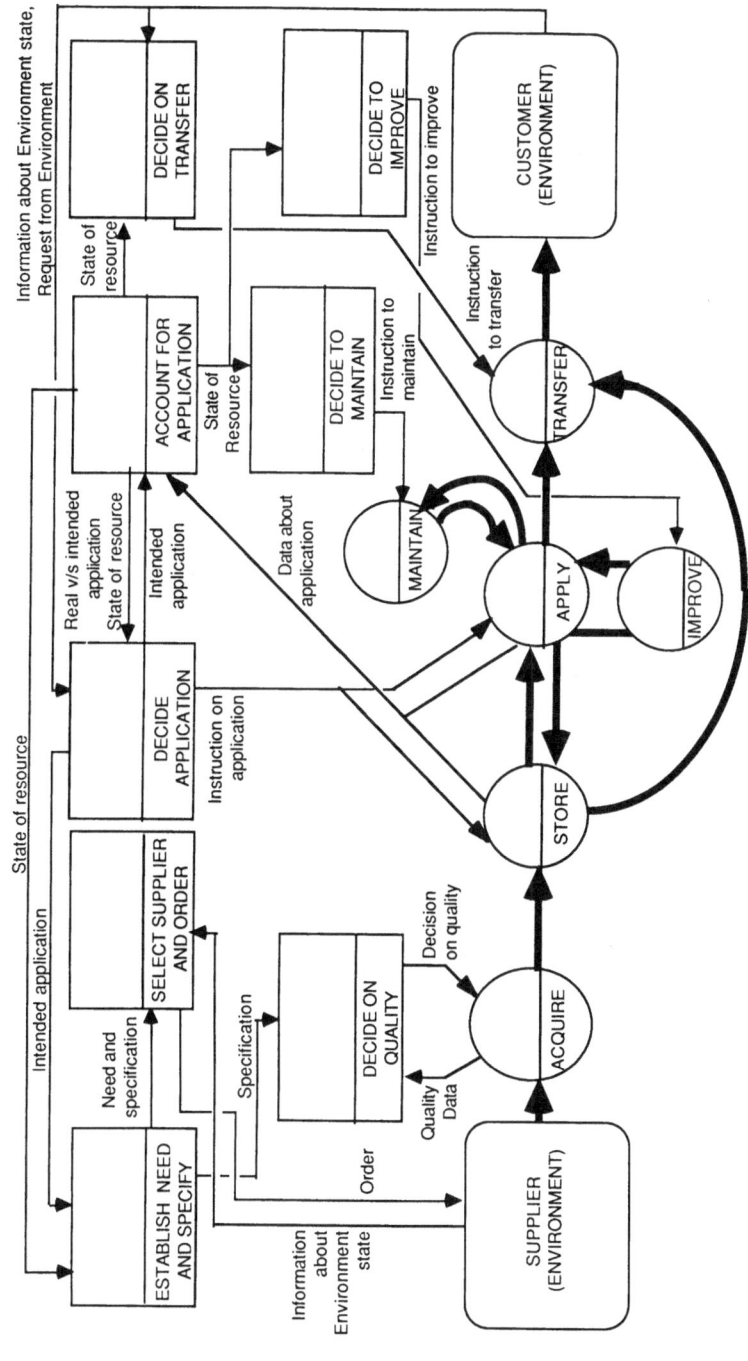

Figure 3. Generalized Processes and Functions and Flows of Information.

151

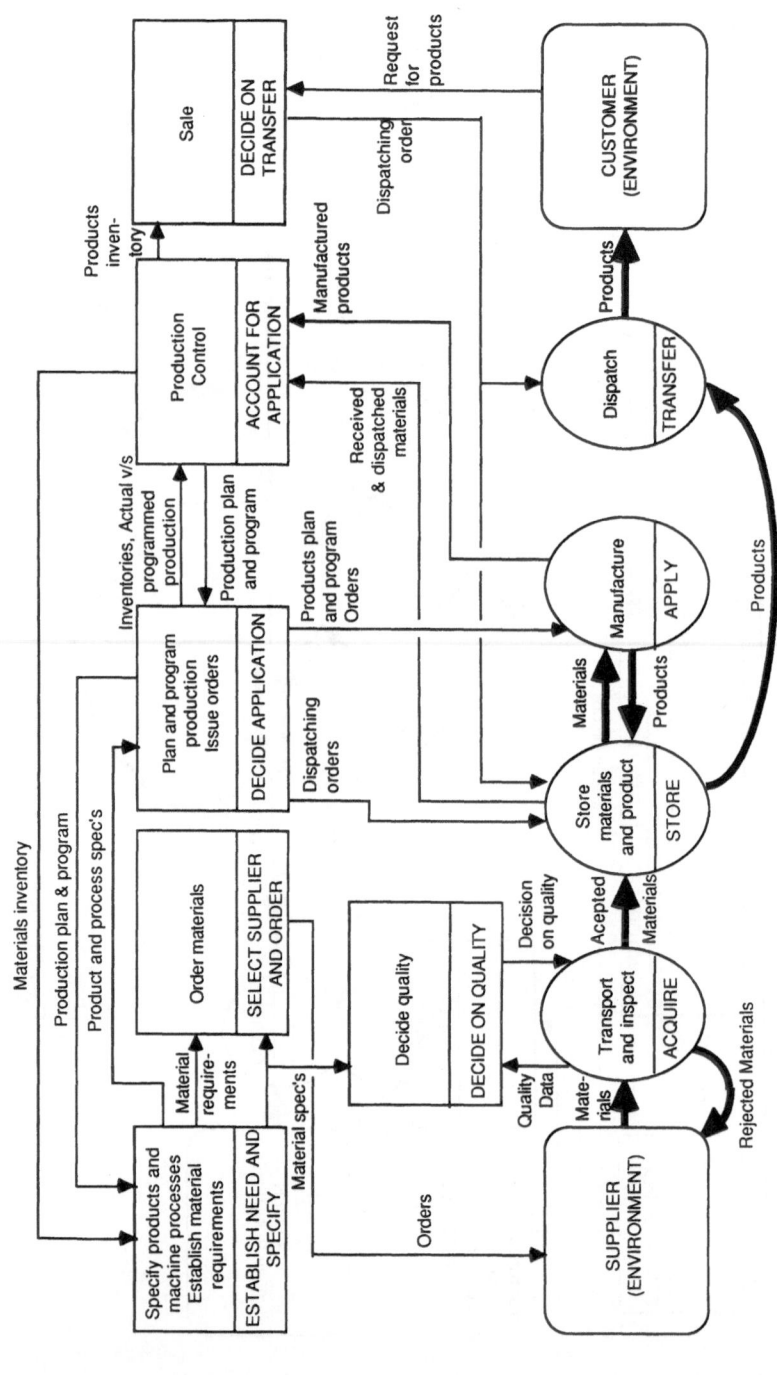

Figure 4. An Example: Materials and Production Management (Simplified).

Table 3

Generalized Functions Needed for Generalized Processes

GENERALIZED PROCESS	GENERALIZED FUNCTIONS
Acquire	Establish Need and Specify, Select Supplier and Order, Decide on Quality
Store	Decide Application (of stored resources)
Apply	Decide Application (present and possibly future; may include planning and programming), Account for Application (determine state of application of resources)
Improve	Decide to Improve
Maintain	Decide to Maintain
Transfer	Decide on Transfer

The other known attempt to identify what we have called generalized functions is BIAIT's Information Handling Disciplines (IHD). Despite their name, these IHD are decision and data processing functions that may occur in Information Systems. There are around 50 and were derived from an empirical study made at IBM, details of which are not known. According to BIAIT, the occurrence of these IHD in a particular case depends on the characteristics of the business where the Information System exists (Carlson, 1979; Kerner, 1979).

Other authors have identified stages in the product/resource life cycle (Zachman, 1979; Ives and Dearmonth, 1984) which are similar to some of the Processes and generalized functions we have defined. This is not surprising since our regulation model can also be thought to exist to manage Resources (including products) through their life cycles (from input to the Organization to exit). These product/resource life cycle stages have been used by BSP (Zachman, 1979) and Ives and Dearmonth (1984) to establish information requirements in a similar fashion to what we will propose in the next section.

Our set of generalized functions pretends to be minimally sufficient, in the sense that this is the least number of functions that allows representing any problem of regulation of Resources in an Organization. Of course we cannot prove this, but we have performed hundreds of tests of this model on actual cases that partially validate our presumption. (See Appendix 1 for a partial list of cases to which all the ideas in this paper have been applied).

The Information System

Now the question is which part of the generalized resources regulation model (Organization model) is the Information System.

It is clear from the above model that information manipulation (processing) and flows are basically a means to:

i) Collect information, determine and inform state of Processes to regulation functions.

ii) Convey orders and instructions about regulation operations or actions to be carried upon Processes.

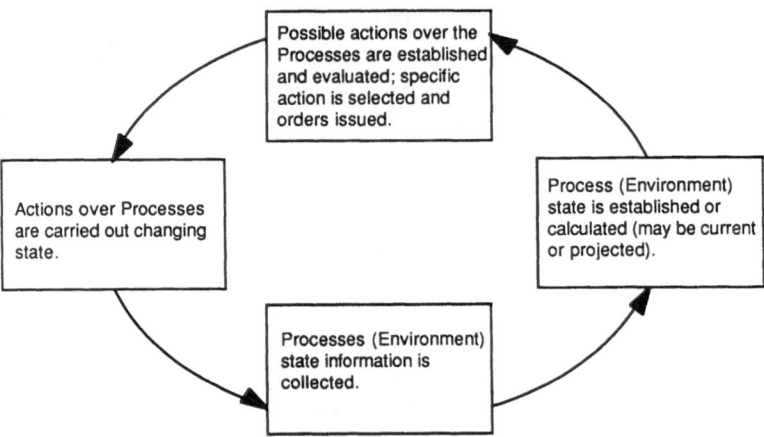

Figure 5. Chain of Consequences Linking Processes
and Regulation Functions.

iii)　　Communicate regulation functions to each other.

iv)　　Calculate, project, evaluate, analyze, etc., consequences of planned actions within certain regulation functions, particularly Decide Application and Establish Need and Specify; e.g., establish material requirements based on a production plan in the example in Figure 4.

v)　　Collect information about Environment state and, within certain functions, forecast future state.

Hence, information processing and flows hold together regulation functions and Processes and communicate them to the Environment. Thus, the only natural way to define the Information System is to make it coincident with the full Organization model in Figure 3. The only constraint is that information has to be formalized, i.e., designed to achieve a certain purpose. In this way, information processing and flows will always be part of the logical chain of consequences shown in Figure 5. This chain is a more general version of the classical feedback loop since, in this case, not only error correcting actions based on current state are allowed, but anticipation is permitted based on projected state of Environment and/or Processes.

This chain is also related to information value, since flows between and processing of information within functions are only justifiable if the whole chain produces the desired effect on the Processes. I.e., all information and decision costs associated to the chain must be balanced against the benefits generated by better Process regulation due to the existence of the chain. This further supports the idea that information, decision and actions (results) over Processes cannot be separated and must constitute a unique system.[4] This we consider the Information System of the Organization.

This approach is also related to organizational coordination structures defined by Malone (1987) as patterns of decision-making and communications among a set of actors (our Processes and functions) that perform tasks in order to achieve goals. Thus, Information Systems in our definition are also coordination structures.

From the model above, we may conclude that there are separate IS for the different resources that an Organization manages (regulates) and this is a frequent situation in practice. However, there is no reason to impose this constraint. IS for different resources can and should be integrated in many cases. To visualize how this occurs, we have to represent each Resource IS in aggregate terms (with no detail) in the same graph, as shown in Figure 6. Then integration among them is shown by means of the information flows between each pair of systems. For example, in Figure 6 we show some of the possible relations (integration) between Materials, Money, Human Resources and Assets IS within a Production

---

[4]This is also supported by the ideas about information value developed by Marschack (1968).

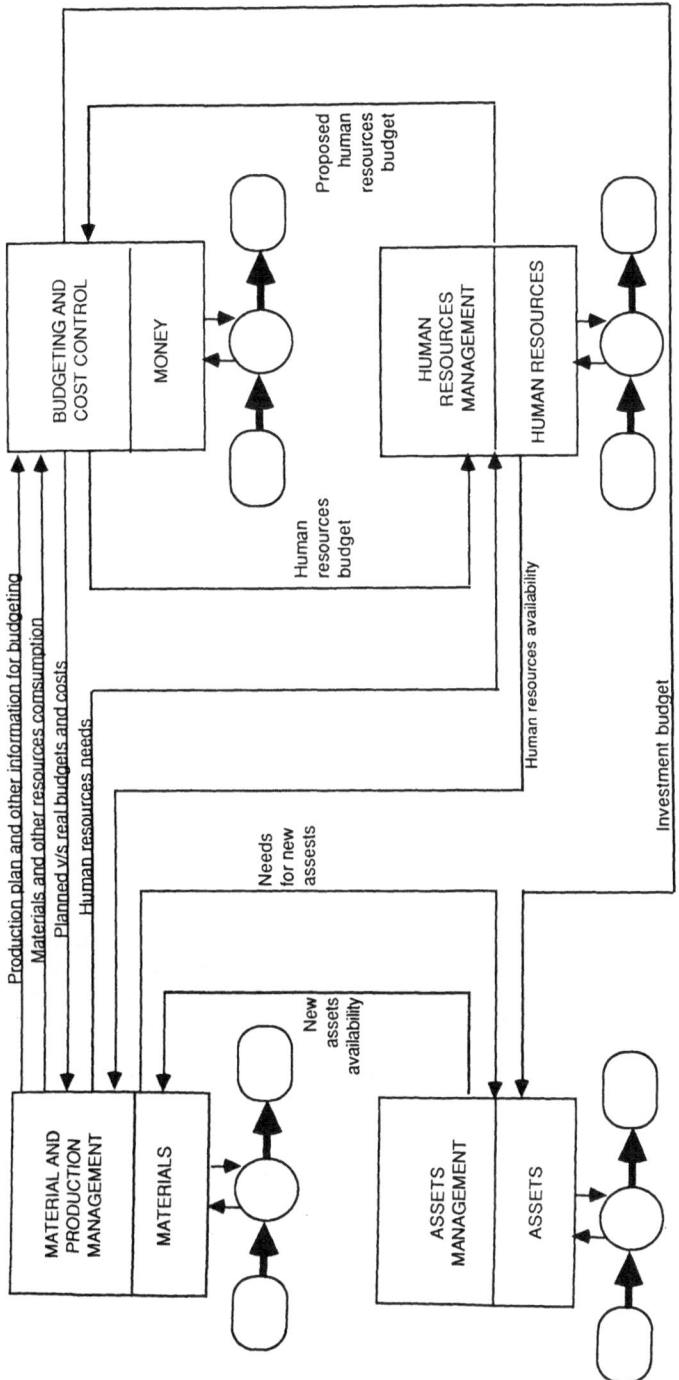

Figure 6. Integration of Resources IS.

Production plan and other information for budgeting

Materials and other resources consumption

Planned v/s real budgets and costs

Human resources needs

BUDGETING AND COST CONTROL

MONEY

Proposed human resources budget

HUMAN RESOURCES MANAGEMENT

HUMAN RESOURCES

Human resources budget

Human resources availability

Investment budget

Needs for new assests

New assets availability

MATERIAL AND PRODUCTION MANAGEMENT

MATERIALS

ASSETS MANAGEMENT

ASSETS

155

Management context. An important assumption in Figure 6 is that all activities within the context can be assigned to one of the Resource IS. This is not always true, since there are cases where activities are shared by two or more Resource IS. This is the case, for example, of the maintenance of an integrated data base that contains information that is used by two or more Resource IS. Another example is the activity of a high level executive committee that sets joint policies in the production, budget, and human resources areas. This type of activity must be considered as a global function in the sense that it interacts with at least two Resource IS but has an identity different from them. These activities, that exist mainly for integration and coordination of the several Resource IS, must be represented separately as another box in a diagram as the one in Figure 6, that interacts by means of information flows with the different Resource IS.

MODEL BASED REQUIREMENT DETERMINATION : EXTERNAL DESIGN

In this section we show how the generalized IS model can be used to determine the requirements for any particular IS and derive alternative IS structures.

We define as requirements the specification of how regulation functions will be performed, possibly by establishing policies, rules, and procedures, and the information processing and flows needed to support such functions. The information processing and flows that will be computerized correspond to the usual concept of information requirements.

It is obvious that alternative ways of implementing the regulation functions will create the need for different sets of information processing and flows. So, according to the IS definition previously given, we may have alternative designs or structures of an IS for a given situation. The problem of establishing such designs is called External Design (Barros, 1975) to distinguish it from the problem of computer subsystem or internal design.

Now, in generating these alternative IS designs or structures, or doing External Design, Organization design theory is applicable as we will show.

In approaching the development of a particular IS we start as usual with a current situation. The generalized model tells us what Processes and regulation functions may exist in such a situation. By matching current activities within the scope of the situation with generalized Processes and functions, it is very easy to generate a model for the current situation.

In order to exemplify the concepts above, we show in Figure 7 the current situation model for a problem in material management. This example has been deliberately kept simple to facilitate understanding, and, so, it covers just a part of only one resource regulation problem. There are no limitations in the model we discussed in Section 2 to fully cover one resource regulation and even the regulation of several resources interacting in a complex way. Also, the example emphasizes resource requisition, but there is no inherent limitation to expand the problem to consider resource utilization and services or goods production.

The current situation is characterized by very simple rules and limited information requirements. Thus, replenishment is decided by comparing Material inventory to a Reorder Point and, if the former is less or equal than the latter, issuing an Order for a Lot Size. Notice that the only basis for reorder criteria is Material requirement based on historical consumption (Dispatched material).

There are many other details which we do not consider for the time being, e.g., how is the material forecast done. We will come back to this when we quantitatively model these situations in order to be able to evaluate them. In particular we will consider the dynamics of the problem, e.g., the time frame in which decisions are made.

In this simple example just one level of diagramming is enough to fully represent the situation. In more complex situations several levels of diagramming can be used by hierarchically decomposing functions in the style of Structured Analysis (De Marco, 1978; Ross, 1977).

Now, given a model for the current situation, we can generate alternatives by discovering regulation functions or relationships absent or imperfectly implemented with respect to the generalized IS model.

Consider the material management example. Notice that material forecast is based on just historical consumption information (Dispatched material). Now the general model in Figure 3 indicates that there may be an obvious relationship between the decision on what to apply the Resource to (Decide Application) and material (Resource) required (Establish Need and Specify). Hence an alternative based on this observation, shown in Figure 8, will explicitly introduce within the system the function Determine Manufacturing Plan (Decide Application) and link it to Compute material requirement (Establish Need and Specify) by means of the Manufacturing Plan. Then material required will be computed strictly for

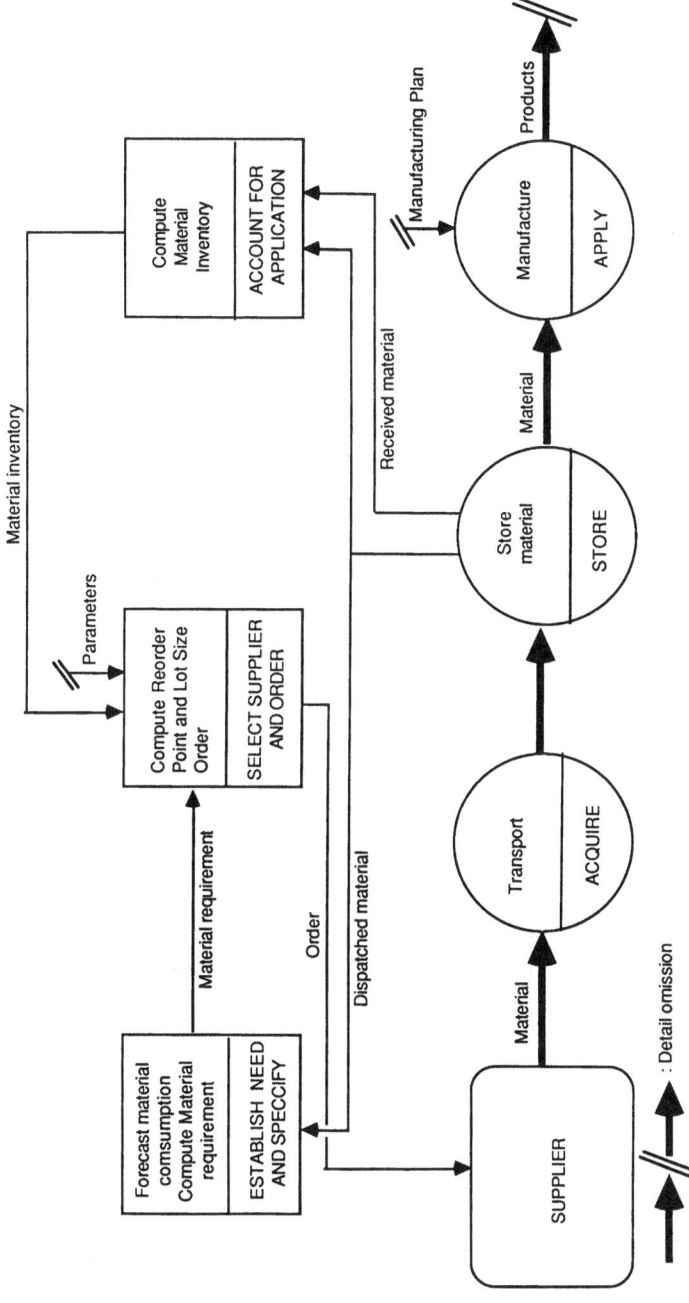

Figure 7. Current Situation Model for Material Management Problem.

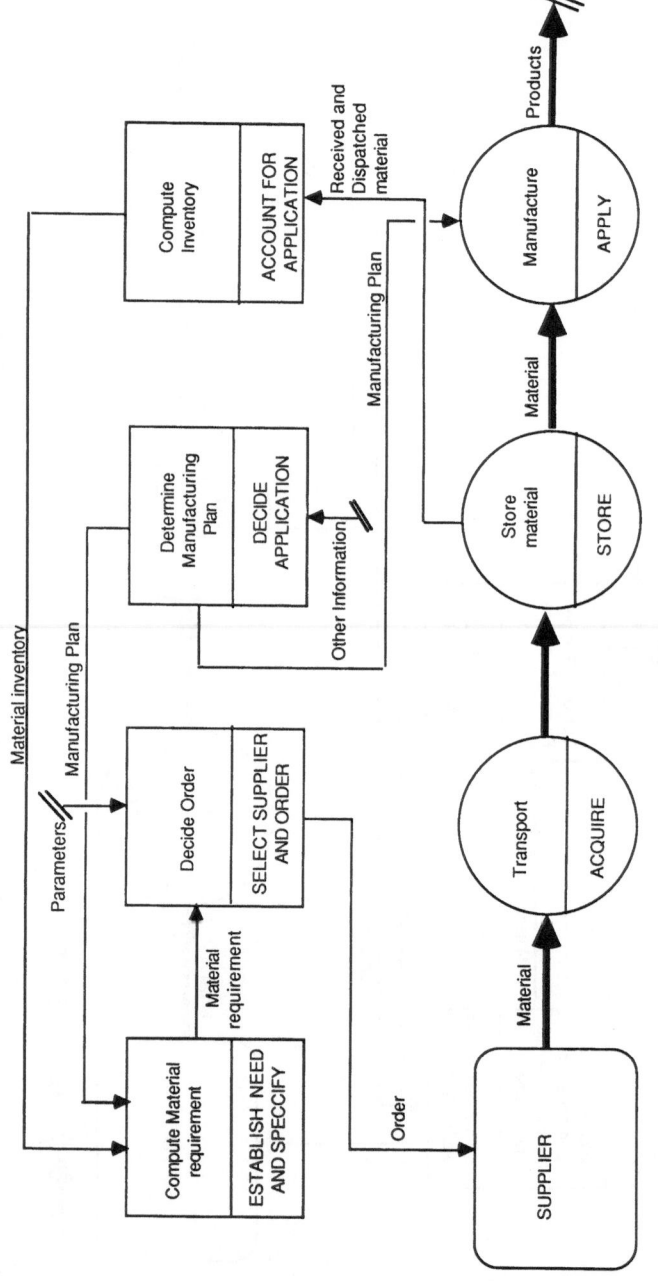

Figure 8. Model for Alternative in the Material Management Problem.

the needs of the Manufacturing Plan and ordering made accordingly, instead of basing the decision on just historical material consumption.[5]

Searching for alternatives can be guided by Organization design theory (Gailbraith, 1977). As detailed elsewhere (Barros, 1987), different implementations of functions and relationships with corresponding sets of information requirements demand different degrees of coordination and organizational structures. These in turn will produce different consequences in terms of results achieved (measured as the quality of regulation in our terminology). But coordination can be approached with two types of mechanisms. On the one hand, we can reduce interaction, hence the need for coordination and flow of information, among units by using slack resources (e.g., buffer inventories and backlogs) and unit self-containment. On the other hand, we can increase the capacity to coordinate by providing more information and coordinating agents, like assistants, staffs and lateral roles, e.g., liaisons (Gailbraith, 1977).

As is usual in IS, in the example we have presented, the alternative goes in the direction of increasing the capacity to coordinate and reducing the use of slack resources. Thus, the computing of Material requirement based on an explicit Manufacturing Plan, as shown in Figure 8, will improve coordination between manufacturing and requisition of materials. This will mean a reduction of the slack resources material inventory and/or delays in product orders satisfaction for, in the current situation, excess inventory has to be maintained to meet unforeseen demand or if not so, lack of material inventory may prevent from satisfying products orders. The better adjustment between material needs and requisition produced by the alternative will mostly eliminate these problems.

Of course these coordination arguments for the alternative we are giving a posteriori can be used a priori in their generation. In addition, it is obvious that the identification of slack resources affected by the alternatives is a key factor in the evaluation we will attempt in the next section.

As further examples of generating alternative IS designs we include in Table 4 a small sample of our experience in this subject.

Alternative IS designs or structures are also related to the idea of coordination structures as defined by Malone (1987). Though Malone refers to the macro structure of an Organization, he makes specific micro-level assumptions about how decisions are handled and to the amount of information (messages) required. Different sets of assumptions lead to different generalized "pure" structure types: product hierarchy, decentralized market, functional hierarchy and centralized market. Thus, for example, in a product hierarchy decisions about tasks (Processes) are decentralized in a product manager for each line of products and messages flow only among a product manager and the processors he directs. It is evident that these types can be considered as general patterns of coordination one can use for an Organization as a whole, and that each type will generate different IS designs. For instance, consider the problem of material management (procurement) for the manufacture of all Organization's products. The product hierarchy design will define an independent material management IS for each product line. Alternatively, we have the possibility of just one material management IS (functional hierarchy) which unifies and satisfies the material requirement for all lines of products.

Malone (1987) analyzes different types of structures in terms of production, coordination and vulnerability costs. Rough approximations to these costs allow an approximate evaluation of the desirability of each structure for a given situation. Hence, Malone's ideas appear to be a good way to screen possible general alternative macro structures for the Organization Information System. Then the generalized IS model and the evaluation procedure we will develop later will allow the detailing of the alternative IS structures and select the most cost-effective one.

Another idea from Organization theory that can be of help in generating alternatives is contingency theory (Lorsch and Lawrence, 1972; Melcher, 1976). As explored elsewhere (Barros 1984, 1987), guidelines derived from this theory can also help in searching for alternatives, taking into account Organization structural variables such as size, work flow characteristics, task programming and spatial-physical factors (Melcher, 1976).

---

[5]In this example, current situation and alternative correspond to simplifications of policies very much used in practice: the first to a ROP (Reorder Point) policy and the second to a MRP (Material Requirements Planning) policy.

Table 4

Typical Approaches for Various Degrees of Coordination

Problem Area	Approaches generated or seen in practice for alternatives with degree of coordination			Slack resources affected by increased coordination.
	Low	Medium	High	
Production Planning (to stock)	Short run (a week to a month) replenishment rule of finished products inventory, e.g. produce a lot of product when inventory reaches a reorder point	Short to medium range (few months) sales forecast. Use of a Manufacturing Requirements Planning (MRP) package to determine production plan to meet the forecast	Medium range (up to a year) planning based on a Linear Programming (L.P.) model	Products inventories decrease Lost sales decrease Backlog decreases Capacity utilization increases
Finantial Planning	Day to day cash management based on current availability or deficit	Short run (one month) cash flow forecast based on current accounts receivable and payable	Medium range (up to one year) cash flow forecast based on explicit finantial model of Organization. Decision Support System (DSS) capability to evaluate different finantial management alternatives.	Unused cash decreases Emergency loans at high interest decrease Delay in payments to suppliers decreases
Equipment Maintenance	Maintain when equipment fails	Preventive maintenance based on fix periodic replacement of parts	Equipment monitoring and maintenance determination by using failure models	Available capacity increases
Budgeting	Budget generated on historical basis (previous budget plus adjustments)	Budget negociated according to planned level of activity	Budget generated based on an explicit model that relates income and expenses to planned level of activity	Unnecessary expenses decrease

Basis of Modeling

Modeling the IS essentially means modeling of the Processes.[6] There are several ways in which we can model a Process, e.g., using Petri Nets (Peterson, 1977) or Finite State Machines (Minsky, 1967). We have chosen the approach that follows due'to the fact that it can be supported by easily available software packages, as we will show later, and that it can be related to most of the modeling work that has been done in OR/MS.

A Process is characterized at a given point in time by state variables. A given state is defined by a specific assignment of values to the state variables.[7]

Changes of or transitions between states are specified through an action function[8] which for a given initial state establishes an immediate succeeding state for the Process. Of course, by repetitive application of the action function we can generate a simulated behavior, or a sequence of states, starting from a given initial state.

This basic model obviously relates to the graphic regulation model of Section 2. Thus, certain regulation functions as Account for Application exist for computing state of Processes' others, like Decide Application, are for actually generating action functions, i.e. taking action based on current state to carry a Process to a certain new state.

We specify an action function by defining:

Yt : state of a Process at time t (given values of a vector of state variables or variable set at time t).

Xt : values of the vector of action or decision variables that affect state of a Process (decision variables are the ones that can be set freely by regulation functions).

Then:

$$Yt+1 = F(Yt, Xt) \tag{4-1}$$

where F is a vector function that assigns a successor state to an initial state for given values of the decision variables.

Now the determination of Xt can be done in many ways, depending on the characteristics of the problem and degree of realism we wish to include in the model; for example:

i)   Deterministic Error Correction

$$Xt = G(Yt, Yt\text{-}1, Yt\text{-}2,....., YO) \tag{4-2}$$

I.e., values of decision variables only depend on current or past state, which corresponds to the usual feedback control or regulation by error scheme. This is the Systems Dynamics approach proposed by Forrester (1961, 1970) and implemented by the software Dynamo (Pugh, 1961). In Systems Dynamics terminology, 4-1 are the Level equations and 4-2, the Rate equations.[9]

ii)   Deterministic Anticipation-Simple

---

[6]A recent alternative approach for modeling IS is Malone's (1987). However, as it is mentioned in the text, it only provides rough approximations to costs that are good for screening but not for the detail evaluation we attempt here.

[7]This characterization is similar to the one that has been used for computer processes (Horning and Randell, 1973).

[8]Here, we are talking about mathematical functions, which are not to be confused with the regulation functions previously defined.

[9]Notice that the class of all Systems Dynamics models is part of our approach, including the possibility of solving them with the software we will describe later.

$$Xt = G(Yt, Yt\text{-}1, Yt\text{-}2,..., YO;\ Yt+1,...,YT) \qquad (4\text{-}3)$$

where Yt means projected future state, T is the horizon and G is a vector of close-expression mathematical functions.

iii) Deterministic Anticipation-Algorithmic

Here G is not a vector of close-expression mathematical functions, but the result of an algorithm.[10] E.g., this will be the case when functions in G form a system of simultaneous equations for the determination of Xt or when Xt is the solution of a Mathematical Programming optimization problem. In these cases one finds that in projecting a future state one must also establish future decisions. Hence, current decision is based on projected future decisions. This is the case, for example, in production smoothing where under seasonal demand today's production must consider future production and its relationship to future peak demand. This leads to the concept of simulation over a rolling horizon, i.e., at time t one solves equations 4-3 considering projected decisions up to the horizon T, then after implementing the decision for the next period one advances time one unit, collects new data about Processes, update state, again solves 4-3 for t + 1 and so on. Considering the effect of future decisions on today's decision also means forecasting future values for parameters which have not been explicated in equations 4-1 to 4-3. For example, in production smoothing this means forecasting product sales for each period of the horizon. Note that this type of specification for G allows use from very simple heuristics to complex OR/MS models.

iv) Stochastic

Since forecasting is subject to error, one can have a better representation of reality by representing future values of parameters as stochastic instead of deterministic variables. In this case decision variables must be determined under uncertainty based on the probability of occurrence of future states and system's behavior also established in a probabilistic way.

Up to now we have implicitly assumed time as discrete. If we wanted no loss of state information, the time increment should be variable and determined by the time interval between events that change Process state. However, we will choose to consider time increments as fixed, but as small as necessary to avoid loss of state information. The reason for this is that the available software that we will use for implementing IS models, can only accept discrete time increments.

Tools for Modeling

The purpose in modeling an IS is to be able to accurately represent a given alternative and to calculate its organizational effectiveness by simulating its behavior. This is geared to make a cost-effectiveness analysis of the alternative to determine if it is preferable to the current situation or to other possible available alternatives. Hence, we need tools for implementing models of the type discussed in the previous section, that allows as quick and effortless an evaluation as possible. Fortunately, these tools already exist, though they have been developed for other purposes. They are the modeling software packages available for building DSS (Reiman and Waren, 1985).[11] These packages use as a calculation paradigm a matrix where columns usually represent time (in discrete increments) and rows or lines are items, such as states, decision variables or parameters, to be projected in time. They contain powerful expressions and modules that allow specifying how an item is to vary in time and also to "solve" the specifications. For example IFPS, one of the leading packages of this type, has, among other facilities, built-in routines to project parameters under various assumptions, e.g., linear and non linear regression; provides a simple logic for specifying conditional values for decision variables; allows to specify and solves linear and non-linear systems of equations for Yt and Xt; allows to specify and solves linear and integer Mathematical Programs for establishing Yt and Xt; permits the specification of parameters as stochastic variables and determines probability distributions of Yt by means of Montecarlo simulation; all this in a very friendly environment where data and model management are very much facilitated. For example, the problems of matrix generation and report production when solving a Mathematical Program are easily handled with the built-in facilities of the package (Execucom Systems Corp., 1983, 1987; Roy, Lasdon and Lordeman, 1986).

Hence, these packages make it possible to build a model and to simulate an alternative under

---

[10]Formally, it can also be the result of a heuristic.

[11]In a limited sense, spreadsheets like LOTUS 1-2-3 are also in this class.

consideration in very little time, usually a few days, and calculate the results it would produce if applied in practice, thus evaluating its effectiveness.

We have extensively tested this scheme with alternatives for a variety of IS using IFPS. In Appendix 1 we give a partial list of the cases we have developed. In all instances, the approach has worked quite well making the quantitative evaluation of alternatives possible. In the next section, we give examples of the application of the approach.

Modeling Examples

The model of the material management problem shown in Figures 7 and 8 is developed below.

In the current situation in Figure 7, the material forecast in done by using exponential smoothing on the historical consumption (Johnson and Montgomery, 1974). Lot size and reorder point are calculated according to the usual formulas (Johnson and Montgomery, 1974) and appropriate values for parameters in these formulas are given. Simulation of this situation will be performed to try to satisfy the material needs for a given Manufacturing Plan, over a horizon of 12 months. However, in this case, no knowledge about this plan is used in making decisions. A model that simulates the behavior under these conditions is given in Figure 9, together with the results obtained for given data. The model clearly separates the implementation of an action function of the type 4-1 in the first block, the projection of future states in the second, and the implementation of a decision function of the type 4-3 in the third block. Notice that this model quantitatively describes a regulation cycle of the type shown in Figure 5.

In the alternative given in Figure 9, the basic idea is to make explicit use of the Manufacturing Plan to anticipate material requirements (in the function Compute material requirements) over the planning horizon. Based on these anticipated requirements, the decision about an order will be based on the Silver Meal (Silver and Meal, 1969) heuristic for the so-called Dynamic Lot Size. A model that simulates this alternative together with the results for a 12 month horizon is given in Figure 10. Of course, in this case the affected slack resource is inventory and it is seen that it is greatly reduced with respect to current situation, with less backorders. Also overall cost is reduced with respect to such situation.

There are many ways in which above models can be extended. For example considering some variables as stochastic, such as lead time and consumption; introducing optimization in the decisions with an optimizing algorithm for the Dynamic Lot Size (Johnson and Montgomery, 1974) and a Linear Programming model for the manufacturing plan (Roy, de Falomir and Lasdon, 1982). Also, rigorous statistical procedures, e.g., replication, can be used to obtain valid estimates of effectiveness improvements over the life of the system.

Alternative Evaluation

It is clear that by modeling a given alternative structure we can measure the Organization effectiveness, e.g., slack reduction, the alternative will induce in practice under given conditions. This will allow the comparison of the effectiveness of this alternative with respect to current situation or to other alternatives. Difference of effectiveness of an alternative with respect to a given base situation represents the value the alternative has with respect to that situation. This is what Marschack (1968) calls information value. Of course, this value is not only associated to the (possibly new and better) information the alternative is using, but also to, as Marschack's theory makes clear, the decision rules the alternative uses. Hence, our method represents a practical way to measure "information value" and implement the ideas proposed by Marschack.

Information value or the value associated to a given alternative should then be compared with the cost of going from the base situation to the alternative. Cost determination includes the specification of the regulation and information processing functions that will the be computerized, and the estimation of development cost by a suitable methodology, such as function points (Albrecht and Gaffney, 1983). If cost is less than the discounted value generated over the life of the system, then the alternative is cost-effective and is worth implementing. Otherwise it should be discarded.

CONCLUSIONS

In this paper we have tried to show that IS exist in Organizations to regulate their processes. This point of view has allowed us to define what an IS should be in terms of general validity to accomplish such regulation. Thus, we have developed a model that includes generalized functions to regulate generalized Processes through flows of information, which can serve as a basic pattern to approach the design of any IS.

From the generalized IS model, we conclude that the design problem in IS consists in searching

COLUMNS 1..12
\\
\\   PROCESS STATE DETERMINATION BASED ON PREVIOUS ACTION.
\\
MANUFACTURING PLAN=900,1150,1050,950,1050,1200,1300,1500,1050,900,1000,1000
DISPATCHED MATERIAL= MANUFACTURING PLAN * MATERIAL UNIT COMSUMPTION
RECEIVED MATERIAL = PREVIOUS ORDER
MATERIAL INVENTORY = INITIAL INVENTORY - DISPATCHED MATERIAL,'
                      PREVIOUS + RECEIVED MATERIAL - DISPATCHED MATERIAL
\\
\\   PROJECT FUTURE STATE.
\\
MATERIAL FORECAST = DISPATCHED MATERIAL, '
                    PREVIOUS * (1 - ALPHA) + DISPATCHED MATERIAL * ALPHA
MATERIAL REQUIREMENTS = MATERIAL FORECAST
INVENTORY FORECAST = MATERIAL FORECAST * LEADTIME + SS
\\
\\   DECISION BY DETERMINISTIC ANTICIPATION SIMPLE.
\\
ORDER = IF INVENTORY FORECAST > = MATERIAL INVENTORY THEN Q ELSE O
Q = ROUND (XPOWERY (2 * A * MATERIAL FORECAST / IC, 0.5))
\\
\\   SUMMARY OF EFFECTIVENESS.
\\
AVERAGE INVENTORY = MEAN (MATERIAL INVENTORY [1], MATERIAL INVENTORY)
NUMBER OF ORDERS = IF ORDER > O THEN PREVIOUS + 1 ELSE PREVIOUS
TOTAL BACKORDERS = IF MATERIAL INVENTORY < O THEN PREVIOUS + 1 ELSE PREVIOUS
TOTAL COST = NUMBER OF ORDERS * A + AVERAGE INVENTORY * IC
\\
\\   PARAMETERS.
\\
A = 500
INITIAL INVENTORY = 0
SS = 0
LEAD TIME = 1
ALPHA = 0.7
MATERIAL UNIT CONSUMPTION = 0.1
IC = 2

	1	2	3	4	5	6
MANUFACTURING PLAN	900	1150	1050	950	1050	1200
DISPATCHED MATERIAL	90	115	105	95	105	120
RECEIVED MATERIAL	0	212	232	0	222	0
MATERIAL INVENTORY	-90	7	134	39	156	36
MATERIAL FORECAST	90	108	106	98	103	115
MATERIAL REQUIREMENTS	90	108	106	98	103	115
INVENTORY FORECAST	90	108	106	98	103	115
ORDER	212	232	0	222	0	240
Q	212	232	230	222	227	240
AVERAGE INVENTORY	-90	-42	17	23	49	47
NUMBER OF ORDERS	1	2	2	3	3	4
TOTAL BACKORDERS	1	1	1	1	1	1
TOTAL COST	320	917	1074	1545	1598	2094

	7	8	9	10	11	12
MANUFACTURING PLAN	1300	1500	1050	900	1000	1000
DISPATCHED MATERIAL	130	150	105	90	100	100
RECEIVED MATERIAL	240	0	267	0	221	0
MATERIAL INVENTORY	146	-4	158	68	189	89
MATERIAL FORECAST	125	143	116	98	99	100
MATERIAL REQUIREMENTS	125	143	116	98	99	100
INVENTORY FORECAST	125	143	116	98	99	100
ORDER	0	267	0	221	0	223
Q	250	267	241	221	223	223
AVERAGE INVENTORY	61	53	65	65	76	77
NUMBERS OF ORDERS	4	5	5	6	6	7
TOTAL BACKORDERS	1	2	2	2	2	2
TOTAL COST	2122	2606	2629	3130	3153	3655

Figure 9. Model for Current Situation - Material Management Problem.

COLUMNS 1..14
\\
\\ ` PROCESS STATE DETERMINATION BASED ON PREVIOUS ACTION.
\\
MANUFACTURING PLAN = 900, 1150,1050,950, 1050, 1200, 1300, 1500, 1050, 900,1000,1000
DISPATCHED MATERIAL = MANUFACTURING PLAN * MATERIAL UNIT CONSUMPTION
RECEIVED MATERIAL = PREVIOUS ORDER
P1: MATERIAL INVENTORY = INITIAL INVENTORY - DISPATCHED MATERIAL, '
                   PREVIOUS + RECEIVED MATERIAL - DISPATCHED MATERIAL
\\
\\ PROJECT FUTURE STATE.
\\
P2: MATERIAL REQUIREMENT GROSS = MANUFACTURING PLAN * MATERIAL UNIT
                         CONSUMPTION
\\
\\ DECISION BY DETERMINISTIC ANTICIPATION-ALGORITHMIC.
\\
CTE = 2 * A/IC
T = IF (PREVIOUS P1: + PREVIOUS ORDER) > = (P2: + FUTURE 1 P2:)'
     THEN 0'
     ELSE IF (MAXIMUM (0, FUTURE 1 P2: - MAXIMUM (0,'
          PREVIOUS P1: - P2: + PREVIOUS ORDER))) > = CTE'
        THEN XPOWERY (CTE / MAXIMUM (0, FUTURE 1 P2: - '
         MAXIMUM (0, PREVIOUS P1: - P2: + PREVIOUS ORDER)), 0.5) '
     ELSE IF (4 * MAXIMUM (0, FUTURE 2 P2: -MAXIMUM (0, PREVIOUS P1: + '
         PREVIOUS ORDER - P2: - FUTURE 1P2:))) > = CTE'
        THEN XPOWERY (CTE / MAXIMUM (0, FUTURE 2 P2: - MAXIMUM (0 , '
         PREVIOUS P1: + PREVIOUS ORDER - P2: - FUTURE 1 P2:)), 0.5)'
     ELSE 2
Q = IF T < = 1 THEN MAXIMUM (0, FUTURE 1 P2: - MAXIMUM (0,'
         PREVIOUS P1: - P2: + PREVIOUS ORDER)),
     ELSE IF T < = 2 THEN MAXIMUM (0, FUTURE 1 P2: - '
         MAXIMUM (0, PREVIOUS P1: - P2: + PREVIOUS ORDER)) + '
         (T-1) * MAXIMUM (0, FUTURE 2 P2: - MAXIMUM (0, '
         PREVIOUS P1: + PREVIOUS ORDER - P2: - FUTURE 1 P2:))'
     ELSE 0
ORDER = Q
\\
\\ SUMMARY OF EFFECTIVENESS.
\\
AVERAGE INVENTORY = MEAN (MATERIAL INVENTORY [1], MATERIAL INVENTORY)
NUMBER OF ORDERS = IF ORDER > O THEN PREVIOUS + 1 ELSE PREVIOUS
TOTAL BACKORDERS = IF MATERIAL INVENTORY < O THEN PREVIOUS + 1 '
                 ELSE PREVIOUS
TOTAL COST = NUMBER OF ORDERS * A + AVERAGE INVENTORY * IC
\\
\\ ` PARAMETERS.
\\
A = 500
INITIAL INVENTORY = 0
SS = 0
LEADTIME = 1
ALPHA = 0.70
MATERIAL UNIT CONSUMPTION = 0.1
IC = 2

	1	2	3	4	5	6
MANUFACTURING PLAN	900	1150	1050	950	1050	1200
DISPATCHED MATERIAL	90	115	105	95	105	120
RECEIVED MATERIAL	0	220	185	0	225	0
MATERIAL INVENTORY	-90	15	95	0	120	0
MATERIAL REQUIREMENT	90	115	105	95	105	120
T	2.0	2.0	0.0	2.0	0.0	1.9
ORDER	220	195	0	225	0	254
AVERAGE INVENTORY	-90	-38	7	5	28	23
NUMBER OF ORDERS	1	2	2	3	3	4
TOTAL BACKORDERS	1	1	1	1	1	1
TOTAL COST	320	925	1013	1510	1556	2047

	7	8	9	10	11	12
MANUFACTURING PLAN	1300	1500	1050	900	1000	1000
DISPATCHED MATERIAL	130	150	105	90	100	100
RECEIVED MATERIAL	254	131	0	190	0	200
MATERIAL INVENTORY	124	105	0	100	0	100
MATERIAL REQUIREMENT	130	150	105	90	100	100
T	2.0	0.0	2.0	0.0	2.0	0.0
ORDER	131	0	190	0	200	0
AVERAGE INVENTORY	38	46	41	47	43	47
NUMBER OF ORDERS	5	5	6	6	7	7
TOTAL BACKORDERS	1	1	1	1	1	1
TOTAL COST	2575	2592	3082	3094	3585	3595

Figure 10. Model of Alternative - Material Management Problem.

165

for alternative structures, including policies and rules for decision functions and associated information processing and flows; i.e., the design of the organizational components within the scope of the IS. We call this design External Design (Barros, 1975), to distinguish it from the problem of internal or software design. External Design has been shown to be a way to ascertain IS requirements.

Linking the problem of External Design to the ideas of modern Organization theory has also provided us with criteria to generate alternative structures that would most likely increase Organization effectiveness. This raises the problem of evaluating such alternatives. The modeling approach explained above provides a way to perform this evaluation and to assure that the External Design we arrive at is cost-effective. This type of evaluation also changes the focus for IS justification in practice, from efficiency improvements usually coming from personnel reductions to effectiveness improvements. The latter comes from better Process regulation which is, according to our approach, the real purpose of IS.

REFERENCES

Albrecht, A. J., and Gaffney, J. E., 1983, Software Functions, Source Lines of Code, and Development Effort Prediction: A Software Science Validation, *IEEE Trans. Software Eng.*, Vol. SE-9, pp. 639-648.

Alford, M., 1985, SREM at the Age Eight: The Distributed Computing Design System, *Computer*, Vol. 18, pp. 36-46.

Ashby, R. W., 1970, *An Introduction to Cybernetics*, Chapman & Hall Ltd, London.

Barros, 0., 1975, Some Ideas on a Methodology for the Logical Design of Information Systems, *Management Datamatics*, Vol. 4, pp. 49-56.

Barros, 0., 1984, *Alternative Architectures in Information System Design in Beyond Productivity: Information Systems for Organizational Effectiveness*, Th.M.A., Bemelmans, ed., North Holland, Amsterdam.

Barros, 0., 1987, Information Requirements and Alternatives in Information System Design, *Information Systems*, Vol. 12, pp. 125-136.

Beer, S., 1972, *Brain of the Firm*, Allen Lane, The Penguin Press, London.

Berzins, V., and Gray, M., 1985, Analysis and Design "MSG.84: Formalizing Functional Specifications", *IEEE Trans. Software Eng.*, Vol. SE-11, pp. 657-670.

Cameron, J. R., 1986, An Overview of JSD, *IEEE Trans. Software Eng.*, Vol. SE-12, pp. 222-240.

Carlson, W. M., 1979, Business Information Analysis and Integration Technique (BIAIT) - The New Horizon, *Data Base*, Vol. 10, pp. 3-9.

Chen, P. P., 1976, The Entity-Relationship Model - Toward a Unified View of Data, *ACM Transactions on Data Base Systems*, Vol. 1, pp. 9-36.

Davis, G. B., 1982, Strategies for Information Requirements Determination, *IBM Syst. J.*, Vol. 21, pp. 4-30.

De Marco, T., 1978, *Structured Analysis and System Specification*, Yourdon Press, New York (1978).

Emery, F. E., 1979, *Systems Thinking*, Penguin Books, Baltimore.

Emery, J. C., 1969, *Organizational Planning and Control Systems*, MacMillan, New York.

Execucom Systems Corp., 1983, *IFPS/Optimum User's Manual*, Rel. 3.0, Austin, Texas. Execucom Systems Corp., 1987, *IFPS User's Manual*, Rel. 11.0, Austin, Texas.

Forrester, J., 1961, *Industrial Dynamics*, The MIT Press, Cambridge, Mass.

Forrester, J., 1970, *Principles of Systems*, Wright Allen Press, New York.

Gailbraith, J. R., 1977, *Organization Design*, Addison-Wesley, Reading, Mass.

Hamilton, M., and Zelding, S., 1976, Higher Order Software - A Methodology for Defining Software, *IEEE Trans. of Software Eng.*, Vol. SE-2, pp. 9-32.

Horning, J. J., and Randell, B., 1973, Process Structuring, *Computer Surveys*, Vol. 5, pp. 5-30.

Ives, B., and Dearmonth, G. P., 1984, The Information System as a Competitive Weapon, *Comm. ACM*, Vol. 27, pp. 1193-1201.

Johnson, L. A., and Montgomery, D. C., 1974, *Operations Research in Production Planning Scheduling and Control*, Wiley, New York.

Kerner, D. V., 1979, Business Information Characterization Study, *Data Base*, Vol. 10, pp. 10-17.

Lorsch, J. W., and Lawrence, P. R., 1972, *Organization Planning*, Richard Irwin and The Dorsey Press, Homewood, Illinois.

Malone, T. W., 1987, Modeling Coordination in Organizations and Markets, *Management Science*, Vol. 33, pp. 1317-1332.

Marschack, J., 1954, *Towards an Economic Theory of Organization and Information, Decision Processes*, Thrall, R. M., Commbs, G. H., and Davis, R. L., eds., Wiley, New York.

Marschack, J., 1968, Economics of Inquiring, Communicating and Deciding, *American Economic Review*, Vol. 58, pp. 1-8.

Martin, J., and Finkelstein, C., 1981, *Information Engineering*, Savant Institute, London.

Melcher, A. J., 1976, *Structure and Process of Organizations*, Prentice Hall, Englewood Cliffs, N.J.

Minsky, M., 1967, *Computation: Finite and Infinite Machines*, Prentice Hall, Englewood Cliffs, N.J.

Peterson, J. L., 1977, Petri Nets, *Computing Surveys*, Vol. 9, pp. 224-252.

Pugh, A. L., III, 1961, *Dynamo User's Manual*, The MIT Press, Cambridge, Mass.

Reiman, B. C., and Waren, A. D., 1985, User-oriented Criteria for the Selection of DSS Software, *Comm. ACM*, Vol. 28, pp. 1966-1980.

Ross, D. T., 1977, Structured Analysis (S.A.): A Language for Communicating Ideas, *IEEE Trans. Software Eng.*, Vol. SE-3, pp. 16-34.

Roy, A., De Falomir, E. E., and Lasdon, L., 1982, An Optimization-Based Decision Support System for a product Mix Problem, *Interfaces*, Vol. 12, pp. 26-33.

Roy, A., Lasdon, L. S., and Lordeman, I., 1986, Extending Planning Languages to include Optimization Capabilities, *Management Science*, Vol. 32, pp. 360-373.

Silver, E., and Meal, H,. 1970, A Simple Modification of the EOQ for the Case of Varying Demand Rate and Discrete Opportunities for Replenishment, *Production and Inventory Management*, Vol. 14, pp. 64-73.

Simon, H., 1970, *The Sciences of the Artificial*, MIT Press, Cambridge, Mass.

Verrijn-Stuart, A. A., 1986, Themes and Trends in Information Systems, *Trens in Information Systems*, Langefors, B., Verrijn-Stuart, A. A., and Bracchi, G., eds., North Holland, Amsterdam.

Yourdon, E., and Constantine, L. L., 1979, *Structured Design*, Prentice Hall, Englewood Cliffs, N.J.

Zachman, J. A., 1979, Business Systems Planning and Business Information Control Study: A Comparison, *IBM Syst. J.*, Vol. 21, pp. 31-53.

Zave, P., 1982, An Operational Approach to Requirements Specification for Embedded Systems, *IEEE Trans. Software Eng.*, Vol. SE-8, pp. 250-269.

APPENDIX 1

PARTIAL LIST OF CASES CONSIDERED IN THIS WORK

1. One-year L.P.-based production and financial planning in a wine industry.

2. Credit management for a manufacturing and distribution company.

3. Personnel management in an engineering firm.

4. Student management in a University.

5. Patient management in a hospital.

6. Assets management in a large mining company.

7. Optimized water-resource and energy management in an electric power company.

8. Books management in a library.

9. Case management in a lawyer's studio.

10. Truck management in a transportation firm.

11. Maintenance management for a large truck fleet in a mining company.

12. Financial planning in a retailer firm.

13. Production process management in a mining company.

14. Personnel management in a private shipping firm.

15. Planning and budgeting in an engineering and building company.

STATIC VS. DYNAMIC INFORMATION SYSTEMS MODELING:

A COOPERATION BASED APPROACH

Maurizio Panti and Alessandro Cucchiarelli

Università degli Studi di Ancona, Facoltà di
Ingegneria, Istituto di Informatica, Via Brecce
Bianche, 60131 Ancona (Italy)

Abstract: Today's approaches to information systems modeling are based on different views of the communication process with respect to the office organizational levels (i.e., top, middle, and operative). These views imply different constraints on information access (rigid and predefined for the lowest level, free and unstructured for the highest) and justify the need for a large set of not homogeneous and not fully integrated information processing tools. This paper, by considering that modeling the information system means modeling the office system, shows how a model of office activities founded on a cooperative approach can unify the communication process between the various organizational levels and can capture the dynamic aspect of the information interchange process in a natural way. In our perspective, the unifying paradigm is communication and not activities because activities are not homogeneous characteristics. The proposed model takes into account the functional characteristics of the sender/receiver in the office communication system. This means that the communication links must match the dynamic characteristics of the office. In this way, we overcome the static constraints imposed by the structural approach.

INTRODUCTION

For many years the increasing demand for automation of information systems has made it necessary to have conceptual instruments with which to represent and guide the different phases of the automation process: from the plan to the realization to the managing. Such instruments are based on the information system model as defined in different works by Forrester (1961), March (March and Simon, 1963), Blumenthal (1969), and Anthony (1965), and are linked to the general system theory. On this model, they have defined the techniques of analysis and planning of the automation and the same information system upon which they are founded. Special attention was paid to management information systems (MIS) (Davis, 1974; Aiello, Nardi and Panti, 1984; Hellis, 1983), thus supplying an interesting range of reference models able to handle the information used for decision making or control activities. Thus, the typical process activity was left to the simple definition of norms and procedures.

In our opinion, until now, the attention was focused on the information needs of decision makers, without excessive consideration of the executive levels in data treatment and, therefore, the handling of global data was not homogeneous. This tendency towards separation has been newly shown, and on a larger scale, when it has been attempted to automate the treatment of text and graphic data. Even though such data is a prominent part of the global information flow within a companies' information system it is not possible to handle such data with the same information managing tools used for the automation of MIS. Therefore, a new field of interest has been developed, Office Automation, born out of the necessity to increase the productivity of the 'white collar workers' (Tsichritzis et al., 1987), because a part of their work is dedicated to the treatment of data other than numbers or letters. They are, therefore, unable to take advantage of the traditional EDP systems because of the lack of integration with the so-called 'productivity tools'. They were designed to increase the man-machine interaction and to make easier the communication process among and inside organizational levels.

Empirical Foundations of Information and Software Science V
Edited by P. Zunde and D. Hocking, Plenum Press, New York, 1990

169

In an information system, communication has two forms:

A.   Structured, that which is completely handled using predefined channels.
B.   Unstructured, that which is interpersonal, unpredictable and not normalized.

Both contribute towards the managing of the activities, even if they are different forms and levels of importance, because an office is an open and cooperative system (Hewitt, 1986) and the unstructured communication plays a significant role in the carrying out of the activities, especially relative to the procedural aspect such as 'how can I do it?'. However, in organizations, structured communication is the officially accepted form and based on this and managing the project and development of tools for information handling are directed. In this way, because of the need of predefined communication channels, it is difficult to reconfigure dynamically the information flow.

OFFICE SYSTEM AND INFORMATION

It is possible to consider different points of view to describe an office: many papers have been written to explore this argument, and the principal approaches are discussed by Bracchi (Bracchi and Motta, 1986). Our approach defines an office as a set of agents that cooperate to solve tasks and a set of relations that join agents together with respect to definite activities. So, if we use set A to identify the agents in the office and set R for the relations, we can say that the office O is

$$O = \{A, R\} \tag{1}$$

Considering a deeper level of description, each agent is uniquely identified by its functionalities, i.e., by the activities it is able to perform without needing further explanation. In this way, each role in the office is mapped into a set of functionalities that defines the procedural ability of the relating agent. It is possible to summarize the previous concept using the expression

$$a_i = \bigcup_{j=1}^{m} f_{ij}$$

where

a_i = agent - i - of the office
f_{ij} = functionality - j - of the agent - i -

But, from

$$A = \bigcup_{i=1}^{n} a_i$$

follows that

$$A = \bigcup_{i=1}^{n} \bigcup_{j=1}^{m} f_{ij} = F \tag{2}$$

where F is the set of functionalities defined for the roles in the office A.

Expression (2) means that, from a modeling point of view, describing the office agents means characterizing the set of functionalities of the office itself. This step is justified by the consideration that our scope is to model the office at the level expressed by (1), without considering the structure of the components in details, but only the item we use to define them. For this reason we leave unexpressed in (2) the relation that links functionalities to each agent (in other words, the "role" of the agent in the office), showing only the set of all functionalities defined in the office.

We can now start considering the relations among agents, underlining the fact that, in our perspective, such kinds of relations are not statically defined, but are links with the agents involved in a certain task at a certain moment. This means that agent A is linked by relation r_i to agent B only to carry out the task t_1, not for other tasks. Using a simple expression, we can say that

$$R = \bigcup_{i=1}^{k} r_i$$

where r_i is the relation - i - that links agents that are performing the same task.

By the previous considerations, it is possible to modify the expression (1) in the following way

$$O = \{F, R\} \tag{3}$$

that expresses the possibility to characterize an office starting from its functionalities and from the relations that link its functional elements (i.e., the agents).

We now want to consider the office information system, seen as composed by a set of means and a set of procedures, that define how to use the means to carry out a certain activity. In this perspective, we can represent the information system IS as

$$IS = \{M, P\} \tag{4}$$

For each means m_i it is possible to specify the set of functionalities it has, that characterize the means with respect to its ability to carry out certain tasks, so that

$$M = \bigcup_{i=1}^{h} m_1$$

where

$$m_i = \bigcup_{j=1}^{k} f_{ij}$$

in this way

$$M = \bigcup_{i=1}^{h} \bigcup_{j=1}^{k} f_{ij} = F$$

where F is the set of functionalities of the means that compose the information system. In a broad sense, procedures define the application sequence of functionalities able to achieve certain results: in other words, they link together different means to carry out certain tasks, so that, considering our goal to model the information system defining its main items (i.e., M and P in (4)), we can represent each procedure using the relation it performs among the involved means. From this consideration, defining p_i as the general procedure in our information system, we can write

$$p_i = r_i$$

where r_i is the relation that holds among the means involved in the procedure - i -.

In this way it is possible to say that

$$P = \bigcup_{i=1}^{k} p_i = \bigcup_{i=1}^{k} r_i = R$$

with

R = set of relations defined in the information system

Coming back to (4), now it is possible to transform that expression into

$$SI = \{F, R\} \tag{5}$$

that expresses the capability of modeling an information system defining the set of functionalities related to its means and the relations among the means themselves.

The comparative analysis of (5) and (3) shows how it is possible to model even an office system as well as an information system by modeling the functionalities of agents in the environment (agents for

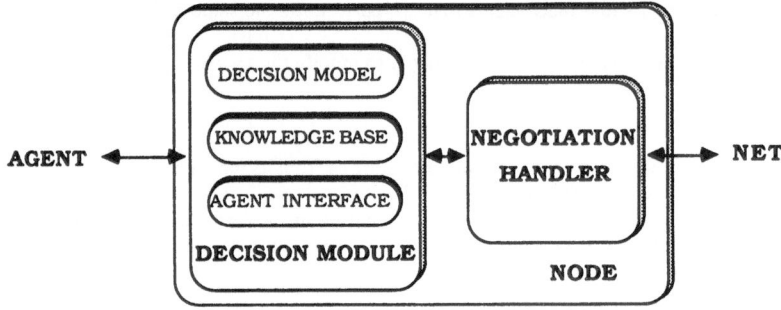

Figure 1. The Node Internal Structure.

the office, means for the information system) and the relations among them. This allows us to justify the step that modeling the information system means modeling the office system and that the information system defined in (4) is the office.

DYNAMIC OFFICE/INFORMATION SYSTEM MODELING

The procedure to carry out a task (making a decision or writing a letter) can frequently change because of different situations (new machines/agents, new data, new rules, new laws), and this requires the ability of the office agent to dynamically change its knowledge about the task and to reconfigure the data flow/structure to fit the new situation. The need of a dynamical approach to activities modeling also arises from the consideration that different office agents may have the ability to solve a particular task, but for each task only a subset of them is selected to carry it out, and the choice among different agents is made considering the best performance offered, in terms of work quality and solution speed, or simply in terms of relative workload. In this perspective of dynamic office/information system, each office task can be seen as being composed by subtasks that different people can do, so that different people can work together to solve the problem (Barber, 1983; Woo and Lochovsky, 1986). In addition, because the greatest part of office tasks are not well structured activities, the heuristic approach to their solution is preferable, in terms of efficiency and solving power.

From the previous considerations, we decided to model the information system by modeling the office system, using a net of workstations, each one with the ability to communicate with the other to form a work-team for office-task solution, and to carry out certain tasks autonomously, using a knowledge based system easy to build up and modify adapting itself to the human agent. In this perspective, the task solving process (define a job, select the agent and assign the task) needs communications capability among nodes of the net, and also efficient tools to speed-up the assignment and subsequent collection of the results. The negotiation mechanism (Davis and Smith, 1984) is a good approach to fulfill the highlighted requirements with a high level communication protocol to obtain an office task negotiation as efficiently as possible (Panti and Cucchiarelli, 1986). In this way, when a task is generated/assigned by/to a node, it can be solved by the node itself and, if it does not have the ability, by one of the other nodes in the net through a help request that starts the negotiation process, allowing the node to assign the task and, after a report reception, to carry it out.

The office is a dynamic structure not only with respect to the information flow, but also in terms of knowledge transfer among the different agents. Considering the frequent changes in office tasks (for example in changing forms or their compilation procedure), we gave the node the ability to change its knowledge in a simple way, by changing the "task template", the description, into the knowledge base of the node, as to how that task can be solved (Panti and Cucchiarelli, 1986), now, when the node must solve the task, it uses the updated procedure. Moreover, the new knowledge must be transferred through the net to other nodes able to do the task, and it is also possible to use the negotiation mechanism for this transfer, giving the node the ability to autonomously increase its knowledge. In this case, there is a knowledge transfer between a node that knows how to solve the task and another node that does not, through a particular mechanism able to transfer knowledge only among agents with the same hierarchical level in the office. In this perspective, the hierarchical attribute given to an office node defines its role. Each node has the ability to modify its knowledge base, even if this may be done only under defined conditions and is permitted to selected people (for example, knowledge manager of the office structure): so, the knowledge is inserted into the system through the nodes and is transferred inside it through the net.

It is important to underline that the task solution activity based on cooperation by negotiation matches some of the main requirements of the dynamical office environment allowing:

A.   A dynamic work assignment to the nodes, through the ability to consider the current workload of the office components.

B.   An easy upgrading of the office, by simply adding/removing nodes.

C.   An easy update of the office structure by changing the role of the nodes modifying their knowledge base.

Figure 1 defines the internal structure of a node in the office system. The decision module, with its capability to solve tasks in the perspective of cooperation with the human agent and the net, is the core of the node, interfacing itself with the net, through the negotiation handler.

NODE STRUCTURE: THE DECISION MODULE

The decision module defines and executes all the necessary actions to carry out a task using the following components:

A.   The decision model
B.   The agent interface
C.   The knowledge base

Inside the module, the *decision model*, defines the general procedure for task solution, that is common to all nodes because the general guidelines of this activity are the same for all the office components. From the node viewpoint, each task can be classified as "complex" or "simple", considering how simple a task is the node can autonomously carry out or how complex a task is that lacks this characteristic. A complex task assigned to a node can be solved only after it's been reduced to a collection of simple tasks. If the node knows which subtasks composes the main task, but ignores how to carry out a particular subtask, the decision module asks for the help of the net, and uses the negotiation handler to search for some other nodes able to carry out the subtask. Using this decision model the node decision module acts autonomously to send/receive messages to/from the net (using the negotiation handler) and to solve the tasks that have no need of human support. The agent is involved only to solve tasks that need information not stored in the office system knowledge base or to give him the control on critical tasks, requesting his approval.

For this reason we have defined an *agent interface*, a friendly front-end between the man and the node: during the work the agent interface handles the communication between agent and the node decision module, using standard input and output procedures, to create an homogeneous and task independent environment with respect to the agent.

The *knowledge base* of the decision module contains the representation of the node procedural ability, i.e., the knowledge that allows the node to transform the description of each task it is able to carry out in a collection of subtasks. In this perspective we can assign the role of an office node as simply defining its knowledge base, i.e., assigning to it the procedural ability to carry out only particular tasks. We can consider two different points of view when speaking about knowledge: the global one, by which the knowledge identifies all the tasks the office is able to do, and the node point of view, which sees the node knowledge base as a description of all the tasks the particular node can do. With respect to the whole system, we can identify global knowledge as the union of all the knowledge bases of the nodes: the system can only do what all the nodes can do. We can easily modify the system knowledge base by simply modifying the knowledge base of the node, adding, deleting or changing the rules that define how to solve a task. For example, if the office needs a new agent with the ability to solve problems unknown by the existing agents, we can simply add a new node to the office net, with a knowledge base that contains the necessary information, to
perform the update.

NODE STRUCTURE: THE NEGOTIATION HANDLER

The information interchange among the nodes of the system is made through a bus link that each node has contact to send or receive data. From the office system point of view, the mechanism of information interchange can be seen as a task solution: every time a node asks for something, it asks for someone who can solve the task

- Give information about something

All the information exchange through the net is tasks proposal and solution. From the node decision module point of view, the net is a gate to the office environment, a world that can propose and carry out tasks. Each request for a task solution is made by the node using the negotiation mechanism: when a node needs to solve a task and lacks the ability to do it, it asks for a partner among the other system components to find somebody who can help it to carry out the task.

We can characterize the negotiation mechanism by looking at the four main phases that compose it: the task announcement, the bid emission, the award sending and the report reception. At the beginning, the node that proposes the task (manager) sends a message to all the nodes of the system: this message contains a brief description of the work and some necessities about the way in which it must be carried out. At this point, all the nodes that have the ability to carry out the proposed task (potential contractors) send the manager a bid message which contains a description of the work quality they can offer; then the manager analyses the offers, choses the node to assign the task and sends it an award. When the assigned task is completed, the contractor sends the manager a report with the results of the work and the task solution process ends.

In order to work properly in our office environment, each node only needs to know how to handle the messages received from the net and how to send them; there is no need to know anything about the office components because the other side of the net is like a black-box from the node point of view: when it asks for something, from the black-box someone replies and qualifies itself. In this way, it is possible to expand the system by simply adding a node that only has to know the information interchange protocol. The negotiation handler receives the input data and sends the output to the node decision module that is not involved in the negotiation process: when the decision module needs to send a task to be solved into the net, it sends the description of the task and other information about it to the negotiation handler (the expected time for solution, the report form,...). At this point, the whole negotiation process is managed by the negotiation handler that returns all the information sent by the contractor at the end of the work to the decision module. The information about the task to solve is sent to the contractor only after the award (if received). At this point the decision module carries out the task and sends the results to the negotiation handler, allowing the report emission. To work properly, the negotiation handler needs access to the decision module knowledge base, to autonomously investigate the capability to evaluate the proposed tasks.

CONCLUSIONS

The system proposed accomplishes a more "natural" model of communication (i.e., interaction among agents) able to satisfy the company's operative needs. The capability to homogeneously transmit "data" and "procedural knowledge" allows the necessary flexibility to adapt the information system to the frequent changes to which it is subjected. Such changes may be objective, due to the addition or subtraction of communication channels, or subjective, relative to not rigidly predefined information needs. In such a way our system includes the concept of an "individual productivity tool" without explicitly defining those same tools, overcoming the problem of integration with the traditional EDP, that is one of the major problems debated in past few years.

Some problems are still open and we are working on them. Among the most interesting of these for future research, we consider the task representation language, the man-machine interface, and the problems arising from the managing of distributed knowledge.

REFERENCES

Aiello, L., Nardi, D., and Panti, M., 1984, Modeling the Office Structure: A First Step Towards the Office Expert System, *ACM-SIGOA*, Toronto.

Anthony, R. N., 1965, *Planning and Control System, A Framework Analysis*, Harward, U.P., Cambridge.

Barber, G., 1983, Supporting Organizational Problem Solving with A Workstation, ACM-TOIS, Vol. 1, No. 1.

Blumenthal, S. C., 1969, *Management Information Systems: A Framework for Analysis*, Prentice-Hall, Englewood Cliffs.

Bracchi, G., and Motta, G., 1986, *Sistemi informativi ed imprese*, Franco Angeli.

Davis, G. D., 1974, *Management Information Systems. Conceptual Foundations, Structure, and Development*, McGraw-Hill, New York.

Davis, R., and Smith, R. G., 1984, Negotiation as a Metaphor for Distributed Problem Solving, *Artificial Intelligence*, Vol. 20, No. 1, January 1984.

Forrester, J., 1961, *Industrial Dynamics*, MIT Press, Cambridge.

Hellis, C., 1983, Formal and Informal Models of Office Activity, *Information Processing '83*.

Hewitt, C., 1986, Offices Are Open Systems, *ACM-TOIS*, Vol. 4, No. 3.

March, J. G., and Simon, H. A., 1963, *Organizations*, Jon Wiley & Sons Inc.

Panti, M., and Cucchiarelli, A., 1986, An Office Information System Model Based on a Contract Net, *IASTED International Symposium of Computer and Their Application for Development*, Taormina, Italy.

Tsichritzis, D., Fiume, E., Gibbs, S,. and Nierstrasz, O., 1987, KNO's: Knowledge Acquisitions, Dissemination, and Manipulation Objects, *ACM-TOIS*, Vol. V, No. 1, January 1987.

Woo, C. C., and Lochovsky, F. H., 1986, Supporting Distributed Office Problem Solving in Organizations, *ACM-TOIS*, Vol. 4, No. 3.

ARCHITECTURAL MODELING OF COMPLEX INFORMATION SYSTEMS

Konrad C. King and Linda J. Bellerby, Ph.D.

The Boeing Company
Vienna, Virginia

Abstract: This paper describes ongoing research, development, and application of architectural models to the design and life cycle support of complex information systems. The purpose of this development work is to define an overarching conceptual framework to rationally partition a complex problem and to integrate the solution components into a cohesive system. Experience at Boeing showed that no single architectural model is adequate to capture the complex interdependencies inherent in large information systems. This led to an approach that creates a distinct architecture for defining the problem (Requirements Architecture) and another for the projected solution (Solution Architecture). The complex mapping between the two distinct architectural models is analogous to the systems engineering allocation process.

The results achieved to date are described in terms of: (1) the rationale and benefits for defining a complex systems architecture which is distinct from the traditional approaches used to define applications systems; (2) the formal dimensioning used to define and characterize an entire systems domain; and (3) the complex mapping between the two architectural models.

The development work incorporates such disciplines as systems engineering, knowledge engineering, and set theory together with an experience base of heuristics. The current work focuses on defining structures which lend themselves to formal hypothesis testing.

INTRODUCTION

This paper describes ongoing research, development and application of architectural models to the design and life cycle support of complex information systems. The purpose of this development work is to define an overarching conceptual framework to rationally partition a complex problem and to integrate the solution components into a cohesive system. Experience at Boeing showed that no single architectural model is adequate to capture the complex interdependencies inherent in large information systems. This led to an approach that creates a distinct architecture for defining the problem (Requirements Architecture) and another for the projected solution (Solution Architecture). The complex mapping between the two distinct architectural models is analogous to the systems engineering allocation process.

The results achieved to date are described in terms of: (1) the rationale and benefits for defining a complex systems architecture which is distinct from the traditional approaches used to define application systems; (2) the formal dimensioning used to define and characterize an entire systems domain; and (3) the complex mapping between the two architectural models.

The development work incorporates such disciplines as systems engineering, knowledge engineering, and set theory together with an experience base of heuristics. Future work will focus on defining structures which lend themselves to formal hypothesis testing.

Statement of Problem

The current investment in large scale, automated information systems has not realized expected improvements in productivity and decision quality. Instead public and private enterprises are confronted with a myriad of "islands of automation" arrayed as isolated and non-interoperable systems at all levels of the organization. The competitive and resource availability pressures facing most enterprises require increased integration between these systems. The challenge is to provide integrated systems with a scope of data sharing and interoperability that matches the breadth and depth of the entire enterprise.

The information systems professionals charged with providing solutions to enterprise-wide information management are faced with a new set of problems. The experience base they draw upon is derived from the development of systems which are independent, functionally bound and non-extensible applications. The concepts and methods which work in the traditional systems development environment are not necessarily applicable to large scale complex systems.

A common approach has been to apply familiar analytic frameworks such as structured programming and relational data modeling paradigms. Other approaches emphasize development practices such as prototyping or reusable programming languages (e.g., ADA). While these approaches have made significant contributions to systems development methodology, they are not comprehensive enough to serve as an architectural framework for designing large scale, complex information systems. New approaches are needed to deal with the increased complexity of the emerging mega-systems which must transcend traditional functional and data sharing boundaries.

Motivation for an Architectural Model

This paper presents an architectural model that provides the basis for analyzing requirements and designing solutions to large scale systems. In order to be useful within the complex systems environment the architectural model must have the following attributes:

- Exhibit stability over time with respect to the definition of architectural elements and their interrelationships;

- Provide a framework to rationally partition the problem;

- Provide the basis for requirements traceability;

- Permit the identification and assessment of very-high level alternatives for understanding the problem as well as directing its solution;

- Demonstrate a unified approach for addressing engineering, development and implementation considerations throughout the life cycle of complex systems; and

- Provide a framework for defining complex dependencies between system components.

Architectures which exhibit the above characteristics provide a frame of reference for incorporating emerging technologies throughout the system life cycle. A significant challenge for any architecture is to reflect an understanding of both the direction and pace of technology developments. Some product areas, such as workstation hardware, have exhibited very rapid changes in their technology base. Other product areas, such as database management systems, take many years of deliberate development to reach maturity. A robust architec-tural model can support incremental developments which exploit leading edge technologies while avoiding bottlenecks caused by the failure of key technologies to mature as anticipated.

CURRENT APPLICATIONS OF INFORMATION SYSTEM ARCHITECTURES

During the past decade a number of significant efforts have been undertaken to formulate architectural models to help manage complex system environments. The following sections describe the results of three initiatives which have been underway for several years. Each of these represent relatively mature efforts which have been implemented on an enterprise-wide basis.

Army Information Architecture

The Army has employed the concept of architecture to establish a family of top level frameworks for each of its information resource management domains. These domains include strategic, tactical and sustaining base activities. The most highly developed architectural model addresses the sustaining base with primary emphasis on the information management assets required to pay, supply, maintain, fund, and account for the Army in garrison.

For this sustaining base, the Army has articulated a three-tiered architecture of regionalized data centers (tier 1), installation level processing centers (tier 2), and individual workstations (tier 3). It has employed this framework to establish system software standards and data interchange standards and to allocate application functionality. The Army has been less successful in mapping a global data sharing strategy to the tiered structure. This is due primarily to the enormous investment in third generation applications which make it difficult to implement data sharing strategies. At present, data is likely to be transmitted rather than shared.

The Army approaches implementation by establishing an objective architecture for the limit of the planning horizon, a current target architecture for mid-term initiatives and a baseline architecture for the existing investment. As highlighted under the previous topic, we believe that a single framework should suffice for all implementation efforts.

Both the Army and the Air Force have adopted characterizations of architectural perspectives which are referred to as information architecture, functional architecture, and geographic/technical architecture. The balance of this paper will present an alternative characterization in terms of a requirements architecture, which addresses many of the information and functional views, and a solution architecture which roughly corresponds to geographic/technical issues.

Air Force Information Systems Architecture

In many respects the Air Force Information Systems Architecture parallels closely the directions reported in this paper. The Air Force architecture explicitly recognizes the distinction between requirements and solution components. It also emphasizes the pivotal role provided by directional goals, policies, technology migration, and standards. It provides for multi-dimensional user operational views (i.e., space, airborne, fixed site and deployable) as well as systems views (i.e., end-user, dedicated, shared, gateway, and long-haul).

The primary difference between the Air Force doctrine and the architectural framework proposed in this paper is one of scope. The Air Force Information Systems Architecture is intended as a framework to accommodate all of its systems rather than to address a single program or initiative. In this regard it does not mandate, nor even strongly support, globally shared information assets. Instead, the Air Force delegates significant architectural responsibility to various subordinate organizations and technical support activities.

The Air Force Information Systems Architecture offers a significant contribution to the overall management and missionoriented direction of enterprise-wide information systems. A number of the dimensional models provide useful high level perspectives.

Boeing Network Architecture

Boeing established a corporate interconnect strategy in 1979 to contain the proliferation of incompatible computing systems and to manage future computing growth. The interconnect strategy, referred to as the Boeing Network Architecture (BNA), (Milholland and Roberts, 1985) promotes development of networked computing systems. The objective of the strategy is to permit information access and sharing across strategic computer systems regardless of application, terminal type or geographic location. BNA is a master plan for electronically integrating geographically dispersed data centers, offices and factory systems. It takes into account strategic requirements, user needs and developments in evolving standards as well as technology trends. Boeing has found that architecture models help provide clarity and a common basis for understanding. The models serve as a common frame of reference for all aspects of the technology. These models also serve as the basis for extending internal architectural practices to major information systems integration contracts in the federal marketplace. The preliminary results of this work are described in this paper.

MODEL STRUCTURE

Foundation Concepts and Terminology

Within the context of this paper architecture is defined as:

A set of rules and a space of objects which comprise a system, where the rules govern the interactions among the (classes of) objects, together with a classification scheme for partitioning the object classes in order to further define constraints on the interactions.

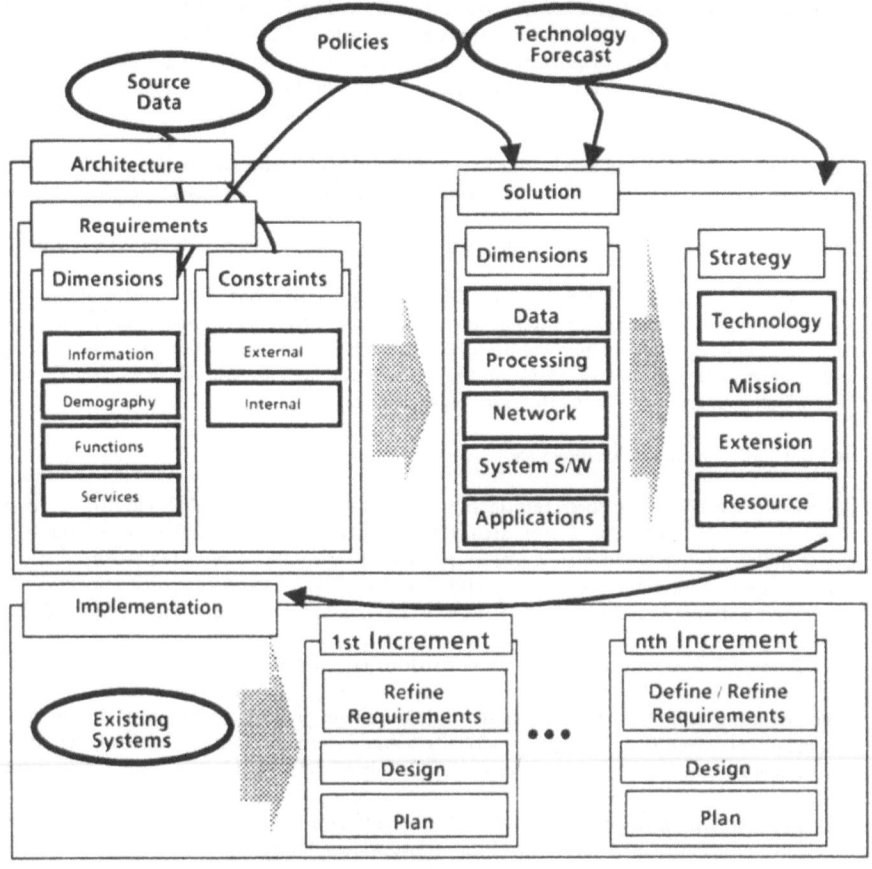

Figure 1. Overview of Information Systems Architecture
Model Showing Principal Dimensions.

An architecture is therefore viewed as independent of any specific product implementation.

The discussion that follows frequently refers to attributes such as large (versus small), complex (versus simple) and enterprise-wide (versus single use). These terms are used to imply a scope of system problems suitable for architectural models. Many systems are considered large because they contain many lines of code, complex computational algorithms, or large databases. However, these systems would benefit little from the application of architectural models. The systems of interest are those with complex interactions between system components, many user classes, and a high degree of technological uncer-tainty initially or over time.

Another class of systems which lend themselves to architectural treatment are those where optimization across all design elements is important. In narrowly focused, single-use applications, it is possible to locally optimize on a particular characteristic such as performance or development schedule. In systems with a large number of diverse users and usages, the imperative is to provide adequate service to all users. In a design environment where decisions relating to highly specialized technical areas can have profound impact on the entire user community, it is essential that a top-level framework exist to identify and reconcile potential conflicts.

As shown in Figure 1, a fundamental concept underlying the architectural model is the differentiation between the architecture used to define the problem (Requirements Architecture) and that used to define the projected solution (Solution Architecture). Each of these architectures is defined by a set of objects, called dimensions, necessary and sufficient to bound and characterize the problem or solution. Each dimension in turn is decomposed into partitions. Both dimensions and partitions are characterized by identifying those attributes which each have in common, as well as those attributes which differentiate them. Architectural dimensioning and partitioning are discussed further in subsequent sections.

Analyzing the correctness, completeness, or priority of requirements needs to be done independent of solution considerations. A common deficiency of requirement statements for information systems is that they are expressed in solution terms (e.g., performance or product requirements). The danger is that key characteristics of the requirements domain will be omitted and that a complete view of systems users, functions performed, and decisions made will not be obtained. Requirements defi- nition should state what the system must do, not how it should work. The decision of what to automate and how to automate should be the responsibility of the architect and designers based on the goals and priorities of the supported community.

Dimensioning the Architecture

Dimensions are a means of providing distinct views of the entire system from a series of perspectives. Each perspective focuses on a particular aspect of the system. An architecture for a building might include dimensions for the plumbing, wiring, ventilation, or masonry. The architect selects dimensions which will aid users and designers in understanding what the system must do and how it will be built. The number and type of dimensions selected is a function of the scope and complex- ity of the target system.

Dimensions which have proved useful in defining the Requirements Architecture include information objects, user demography, supported mission functionality and information services. These dimensions clarify what information the system must provide, who will use the system, what job functions users perform, and what capabilities they need to support those functions. From the solution side, typical dimensions include data, processing environment, network, and various classes of software. These dimensions provide solution views which designers must integrate to deliver desired capability.

The criteria for addressing a particular dimension are a function of the scope and freedom to impact various aspects of the problem. If the target system is to use an existing database, will be hosted on an installed processing suite or will communicate over an existing network, there is little need to develop a formal model of data, processing or network solution dimensions. Similarly, if the processing is constrained to be accomplished at a single location there is no justification for architecting the distribution of processing, data, or network communications.

Partitioning the Dimensions

In developing architectural models of complex systems it frequently is necessary to define sub-dimensions in order to capture important architectural distinctions. These subdimensions are called partitions. A classic example is partitioning the processing dimension of the Solution Architecture into three tiers which cover enterprise-wide, organizational and individual processing environments. Partitioning should yield unambiguous and non-overlapping clusters in each dimension.

The value of a partitioning scheme lies in its ability to provide a meaningful aggregation of requirements as well as a foundation for a strategy to implement the solution. Although partitioning detracts from the simplifying goal of architecture, it is a necessary part of defining complex environments.

REQUIREMENTS ARCHITECTURE

The Requirements Architecture provides a framework to identify, organize, validate, and refine requirements at the overall system level. The organization of requirements is achieved through dimensions such as information, user demography, supported mission functionality, and information services. In contrast to the body of requirements addressed by these dimensions, there exists a set of technical requirements which are referred to as constraints. While requirements focus on what the system must do to deliver information to users in support of business processes, constraints focus on design restrictions. For example, a requirement that a system must comply with the GOSIP standards constrains the type of network solution that can be implemented.

The following sections describe the four dimensions of the Requirements Architecture and the classification of constraints.

Information Dimension

In most modern information systems, information and its underlying representation as data provide the coupling between all system components. The value of most systems is measured by their ability to present information at the right time, to the right decision maker, in a useful form. In fact, it is the value of information that offsets a system's acquisition and operational costs.

181

We believe that the information dimension of a Requirements Architecture matches most directly the intended scope of the ANSI SPARC three schema model for database management standardization. An even closer fit is achieved with Niesen's non-lexical object types (nolot) where concepts are totally free of representational issues.

Theoretical and methodological developments during the past 15 years have resulted in objective techniques for information definition and analysis. Information analysis techniques such as Codd's relation model, Tasmania (RM/T) (Codd, 1979) or Nijssen's Information Analysis Model (NIAM) (Nijssen, 1980) can yield essential and replicable insights into requirements definition. These techniques can be used to partition the information dimension into qualitatively distinct information objects or entities. The data represented by each partition can be counted and sized and input to capacity and performance estimates.

When dealing at an architectural level, information analysis should be limited to a finite number of operational primitives. Additional levels of detail can be derived during detailed system design.

User Demography Dimension

Traditional system development methods do not provide an explicit framework for understanding the ubiquitous user. Historically, the design of batch systems was not dependent upon a user's direct interaction with components of the system. The nature of a user's interaction with automated systems is now a critical aspect of that system's design.

User demography focuses on individual usage style, organizational context, and geographic location. Individual usage style is differentiated into such elements as the experience of the user (naive, casual, frequent, expert), his primary interaction with the system (supplies data, consumes information), or nature of the supported task (uses the system to do work, does work and tells the system, system tells user how to do the work). Usage style characteristics map to the MANPRINT (Manpower and Personnel Integration) view of an individual at the controls of the system. Usage style is one of the less developed aspects of Requirements Architecture and requires additional work.

Organizational context provides some of the richest insights into what an information system should do. Individuals bring to, or get from, a system only what their job position directs. Organizational context articulates and delimits missions, charters, objectives, goals, responsibilities, activities, functions and information usage flows which are critical to defining system requirements.

Geography is peculiar to those problem domains whose elements are significantly dispersed. Geographic location includes the notion of proximity in such terms as work unit, building, campus, metropolitan, regional, continental, or global. Geography can also be expressed in terms of fixed, relocatable, or mobile.

While user demography is useful in its own right, it is particularly significant in combination with the other requirements dimensions. It also serves as one of the significant traceability mappings to the Solution Architecture.

Mission Functionality Dimension

In traditional information systems supported functionality (e.g., budgeting, payroll, shop floor control) represented the principal dimensioning for both requirements and solutions. These systems were packaged in the form of application systems or subsystems. Even in large scale systems functionality remains a critical dimension enabling users to locate and trace their requirements. This traceability must be maintained even though the system is attempting to achieve a high degree of functional integration in a solution.

Requirements analysis frequently confuses the functions the system should support with the functions the system should per-form. This dimension is concerned exclusively with the sup- ported functionality. The Solution Architecture addresses the functions the system should perform.

The predominant contribution of modern information systems is to favorably impact the quality and timeliness of decisions made relative to achieving organizational goals. Effective systems must therefore be based on a thorough understanding of the functions performed and the decisions which are made to further organization missions. This dimension is particularly useful in facilitating close interaction between the system user and the system designer.

From another perspective, information systems historically have eluded cost benefit accounting. This results to a large extent from the failure to explicitly relate information systems requirements to improvements in achieving organizational goals. As long as information system performance is measured and accounted for in cycles, cylinders and pages as opposed to mission accomplishment or bottom line contribution, solutions will fall short of real expectations.

In defining functionality requirements, the supported user community should define the functions they perform as well as the criteria they use to measure success. When matrixed with the organizational structure established under the user demographics dimension, a sound hierarchical decomposition of the supported mission can be developed down to the individual job classification. However, we must caution against the direct translation of organizational structure into the Solution Architecture. This tends to encourage functional bounding of systems when the objective is to achieve cross-function information sharing.

Information Services Dimension

Of all the requirements dimensions, information services is the least developed and, at present, the most elusive. In one sense, this dimension is a synthesis of the other three. In another sense, the information services dimension forms the most direct path to the solution with particular emphasis on application functionality. Our current view of information services is expressed in terms of a data services view, a user services view, and a system functional view.

From an information requirements perspective, a system either provides information primitives acquisition or information derivatives exploitation services. In the first instance the system furnishes services to acquire raw observations in the form of information primitives from external suppliers (persons or other systems). In the second case the system exploits previously acquired information primitives to deliver information packaged and presented to support actions, decisions, etc. Employing this acquisition/exploitation model against the subject-oriented information dimension establishes:

- A specific (at least one and hopefully only one) acquisition service is defined for each primitive relation, subject, entity, etc. in the information model

- An array of exploitation services are defined where information is needed to support functional mission elements

- Exploitation services are defined in the form $y = f(x)$ where y is the product, f is the service and x is the set of information primitives from which y is derived, selected, calculated.

Constraints Model

In addition to the dimensions described above, the Requirements Architecture must address requirements expressed as internal and external constraints. Internal constraints are restrictions on design decisions pertaining to how the system will be designed, built, and operated. External constraints are limitations imposed on the system as a whole from its environment.

Internal constraints typically provide direction on how, or how well, the system must achieve its goals. The following scheme provides a useful way to partition internal constraints:

- Performance constraints (e.g., measures of efficiency, integrity, reliability, supportability, survivability, usability, and availability);

- Design constraints (e.g., measures of correctness, controlability, maintainability, and verifiability);

- Extensibility constraints (e.g., measures of expandability, flexibility, interoperability, portability, and reusability);

- Security and data integrity constraints (e.g., measures of accountability, authenticity, authority, and sensitivity); and

- Operational constraints (e.g., measures of manageability, operability, simplicity, and usability).

External constraints tend to reflect non-technical issues such as economic or market considerations. They are usually imposed on the system from external sources and therefore are not under the control of the system manager. External constraints may include:

- Funding or other budgetary limitations;

- Interoperability with information systems outside the scope of the program;

- Maturity of the available technology;

- Schedule for accomplishment of results;

- Environmental capability of the supported organization, with its personnel and material resources, to employ, and sustain the solution; and

- Legislative constraints which are legally or administratively binding on the supported program.

By definition, constraints on the solution are always expressed in terms of the solution not the requirements. In identifying constraints, we have found it useful to employ the same dimensioning used for the solution architecture. For example, the requirement to use POSIX is an internal design constraint being placed on the system software dimension of the Solution Architecture. A well-defined constraint should map directly into a specific dimension and partition of the Solution Architecture.

Constraints can represent a rational approach to building and sustaining an orderly data processing environment. Constraints provide a vehicle to specify standards which promote information sharing and system interoperability. However, overly constrained solutions tend to be higher risk and more costly than minimally constrained solutions. Carefully defined and objectively supported trade-off studies often can identify areas where rigidly defined internal constraints can be relaxed with minimal impact on overall system performance. Trade off studies also should be performed on constraints which have been identified as major cost drivers.

We have found the distinction between dimensioned requirements and constraints to be an extremely useful scheme which allows the architect to focus on a limited and well organized set of requirements. Experience with complex systems has shown that approximately 80% of the stated requirements are classified under the constraints portion of the Requirements Architecture rather than the requirements dimensions.

SOLUTION ARCHITECTURE

The dimensions of the Solution Architecture correspond closely to the disciplines, skills, and product sets which will be used to design, build, install, operate and maintain the solution. The solution Architecture dimensions and partitions reflect the elements to which requirements and constraints are allocated. The solution strategies which meet those requirements can then be assessed in terms of feasibility, cost and scheduling.

Solution Architecture dimensions are selected based on the scope and degree of design freedom inherent in the overall concept of operations. Partitions are selected to form the basic building blocks as well as the inter- and intra-system interfaces needed to deliver required system services.

In order for the architecture to serve as a useful framework for subsequent detailed design, the dimensions and partitions should be described in the following terms.

- Characterize each partition in terms of the allocated dimensional and constraint requirements;

- Identify the applicable system design, development, operational, and sustainment policies and objectives;
- Cite relevant standards and conventions;

- Assess technology and its expected evolution as it pertains to the dimension/partition;

- Justify the adopted partitioning scheme in terms of the architectural trade off studies performed; and

- Characterize the interaction of each partition with other dimensions and partitions.

The following sections describe a set of Solution Architecture dimensions which have been used on several large scale information system programs. The dimensions are data, processing environment, network, system software environment, and application software.

Data Dimension

Although there is no inherent order in defining the dimensions of the Solution Architecture, modern complex systems typically employ a data-centered strategy in their development and execution. Consequently, the data dimension is the preferred focal point for the Solution Architecture. This dimension focuses on how physical data packages are allocated across and within processing sites.

Partitioning the data dimension must consider the degree of data centralization/decentralization that is required to achieve data base access requirements. The structure of the partitioned data must provide a faithful implementation of the information objects defined in the Requirements Architecture. As with other elements of the solution architecture, it is important that the partitions selected be capable of describing the solution environment of tomorrow as well as the various increments through which it may pass.

Processing Environment Dimension

The processing environment dimension maps the various classes of generic computing, storage and peripheral equipment into a multi-tiered structure. A typical partitioning of this dimension includes a three-tier structure encompassing enterprise-wide, organizational and individual processing suites. The tiers represent different levels of data sharing and are not necessarily related to the size of the processor. This structure provides the basis for allocating functionality and defining site configurations. As systems evolve to support a global community of users, the old patterns of processor configuration must be re-examined.

Consistent with our overall data-centered architectural approach, the physical data packaging established in the data dimension provides the basis for determining the equipment needed to acquire, store, and process that data. The number and location of processing sites are is driven by the demographics of the supported population.

The primary objective of the processing environment dimension is to facilitate a heterogeneous, non-vendor specific implementation across all tiers. This provides the basis for increased competition in procuring equipment and technology infusion over the system life cycle. Sufficient interoperability across tiers should be provided to permit the migration of data, software utilities, and applications between sites.

Network Architecture

The network dimension describes connectivity and transportation between and within processing sites. The partitioning strategy for this dimension is based on the geographic scope of connectivity. A typical scheme might include partitions for local area, metropolitan area, continental, and international connectivity. Solution strategies for achieving this connectivity could include a combination of terrestrial, satellite, optical and non-electronic media such as overnight mail.

Since the primary data interchange is between hardware nodes, the processing environment dimension is one of the primary reference points for constructing alternatives for network topologies. Network capacity requirements, on the other hand, are driven by the data volumes to be acquired or consumed by each node.

System Software Environment Dimension

This dimension addresses the allocation of software support functionality across the processing environment dimension. In our attempt to provide a rigorous framework for solution architecture, system software has proved to be the least orderly dimension. In general, we use the criteria that all software which is not application specific belongs to the system software dimension.

Multiple partitioning strategies have been used for this dimension. One approach is to use commonly accepted classes of general purpose software such as operating systems, data management systems, and productivity tools. Most partitioning schemes focus on a spectrum of machine-oriented through useroriented system services. Using notions such as level of abstraction remain to be explored.

In relating the systems software dimension to requirements, we have found that requirement statements contain a preponderance of internal constraints which map closely this dimension. From the perspective of other solution dimensions, the primary influence is exerted by the processing dimension which bounds the requirement for operating systems. The network dimension provides the requirement for network software access methods. Finally, the applications software dimension, when fully developed during the design process, invariably results in the identification of "common" processes required to support missionspecific functions.

Application Software Dimension

This dimension of the Solution Architecture addresses applications software that provides direct support to specific functional disciplines. This dimension provides the basis for allocating user-specific

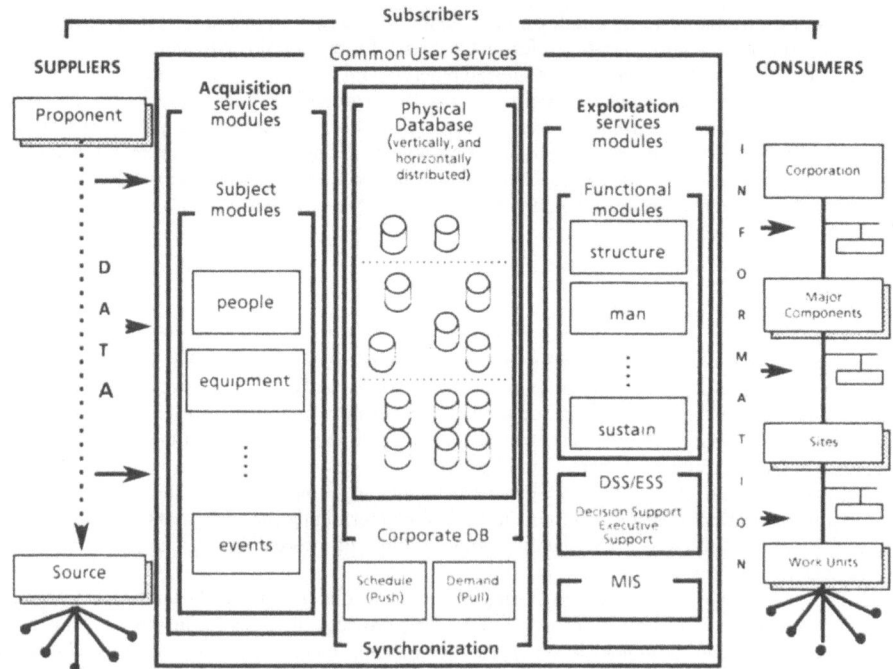

Figure 2. Application Software Architectural Model.

functionality across the processing architecture. The application software dimension is used to address domain specific processes in a data-centered architecture. The modeling of this dimension as illustrated in Figure 2 follows some of the efforts reported by Appleton (Appleton, 1986) on information asset management.

The data-centered view defines processes from the perspective of data. From this perspective, a process either acquires data to be stored or exploits data that has been stored. This contrasts with the conventional approach of describing data from a perspective of a process (input to a process or output from a process).

The model has been further enhanced by adding a third partition, synchronization, to address the vertical and horizontal distribution of data. Synchronization is the general concept which ensures the currency, validity and integrity of data distributed throughout the architecture. In an ideal world this would occur transparently from the perspective of users and system developers. Until that objective is achievable, this model facilitates definition of all application functions required to synchronize data through replication or summarization/extraction. Ultimately the synchronization function will atrophy leaving simple, easily maintained acquisition and exploitation application software.

IMPLEMENTATION STRATEGY

Although implementation strategies are not an explicit part of the architecture model, they should play a significant role in its definition. This is particularly true where the target system will be implemented over time. A common approach is to provide for an incremental implementation where the first increment establishes a baseline of useful capability. Subsequent increments add new capabilities or improve the integration of existing capabilities.

The architectural model described above facilitates incremental system evolution by providing traceability between user requirements and the solution defined for each increment. The architectural model also directs the deployment of new technology as required to meet new requirements.

QUALITATIVE ASSESSMENT OF ARCHITECTURES

During the course of our work with large scale information systems we have developed several measures to test either the overall quality of an architecture or to compare alternative architectures. Foremost among these tests is the subjective measure of the degree to which a given architectural formulation approaches the objectives of simplifying, unifying and rationalizing the problem. These tests are usually performed in two stages. First we assess the accuracy and soundness against each attribute to remove such errors as over-simplification, unsupported unification, or unsound rationalization. Second, we apply an absolute assessment of adequacy in the form of questions such as: Is it simple enough? Is it sufficiently unified? Do we understand the supporting rationale? Only at this stage do we feel prepared to compare alternatives or assert that using an architectural approach will justify the effort.

A measure of the accuracy of separating requirements from solutions derives from a heuristic observation of successful complex systems and a subjective assessment of how complex systems fail to achieve desired results. Simply stated, the heuristic holds that "if the solution looks anything like the problem, the architect has failed to understand one or the other, or both". The most straight forward illustration of this condition is where solutions are defined and implemented along purely functional boundaries such as payroll, personnel, finance, or supply. Such systems typically fail to provide for information sharing across system boundaries. Conversely, requirements which are phrased in terms of programs to be written, files to be maintained, or computers to be installed, on the one hand tend to omit crucial information about the skill levels of users, the goals of their parent organizations or potential information needs for future extensions. Additionally, these kinds of requirements tend to constrain the application of optimal or directional technologies.

TOPICS FOR FURTHER RESEARCH

Spectral Dimensioning

Traditional batch processes with their daily, weekly, monthly run streams and their old master/new master serial tape architectures simplified the challenge of dealing with issues of currency, effectivity, retrospection and prospection by offering a very limited repertoire of time-based models. Interactive systems, vertically integrated user communities, write-once media, and the general direction to manage enterprise wide information needs, challenge future systems to deal consistency with the time dimension of data. Where once dates where recorded on paper labels or entered by console operators from run sheets, they must now be an explicit element of the information base.

We see a need to develop a rich model for defining and explicitly expressing the spectral attributes that characterize classes of objects likely to be addressed by information systems.

Information Services Model

Beyond a basic characterization of styles as reactive, integrated, and proactive, we have not identified other classes or attributes of styles. We are confident that the taxonomy, while rich, is both knowable and could be extremely useful. The application of research which has been conducted in areas such as cognitive decision making styles can improve the characterization of this dimension. One of our principal concerns is that characterizations conform to the definitional imperative of requirements and avoid constraining design solutions.

Goal Directed Architectures

Our initial work in describing supported functionality has focused on what the supported organization did rather than why it did it. More recently we have encountered complex systems programs that challenged the information systems architect to improve the productivity of personnel rather than merely automating existing processes. The objective is to design systems that contribute significantly to meeting the organizations goals.

We believe that this is a proper challenge for information systems and the architecture should properly describe goals in its requirements and describe how general or specific feature of the solution contributes to their achievement. Articulating those goals in a form that will support the general traceability afforded by the architecture remains a significant challenge.

System Software Environment Model

As discussed earlier, we believe the system software environment model to be one of the least amenable to unambiguous partitioning. Our suspicion is that the evolutionary growth of such elements as operating systems, database management systems, productivity tools and security monitors have led to packaging which is more historical and market-driven than it is rational. We believe that considerable work must and should be done to bring objectivity and comparability to the process of choosing between alternative design approaches for this dimension.

AN ACTION PROGRAM FOR INFORMATION SYSTEMS ARCHITECTURE

User Initiatives

As discussed in the beginning of this paper, the primary impetus of complex information systems, and hence of architecture to support them, has been the vision of public and private enterprise leadership. This vision holds that the community of information systems practitioners ought to be capable of crafting system solutions that deliver usable, relevant information. Although there has been repeated failure to deliver these solutions, management must recognize the tremendous intellectual and management challenges presented, must more sharply assess the criticality to institutional success and survival, and must allocate the appropriate resources and attention.

Vendor Initiatives

The hardware. software and service offerings in support of enterprise-wide information systems initiatives have until very recently, been characterized by an entrepreneurial strategy of creating proprietary, non-interoperable environments. Under these conditions migration across vendor product sets was extremely difficult. Recently influences external to the market have begun to counteract this tendency. Of particular note has been the Open Systems Interconnection initiative supported by an alliance of international standards activities and a number of major automation users such as the Manufacturing Automation Protocol and Technical Office Protocol (MAP/TOP) Users Group. These efforts have been joined by associations of major vendors such as the Corporation for Open Systems (COS) and the Open Systems Foundation (OSF) in promoting the level of interchange and interoperability essential to realizing the benefits expected for enterprise-wide information systems. All parties with a stake in the success of large scale information systems must vigorously promote and support these initiatives.

Standards Initiatives

Just as automation product vendors are challenged to aggressively mold their offerings to conform to standards, it is incumbent on the standards community to assure that new standards are based on intellectually sound models of how information systems should be built and operated. It has been observed that the only thing worse than no standard is the wrong standard. The absence of a standard merely encourages the market to continuously seek new, and potentially better ways to meet real problems with affordable solutions. The presence of the wrong standard universally inhibits development and inquiry of sound solutions. Premature and inappropriate standards, more than most other factors, have led to an information systems industry which is marginally productive and costly to maintain. To counteract this influence, the standards community must institutionalize a more adaptive and intellectually rigorous approach to the setting and proliferation of conventions and protocols.

Professional Initiatives

The final challenge to realizing successful complex information systems benefits is a purely intellectual challenge. In the work we have observed, we are struck by the lack of a rich. well-articulated, and complementary framework of models for comprehensively and objectively reasoning about such systems. We believe that academics, in partnership with senior practitioners, have a special and specific obligation to accept@ the task of discovering, articulating, and sharing these architectural models. With a less than sterling track record of complex system implementation successes, this process will be extremely challenging and will require contributions from all members of the community.

REFERENCES

Appleton, D., 1986, Very Large Projects, *Datamation*, January 15, 1986.

Codd, E., 1979, Extending the Data Base Relational Model, *Proceedings of ACM-SIGMOD International Conference on Management of Data*, Boston, MA, June 1979.

Department of the Army Pamphlet 25-1, Army Information Architecture.

Headquarters, U. S. Air Force, Letter, Subject: Air Force Information Systems Architecture, May 8, 1985.

Milholland, T., and Roberts, G., 1985, Boeing Rolls Out 'Ultimate' Network, *Computerworld*, November 4, 1985.

Nijssen, G., 1980, *A Framework for Advanced Mass Storage Applications*, Medinfo North-Holland.

APPENDIX: KEE BACKGROUND INFORMATION

KEE is an object-oriented programming environment developed for AI research and application. Its ancestral roots stem from LOOPS and Smalltalk. Unlike Smalltalk, it is implemented on top of LISP rather than built from scratch, yet like its ancestors, the emphasis is on the use of objects in an interface.

Modules in KEE are called *knowledge bases*. A knowledge base consists of one or more *units*, where a unit is the main data structure in KEE and corresponds to objects from other object-oriented systems. Each unit has a unique name within a knowledge base and units are composed of *slots*. A slot is thus equivalent to an attribute or field in a tuple. Slots may be viewed as sets of objects or there may be order imposed upon the objects via a slot. The values of a slot may be non-atomic, thus objects can point to one another through slot values. Also, a slot may have data type restrictions and impose requirements for a minimum or maximum cardinality.

Users may add other attributes to slots through *facets*. Facets are essentially attributes on attributes. Everything in KEE is implemented using units, so classes and instances are units in KEE. Rules, knowledge bases, and graphic icons are also units. Since classes are implemented as units, their definition is dynamically extensible by sending messages. Consequently, certain types of optimizations are ruled out because there is not a semantic distinction between different types of objects: they are all units.

KEE has a wide spectrum of functionality and there are seven components of KEE that form somewhat novel primitives in a SEE. First, the inheritance mechanism in KEE is quite flexible. There are two completely different types of in- heritance. One type is slot inheritance where the developer may decide whether or not a slot is inherited from one class to another class or instance. The other type of inheritance involves values. In this case, when the slot itself is inheritable, the values to t, Letter, Subject: Air Force Information Systems Architecture, May 8, 1985.

A MANAGEMENT MODEL FOR EFFECTIVE INFORMATION-USE IN RESEARCH WORK

Aatto J. Repo

Telematics
Finnish PTT
Helsinki, Finland

Abstract: An idea of a dual approach to the value of information is briefly presented. The approach uses simultaneously exchange values of information products and services in the markets and value-in-use of information and knowledge for research or any other information work. At the present low economic awareness of scientists one cannot use pure economic measures in monitoring the value of information for research work. In a series of case studies we have studied value-in-use of information thoroughly at the Technical Research Centre of Finland (VTT). Information seeking and use, and the quality of twelve research projects have been analyzed. A questionnaire on the general information seeking and use patterns of the scientists at VTT has been completed. In addition, data on time-allocation for the information activities in the research projects was collected. A model of the actions to be taken for effective information seeking and use has been developed from the data. The model has been analyzed and developed further in the interviews of the research managers at VTT. As a result we have a model of six actions to be taken by the research managers: (1) ensure that results of the research are 'published'; (2) ensure that there is a rich information environment; (3) encourage joint efforts in information seeking and use; (4) ensure that the information found is actually put to use; (5) improve the seeking of methodological information; and (6) ensure that the time used for information seeking and use is appropriate to the research task. These actions optimize the value-in-use of information in a research process.

INTRODUCTION

The economics and value of information are analyzed in this study. Efforts are made to deepen our understanding of the phenomenon. Our approach could be characterized as a phenomenological or hermeneutic approach, where by means of the case studies and the analysis of the literature, the nature of the practical value of information is identified. It is our belief that practical information-use situations give the best starting point for the analysis (Repo, 1986; 1987(a); 1987(b); 1988). This is somewhat different approach from most of the recent studies which have often been motivated by the need to argue for the importance of some particular information systems, information services, information products and even information professionals. The Special Libraries Association study, President's Task Force on the Value of Information Professional (1987), provides a good summary of the latest approaches in the field of information science. Although such studies as those collecting examples of the usefulness of certain information services are undoubtedly necessary and useful for the providers of those services, they still leave rather a vague picture of the value analyses in general.

VALUE OF INFORMATION: SOME THEORETICAL FINDINGS

There are three paradigms 'ruling' the research of the value of information: the economic paradigm, the cognitive paradigm and the information theory paradigm. Interestingly, economists have concentrated their recent interest around the information theory paradigm and the economic paradigm is

Empirical Foundations of Information and Software Science V
Edited by P. Zunde and D. Hocking, Plenum Press, New York, 1990

191

only used in some empirical studies. Information scientists mainly use the cognitive or economic paradigms. Although there have been a few attempts to cross the boundaries of the paradigms, the main part of the research is completed under one paradigm. For instance, those information scientists who are studying information markets and information management clearly emphasize basic economic thoughts. Other information scientists who study, say, the use of information and information systems usually stress the cognitive paradigm.

While economists have failed to introduce useful practical means to measure the value of information in spite of research based on information theory, the research in information science seems to split into two groups. There are those who believe strongly in economics. After the failed attempts in using cost-benefit analysis there is the information accounting and budgeting boom at the organizational level, better known as the Information Resource(s) Management (IRM) approach. On the other hand, there has been much research on the use of information, which, at best, applies a cognitive approach.

We arrived at the conclusion from the literature review that it is necessary to organize research on the value of information by using the economic and cognitive approaches simultaneously (Repo, 1988). Neither of them describes the phenomenon fully alone. By simplifying, one can introduce a dual approach to the value of information for practical studies:

1. The exchange value of information products, services, channels and systems should be studied using economic methods.

2. The value-in-use of information should be studied using the cognitive approach which takes the user, the use and the effects of the use of information into consideration.

The specifications of the value concept are used in the study for analyzing the value of information. Values can be divided into philosophical values and practical values. Philosophical values provide a background for our behavior, but they are hard or sometimes even impossible to detect. We concentrated on practical values further divided into value-in-use and exchange values. The value-in-use, the main interest in our study, describes the value of information from the information user's and *use* viewpoint. The exchange value considerations are needed when we want to compare values either in comparison with the values of information channels, services or products in an information need situation, or in a marketing situation for determining the price for a piece of information, information product or information service.

The value-in-use of information can only be stated by the user of information, while he is performing his knowledge-work task and sometimes from the results of the task. In order to avoid subjectivism, the basis for determining the value of information even from an information-use viewpoint has to be in the knowledge-work itself. Studying the value-in-use of information in practice is a demanding task. Objective value-in-use is usually impossible to measure in full. Only some indicators may be available from individuals as to how the information influenced the task and the results (subjective value-in-use). It is also necessary to study the expected subjective value-inuse because it provides possibilities to study valuing processes of individuals, while they value information products and services. For value data we have to ask the actual users, but their estimates can be more accurate if we distinguish between the kinds of information they need.

To summarize the theoretical findings:

1. There is no sense in trying to measure the total value of information; different viewpoints and observation levels impose different emphases.

2. One should speak of the value of information at the user level only in terms of value-in-use. Because the value-giving situation of information products and services is need-oriented, expected value-in-use studies are necessary. Reference to use values in money terms makes it easy to intermix value-in-use with exchange values. Only seldom is it possible to derive exchange values from objective value-in-use.

3. The organization, or the community more generally, provides the framework for knowledge work and it operates with exchange values. There are seldom real measurements for such a concept as the value-in-use of information at the organizational level. Should we only speak of the exchange values of information products, services, systems and channels? But even this proves difficult because scientists, managers, etc. are not used to thinking of information as a commodity.

4. When the value of information is studied in an organization, the information-use contexts have to be examined thoroughly. In addition, the information users' opinions about

information needs in particular use situations have to be studied. The examples of value-in-use have been the most useful tools available so far.

THE VALUE OF INFORMATION IN ORGANIZATIONAL SETTINGS: A FRAMEWORK FOR MANAGING INFORMATION-USE

Starting Points

An organizational setting, a technical research center, was thought to provide ideal surroundings for testing our approach to the value of information. A set of case-studies and other data collections were set up for developing a comprehensive understanding of the economics and the value of information seeking and use at the Technical Research Center of Finland (VTT). The practical management questions to be answered were: How can one make the use of information optimal, and what kind of methods can be developed for monitoring the use of information?

The case-studies by Allen (1977), and Bitz and Owen (1981) largely influenced the settings for the studies. The U.S. studies of the value of information by King Research Inc. (King et al., 1982; Roderer et al., 1983) encouraged the collecting of empirical measures of the exchange values of information. In addition, several surveys on engineering research had an impact on our studies. However, our interest in the use of information in research work meant that the common surveys on the use of information systems, channels and services were not of much help.

The value-in-use of information for the research projects was the main point of interest in our study. We found evidence to suggest that it is not possible to collect statistical data on the value-in-use of information inputs and find their influence in the results of the research. Although there were some individual examples, they were not generally useful. Obviously the European research tradition is quite different from that in the United States. This meant that we were forced to neglect the approach mentioned earlier which had been successfully applied by King Research Inc.

Our dual approach meant that we were also looking for evidence of the exchange values of the information services and information products used. These efforts failed. We consider our dual approach valuable in the light of the several reasons for the failure:

1. The scientists and even research managers are not used to thinking about information products and services in monetary terms. The main reason for this is that the costs of using these products and services - they think - are of minor importance and that usually they are so specialized that the comparison of different products and services is difficult. The scientists have also been accustomed to 'free' information services from teachers and university libraries when they were students.

2. Information markets are developing, but they are not yet sufficiently developed. Top level research groups have to get into the situations where information and knowledge are exchanged with other (international) research organizations. This means that the scientists get the information and knowledge before it enters the market. This may be the case even in the future in spite of the developing information market, because of the new means to perform co-operative research and, also, because of increasing international co-operation in technical research. In other words, much of the important information exchange takes place outside the information market and thus the research managers do not see the exchange value considerations as being important.

3. The earlier mentioned European tradition in research probably hinders thinking in terms of exchange values when considering information products and services. This situation is bound to change when there are more comparable information products and services available on the market.

The problems on the market side of the exchange value studies meant that we concentrated upon collecting data on the costs of information-use. This proved rewarding in providing interesting data and, also, in motivating the research managers to start thinking of information seeking and use as an important part of their management practices.

In this section the findings of the VTT study are summarized. The views of scientists and managers are put together. The idea is to give the reader the frame of reference for the model in the next section. The model describes the management actions needed to ensure effective information-use in research work.

Costs of Information Seeking and Use. The scientists and managers tend to underestimate the importance of the costs of information seeking and use. The main reason for this is that only seldom are the costs of a project shown in the project budget. The accounting practice at VTT is that only foreign travel and some services acquired from the Information Service (for instance, online services included, but circulation of periodicals excluded) are clearly seen in the projectaccount. At present these 'direct' costs of information-use at VTT are a few thousand Finmarks (1 $ = 4 FIM), less than 5% of the project budget on average.

The often omitted labor expenses constitute the biggest share of the costs. The time study of the project heads at VTT showed that information seeking from literature took 9% of the total time used for the project and reading took 12%. Communication took 26%. This means that nearly half of the time is used for information seeking and use. It is worth noting here that VTT with her 2600 employees has a central national task in creating, maintaining and developing technical expertise for Finnish industry. When research work is made more effective, the time used for information activities has to occupy the central role. Better information services and better support in communication could easily offset the costs of the investments in the form of saved time. Still, the key to this problem area is how to make scientists work more effectively and use all the support available whenever needed.

The time usage statistics raised mixed feelings among the heads of the laboratories. For the majority, the statistics came as a surprise and their main concern was the small proportion of actual research (under one third of the total time used). Nearly one fifth received ideas for further studies and actions in their laboratories, but one fifth doubted whether the research work could be made more effective by rationalizing the time usage.

Benefits from the Use of Information. After counting the costs one would like to see the benefits gained. Unfortunately, only seldom can one find clear-cut connections between information-use and the results of the research. Sometimes a new piece of information gives a clearly noticeable new and 'better' direction for the research, but usually new information flows continuously to the research process in the form of documents, advice from the experts and colleagues, etc. New information and knowledge join the earlier knowledge, and it is afterwards hard to isolate the role an individual piece of information has had in the research work.

Some scientists gave examples where the piece of information had a central role in the research process. The benefits from the use of information could be measured, for instance, in the following cases:

- an online search saved time in planning a visit to a research organization and, also, in planning a project;

- a visit to a foreign research organization gave new information which saved time in an ongoing project;

- a personal contact with an expert saved time (several responses); and

- a current awareness service picked out a piece of information which improved the result of a project substantially.

The examples of the benefits gained from a piece of information are important in describing the value of an individual information channel. These few examples are not of much help in developing the information seeking and use practice for research work. The use of information as a part of research work must be studied more thoroughly.

Information Seeking and Use. Information and knowledge come to a research project with the scientists appointed to work in the project. New information is acquired during the project. To a certain extent new information comes also with new equipment and software used. In the twelve projects studied thoroughly at VTT, the results were partly based on the earlier knowledge of the project groups. A senior scientist, usually a project leader, has often taken part in the planning and development of its idea. His responsibility has been the seeking and use of new information. Less experienced scientists work as assistants in the projects. This general working pattern means that senior scientists generate and direct information behavior in the research groups and the laboratories.

Personal contacts and periodicals are the most frequently used and the most important sources of new information. Research reports, books and other documents are also much used, contrary to the impression given by some U.S. studies (e.g., Allen, 1977). Online searching is less often used. It is also rated quite low in spite of a lot of efforts the Information Service has made to promote it. The senior scientists emphasized how the best documents for the research are often found through personal contacts. The scientists rated the main channels of information in the following order. The average numbers of use are shown in parentheses:

1. International and national contacts (10 important international and 10 important national contacts per project, 2 international business trips per scientist per year),

2. Scanning and reading of periodicals (13 periodicals per scientist),

3. Visits to library (24 visits per scientist per year),

4. Abstract journals (3 journals per scientist), and

5. Online searches (1.4 searches per scientist per year).

The heads of the laboratories generally emphasized that online searching should be used more and thought that it should be second in rating to contacts. The managers would also like to put the libraries at the end of the list as their use was considered time-consuming. (Meaning large special libraries here. Most managers acknowledged the need for a small reference library in the laboratory).

There are three major factors influencing the use of information in a research project: scientists, tasks and the types of information needed.

The scientists fall into groups ranging from 'information rich' (or gatekeepers) to 'information poor'. The gatekeepers frequently use various channels and sources whereas the few sources 'information poor' use are used only occasionally. These scientists are more interested in such work as laboratory experimenting and programming. In the case-studies at VTT we found a fairly even number of scientists in both groups. Another related phenomenon was also observed: some scientists prefer the procedural approach to their problem solving while others are theoretically oriented. There was much evidence that information seeking and use patterns are heavily dependent on the attitudes and working practices of individuals (for discussions on the attitudes of engineers, see Nagus (1982). The nature of the project, laboratory or working experience had less influence on the behavior. It looks as though the optimum research group consists of the most heterogeneous set of individuals. This was also emphasized by the heads of the laboratories. Although the lack of gatekeepers in a research group is likely to cause problems, there is also a need for 'workers' and these abilities are not always found in the same person.

The case studies of twelve research projects demonstrated that the use of external information is essential in the research projects of VTT and less effort goes into generating new knowledge and information. This is probably a true observation (supported by the time usage data) although the research programmes, from which the projects come, emphasize the new areas of research at VTT. In these circumstances, effective information seeking and use is vital.

The seeking and use of factual information differs from seeking and use of methodological information. The seeking and use of factual information seems to be quite straightforward, although often cumbersome: for instance, by the series of laboratory tests or already documented test results. The seeking and use of methodological information is much more demanding; it is often a time-consuming learning process. It seems to be especially important to use rich channels and sources here. Personal contacts proved to be competing successfully with 'official' intermediaries. It is far more useful to get a list of readings from a colleague than through, for instance, an online search. The former list includes an expert's knowledge of the useful readings while the latter is a more random selection of readings available in a set of databases. Additionally, experts and colleagues were useful in teaching the use of methods, and in supporting the selection of methods for the research project.

The information deluge is much talked about in the private sector and within governmental organizations also. However, in the research organization the problem seems to exist in finding good and detailed enough information. The scientists and the research managers have become used to the situation where only half of the acquired information proves to be partially useful and only a small percentage of it is generally useful. 'Waste' scanning and screening is a part of the research process, if there are no clear solutions for the research tasks at hand in one's range of vision.

Action to Be Taken for Effective Information Seeking and Use

We used the input-output model of a research process as a basic frame in our analyses of the

```
INPUTS   ===>   RESEARCH PROCESS   ===>   OUTPUTS

   õ            õ                          1. Ensuring
   V            õ                             adequate
                õ                             documentation.
2. Ensuring that õ
   there is rich  õ
   information    õ
   environment.   õ
                  õ
3. Encouraging    V
   joint efforts
   in information  4. Ensuring that the
   seeking and        information found
   use.               is actually put to use.

5. Improving the
   seeking of
   methodological  6. Ensuring that time used
   information.       for information seeking
                      and use is appropriate
                      to the project.
```

Figure 1. Management Actions for Optimizing the Value-
in-use of Information for Research Work.

research work. The 'black box' of the research process is opened by monitoring information seeking and use for the process. When it became clear that only cost-data of the use of information can be produced for statistical analysis, the cost-benefit analysis of information-use had to be discarded. By collecting descriptive data about the use of information in the research processes and data on the quality of research results, we developed an elaborate input-output model of the management actions for promoting effective information behavior. These actions optimize the value-in-use of information for research tasks.

The model was developed for the benefit of management. For this reason, only the most important actions are included. The model was submitted to VTT laboratory heads for comments and alterations and is presented in Figure 1. All the actions were seen as useful in monitoring the effectiveness of information seeking and use. The actions are rated in Figure 1 according to the importance the managers placed on them.

The most important and also the most common way of ensuring the effective use of information in the research process is to monitor the documentation of research. The quality and variety of the documents produced were the major concern of the research managers. However, it was emphasized that publications are only one result of the research and usually equipment, software, etc. are more important results.

Ensuring that there is a rich information environment for the research groups was thought to be the second most important action in managing the use of information. A variety of information channels, information systems, information services and information products should be available, and the scientists should have the abilities to use them efficiently. New effective means should be adopted quickly. In this respect the scientists do not seem to be as progressive as the managers.

Thirdly, one should encourage joint efforts in information seeking and use. The idea of working in pairs (senior and junior scientists working together) and, more generally, heterogeneous research groups were considered worth aiming for. There are two demands ensuing from this: the research groups must be big enough (this presupposes that the research tasks are large enough); and there must be enough time for appropriate communication.

Ensuring that the information is put to use is the fourth in importance of the management actions. The personal filing practices should be developed for effective use of collected documents, notes, etc. The fact that the scientist has to screen and scan a lot of documents for his research work was acknowledged by the managers, but the use of acquired information was generally seen to be too low.

Improvement of the seeking and use of methodological information comes next in importance for the managers. The rich channels were considered important. Colleagues and outside experts are essential in advising the projects in methodological problems. It was considered vital for the development of research groups that sufficient effort be put into the seeking and use of new methodological information.

Table 1

Data Collection for the Action Model For Effective Information Seeking and Use in Research

Data Collection	Indicator
All/sample of the projects ended in a certain year, an interview/ questionnaire to the heads of the projects.	Contacts in the projects Size and nature of the project staff How method information is sought The use of article copies Documentation data
All/sample of the ongoing projects in the laboratory, a time-allocation study to the scientists working on the projects.	Time used in - information seeking - reading - communication/in - communication/outside - research - project-bureaucracy - documentation
All/sample of the scientists in the laboratory, a questionnaire.	Foreign traveling Periodicals reading Online searches done Abstract journals read Visits to library made
All/sample of the scientists in the laboratory, an interview/ questionnaire.	Ideas for developing Information Seeking and Use

Sixthly, the manager has to ensure that time used for information seeking and use is appropriate for the project.

There is a clear need for producing time-allocation data on the work of the research groups for management purposes. These data are useful in convincing the managers of the importance of information activities in research work. They are, also, needed as a background information when rationalizing efforts to support the working patterns of scientists are made.

The model can be used in developing the effectiveness of information seeking and use in research groups and research laboratories. Detailed data have to be collected about the information seeking and use patterns of the scientists. Table 1 summarizes the data collection methods suitable for a research laboratory. It is a modification of the data collection of this study.

In practice, the methods have to be modified according to local needs and interests. The heads of the laboratories at VTT were interested in different things, some in time-usage and others in the facts about information seeking and use in the projects. The majority felt that it is not necessary to collect all the data listed in the Table below when VTT level data are already available. It was generally emphasized that after data collection the results must be discussed in a seminar for the managers and the scientists of the laboratory. It is also important that the representatives of the information service and other units supporting the information seeking and use should participate in the development.

At organizational level, the following actions are needed for more effective information seeking and use (a research organization, recommendations based on VTT data):

1.	Research has to be developed in large enough units and the time scale of research has to be 5-10 years. This provides the possibility of building information seeking and use practices in the research group that are not totally dependent on the abilities of certain scientists, but the responsibilities can be shared by group members. Issues of information seeking and use need to have a more recognized role in the development of research groups.

2. The research units (laboratories) have to monitor and develop their information seeking and use patterns and abilities more consciously as an important part of the management practice. Local data collection and discussions are needed from time to time to remind the scientists and managers of the importance of these issues.

3. The parent organization needs to give good support to communication between the research units in the organization and to their national and international contacts. Electronic mail and international networks are the most important development targets at present. Although progressive research organizations use these systems already, their broader use is just beginning.

4. The information service unit has to offer scientists a variety of services the use of which is flexible. Instead of general services one should develop more tailored services for the research units and even for the individual scientists. In order to be able to offer cost-justified services, the information service unit has developed systems which broaden self-service.

CONCLUSIONS

Information seeking and use practices vary. The behavior of the scientists and the working patterns in the laboratories are the result of a complex set of influencing factors. These include the field of research, the personnel structure, the age and the size of a research unit, the nature and the size of a research project, etc. Thus, generalizations from the VTT data at this level of detail must be made with caution. However, the earlier studies on engineering research support the findings at the general level, although because of somewhat different approaches closer comparisons are not possible (Allen, 1977; Bitz and Owen, 1981; Gralewska-Vickery, 1976; Shuchman, 1981).

We developed a model for use in management. This meant that we had to do without Allen's (1977) longitudinal studies as well as without 'laboratory tests' of the information-use proposed by Bitz and Owen (1981) because, in management, to use those studies would burden the scientists too much. On the other hand, the surveys of the use of information channels, like Shuchman (1981) did, are not useful alone.

In future research on the value of information we suggest more specific goal setting and definitions of what values are actually being studied and measured. Research in the area is certainly needed, but in order to gain more reliable and more easily comparable results the basic approach has to be clearer.

Information is acquired in the form of information products and services. The value of information is fully explicated in its use. This means that the cognitive processes of individuals involved in information tasks, and such issues as time for learning about the use of different types of information, and time for actual use, have to be studied.

It seems that, in practice, a case study approach is the only means at present available for studying the value of information deeply enough. Data have to be collected from information work and individuals performing the work using several collection techniques (interviews, questionnaires, diaries, content analysis, etc.). The model developed in this study has to be applied to other areas, such as company research units and other research organizations. Furthermore, it would be interesting to see how useful the dual approach and the model would be in analyzing the economics and value of information seeking and use in other areas, such as planning, marketing, etc. in the private sector. The success in these areas would mean that we would then be able to give better tools for the managers to monitor the economics and value of information seeking and use than those occasional studies of the economics of individual services which have provided the best results until now. But, at first the managers need to be 'awakened' to the importance of these activities, and here time allocation studies such as those reported in this thesis are surely needed.

Two research ideas have been developed from our studies. The first one deals with the seeking and use of international information in a set of Finnish high tech companies. The basic interest is supposed to focus on the information concerning both marketing and innovations because they both are essential for the success of the companies. The approach developed in our studies at VTT is planned to be used in a modified form: case studies should burden the participating organizations as little as possible. On the other hand, there are needs to deepen our analysis. One particular point for this is in studying more thoroughly the types of information sought and used, and the corresponding time needed. So, the role of time allocation study would be an integrated part of other data collections.

Another idea is to apply our approach in analyzing the information work in public administration. The idea here is to study the information seeking and use behavior of civil servants. The key-tasks of a set of civil servants are planned to be analyzed for developing more effective information seeking and use behavior.

REFERENCES

Allen, T. J., 1977, *Managing the Flow of Technology: Technology Transfer and the Dissemination of Technological Information Within the R&D Organization*, The MIT Press, Cambridge, Massachusetts.

Bitz, A. S., and Owen, B. S., 1981, *An Approach to the Potential Importance of Information in Engineering*, British Library R&D Report 5603, London.

Gralewska-Vickery, A., 1976, Communication and Information Needs of Earth Science Engineers, *Information Processing and Management*, Vol. 12, p. 251.

King, D. W., Griffiths, J.-M., Roderer, N. K. and Wiederkehr, R. R. V., 1982., *Value of the Energy Data Base*, Technical Information Center, United States Department of Energy, Oak Ridge, Tennessee.

Nagus, A. E., 1982, *Repackaging of Engineering Information for Manufacturing Industry*, British Library R&D Report 5725, London.

President's Task Force on the Value of the Information Professional, 1987, *Special Libraries Association 78th Annual Conference*, Anaheim, California, June 10, 1987.

Repo, A. J., 1986, The Dual Approach to the Value of Information: An Appraisal of Use and Exchange Values, *Information Processing & Management*, Vol. 22, No. 5, p. 373.

Repo, A. J., 1987(a), Economics of Information, *Annual Review of Information Science and Technology*, Williams, M. E., ed., Elsevier Science Publishers, Amsterdam.

Repo, A. J., 1987(b), Pilot Study of the Value of Secondary Information: Discussions From the Viewpoints of Information Providers and users, *Aslib Proceedings*, Vol. 39, No. 4, p. 135.

Repo, A. J., 1988, *An Approach to the Value of Information: Effectiveness and Productivity of Information Use in Research Work*, PhD Thesis, The University of Sheffield, Department of Information Studies, Sheffield (manuscript).

Roderer, N. K., King, D. W. and Brouard, S. E., 1983, *The Use and Value of Defense' Technical Information Center Products and Services*, Defense Technical Information Center, Alexandria, Virginia.

Shuchman, H. L., 1981, *Information Transfer in Engineering*, The Futures Group, Glastonbury, Connecticut.

SOFTWARE IMPLEMENTATION AND APPLICATIONS OF THE

GENERALIZED INFORMATION SYSTEM

L. R. Medsker, J. M. Gardner, M. C. Yovits, and
R. M. Kleyle

Indiana University-Purdue University at Indianapolis
Indianapolis, IN 46223

Abstract: We have previously developed a powerful and flexible model to describe information flow based on the concept of a Generalized Information System (GIS). Recently, we have expanded and enhanced the capabilities and understanding of this system. We define information in terms of its effect on the uncertainty in making decisions, and we develop simple, useful relationships and parameters that provide a formal and quantitative framework for describing the flow of information. One new concept is an information measure, which indicates quantitatively the change in a DM's certainty for making a decision after the receipt of a document, message, or other data. Another concept is the information profile, which is a measurable relationship that shows how much a particular document can improve effectiveness of various decision makers. In addition to our interest in establishing the foundation of a general information science, our goals include the development of applications our model to practical situations. We report here on the systematic design and development of software that is being used for simulations of mathematical formulations of our model, for experiments to collect data to test our model, and for the development of applications. A first use of this software is a "game" by which human subjects are presented with problems and are asked to make decisions. This paper describes the software system and prototype experiments.

INTRODUCTION

We have been developing a powerful and flexible model (Yovits, Foulk, and Rose, 1981) based on the concept of a Generalized System (GIS) and have recently expanded and enhanced capabilities and understanding of this system (Yovits and Foulk, 1985; Yovits, de Korvin, Kleyle, and Mascarenhas, 1987(a), 1987(b)). In this model of information flow, we define information in terms of its effect on the uncertainty associated with decision making, and we develop simple, useful relationships parameters that provide a formal and quantitative framework for describing the flow of information. This approach also relates to the effectiveness of decision makers in a particular situation; thus, we also define explicitly and quantitatively the term, decision maker effectiveness (DME).

The GIS model follows from the intimate connection between information and its use by a decision maker (DM) who must choose best course of action (COA) from among many available ones. Information is related to the DM's certainty regarding the choice of a COA, and the certainty is given by the DM's probability distribution for choosing the various COA's. In this model, a DM becomes more effective and more confident by making use of feedback resulting from decisions made.

Of course, in a real situation the DM has access to external input such as documents, messages, and other data, which we treat as sources that give rise to information by changing the DM's internal information state. Part of our recent work (Yovits, de Korvin, Kleyle, and Mascarenhas, 1987(a), 1987(b)), has focused on the relationship between external messages or documentation received by the DM and the feedback results. One important concept is the information profile, which is a measurable relationship that shows how much a particular message or document can improve the effectiveness of various decision makers.

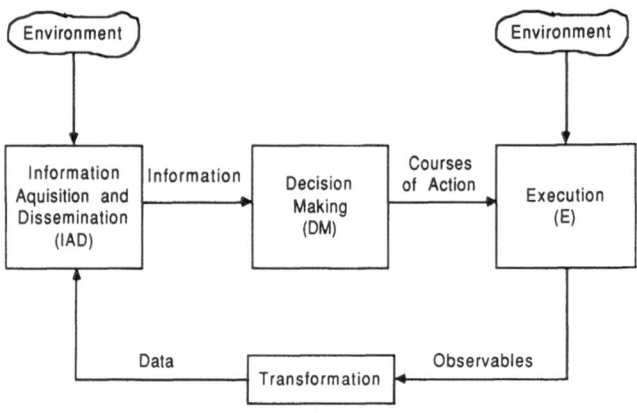

Figure 1. The Generalized Information System Model.

In addition to theoretical interests in establishing the foundation of a general information science, we have developed software that is being used for simulations of mathematical formulations of our model, for experiments to collect data to test our model, and for the development of applications. One use of this software is a "game" by which human subjects are presented with problems and are asked to make decisions. The results will be used to verify and refine our model and to determine actual information profiles.

This article describes our software system for studying the GIS model. A goal has been an experimental design that is sufficiently flexible to allow the measurement of the various quantities in our theoretical work. The results of preliminary experiments show that parameters of our model are significant in describing characteristics of decision makers. We also describe prototype experiment that could show the feasibility of using our software to measure quantities of information that are used by decision makers.

GIS MODEL

Our approach, briefly summarized here, is described in detail in previous work (Yovits, Foulk, and Rose, 1981). We begin with the model of a Generalized Information System (GIS) as shown in Figure 1, which follows from our assumed connection between information and decision making. On the basis of the current assessment of a total situation, the DM tries to make the best choice from among many COA's. As the DM makes more decisions and obtains feedback, the DM becomes more effective and confident, developing a more realistic model of the situation. In addition, external information could modify the DM's decisions, as we have discussed in recent work (Yovits, de Korvin, Kleyle, and Mascarenhas, 1987(b)). To illustrate this model, we have provided examples in Yovits, Foulk, and Rose (1981) of how the model could describe decision making by a physician, economist, farmer, and baker. In our initial approach a closed system (i.e., no external sources), the DM chooses a COA_i with a certain selection probability $P(a_i)$, which is a function of the DM's assessment of the overall worth (which we call the expected value, EV_i) of choosing COA_i. As the DM's effectiveness increases, the probability of choosing the COA with the greatest EV becomes greater until the DM becomes certain about the choice of the best COA. Even though most DM's probably do not actually think in mathematical terms, we believe that our analytical approach is descriptive of the mental models used by DM's, so we utilize it for simplification in establishing relationships about the way information affects decision making. The use of a more complex model of decision making should give similar results on the particular aspect of information usage, which is the object of our work.

When a DM executes a COA, some outcome value results. Choosing any one of, for example, four COA's results in one of four possible outcome values, given in V*, which occur with probabilities given in W*. Thus, the DM has to experiment by choosing various COA's to learn which one is, on the average, the best. The best COA will have the highest actual expected value. However, the DM does not know this value until a sufficient number of choice-feedback cycles allow the DM to become more effective. Until then, the DM has a subjective expected value that approaches the actual limit as time goes on. This limit on expected values is denoted by EV_i^*, where i designates the particular COA. The performance of a DM

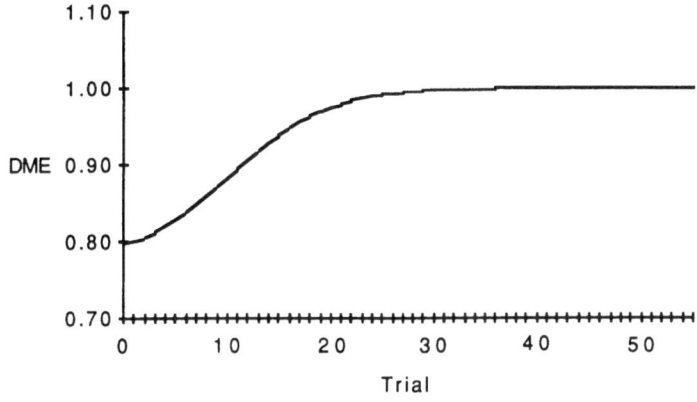

Figure 2. Sample Calculated DME Curve. (For Details of the Calculation and Typical Parameters, see Yovits et al. (1985).

is given by the DM effectiveness, DME, which is a dimensionless quantity that ranges from zero to one. A typical DME curve is shown in Figure 2.

As mentioned earlier, we have related information, denoted by I, to the certainty that the DM has when choosing a COA. This certainty is some function of the DM's subjective probability distribution, which we call the information state. In other articles (Yovits, de Korvin, Kleyle, and Mascarenhas, 1987(a), 1987(b)), we show the functional relationships a) for the case where the set of viable COA's is known, but the relative expected values are not, and (b) where the, possibly many, COA's have not been narrowed down to the ones that are really viable.

External information will have a different effect on DM's with different DME's. Therefore, we have developed a relationship for what we call a document's information profile, which is the change in DME due to the external information. Since DM's with different effectiveness levels may access the same document, this change in DME should be a function of DME (see Figure 3 for a typical profile). We are developing experimental studies in which the DM considers external information such as documents, books, and reports so that we can measure the way it changes the decision maker's effectiveness. In this way, information profiles can be established for specific documents to provide quantitative measures of their usefulness.

THE SOFTWARE SYSTEM DESIGN

An important phase of our research program is the development of software systems for both simulations and experiments that will be needed for further theoretical development and for the study of

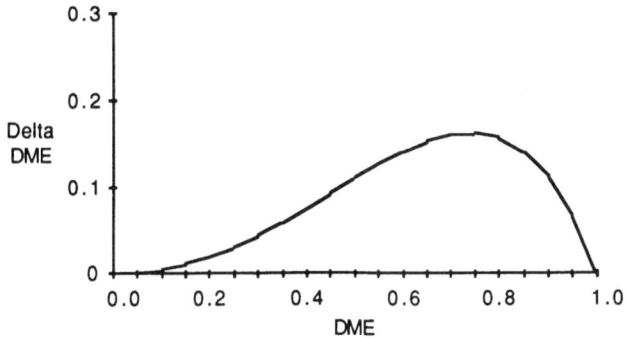

Figure 3. A Typical Information Profile.

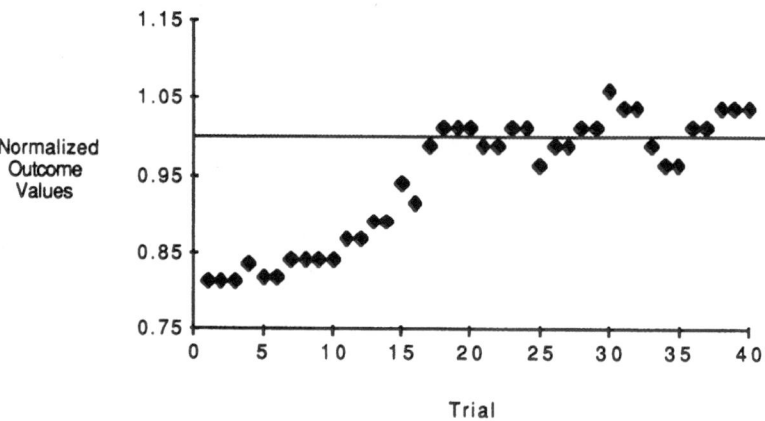

Figure 4. Sample Data on Outcome Values Resulting
From Choices of COA Made by a Subject.

potential applications. We are developing a software system that will provide a framework that will follow the information flow process as described by the GIS model and have tested it against the earlier experimental work of Yovits, Foulk, and Rose (1981).

The systems are being developed in the UNIX environment on an AT&T 3B2 computer. The software development and testing is facilitated by use of the UNIX make utility and the modular design of the system. The software has been designed to provide a flexible, modular system that will allow us to isolate and study certain theoretical points or to collect data on specific aspects of decision making. The system is planned to evolve as additional features are added to our model and to be usable for an extended period. An important design requirement is the ability to readily test new ideas without writing software from scratch. We also intend to use this system as the basis for developing useful applications of our model.

We are currently developing and using fundamental aspects of the software with the aim of expanding the system in three areas: (1) We want to use simulations to provide guidance for the theoretical and experimental work on issues such as the nature of the unstructured region where the DM must learn which of the many COA's are actually viable and worth considering; (2) Among the many application areas, we are exploring ideas in the areas of artificial intelligence and expert systems and in database organization and design using our measure for the value of data to provide a more effective database; and (3) We plan to do experiments to examine in more detail our theoretical results and the significance of the model in real decision making situations.

Our software is the basis for a data collection system that is being used in experiments with real decision makers. This application of our basic system simulates some parts of the decision making environment, but also includes interface modules for input by the DM and for storing and managing the data. Future enhancements will allow interruptions from the information flow and decision making process to ask questions about the DM's strategies and to allow for external sources to be used. Thus, subjects at terminals can receive partial information or clues at controlled points during a session. The experiments described below are prototype studies that will be used to test and modify the experimental design for a larger study.

The human subjects participating in the initial experiments will be staff and students from our department who volunteer to play the "games". The subjects will be given various problems from Yovits and Foulk (1985) via the terminal, some for practice and others so that we can collect data on their decision making processes. The rows of the problem matrices, and, therefore, the COA's, will be changed randomly from one experiment to the next to avoid predictable patterns for the favored COA.

The terminal screens seen by the subjects will be supplemented by verbal explanations by a research assistant. The first screen introduces the subject to the session and collects the identification number, which is also used as the seed in a random number generator. Next, the subject enters the first guess of a COA and then sees the result displayed on the screen. The system chooses a value from those in the row of the matrix V^* corresponding to the COA chosen by the subject. The particular outcome value is randomly selected, but weighted according to the probabilities in matrix W^*. Thus, over enough trials, the subject can learn which COA gives the best overall results. In the last screen, the subject finally decides

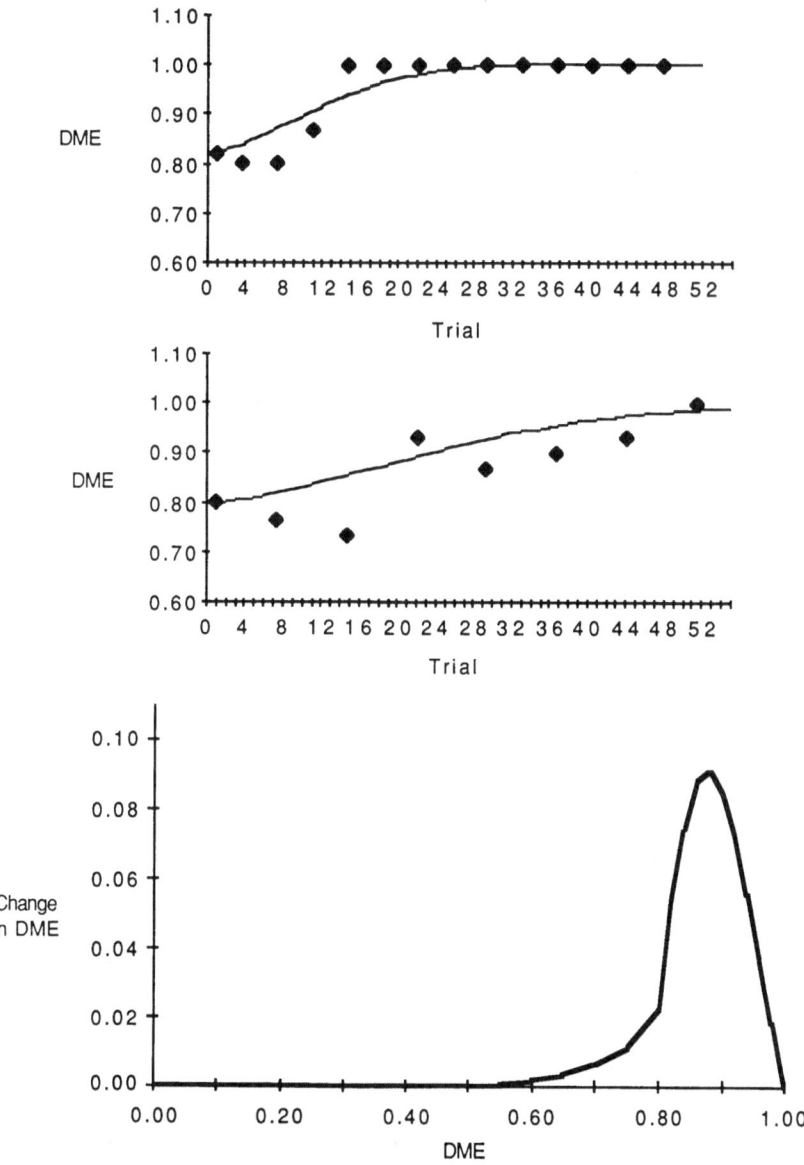

Figure 5. Sample Data for Experiments with Human Subjects. In the First Two Plots, the Subject was/was not, respectively, Given External Information. The Third Plot is Derived From the Fits to Those Data and is the Difference in DME's Over the Range of DME Values.

to choose a COA that is believed to be the best, and the system shows a message to tell the subject if the choice was correct.

In the prototype experiments on the determination of information profiles, subjects who have practiced sufficiently will be given two problems. In the first, they are given one using a fairly difficult matrix. In the second, which is actually the same problem with rows in a different order, they are given the hint that a particular COA is not good. The comparison of their decision making performance in these two situations will form the basis for generating an experimental information profile and demonstrating the feasibility of the data analysis technique.

SAMPLE RESULTS

The results of an experimental session is a series of (COA, outcome value) pairs as a function of trials by the subject. The outcome values for the same choice of COA can be different due to the statistical nature of the problem (as given in the matrix W'). Figure 4 illustrates this point, showing normalized outcome values from a sample experiment. In this display, data are averaged over sequences of four COA's. Note that even after the best choice of COA is found, further selections of that COA (from simulations) give fluctuating outcome values for the reason explained above.

The sample data were analyzed by first plotting the experimental DME values as a function of trial. The DME's were found by considering sequential sampling groups of (e.g., four) COA's and calculating a selection probability distribution from the fractions of 1's, 2's, 3's, and 4's chosen in that sample. The experimental DME was then derived from the expression

$$DME_{expt} = \sum_{i=1}^{m} P_{expt}(a_i) \ EV_i^* / EV^* (\max)$$

where $EV^*(\max)$ is the largest of the EV's among the various COA's.

As can be seen in Figure 5, the DME data shows the general features predicted from the model, as shown by the solid curves. From the best fits to the data for experiments with and without external information, we can see that the DM's performance improved when the hint was given. Although this would be expected, the point of these feasibility experiments was to develop the data collection and analysis techniques. In further experiments, more interesting and significant external sources will be used for generating information profiles. The result of the prototype experiment is the profile curve in Figure 5, which gives the difference in DME as a function of DME.

SUMMARY

We have designed experiments to study and modify our experimental software and our procedures for measuring the use of information by decision makers. We are currently refining the interface to human subjects, determining the best experimental procedure, and developing a data analysis technique that will allow us to derive experimental information profiles.

Future work is planned to collect significant amounts of data in experiments with human decision makers so that profiles can be determined for various types of external sources. We aim in this way to show the usefulness of our model and associated concepts and parameters in real situations.

REFERENCES

Yovits, M. C., and Abilock, J. G., 1974, A Semiotic Framework for Information Science Leading to the Development of a Quantitative Measure of Information, *Information Utilities, Proceedings of the 37th ASIS Annual Meeting*, Vol. 11, Atlanta, Georgia.

Yovits, M. C., Foulk, C. R., and Rose, L. L., 1981, Information Flow and Analysis: Theory, Simulations, and Experiment, Part I. Basic Theoretical and Conceptual Development, Part II. Simulation, Examples, and Results, *Journal of the American Society for Information Sciences*, Vol. 32, pp. 187-210.

Yovits, M. C., and Foulk, C. R., 1985, Experiments and Analysis of Information Use and Value in a Decision-Making Context, *Journal of the American Society for Information Sciences*, Vol. 36, pp. 63-81.

Yovits, M. C., de Korvin, A., Kleyle, R., and Mascarenhas, M., 1987(a), Information and Its Relationship to Decision Making: The Information Profile and Other Quantitative Measures: A Brief Summary, *Proceedings of Third Symposium on Empirical Foundations of Information and Software Science*, Plenum Publishing Corp., Denmark, pp. 231-241.

Yovits, M. C., de Korvin, A., Kleyle, R., and Mascarenhas, M., 1987(b), External Documentation and Its Quantitative Relationship to the Internal Information State of a Decision Maker: The Information Profile, *Journal of the American Society for Information Science*, Vol. 38, No. 6, pp. 405-419.

V. MODELING HUMAN-MACHINE INTERACTION

BUILDING A USER MODELLING SHELL

Dianne Murray

Division of Information Technology and Computing
National Physical Laboratory
Teddington
United Kingdom. TW11 0LW

Abstract: Previous research into the specification and implementation of an Embedded User Model (EUM) within a number of small adaptive systems has lead to the recognition of the need for a software toolkit for constructing such models. This "User Modelling Shell" is similar to the concept of an Expert System Shell and will provide both generic and individual user models suitable for different types of interaction and application.

A description of the requirements of a User Modelling Shell is presented, together with consideration of the form of the EUMs themselves. The practical issues which present themselves include the question of where to site the User Model within either a general User Interface Management System or within certain system architectures; that of which type of user features can be modelled in an appropriate form; the problems of eliciting user information, and the evaluation both of the User Modelling Shell and the adaptive systems themselves.

INTRODUCTION - WHY WE NEED ADAPTIVE SYSTEMS

The human interface to a computer system is not only manifest at the physical level of screen and display or input, and output medium, but also at the wider levels of the 'environmental context' and 'cognitive ergonomic' interaction. Table 1, based upon a table presented by Rasmussen (1987) shows five broad levels of interaction in Human-Computer systems:

Table 1

Levels of Abstraction

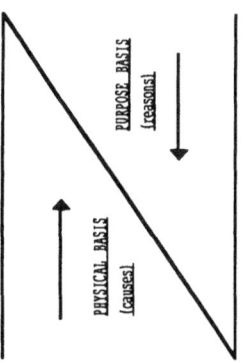

FUNCTIONAL PURPOSE
System and user goals, intentions.

ABSTRACT FUNCTION
Task structure; work organisation.

GENERALISED FUNCTION
Applications and functions.

PHYSICAL FUNCTIONS
Screen displays; I/O devices.

PHYSICAL FORM
Ergonomic and environmental setting.

Empirical Foundations of Information and Software Science V
Edited by P. Zunde and D. Hocking, Plenum Press, New York, 1990

209

Table 2

Categories of Adaptivity (Edmonds, 1987)

	On Request	Prompted	Automatic
Common User Errors			√
User Characteristics		√	√
User Performance	√	√	
User Goals	√	√	
Information Environment	√		

A human-computer dialogue can cover interaction aspects such as the manner in which information is arranged, presented, and modified by a set of application programs or the style of the interactive dialogue between user and system, including that of the interpretation of user errors and unexpected actions.

One way in which to deal with different physical environments and individual requirements is to provide a 'customizing' facility or 'adaptable interface' which provides either the user or the system with the ability to alter and tailor facets of system behavior such as command sets, default settings or error responses. These can be modified to suit an individual's personal preference or can be fixed at preset levels. An extension of customization is the provision of an 'adaptive interface' which provides the system with an integrated knowledgebase about both individual and generic users. This feature enables an inference engine within the computer system to make decisions on the basis of user behavior and characteristics and to alter aspects of the interaction style and features to meet more closely the task and personal needs of specific users. Systems which can amend their user knowledge base, dynamically alter interactions on the basis of dynamic information, and modify their own behavior as a co-operative rational 'other agent' or a dialogue partner are 'self-adaptive systems'.

Both the feasibility and characteristics of this type of system have recently been investigated (Benyon, Innocent and Murray, 1987; Benyon, Murray and Milan, 1987; Benyon and Murray, 1988) while others have identified taxonomies of adaptivity (Totterdell et al., 1987; Edmonds, 1987). Edmonds has drawn up a categorization of current adaptive responses in which he distinguishes between 'on request'; 'prompted' and 'automatic' adaptation to user actions and characteristics, and to environmental features, as in Table 2 presented above.

Table 3

Levels of Adaptivity (Totterdell et al., 1987)

Level 1 Systems - produce a change in output in response to a change in input.

Level 2 Systems - include an evaluation function which selects from a range of possible outputs.

Level 3 Systems - include a mechanism for monitoring the effect of the selected strategy on the environment and altering the evaluation function appropriately.

Level 4 Systems - possess an internal model of the environment in addition to an evaluation function and use the predictive capability of the model to select an appropriate response.

Level 5 Systems - inherit knowledge from previous generations and adapt before they come into existence.

Table 4

Adaptivity in HCI Systems

	Customizable (Level 1)	Adaptable (Level 2, 3)	Adaptive (Level 3, 4)
Physical Form	✓		
Physical Functions	✓	✓	
Generalized Function	✓	✓	
Abstract Function		✓	✓
Functional Purpose			✓

Totterdell et al. (1987) have identified five levels of adaptivity which range from systems which include evaluative and monitoring features to those which include a model of the environment, a predictive capability and a knowledge-inheritance mechanism, as in Table 3.

Merging these two with the HCI aspects identified earlier, it appears that Level 4 self-adaptive systems can provide automatic adaptation to the generalized information (but not the physical) environment and to user goals at the levels of Functional Purpose and Abstract Function. Level 5 systems are akin to cybernetic entities which have their own goals and can act as autonomous rational other agents (Kiss, 1987). A new taxonomy is presented in Table 4.

All life encompasses change and users of a computer system are always, in one sense, learners - skills are constantly being developed and new facets of applications or other ways of achieving a task are recognized. Even 'expert' users can hone their actions as they practice a routine cognitive skill. The provision of adaptive computer systems should benefit all types of user since the interface to the application being used will be tailored to individual requirements, skills and preferences. This is quite different from current approaches to systems design which requires human adaptation to the conventions of an inflexible and pre-specified interaction paradigm. In general, systems which could be customized or given an adaptive capability are public information systems such as databases, interactive media systems and electronic mail, or are interfaces to standard generic applications. Those which can be made adaptive are the class of co-operative 'intelligent advisers' such as tutoring systems, natural-language dialogue interfaces, intelligent help systems, co-operative expert systems, advanced programming environments and multiagent multi-user systems.

One means of providing generic and customizable interfaces to public information facilities is through the use of an individual database (held in a 'smart card' or a portable disk) which contains profile data about a user. This personal profile could drive a number of computer interactions through a customized interface, operating within the mechanisms to be discussed later in this paper.

MODELS FOR ADAPTIVE SYSTEMS

User Models

An adaptive interface requires a 'User Model' of an individual user's behavior, responses and intentions in order to provide data for evaluative functions and its predictive capacity. In order to adapt at an affective and cognitive level, this model should contain some weighted data on personal 'cognitive' features as demonstrated by both overt and implied behavior. Further user details could be inferred from patterns of usage and log sequences or could be explicitly provided by profile information.

Such information would be used as data for a system's model which would be of a similar construction to the inference engine of an expert system, encompassing production rules and an evaluative function as in the Level 4 systems identified earlier. This model will drive and amend the interaction and the interface features presented to the user, based on personal and behavioral information derived from a profile and by continually monitoring the interaction - making predictions of users' intentions and comparing actual performance against what is known about the user's skills and natural preferences.

Models which enable adaptive interactions are termed 'Embedded User Models' or EUMs (Murray, 1987; 1988). They are a class of User Model holding information about user characteristics or about the behavior of an individual when using an interactive computer system. This knowledge is used to provide adaptivity, either by intervention or by co-operative agreement with a user. In contrast to other 'mental' models or designers' models, which are intangible and implicit, EUMs are explicit representations of user features and decisions and can be instantiated as part of system software or as a feature of a User Interface Management System (UIMS).

A 'User Profile' holds relevant details and user information in a form to be updated and removed at the end of a session. It feeds parameters to the system-maintained dynamic models at the onset of an interactive session and provides data for a Shared Knowledge Base accessible to all models.

Other explicit models which are required to provide adaptivity and adaptability are those concerned with managing the user interface and the interaction with an application package. These are 'Application' and 'Expert Models' and are discussed below.

Application Models

If the set of interactions throughout a system is regarded as involving three co-operating processors (the human, an interface processor and a task processor), both task and interface processors can function as forms of User Models. The task and dialogue can be further separated to provide an Application Expert' based upon the user's view of the semantics of the application. A model of the task must be derived from the system designer, or from some expert, in which case the type of Application Model described by Alty and McKell (1986) in a co-operating architecture appears suitable. The role of the former is to guard the application, to provide a filter for an input and dialogue controller, and to act as a source of advice and guidance for a User Model (i.e., to provide an 'expert' view of the application).

The Application Model can be expanded within the context of a Supervisory Control System. Alty and Mullin (1987) review methods of achieving functional separation of interface features so that sets of actions can be logged, different dialogue sequences provided and dialogue changed without altering the application code. Decisions about different users are given to the User Model and decisions on task-specifics and inter-dependencies are the province of the Application Model. Interface presentation details are the responsibility of a Presentation System.

The functions of the various parts of the system are shown below:

- *Presentation System*
  Responsible for interface actions and hardware-dependent operations, controlling the physical realization at the interaction level.

- *Application Model*
  Explicit task representation.

- *Dialogue System*
  Controls communications between all modules and contains general information about objects and presentation styles, together with application-dependent knowledge.

- *User Model*
  Advisor to the Dialogue System on interaction or tutorial style, accessing knowledge of specific users. Plan interpreter mapping onto actual application realizations.

Alty and Mullin discuss the provision of additional facilities such as context-specific help and conclude that the Dialogue System interacts with more than one Application Model. Internal and external Application Models may be supplemented by a model specifically related to operator conversations with the system. They propose application-dependent 'Dialogue Assistants' whose function is to converse with the internal models but which are also capable of monitoring output from the User Model in order to fulfill user plans and goals.

Tutoring System Models

Another distinct set of system models which provide mechanisms for both monitoring and assessing user actions comes from work on Intelligent Tutoring Systems (ITS). The rationale of computer-based teaching systems is that, for given student and subject situations, a computer system can control for the variance of human teaching and can determine how to provide individualized instruction in a constrained subject domain.

In order to reduce the gap between a user's knowledge state and the codification of some expert's knowledge, or 'goal state', the ITS must be able to distinguish between a number of domains, especially that of domain-specific expertise and that of tutorial strategy. ITS are intelligent systems which must be able to reason;   to recognize errors and misconceptions;   to monitor and intervene when necessary at

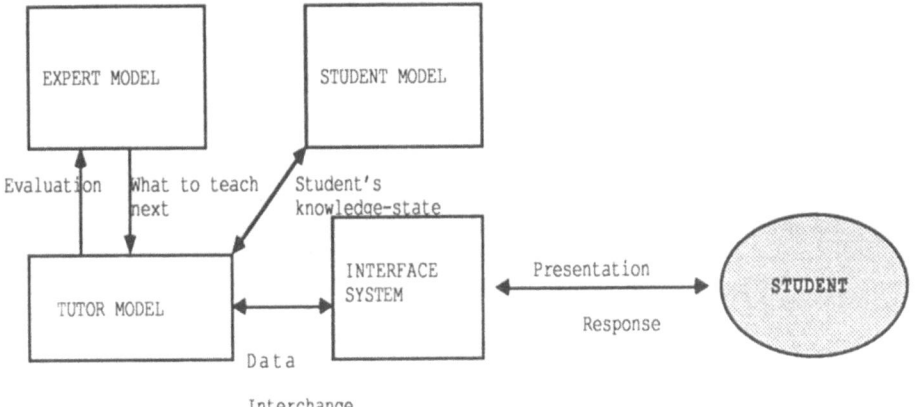

Figure 1. Constituents of Intelligent Tutoring Systems.

different levels of explanation; and to generate problems on a given set of instructional guidelines.

To fulfill these requirements they must have a number of distinct features as shown below, some of which bear a great resemblance to the requirements for adaptive systems identified in Table 3:

- The subject domain should be structured as a knowledge-base;

- Tutorial strategies should exist as a separate rule-base operating on this knowledge-base;

- The student's state of knowledge must be represented in some form;

- There must be some evaluative function;

- The interaction must be dynamically generated, not pre-defined;

- The interface must be coherent to the student.

These functions can be combined in a number of ways and in different architectures, but all have the same basic components, which is shown diagrammatically in Figure 1.

The 'Expert Model' is a representation of the knowledge to be imparted to the student, together with the explanatory facility for remedial intervention. It may also contain an error recognition and evaluation feature, and a problem-solving model (these features may also be sited in sub-models, or as part of the Tutor Model, or as separate elements).

The 'Tutor Model' arranges for the particular teaching strategy, initiates remedial actions, and monitors and assesses performance in conjunction with the evaluative function. Problem-generation from the knowledge-base will offer a sequence of problems, adapting the difficulty level on the basis of previous performance, but will also present new problem classes and review or practice already known items.

The 'Interface Controller' arranges the relevant output and accepts student input. The 'Student Model' holds the representation of the Student's current knowledge-state.

Student Models

As Sleeman and Smith (1981) indicate, Student Models have a number of requirements: they must be executable and predictive; they must be able to be easily changed in order to show developments in learning stages; they must have some algorithm for tackling problem-solving, and they must be readily appreciated by participants.

The distinction between a Student Model and other types of model hinges on the use to which the model is put, its location within the UIMS and relationship to the Interaction Models (Application Models and Dialogue Filters). The purpose of the model is at issue here. A Student Model contains a history of task performance and some very specific representation of the state of that individual's knowledge in a specific subject area. Some of this may be held in the form of a User Profile and can have other uses in CBT management and score-keeping.

Models for Adaptive Systems: Summary

The various types of model which have been identified are all necessary to build a realistic adaptive system with a workable Embedded User Model. They will have to cooperate in a dynamic fashion after inheriting or accepting data from a shared knowledge-base and will all operate on different aspects of user information. To do so, they must be distinguished in some way from each other and Table 4 offers some definitions.

The architecture of systems with Embedded User Models is discussed in detail in the next section of this paper and some of the methods of operation and data to be operated upon are presented.

HOW WILL ADAPTIVE SYSTEMS WORK?

The User Profile

This model deals with features such as influences on user behavior which could be of the following type:

- Social/attitudinal aspects;

- Skills and domain knowledge;

- Task Perception;

- System Experience;

- Past history; and

- Constraints.

More specific and detailed information about individuals could take the form of:

- Static personal features (age, sex etc.);

- Past inputs, usage history and user log (possibly based on statistical methods and standard distributions);

- Management information

  - domain-specific details
    (scores, interrupted log etc);

  - generic 'relevant' background and skills
    (some derived from the current interaction session,
    some from user histories);

- Background computing experience;

- General task or application skills and experience;

- Application-specific skills and experience;

- Individual preferences for screen layout and interaction modes;

- Volatile personal, affective and conative information to feed the Embedded User Model.

The Embedded User Model

Since this information predicts user behavior when working with an interactive computer system or within a specific task environment, it requires a more rigorous definition. It is, however, closely allied to the task and domain area and is likely to be a volatile target necessitating experimental investigation (see Benyon and Murray, 1988; Murray and Benyon, 1988 for a discussion of these issues).

An example of the difficulties which can be encountered is the issue of *cognitive style* (Fowler and Murray, 1987) which can reside in both models, and is seen as pertaining to learning characteristics and modes of information integration. A Profile feature could emphasize the gross differentiation between broad and generalizable ways of solving problems in order to modify the overall display parameters. A feature in the EUM could use this data to generate questions in keeping with an individual's preferred problem-solving strategy as matched against dynamic inferences made about the consistency or validity of that strategy. Another potentially important facet of individual variation is that of learning style, investigated by van der Veer et al. (1985) and van Muylwijk et al. (1983) on educational projects in the Netherlands into the provision of better individually-tailored interfaces. A number of other aspects of cognitive function have been suggested as parameters to amend the human-computer interface and a list is presented below:

- learning style (van der Veer et al., 1985)

- cognitive style (Fowler and Murray, 1987)

- spatial ability (Vicente and Williges, 1987)

- task/system expertise (Fowler et al., 1987)

- short-term memory (Benyon, Murray and Milan, 1987)

- learning strategy (Neal, 1987)

- risk-aversion (Neal, 1987)

- levels of attention and confidence, aggressivity in tool use (Neal, 1987).

While specific values and scores could be given to each of these features, they are probably better instantiated in an AI knowledge representation schema and controlled by production rules. If values are a suitable representation then one possible implementation strategy is that of 'stereotypes', as in the GRUNDY model (Rich, 1979). Stereotypes represent a structured collection of traits or characteristics, stored as facets, to which is attached a value, a confidence-level and rationale. Some traits are triggers and have an attached probability rating which can mediate or inhibit firing of a whole stereotype.

- Stereotypes can, therefore, model canonical users on a variety of dimensions, and can move between individual stereotypes (also called the 'User Synopsis') either on the basis of confidence levels or with some form of conflict resolution or other agent's goals recognition strategy.

While many issues in using stereotypes need to be tackled, notably that of the spread of activation and the precise means of conflict resolution, it would seem to be the most useful technique investigated so far. The differentiation between Embedded User Models and User Profiles', and a description of the different forms of data which each could hold, together with distinct functions and purpose, as presented in Table 5, would be feasible within such a structure. The separable systems architecture which this would entail is presented in detail in the next Section.

REPRESENTATIONAL ASPECTS

There are a number of possible ways of describing both student and expert knowledge states. Strategies include those for modelling of the task, the user, and the level of tutorial assistance required. A classification of the types of representation has been drawn up by Goldstein (1979).

The 5-way classification is as follows:

- *symbolic* (explanatory and descriptive 'glass-box' techniques) versus *quantitative* (predictive 'blackbox' techniques);

Table 5

Contents and Purposes of Models

Model Type	Purpose	Contents
Embedded User Model	Assess user status Determine interaction parameters	User characteristic
Student Model	Represent Student knowledge-states	Knowledge-base
User Profile	Provide customization Arrange tailored start-up interface Feed data to EUM and Shared Knowledge Base	Personal information
Tutor Model	Interpret user actions Assess extent of 'learning' and determine next move Direct progress on basis of feedback from other models	Strategy rule-base
Expert Model	Hold embedded "goal-state"	Knowledge-base
Application Model	Filter for separable functions in UIMS Communications Controller	Task and Communication details

- *performance* (user sampling by monitoring, statistical analysis or recording collective expertise) versus *cognitive and symbolic* (models elicited and used in Knowledge Engineering);

- *skilled* (behavioral, measured by standard of performance) versus *unskilled* (erroneous performance and buggy models in genetic graph representations);

- *static* (differential subset of an expert model within a closed-world assumption) versus *dynamic* (as in plan and goal recognition);

- *single* versus *composite*.

These can all be represented in a variety of forms such as finite automation overlay, skill and buggy models; graphs, trees and networks; adaptive and self-improving or game-playing procedures; AI-based planning techniques, frames and scenarios; goal-recognition and explanation-based methods; stereotypes, or skill, knowledge and population characteristics including canonical models and double or multiple stereotypes.

In particular, some techniques and mechanisms for assessing student knowledge states, expertise and learning behavior and for providing evaluative functions can be illustrated:

- Measure against set questions and examples;

- Express knowledge through the level of application of sub-problems or concepts when answering questions (represented by values derived from a function and equivalence classes, or in matrix form);

- Roughly measure 'understandability' as an approximation on the problem;

- Evaluate by summing the cost functions associated with various transformations and the operations performed in order to reach a given solution;

- Generate problems in the type of rule to be applied and within the user's difficulty level;

- Model explanation as a frame-based representation;

- Production rules simulating problem-solving (e.g., general, specific, correct or deviated).

A relevant line of research is that of 'High-Level Dialogues' (Kiss, 1986, 1987) in identifying three dimensions of HCI which are pertinent to this discussion:

- Cognitive (pertaining to psychology, AI and cognitive science);

- Conative (pertaining to goals and plans);

- Affective (pertaining to other agents).

Basic questions relating to identification of user goals are in the scope and possible extent of the goals identified, together with the available user plans. Such plans will be based upon the primitive actions underlying goals and will be expressed in some specific manner. Both the language formalism used to communicate user goals to the system, and the system's mechanisms for reasoning about user goals within a given representation schema are issues which must be addressed at the outset when specifying the system to be implemented.

If a User Model is regarded as an autonomous other agent, then the question arises of how best to assist that user, by *teaching* (i.e., acting autonomously FOR the user), or *telling* (i.e., acting cooperatively WITH the user). Extensions to this distinction highlight problems of dialogue management and legality or permissibility. A User Model, if it is an agent, must have goals and must hold a relationship with the user. Such a relationship may be one of indifference, of conflict, or of cooperation. Autonomy and rationality are necessary and desirable to provide 'intelligent assistants'. They would undertake the delegation of tasks. This, however, raises problems in the area of control. In an adaptive system, or any interface achieving customization, both agents' needs and requirements have to be communicated over a period of time, or over a number of distinct sessions.

PROGRAM FOR A USER MODELLING SHELL

A two-year project to produce a development environment for the creation and testing of Embedded User Models within the types of system identified earlier has just started. The systems developed will be tested as prototypes to allow in-depth exploration of the mechanisms and capabilities of adaptive interfaces, and to identify and quantify the problems of introducing adaptivity into real-life human-computer interfaces.

The areas of difficulty met with so far have been in eliciting domain knowledge from experts and in representing knowledge about the user in some realistic and workable manner. What is now required is a means of enhancing user modelling expertise with a tool which can assist in the design of adaptive interfaces. A User Modelling Shell is being designed and will be built as part of a toolkit for constructing EUMs through elicitation of both designer's and user's knowledge of an individual's conative and affective characteristics.

It is intended to produce software which can act as a specific EUM for a particular application requirement within the general architectural outline indicated. It will thus, also, function as a designer's tool (Murray and Benyon, 1988) to enable early prototyping and iterative design practices to be applied to the construction of customizable and adaptive interfaces driven by a model of the user. It will also have the

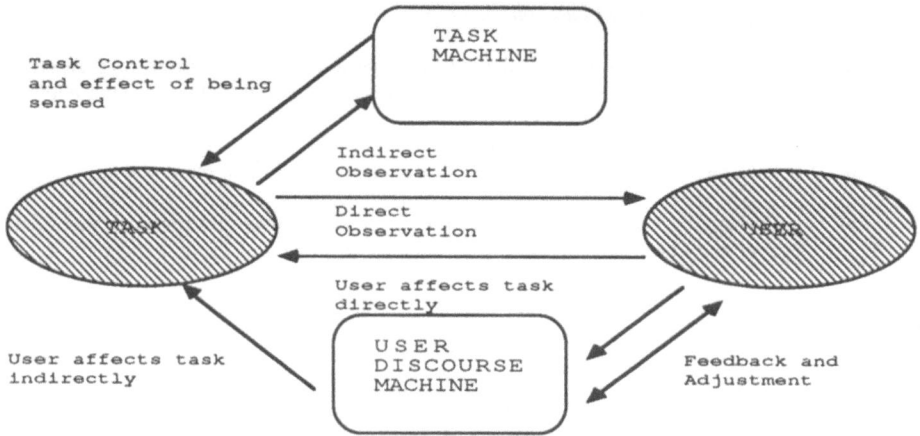

Figure 2. User Discourse Machine.

capability of providing generic user models suitable for different types of interaction or a range of applications.

Although investigations of aspects such as cognitive style (Fowler and Murray, 1987) and personal characteristics (Benyon, Murray and Milan 1988) have been undertaken, the relationship between those identified as meriting attention and the humancomputer interaction aspects is poorly understood. Experimental work does not easily generalize to other areas, and the measurement of such characteristics is fraught with argument and discrepancies. One important issue is to isolate some characteristics or combination of characteristics which are
salient to HCI or to a class of interactions in general.

Suitable features are those which significantly affect the success of the interaction of intermediate or discretionary classes computer users; those which can be inferred or otherwise elicited from the user in an unobtrusive way, and those which can be used to dynamically adapt the interaction to provide more suitable dialogue for that individual.

Aspects of individual cognitive style will be pursued with emphasis on how this can be represented in a form which is subtle enough to provide a basis for adaptivity. At present HCI guidelines distinguish only crude classes of users such as novices and experts - this will be extended to take account of individual, identifiable and measurable HCI guidelines. Experimental work will be targeted to the elicitation of empirical evidence, and to act as demonstrators for the knowledge elicitation and representation raised during the development of the User Modelling Shell and will follow the broad lines described in an earlier Section.

Evaluation of the developed systems at all stages, including that of early evaluation of designs will be essential. Evaluation methodologies have been developed in another project and will be tested against the prototypes from this project. In this situation, they are based upon psychologically-derived techniques which are also employed as Knowledge Elicitation strategies (Howard and Murray, 1987(a), 1987(b); Hart, 1986) or upon developments in Multi-Dimensional Scaling in order to maintain a close coupling with the AI aspects of building a User Modelling Shell.

OUTLINE ARCHITECTURE

A possible architecture for an adaptive system to be built with such a User Modelling Shell and which incorporates the various models discussed earlier is presented in Figure 3. It has as a basis a 3-way model of Human-Computer Interaction, as in the Figure 2, as originally described by Card (1984). It is a triple-agent model which can provide adaptivity and customization at the automatic and prompted levels and comprises two intelligent agents (the User and the System). Both hold models of the other agent and engage in cognitive, conative and affective goal-directed interactive conversations based on joint access to shared task description.

The outline for a system with an Embedded User Model expands upon this and takes the form of a schematic diagram. It is still in the process of further refinement and, as such, open to further refinement.

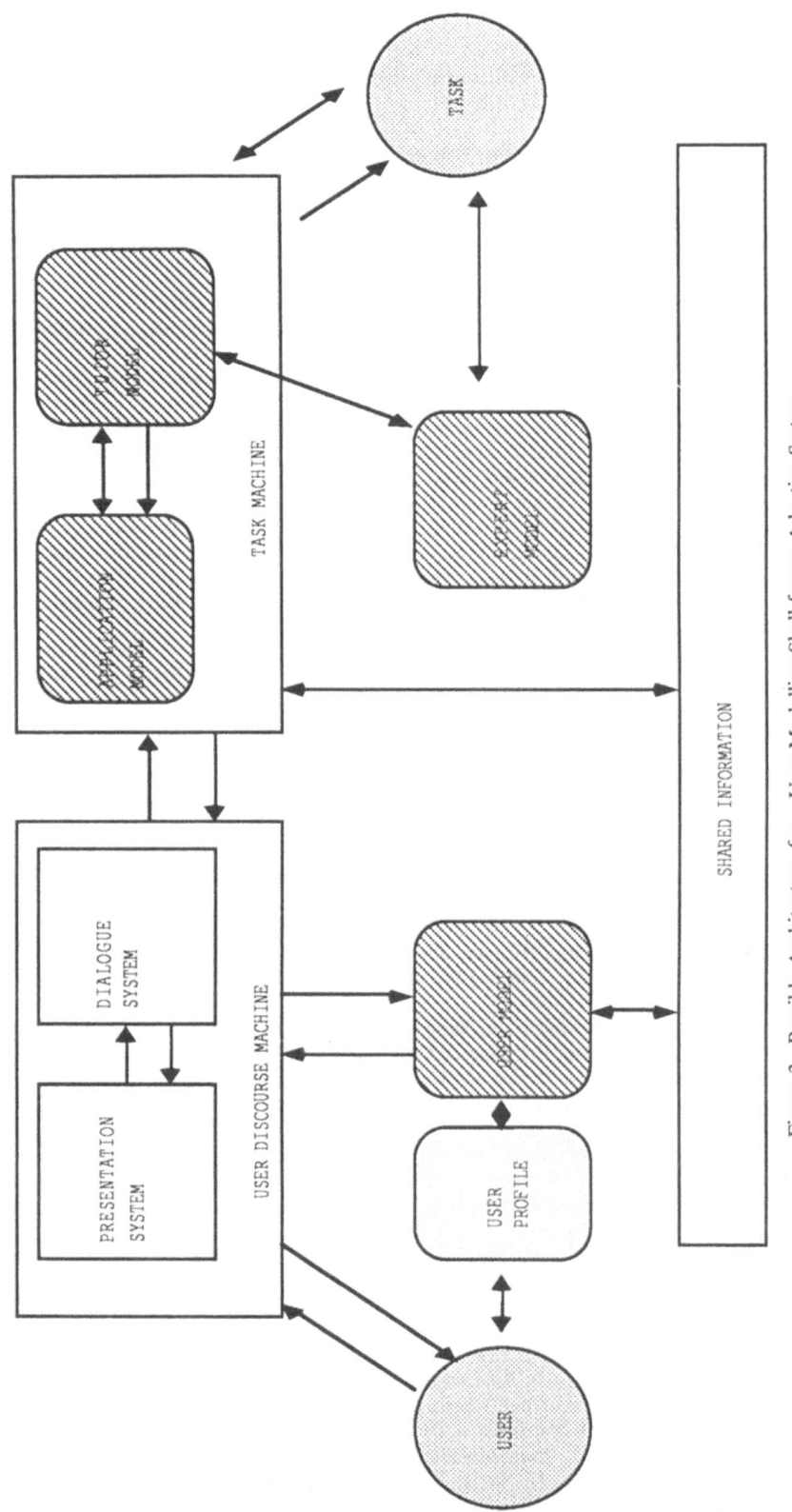

Figure 3. Possible Architecture for a User Modelling Shell for an Adaptive System.

219

REFERENCES

Alty, J. L., and McKell, P., 1986, Applications Modelling in a User Interface Management System, *People and Computers: Designing for Usability*, Harrison, M. D., and Monk, A. F., eds., Cambridge University Press, London.

Alty, J. L., and Mullin, J., 1987, The Role of the Dialogue System in a User Interface Management System, *Proc. Interact '87, Second IFIP Conference on Human-Computer Interaction*, Bullinge, H-J., and Shackel, B., eds., North Holland, Amsterdam.

Benyon, D., Innocent, P., and Murray, D. M., 1987(a), System Adaptivity and the Modelling of Stereotypes, *Proc. Interact '87, Second IFIP Conference on Human-Computer Interaction*, Bullinge, H-J., and Shackel, B., eds., North Holland, Amsterdam.

Benyon, D., Murray, D. M. and Milan, S., 1987(b), Modelling Users' Cognitive Abilities in an Adaptive System, *Proc. 5th Symposium EFISS*, Risø National Laboratory, Denmark, November 1987, Rasmussen, J., and Zunde, P., eds., Plenum Publishing, New York, in press.

Benyon, D. and Murray, D., 1988, Experiences with Adaptive Interfaces, *Computer Bulletin*, Vol. 30, No. 3.

Card, S. K., 1984, Human Factors and the Intelligent Interface, *Combining Human Factors and AI: A New Frontier in Human Factors*, Kohl, G., and Nassau, S. S., eds., Proc. Symposium sponsored by the Metropolitan Chapter of the Human Factors Society, New York, November 15th, 1984.

Edmonds, E. A., 1987, Adaptation, Response and Knowledge, *Knowledge-Based Systems*, Vol. 1, No. 1.

Fowler, C., and Murray, D. M., 1987, Gender and Cognitive Style Differences at the Human-Computer Interface, *Proc. Interact '87, Second IFIP Conference on Human-Computer Interaction*, Bullinge, H-J., and Shackel, B., eds., North Holland, Amsterdam.

Goldstein, I., 1979, The Genetic Graph: A Representation for Procedural Knowledge, The Evolution of Procedural Knowledge, *Int. Journal of Man-Machine Studies*, Vol. 11.

Hart, A., 1987, *Knowledge Acquisition for Expert Systems*, Kogan Page, London.

Howard, S. and Murray, D. M., 1987(a), A Taxonomy of Evaluation Techniques for HCI, *Proc. Interact '87, Second IFIP Conference on Human-Computer Interaction*, Bullinge, H-J., and Shackel, B., eds., North Holland, Amsterdam.

Howard, S. and Murray, D. M., 1987(b), *A Survey and Classification of Evaluation Techniques for HCI*, NPL DITC Report 94/ 87, National Physical Laboratory, Teddington.

Kiss, G., 1986, *High-Level Dialogues in MMI: Final Report on the Alvey Survey Project*, The Alvey Directorate, London.

Kiss, G., 1987, Contribution to: M. Cooper and D. Dodson, eds., Alvey Knowledge-Based Systems Club, Intelligent Interfaces Special Interest Group, *Proc. of the Second Intelligent Interfaces Meeting, May 28-29th 1987*, London.

Murray, D. M., 1987, Embedded User Models, *Proc. Interact '87, Second IFIP Conference on Human-Computer Interaction*, Bullinge, H-J., and Shackel, B., eds., North Holland, Amsterdam.

Murray, D. M., 1988, *A Survey of User Modelling Definitions and Techniques*, NPL DITC Report, National Physical Laboratory, Teddington.

Murray, D. M., and Benyon, 1988, Models and Designers' Tools for Adaptive Systems, presented at 4th European Conf. on Cognitive Ergonomics, Cambridge, UK, September 1988.

Neal, L. R., 1987, Cognition-Sensitive Design and User Modelling for Syntax-Directed Editors, *Human Factors in Computing Systems and Graphics Interface*, Carroll, J. M., and Tanner, P. P., Proc. CHI+GI '87, ACM.

Rasmussen, J., 1986, *Information Processing and Human-Machine Interaction*, North-Holland.

Rich, E., 1979, User Modelling Via Stereotypes, *Cognitive Science*, Vol. 3.

Sleeman, D., 1985, UMFE: A User Modelling Front-End System, *Int. Journal of Man-Machine Studies*, Vol. 23.

Sleeman, D. and Smith, M. J., 1981, Modelling Student's Problem Solving, *Artificial Intelligence*, Vol. 16.

Totterdell, P. A., Norman, M. A., and Browne, D. P., 1987, Levels of Adaptivity in Interface Design, *Proc. Interact '87, Second IFIP Conference on Human-Computer Interaction*, Bullinge, H-J., and Shackel, B., eds., North Holland, Amsterdam.

Van der Veer, G. C., Tauber, M., Waern, Y. and van Muylwijk, B., 1985, On The Interaction Between System and User Characteristics, *Behavior and Information Technology*, Vol. 4, No. 4.

Van Muylwijk, B., Van der Veer, G. C., and Waern, Y., 1983, On the Implications of User Variability in Open Systems, *Behavior and Information Technology*, Vol. 2, No. 4.

Vicente, K. and Williges, R.C., 1987, Visual Momentum as a Means of Accommodating Individual Differences Among Users of a Hierarchical File System, *Proc. 5th Symposium EFISS*, Rasmussen, J., and Zunde, P., eds,. Risø National Laboratory, Denmark, (Plenum Press, in press).

EVALUATION OF HUMAN-COMPUTER INTERFACE DEVELOPMENT TOOLS:

PROBLEMS AND PROMISES

Deborah Hix

Virginia Tech
Department of Computer Science
Blacksburg, VA 24061

Abstract: The computer industry has seen an explosive emergence of user interface management system (UIMS) toolkits in the last few years. However, there are no standards for the components of such toolkits, and no procedure for systematically evaluating or comparing these toolkits. With their proliferation, *ad hoc* evaluations and comparisons are constantly being done, without a formal, structured approach.

This paper will describe several of the problems involved in developing an evaluation procedure for UIMS, and will report on research that is showing promise as an evaluation procedure that produces quantifiable criteria for evaluation and comparing UIMS. Such a procedure could be used, for example, for choosing a UIMS for a particular human-computer interface development environment.

The procedure we have developed generates ratings for two dimensions:

- Functionality of the UIMS being evaluated, and
- Usability of the UIMS being evaluated.

Functionality refers to what the UIMS can do; that is, what interface styles, techniques, and features it can be used to produce. Usability refers to how well the UIMS does what it can do in terms of ease of use (a subjective, qualitative rating of how easy the UIMS is to use) and human performance (an objective, quantitative rating of how efficiently the UIMS can be used to perform a task).

A significant by-product of this research is a practical taxonomy of types of human-computer interfaces, including interaction styles, features, and hardware, in addition to a taxonomy of types of interface development support provided by UIMS, and general characteristics of UIMS.

1.   INTRODUCTION

1.1 Motivation For An Evaluation Procedure For Human-Computer Interface Development Tools

The computer industry has seen an explosive emergence of interactive tools for human-computer interface development in the last few years. Such tools are the focus of intense interest in both the research and commercial arenas. However, there is no extant procedure for systematically evaluating or comparing these tools. With their proliferation, ad hoc evaluations and comparisons are constantly being done, but without a formal, structured approach.

There are numerous problems associated with performing valid and reliable evaluations of such tools. This paper discusses these problems and why they make development of a structured evaluation procedure so difficult. It concludes by reporting on research that is showing promise as an evaluation procedure that produces quantifiable criteria for evaluating and comparing human-computer interface development tools. Results of an empirical pretest of this procedure indicate that it has potential for providing valid and reliable results across different tools and different evaluators. This work is ground-

Empirical Foundations of Information and Software Science V
Edited by P. Zunde and D. Hocking, Plenum Press, New York, 1990

221

breaking research, representing one of the first attempts to produce a structured, quantitative approach to the evaluation of human-computer interface development tools.

1.2 Related Work.

Development of procedures for evaluating other kinds of software has preceded our work. For example, a methodology for standardized evaluation of text editors was based on classification of possible editing tasks, as well as both quantitative and qualitative evaluation of dimensions such as time to perform tasks, error costs, learning time, and functionality (Roberts and Moran, 1983). Validation has been done both through their own use of the methodology and through replication studies (Borenstein, 1985). A methodology for evaluation of software packages, particularly commercially available systems, based on criteria such as performance documentation, and support, has also been developed and successfully used (Cohill, Pilitsis, and Gilfoil, 1988).

2. PROBLEMS IN EVALUATING HUMAN-COMPUTER INTERFACE DEVELOPMENT TOOLS

A surprising number of problems arise when one attempts to develop a formal, structured evaluation procedure for human-computer interface development tools.

2.1 Definition of a Human-Computer Interface

At the heart of the difficulty of developing an evaluation procedure for human-computer interface development tools is the central problem of determining "what is a human-computer interface?". Such terms and acronyms as *human-computer interface, user interface, human-computer dialogue,* and simply *dialogue* are used relatively interchangeably in this fast-growing area. Some define the dialogue to be just the two-way flow of symbols between human and computer, while others define it to include the hardware (input/output) devices as well. Behavioral scientists sometimes refer to cognitive aspects -- what the human is thinking -- and/or gestural aspects -- what the human is doing -- of human-computer interaction. In this paper we shall use the term *human-computer interface* to refer to the two-way flow of symbols (the communication) between human and computer, as well as all hardware devices and (non-application) software that support this communication. This interface typically does not, especially from a computer science viewpoint, include cognitive or gestural activities.

2.2 Definition of a Human-Computer Interface Development Tool

If the terminology for what is occurring when a human uses a computer is confusing, then the terminology for the software that allows development of this human-computer interface is impossible. A plethora of terms has emerged, including *user interface development tools* or *user interface development toolkits, user interface development environments, human-computer interface development environments,* and -- probably the most prevalent -- *user interface management systems* or *UIMS*. As with the "interface versus dialogue" ambiguity, there has been a "tool versus toolkit versus UIMS" ambiguity. A *tool* generally refers to anything from a complete interface development environment to a single library routine for a specific interface feature, while a *toolkit* now is generally accepted to be a library of callable program routines to produce low level interface features. A UIMS is an integrated set of high-level interactive programs for designing, prototyping, executing, evaluating, and maintaining human-computer interfaces. However, there seems to be a trend away from use of the term UIMS, with its implication of more functionality than many of these tools provide. In this paper we shall use the phrase *human-computer interface development tool* as the more general term to refer to these design-time/run-time software systems for developing human-computer interfaces.

2.3 Classification of Standard Tool Components

Because it is difficult to define what a human-computer interface is, it is therefore difficult to determine what the components of tools for developing that interface should be. There is, in fact, no clearly identified set of interface classes that such tools should be able to produce. Such a classification would encompass all kinds of styles, interaction techniques, and features that could exist across all interfaces. It would include all possible hardware -- both input and output -- devices. In addition to simply being able to produce all kinds of interfaces, a tool should afford some development support and guidance for its user. Such support would include prototyping capabilities within the tool, help and documentation for using the tool, and even automated project management. Finally, there are general desirable characteristics of human-computer interface development tools, such as integration and consistency across the entire tool and reusability of parts of the interface produced using the tool. Establishing a classification structure within which to perform the evaluation is itself a non-trivial task, given the amazing variety of "things" found in interfaces and interface development tools.

2.4 Salient Dimensions for Evaluation

Determining salient dimensions for evaluating and comparing human-computer interface development tools is another critical problem. If reasonable evaluation criteria are not chosen, the procedure for evaluation will not produce useful results. Possibilities for dimensions include:

- functionality of the tool,
- usability (ease of use) of the tool,
- ease of learning the tool,
- user performance (time to perform tasks) with the tool,
- errors made using the tool,
- system performance (run-time speed) of the tool,
- documentation (both on-line and hardcopy) for the tool,
- available support (service) for the tool, including upgrades,
- cost of the tool, and
- hardware upon which the tool runs.

Several of these dimensions are especially difficult to deal with. For example, functionality measures the number of interface styles, features, techniques, devices, and so on, that a tool can produce. However, as discussed above in Section 2.3, there is no classification of all the styles, features, and devices that are currently found in interfaces, nor the kinds of support and general characteristics that are desirable in such tools. Determining what level of detail to include in the functionality structure is also difficult; too high a level gives too little discriminating power and too low a level can overwhelm with details. As another example, usability is a poorly understood aspect of evaluation in the human-computer interaction area. Usability is sensitive to the skill level of the user (or evaluator) of the tool, the environment within which the tool will be used (or evaluated), the task/application domain, and so on. Including ease of learning as a dimension necessitates training tests, considerably lengthening the tool evaluation process. Similarly, run-time performance of the tool is a problematic dimensions, since such measurements are very difficult to obtain and are host system dependent. Further, the important issue is the tool user's (or evaluator's) overall perception of the run-time performance. A tool with slow response will indirectly show up in usability ratings. Even interactions among dimensions can cause unexpected problems. For example, it might be possible to directly compare functionality scores across several tools, but not usability scores. In order to compare usability scores across several tools, those tools must have identical functionality. That is, they must do exactly the same things -- a very unlikely occurrence. Comparing usability scores across several tools out of context from functionality scores can be dangerous.

2.5 Measurability and Quantifiability of Results of Evaluation

Closely related to selection of salient dimensions for evaluation is how to measure and quantify those dimensions. In particular, removal of subjectivity is important. Measuring usability is still generally an unsolved problem in the human-computer interaction field. Measuring usability, of necessity, requires the evaluator to make a subjective rating of the tool's usability. Subjective data can be very valuable. However, the potential exists for inconsistent data if evaluators are not provided with clearly, consistently defined rating scales for a usability dimension. A numerical scoring technique, for example to provide sums and averages that have meaning, is also desirable. The numerical results need to have discriminating power; that is, significant differences in tools should be reflected in the results. Putting metrics on the various evaluation dimensions is a non-trivial problem.

2.6 Establishing a Core Set of Functions

Often evaluation procedures include use of a core set of functions. For a particular type of tool, that core set would represent basic interface functions that such a tool should be able to produce -- without which a tool cannot accomplish "useful work". Producing such a core set for human-computer interface development tools would require a great deal of empirical work, observing numerous varieties of human-computer interfaces and tools to determine those "things" that occur most frequently.

2.7 Specification/Implementation Techniques

Human-computer interface development tools use a wide variety of techniques for specification and implementation of human-computer interfaces. These techniques include writing various kinds of programming code, using linguistically-based notations, developing graphically-based representations, and using direct manipulation of symbols to specify and implement an interface. Some tools may use more than one of these types of techniques. The "flavor" of the tool is heavily influenced -- as it may be its learnability and usability -- by the type of specification and implementation techniques it uses.

2.8 Acquisition of Human-Computer Interface Development Tools

It is essential for valid and reliable results that the software and hardware under evaluation be available for extended "hands-on" use by the evaluator. Any attempt to collect data that could be determined from sources such as marketing glossies, demonstrations, videotapes, and documentation will likely be unsatisfactory; without the "real thing" (actual software and hardware), information obtained from such sources cannot be verified. While some inferences about some dimensions such as functionality and usability can be made from these sources alone, the results of an evaluation procedure are most useful only when they are produced as a result of "hands-on" experience with the tool being evaluated. However, a "catch-22" situation can arise in the case of comparative evaluation of tools, with a goal of selecting one of them for a particular environment: the tool cannot be adequately evaluated without acquiring it, but one does not initially know which tool to acquire. Costs for human-computer interface development tools vary dramatically, and can be quite high.

2.9 Inherent Complexity

Human-computer interfaces are inherently complex; therefore, human-computer interface development tools are inherently complex software systems. Using such a tool, the variety of tasks that can be performed is large and difficult, and few events occur often enough to obtain reliable measures, posing a problem in comprehensively evaluating the tool.

2.10 Selection of Evaluators

An appropriate evaluator is needed for performing the evaluation procedure. But the proper type of person can be hard to find. This person should be someone who uses these types of tools and is familiar with several of them, if possible. Such a trained, experienced person will, for example, be more likely to give reliable, consistent usability ratings. An evaluator should be able to exhibit, perhaps through performance of some baseline tasks using the tool(s) being evaluated, a minimal measurable level of expertise with each tool under evaluation.

2.11 Magnitude of the Evaluation Effort

Related to the selection of evaluators is the magnitude of the effort involved in a formal, complete evaluation of a human-computer interface development tool. The process is costly, involving an appropriately experienced person for a significant amount of time.

2.12 Environment Sensitivity of the Evaluation Procedure

Some dimensions for evaluation can be environment-sensitive. That is, the environment in which a particular tool is to be used can influence the type of tool best suited for that environment. For example, a tool that can produce interfaces that use a mouse seems to be mandatory in most common human-computer interface environments, but would not be as necessary for an interface being developed for a low-gravity situation in which a mouse might be less desirable. This problem suggests that appropriate dimensions be adjustable for environment sensitivity.

2.13 Acceleration of Technological Advances

The speed with which technological advances are occurring in the human-computer interface realm can render an evaluation procedure for tools worthless even before it has been shown to be useful. An evaluation procedure should, therefore, be easily adaptable and extensible to new interaction styles, techniques, features, devices, and so on.

2.14 Evaluation of the Evaluation Procedure

As discussed earlier (in Section 1.2), procedures have been successfully developed and applied to evaluation of other kinds of software (e.g., text editors). However, little research has been done in the area of evaluation of human-computer interface development tools. As such procedures are developed, in order for them to be scientifically sound, they must be shown to produce reliable (replicable) and valid results. Statistically determining reliability and validity of an evaluation procedure is a lengthy, time-consuming process involving use of the procedure with a variety of tools and a variety of evaluators.

3. PROMISES FOR EVALUATING HUMAN-COMPUTER INTERFACE DEVELOPMENT TOOLS

We have developed an evaluation procedure that results in quantifiable criteria for evaluating and comparing human-computer interface development tools. The goal of such a procedure is to provide valid and reliable numeric data through a standardized technique for evaluation and comparison. Such data could be used, for example, for choosing a tool for a particular human-computer interface development environment. It is important to remember that this procedure has been developed to evaluate human-computer interface development tools, and not the human-computer interfaces that they produce.

3.1 Overview of The Evaluation Procedure

The evaluation procedure we have developed revolves around "hands-on" use of the tool to be evaluated. First, the tool(s) must be acquired. After learning the tool, the evaluator completes a lengthy (28 page) detailed form that is organized around two dimensions: *functionality*, which refers to what the tool can do (what interface styles, techniques, and features it can be used to produce) and *usability*, which refers to how well the tool does what it can do, in terms of ease of use (a subjective, qualitative rating of how easy the tool is to use) and human performance (an objective, quantitative rating of how efficiently the tool can be used to perform a task). The evaluator then performs calculations (using an automated spread sheet that exactly reflects the evaluation form) to determine summary scores, and transfers these scores to an executive summary section. Finally, if desired, the evaluator performs benchmark interface development tasks, completing the evaluation. An important feature of the evaluation procedure is a detailed glossary of definitions for every item in the evaluation form, as an aide in reducing ambiguity and interpretation of terms across evaluators.

The functionality dimension is divided into three areas: *types of interfaces* this tool can produce, including interaction styles (e.g., menus, forms, typed string inputs, and windows), features of interfaces (e.g., animation, adaptive dialogue, types of navigation, defaults, graphics, spelling checking, and so on), and all sorts of hardware (I/O) devices; *types of support* provided for using this tool and for supporting the general process of interface development (e.g., rapid prototyping, evaluation, access to a database management system, interface libraries, help, documentation, and so on); and *general characteristics* of this tool, such as consistency, integration, and reusability of interface components.

The usability dimension is measured with two methods: *subjective evaluation* measures ease of use for each of the three areas of the functionality dimension (i.e., the evaluator indicates on the form, for each function the tool can produce, whether the tool was hard, adequate, or easy to use to produce that function); and *objective evaluation* measures human performance using a set of suggested benchmark interface development tasks that can be customized as needed for a particular interface environment.

For the types of interfaces the tool can produce, the evaluator also indicates the primary type of specification/implementation technique the tool uses to produce individual functions. Techniques from which the evaluator can choose include *textual language coding*, such as with a conventional programming language or specialized dialogue language; *direct manipulation* of objects or graphics; and *other techniques* such as manipulation of tables, rules, or form-filling.

3.2 Output of the Evaluation Procedure

Several numbers result for each tool that is evaluated using this procedure. A *functionality rating (percentage)* is an indicator of the number of functions the tool provides. For example, a functionality rating of 85% indicates that the tool supports 85% of the functions listed in the evaluation form. A *usability rating (percentage)* is an indicator of the ease with which supported functions can be produced with the tool being evaluated. A usability rating of 32% would be low, indicating that a tool is rather difficult to use. A *specification/implementation technique rating (percentage)* is an indicator of the degree to which a specific technique is used in the tool as the mechanism for producing the various functions of an

225

2.14 Evaluation of the Evaluation Procedure

As discussed earlier (in Section 1.2), procedures have been successfully developed and applied to evaluation of other kinds of software (e.g., text editors). However, little research has been done in the area of evaluation of human-computer interface development tools. As such procedures are developed, in order for them to be scientifically sound, they must be shown to produce reliable (replicatable) and valid results. Statistically determining reliability and validity of an evaluation procedure is a lengthy, time-consuming process involving use of the procedure with a variety of tools and a variety of evaluators.

3. PROMISES FOR EVALUATING HUMAN-COMPUTER INTERFACE DEVELOPMENT TOOLS

We have developed an evaluation procedure that results in quantifiable criteria for evaluating and comparing human-computer interface development tools. The goal of such a procedure is to provide valid and reliable numeric data through a standardized technique for evaluation and comparison. Such data could be used, for example, for choosing a tool for a particular human-computer interface development environment. It is important to remember that this procedure has been developed to evaluate human-computer interface development tools, and not the human-computer interfaces that they produce.

3.1 Overview of The Evaluation Procedure

The evaluation procedure we have developed revolves around "hands-on" use of the tool to be evaluated. First, the tool(s) must be acquired. After learning the tool, the evaluator completes a lengthy (28 page) detailed form that is organized around two dimensions: *functionality*, which refers to what the tool can do (what interface styles, techniques, and features it can be used to produce) and *usability*, which refers to how well the tool does what it can do, in terms of ease of use (a subjective, qualitative rating of how easy the tool is to use) and human performance (an objective, quantitative rating of how efficiently the tool can be used to perform a task). The evaluator then performs calculations (using an automated spread sheet that exactly reflects the evaluation form) to determine summary scores, and transfers these scores to an executive summary section. Finally, if desired, the evaluator performs benchmark interface development tasks, completing the evaluation. An important feature of the evaluation procedure is a detailed glossary of definitions for every item in the evaluation form, as an aide in reducing ambiguity and interpretation of terms across evaluators.

The functionality dimension is divided into three areas: *types of interfaces* this tool can produce, including interaction styles (e.g., menus, forms, typed string inputs, and windows), features of interfaces (e.g., animation, adaptive dialogue, types of navigation, defaults, graphics, spelling checking, and so on), and all sorts of hardware (I/O) devices; *types of support* provided for using this tool and for supporting the general process of interface development (e.g., rapid prototyping, evaluation, access to a database management system, interface libraries, help, documentation, and so on); and *general characteristics* of this tool, such as consistency, integration, and reusability of interface components.

The usability dimension is measured with two methods: *subjective evaluation* measures ease of use for each of the three areas of the functionality dimension (i.e., the evaluator indicates on the form, for each function the tool can produce, whether the tool was hard, adequate, or easy to use to produce that function); and *objective evaluation* measures human performance using a set of suggested benchmark interface development tasks that can be customized as needed for a particular interface environment.

For the types of interfaces the tool can produce, the evaluator also indicates the primary type of specification/implementation technique the tool uses to produce individual functions. Techniques from which the evaluator can choose include *textual language coding*, such as with a conventional programming language or specialized dialogue language; *direct manipulation* of objects or graphics; and *other techniques* such as manipulation of tables, rules, or form-filling.

3.2 Output of the Evaluation Procedure

Several numbers result for each tool that is evaluated using this procedure. A *functionality rating (percentage)* is an indicator of the number of functions the tool provides. For example, a functionality rating of 85% indicates that the tool supports 85% of the functions listed in the evaluation form. A *usability rating (percentage)* is an indicator of the ease with which supported functions can be produced with the tool being evaluated. A usability rating of 32% would be low, indicating that a tool is rather difficult to use. A *specification/implementation technique rating (percentage)* is an indicator of the degree to which a specific technique is used in the tool as the mechanism for producing the various functions of an interface. A typical result might be that object manipulation is used 62% of the time for producing interface. A typical result might be that object manipulation is used 62% of the time for producing interfaces, and textual programming used the remaining 38% of the time. Unfortunately, because of space limitations, detailed examples of real data must be omitted. There are, however, some partial results given in Section 4.4.

A completed evaluation report consists of the following parts:

- A *general description* of the tool being evaluated;

- Information about *sources* used in preparing the evaluation;

- An *executive summary* of the summary functionality and usability ratings for each of the three main parts -- types of interfaces, types of support, general characteristics -- of the form;

- A *detailed evaluation* of functionality and usability dimensions for each of the three areas, which is used to compute the summary functionality and usability ratings; and

- A *glossary* that contains definitions of every item in the form.

4.   RESULTS OF PRETESTING THE EVALUATION PROCEDURE

In order to begin determining the efficacy of our work in evaluating human-computer interface development tools, we conducted a preliminary test of the tool evaluation procedure, using it to evaluate three different tools. The goals of this test were not actually to evaluate the tools, but rather to "debug" the evaluation procedure, to obtain an indication of whether the procedure provides useful information (a validity check), and whether it provides consistent results (a reliability check).

4.1 Method

Copies of the evaluation form were distributed to three members of our Dialogue Management Project research group. These evaluator subjects have each been active researchers in human-computer interaction, particularly in the area of tools, for more than three years. The tools that were evaluated were Apple Macintosh's *HyperCard*, Telerobotic's *CourseBuilder*, and Dan Bricklin's *Demo* Program. First, the evaluators completed evaluation reports for their randomly assigned systems. Then, we performed a between-evaluator comparison of results to determine what the between-evaluator differences were (how consistent the final ratings were for the same tool across different evaluators). Finally, all evaluators were interviewed to determine what problems they had encountered while using the procedure, to determine what caused between-evaluator differences, to discuss whether or not they considered the tool evaluation results useful and trustworthy, and to see what they felt the results meant.

4.2 Reported Results

Evaluator subjects reported that they spent from six to eight hours learning each of the tools, and two to three hours completing the evaluation form and its calculations. Evaluators felt that the results fairly presented the capabilities of the tools, and that the executive summaries provided useful information. They were also pleasantly surprised that the comparison of different evaluators' numeric results across different tools showed remarkable agreement.[1] All felt the form provided a structured, consistent mechanism for both evaluating human-computer interface development tools and presenting results for those evaluations.

Examination of evaluation details revealed several instances where one evaluator marked a function "not possible" while a different evaluator marked it otherwise. Upon questioning the evaluators, this turned out to be due to different interpretations of the definition of the particular function, and, interestingly, to evaluator differences in expertise with the tool. That is, one evaluator found a way to produce a particular function using the tool, while the other evaluator did not. There was somewhat greater variation in the usability ratings than in the functionality ratings.

---

[1] These numeric data, even when condensed, are too voluminous to present here. They are available in their entirety in Hix (1987). Partial results are presented in Section 4.4.

4.3 Conclusions and Discussion

These between-evaluator results were substantially more similar than we expected. We anticipated the possibility of quite discrepant numerical results across different evaluators for the same tool, since this was the first time the evaluation procedure had been used. However, *results of our preliminary test comparisons indicate that this procedure for evaluating human-computer interface development tools has potential for providing valid and reliable results across different evaluators.*

During analysis of the between-evaluator results, we found two major causes of discrepant final ratings:

- Differences in interpretation of definitions in the glossary, and
- Differences in expertise level of different evaluators in using the same tool.

Differences in interpretation of definitions leads to two main conclusions: details in the glossary must be expanded, and the need for evaluator training must be explored. Differences in expertise level can be mitigated by making comparisons across different tools based on only one evaluator's results. When this is not feasible, the conclusion is that evaluators should be consistently trained to a predetermined level of proficiency. However, producing such a training session is itself a major undertaking.

4.4 Example: Interpretation of Results

In order to show how output of our evaluation procedure can be interpreted and used to choose a tool for a particular environment, we will present a hypothetical example comparing three tool evaluations. Several assumptions[2] will be made for this example:

- The evaluation procedure produces valid and reliable results,
- A difference of 10 percentage points is significant for functionality ratings, and
- A difference of 20 percentage points is significant for usability ratings.

In addition, requirements for selecting a tool for our hypothetical environment include:

- The chosen tool must be capable of producing menus, forms, and simple typed input,
- The chosen tool must be easy to use, and
- Use of the chosen tool must require only minimal textual programming skills.

The first step in the selection proces is to quantify these criteria. We will do this by arbitrarily choosing the following ratings to satisfy, respectively, each of the three requirements:

- A minimum functionality rating of 50% for menus, forms, and simple typed input;
- A minimum overall usability rating of 50%; and
- Less than one-third of a tool's functions must be programmed textually.

We can now compare the three tools evaluated in our preliminary tests using actual evaluation results to make our comparisons. Figure 1 presents the necessary information, extracted from the appropriate executive summaries.

Comparison of functionality ratings. We see immediately that CourseBuilder cannot generate forms, while HyperCard and Demo satisfy the 50% functionality requirement for forms. Thus, we eliminate CourseBuilder from the set of alternatives. HyperCard can generate more kinds of menus and forms than Demo can and the difference in the appropriate functionality ratings are more than 10%. They both have identical functionality ratings of 25% for generating typed input, failing our functionality requirement of 50% for typed input. This is because the final rating is calculated using all individual items found under the typed input category. Since our requirement was only for simple typed input, we must look at the detailed portion of the evaluation form. This shows that the 25% rating is the result of each tool being capable of generating simple typed input, which satisfies that part of our functionality criterion. Thus, from these results, we can say that HyperCard is functionally superior to Demo, at least according to the requirements we set forth.

---

[2]It must be understood that these are assumptions and are not claims that can be made about our evaluation procedure. The ability to provide such claims is a large part of our current research.

	MENUS	FORMS	TYPED INPUT	TEXTUAL PROGRAMMING
HyperCard				
functionality	90%	75%	25%	29%
usability	70%	93%	67%	
CourseBuilder				
functionality	80%	0%	75%	0%
usability	100%	Not applic.	78%	
Demo				
functionality	80%	50%	25%	0%
usability	58%	50%	67%	

Figure 1. Actual Partial Final Functionality and Usability
Ratings for the Three Tools Used in the Pretest.

Comparison of usability ratings. A comparison of the usability ratings reveals that HyperCard is considerably easier to use for producing menus and forms (both these exceed our 20% different requirement) than Demo. They have identical usability for producing simple typed input. Interestingly, note that CourseBuilder has higher usability ratings than either HyperCard or Demo for both menus and typed input. Thus, if the selection requirements had been different (e.g., favoring usability over functionality or with a less stringent functionality requirement for forms), CourseBuilder might not have been eliminated so quickly.

Comparison of textual programming requirements. Our results show that Demo requires no textual programming whereas HyperCard requires textual programming skills 29% of the time. Our selection criterion states that a textual programming rating of less than 33.3% is acceptable, so both HyperCard and Demo satisfy this requirement. (So, would CourseBuilder, too, had we not already eliminated it from consideration).

Final decision. HyperCard has higher functionality and usability ratings than Demo, and fall within the acceptable limit of required textual programming effort. Thus, we would recommend HyperCard as the more appropriate tool, given the assumptions and selection requirements stated at the beginning.

5. SUMMARY AND FUTURE RESEARCH

We have discussed numerous problems involved in developing a structured, formal procedure for evaluating human-computer interface development tools. We have also presented an evaluation procedure that attempts to overcome some of these problems. It produces quantifiable ratings for the functionality and usability of such a tool. We have pretested this procedure using three evaluator subjects and three tools, and the results are promising -- enough so that we have made revisions to the procedure and are currently conducting a formal empirical study involving different human-computer interface development tools and more evaluator subjects to determine statistically whether the results of the procedure are indeed valid and reliable.

Our evaluation procedure is ground-breaking research, representing one of the first attempts to produce a structured, quantitative approach to the evaluation of human-computer interface development tools. Our goal is that this embryonic research will eventually result in a rigorous, trusted methodology for evaluating human-computer interface development tools. We have just begun understanding the real problems and promises involved in developing such a methodology.

ACKNOWLEDGEMENTS

The author would like to thank members of the Dialogue Management Project who participated in this research, especially Dr. H. Rex Hartson, Antonio Siochi, Eric Smith, and Matt Humphrey. Andy Cohill also provided valuable input during the early stages of its development. JoAnne Lee Bogner helped greatly with formatting of the manuscript. This research was funded by the Software Productivity Consortium and the Virginia Center for Innovative Technology.

REFERENCES

Borenstein, N. S., 1985, The Evaluation of Text Editors: A Critical Review of the Roberts and Moran Methodology Based on New Experiments, *Proceedings of the CHI '85 Conference*, San Francisco, CA, April 1985, pp. 99-105.

Cohill, A. M., Gilfoil, D. M., and Pilitsis, J. V., 1988, Measuring the Utility of Application Software, *Advances in Human-Computer Interaction*, Volume 2, H. R. Hartson and D. Hix,, eds., Ablex Publishing Corp., Norwood, NJ, pp. 128-158.

Hix, D., 1987, *An Evaluation Procedure for Human-Computer Interface Development Toolkits*, VPI&SU Department of Computer Science Technical Report, October 1987.

Roberts, T. L., and Moran, T. P., 1983, The Evaluation of Text Editors: Methodology and Empirical Results, *Communications of the ACM*, Vol. 26, No. 4, April 1983, pp. 265-283.

MODELLING HUMAN MACHINE INTERACTION: TECHNIQUES FOR

PREDICTION OF PERFORMANCE

Ömer Akin, Professor

Department of Architecture
Carnegie-Mellon University
Pittsburgh, PA 15213

Abstract: Human computer interaction (HCI) is an integral part of computer programming (CP). Viewing computer system design as an integrated process including both HCI and CP, it is possible to advance the quality of satisfaction of users with computer systems. Key issues in HCI design include specification of system performance expectations, analysis of performance prediction during design, and analysis of system performance after implementation. In current HCI literature, these issues have given rise to several methods of specification and prediction of system performance after implementation. In current HCI literature, these issues have given rise to several methods of specification and prediction of system performance. These methods fall under three categories: keystroke models, unit-task models and simulations. The advantages and disadvantages of these three categories of methods are discussed and contrasted.

ISSUES OF SYSTEM DESIGN

A central ingredient of system design is to provide a functionality for performing a set of tasks at a certain level of proficiency. This functionality has two principal ingredients. One is the performance of the desired task by the computer. And the other is the enabling of the user to direct the computer to perform the task in a manner that is compatible with his needs. The former function is generally considered as the essence of computer programming (CP), and the latter the essence of human computer interaction (HCI).

As system designers configure computer programs they also shape, advertently or inadvertently, the HCI aspects of the system and vice versa. Decisions made in the interest of one can make it easy or difficult to deal with the other. Often the choices to be made present obvious tradeoffs between goals related to task functionality versus graceful interaction of systems and users.

Consequently, the other central ingredient of system design has to do with designing for performance at a certain level of proficiency for a certain group of users. Basically, there are two major categories under which user skills are calibrated, ergonomic or motor-perceptual and cognitive requirements of users. The former deals with the efficient and stress-free use of the computer and its peripherals in performing tasks (Roberts, 1979). The latter deals with the compatibility of the agreement between the cognitive models of the user and the structure of the program at the user's disposal (Black and Sebrechts, 1981; Norman, 1983).

HCI is a difficult aspect of any system design, even in cases where there is adequate attention paid to these issues. One reason for this is that the dynamics between the user and the system, both at the motor and cognitive levels, is difficult to predict. As is the case in other real world systems, there are too many factors to take into account during the design stage. Furthermore, as the users begin to interact with implemented systems, adaptation to the new situation may result in the modification of the user's normal behavior. This introduces behaviors initially unexpected by system designers, and, thus, problems not initially part of design intentions.

Empirical Foundations of Information and Software Science V
Edited by P. Zunde and D. Hocking, Plenum Press, New York, 1990

231

ISSUES OF HUMAN-COMPUTER INTERFACE DESIGN

The principal goal of HCI design then is to manipulate the compatibility of user parameters and system features to minimize the aberrations that are possible, probable or manifest due to use. This occurs during three distinct design related activities: 1) specification of performance expected from a new system based on evaluation of existing systems; 2) analysis of performance prediction during the initial design phase; and 3) analysis of performance in existing systems.

The first activity is the prevalent form of HCI research. The majority of studies analyzing a form of user interface deal with studying an existing system and developing strategies for future systems which concern a similar set of tasks, users or functionalities -- for example, file transactions (Hayes, 1984), file management (Akin, Baykan, and Rao, 1988), text editing (Card, 1978; Roberts, 1979), error messages (Brown, 1983), and a mail system (Akin and Rao, 1985).

The second activity is less common, primarily due to the difficulty of evaluating a system during design, that is before it is operational, with any degree of accuracy. The options in this category include prediction of performance based on simulations (Akin, Lai, and Rao, 1988; Card, 1978), productions systems (Reisner, 1981) and analytical "keystroke" models (Card, Moran and Newell, 1979).

The third activity has traditionally led to the development of front end systems specialized in HCI problems. The obvious difficulty of this approach is that the CP and HCI are not integrated and, consequently, inefficiencies in system design are inevitable. Some of these front ends are envisioned as remedies to existing programs (Hayes, 1984) and others as universal front ends for large classes of systems (Hayes and Szekely, 1983; Moran, 1978).

DESIGN PROCESS MODELS

Prediction of user interaction during the design activities outlined above naturally requires different models and methods of analysis. Let us summarily review some of the critical phases of design and implementation where some of these methods of specification and prediction have been used.

Specifying Performance Expectations

This is one of the most ill-structured stages in HCI design. Most researchers rely on general knowledge and experience in specifying the initial expectations for a system's interface function. Miller (1979) emphasizes the importance of the task and its goals and refers to the tradeoffs necessary between economic, psychological and cost variables in order to optimize the performance of a given system. Moran (1978) in his discussion of CLG (Command Language Grammar) stresses the design of the user interface as the mediator between the structure of the interface and the psychology of the user. Black and his associates (Black and Sebrechts, 1981) underscore the importance of mental models of the structure of a system for the user.

Greater specificity in performance expectations requires the calibration of the performance of operational computer systems in a task category and the establishment of performance benchmarks to be met in the design of new systems.

Analysis of System Performance

A number of studies have calibrated the performance of existing systems both qualitatively and quantitatively. Akin and his associates (Akin and Rao, 1985) have studied a mail system called RdMail, and showed inefficiencies which result from the specialization of commands and the variances in the skill levels of users. Their analysis was based on decomposing user protocols into command segments and mapping these segments into standard mail tasks. Card (1978) and Roberts (1979) on the other hand have used a higher resolution analysis of their data decomposing user's text editing behavior into individual keystrokes. From these they were able to predict the time required to perform standard tasks in the context of a number of comparable text editing systems.

These findings generally provide useful information for developing new systems or new interfaces for existing systems which can hopefully circumvent the problems found in their precursors. However, often new generation systems start with radically different hardware and system performance assumptions and, consequently, require entirely different insights about design. Thus, the more valuable sort of analysis for HCI, and also the more difficult one, deals with the prediction of performance in a system which is being designed.

Predicting System Performance From Designs

The most significant accomplishments to date in this area have been the contributions of Card, Moran and Newell (1983) described in their book titled, "The Psychology of Human-Computer Interaction". Based on their own work and work by others, the authors show analytical methods of performance prediction, at different levels of resolution. The keystroke model is shown to be a powerful tool for accurately predicting task performance. In addition, they developed a model called unit-task to calibrate performance of users at a higher level of resolution. The two models provide a basis for the "engineering" of HCI systems with a degree of precision which resembles engineering design applications in other fields.

Another method which permits design prediction of performance of system designs is simulation of some aspect of a design without actually implementing it. Card (1978) uses simulation to predict system behavior once the keystroke level analysis is complete. Another example of simulation as a predictive tool is used in Akin's work (Akin, Baykan, and Rao, 1988; Akin, Lai, and Rao, 1988) in designing a syntax for an automatic interpreter for speech input of graphics information. By generating samples of phrases and statements from an initial syntax expressed in BNF notation, authors were able to refine the syntax to the level where it produced phrases and statements to match user statements with accuracy at the 80 to 90 percentile level.

Yet another form of verification of the logical structure of system designs is illustrated in Reisner's work (1981). Using formal descriptions of alterative graphics systems, the author was able to show the performance differences which would occur between alternative designs once they were implemented.

ANALYTICAL MODELS

Analytical models for prediction of performance illustrated in the above review fall under three categories: GOMS or keystroke models (Card, Moran, and Newell, 1983), unit-task models, and simulation models (Card, 1978; Akin, Baykan, and Rao, 1988; Akin, Lai, and Rao, 1988).

GOMS or Keystrokes

Card and associates (Card, Moran, and Newell, 1983) have broadly described a class of models named after the four components of which it consists: goals, operations, methods for achieving goals, and selection rules for choosing among competing methods. GOMS models enable the analysis of a given task into these four categories and, therefore, provide a structure for reconstituting them into sequences representing different computer functionalities. By estimating the time required to fulfill each component, it is possible to predict or explain user efforts at the console for a variety of functions.

The keystroke model is a special case of the GOMS model. It is concerned with the prediction of user time at the computer in terms of manual work including mental effort needed to undertake the manual work and computer response time. Predictions of this method have been calibrated against human users in text editing execution time. Consequently, it has been used to estimate efficiency of alternative system configurations and algorithms in performing standard tasks. Once reliable estimates for operators, such as Keystroking (K), Pointing (P), Homing (H), Drawing (D), Mental task (M), and System response (R) are available, this method can be used as a design tool to evaluate efficiency of alternative approaches and, ultimately, help choose between them.

Unit-Tasks

GOMS type analysis can also be used in looking at higher level aggregations of operations. Card and his associates (Card, Moran, and Newell, 1983) show that tasks, such as page- layout, can be disaggregated into smaller tasks, such as processing new page, headings, figures, footnotes, indentations, text fonts, and references. By estimating the time required for each subtask, then they were able to estimate time required to execute alternative system functions.

Like the GOMS models, the unit-task models can show efficiencies or inefficiencies in computer system design. Akin and his associates' (Akin and Rao, 1985) study of electronic mail illustrates this point from the empirical point of view. They decomposed the user operations into high level tasks, such as reading text from the screen, typing, waiting for display of text, waiting for system response, as well as low level tasks, such as typing each system command and its parameters. By analyzing command usage and time taken at the console to execute a set of standard functions, they were able to show that experts while using a very large set of specialized commands were no more efficient than regular users who relied on a handful of general purpose commands.

233

Because the design of the system commands are not sufficiently developed or are subject to change, certain aspects of system design do not permit the kind of detailed analysis reviewed above. In these cases simulations prove to be more effective. Card (Card, Moran, and Newell, 1979) in testing the GOMS model had utilized a simulation model to replicate user behaviors. His simulation accurately predicts operation types, operation sequences, and processing times for standard text editing functions.

In developing a syntax for natural language input of graphic information, Akin (Akin, Baykan, and Rao, 1988; Akin, Lai, and Rao, 1988) built a simulation model to replicate statements used by human subjects to give verbal directives as inputs for graphics systems. The simulation technique used was twofold. By collecting data from users, they simulated the system being designed as a hybrid human-computer system in which the natural language understanding was done by an operator. By testing and refining the syntax developed for system design, they used simulation techniques to approximate subjects' statements. With the aid of repeated refinements on the syntax represented in BNF notation, they were able to increase the number of statements matching subjects' statements to 80% of all randomly generated statements.

CONCLUSIONS

Human computer interaction (HCI) is an integral part of computer programming (CP). Viewing computer system design as an integrated process including both HCI and CP, it is possible to advance the quality of user satisfaction with computer systems.

Key issues in HCI design include specification of systems performance expectations, analysis of performance prediction during design and analysis of system performance after implementation. In current HCI literature, these issues have given rise to several methods of specification and prediction of system performance. These methods fall under three categories: keystroke models, unit task models and simulations.

Keystroke models provide reliable predictions of alternative system designs, but, require that the system being calibrated be completely specified or implemented. This limits its use as a design diagnostics technique. Unit-task models are useful in performing similar predictive analyses with higher level system functions. They have similar advantages and disadvantages as do the Keystroke models.

Simulation models, while not fully exploited as a predictive technique, have promise as design diagnostic tools. Their advantages include application in cases where virtually no implementation exists, being instrumental in exposing some of the unpredictable aspects of HCI, requiring little system specification and yielding results, expediently. On the other hand, their results are not as reliable and accurate as those of the two previous models. Nevertheless, simulation models remain one of the least explored and most promising approaches to analytical modeling of HCI.

REFERENCES

Akin, Ö. and Rao, D.R., 1985, Efficient Computer-User Interface in Mail Systems, *International Journal of Man-Machine Studies*, Vol. 22, pp. 587-611.

Akin, Ö., Baykan, C., and Rao, D. R., 1988, Structure of a Directory Space: A Case Study with a UNIX Operating System, *International Journal of Man-Machine Studies* (forthcoming issue).

Akin, Ö., Lai, R. C., and Rao, D. R., 1988, A Syntax for Natural Language Interface with Computer-Aided Drawing Systems, Working paper, Laboratory for Design Information Processing, Department of Architecture, Carnegie-Mellon University, Pittsburgh, PA.

Black, J. B., and Sebrechts, M. M., 1981, Facilitating Human-Computer Communication, *Applied Psycholinguistics*, Vol. 2, pp. 149-177.

Brown, P. J., 1983, Error Messages: The Neglected Area of the Man/Machine Interface? *Communications of the ACM*, Vol. 26, No. 4, pp. 246-249.

Card, S. K., 1978, *Studies in the Psychology of Computer Text Editing Systems*, Research Report #SSL-78-1, XEROX Palo Alto Research Center, Palo Alto, CA.

Card, S. K., Moran, T. P., and Newell, A., 1979, *The Keystroke-Level Model for User Performance Time With Interactive Systems*, Research Report #SSL-79-1, XEROX, Applied Information Processing Psychology Project, Systems Science Laboratory, Palo Alto Research Center, Palo Alto, CA.

Card, S. K., Moran, T. P., and Newell, A., 1983, *The Psychology of Human-Computer Interaction*, Lawrence Erlbaum Associates, Hillsdale, New Jersey.

Hayes, P. J., 1984, *Executable Interface Definitions Using Form Based Interface Abstractions*, Research

Report #CMU-CS-84110, Department of Computer Science, Carnegie-Mellon University, Pittsburgh, PA.

Hayes, P. J, and Szekely, P. A., 1983, *Graceful Interaction Through the COUSIN Command Interface*, Research Report #CMU-CS-83-102, Department of Computer Science, Carnegie-Mellon University, Pittsburgh, PA.

Miller, R. B., 1979, The Human Task as Reference for System Interface Design, *IEEE Transactions on Machine Systems*, pp. 97-100.

Moran, T. P., 1978, *Introduction to the Command Language Grammar*, Research Report #SSL-78-3, XEROX, Applied Information Processing Psychology Project, Systems Science Laboratory, Palo Alto Research Center, Palo Alto, CA.

Norman, D. A., 1983, Design Rules Based on Analyses of Human Error, *Communications of the ACM*, Vol. 26, No. 4, pp. 254-258.

Reisner, P., 1981, Formal Grammar and Human Factors Design of an Interactive Graphics System, *IEEE Transactions on Software Engineering*, Vol. SL-7, No. 2.

Roberts, T. L., 1979, *Evaluation of Computer Text Editors*, Research Report #SSL-79-9, XEROX, Applied Information Processing Psychology Project, Systems Science Laboratory, Palo Alto Research Center, Palo Alto, CA.

A MODEL OF THE OPERATOR'S TASK IN DIAGNOSTIC PROBLEM SOLVING

Vijay Vasandani and T. Govindaraj

Center for Human-Machine Systems Research
School of Industrial and Systems Engineering
Georgia Institute of Technology
Atlanta, Georgia 30332

Abstract: In supervisory control of complex dynamic systems a major part of the problem solving activity is concerned with fault diagnosis. Therefore, operator training for diagnostic problem solving is essential to ensure competent performance. Intelligent computer aids and operator associates can be very effective for training operators in a variety of domains. Development of such computer aids depends on the availability of suitable models of the operator's task. The task model must incorporate the structure, functions, and behavior of the system in an appropriate form. This paper proposes a methodology for building a normative model of the operator's task. The proposed model supports qualitative reasoning for schema instantiation based on qualitative values of the system state. The choice of qualitative reasoning makes the model consistent with how human operators function while diagnosing faults. The model uses level of abstraction inherent in the dynamic systems to decompose the operator's fault diagnosis task into a hierarchy of functions. An application of the model to an existing marine power plant simulator is also presented.

INTRODUCTION

In supervisory control of complex dynamic systems, fault diagnosis forms a major part of problem solving activity. Fault diagnosis of complex dynamic systems depends on the operator's use of system knowledge at multiple levels of abstraction and detail (Rasmussen, 1985). Efficiency of troubleshooting depends upon timely compilation, integration, and organization of appropriate pieces of operational information about components on the basis of observed symptoms. Even if the oprators ar familiar with the fundamentals of system operation, difficulties arise during troubleshooting and diagnostic problem solving due to their inability to combine symptom information with mental resources concerning system knowledge. Performance is adversely affected by ineffectiveness of control or problems with the metacognitive aspects of the operators' fault diagnosis and problem solving behaviors. Operator training that helps organize system knowledge and operatonal information including symptom-cause relations is, therefore, essential to ensure competent performance.

Training programs should help the operators learn and organize relevant system knowledge to facilitate diagnostic problem solving. Since training on actual systems is usually very expensive, simulators are often used where a wide range of failure conditions are to be simulated. Training simulators combined with intelligent computer aids assume an important role in many training programs. Development and successful implementation of effective computer aids in a training program for large, complex, dynamic systems depends on the availability of:

(1)   a simulation methodology that has cognitive compatibility with the operator under training, and,

Empirical Foundations of Information and Software Science V
Edited by P. Zunde and D. Hocking, Plenum Press, New York, 1990

237

(2)   a normative model of the operator's task that promotes understanding of the task, guides instructional strategies and provides the computer aid with means to infer the student's actions.

In this paper, we describe an architecture for modeling an expert operator's diagnostic problem solving task. The model of an expert's task constitutes the expert module, one of three essential components of an intelligent tutoring system (ITS). The other two comopnnets are the student module and the instructional module. The student module contains a model of a student's current level of competence. Finally, the instructional model is designed to sequence instructions and tasks based on the information provided by task and student models.

Details of the model, including an application to a marine power plant simulator, are provided below following a brief discussion of the qualitative approximation methodology used in developing the simulator.

SIMULATOR METHODOLOGY

Qualitative approximation (Govindaraj, 1987) provides a convenient, practical means of designing simulators of complex dynamic systms. In qualitative approximation, a combination of bomttom-up and top-down approaches to modeling system dynamics is used. This is in sharp contrast to qualitative reasoning models in AI (Reiger, 1975; Reiger and Grinberg, 1977; de Kleer and Brown, 1981, 1984; Forbus, 1984; Kuipers, 1984, 1986; Kuipers and Kassirer, 1984; Stevens, 1982) that follow a bottom-up approach, starting from formal, detailed representation of lower level components without considering the overall system functions. For the most part, the qualitative reasoning models are concerned with stead state phenomena. Only the sequence of operations are described iwthout regard to their exact time relationships. These models provide a means of representing a physical device, though not necessarily convenient means of representing a complex, interconnected dynamic system with continuous states for the purpose of fault diagnosis training. Qualitative approximation is based on a hierarchical description of dynamic systems, where primitives that approximate the functions of the component are at the lowest level. The primitives provide qualitative states that describe the evolution of the systm. Using this methodology, large systems can be simulated with moderate amount of computational power due to reduced computational requirements. QSteam, an application of qualitative approximation techniques, simulates the dynamics of system states of a marine power plant under a number of failure situations. Qualitative measures such as "low pressure", "temperature slightly high" are used to describe the system states. Basic principles of the design methodology and details of the simulator are described in Govindaraj (1987).

A NORMATIVE MODEL OF AN OPERATOR'S DIAGNOSTIC TASK

Constructing an expert module for an ITS depends on the availability of (1) appropriately structured domain knowledge, and (2) knowledge of strategies for fault diagnosis. Together, the domain knowledge and strategies constitute a normative model of the operator's diagnostic problem solving task. The instructional module uses this normative model to train students to use proper strategies in diagnostic problem solving, and perhaps for inferring the student's actions. The normative model should, therefore, capture the organization of system knowledge and the strategies used by an expert operator. Requirements and features of the normative model are described in this section

Construction of a normative model of operator's diagnostic task requires a thorough understanding of operator's strategies. During troubleshooting, an operator normally starts by considering higher level system functions, using patterns established during prior experience and training. Simple pattern matching, when possible, is the fastest means of troubleshooting (Rasmussen, 1981). However, such an approach, usually based on shallow or surface knowledge concerning causes of failure and symptoms, is inadequate for difficult problems. Recourse to detailed knowledge of basic principles, structure, behavior, and functions of the system is necessary, at least during parts of the troubleshooting exercise, when any portion of the symptom cannot be explained in terms of simple pattern matching alone. Judicious choice of lower level modules for reasoning and detailed investigation become necessary for an efficient fault diagnosis and problem solving process.

Rasmussen (1986) has characterized two diagnostic search strategies in problem solving: (1) symptomatic search, and (2) topographic search. Symptomatic search is a highly economical strategy where a successful association between cause and effect is generated based on prior experience. A failure to identify a match between observed symptoms and plausible case based on prior experience leads to topographic search. In topographic search, fault diagnosis is guided by causal reasoning and is often less

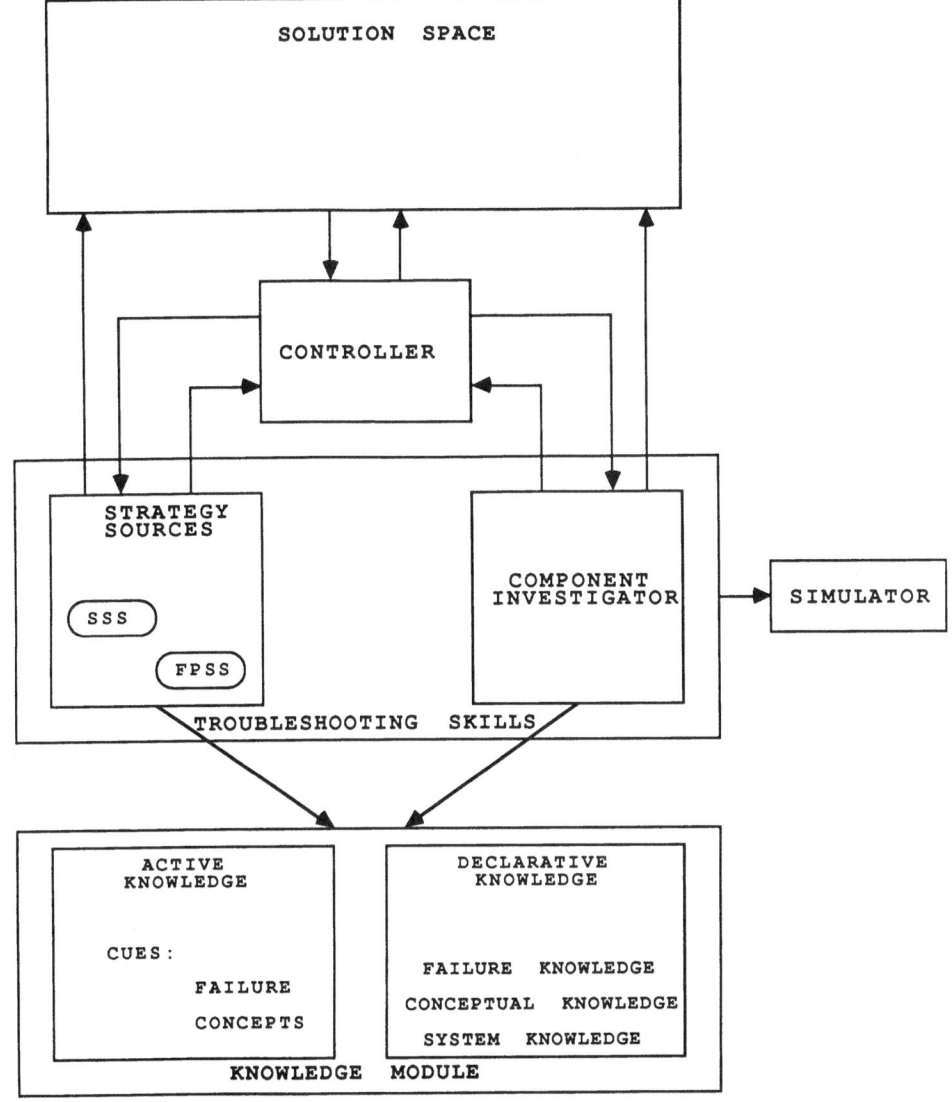

Figure 1. Model Architecture.

economical than symptomatic search. Topographic search utilizes the system knowledge in causal reasoning and deductive processes to generate a hypothesis about failed components. The hypothesis is tested by comparing the model of normal behavior of suspected component to its behavior in the abnormally functioning system. Neither symptomatic nor topographic strategy is adequate by itself to complete the task. An operator usually switches between the two search strategies, adopting topographic search only if symptomatic tests are inconclusive. Various attempts at modeling operator's knowledge and task strategies have been made. The resulting models can be categorized as either macro or micro models.

Macro models of fault diagnosis such as the one proposed by Rouse and Hunt (1984) successfully classify diagnostic behavior, but make no attempt at specifying how knowledge is organized by the operator and what mechanisms are used to arrive at the actions observed. Some micro models (Clancey, Shorliffe, and Buchanan, 1979; Kolodner, 1983; Kolodner and Kolodner, 1984), on the other hand, attempt to identify the essential components of medical diagnosis behavior. The expert "Profile", in IMTS (Towne and Munro, 1988), is a good example of modelnig diagnositic expertise in a corrective maintenance domain. Profile models an expert troubleshooter and allows IMTS to demonstrate diagnostic strategies on a simulator of a helicopter's bladefolding subsystem. A similar model of a troubleshooting task has been proposed by

239

```
Active-Knowledge  :  object

       :  seen-symptoms       ::  instance  of  symptom-vector

           :  symptom              ::  instance  variable
           :  cue                  ::  instance  variable

       :  known-concepts      ::  instance  of  concept-vector
           :  cue                  ::  instance  variable



    Example

  Active-Knowledge


    :  seen-symptoms

        :  symptom    ::(Condenser  main  vacuum  pressure  low
                                             alarms  sounds)
        :  cue        ::  (FailedCp.Pump  FailedVp.Pump)


    :  known-concepts

        :  cue        ::  (low-pressure)
```

Figure 2. Example of Active Knowledge Representation.

Govindaraj and Su (1988) which accounts for observations of fault diagnosis performance on a marine power plant simulator. Another type of micro model is OFMSPERT (Rubin, Mitchell, and Jones, 1987). Using a blackboard architecture, OFMSPERT is used to dynamically infer the operator's intentions, given operator actions, and the state of the system. These micro models fit into the scheme of an intelligent tutoring system better than macro models, because they incorporate structuring of system knowledge, provide explanations, and are more compatible with the operator strategies.

This section provided an overview of strategies and models of diagnostic problem solving. An architecture for modeling an operator's fault diagnostic performance which is consistent with the requirements of an intelligent tutoring system is proposed in the next section. The architecture deals with issues of system knowledge representation and application of strategies employed by experts in troubleshooting large, complex, dynamic, engineering domains.

MODEL DESCRIPTION

The proposed model of fault diagnostic performance divides the problem solving framework into five major constituents: (1) knowledge module; (2) strategy sources; (3) component investigator;

```
FAILURE  KNOWLEDGE


    Failed Component                :: instance of Failure-vector

        : failures                  :: instance of schema

            : component-name        :: instance variable

            : component-type        :: instance variable

            : symptom               :: instance variable

            : cause                 :: instance variable

            : fluid-path            :: instance variable

            : cause-effect-association :: instance variable


    EXAMPLE

    Failed Cp.Pump

        : failures
            : component-name        :: Cp.Pump
            : component-type        :: (heat-exchanger closed-vessel)
            : symptom               :: (Condenser main vacuum low
                                              pressure alarm sounds)
            : cause                 :: (broken flexible coupling)
            : fluid-path            :: (steam-condensate)
            : cause-effect-association
                        ::
                    (((low condensate discharge pressure)
                      (36 pressure Cpdv.Valve Gec.Condenser low))
                     ((high condensate level in condenser)
                      (60 level Condenser hw.Well high))
                     ((low vacuum in condenser)
                      (27 pressure Condenser Vp.Pump low))
                     ((high LP Turbine Temperature)
                      (55 temperature Lpt.Turbine Condenser high))
                     ((low water level in deaerator)
                      (58 level dft.Tank dfthlt.Transmitter S-low))
                     ((low water pressure in deaerator)
                  (19 pressure dft.Tank dfthlt.Transmitter S-low)))
```

Figure 3. Example of Declarative Knowledge Representation for a Failed Component.

(4) controller; and (5) solution space (See Figure 1). The knowledge module contains the domain specific knowledge and the strategy source organizes the knowledge about troubleshooting strategies. The component investigator contains procedural knowledge required to verify state variable values for a suspected component. The controller coordinates the operations of the strategy sources and the component investigator by making information available on a type of blackboard called solution space. Details are provided below.

```
┌─────────────────────────────────────────────────────────────────────┐
│                                                                       │
│  CONCEPTUAL    KNOWLEDGE                                               │
│                                                                       │
│                                                                       │
│  A-CONCEPT          :: instance of concept                            │
│                                                                       │
│                                                                       │
│      : concept-name          :: instance variable                     │
│      : cause-of-concept      :: instance variable                     │
│                                                                       │
│                                                                       │
│  EXAMPLE                                                              │
│                                                                       │
│                                                                       │
│    low-pressure                                                       │
│                                                                       │
│      : concept-name     :: low-pressure                               │
│      : cause-of-concept :: ((specific-course pressure controller)     │
│                             ((concept (vacuum leak-in)                 │
│                                       (water leak-out)                 │
│                                       (gas leak-out change-in-phase))) │
│                             ((system-state (closed-vessel              │
│                             (water water level water low)              │
│                             (gas-water gas level water low)            │
│                             (vacuum-condensate vacuum level            │
│                                       condensate high))))              │
│                                                                       │
└─────────────────────────────────────────────────────────────────────┘
```

Figure 4. Example of Declarative Knowledge Representation for a Working Concept.

1.   **Knowledge Module**

The knowledge module consists of static knowledge organized into two distinct components: (1) active knowledage, and (2) declarative knowledge. The motivation to organize knowdledge as presented below comes from our desire to capture the skills of expert operators in a manner that may prove useful to train novice operators.

Active Knowledge is the component of an operator's knowledge that gets activated when symptoms of failure are first observed. It is activated to fetch specific instances of seen failures, familiar working concepts, and procedural knowledge from long term storage. Active knowledge contains cues to information about failures that have been observed by the operator in the past. These cues provide possible explanation for some of the obvious symptoms noticed during a troubleshooting session. In addition to these cues, active knowledge contains cues to compiled conceptual knowledge in the "declarative" section. Compiled conceptual knowledge refers to basic principles of system operation that any operator is expected to learn during the course of formal education and job-specific training (See Figure 2).

The second component of knowledge module, "declarative knowledge", contains three types of knowledge structures: (1) information about plausible faulty behavior of various components, (2) working concepts derived from the first principles, and (3) the organization of the components in the system. The first type has detailed information about plausible faulty behavior of various components. An example is shown in Figure 3, which corresponds to a failed condensate pump. Embedded into this structure is the causal and temporal relationships between different states of the system as the effects of a fault propagates through the system. The use of these relationships by experts were noticed in the experimental studies conducted by Govindaraj and Su (1988). The causal links between different states of the system defines a systematic approach for understanding fault propagation. This approach of using causal relationships is desirable because in addition to providing information about the affected guages, it explains the abnormal behavior. The temporal relationship between the states of the system as presented in these structures, implicitly outlines a plan for investigating the failure, and, hence, fits the description of a schema. For instance, the schema of a possible failure in the condensate pump shown in Figure 3 stores the temporal and causal

The second component of the knowledge module, "declarative knowledge", contains three types of knowledge structures: (1) information about plausible faulty behavior of various components, (2) working concepts derived from first principles, and (3) the organization of the components in the system. The first type has detailed information about plausible faulty behavior of various components. An example is shown in Figure 3, which corresponds to a failed condensate pump. Embedded into this structure is the causal and temporal relationships between different states of the system as the effects of a fault propagate through relationships between system states in the slot for "cause-effect-association". The failure of the condensate pump results in low condensate discharge pressure and an increase in condensate level in the condenser. High condensate level leads to a drop in vacuum in the condenser causing the steam temperature at LP Turbine outlet to be higher than normal. With time the effects of low condensate discharge pressure propagate to the deaerator where there is a drop in both the water level and pressure. FailedCp.Pump in Figure 3 is shown as a vector of such schemas to account for the various ways in which a single component, i.e., a condensate pump in this case, can possibly fail.

The second knowledge structure organizes working concepts derived from first principles. These concepts are represented as objects which are defined by a collection of propositions and act as compiled conceptual knowledge. Concepts are represented throughout this discussion using the states resulting from failures as the reference. An example of the concept "low-pressure" is shown in Figure 4. The "cause-of-concept" slot in each concept stores the general explanation for the cause of the concept. The explanation may be provided by a specific cause, or a specific state of the system or even another concept.

The third knowledge structure in declarative knowledge pertains to the organization of the components in the system. This knowledge structure organizes the structure of the system at a functional level of abstraction. The functional organization identifies a collection of componnts forming a subsystem needed to satisfy a higher level function or goal of the system. Examples of such subsystems are the steam generation subsystem, steam condensation subsystem, and the power generatoin subsystem. Within each functional level, a relational structure connects modules at an appropriate lvel of aggregation. The relational structure identifes a collection of components, in the sequence they appear along the same fluid path. Examples of some fluid paths in a power plant are steam-condensate, cooling-water, lube-oil and fuel-oil. A particular component may appear under more than one functional subsystem and, also, under more than one fluid path. This is evident from the example of the condenser in Figure 5.

During the course of a single fault diagnosis session, knowledge in the knowledge module remains static. It may, however, be altered or updated at the end of the task by an activated learning module to capture the effects of experience. This learning module is still under development.

2.   Strategy Sources

The strategy sources constitute the functional knowledge of two important constituents of a fault diagnosis task: (1) symptomatic search, and (2) topographic search (Rasmussen, 1986). To perform symptomatic search, a set of symptoms is used as a template to be matched against a mental library of abnormal system conditions. In topogrpahic search for a fault, normal system response is compared to observed response in the abnormally functioning system. Failure is found by determining the location of mismatch between the predicted and the observed system states. In carrying out their roles, the strategy sources access information from the knowledge module and post the results on the solution space. Currently, there are two strategy sources, one that supports symptomatic search and the other that aims for a solution using concepts derived from thermodynamics. More specialized strategy sources may be added later.

3.   Component-Investigator

Using the failure schemas of components, the component investigator performs a verification task to confirm whether the guages supposedly affected by the hypothesized failure do indeed display abnormal readings. Irrespective of the outcome of the verification task, the component-investigator also posts the results of each of the tests it conducted on the solution space for assessment by the controller.

4.   Controller

The controller is responsible for coordinating the functions of the other modules. The controller knows the capabilities of its strategy sources and component investigator which come under its domain of control. It uses the information displayed on the solution space along with some built-in heuristics to delegate authority and instruct the strategy sources and the component-investigator.

5.   Solution Space

The solution space is a dynamic, global data structure where a set of partial solutions, tests to conduct, results of the tests, and the current hypotheses are constantly displayed (Figure 6). The strategy sources and the component-investigator add, delete, and modify entites on the solution space to keep the

```
SYSTEM    KNOWLEDGE


A-SUBSYSTEM              :: instance of SubSystem

  :fluid-components   :: instance variable



    EXAMPLE

    Steam-Condensation

       : fluid-component

          :: ((Saltwater (Sea)
                    (.. ..) (.. ..) (- - - - - - -
                    (condenser  (heat-exchanger  closed-vessel))
                    (.. ..) - - - - - -) (Sea)))
               ((steam-condensate  (power-generation
                    (.. ..) (.. ..) (- - - - - -
                    (LP-Turbine (S urceSink))
                    (condenser (heat-exchanger closed-vessel))
                    (CP.Pump (controller))
                    (.. ..) (.. ..) - - - - - -)
                    (steam-generation))))
```

Figure 5. Example of Declarative Knowledge Representation for Organization of System Components.

controller up-to-date about the progress being made on the task. When a tutor module is added later, it too will have access to information being displayed on the solution space to guide its instructional strategy.

The architecture of the model of fault diagnosis is being used to build an application in the marine power plant domain. Details of this application are described below.

PET: AN APPLICATION OF THE MODEL

Power plant Expert Troubleshooter (PET) is an application of the model currently being implemented to work in conjunction with QSteam, the marine power plant simulator mentioned earlier. QSteam incorporates realistic failures and system schematics to simulate failure situations in a marine power plant. PET conducts fault diagnosis on this simulator. Both PET and the human interacting with QSteam have access to the same set of simulator commands, guage information, and symptom information. The following example illustrates the functions of PET.

EXAMPLE

OBVIOUS SYMPTOM: Condenser main vacuum low pressure
                alarm sounds

ACTUAL FAULT: Failure of condensate pump

When the failure occurs, the obvious symptoms are posted on the solution space. The controller begins the diagnostic process by activating the symptomatic strategy source after it learns about the obvious symptom from the solution space. The function of the symptomatic strategy source (SSS) at this stage is to find a match between the observed symptom and the seen-symptoms contained in "active knowledge". The result of the search is posed on the solution space before control is shifted back to the controller. Two cases are discussed below. They correspond to: (1) a previously seen symptom, and (2) a previously unseen symptom.

244

```
┌─────────────────────────────────────────────────┐
│                                                   │
│    SOLUTION  SPACE                                │
│                                                   │
│                                                   │
│    : mode                                         │
│                                                   │
│    : observed symptom                             │
│                                                   │
│    : symptom recognized                           │
│                                                   │
│    : recognized-key-words                         │
│                                                   │
│    : component-where-symptom-observed             │
│                                                   │
│    : fluid-path-indicated-by-symptom              │
│                                                   │
│    : possible-explanations                        │
│                                                   │
│    : explanations-already-investigated            │
│                                                   │
│    : explanation-being-investigated               │
│                                                   │
│    : hypothesis-presently-supported               │
│                                                   │
│    : component-under-investigation                │
│                                                   │
│    : fluid-path-under-investigation               │
│                                                   │
│    : gauges-to-test-and-expected-results          │
│                                                   │
│    : test-results-observed                        │
│                                                   │
│    : most-likely-cause                            │
│                                                   │
└─────────────────────────────────────────────────┘
```

Figure 6. Solution Space: A Global Data Structure.

CASE 1: The symptom is recognized as one that has been seen before.

The controller reactivates the SSS enabling it to proceed further. The SSS uses the seen symptoms cue to retrieve failure schemas corresponding to the failed component. It is possible that more than one failure scheme are retrieved; and of the retrieved schemas one or none may explain the actual cause of the observed symptom. In either case, an initial hypothesis is formed and is posted on the solution space next to the slot marked "Hypothesis-presently-supported". The hypothesis is a list of pointers to failure schemas of components suspected to have failed. A malfunctioning condensate pump or vacuum pump are two of the many ways to explain the symptom observed in the selected example, The hypothesis may thus contain references to one or both of these causes.

Next, the controller prompts the component investigator into action, which investigates each of the suspected components in the hypothesis, one at a time. The component investigator, with the help of failure knowledge, plans a series of gauge-checks, and posts the results of each gauge-check on the solution space. The controller compares the results from the hypothesized failure to the actual results and, if all its predictions are met, identifies the suspected component and terminates the diagnosis. The controller may also terminate the diagnostic process as soon as it has sufficient evidence to reject the suspected components from its hypothesis. As soon as the investigation of a component is completed, the name of that component is eliminated from the list of components in "Hypothesis-presently-supported" in the solution space. In the event that no component in the suspected set satisfactorily explains the observed symptom, the controller looks for an alternative strategy source. Further analysis in this case will proceed along the same lines as indicated for Case 2.

For the example under consideration, the presence of FailedCp.Pump in the hypothesis at the end of the symptomatic search would solve the problem and lead to a successful termination of the diagnostic task. Presence of FailedVp.Pump alone in the hypothesis, on the other hand, would lead to an impasse only to be resolved later through the application of an alternative strategy source originating from basic concepts.

Symptoms and test results observed during investigations, both normal and abnormal, always remain posted on the solution space. Their presence there enables the controller to reason using forward and backward reasoning techniques to refine the hypothesis about suspected components.

Case 2: The symptom is not recognized as one that has been sen before or when symptomatic search fails to provide a satisfactory explanation for the observed symptom.

The first step for the "first principle strategy source" (FPSS) involves identifying some of the keywords as they appear in the description of the symptom. The three key items that the system tries to recognize are: (1) name of the component where signs of the failure are reflected, (2) the fluid path which is likely to contain the affected component, and (3) the system state that has become the cause of concern. For the example considered, the three keywords are condenser, vacuum, and low-pressure, and these are displayed on the solution space.

The steps below describe the process of diagnosing the fault for the example:

1. (a) The controller analyzes the information displayed on the solution space and proceeds to investigate each possible cause. The first cause is very specific and focuses suspicion on all pressure controllers in the affected fluid path.

    (b) Using system knowledge, the model finds all pressure controllers in the vacuum path adjacent to the condenser. The search is confined to a space around the condenser since the symptom has been observed near that component.

    (c) A new hypothesis of pointers to failure schemas of all such components is formed and displayed on the solution space.

    (d) Investigation of the components in the hypothesis list proceeds in the manner described earlier in Case 1.

    (e) If no knowledge about the failure of a suspected component is available in declarative knowledge, the component is removed from the list of suspected components. However, the name of the component is retained as a probable cause for failure. This action gives the model the ability to terminate the diagnostic task gracefully after providing a reasonable explanation, if its present knowledge is not adequate for diagnosis.

    (f) If there are no pressure controllers to be found in the vacuum path, the controller switches attention to the second cause.

2. (a) The second probable cause is best explained in terms of another concept - "leak-in". A search through "leak-in" concept yields activated failure schemas of all components that explain leaking behavior in the vacuum path.

    (b) Steps 1(c) through 1(f) are repeated for components in the revised list of hypothesis formed in step (a).

3. (a) Explanation using first principles does not always help the model to hypothesize a specific failure, but may provide a direction for backward reasoning. This explanation establishes a causal link between observed abnormalities and some other abnormality. For example, in the cases considered, the abnormally high condensate level could explain the low vacuum in the condenser.

    The model next tries to confirm if the condensate level is in fact high. If the level is found to be high, the list of symptoms is revised and the model recurses through the entire process described above. Heuristics such as those favoring the activation of schemas with higher number of preconditions satisfied can help the controller resolve conflicts when more than one schema bids to explain the new set of symptoms.

Finally, on exhausting all hypotheses and avenues of further progress, the model provides the contents of "most-likely-cause" on the solution space as an explanation for the observed symptom. The state of the solution space at the end of an unsuccessful diagnostic task provides an opportunity for a learning module to build a new failure frame. This learning is possible because even though the model was unsuccessful in diagnosing the fault, information about abnormal readings of affected gauges was generated and displayed on the solution space. This information combined with input from a human expert could possibly be used to build a new knowledge structure for the new failure. Development of such a learning module is neither a trivial nor straight forward task.

SUMMARY

An architecture for modeling an expert operator in diagnostic problem solving was proposed. Fault diagnosis is a major problem solving activity in the supervisory control of complex dynamic systems. The model described here, combined with intelligent computer aids, can help operators acquire good problem solving skills when used with appropriate training simulators. Simulators designed via qualitative approximation and intelligent computer aids developed using the expert operator model described in this paper can be very effective due to a high degree of cognitive compatibility with trainees. This paper concludes with a brief description of an application of the model of diagnostic problem solving to a marine power plant simulator.

ACKNOWLEDGEMENTS

The authors wish to express their gratitude for the support and encouragement provided by Drs Susan Chipman and Michael Shafto. Their research is supported by a contract from Manpower R & D Program, Office of Naval Research under contract number N00014-87-K-0482. Contract monitor is Dr. Susan E. Chipman.

REFERENCES

Clancey, W. J., Shorliffe, E. H., and Buchanan, B. G., 1979, Intelligent Computer-Aided Instruction for Medical Diagnosis, *Proceedings of the Third Annual Symposium on Computer Applications in Medical Computing*, Silver Springs, MD, pp. 175-183.

de Kleer, J., and Brown, J. S., 1981, Mental Models of Physical Systems and Their Acquisition, *Cognitive Skills and Their Acquisition*, Anderson, John R., ed., Lawrence Erlbaum Associates, pp. 285-309.

de Kleer, J., and Brown, J. W., 1984, A Qualitative Physics Based on Confluences, *Artificial Intelligence*, Vol. 24, No. 1-3, pp. 7-83.

Forbus, K. D., 1984, Qualitative Process Theory, *Artificial Intelligence*, Vol. 24, No. 1-3, pp. 85-168.

Govindaraj, T., Su Yuan-Liang, D., 1988, A Model of Fault Diagnosis Performance on Expert Marine Engineers, *International Journal of Man-Machine Studies*, to appear.

Govindaraj, T., 1987, Qualitative Approximation Methodology for Modeling and Simulation of Large Dynamic Systems: Applications to a Marine Steam Powerplant, *IEEE Transactions on Systems, Man, and Cybernetics*, Vol. SMC-17, pp. 937-955.

Kolodner, J. L., 1983, Maintaining Organization in a Dynamic Long Term Memory, *Cognitive Science*, Vol. 7, No. 4, pp. 243-280.

Kolodner, J. L., 1983, Reconstructive Memory, *Cognitive Science*, Vol. 7, No. 4, pp. 281-328.

Kolodner, J. L., and Kolodner, R. M., 1984, An Algorithm for Diagnosis Based on Analysis of Previous Cases, *Experience in Problem Solving: A Trilogy of Papers*, GIT-ICS, 84/16, School of Information and Computer Science, Georgia Institute of Technology.

Kuipers, B., 1984, Commonsense Reasoning about Causality: Deriving Behavior from Structure, *Artificial Intelligence*, Vol. 24, No. 1-3, pp. 169-203.

Kuipers, B., 1986, Qualitative Simulation, *Artificial Intelligence*, Vol. 29, No. 1-3, pp. 289-338.

Kuipers, B., and Kassirer, J. P., 1984, Causal Reasoning in Medicine: Analysis of a Protocol, *Cognitive Science*, Vol. 8, No. 4, pp. 363-385.

Rasmussen, J., 1981, Models of Mental Strategies in Process Plant Diagnosis, *Human Detection and Diagnosis of System Failures*, Rasmussen, J., and Rouse, W. B., ed., Plenum Press, New York.

Rasmussen, J., 1985, The Role of Hierarchical Knowledge Representation in Decision Making and System Management, *IEEE Transactions on Systems, Man, and Cybernetics*, Vol. SMC-15, No. 2, pp. 234-243.

Rasmussen, J., 1986, *Information Processing and Human Machine Interaction: An Approach to Cognitive Engineering*, North-Holland, New York.

Rieger, C., 1975, The Commonsense Algorithm as a Basis for Computer Models of Human Memory, Inference, Belief, and Contextual Language Comprehension, *Proceedings of the Conference on Theoretical Issues in Natural Language Processing*, Cambridge, MA, pp. 180-195.

Rieger, C., and Grinberg, M., 1977, The Declarative Representation and Procedural Simulation of Causality in Physical Mechanisms, *Proceedings of the Fifth International Joint Conference in Artificial Intelligence*, Cambridge, Mass.

Rouse, W. G., and Hunt, R. M., 1984, Human Problem Solving in Fault Diagnosis Tasks, *Advances in Man-Machine Systems Research*, Rouse, W. B., ed., JAI Press, Vol. 1, pp. 195-222.

Rubin, K. S., Mitchell, C. M., and Jones, P. M., 1988, Using a Blackboard Architecture for Dynamic Intent Inferencing, *IEEE Transactions on Systems, Man, and Cybernetics*, Vol. 3, pp. 1150-1153.

Steven, A., 1982, *Quantitative and Qualitative Simulation in Portable Training Devices*, Bolt Beranek and Newman Inc., for National Academy of Sciences.

Towne, D. M., and Munro, A., 1988, Intelligent Maintenance Training System, *Intelligent Tutoring Systems: Lessons Learned*, Psotka, Joseph, Massey, L. Dan, and Mutter, Sharon A., eds., Lawrence Erlbaum Associates Publishers, Hillsdale, NY.

INTENT INFERENCING WITH A MODEL-BASED OPERATOR'S ASSOCIATE

Patricia M. Jones, Christine M. Mitchell,
and Kenneth S. Rubin*

Center for Human-Machine Systems Research
School of Industrial and Systems Engineering
Georgia Institute of Technology
Atlanta, GA 30332

*ParcPlace Systems
2400 Geng Rd.
Palo Alto CA 94303

Abstract: This paper describes a portion of the OFMspert (Operator Function Model Expert System) research project. OFMspert is an architecture for an intelligent operator's associate or assistant that can aid the human operator of a complex, dynamic system. Intelligent aiding requires both understanding and control. This paper focuses on the understanding (i.e., intent inferencing) ability of the operator's associate. Understanding or intent inferencing requires a model of the human operator; the usefulness of an intelligent aid depends directly on the fidelity and completeness of its underlying model. The model chosen for this research is the operator function model (OFM) (Mitchell, 1987). The OFM represents operator functions, subfunctions, tasks, and actions as a heterarchic-hierarchic network of finite state automata, where the arcs in the network are system triggering events. The OFM provides the structure for intent inferencing in that operator functions and subfunctions correspond to likely operator goals and plans. A blackboard system similar to that of HASP (Nii et al., 1982) is proposed as the implementation of intent inferencing function. This system postulates operator intentions based on current system state and attempts to interpret observed operator actions in light of these hypothesized intentions.

The OFMspert system built for this research is tailored for the GT-MSOCC (Georgia Tech Multisatellite Operations Control Center) simulation. The GT-MSOCC OFMspert has been the subject of rigorous validation studies (Jones, 1988) that demonstrate its validity as an intent inferencer.

INTRODUCTION

Computational representations and models have been constructed for "understanding" human behavior in many applications, e.g., understanding natural language (Winograd, 1972) and understanding stories (Schank and Abelson, 1977). Artificial intelligence has developed many representational formalisms and control strategies that are intended to mimic "intelligent" behavior (cf Cohen and Feigenbaum, 1982). In the field of human-machine systems research, AI techniques offer powerful methodologies for understanding human behavior in the context of human-machine interaction.

Our particular concern is with human-machine interaction in the control of complex dynamic systems (e.g., nuclear power plants). Such systems are highly automated; thus, the human operator acts as a supervisory controller (Sheridan and Johannsen, 1976; Rasmussen, 1986; Wickens, 1984). Supervisory con-

Empirical Foundations of Information and Software Science V
Edited by P. Zunde and D. Hocking, Plenum Press, New York, 1990

249

trol typically consists of routine monitoring and fine-tuning of system parameters. However, in the event of abnormal or emergency situations, the human operator is expected to detect, diagnose, and compensate for system failures. The ability of a supervisory controller to cope with such situations can be severely limited. Wickens (1984) cites several problems with supervisory control: an increased monitoring load; a "false sense of security" whereby the operator trusts the automation to such an extent that any human intervention or checking seems unnecessary; and "out-of-the-loop familiarity" that implies a reduced ability to cope with non-routine situations.

An important question then becomes how to improve system performance and safety in supervisory control. The answer is not to automate the human out of the system; today's technology cannot match the human's ability to cope with uncertain and novel situations (Chambers and Nagel, 1985). Rather, automated systems must support the human operator. Given that the human will remain an integral part of a complex system, a potential approach to advanced automation is that of "amplifying" rather than automating human skills (Woods, 1986).

The OFMspert (Operator Function Model Expert System) project is an effort to develop a theory of human-computer interaction in supervisory control. OFMspert itself is a generic architecture for a computer-based operator's associate. The operator's associate (and similarly, the Pilot's Associate (Rouse et al, 1987; Chambers and Nagel, 1985)) represents a design philosophy that allows the human to remain in control of a complex system. The computer-based associate is a subordinate to which the human operator can delegate control activities. The associate also actively monitors system state and operator actions in order to provide timely, context-sensitive advice, reminders, and suggestions. The intent is to provide intelligent support for the human operator.

The intelligence and utility of the operator's associate rest on its abilities to understand the operator's current intentions in order to provide context-sensitive advice and assume responsibility given for portions of the control task. Models of human machine interaction offer a variety of frameworks for understanding human behavior (i.e., inferring intentions) in the control of a complex dynamic system (see Jones and Mitchell (1987), and Jones (1988) for a review). Knowledge-based problem solving strategies are tools for implementing and reasoning with the knowledge represented in the human machine interaction model. OFMspert combines a particular human-machine interaction model (the operator function model (OFM) (Mitchell, 1987)) and knowledge-based problem solving approach (the blackboard model of problem solving (Nii, 1986)) to provide the understanding capability necessary for an effec- tive operator's associate (Rubin, et al., 1987). In the next sections, the OFM and the blackboard model of problem solving are described. Next, ACTIN (Actions Interpreter), the intent inferencing component of OFMspert, is discussed, along with a detailed example of how ACTIN infers operator intentions dynamically. Finally, experimental results that validate ACTIN's intent inferencing ability are considered.

THE OPERATOR FUNCTION MODEL

The operator function model (OFM) (Mitchell, 1987) provides a flexible framework for representing operator functions in the control of a complex dynamic system. The OFM represents how an operator might organize and coordinate system control functions. Mathematically, the OFM is a hierarchic-heterarchic network of finite-state automata. Network nodes represent operator activities as operator functions, subfunctions, tasks, and actions. Operator functions are organized hierarchically as subfunctions, tasks, and actions. Each level in the network may be a heterarchy, i.e., a collection of activities that may be performed concurrently. Network arcs represent system triggering events or the results of operator actions that initiate or terminate operator activities. In this way, the OFM accounts for coordination of multiple activities and dynamic focus of attention.

Historically, the OFM is related to the discrete control modeling methodology (Miller, 1985; Mitchell and Miller, 1986). The OFM is distinguished by its modeling of both manual and cognitive operator actions in the context of system triggering events. Manual actions are system reconfiguration commands. Cognitive actions include information gathering and decision making that are typically supported by information requests.

The OFM is a prescriptive model of human performance in supervisory control. Given system triggering events, it defines the functions, sub-functions, tasks, and actions on which the operator should focus. Used predictively, the OFM generates expectations of likely operator actions in the context of current system state. Used inferentially, the OFM defines likely operator functions, subfunctions, and tasks that can be inferred based on operator actions and system state. Thus, the OFM for a particular domain defines the knowledge needed to perform intent inferencing. What is needed next is a problem solving strategy to use this knowledge.

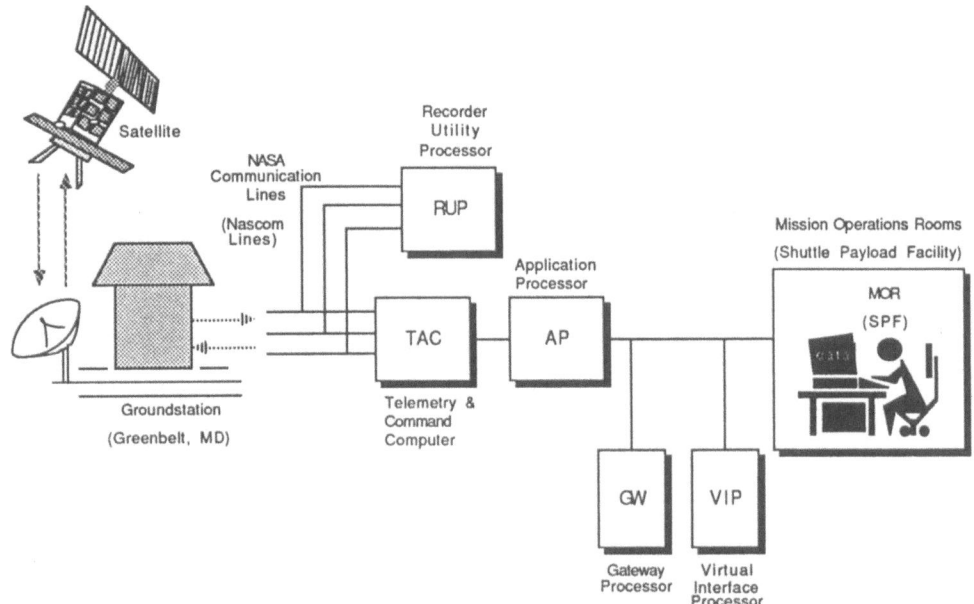

Figure 1. Multisatellite Operations Control Center (MSOCC).

THE BLACKBOARD MODEL OF PROBLEM SOLVING

OFMspert's intent inferencing component, called ACTIN (Actions Interpreter), uses the HASP blackboard model of problem solving (Nii et al, 1982; Nii, 1986). The HASP blackboard is one of the few artificial intelligence systems that explicitly addresses real-time problem solving in dynamic environments.

The blackboard model of problem solving consists of three components: the blackboard, knowledge sources, and blackboard control. The blackboard is a data structure on which the current best hypothesis of the solution is maintained and modified. The hypothesis is represented hierarchically, at various levels of abstraction, and evolves incrementally over time as new data become available or old data become obsolete. Domain-specific knowledge is organized as a collection of independent knowledge sources. Knowledge sources are responsible for posting and interpreting information on the blackboard. Blackboard control applies knowledge sources opportunistically; that is, in either a top-down or bottom-up manner, depending on what is more appropriate in the current context.

The blackboard model of problem solving is compatible with the knowledge represented in the OFM. Both models use a hierarchical representation. The blackboard knowledge sources provide a modularity that naturally represents much of the domain knowledge contained in the OFM arcs. The opportunistic control strategy offers the dynamic flexibility necessary for inferring intentions in real time. ACTIN combines the OFM representation of domain knowledge and the blackboard model of problem solving to dynamically construct and assess current operator intentions.

ACTIONS INTERPRETER (ACTIN)

ACTIN's blackboard represents operator intentions as a hierarchy of goals, plans, tasks, and actions that correspond to the OFM's hierarchy of functions, subfunctions, tasks, and actions. Goals are currently instantiated functions, plans are currently instantiated subfunctions, and so on. In some respects, ACTIN is a process model that uses the blackboard problem solving method to build a dynamic representation of current operator intentions based on the OFM's static knowledge (Wenger, 1987).

The general mechanism for the blackboard approach to intent inferencing is as follows. Given an OFM, currently hypothesized goals, plans, and tasks (GPTs) or sometimes additional plans and tasks (PTs) for an existing goal are placed on the blackboard in response to system triggering events. The blackboard incorporates operator actions into the representation with opportunistic reasoning. Thus, actions can be immediately interpreted as supporting one or more current goals, plans, and tasks; and goals, plans, and tasks can be inferred on the basis of operator actions.

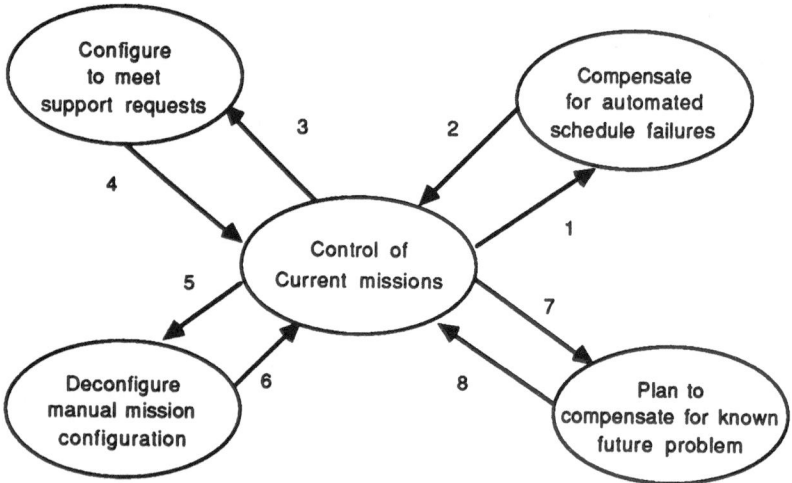

1. Error message received from the automatic scheduler.
2. Compensation completed or unable to compensate.
3. Unscheduled support request received by the operator.
4. Request configured or unable to meet the request.
5. Message received that a manually configured mission is completed.
6. Deconfiguration completed.
7. Operator summons schedule and/or mission template pages when no
   other triggering event takes place.
8. Terminate planning function.

Figure 2. GT-MSOCC Operator Functions.

Construction knowledge sources are responsible for building the representation of goals, plans, tasks, and actions. These knowledge sources can further be characterized as either model-driven or data-driven. Model-driven knowledge sources are those that post GPT information on the blackboard in response to system triggering events as defined by the OFM. Data-driven knowledge sources are those that post operator actions and attempt to infer support for any current tasks on the blackboard. Data-driven knowledge sources may also postulate GPT information on the basis of operator actions. Assessment knowledge sources are responsible for evaluating the extent to which operator actions support currently hypothesized goals, plans, and tasks. Assessments are always made in the context of a particular goal or plan which forms the context for possible advice or reminders.

In order to illustrate ACTIN's dynamic intent inferencing, it is first necessary to describe the application domain for which our OFMspert was built: the Georgia Tech Multisatellite Operations Control Center(GT-MSOCC). After describing GT-MSOCC and its OFM, an example of ACTIN's intent inferencing is presented.

GT-MSOCC: APPLICATION DOMAIN

GT-MSOCC is a real time, interactive simulation of MSOCC, a NASA ground control station for near-earth satellites (Mitchell, 1987). MSOCC is a facility for capturing and processing data sent by satellites (see Figure 1). GT-MSOCC is a research domain designed to support theoretical and empirical research on human-computer interaction in the context of a complex dynamic system. It is a high fidelity simulation of the operator interface to an actual NASA ground control system. For more detail, see Mitchell (1987).

GT-MSOCC operator activities are defined by the GT-MSOCC OFM. At the highest level of the GT-MSOCC operator function model are major operator functions and the system events that cause the operator to transition among functions (see Figure 2). This level of description represents operator goals in the context of current system state. The arcs define system events that trigger a refocus of attention or the addition of a function to the current set of operator duties.

Table 1

GT-MSOCC Goals, Plans, Tasks, and Actions

Goals	Plans	Tasks	Actions
Control current mission CCM	Monitor software (MSW)	Check MOR (CMOR)	telem
		Check endpoints (CEND)	rup/gw/vip/cms telem
	Monitor hardware (MHW)	Check hardware (CHW)	--
Manual Configure Request CCN	Check system constraints (CSC)	Check current number of missions (CCNM)	--
		Check mission schedule (CMS)	msocc sched, msn scheds
		Check scheduled number of missions (CSNM)	msocc sched,pending
	Check mission requirements (CMR)	Check mission template (CMT)	msocc sched, msn scheds
	Identify candidate hardware (ICH)	Find current (FCUR)	--
		Find unscheduled (FUSC)	equip scheds, avails
	Answer question (ANQ)	Execute answer(XAN)	operator answer
		Execute configure (XCON)	manual config. (MCON) events
Compensate for Schedule Failure CFSF	Reconfigure (RCON)	Find duration (FDUR)	telem, pending
		Execute reconfigure(XRCO)	man. reconfig (MRCO), events
		For each equipment: Find current (FCUR)	--
		Find unscheduled (FUSC)	equip scheds, avails
———	Manual Deconfigure Request (DCON)	Execute deconfigure (XDCO)	man. deconfig(MDCO), events
———	Troubleshoot (TBLS)	Check endpoints (CEND)	gw/rup/cms/vip telem
		Check interior (CIN)	nas/tac/ap/modlan telem
———	Replace(HRPL or SRPL)	Find duration (FDUR)	telem, pending
		Find current (FCUR)	--
		Find unscheduled (FUSC)	equip scheds, avails
		Execute replace(XRPL)	replace (RPL)

The default high-level function is to control current missions. This involves the subfunctions of monitoring data transmission and hardware status, detection of data transmission problems, and compensation for failed or degraded equipment. Each subfunction is further defined by a collection of tasks, which in turn are supported by operator actions (system reconfiguration commands or display requests).

System triggering events cause the operator to focus attention on other high-level functions. An unscheduled support request causes the operator to shift to the "configure to meet support requests" function. An error message from the automatic scheduler causes the operator to transition to the function compensate for the automated schedule failure. A request to deconfigure a mission causes the operator to shift to the function of deconfiguring a manual mission configuration. Finally, the operator may engage in long-term planning in the absence of other system triggering events. Upon the termination of these other functions, the operator resumes the default control of current missions function. Functions may be terminated by their successful completion or the determination that they cannot be completed.

In this section, a detailed example of ACTIN's intent inferencing is provided in the context of GT-MSOCC. Table 1 shows the organization of GT-MSOCC goals, plans, tasks, and actions, as defined by the GT-MSOCC OFM. Given system triggering events, ACTIN's model-driven knowledge sources post the appropriate goal, plan, and task (GPT) structures on the blackboard. When operator actions occur, ACTIN's data-driven knowledge sources post actions on the blackboard and attempt to "connect" the actions to tasks which they support. This "connection" between actions and tasks defines ACTIN's intent inferencing capability.

The knowledge of appropriate inferences of intent is contained in a data structure that matches actions to task types. Data-driven knowledge sources consult this structure to determine that task type(s) that a current operator action can support. They then search the blackboard's task level of abstraction for those types, and connect the action to all appropriate tasks.

To illustrate ACTIN's dynamic construction of operator intentions, consider the following scenario from GT-MSOCC. The scenario is described in terms of GT-MSOCC system events and operator actions, which then cause activity on the blackboard. ACTIN's intent inferencing results in statements written to a logfile. In the accompanying figures, the current blackboard structure is shown, along with ACTIN's inferences of intent.

1). The PM mission is automatically configured. ACTIN's model-driven knowledge sources post the goal to control the current mission (CCM) for PM. This goal is comprised of two plans: to monitor data transmission or software (MSW) and to monitor hardware status (MHW). Each plan is composed of one or more tasks. The monitor software plan consists of two tasks: to check data flow at the MOR (CMOR) and to check data flow at endpoint equipment (CEND). The monitor hardware plan consists of the single task to check hardware status (CHW). This entire GPT structure defines the control of current mission function prescribed by the OFM. When PM is configured, ACTIN's knowledge sources retrieve the control of current mission GPT structure, fill in mission-specific information (e.g., the name of this particular mission is PM), and post the structure on the blackboard. The resulting blackboard is shown in Figure 3(A).

2). Another mission (Geographic Explorer, or GEO) is configured. In the same way the control of current mission GPT was posted for PM, a control of current mission GPT for GEO is also posted. The resulting blackboard is shown in Figure 3(B).

3). The operator requests the main telemetry page ("telem"). ACTIN's data-driven knowledge sources determine that the current action type is "telem" and that actions of this type potentially support the tasks of checking the MOR(CMOR) and finding the duration (FDUR) of current missions. Upon examining the tasks level of the blackboard, the knowledge sources find that two eligible tasks are posted: the CMOR tasks for PM and GEO. Thus, the "telem" action is posted and connected to the CMOR tasks. The resulting blackboard is shown in Figure 3(C).

4). The operator requests the gateway telemetry page ("GwTelem"). ACTIN's data-driven knowledge sources determine that the current action type is "GwTelem" and that actions of this type potentially support the tasks of checking the endpoint (CEND) of current missions. Upon examining the task's level of the blackboard, the knowledge sources find that two eligible tasks are posted: the CEND tasks for PM and GEO. Thus, the "GwTelem" action is posted and connected to the CEND tasks. The resulting blackboard is shown in Figure 3(D).

5). One of the components used by PM experiences a hardware failure. The component in this example is RUP2. Upon the occurrence of this triggering event, ACTIN's model-driven knowledge sources post a Plan to replace the failed component, along with the four associated tasks of finding a currently available replacement (FCUR), finding the duration of the mission (FDUR), finding an unscheduled replacement (FUSC), and executing the replace command (XRPL). The resulting blackboard is shown in Figure 3(E).

6). The operator again requests the main telemetry page. This time ACTIN's knowledge sources determine that this action can support three tasks on the blackboard: FDUR for RUP2 and CMOR for both PM and GEO. The resulting blackboard is shown in Figure 3(F).

7). The operator requests the schedule for RUP1 ("Rup1Sched"). ACTIN's data-driven knowledge sources determine that the current action type is "Rup1Sched" and that actions of this type potentially support the task of finding unscheduled equipment (FUSC) for RUP components. Upon examining the tasks level of the blackboard, the knowledge sources find that one eligible task is posted: the FUSC task for RUP2. Thus, the "Rup1Sched" action is posted and connected to the FUSC task associated with the RUP2 replace plan. The resulting blackboard is shown in Figure 3(G).

8). Finally, the operator requests the schedule for NAS5. ACTIN's data-driven knowledge sources determine that this request potentially supports finding unscheduled NAS components (i.e., the FUSC task associated with any NAS component). However, although a FUSC type task is Posted, it is not associated with a NAS type component. ACTIN is unable to interpret this request as supporting any current tasks. Thus, the "Nas5Sched" request action is posted, but not connected to any current tasks. Figure 3(H) illustrates the resulting blackboard.

Several characteristics of ACTIN's interpretation algorithm are notable. First, actions are immediately connected to whatever appropriate tasks exist on the blackboard *at the time the actions are posted*. Connection links are not inferred after the action is posted.

Another important feature is ACTIN's property of maximal connectivity. That is, ACTIN interprets actions in the broadest possible context, assuming that the operator is extracting the maximum amount of information from the display pages requested. In the example above, ACTIN inferred that the second telem action supported all current CMOR tasks as well as the FDUR task for RUP2. Thus, the operator is "given the benefit of the doubt" in the evaluation of performance.

The evaluation of operator performance is performed by knowledge sources that assess the degree to which operator actions support current tasks (and by extension, plans and goals). ACTIN schedules assessments periodically in the context of particular goals or plans. In the example above, ACTIN schedules separate assessments for the control of current mission goals for PM and GEO, and the replace plan for RUP2. Assessments note the number of supporting actions and the time at which those actions occurred. The assessments for PM and GEO would note that the CMOR task is supported by two actions and the CEND task is supported by one action. RUP2's replace plan assessment would state that one action supports the FDUR task and one action supports the FUSC task. The results of these assessments are written to a logfile.

To summarize, the proposed model for intent inferencing uses the OFM methodology to postulate operator functions, subfunctions, and tasks on the basis of current system state and observed operator actions. This model has been implemented using a blackboard architecture. This structure, of which the scenario described in this section is an example, defines the context for intent inferencing.

The OFM and its implementation in ACTIN is an example of "the middle ground" in theory construction in cognitive science (Miller, Polson, and Kintsch, 1984). The theory has well-defined structures and processes to "support both the instantiation of the theory as an executable computer program and qualitative experimental studies of the theory" (Miller, Polson, and Kintsch, 1984, p. 13).

In the next section the validation of the proposed model is explored. A two-stage framework for validation is proposed, and experimental results are briefly discussed.

EXPERIMENTAL VALIDATION

Validation of intent inferencing assures that the system is correctly inferring the intentions of the human operator. Within the context of the OFM structure of intentions, this means that the system infers support for the same tasks (and by extension, plans and goals) as the human, given the same set of operator actions. The "human" in this case can be a human domain expert performing a post hoc analysis, or the human operator giving an (on-line) account of intentions. Thus, the proposed two-part framework for the validation of intent interferencing is 1) comparison of expert and OFMspert analyses; and (2) comaprison of concurrnet verbal protocols and OFMspert analysis (see Jones, 1988, for more details).

The experimental validation of ACTIN's intent inferencing was conducted in two studies. In Experiment 1, a domain expert's interpretations of operator data were compared to ACTIN's interpretations of those same actions on an action-by-action basis. In Experiment 2, verbal protocols were collected from GT-MSOCC operators while they were controlling GT-MSOCC. Statements of intentions for each tion were compared to ACTIN's interpretations.

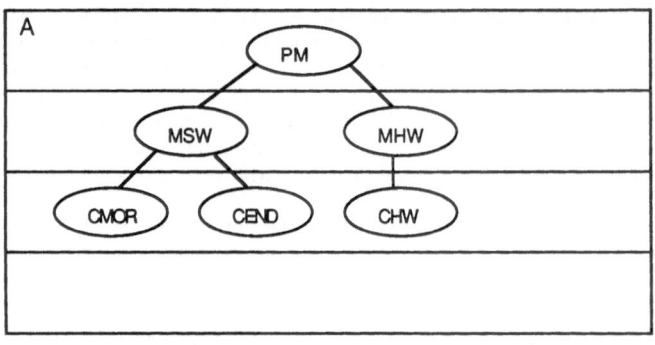

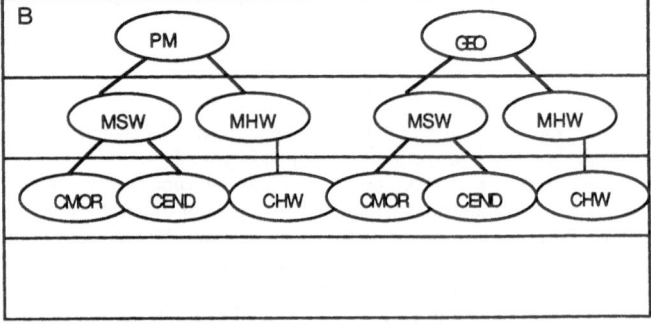

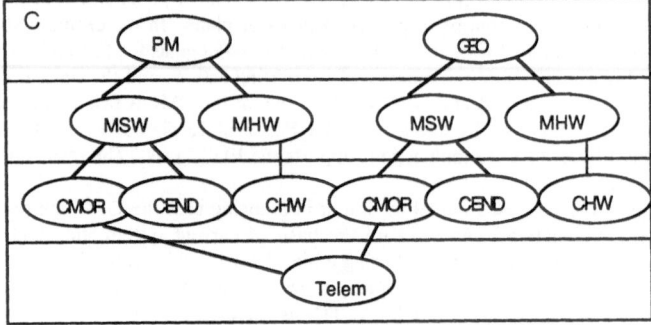

Telem is interpreted as supporting CMOR for PM, CMOR for GEO

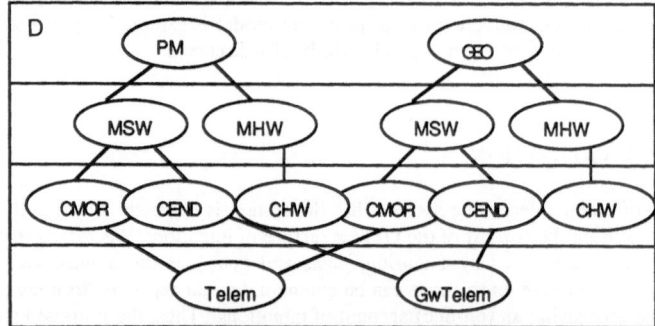

GwTelem is interpreted as supporting CEND for PM, CEND for GEO

Figure 3. (A) Blackboard after PM is configured.
(B) Blackboard after GEO is configured.
(C) Blackboard after Telem Page Request.
(D) Blackboard after GwTelem Page Request.

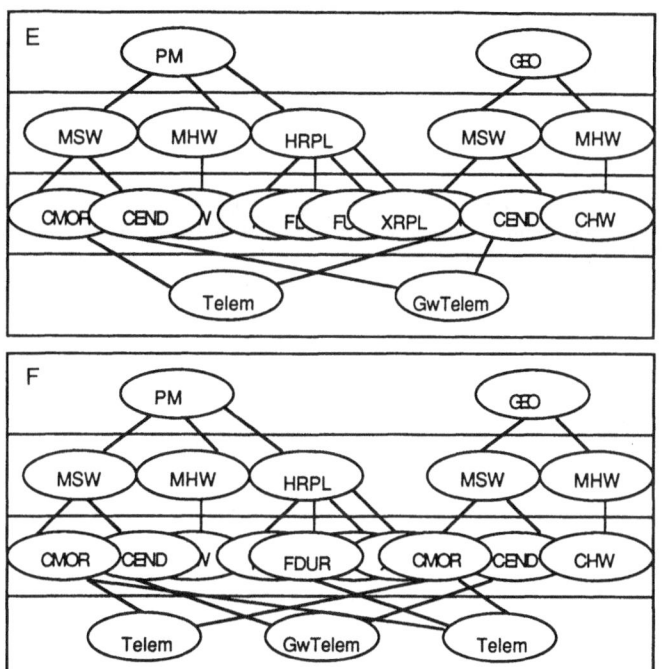

Telem is interpreted as supporting CMOR for PM, CMOR for GEO, FDUR for RUP2

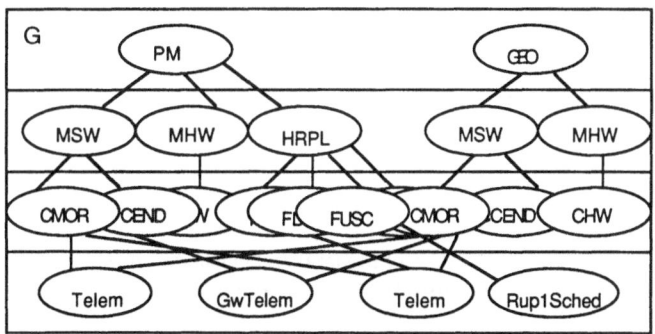

Rup1Sched is interpreted as supporting FUSC for RUP2

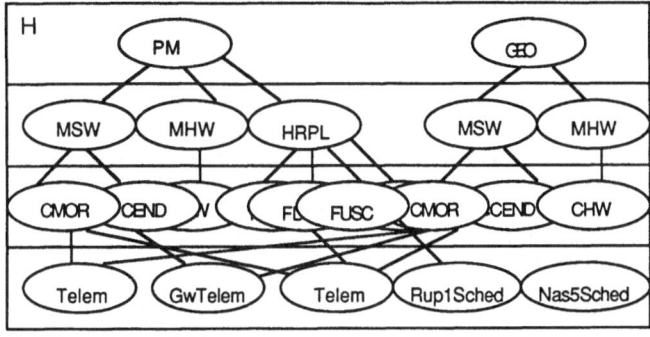

Unable to connect Nas5Sched

Figure 3. (E) Blackboard after RUP2 Hardware Failure.
(F) Blackboard after Telem Page Request.
(G) Blackboard after RUP1 Schedule Request.
(H) Blackboard after NAS5 Schedule Request.

The results of these studies are discussed in detail in Jones (1988). Overall, the results showed that ACTIN's intent inferencing ability compared favorably to inferences made by a domain expert and statements from verbal reports.

ACKNOWLEDGEMENTS

This research was supported by NASA Goddard Space Flight Center Contract Number NAS5-28575 (Karen Moe and Walt Truszkowski, technical monitors) and by NASA Ames Research Center Grant Number NAG-413 (Dr. Everett Palmer, technical monitor), awarded to Dr. Christine M. Mitchell.

REFERENCES

Chambers, A. G., and Nagel, D. C., 1985, Pilots of the Future: Human or Computer? *Communications of the ACM*, Vol. 28, No. 11, pp. 1187-1199.

Cohen, A., and Feigenbaum, E. A., 1982, *The Handbook of Artificial Intelligence*, Addison-Wesley, Reading, Mass.

Jones, P. M., 1988, *Constructing and Validating a Model-Based Operator's Associate for Supervisory Control*, Report No. 88-1, Center for Human-Machine Systems Research, School of Industrial and Systems Engineering, Georgia Institute of Technology, Atlanta, GA.

Jones, P. M., and Mitchell, C. M., 1987, Operator Modeling: Conceptual and Methodological Distinctions, *Proceedings of the 31st Annual Meeting of the Human Factors Society*, Volume 1, pp. 31-35, Santa Monica, CA.

Miller, J. R., Polson, P. G., and Kintsch, W., 1984, Problems of Methodology in Cognitive Science, *Method and Tactics in Cognitive Science*, Kintsch, W., Miller, J. R., and Polson, P. G., eds., Lawrence Erlbaum Associates, Hillsdale, NJ.

Miller, R. A., 1985, A Systems Approach to Modeling Discrete Control Performance, *Advances in Man-Machine Systems Research*, Volume 2, Rouse, W. B., ed., pp. 177-248, JAI Press, New York.

Mitchell, C. M., 1987, GT-MSOCC: A Research Domain for Modeling Human-Computer Interaction and Aiding Decision Making in Supervisory Control Systems, *IEEE Transactions on Systems, Man, and Cybernetics*, Vol. SMC-17, pp. 553-572.

Mitchell, C. M., and Forren, M. G., 1987, Multimodal User Input to Supervisory Control Systems: Voice-Augmented Keyboards, *IEEE Transactions on Systems, Man, and Cybernetics*, Vol. SMC-17, pp. 594-607.

Mitchell, C. M., and Miller, R. A., 1985, A Discrete Control Model of Operator Function: A Methodology for Information Display Design, *IEEE Transactions on Systems, Man, and Cybernetics*, Vol. SMC-16, pp. 343-357.

Mitchell, C. M., and Saisi, D. L., 1987, Use of Model-Based Qualitative Icons and Adaptive Windows in Workstations for Supervisory Control Systems, *IEEE Transactions on Systems, Man, and Cybernetics*, Vol. SMC-17, pp. 573-593.

Nii, H. P., Feigenbaum, E. A., Anton, J. J., and Rockmore, A. J., 1982, *Signal-to-Symbol Transformation: HAS/SIAP Case Study*, Heuristic Programming Project, Report No. HPP-82-6, Heuristic Programming Project, Stanford University, Stanford, CA.

Nii, H. P., 1986, Blackboard Systems, *AI Magazine*, Vol. 7-2, Vol. 7-3.

Rasmussen, J., 1986, *Information Processing and Human-Machine Interaction: An Approach to Cognitive Engineering*, North-Holland, New York.

Rouse, W. B., Geddes, N. D., and Currey, R. E., 1987, An Architecture for Intelligent Interfaces: Outline of an Approach to Supporting Operators of Complex Systems, *Human-Computer Interaction*, Vol. 3.

Rubin, K. S., Jones, P. M., and Mitchell, C. M., 1987, *OFMspert: Application of a Blackboard Architecture to Infer Operator Intentions in Real Time Decision Making*, Report No. 87-6, Center for Human-Machine Systems Research, School of Industrial Systems Engineering, Georgia Institute of Technology, GA. Also *IEEE Transactions on Systems, Man, and Cybernetics*, to appear.

Schank, R. C., and Abelson, R. P., 1977, *Scripts, Plans, Goals, and Understanding*, Lawrence Erlbaum Associates, Hillsdale, NJ.

Sheridan, T. B., and Johannsen, G., 1976, *Monitoring Behavior and Supervisory Control*, Plenum, New York.

Wenger, E., 1987 *Artificial Intelligence and Tutoring Systems*, Morgan Kaufmann, Los Altos, CA.

Wickens, C. D., 1984, *Engineering Psychology and Human Performance*, Charles Merrill, Columbus, OH.

Winograd, T., 1972, *Understanding Natural Language*, Academic Press, New York.

Woods, D. D., 1986, Cognitive Technologies: The Design of Joint Human-Machine Cognitive Systems, *The AI Magazine*, pp. 86-92.

COMPUTER AIDED DECISION MAKING USING UNCERTAIN AND IMPRECISE INFORMATION

E. Czogala and J.Chmielniak

Silesian Technical University
Pstrowskiego 16
44-100 Gliwice, Poland

Abstract: In many decision situations, especially in an uncertain and imprecise decision making environment, the decision criteria, such as objective functions, restrictions or goals are often modeled by means of a concept of a probabilistic set. A probabilistic set C of **X** is essentially defined by its defining function $C : X \times \Omega \rightarrow [0,1]$ where X represents a set of feasible alternatives and Ω stands for a space of elementary events.

Aggregating all decision criteria sets by means of various operations on probabilistic sets (such as triangular norms, compensatory operations, averaging operations and so on) the final decision probabilistic set has to be found.

Taking into account the distribution function description of the probabilistic set, we can obtain the basic characteristics (e.g., mean value, variance, etc.) of each alternative. According to given criteria (e.g., criteria based on the concept of stochastic dominance, mean-variance criterion and others), we can make the final choice of the best alternative.

FUZZY SETS IN DECISION MAKING

The concept of fuzzy set was applied to decision making by Bellman and Zadeh (1970) first and continued by many authors (Czogala, 1988; Czogala and Hirota, 1986; Kacprzyk, 1983; Takegushi and Akashi, 1984; Wrather and Yu, 1982; Yager, 1984).

In conventional multi-criteria decision making problems we usually start with a finite set **X** of N possible elements (alternatives, variants) $x_i \in X$ and M real valued criteria $C_1,...,C_M$. The criteria $C_j (j = 1,...,M)$ are considered as fuzzy sets defined by the respective membership functions

$$C_j : X \rightarrow [0,1] \tag{1}$$

or

$$x_i \rightarrow C_j(x_i) \quad \forall\, i,j \in N \tag{2}$$

In fuzzy approach $C_j(x_i)$ may indicate the degree to which x_i satisfies the criterion (objective function, restriction or goal) C_j.

In decision making tasks, an aggregation of decision criteria plays a significant role when one desires to satisfy more than one criteria. Fuzzy sets representing criteria may be aggregated using various aggregation operators. We can join fuzzy sets by means of such general operators as triangular norms (Czogala and Hirota, 1986) with their properties like monotonicity, commutativity, and associativity or even operators of the "compensatory and" type (Zimmerman and Zysno, 1980) without associativity property. Aggregating criteria by means of binary operators, we may obtain the final fuzzy decision set D in the form:

$$D = \ldots \cdot\left(\left(C_1 o_{p_1} C_2\right) o_{p_2} C_3\right) \cdots o_{p_{m-1}} C_M \tag{3}$$

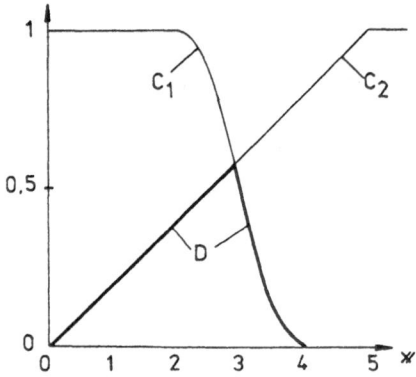

Figure 1. Fuzzy Criteria and Decision Set.

where o_{p_k} (k = 1,2.....M-1) stands for the general aggregation operator depending on parameter p_k for each $x_i \in X$.

The problem of evaluating the optimal alternatives which arises now may be solved in many ways, using various criteria. From the decision set D we can determine the set of elements having the highest degree of preference i.e.:

$$M = \{x_{opt} \in X \mid D(x_{opt}) = \max_{x \in X} D(x) \} \tag{4}$$

or

$$x_{opt} = \frac{\int_x^x D(x) \, dx}{\int_x D(x) \, dx} \tag{5}$$

Where in last formula x_{opi} is respected to be the center of gravity of the decision set D.

An important feature of this approach is worth noticing, namely the symmetry between the criteria which allows treatment of all of them in the same way.

As an illustration of that let us consider a simple example assuming that two criteria are expressed as:

C_1 : x should be "fuzzy greater than 0"
C_2 : x should be "fuzzy less than 4"

where

$$C_1(x) = \begin{cases} 0 & x \le 0 \\ x/5 & 0 \le x \le 5 \\ 1 & x \ge 5 \end{cases} \tag{6}$$

$$C_2(x) = \begin{cases} 1 & x \le 2 \\ 1 - 2((x-2)/2)^2 & 2 \le x \le 3 \\ 2((x-4)/w)^2 & 3 \le x \le 4 \\ 0 & x \ge 4 \end{cases} \tag{7}$$

Both these sets and the fuzzy decision set D taken as an intersection of the criteria, i.e.,

$$D(x) = \min(C_1(x), C_2(x)) \tag{8}$$

are shown in Figure 1.

According to formula (4) we have $x_{opi} = 3$.

PROBABILISTIC SETS IN DECISION MAKING

We also start here with a finite set **X** of N feasible elements (alternatives) x_i, and M real valued criteria $C_1,...,C_M$. The criteria C_j (j = 1,...,M) are considered as probabilistic sets (Czogala and Hirota, 1986), i.e.

$$C_j : X \times \Omega \rightarrow [0,1] \tag{9}$$

or

$$(x_i, \omega) \rightarrow C_j(x_i, \omega) \qquad \forall \ i,j \in N \tag{10}$$

where Ω stands for a set of elementary events ω.

In terms of probabilistic distribution function description of probabilistic sets we usually consider two forms of that function, i.e., a continuous case and a discrete case. Probabilistic sets C_j are aggregated by various aggregation operators. We can also join probabilistic sets by means of such general aggregation operators as triangular norms with their properties like monotonicity, commutativity and associativity or operations as "compensatory and" without associativity property (Zimmerman and Zysno, 1980). The final probabilistic decision set D may be written in the form as previously:

$$D = \dots ((C_1 o_{P_1} C_2) o_{P_2} C_3) \dots o_{P_{M-1}} C_M \tag{11}$$

We may describe the set D in terms of distribution functions using respective joint distribution function, i.e.,

$$F_D(z) = F_{(\dots((C_1 o_{P_1} C_2) o_{P_2} C_3) \dots o_{P_{M-1}} C_M)}(z) \tag{12}$$
$$\forall \ x_i \in X, \ z \in [0,1]$$

The final form of this function depends on the input information and on the operations taken into account. Very often the only information we have is the distribution function of each particular set i.e., $F_{c_j}(z)$ (of course for each alternative $x_i \in X$), which is in fact the marginal distributon function. In those cases we will assume independence of the input probabilistic sets in order to get the distribution function of the final decision set D. It should be mentioned here that it is possible to get a general description of the input sets.

If we have the distribution function of the decision set we can easily determine the respective mean value

$$E(D) = \int_0^1 z \ df_D(z) \tag{13}$$

and the variance

$$V(D) = \int_0^1 (z - E(D))^2 \ df_D(z) \tag{14}$$

and higher moments for each element $x_i \in X$.

Variance is also called vagueness in terms of probabilistic sets. The mean and variance values are used with various criteria to choose the best element, i.e., criteria based on stochastic dominance or mean-variance criteria based on the inequalities (Wrather and Yu, 1982):

$$E(D)(x_i) \geq E(D)(x_j), \qquad V(D)(x_i) \leq V(D)(x_j) \qquad \forall \ i \neq j \tag{15}$$

with at last one inequality holding strictly.

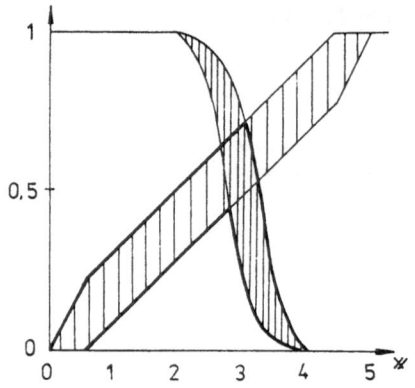

Figure 2. Probabilistic Criteria and Decision Set.

As in fuzzy approach we will give here an example to illustrate the above considerations. Assume the criteria are expressed as

C_1 : x should be "probabilistic greater than 0"
C_2 : x should be "probabilistic less than 4"

where the mean values of probabilistic sets of these criteria are fuzzy sets of the example given in fuzzy approach. These probabilistic sets and probabilistic decision set are illustrated in Figure 2.

PROBABILISTIC DESCRIPTION OF THE DECISION SET

The general formula for a distribution function of a decision probabilistic set composed of two probabilistic sets X and Y may be written as follows (Czogala and Hirota, 1986):

$$F_D(z) = \int\int_{D_z} f_{XY}(x, y) \; dx \; dy \qquad (16)$$

where $D_z = \{(x,y) ; x \, o_p \, y \le z, a \le x \le b, c \le y \le d \}$ - denotes the integral domain and $f_{XY}(x,y)$ stands for the respective joint density function of the input sets.

We can take a density function as a continuously distributed in a rectangle $[a,b] \times [c,d]$

$$g_{XY}(x, y) = \begin{cases} f_{XY}(x, y) & if \; a \le x \le b, \; c \le y \le d \\ 0 & otherwise \end{cases} \qquad (17)$$

satisfying the equality:

$$\int_a^b \int_c^d g_{XY}(x, y) \; dx \; dy = 1 \qquad (18)$$

or for the discrete case, which seems to be the more practical one, we take:

$$f_{XY}(x, y) = \begin{cases} \sum_{i=1}^m \sum_{j=1}^n w_i v_j \, \delta(x-x_i) \, \delta(y-y_j) & if \; x_i \in [a,b] , \; y_j \in [c,d] \\ 0 & otherwise \end{cases} \qquad (19)$$

where symbol $\delta(x)$ denotes Dirac's pseudo-function and w_i, v_j, stand for the respective probabilities which fulfill the equalities:

262

Table 1

Alternatives and Critera for the Example

Alternatives	x_1	x_2	x_3
Criterion 1	0.3	f_1	p_1
Criterion 2	0.5	f_2	f_4
Criterion 3	0.7	f_3	p_2

where

f_1 is normal density function on [0.2,0.6] m=0.4 σ^2=0.1

f_2 is uniform density function on [0.1,0.7]

f_3 is exponential density function on [0.5,1] λ=0.8

f_4 is exponential density function on [0.3,0.8] λ=0.4

p_1 are discrete probabilities p(0.5)=0.5, p(0.7)=0.5

p_2 are discrete probabilities p(0.3)=0.6, p(0.6)=0.4

$$\sum_{i=1}^{m} w_i = 1, \qquad \sum_{j=1}^{n} v_j = \tag{20}$$

Particularly w_i = 1/m and v_j = 1/n.

Taking into account the assumption of the independence of the respective random variables we can calculate the probabilities $p(z_k)$ where $z_k = x_i o_p y_j$ (k = 1,...,l) where l ≤ m*n.

$$p(z_k) = P(D=z_k) = P(Xo_{pY}=z_k) = \sum_{i,j:x_i o_p y_j = z_k}^{P} (X=x_i) P(Y=y_j) = \sum_{i,j:x_i o_p y_j = z_k}^{w_i} v_j \tag{21}$$

The density function of D can be calculated as follows:

$$f_D(z) = \sum_{k=1}^{l} p(z_k) \delta(z-z_k) = \sum_{k-1}^{l} \sum_{i,j:x_i o_p y_j = z_k} w_i v_j \delta(z-x_i o_p y_j) \tag{22}$$

The distribution function of D can be obtained in the form:

$$F_D(z) = F_{Xo_pY}(z) = \sum_{k:z_k<z} p(z_k) \tag{23}$$

Mean and variance are calculated as follows:

$$E(D) = \sum_k z_k\, p(z_k) \tag{24}$$

$$V(D) = \sum_k (z_k - E(D))^2\, p(z_k) \tag{25}$$

For continuous density function we can write the formulas:

$$p_{i.} = \int_{x_i-h/2}^{x_i+h/2} \int_{c}^{d} f_{XY}(x,y)\ dx\ dy = \int_{x_i-h/2}^{x_i+h/2} f_X(x)\ dx \tag{26}$$

Table 2

Ordered Results of the Example

	mean	variance
x_2	0.425	0.007
x_3	0.418	0.010
x_1	0.410	0.000

$$p_{.j} = \int_a^b \int_{y_j-h/2}^{y_j+h/2} f_{XY}(x,y) \; dx \; dy = \int_{y_j-h/2}^{y_j+h/2} f_Y(y) \; dy \qquad (27)$$

The marginal probability $p_{i.}$ corresponds to w_i and p_j to v_j. Using the assumption of independence the obvious equality holds true:

$$P_{ij} = P_{i.}.P_{.j} \qquad (28)$$

Discretizing the continuous case we may combine both cases (i.e., a discrete case and a continuous one) applying various aggregation operations in a unified computer algorithm.

NUMERICAL EXAMPLE

Let us consider a case of three alternatives for which the input data are discrete, continuous and mixed (Table 1).

It is assumed that there are three criteria joined into one probabilistic set. Table 2 presents the ordered results obtained by means of the "compensatory and" operation:

x o$_p$ y = (1-p)*min(x,y) + p*max(x,y)

The same value of parameter p (i.e., p=0.2) is taken for both aggregations.

CONCLUDING REMARKS

Very often a decision maker faces a problem of choosing among elements (alternatives). In this paper, it is assumed that all the elements in the choice set can be characterized by a finite number of various criteria. The uncertainty is represented by a finite number of various criteria. The probabilistic sets representing criteria are aggregated by different connectives in order to obtain the final decision set which is a probabilistic set as well. Some empirical works (Zimmerman and Zysno, 1980) indicate that t-norms are not very appropriate to model human use of the "and", so the compensatory operators seem to be more adequate in human decision making. However, here we have to point out again that these operators have no associativity property. It should be also mentioned that the described algorithm can be easily used for multi-criteria and multi-stage decision making problems too.

REFERENCES

Bellman, R., and Zadeh, L. A., 1970, Decision Making in a Fuzzy Environment, *Management Science*, Vol. 17, pp. 141-164.

Transactions on Systems, Man, and Cybernetics, Vol. 14, No. 4, pp. 618-625.

Wrather, C., and Yu, P. L., 1982, Probability Dominance in Random Outcomes, *Journal of Optimization, Theory, and Applications*, Vol. 36, No. 3, pp. 315-334.

Yager, R. R., 1984, Fuzzy Subsets with Uncertain Membership Grades, *IEEE Transactions on Systems, Man and Cybernetics*, Vol. 14, No. 2.

Zimmerman, H. J., and Zysno, P., 1980, Latent Connectives in Human Decision Making, *Fuzzy Sets and Systems*, Vol. 4, pp. 37-51.

VI. MODELS OF LANGUAGE USE

STATISTICAL MODELS OF LANGUAGE USE

Ian H. Witten and Timothy C. Bell*

Department of Computer Science
University of Calgary
Calgary, Canada T2N 1N4
(403) 220-6780
ian@cpsc.calgary.cdn

*Department of Computer Science
University of Canterbury
Christchurch 1, New Zealand
(64-3) 642352
..!watmath!cantuar!tim

Abstract: An oft-cited model of word frequency in natural language is the Zipf distribution, held by some to account for the fact that common words are, by and large, shorter than rare ones through a principle of "least effort". It is beginning to re-emerge as a model of artificial language too; for example, command usage in computer systems. However, it has been established that Zipf's law is very easily achieved by simple random processes. This paper examines random models of both word and letter production, derives the associated rank/frequency relationships, and compares them with those found in naturally-occurring English text. The result shows that Zipf's distribution arises from purely random sources, and questions the validity of interpretations of observed hyperbolic rank/ frequency distributions as manifestations of purposeful, or even evolutionary, behavior.

INTRODUCTION

It has often been noticed that when words occurring in natural-language texts are tabulated in rank order and their frequencies plotted, the hyperbolic shape of Figure 1(A) is obtained. The effect is characterized by the fact that the product of rank and frequency remains approximately constant over the range. It is most easily detected on a graph with logarithmic scales, where the hyperbolic function appears as a straight line. Replotting the word frequencies on log scales produces the remarkably straight line of Figure 1(B). Similar shapes are obtained from the distributions of other naturallyoccurring units such as letters in text and references to articles in journals.

These effects were popularized 40 years ago by a book entitled *Human Behavior and the Principle of Least Effort* (Zipf, 1949). Its author, the American philologist George Kingsley Zipf (1902-1950), collected a remarkable variety of hyperbolic laws in the social sciences. Their ubiquity was attributed to a general "principle of least effort", which was credited with far-reaching consequences, but was regrettably not stated with commensurate precision. He also wrote of a fundamental governing principle that determines the number and frequency of usage of words in speech and writing, and associated this with the least-effort principle; although the details of how the latter was supposed to explain the former are not clear.

Although the Zipf law is not exact, it is a good enough approximation to natural language phenomena to demand an explanation. Moreover, we have observed that the same hyperbolic distribution is beginning to re-emerge as a model of artificial language and user behavior; for example, command usage

Empirical Foundations of Information and Software Science V
Edited by P. Zunde and D. Hocking, Plenum Press, New York, 1990

269

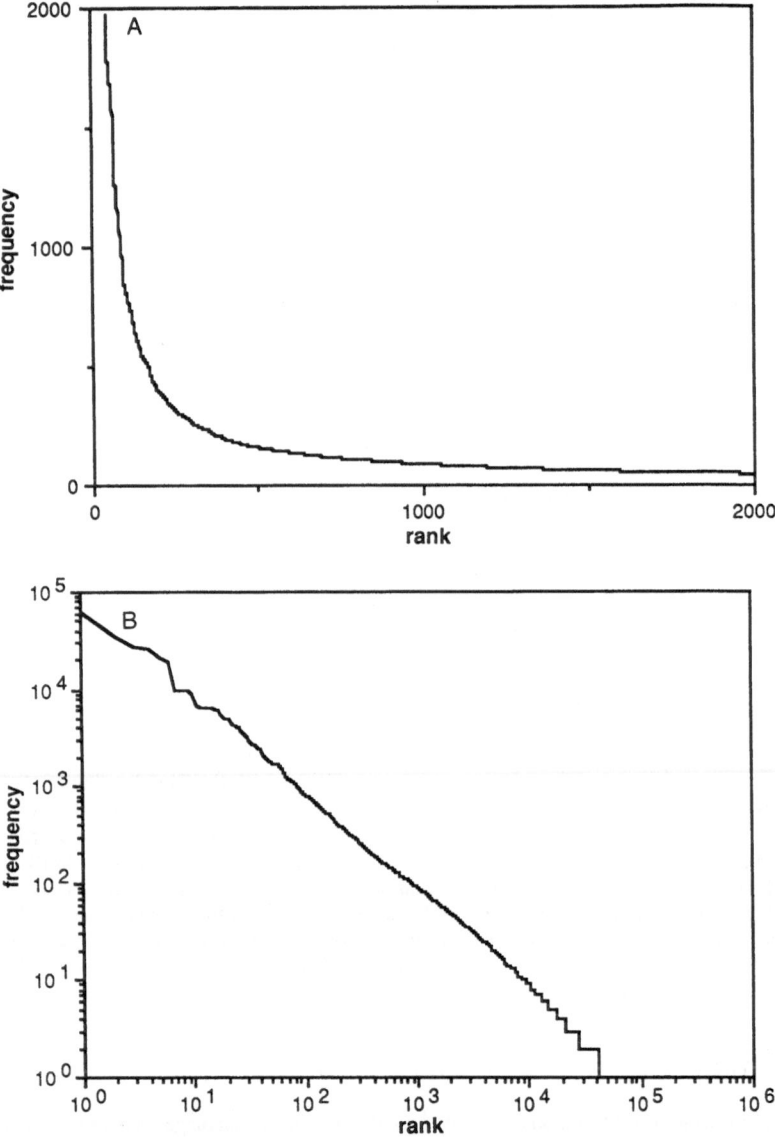

Figure 1. (A) Word-Frequency Data From a Million Words of English Text.
(B) The Same Data Plotted on Logarithmic Scales.

in computer systems (e.g. Peachey, Bunt, and Colbourn, 1982; Witten, Cleary, and Greenberg, 1984; Ellis and Hitchcock, 1986). The principle of least effort is sometimes cited tool although it is not quantitative enough to carry much explanatory weight.

However, teleologically-based explanations of Zipf's law may be unnecessary, for it seems that in many situations it is very easily achieved by simple random processes. It was shown some time ago that the hyperbolic distribution of word frequencies is a direct consequence of the assumption that letters are generated according to a simple random process, although this does not appear to be widely known. In this paper we recapitulate this result and compare the predicted word distribution with that obtained from a large corpus of naturally-occurring English. We also examine a simple random model of letter production, deriving the associated rank/frequency relationship. While the resulting distribution differs from the Zipf law, it provides an excellent fit to the letter distribution observed in English--much better than Zipf's.

Table 1

Word Statistics From the Brown Corpus

word	% prob	digram	% prob	trigram	% prob
the	6.15	of the	0.95	one of the	0.03
of	3.54	in the	0.55	as well as	0.02
and	2.70	to the	0.33	the United States	0.02
to	2.51	on the	0.23	out of the	0.02
a	2.14	and the	0.21	some of the	0.02
in	1.90	for the	0.17	the end of	0.01
that	0.97	to be	0.16	the fact that	0.01
is	0.95	at the	0.15	part of the	0.01
was	0.94	with the	0.14	to be a	0.01
for	0.86	of a	0.14	of the United	0.01
with	0.68	that the	0.13	a number of	0.01
as	0.65	from the	0.13	end of the	0.01
he	0.65	by the	0.13	members of the	0.01
The	0.64	in a	0.13	in order to	0.01
his	0.63	as a	0.09	the use of	0.01
be	0.61	with a	0.09	that he had	0.01
on	0.61	is a	0.08	the number of	0.01
it	0.54	it is	0.08	most of the	0.01
had	0.50	of his	0.08	side of the	0.01
by	0.49	was a	0.08	that he was	0.01
at	0.49	is the	0.08	in front of	0.01
I	0.44	had been	0.07	and in the	0.01
not	0.41	for a	0.07	there is a	0.01
are	0.41	it was	0.07	of the most	0.01
from	0.41	he was	0.07	It was a	0.01
or	0.40	into the	0.07	One of the	0.01
have	0.38	as the	0.07	there was a	0.01
...	...	...	...	...	...

number of units	100237		539929		884371
entropy (bits/word)	11.47		6.06		2.01
entropy (bits/letter)	1.95		1.03		0.34

NATURAL WORD DISTRIBUTION

The distribution of Figure 1 was obtained from a collection of American English text known as the Brown corpus, which was drawn from printed sources published in the U.S. in 1961 and has been widely used in studying language statistics. Its 500 separate 2,000-word samples total just over a million words of natural-language text representing a wide range of styles and authors, from press reporting through belles lettres, from learned and scientific writing through love stories.

Figure 1 is effectively a sorted histogram of word counts. However, counting words is complicated by the difficulty of defining what a "word" is. For the purpose of text analysis, words are generally considered as sequences of non-space characters. Thus "letter", "letters", "lettering", and "lettered" are each counted separately. Generally, upper-case letters are mapped to the corresponding lower-case ones. Homographs (like verbal "can" and noun "can") will appear as the same word, and variants of spelling (like "cannot," "can't," and "can not") as different ones (in the last case, as two separate words). Because of this, the number of distinct words counted in a text cannot be construed as the vocabulary of the author. There are a multitude of small matters that must be resolved when analyzing text into words--the treatment of hyphens and apostrophes; numbers expressed as digits; proper names; acronyms; words without vowels; and so on. Each analysis program takes its own stand on such matters, and consequently different word counts are often obtained for the same body of text. Fortunately, these small discrepancies do not have a noticeable effect on statistical models of language, and are effectively masked by the logarithmic scale on which rank/frequency graphs are usually plotted.

Table 1 shows the frequencies of the most popular few words in the Brown corpus, the complete data being plotted in Figure 1. Here a word is taken to be a longest contiguous group of characters separated by spaces, and multiple spaces are ignored. Although this definition is not ideal (for example, the token "end" is distinguished from the token "end;"), it is highly pragmatic, and because information content is invariably measured on a logarithmic scale, as entropy, the results produced are similar to other definitions such as contiguous groups of *letters*. Using our definition, the Brown corpus contains a total of 1,014,941 words, and 100,237 different ones. The average word length is 4.9 characters (plus one space). This is a little higher than the generally accepted figure of 4.5 because punctuation is frequently appended to "words".

Short function words appear much more often than content words like nouns and verbs. The most frequent 5-letter word in the Brown corpus is "which", the first 6-letter one "should", the first 7-letter one "through" the first 8-letter one "American", the first 9-letter one "something", the first 10-letter one "individual", the first 11-letter one "development". The 100 most frequent words account for 42% of the words in the corpus, but only 0.1% of its 100,237 different words. Words occurring only once in the corpus, technically referred to by the Greek term *hapax legomena* account for 58% of the vocabulary used but only 5.7% of words in the text (although with an average length of 8.4 characters, they represent 9% of the characters in the text.) Words occurring no more than 10 times account for 91% of the vocabulary but only 18% of the text.

Not every word in the corpus can be found in an English dictionary. Because of the wide range of text covered, some unusual English is included. For example, a quote from a soldier's letter contains the sentence:

"Alf sed he heard that you and hardy was a runing together all the time and he though he wod gust quit having any thing mor to doo with you for he thought it was no more yuse."

Despite its unusual style, this sentence is a part of English literature, and is a salutary reminder that any model of English should have a small allowance for any sequence of characters.

Also shown in Table 1 are word-level digram and trigram frequencies of the corpus. The high-frequency digrams are clearly those that come immediately to the fingers of a skilled typist. In the trigrams, the culture-dependent content of the corpus begins to show, with the appearance of phrases like "the United States" and "members of the".

ZIPF'S LAW

Zipf's law states that the product of rank and frequency remains constant, that is, the probability of the unit (e.g., word) at the r'th rank is

$$p(r) = \frac{\mu}{r} , \quad r = 1, 2, \ldots, N.$$

Because the sum of the probabilities must be one, the normalizing constant μ for a vocabulary of N words can be calculated as

$$\mu \propto \frac{1}{\log_e N + \gamma} ,$$

where $\gamma = 0.57721566$ is known as the Euler-Mascheroni constant. This is a good approximation for appreciable values of N.

A number of other hyperbolic distributions have been studied. Zipf's law dictates that the frequency of the second most popular item is half that of the highest-ranking one, the third item is one third, and so on, so that relative frequencies form the series 1, 1/2, 1/3, ... The distribution is often described as "harmonic," because the same law governs the frequencies of natural harmonies in music. But empirical data often does not exhibit this characteristic exactly. To improve the fit of the distribution for small r, a parameter c may be introduced into the denominator. A further parameter B can be added to improve the fit for large r, giving

$$p(r) = \frac{\mu}{(c + r)^B} , \quad r = 1, 2, \ldots, N.$$

272

According to Mandelbrot (1952), whose name this distribution bears, B>1 in all the usual cases, and he defined 1/B to be the "informational temperature" of the text, claiming that it is a much more reliable estimate of the wealth of vocabulary than such notions as the "potential number of words". Other hyperbolic laws close relatives of the Zipf distribution, have been studied, including the lognormal (Carroll, 1966, 1967) and Bradford (Fairthorne, 1969) distributions.

When r=1 in Zipf's law, p(r)=μ, and so the normalizing constant can be estimated from the y-intercept of the rank/frequency graph. A straight-line approximation to the curve of Figure 1(B) has a y-intercept of around 90,000. Expressed as a fraction of the million-odd words in the corpus, this becomes 0.09. This is a little lower than Zipf's estimate of μ=0.1, which he obtained from the log rank-frequency plot of word data from James Joyce's monumental 260,000-word novel *Ulysses*. Zipf also obtained approximately the same value from a much smaller sample taken from American newspapers. Since the vocabulary used in the Brown corpus is N=100,237 words, the above normalization formula gives a value of μ=0.083, while the fact that Joyce used N=29,899 different words puts the value at μ=0.092. However, these estimates may be less reliable since they depend on only one parameter, vocabulary size, and not on the actual distribution itself. It is apparent that the value of N is extraordinarily sensitive to μ; using Zipf's estimate of μ=0.1 leads to N=12,500 different words instead of Joyce's 29,899!

In many applications, the entropy of the word distribution is important. The entropy of the Zipf distribution can be obtained from

$$\sum_{r=1}^{N} - \frac{\mu}{r} \log \frac{\mu}{r} \approx \frac{\mu (logN)^2}{2 \log e} - \log \mu$$

This leads to an estimate for the entropy of the word distribution in the Brown corpus of 11.51 bits per word, which is remarkably close to the actual value given in Table 1 of 11.47. This contrasts with the 16.61 bits that would be required to specify one out of the 100,237 different words used in the Brown corpus if their distribution were uniform.

A RANDOM GENERATIVE MODEL FOR WORDS

A simple generative model of text has spaces occurring 18% of the time (which accounts for the average word length In English of 4.5 characters), while letters are generated randomly with equal frequency. This model was first proposed by Miller, Newman, and Friedman (1957):

"[Imagine that] a monkey hits the keys of a typewriter at random, subject only to these constraints:

-- he must hit the space bar with a probability of p and all the other keys with a probability of 1-p, and

-- he must never hit the space bar twice in a row.

Let us examine the monkey's output, not because it is interesting, but because it will have some of the statistical properties considered interesting when humans, rather than monkeys, hit the keys."

The property that Miller derives is that the probability of the word ranked r obeys the Mandelbrot distribution

$$p(r) = \frac{0.11}{(0.54 + r)^{1.06}} ,$$

where the constants are based on the assumptions p=0.18 and a 26-letter alphabet. This is very close to Zipf's model for Ulysses. As Miller tartly observes, "research workers in statistical linguistics have sometimes expressed amazement that people can follow Zipf's law so accurately without any deliberate effort to do so. We see, however, that it is not really very amazing, since monkeys typing at random manage to do it about as well as we do."

The result basically depends on the fact that the probability of generating a long string of letters is a decreasing function of the length of the string, while the variety of long strings is far greater than the variety of short strings that are available. Consequently both the rank of a word and its frequency are determined by its length, for the monkeys, and, as Zipf and many others have observed, for English too. And the nature of the dependence is such that the product of rank and frequency remains roughly constant.

273

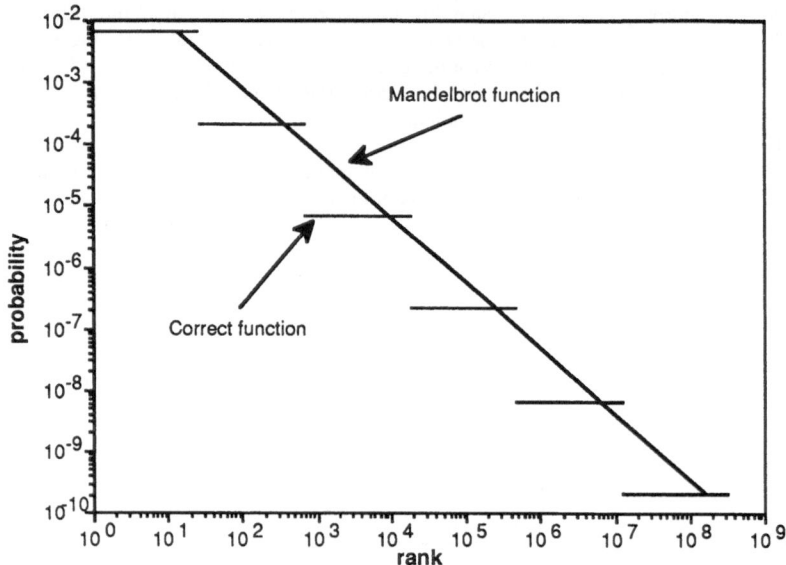

Figure 2. Rank-Probability Graph for Words Generated by Miller's Monkeys.

Miller's analysis of the text produced by monkeys assumes that letters are equiprobable, so the most common words are "a", "b", ... "z", each of which is equally likely to occur. This means that the words of rank 1 to 26 have the same probability, whereas the Mandelbrot formula shows a steady decrease. Likewise, the two-character words, which have rank 27 to 702, are equiprobable, and so on. Thus the correct rank- frequency relationship is a series of plateaus, shown on the probability frequency graph of Figure 2. The function derived by Miller passes through the average rank of each plateau, as shown. In this stepped rank/frequency distribution, the first 26 places are occupied by 1-letter words each of frequency 0.855% (for a total of 22%), the next 26^2 by 2-letter words each of frequency 0.026% (for a total of 17%), and so on. Although the center of each step lies exactly on the derived curve, the discrete nature of the distribution differs markedly from Zipf.

This discrepancy is attributable to the assumption that letters are equiprobable. The use of natural single-letter frequencies (or frequencies from the simple letter model mentioned above) smooths off the

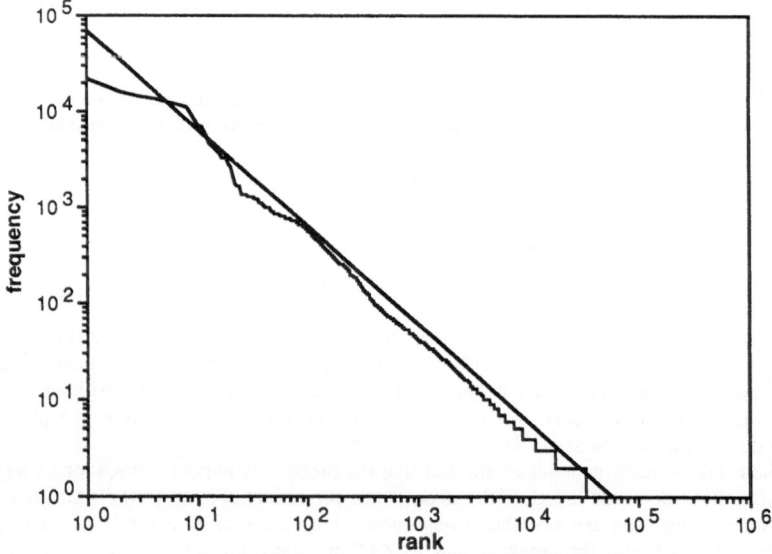

Figure 3. Rank-Frequency Graph for Words in Order-0 Random Text.

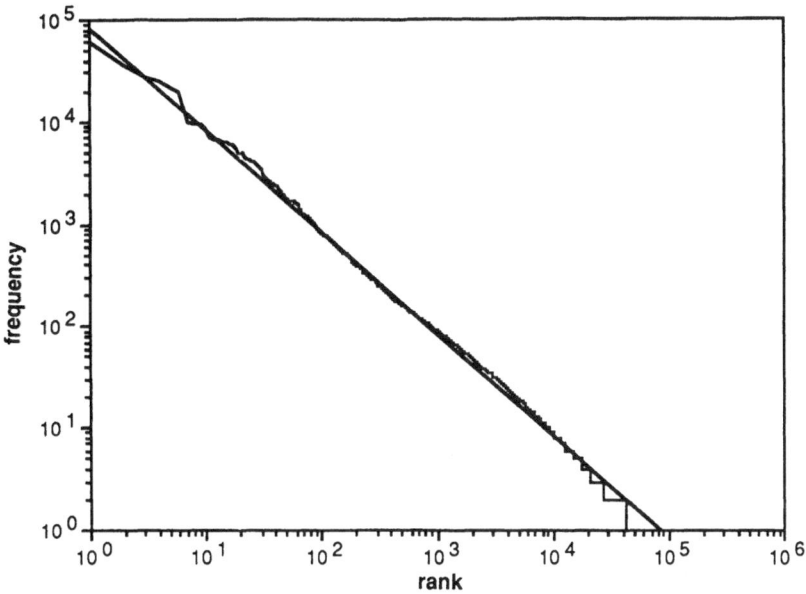

Figure 4. Word-Frequency Data From the Brown Corpus, Along with Zipf.

steps. If the monkeys are trained to strike each key with a frequency corresponding to its probability in English text, the plateaus are eroded so that the curve follows the Mandelbrot function very closely. Figure 3 shows the curve for a sample of a million words produced in an actual experiment with specially-trained monkeys[1], with the Zipf-Mandelbrot relation superimposed (they are indistinguishable at this scale).

The Zipfian behavior of this simple model is as remarkable as Miller's original observation, for it is based on random text obtained from an order-0 Markov model, which bears little resemblance to English. Here, for example, is a sample of text generated from this model, using single-letter probabilities taken from the Brown corpus.

> fsniaad ir lntns hynciaais oayimh t n at oeotc fheotyi t afrtgt oidts wrr thraeoe rdar ceg pso isemahntaweei t etaodgdna em r n nd fih an f tpteaanmas ss n tbar o be um oon tsrcs et mi ithyoitt h u ans w vsgr tn heaacrd erfdut y c am hra ieodn nyersoto oea nlorseo j r s t w ge g ikde 1 eeiahednn ngaosl dshoo +h seelm os threen nrgifeoedsoht tgt n ti a issninabih nhte bs co efhetntoilgevtnnadrtssaa ka dfnssiivb kuniseeaol h acdchnr onoal ie a lhehtr webolo aere mblefeuom eomtlko h oattogodrinl aw lbe.

Although characters appear in their correct proportions, no relationship between consecutive characters has been captured. While this can be corrected by using higher-order statistics, such sophistication is unnecessary for achieving the Zipf relationship.

Despite its statistical explanation in terms of a random process, the fact remains that the Zipf law is a useful model of word frequencies. Figure 4 reproduces the graph of Figure 1b, showing frequency against rank for the N = 100,237 different words in the Brown corpus, along with the Zipf model with normalizing constant calculated from $\mu = 1/(\log_e N + \gamma) = 0.08270$. Towards the end of the main line of data points the observed frequencies slope downwards marginally more steeply than the model, indicating that the Mandelbrot distribution with B slightly greater than unity may provide a better fit. Moreover the data seem flatter than the Zipf curve towards the left, an effect that could be modelled by choosing c>0, but is more likely a remnant of the first plateau seen in Figures 2 and 3.

---

[1]Computer-simulated ones.

Table 2

Letter Statistics From the Brown Corpus
("-" signifies a space character)

letter	% prob	digram	% prob	trigram	% prob	tetragram	% prob
-	17.41	e-	3.05	-th	1.62	-the	1.25
e	9.76	-t	2.40	the	1.36	the-	1.04
t	7.01	th	2.03	he-	1.32	-of-	0.60
a	6.15	he	1.97	-of	0.63	and-	0.48
o	5.90	-a	1.75	of-	0.60	-and	0.46
i	5.51	s-	1.75	ed-	0.60	-to-	0.42
n	5.50	d-	1.56	-an	0.59	ing-	0.40
s	4.97	in	1.44	nd-	0.57	-in-	0.32
r	4.74	t-	1.38	and	0.55	tion	0.29
h	4.15	n-	1.28	-in	0.51	n-th	0.23
l	3.19	er	1.26	ing	0.50	f-th	0.21
d	3.05	an	1.18	-to	0.50	of-t	0.21
c	2.30	-o	1.14	to-	0.46	hat-	0.20
u	2.10	re	1.10	ng-	0.44	-tha	0.20
m	1.87	on	1.00	er-	0.39	.---	0.20
f	1.76	-s	0.99	in-	0.38	his-	0.19
p	1.50	,-	0.96	is-	0.37	-for	0.19
g	1.47	-i	0.93	ion	0.36	ion-	0.18
w	1.38	-w	0.92	-a-	0.36	that	0.17
y	1.33	at	0.87	on-	0.35	-was	0.17
b	1.10	en	0.86	as-	0.33	d-th	0.16
,	0.98	r-	0.83	-co	0.32	-is-	0.16
.	0.83	y-	0.82	re-	0.32	was-	0.16
v	0.77	nd	0.81	at-	0.31	t-th	0.16
k	0.49	.-	0.81	ent	0.30	atio	0.15
T	0.30	-h	0.78	e-t	0.30	-The	0.15
"	0.29	ed	0.77	tio	0.29	e-th	0.15
...	...	...	...	...	...	...	...

number of units	94		3410		30249		131517
entropy							
(bits/letter)	4.47		3.59		2.92		2.33

A RANDOM MODEL FOR LETTERS

It is tempting to apply Zipf's relationship to all sorts of other rank-frequency data. For example, the letter, digram, trigram, and tetragram distributions of the Brown corpus, shown in Table 2, are all hyperbolic in form, and it is often assumed that such distributions obey Zipf's law. In fact, however, this law is not a particularly good model of letter frequencies. For example, it gives an entropy of 5.26 for the order zero letter frequencies, whereas the observed value for the Brown corpus is 4.47.

For single-letter frequencies, a more accurate approximation is achieved when the probability interval between 0 and 1 is simply divided randomly into $N = 26$ parts and the pieces assigned to the letters (Good, 1969). The letters should be used in their naturally-occurring order of likelihood, "etaoin ...".

Suppose the unit interval is broken at random into N-1 parts; in other words, N-1 points are chosen on it according to a uniform distribution. If the pieces are arranged in order beginning with the smallest, their expected sizes will be

$$\frac{1}{N} \cdot \frac{1}{N} \, , \quad \frac{1}{N} \, \frac{1}{N} + \frac{1}{N-1} \, , \quad \frac{1}{N} \, \frac{1}{N} + \frac{1}{N-1} + \frac{1}{N-2} \, , \quad \cdots$$

It can be shown that this gives the rank distribution

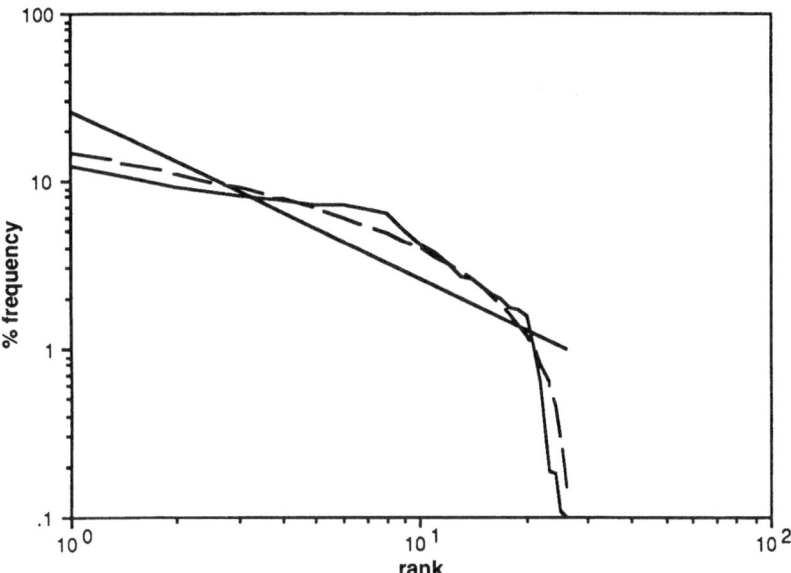

Figure 5. Letter-Frequency Data From the Brown Corpus, Along with Zipf Distribution (Straight Line) and Randomly Assigned Probabilities (Dashed Line).

$$p(r) = \frac{1}{N} \sum_{i=0}^{N-r} \frac{1}{(N-i)} \ ,$$

where p(r) is the probability of the letter of rank r (Whitworth, 1901). It has been observed that letter distributions (and, incidentally, phoneme distributions too) tend to follow this pattern.

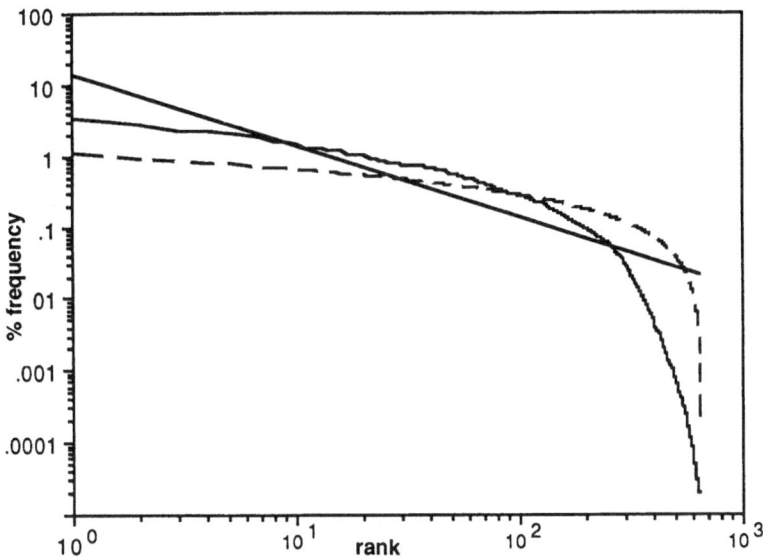

Figure 6. Digram Data From the Brown Corpus, Along with Zipf Distribution (Straight Line) and Randomly Assigned Probabilities (Dashed Line).

277

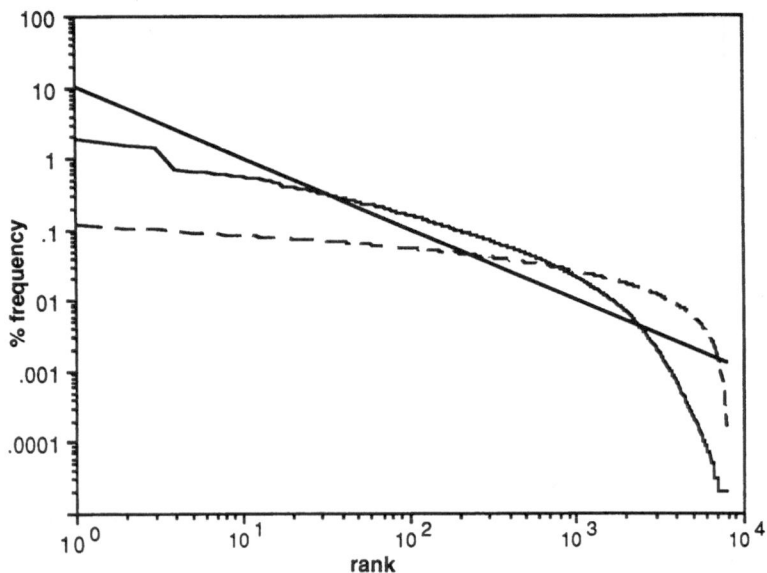

Figure 7. Trigram Data From the Brown Corpus, Along with Zipf
Distribution (Straight Line) and Randomly Assigned
Probabilities (Dashed Line).

Figure 5 plots the letter probabilities of Table 2 (lower case letters only) against rank, on logarithmic scales. The Zipf distribution appears as a straight line, while the dashed line is the random distribution derived above, with N=26. Although the latter appears to follow the data closely, the logarithmic scale masks sizeable discrepancies. Nevertheless it is clearly a much better fit than the Zipf distribution.

The analogous graphs for digrams and trigrams are shown in Figures 6 and 7. Here the number N of units was chosen to be exactly the number of different digrams and trigrams that appeared in the corpus (645 and 7895 respectively) rather than the number of possible combinations ($27^2 = 729$ and $27^3 = 19683$ respectively--27 since digrams and trigrams may include a space character). The first three data points of the trigram graph--the ones before the marked step downwards--all correspond to the sequence " the ". It is apparent that the random distribution follows the curve of the observed one in broad shape, whereas the Zipf plot is linear. However the discrepancies are much greater than in the single-letter case, and neither Zipf nor random model offers a really good fit to n-gram data.

While the broad shape of the random distribution matches the naturally-obtained one better than the Zipf law does, this improvement is not reflected in the entropies of the distributions. The observed entropy of the single-letter distribution is 4.11 bits/letter (this is different from the figure of 4.47 given in Table 2 because that figure is for the full 94-character alphabet whereas this one is for the 26 letters only). In this case the random model matches very well, with an entropy of 4.15 bits/letter--better than the Zipf distribution whose entropy is 3.94 bits/letter. But in the digram case the observed entropy is 6.76 bits/digram, while Zipf gives 7.10 and the random model 7.48; while in the trigram case the figures are 8.43 (observed), 10.13 (Zipf), and 10.29 (random).

CONCLUSION

The Zipf distribution, rationalized by the principle of least effort, appears at first sight to be an attractive model for hyperbolic distributions such as the characteristic rankfrequency relations found throughout language. But in the two cases we have studied, letter and word frequencies, simple random models can match the data as well or better.

Figure 8 shows the result of combining the random letter and word models. Two of the curves show the natural word data from the Brown corpus along with the Zipf model (as in Figure 4. A third replicates the curve of Figure 3, which is obtained when a million words are generated from a random source that

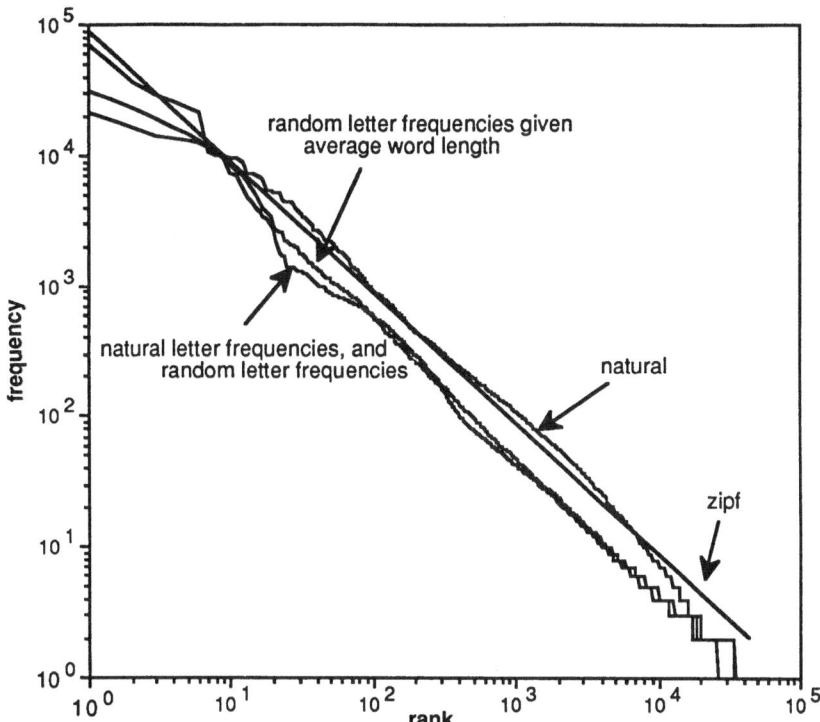

Figure 8. Natural and Synthetic Word-Frequency Data.

generates lower-case letters and spaces according to their natural frequency in English. Apart from the alphabet size, this model has 27 numerical parameters (26 of them independent), corresponding to the frequencies of letters and spaces in English. An almost identical curve is obtained by combining the random model of letters with that of words, in other words, using frequencies generated by the letter model to drive the word model. The final curve, which is a slightly better fit to the natural data, is obtained by giving the space character its naturally-occurring frequency of 18%, and dividing the remaining probability randomly amongst the 26 letters as indicated above. This gives a model with only one numerical parameter (apart from the alphabet size), which is effectively the average word length of English. In the other case, the probability interval is split 27 ways and the largest portion, which turns out to be 14%, is allotted to the space character. The only English-language parameter in this model of word frequency is the alphabet size of 26; yet it offers a remarkably good approximation to the naturally-occurring data distribution.

The results of this analysis show that Zipf's "least effort" principle apparently arises from purely random sources, and questions the validity of interpretations of observed hyperbolic rank/frequency distributions as manifestations of purposeful, or even evolutionary, behavior.

REFERENCES

Carroll, J. B., 1966, Word-Frequency Studies and the Lognormal Distribution, *Proc. Conference on Language and Language Behavior*, Zale, E. M., ed., Appleton-Century-Crofts, New York, pp. 213-235.
Carroll, J. B., 1967, On Sampling From a Lognormal Model of Word-Frequency Distribution, *Computational Analysis of Present-Day American English*, Kucera, H., and Francis, W. N., ed., Brown University Press, Providence, RI, pp. 406-424.
Ellis, S. R., and Hitchcock, R. J., 1986, The Emergence of Zipf's Law: Spontaneous Encoding Optimization by Users of a Command Language, *IEEE Trans. Systems, Man, and Cybernetics*, Vol. SMC-16, No. 3, pp. 423-427.
Fairthorne, R. A., 1969, Empirical Hyperbolic Distributions (Bradford-Zipf-Mandelbrot) for Bibliographic Description and Prediction, *J. Documentation*, Vol. 25, No. 4, December 1969.

Good, I. J., 1969, Statistics of Language, *Encyclopaedia of Information, Linguistics, and Control*, Meetham, A. R., and Hudson, R. A., eds., Pergamon, Oxford, England, pp. 567-581.

Mandelbrot, B., 1952, An Informational Theory of the Statistical Structure of Language, *Proc. Symposium on Applications of Communication Theory*, Butterworth, London, September 1952, pp. 486-500.

Miller, G. A., Newman, E. B., and Friedman, E. A., 1957, Some Effects of Intermittent Silence, *American J. Psychology*, Vol. 70, pp. 311-313.

Peachey, J. B., Bunt, R. B., and Colbourn, C. J., 1982, Bradford-Zipf Phenomena in Computer Systems, *Proc. Canadian Information Processing Society Conference*, Saskatoon, SK, May 1982, pp. 155-161.

Whitworth, W. A., 1901, *Choice and Chance*, Deighton and Bell, Cambridge.

Witten, I. H., Cleary, J., and Greenberg, S., 1984, On Frequency-Based Menu-Splitting Algorithms, *Int. J. Man-Machine Studies*, Vol. 21, No. 21, pp. 135-148, August.

Zipf, G. K., 1949, *Human Behavior and the Principle of Least Effort*, Addison-Wesley, Cambridge, MA.

A SPEECH ACT BASED MODEL FOR ANALYZING COOPERATIVE

WORK IN OFFICE INFORMATION SYSTEMS

Esa Auramäki

University of Jyväskylä
Department of Computer Science
Jyväskylä, Finland

Abstract: In this paper we present the SAMPO-approach for modelling and analyzing office information systems. We emphasize the collective features of office work and the role of communications in coordinating the collective efforts. The approach is based on the language action view where language is seen as a means of doing things. The approach also accepts the fact that collective work includes both harmony and conflict and tries to capture both of these features.

1.   INTRODUCTION

The role of communication in office information systems has been emphasized both in office systems research and in office practice. This implies that the approaches for office systems development should pay careful attention to office communications. The trend to increase computer support for office communications in the form of advanced electronic mail and conferencing systems is also prominent.

Another interesting area is the support for cooperative or collective work (Canning McNurlin, 1986; CSCW86, 1986; Olson, Conway, and Atkins, 1987). Cooperation is a misnomer in the sense that in the normal use of language it neglects the conflicts inherent also in such social work which aims at achieving some common goals. The term cooperation usually excludes also the conflictual or even opportunistic patterns of behavior. In this sense we prefer the term collective work used by Howard (1987). In this paper we shall use the term collective work for denoting a phenomenon where two or more people are striving towards some goal, and where the goal can be negotiated during the collective efforts.

The areas of communications and cooperation are linked together, because communication is needed to coordinate the cooperative efforts (Winograd, 1987). Through communications people try to get things done, they inform themselves and other people about the state of their efforts, they express feelings, beliefs and so on. A communication approach based on speech act theory (Austin, 1962; Searle, 1969; Searle and Vanderveken, 1985) - the SAMPO-approach (a Speech Act based office Modelling aPprOach) - has been suggested in Lyytinen and Lehtinen (1985); Lehtinen & Lyytinen (1986); and Auramäki, Lehtinen, and Lyytinen (1988). Speech act theory as a basis for this approach emphasizes the pragmatic meanings of office communications. Accordingly, the meanings of messages are bound to the context of the message and to the intention of the speaker in using the message.

The approach can be seen as one representative of the language action view Flores and Ludlow, 1980; Winograd, 1987; Hirschheim, 1985; Lyytinen and Lehtinen, 1984; Lehtinen and Lyytinen, 1986; Auramäki, Lehtinen, and Lyytinen, 1988) where the various functions of language are explicitly put under careful analysis. According to that view, language is used to perform some acts. Whenever one expresses an utterance he/she performs an act that is called a speech act. The central contribution of speech act theory based approaches is in the finding that we are doing things with words. We need not be satisfied with systems that only "store words", but we may develop information systems that perform linguistic acts (e.g., make contracts) or at least give support to people to make such acts (e.g., support negotiation). Information in this sense is not considered only as a presentation of "assertives" or "facts", but we use language for many more complicated purposes. Information is not "truth-valued", but we express propositions on several levels of intention and uncertainty.

Another premise of our work is based on the findings concerning work organization. The organizational forms clans (groups), hierarchies and markets have been discussed by Ciborra (Ciborra, 1984). In Ciborra's work information production and use is regarded as elements of coordinative problem solving in partially conflicting organizational settings. The trend from information systems that give personal support to systems that support the work of groups is reported (Canning McNurlin, 1986).

The groups (clans) can be seen as a new organizational form in contrast to the classical hierarchies. In this sense the group organizations set new requirements for information systems when compared with hierarchies. The markets as such have gained much interest in research during the last few years and systems for supporting even strategic market operations have been designed (Malone, Yates, and Benjamin, 1987). Many of those systems which have contributed firms to gain strategic advantage have supported other than pure assertive uses of language, e.g., they have supporting the ordering of flight tickets and accommodation. They have provided the customers with tools that give them support to express directives and the clients with tools that give them support to make promises, permissions, and so on. These features and research findings give support to our belief that information systems can contribute to different organizational forms and that they can give support to more complex communication functions than just to give access to databases or to provide the standard e-mail functionalities.

We also believe that it is important to recognize the conflictual features inherent in organizational life. When designing and implementing information systems we can not clear the conflictual features and many times there is even no need to do that. The conflicts are part of organizational evolution and they can even be a factor that enforces the organization to live. The same concerns strategic or even opportunistic behavior. In business, we play games where opportunism and strategy (in the boundaries of legislation) are an essential part. We ourselves sometimes look for opportunities and we have to react to the moves of our competitors.

SAMPO-approach is oriented towards the development of office information systems. It provides methods for analyzing and describing office communications. The emphasis is on the purposes of communication and the effects of the speech acts. The main methodological phases in SAMPO are called discourse analysis, information modelling (Lyytinen and Lehtinen, 1984; Lyytinen and Lehtinen, 1985) and information systems specification. In this paper we shall deal primarily with discourse analysis.

In section 2 we present the basic concepts related to office collective work, speech acts, and discourses. In section 3 we characterize the fundamental principles of the SAMPO-approach for office analysis. In section 4 we exemplify the use of modelling concepts in describing communications examples in a collective office setting. In section 5 we discuss the possibilities for technical solutions in implementing the speech act based model of an office, and in section 6 we present the concluding remarks and discuss future research directions.

2.   BASIC CONCEPTS

In this section we present the basic concepts of speech act and discourse theories employed in the SAMPO-approach to model office communications. We also discuss the types of office action and especially the nature of collective work and the concepts of harmony, conflict and opportunism in office action.

2.1 The Concept of Office in SAMPO

In SAMPO we emphasize the communication function in offices. The offices are seen as places where people make commitments through communication, i.e., they make promises for future action, they assert things, they direct other people to perform actions, and so on.

Communication as such is not a sufficient reason for the existence of organizations. As noted in Searle (Searle and Vanderveken, 1985) there is a rather limited number of things we can do with language, e.g., one cannot fry an egg with language. Organizations also perform other kinds of acts; they produce physical goods, services, and so on.

The acts can be classified into speech acts and instrumental acts. The instrumental acts are considered mainly as human deeds that may accomplish changes in the "real" physical world. Speech acts are symbolic deeds that result in linguistic expressions. Speech acts and instrumental acts are related; for example, speech acts may trigger instrumental acts (as fulfilling the promise to arrive at a meeting), report of the state of the instrumental acts, and so on (e.g., the stock status).

Speech acts form sequences which are called discourses. Many times an individual speech act can not be fully understood alone, but as a part of the discourse.

282

Table 1

Action Types in Offices

Action Type	Number of Actors	Goal Sharing	Purpose	Objects of Action
Instrumental	1	n/a	Technical control	Physical objects
Strategic	>1	Also conflictual goals	Pursuit of individual interests	People
Communicative	>1	Shared Main goal	Mutual understanding	People
Discoursive	>1	Shared Main goal	Clarification of message validity	People

A more elaborated classification of acts is presented in Lyytinen (1986) and Lyytinen et al (1987). The four action types are presented in Table 1.

In this paper we are interested in how we can model language use in strategic, communicative, and discoursive action. Instrumental action is discussed only through its relation to the speech acts and discourses.

2.2   Concepts of Collective Work

As we noted before we see office work as an activity where people work together in order to accomplish some office tasks. In this collective work they need some coordination and control mechanisms which contribute to the group work efficiency and effectiveness. Communication is the basic mean used in coordinating and controlling the collective efforts. Other forms of coordination are money and shared materials, to name a few.

The verb "to coordinate" is defined in Webster's dictionary to have meanings like set in order, arrange, adjust (various parts) so as to have harmonious action. Thus, in office settings coordination is oriented towards arranging and setting in order office activities.

While performing office activities people may have conflicting goals, they may behave opportunistically, there may be severe power struggles and so on.

According to Bacon (Bacon, 1980), conflict is an opposition and tension between two or more parties due to actual or perceived incompatibility of goals or means of achieving goals. Furthermore, Bacon makes a distinction between conflict and competition. According to him, competition might be considered a controlled and civilized form of conflict and conflict tends to be irrational, personalized, without rules and oriented to destroying rather than winning. As Bacon says, conflict is not good or bad, per se; sometimes it can bring a positive change, increase motivation, etc., but sometimes it may be destructive and dysfunctional. A long list of possible causes of conflicts within EDP functions are listed in Bacon; e.g., task overload in EDP, differences in perception of the role of systems function, difference of values, communication barriers, and scarce resources.

Opportunism is defined in Webster's dictionary as the practice of policy of adapting one's action judgments, etc. to circumstances as in politics, in order to further one's immediate interests, without regard for basic principles or eventual consequences.

In real offices we have conflicts and even opportunism. Thus, we cannot rely on coordination mechanisms that assume pure harmony. We need an approach which recognizes and allows both harmony and conflict. In our examples, we shall concentrate on specifying situations with possible conflicts and with possible opportunism, because we believe these features are not properly understood in current office modelling techniques and methodologies.

Also the systems development process can become an arena of severe conflicts. Actually, there is a wide range of literature concerning the social (and political) nature of the systems development process (see for example the papers in Briefs (Briefs, Ciborra, and Schneider, 1983). Thus, systems development can also be seen as an environment of collective work with both conflictual and harmonic features.

Negotiations are an office function where we have both conflictual and cooperative features. An excellent survey of theories usable in understanding negotiations is presented in Srikanth and Jarke (1986). Interesting disciplines are Game Theory (bargaining), economics (decision making under certainty), process analysis (joint decision making process), sociology, industrial relations (collective bargaining), politics (international negotiations), and psychology (behavioral styles and negotiation strategies). In their paper, Srikanth and Jarke (1986) present a model of negotiation which absorbs ideas from the above mentioned disciplines. They claim that for describing and prescribing negotiation information is needed about the environment, former experience, negotiator needs and values, perceptions and expectations, decision making process, bargaining behavior, and the state of the problem. According to them these components influence and change each other dynamically.

The analysis of power structures might be useful while analyzing the conflict situation. There are various sources of power, e.g., expertise and reputation, control of resources, formal authority, alliances and coalition links with key executives, reward power, and attractiveness of personality and behavioral effectiveness (Bacon, 1980). In our approach, the analysis of power structure is an inherent part of the specification of the speech acts. The analysis of the conditions for successful speech acts enforces one to answer questions like who is authorized to direct and commit, who is getting reports, and so on.

There are several approaches to conflict management. The main alternatives can be classified as a win-win situation, win-lose situation, and lose-lose situation. There are also methods for conflict management, e.g., Integrative Decision Method (IDM) that aims at conflict control and resolution (win-win solution which is acceptable to both parties). The main strategies for conflict management can also be connected to the possible conflict situations identified during the specification of the OIS discourses.

2.3   Speech Acts

A speech act is the basic unit of communication and it involves several sorts of "subacts": propositional acts, illocutionary acts, utterance acts, and perlocutionary acts. An utterance act is the act that a speaker performs by uttering an expression. For example, expressions "John loves Mary" and "Mary is loved by John" when uttered are different utterance acts. An illocutionary act is a basic unit of meaningful human communication; it is always performed when one utters certain expressions with an intention. For example, one can perform illocutions "I promise to write a letter", or "I refuse to pay a bill". When the intention is recognized and the full meaning of the expression has been understood, we say that the illocutionary act has been successful. The understanding of the meaning requires that certain conditions described later are fulfilled (e.g., succeed in achieving illocutionary point, satisfaction of propositional content, preparatory and sincerity conditions). A propositional act is the subsidiary act of illocution. By expressing the propositional content the speaker performs an act of denotation and predication. An example of predication is "writing a letter" and denotation "I" in the previous example. A perlocutionary act is an act involved in uttering that produces effects on the feelings, attitudes, and subsequent behavior of the hearers. Perlocutionary effects are the effects caused by perlocutionary acts. Examples of perlocutionary effect is to get somebody to write a letter as a result of a request to write a letter. Perlocutionary acts are not eventually linguistic and actually perlocutionary effects can be achieved without performing speech acts at all.

Through communication we perform speech acts where we express performatives like to promise, to command, to assert, and so on. These illocutionary acts produce perlocutionary acts and perlocutionary effects. Some of these perlocutions are physical acts (like the delivery of an article), and some deal with more abstract terms (like becoming persuaded).

Illocutionary Acts. In this paper we mainly discuss the illocutionary acts. An elementary illocutionary act consists of context, illocutionary force, and propositional content. All these constituents are important in understanding the meaning of an utterance.

More complex illocutionary acts can be formed from elementary illocutionary acts by using illocutionary connectives which are illocutionary negation (-), illocutionary conjunction (&), and illocutionary conditional (= >).

Content. The term content refers to the propositional content of the message. As we noted above, the propositional act is always a part of the illocutionary act.

Context. The context is defined by the terms speaker, hearer, time, place, and the possible world. The first four terms are self-explanatory. They define a context where a speaker utters something to a

Table 2

Properties of Primitive Illocutionary Forces

Primitive Illocutionary Force	Illocutionary Point	Propositional Content Conditions	Preparatory Conditions	Sincerity Conditions
Assertive illocutionary force	Assertive Point	no	Speaker has reasons for accepting or evidence supporting the truth of the propositional content	Psychological state: belief
Commissive illocutionary force	Commissive point	Propositional content represents a future course of action of the speaker	Speaker is able to perform the act	Psychological state: intention
Directive illocutionary force	Directive point	Propositional content represents a future course of action of the hearer	Hearer is able to carry out the course of action	Psychological state: desire
Declarative illocutionary force	Declarative point	no	Speaker is capable of bringing about the state of affairs represented in the propositional content	Psychological states: desire and belief
Expressive	Expressive	no	no	no

hearer at time t at place p. The speakers and hearers may be real persons, roles carried by persons or person groups depending on the structure and formality of communications.

The possible world refers to the residual features of the context which are relevant to the successful performance of a speech act. The possible world is something which is more than the "actual world" and it enables us to talk about "what could be" (e.g., the future). Typical constituents of the possible world include the presupposed authority of the speaker over the hearer, speaker's and hearer's presuppositions of what has happened and what is possible in the world and so on.

Illocutionary Force. An illocutionary force determines the social relational established (commitments) and the way how the propositional content is related to the world. The social relationships define expectations of agents' future behaviors that bind all parties. An illocutionary force has seven components altogether (Searle and Vanderveken, 1985). In this paper we use four of these components: illocutionary point, propositional content conditions, sincerity conditions, and preparatory conditions.

Illocutionary Point. Each type of illocutionary act has a point or a purpose essential to its being an illocutionary act of that type. For example, the point of a statement is to tell how things are. This point or purpose is called the illocutionary point.

The illocutionary point determines the "direction" in which the propositional content ("word") matches with the world. For example, in "commanding" the "world" is intended to be changed to match with the "word".

Illocutionary points can be classified into just five categories:

(1)   The assertive point tells how the world is (e.g., to state, to predict),

Table 3

Additional Conditional Specifications

Illocution	Propositional Content Conditions	Preparatory Conditions	Sincerity Conditions
Assertives	Proposition about past or future (report) Proposition about past (retroduction) Propositional content has something to do with the speaker (boast: one cannot express pride about things which do not concern him)	The respective status or position of the speaker and the hearer (testify: status of the speaker) Their psychological states (inform: assumption about the state of knowledge of the hearer)	Expressing dissatisfaction (lament) or pride (boast)
Directives	A certain sort of speech act to the original speaker is required (yes-no question)	Allowance of refusal (accept) Prima facie reasons for refusal are allowed (consent) Presupposition that doing the directed thing is good to the hearer (advise) Presuppositions about what is good or bad in general (threaten: presupposition that the act is bad for the hearer)	
Commissives		The responsibilities and abilities of the speakers and the hearers (criticize: presupposition that the hearer is responsible) The surroundings of the discourse (accept: presupposition about the preceding discourse: a speaker has given a directive that allows refusal)	

(2)   The commissive point is to commit the speaker to doing something (e.g., to promise, to agree),

(3)   The directive point is to try to get the hearer to do things (e.g., to order, to request),

(4)   The declarative point is to change the world by saying so (e.g., to christen, to declare), and

(5)   The expressive point is to express the speaker's feelings and attitudes (e.g., to apologize, to condole).

Propositional Content Conditions. The content of an illocution cannot be arbitrary, but must satisfy certain conditions that are called propositional content conditions. For example, the illocutionary point of the sentence "Draw a triangular square" cannot be achieved, because the propositional content is impossible. In the similar vein, the propositional content of invoicing can only refer to payments and not salaries.

Preparatory Conditions. The preparatory conditions specify the states of affairs a speaker must presuppose to obtain in the world if he is to perform the illocutionary act he intends to do. For example, in placing a purchase order the buyer presupposes that the supplier has not gone bankrupt, it has the same address as earlier, it still seems the ordered product, etc.

Sincerity Conditions. The sincerity conditions are used to specify the psychological states a speaker expresses in the performance of an illocutionary force. The basic states are beliefs, intentions, and desires. For example, a speaker who asserts something expresses a belief, a speaker who promises something expresses an intention, and a speaker who directs a hearer to do something expresses desires. A concept related to sincerity conditions is the strength of sincerity conditions. Thus, we can express varying degrees of sincerity in intention, belief, and desire.

Primitive Illocutionary Forces. By analyzing these constituents of illocutionary force Searle and Vanderveken (1985) argue that there are five primitive illocutionary forces, namely primitive assertive, primitive commissive, primitive directive, primitive expressive, and primitive declarative illocutionary force. The general properties and conditions for these primitive illocutionary forces are presented in Table 2. There are also additional conditions specific to illocutions in these primitive classes. The additional conditions presented in Searle and Vanderveken (1985) are listed in Table 3.

An interesting approach to illocutionary (speech) acts is presented by Cohen (Cohen and Levesque, 1987), where they attempt to derive the properties of illocutionary acts from principles of rationality. They question the need to recognize the illocutionary force and argue that many properties of illocutionary acts can be derived from the beliefs, intentions, and other mental states of speakers and hearers. They also question the primitive nature of illocutionary acts. Advantages of their approach include the modelling of a speaker's insincere performance of illocutionary acts, and showing how multiple illocutionary acts can be simultaneously performed with one utterance. However, to us it seems that the constructs behind the illocutionary force definition offer a sufficient tool for analyzing office speech acts.

2.4   Discourse

When studying office communications we are not only interested in individual speech acts, but also on sequences of speech acts. These chains of speech acts are called discourses. The goal of the discourse study is to reveal mechanisms that keep the sentence-flow coherent and allow the discourse to proceed in a rational, rule-governed manner. Discourse concepts are discussed more profoundly in Auramäki, Lehtinen, and Lyytinen (1988) and here we present only a short overview of the possibilities of discourse studies.

Speech acts imply a specific set of alternatives that can succeed them in a speech act pattern. These alternatives form a *stage* in a discourse. For example, a question can open a stage in a discourse where alternatives are: an answer, a clarification request, a refusal, or a counter question. The set of alternatives depends on the purpose of the discourse type.

Stages in speech act patterns can be grouped into two larger *discourse segments*. Segments share a common topicalization and have a subgoal that is relevant in achieving the purpose of the discourse type. Segments drop out parts of the existing topicalization and introduce new ones. Therefore, segments are important to the analysis of the coherency, topicalization and control flow of the discourse.

Moves are speech acts that activate stages in a discourse. They control the flow of the discourse processes. When studying moves, we thus thematize the function of various speech acts for the development of the ongoing discourse.

Topicalization means those aspects in a context of utterance that are put into the focus in a stage of a discourse process. Here the illocutionary force of the act expresses what commitments the act has activated. The propositional content distinguishes objects and their properties that are of interest. Topicalization changes as we change the illocutionary force, the propositional content, or both. The last two introduce usually new discourse segments, whereas the first one deals with the evolution, creation, exchange and reporting of commitments within the same discourse segment.

3. THE SAMPO-APPROACH FOR OFFICE ANALYSIS

The SAMPO view of office systems development is based partly on the planned change of an office. In the planned change mode the office modelling is considered to be beneficial. Of course the restrictions of any modelling approach are recognized: the informal features of an office cannot always be identified or even discovered; some features cannot be described at all; the reasonable level of details of description should be selected and so on. However, we believe that in some cases the carefully planned change approach is reasonable, and that in these cases the speech act based office model could help one to find inconsistent, inadequate (incomplete), and ambiguous features of office communications and to find ways to improve communications. The improvements can be achieved, e.g., through educating people to communicate more effectively, through using new information technology, through developing the organization, and so on. The planning approach does not exclude the more evolutive or adaptive view of change; the plans are just guidelines that make the adaptation more predictable and they help to recognize the need for adaptation. The planning approach examines also the opportunistic and conflictual features of office communications; the speech act specifications are not restricted only to the unpolitical, "rationalistic" uses of language. This is an important feature because many of the strategic level information systems embed opportunism.

Any office analysis should fix what sorts of communications will take place through a formalized OIS. In SAMPO the ISD-process (Information Systems Development) has three phases:

(1)   change analysis, that tries to identify the office problems and potential development areas,

(2)   information systems specification, where the selected (and alternatives for) information system solutions are described, and

(3)   information systems design, where the questions dealing with cost effective design and implementation solutions are discussed.

The SAMPO-approach provides models basically for two phases of information systems specification: discourse analysis and information modelling. In discourse analysis the general structures and purposes of discourses are analyzed and in information modelling we deal with the content and structures of the individual elements of discourses. The discourse analysis methods help also in some subphases of the change analysis (finding areas where the communication practices could be developed). The models provide a basis both for technical and organizational implementations. The models just give guidelines for improving the qualities (coherency, inambiguity, completeness) of the discourse. Sometimes they might also be used in educating the participants of the discourse to communicate more efficiently. Although the models are not technology-oriented, they, however, might be used also in assessing different technical solutions. Current office models do not adequately recognize the possibilities of future technologies such as the "electronic contracting" (Lee, 1988), "electronic promising" (Kimbrough, 1988), and the conversation tools such as Coordinator (Winograd and Flores, 1986; Winograd, 1987) and Information Lens (Malone et al., 1987(a); Malone et al., 1987(b)). We believe that the speech act based modelling approach could help in identifying the need for using such tools and might help in planning proper uses for such tools.

3.1 Discourse Analysis in SAMPO

The purpose of the discourse analysis is to specify well-formed sequences of speech acts for the use of an OIS. Discourse processes that are dysfunctional are identified. The methods of discourse analysis can be used both to analyze current problems in communications and to assess the quality of alternative office designs.

The quality of discourses concerns coherency, completeness, and ambiguity of a discourse process generated within an OIS.

The study of discourse coherency shows how the utterances in a discourse logically connect to each other. A coherent discourse includes only successful illocutions, i.e., those that achieve their purpose. For example, if we receive a request, we must clarify under what conditions it is acceptable to "accept" the request, to make a "counter-offer", to "reject" the request, to "ask for" clarification, etc. The notion of coherence does not reject the possibility for making insincere speech acts, it just helps to make them explicit.

The notion of discourse coherency has been applied in proposed taxonomies of conversations, for example in the conversation taxonomy conversation suggested by Winograd and Flores (1986), conversation for action, conversation for possibilities, conversation for clarification, and conversation for orientation and in the "templates~ (such as a request for action, notice, commitment) discussed by Malone (Malone et al., 1987(a); Malone et al., 1987(b)).

The concept of coherency implies that something must be done if a discourse process turns out to be a non-coherent one. However, the concept of coherence can also be used in identifying and specifying opportunistic behavior. In such discourses we can express beliefs, desires, and intentions where the sincerity conditions of speech acts contain low level degrees of sincerity.

Discourse completeness implies that a discourse is in some sense completely specified. In other words the OIS specification should include all performable speech acts needed to complete the discourse. This implies the analysis of two related aspects of discourse processes. First, we should define all speech acts that are possible on a certain discourse stage. Second, we should define all stages that are needed to terminate a discourse process. A discourse process terminates if no commitments are pending, i.e., they all have in one way or the other been resolved and the topic is closed down. The second aspect of completeness assures that the specification does not include a discourse process which does not reach a terminal stage.

Consider for example "requesting". A "request" is usually followed by an "acceptance". However, a request may also be succeeded by an "counter-offer", "a clarification request", "a request for delaying the answer", "a rejection", "a note that the request should be forwarded to somebody else", etc. (seemingly ad infinitum). All these, and maybe a host of other speech acts, may be needed to make the OIS specification a complete description of the discourse stage. In addition, we must notify what speech acts are needed to make all these possible alternative discourse processes following a "request" to reach an end. For example, "a rejection" after a "request" terminates the discourse process. On the other hand after "a note" a "request" may be forwarded to another person or no "request" is sent out if we cannot find an appropriate person.

A discourse can be more or less ambiguous. Discourse is ambiguous if it is unclear what meanings different terms and predicates obtain in the discourse. Analysis of discourse ambiguity thus sheds light on how clear discourse topics are for discourse participants and how fixed and bounded the topics are. Possible sources of ambiguity are the "tacit knowledge", or the inherent political nature of many office activities where some parties might obtain visible advantages from higher ambiguity.

3.2 Discourse Analysis Methods

Two graphical description methods are proposed. They are supplemented with several tables that delineate in more detail various elements in a discourse.

The graphical methods for describing discourses are:

(1)   a discourse graph, and

(2)   a conversation graph.

Both graphs are directed cyclic networks. Discourse graphs describe the overall structure of the discourse. Conversation graphs aim at describing the dynamic discourse features.

Discourse graphs and conversation graphs describe networks of acts and detect:

(1)   principles needed in the set up and control of commitments;

(2)   inconsistencies in the coordination of commitments; and

(3)   possibilities for organizational development that simplifies communication and control mechanisms.

A discourse graph delineates discourse objects and their properties and relationships. It is a model of an institutionalized discourse and its comprehensive structure. It is used to identify a discourse and its topic. A discourse graph can be seen to represent a partial "script" or "schema" for communications. It defines necessary and sufficient conversation possibilities for each discourse participant. Discourse graphs are represented with the symbols depicted in Figure 1.

A conversation graph describes patterns of speech acts and instrumental acts and their dynamic dependencies. Conversation graphs resemble the templates of Information Lens (Malone et al., 1987(a); Malone et al., 1987(b)) or the kinds of action in Winograd (Winograd and Flores, 1986; Winograd, 1987) by representing open conversation possibilities after each move in a conversation. However, those models limit the interaction to two partners, whereas in SAMPO the number of communicants is not restricted. The conversation graphs are not discussed in more detail here.

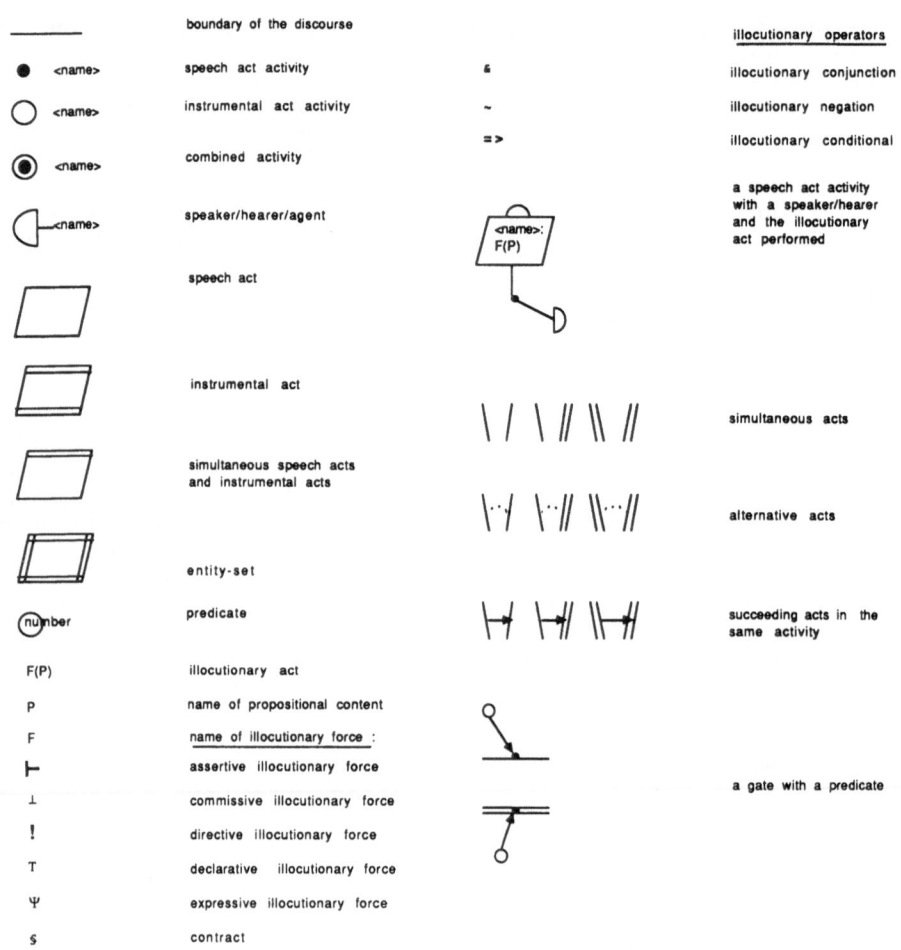

Figure 1. Symbols for Discourse Graphs.

4. MODELLING COMMUNICATIONS BY SAMPO DISCOURSE MODELS

In the sequel we present examples of modelling collective work where also conflictual elements are present. Typical examples of collective work with possible conflicts are system development (see approaches in Briefs (Briefs, Ciborra, and Schneider, 1983)), in setting budget, in politized interactions between production and marketing, in interactions between accountants and the users of financial services, between professionals seeking for autonomy, and bureaucrats who aim at improving control, etc. (Morgan, 1986). Good examples of the consequences of not understanding the power structure and possible conflict sources can be found in the article of Dimino (Dimino, 1983).

In this paper we analyze an example concerning budget planning, but we could as well present an example connected more closely to information service (e.g., the question who gets what information from an information service is very important). The information collected through information service functions is also intended to be used for some purpose, e.g., to be used in budgeting. As pointed out above in our opinion, information is not just something which is true or false, the pragmatic meaning and use of information is the essential feature of information.

In the example we discuss and analyze an office which is organizing a business conference. The conference is connected to an exhibition. The main interest groups are the conference planning group, a representative from the exhibition organization, an advisory group, sponsors, potential customers, hotels, travel agencies, lecturers, organizations that sell addresses from their address registers, magazines, journals, newspapers, press, business, a federation of data processing and so on. There are several levels of organizations in this environment. The organization we are especially interested in is the conference

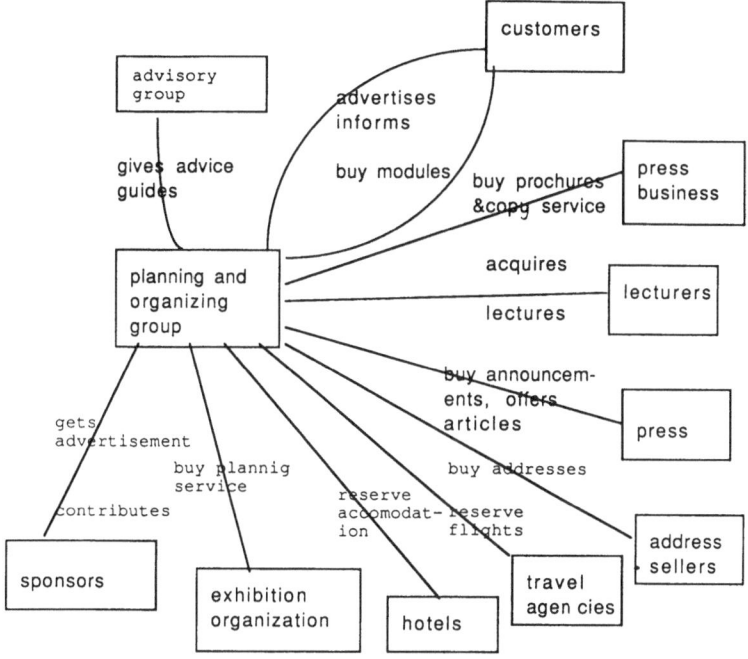

Figure 2. Activities and Interest Groups in Conference Planning and Organizing.

planning group (level 1). Another level consists of the planning group, the advisory group, and the representative of the exhibition (level 2). The level 1 organization is based mainly on shared goals; the aim of their work is to plan the conference program and organize the conference. Collective work on level 2 is based on both shared goals and on individual (possibly conflicting) goals; the exhibition organization buys the conference planning service from the planning group, the planning group and the exhibition organization try to organize the exhibition and the conference as an integrated whole, the exhibition organization finances the organizing of the conference and the possible profits are shared based on a contract between the planning group and the exhibition organization, the advertisement of the conference and the exhibition is performed in cooperation and so on. The advisory group oriented towards securing the quality of the conference and the exhibition, they give advice on topics and on acquiring qualified lecturers, and they get mainly some merits for themselves and possibly to the organizations they represent. The other interest groups listed above can be seen external to the level 2 organization. Thus, there can be seen two levels of an "internal" organization (the organization responsible for the organizing of the integrated whole) and another group of organizations that are "external" to that organization. This implies that we have to model and analyze collective work that is internal to an organization and work that is performed between many organizations. The relationships between these organizational units are depicted in Figure 2.

Figure 2 gives a simplified picture of the actions performed in the collective strives of the planning group and the other interest groups. It is already intuitively easy to imagine that between these groups there are many different goals and many possible sources of conflict. It would not be fair to argue that these groups together form a collective work unit. There are just lots of interest groups involved one way or another in the planning and organizing of the conference. In these interactions lots of possibilities for strategic action exists; e.g., the planning group negotiates on prices with press (advertisement), with press business (copy costs), with travel agencies (the costs of flights for invited foreign lecturers); the planning group negotiates the share of profits with the exhibition group and with the Federation (in this case about the conditions of competition) and so on. Many official contracts are made to guide the cooperation and other forms of work between the parties. Also many assumptions concerning the behavior of the other parties are made not formulated into official contracts. Some action types are strategic and even opportunistic in their nature; e.g., advertisement is in some of its parts oriented towards persuasion and might contain exaggeration; while making contracts with press business (e.g., we promise to distribute free

REVENUES
   Conference fees OTHER REVENUES
   Sponsor contributions
   Advertising contracts
   Others
   Selling of conference bags etc. TOTAL REVENUES

   COSTS
   Lecturer costs (travel, accommodation, lecturing fees)
   Organizing costs (travels, accommodations, wages)
   Information, guidance
   Social security fees
   Announcing
   Advertisement (magazines, direct advertisement)
   Copying
   Refreshment (parties, etc.)
   Representation
   Office costs
   Phone
   Accounting
   Security
   Rents
   Stakeholder outputs
   Others TOTAL COSTS

   PROFIT

Figure 3. Budget Structure

magazines and the press publishes news and free announcements concerning the conference and the lecturers; the planning group itself writes articles of the main themes and important lecturers and the press accepts and publishes the articles) etc. Thus, self-interests of the different groups are an important factor behind the contracts and informal agreements.

This environment contains various information systems of which some can be supported through computerized tools. It is important to note that we are using information to act; we make contracts, we ask people to do things, we promise to do things, we try to persuade people to do things and so on. These information systems are also interrelated in various ways and in a way they all together form a complex information system which aims at supporting the conference (and exhibition) planning and organization. In this paper we do not discuss the division between an information system and some "real" object system. We, however, want to note that the boundary between information system and an object system is quite fuzzy. We just think that in an information system there are the people speaking and acting, language used in speaking, and technology used in implementing computerized tools (see the contexts in Lyytinen, 1986). We make the distinction between performing speech acts and instrumental acts that concern physical things, but it does not seem reasonable to say that this manifests the distinction between an information system and the physical object system (e.g., document transmission through physical or electronic means is considered a part of IS).

When continuing with our example we concentrate in the functions of the planning group and especially in the budget planning. The other functions listed in Figure 2 are discussed only through their relations to budget planning. In the budget we have the cost and revenue components presented in Figure 3.

The planning of the conference involves many kinds of contracts and negotiations. We have a contract, e.g., with the data processing federation (concerns competition); we can freely distribute announcements and brochures through some of the channels of the federation, we use the name of the federation in advertising, and we have a contract concerning scheduling of similar conferences. We have contracts with sponsors which state the conditions of presenting their logos in our advertisements and in the final conference program. With the exhibition organizers we have a contract where we are committed to prepare and implement the conference program and the budget for the conference and the exhibition organizers are committed to take the financial responsibility according to the agreed budget lines. With the lecturers we have contracts which state that the lecturers promise to lecture on agreed topics on agreed times and we promise to pay to them agreed lecturing fees, accommodations, and travels. Thus, we have many kinds of contracts with different partners. Some of them are legally binding, some are based on mutual trust and beliefs. Some of the last mentioned contracts are sensitive to opportunism and conflicts. Thus, the interpretation of a budget as a pure assertive document could cause severe problems in specifying the requirements of a budget planning system. In the following we shall analyze more thoroughly the budget planning and the resulting budget through the speech act and discourse concepts. We want to give some examples of the importance of understanding the whole meaning of speech acts including the illocutionary force when analyzing budget processes in an office.

In budget planning we can identify the following speech acts:

(1)   the exhibition group suggests some budget figures (the sharing of advertisement costs, share of profits)

(2)   the data processing federation presents its requirements for its fixed share and its share of profit

(3)   the planning group (actually the university) presents its requirements for its share of profits

(4)   the planning group commits to use the lecturing fee standards of the data processing federation for domestic lecturers

(5)   the lecturing fees for foreign lecturers are negotiated with the lecturers themselves

(6)   the planning group, the advisory group, and the representatives of the exhibition organization make a decision on the conference fees (many classes of feeing policies)

(7)   the budget planner computes the expected revenues (estimates the number of participants and computes the expected revenues

(8)   the planning group makes contracts with sponsors on contributions and exchanges

(9)   the planning group requests offers from the printing companies (printing the brochures, etc.)

(10) the planning group receives offers from printing component

(11) the planning group selects the best offer

(12) budget planner computes the costs of copying the papers

(13) the budget planner evaluates the other budget items

(14) the planning and organizing group makes a budget draft according to the suggested budget figures

In program planning the following speech acts are performed:

(1)   the advisory group presents its suggestions of program topics and lecturers

(2)   the planning group presents it suggestions of program topics and lecturers

(3)   the exhibition group presents the schedule for the exhibition

The speech acts in program planning discourse and budgeting discourse are interrelated during the earlier budgeting phases; for example, the costs of lecturers depend on the quality and nationality of the lecturer (traveling costs, etc.) and the expected number of conference participants depends on the quality of the program. Thus, the earlier phases of budgeting contain a lot of dynamics. Actually, the first budget versions define just the main lines and the later versions define the limits for individual budget items.

The speech acts presented above are only a part of the whole discourse. However, even this small part illustrates that a document called budget contains several elements that can not be considered truth-valued assertives, but rather are promises, contracts, and even directives. This especially concerns the

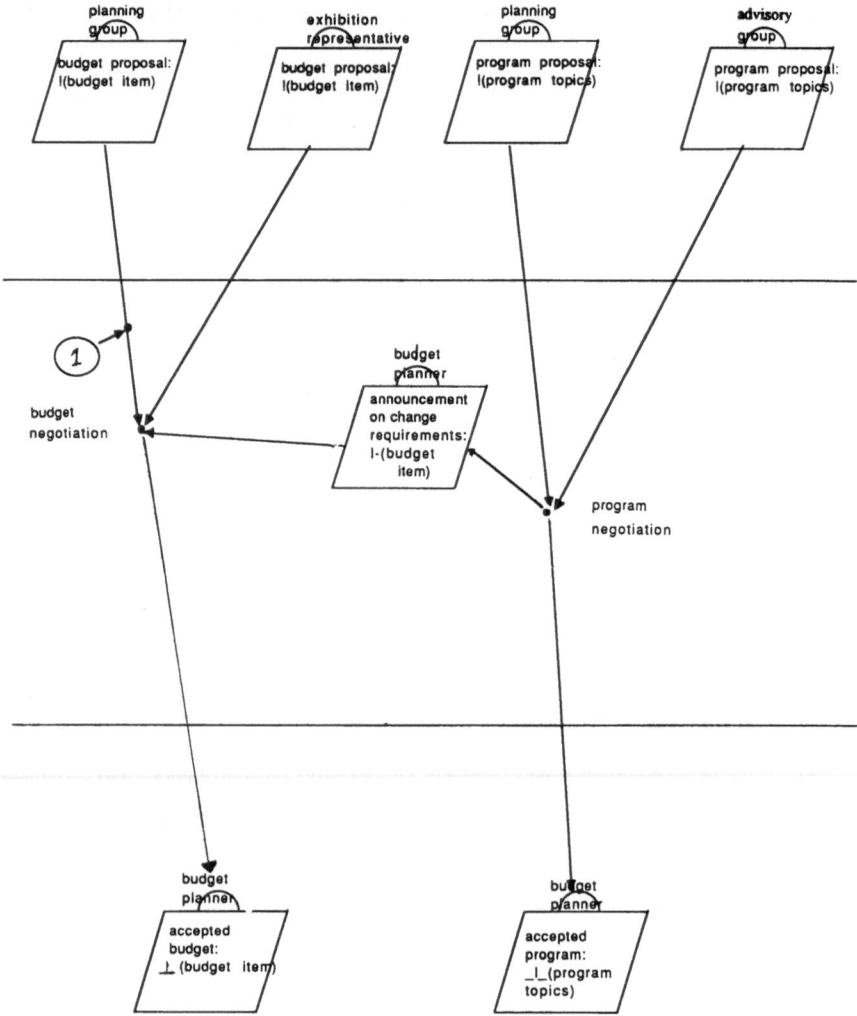

Figure 4. An Example of a Discourse Graph.

earlier versions of the budget, the last version which is the actual budget aimed at guiding the implementation of the conference is stable and contains mainly assertives (predictions) and contracts (that often consist of mutual promises). A part of the budget planning discussed so far is presented by SAMPO discourse graphs in Figure 4. The graph makes explicit some parts of the context of the utterance (the speakers and the hearers), the illocutionary point of the utterance, the name of the propositional content of the utterance and some predicates that control the flow of the discourse. The graph is usually supported by tables that contain more information about the discourse, e.g., speech act tables contain information about the frequency and timing of the speech acts, channels used in communication. The tabular presentations are discussed more thoroughly in Auramäki, Lehtinen, and Lyytinen (1988).

It is important to make the difference between different illocutions; e.g., it helps us to understand that there are budget items that are more certain than others. For example, legal contracts are more certain than just suggested budget figures (directives). Through knowing the binding contracts we can compute the values for certain budget items, but for some other budget items we have to evaluate the uncertainties. It is also important to notice the difference between promises and binding contracts.

It is also important to notice the difference concerning the sincerity conditions of the speech acts. In Table 4 we describe informally the conditions for performing speech acts while making contracts with the exhibition organization.

294

Table 4.

Sincerity Conditions in Making Contracts

SPEECH ACT TABLE: SINCERITY CONDITIONS			
Speech Act	Speaker	Hearer	Sincerity Conditions
Budget proposal/ exhibition group	Exhibition Group	Planning Group	Desire to keep advertisement costs in reasonable state Belief that the suggested revenues can be obtained Desire to minimize the share of costs of the exhibition group Belief that the suggested figures make possible an effective advertisement campaign Intention to maximize the share of the exhibition group of the advertisement costs
Budget proposal/ planning group	Planning Group	Exhibition Group	Desire to keep the costs in reasonable state Desire to minimize the share of costs of the planning group Belief that the suggested figures make possible an effective advertisement campaign Belief that the suggested revenues can be obtained Intention to maximize the share of the exhibition group of the advertisement costs

The sincerity conditions are described by evaluating the beliefs, desires, and intentions of the communicating partners. Thus, for example we can notice the conflicting goals between the exhibition group and the planning group; both parties are trying to minimize their share of costs. This reflects that fact that we are advertising the conference and the exhibition together, but they have their own budgets. In the same way the exhibition group and the conference planning group are trying to maximize their share of profits.

Another interesting area for analyzing the sincerity conditions would be the sponsoring arrangements. Sponsoring arrangements are made during many phases of informal communications. Promises are made and some of them become binding some do not. During the budgeting process we should be able to evaluate the certainty of these promises and thus we could evaluate the certainty of the revenues.

Thus, it is easy to see that the evaluation of the sincerity conditions of the speech acts in budget planning is an important factor. This should also be reflected in the system that is used to support the planning and control of the budget.

5. IMPLEMENTATION CONSIDERATIONS

In this section we discuss the implementation strategies for a speech act based model. First, we discuss the work done on development of computerized tools that support cooperative or collective work. After that we characterize an object oriented approach for implementing speech acts.

In this paper we do not discuss more profoundly the organizational implementation of the model. We just note that while making discourse analysis we try to reveal speech acts where the requirements for successful performance are not met and substitute them with successful speech acts. In the same way the conditions for coherence, completeness, and ambiguity are analyzed and the ineffective discourse structures are substituted for more effective and efficient discourse structures. Altogether this means that we try to develop the discourse structures in a way that serves better the goals of the organization. Sometimes we can use computers to support the discourses, sometimes not.

However, as we noted when discussing these discourse qualities we can also strive towards discourse structures that do not meet the conditions of pure cooperation. Thus, we may also specify successful defective speech acts and incoherent and ambiguous discourse structures. However, in these cases we try to make the goals and the conditions of the discourse explicit.

5.1   On Research On supporting Collective Work by Computerized Tools

In this section we shall summarize some research results concerning computer support for collective group work. We also discuss some logic approaches which do not yet have computer implementations. The proposed logics, however, provide a basis for computerization. Most of this research has been oriented towards cooperative or collaborative work. Quite many of these systems are oriented towards supporting communications and there are several approaches based on the speech act theory.

The approaches that support collective work vary a lot in their nature. Some approaches emphasize cooperation and collaboration and some other approaches also deal with conflicts. Some approaches provide a quite general schema for collective work and some others are more specialized.

Coordinator (Winograd, 1987; Winograd and Flores, 1986) provides support mainly for a conversation type called conversation for action. The support contains a "protocol" for conversation for action and supports queries for state of action (promises that I have made). The Coordinator has its roots in speech act theory. The conversation for action scheme is oriented towards cooperation. Winograd (Winograd, 1987) discusses also other types of conversations such as conversation for clarification, conversation for possibilities, and conversation for orientation. As he says, conversation for clarification might involve negotiation between parties to get a "favorable deal".

Information Lens (Malone et al., 1987(a); Malone et al., 1987(b)) is an advanced approach for supporting information sharing and communication. Like Coordinator it also supports some predefined "protocols" which the user can voluntarily employ. The protocols supported seem mainly support cooperative behavior.

Mediator (Jarke, Jelassi, and Shakun, 1987; Srikanth and Jarke, 1986) is a negotiation support system that recognizes both shared and conflictual goals. Its support contains features like consensus seeking, shared information, joint problem presentation, and communication center. In Srikanth and Jarke (1986) several theories behind negotiation are discussed and also ideas of supporting individual negotiator are presented. Other systems for supporting meetings are NICK (Ellis et al.) and Colab (Stefik et al.).

Lee (1987) discusses electronic contracting which is also an issue related to negotiation. He discusses the underlying conceptual structures of contracts and contracting and presents a logic model that emphasizes temporal, deontic and performative aspects of contracting. Contracting is seen as a generalization of direct exchange that provides the cross-temporal transactions, allowing one party to offer goods or services at one time in exchange for other goods and services at another time. In contracting, more complex negotiations are possible than in exchange markets. In this paper, Lee shows how relative time, absolute time, deontic logic obligation, sanctions, and performatives can be presented in a logic model of contracting. Time logics are used to present deadlines for action in contracts, deontic logic is used to present obligations and permission and the possibly related sanctions. In the paper, both logic and Petri Net presentations of contracts are discussed. In his approach Lee aims at a formal language which can be used in specifying the obligations of the contracting parties and which also supports inferencing (e.g., if a contract is incomplete or if it has contradictory conditions) about contracts.

Koo (1988) describes a commitment-based communication model COMTRAC (COMmitment TRACk) where autonomous office agents cooperate in office environments. The basic modelling concepts are agents who cooperate to accomplish certain tasks based on certain plans. In addition to executing and generating the plans, the agents communicate with one another to coordinate their work and to distribute tasks to other agents. Koo defines a contract as a record of commitments between agents and they typically consist of two bound parties and a set of obligations. Contract is defined through the concepts term and qualification. Term specifies the tasks to be performed, the asker, the doer, and the time when the result is to be achieved. Terms of contract are often negotiated, an asker performs a request to a doer, and the doer can accept the proposal of the asker, reject it, or counter-propose to the asker with a modified proposal. Qualification is the condition that has to be satisfied no later than the time when the obligations in the term are fulfilled. In the model, if the doer does not fulfill the promise, the contract is considered to be breached by that party and the obligations of the other party are no more binding. Related contracts can be grouped into a structure called contract portfolio.

A logic called illocutionary logic has been proposed in Searle and Vanderveken (1985). It has been used for information modelling in Lyytinen and Lehtinen (1984) and in Lehtinen and Lyytinen (1986). Kimbrough (1988) considers illocutionary logic as not theoretically well-developed and suggested the use of more standard logic for presenting the illocutions. He deals especially with the logic of promising. According to him promising is a modal sort of thing and aims at presenting the effect of modal operators in predicate logic. This is done by conditioning on possible worlds and rel-ativizing the conditioned predicates. Thus, the possible worlds can be categorized into worlds where promises are kept and into worlds where promises are not kept.

Attempts to formalize speech acts are made also by Cohen and Levesque (1987), Perrault et al. (1978), and Perrault (1987). In Perrault et al. (1978) they discuss the possibilities of a program to characterize a speaker's capacity to perform speech acts. The specific speech acts discussed are request and inform. Perrault (1987) suggests the use of default logic to deal with speech act consequences and revision of beliefs. A language is proposed through which one can express sentences like "r is true at time t", "x did a at time t", "x believes at time t that p", and "x intends at time t that p". In Cohen and Levesque (1987) an approach for describing communicative action is presented. In the approach the sincerity of an agent is also discussed.

5.2   SAMPO as an Object Oriented Modelling Approach

Object-oriented models have gained much interest in office modelling (Tsichritzis, 1987; Banerjee et al., 1987; Ahlsen et al., 1982). The advantages of object-orientation are the modelling of all conceptual entities with a single concept, liberation from the "tyranny of keys", flexibility to change the model, etc. (Borgida, 1985; Banerjee, 1987).

We do not have space to discuss here the object-oriented paradigm more deeply, but refer to Wegner (1987) for an analysis of object-oriented concepts. However, the class structures, inheritance mechanisms, and the message passing schemes seem to form an essential part of the approaches. SAMPO could be developed to an approach with active, intentional objects. SAMPO provides a communication oriented view of an office and the office objects can be seen as speech acts. SAMPO provides a structure for these objects through the classification into context, illocutionary force, and propositional content.

The intelligence of these objects can be obtained through formalizing the illocutionary force. Thus, the objects could send and analyze messages where the rules for evaluating the illocutionary points (e.g., commissives, directives) and the conditions of success (preparatory, sincerity, and propositional content conditions) are made explicit.

6.   CONCLUSIONS

In this paper we have given a brief outline of a restricted set of the features of the SAMPO-approach for modelling cooperative and collective work in office information systems. The special emphasis in the approach is on office communications. The main concepts of speech act and discourse theories as the background of the SAMPO-approach have been presented and illustrated through examples. Also some consideration concerning computer-based implementation for supporting or automating some features related to the collective/cooperative work have been discussed.

However, much needs to be done in order to get evidence about the benefits of a speech act based modeling approach. We do not currently have much experience in using SAMPO in real offices. Most tests have been carried out by developers of the method in quite small and simple cases. However, it seems to us that SAMPO offers insightful ways to analyze office communications and to design successful and effective office communications. Another deficiency of the model concerns the technical implementation of the model created through SAMPO. Some modern technologies are implementing the model we have discussed in this paper, but in its current state SAMPO does not provide detailed guidelines for the implementation. The object-oriented approach briefly discussed in this paper seems to give good possibilities for making a flexible implementation for the model. Third deficiency of the model relates to the fact that we do not currently have computer support for creating and updating the SAMPO-graphs and other SAMPO-descriptions.

Thus, the main challenges for future work concerning the SAMPO-approach are the field tests of the model, implementation technologies for the model, and computer support for the description techniques.

REFERENCES

Auramäki, E., Lehtinen, El, and Lyytinen, K., 1988, A Speech Act Based Office Modelling Approach, *ACM TOOLS*, Vol. 6, No. 2, April 1988.

Austin, J., 1962, *How to do Things with Words*, Claredon Press, London.

Bacon, J., 1980, Conflict Management in the Systems Environment, *Journal of Systems Management*, February 1980.

Banerjee, J., Chou, H-T, Garza, J., Kim, W., Woelk, D., Ballou, N., and Kim, H-J, 1987, Data Model Issues for Object-Oriented Applications, *ACM TOOLS*, Vol. 5, No. 1, January 1987.

Borgida, A., 1985, Language Features for Flexible Handling of Exceptions in Information Systems, *ACM TOOLS*, Vol. 10, No. 4, December 1985.

Briefs, U., Ciborra, C., and Schneider, L., eds, 1983, *Systems Design For, With, and By the Users*, North-Holland, Amsterdam.

Canning McNurlin, B., ed., 1986, Spotlight on Group Services, *EDP Analyzer*, Vol. 24, No. 11, November 1986.

Ciborra, C., 1984, Management Information Systems: A Contractual View, *Beyond Productivity: Information Systems Development for Organizational Effectiveness*, Bemelmans, Th. M. A., ed., Elsevier Science Publishers B. V., North-Holland.

Cohen, P., and Levesque, H., 1987, *Rational Interaction as the Basis for Communication*, November 24, 1987.

CSCW86, 1986, *Materials of the Conference on Computer Supported Cooperative Work*, Austin, Texas.

Dimino, S., 1983, Corporate Politics and the System's Process, *Journal of Systems Management*, September 1983.

Flores, F., and Ludlow, J., 1980, Doing and Speaking in the Office, *Decision Support Systems: Issues and Challenges*, Fick, G., and Sprague, R., eds., Pergamon Press, Oxford.

Hirschheim, R., 1985, *Office Automation, A Social and Organizational Perspective*, John Wiley and Sons.

Howard, R., 1987, Design and Social Responsibility: The Political Implications of 'Computer Supported Cooperative Work, *Office: Technology and People*, 3, pp. 175-187.

Jarke, M., Jelassi, M., and Shakun, M., 1987, MEDIATOR: Towards a Negotiation Support System, *European Journal of Operational Research*, Vol. 31, No. 3.

Kimbrough, S., 1988, "*On Representation Schemes for Electronic Promising*", a paper presented at the 21st Hawaii International Conference on System Sciences, January 1988.

Koo, C., 1988, A Commitment-Based Communication Model for Distributed Office Environments, *Proc. of Conf. on Office Information Systems*, SIGOIS Bulletin, Vol. 9, No. 2&3, April & July 1988.

Lee, R., 1988, A Logic Model for Electronic Contracting, *Decision Support Systems*, Vol. 4, No. 1, March 1988.

Lehtinen, E., and Lyytinen, K., 1986, Action Based Model of Information Systems, *Information Systems*, Vol. 11, No. 3.

Lyytinen, K., and Lehtinen, K., 1984, On Information Modelling Through Illocutionary Logic, *Third Scandinavian Research Seminar on Information Modelling and Data Base Management*, Kangassalo, H., ed., Acta Universitatis Tamperensis, Ser. B 22.

Lyytinen, K., and Lehtinen, K., 1985, Discourse Analysis as an Information System Specification Method, *Proceedings of the 7th Scandinavian Seminar on Systemeering*, Sääksjärvi, M., ed., Helsinki.

Malone, T., Grant, K., Lai, K-Y, Rao, R., and Rosenblitt, D., 1987(a), Semistructured Messages are Surprisingly Useful for Computer Supported Coordination, *ACM TOOLS*, Vol. 5, No. 2, April 1987.

Malone, T., Grant, K., Turbak, F., Brobst, S., and Cohen, M., 1987(b), Intelligent Information-Sharing Systems, *CACM*, Vol. 30, No. 5, May 1987.

Malone, T., Yates J., and Benjamin, R., 1987(c), Electronic Markets and Electronic Hierarchies, *CACM*, Vol. 30, No. 6, June 1987.

Morgan, G., 1986, *Images of Organization*, SAGE Publications Inc., Beverly Hills, USA.

Olson, J. R., Conway, L., and Atkins, D., 1987, The EXPRESS Project: Research Issues in Building and Implementing a Platform for Collaborative Technologu, *Proc. of the 8th ICIS Conference*, DeGross, J., and Kriebel, C., eds., Pittsburgh, Pennsylvania.

Searle, J., 1969, *Speech Acts - An Essay in the Philosophy of Language*, Cambridge University Press.

Searle, J., and Vanderveken, D., 1985, *Foundations of Illocutionary Logic*, Cambridge University Press.

Srikanth, R., and Jarke, M., 1986, Individual Negotiation Support in Group Decision Support Systems, *Proc. of IFIP WG 8.4 Working Conf. Office Systems: Methods and Tools*, North-Holland.

Tsichritzis, D., Fiume, E., Gibbs, S., and Nierstrasz, O., 1987, Knowledge Acquisition, Dissemination, and Manipulation Objects, *ACM TOOLS*, Vol. 5, No. 1, January 1987.

Winograd, T., and Flores, F., 1986, *Understanding Computers and Cognition, A New Foundation for Design*, Ablex Publishing Company, Norwood, New Jersey.

Winograd, T., 1987, *A Language/Action Perspective on the Design of Cooperative Work*, Report No. STANCS-87-1158, Stanford University, Department of Computer Science, May 1987.

QUANTITATIVE REGULARITIES OF THE DIVERSITY OF LEXICAL MEANING

Pranas Zunde and Hongyi Zhou

School of Information and Computer Science
Georgia Institute of Technology
Atlanta, GA 30332

Abstract: There is a number of extensively tested and confirmed regularities of use of natural language such as rank-frequency distribution (widely known as Zipf's Law) and type-token distribution of words. Most of these regularities are based on formal attributes of words (number of word occurrences, number of different lexicographical types of words, etc.). On the other hand, very little has been done to investigate potential regularities involving semantic attributes of natural language. The focus of the study reported here is on the quantitative aspects of the diversity of referential meaning of linguistic elements which they acquire in the process of overall semantic attribution.

Specifically, the objective was to investigate, for selected languages, the distribution of words and morphemes by the number of their dictionary meanings. Truncated negative binomial, Waring, Yule, Borel, and zeta distributions were selected as the most likely theoretical candidates. Statistical methods were used to evaluate goodness-of-fit of empirical data to these theoretical distributions. Results on the distribution of words by the number of dictionary meanings and on the lexical frequency distribution of morphemes are presented. Best fits to empirical frequencies of words by the number of meanings for English, Spanish, Russian, and Hungarian languages and for English morphemes were obtained to negative binomial, Waring and Yule distribution laws, both across and within the major grammatical categories of words (i.e. nouns, verbs, adjectives).

The results of fitting the frequencies of word associations to theoretical distributions are described. The distributions of word associations for a sample of 67 stimulus words fitted best to truncated negative binomial law with remarkable consistency. Potential generalizations and implications of these findings are discussed.

INTRODUCTION

Whereas considerable amount of research has been done and reported on various syntactic or formal regularities of natural language use such as statistical laws of rank-frequency distribution (widely known as Zipf's law) or type-token distribution, the study of regularities of semantic nature has so far attracted much less attention (Zunde, 1981). In the latter category, most studies focused on correlational dependencies between semantic attributes or between semantic attributes and other features of natural languages (Zunde, 1987). Examples are studies of correlational dependencies of: co-occurrence of word types related in meaning and the distance between them in word tokens (Lewis, Baxendale, and Bennettt, 1967; Korolev, 1977); co-occurrence of synonymous word types in different sentences and the similarity of their contexts (Lewis, Baxandale, and Bennett, 1967); difference in meaning of two morphemes and the similarity of their environments (Harris, 1954; Rubenstein and Goodenough, 1965); number of meanings (senses) of a word type and the frequency of its occurrence (Zipf, 1949; Guiraud, 1965; Guiraud, 1971); number of meanings of a word type and the length in letters of that word type (Baker, 1950); number of meanings of a word type and the number of phonemes in it (Guiraud, 1954); number of lexical meanings of a word type and its rank in a list ordered by nonincreasing frequency of occurrence of word types (Zipf, 1949); number of synonyms of a word type in a given text and the number of occurrences of that word type

Empirical Foundations of Information and Software Science V
Edited by P. Zunde and D. Hocking, Plenum Press, New York, 1990

301

in·jec'tion (*ĭn·jĕk'shŭn*), n. [L. *injectio.*] 1. Act of injecting; esp., the forcible throwing in of a liquid, or aeri-
form body, by means of a syringe, pump, etc.
2. That which is injected; esp., a liquid medicine thrown
into the subcutaneous tissue or a cavity of the body by a
syringe or other instrument; a clyster; an enema.
3. Introduction of a suggestion; a hint. *Now Rare.*
4. *Anat.* a Act or process of injecting vessels or tissues
(see INJECT, *v., 3*). b A specimen prepared by injection
5. *Geol.* The intrusion of molten magma between rocks.
6. *Med.* State of being injected; congestion.

INJECTION: 7 MEANINGS

ink'ber'ry (ĭngk'bĕr'ĭ; -bĕr·ĭ), n.; *pl. -RIES* (-ĭz). a The
holly *Ilex glabra* of eastern North America, with ever-
green oblong leathery leaves, and small black berries; —
called also *gallberry.* b The box brier. c The pokeweed.
d The fruit of any of these plants.

INKBERRY: 4 MEANINGS

Figure 1.   Two Examples of Lexical Items from the English Source Dictionary
and the Number of Their Dictionary Meanings.

in text (Andrukovich and Korolev, 1977); structural similarity and judged similarity of scientific concepts (Johnson, 1969); structural similarity and associative similarity of scientific concepts (Johnson, 1969); meaningfulness of a word and its perceptual stability (Terwilliger, 1968); speed of recognition of meaning related words and their pronunciation (Meyer and Schvaneveldt, 1976; Becker and Killion, 1977); and fraction of cognates shared by two daughter languages and the duration of their development (Edmundson, 1977). The focus of our study described in this paper was on the quantitative aspects of the diversity of referential meaning of linguistic elements, such as words or morphemes, which they acquire in the process of the overall semantic attribution.

OBJECTIVE OF THE STUDY

The main objective of the study was to investigate whether the frequency distribution of English and Spanish words (dictionary entries) by the number of their dictionary meanings and the lexical frequency distribution of English morphemes obey certain probability distribution laws or not. At some given point in time, the state of the process of semantic attribution is captured in dictionaries, both in terms of the variety of the family of lexical items and in the variety of referential meanings attributed to each lexical item. Thus, using dictionaries as the prime source of data of this kind, we studied, first, the distribution of words by the number of their dictionary meanings. The study was limited to English and Spanish languages. Comparisons were also made with reported results for Russian and Hungarian languages. We also studied analogous distributions of morphemes and subclasses of morphemes (suffixes etc.). Studies of frequency distributions of words by the number of their dictionary or lexical meanings were reported by Pap (1967) for Hungarian language, and by Krylov and Yakubovskaya (1977) as well as by Korolev (1977) for the Russian language. Unfortunately, nothing is said there about exclusion or inclusion of certain categories of entries, handling of homograph, method of determination of the number of meanings for a dictionary entry etc., so that only limited comparisons could be made with our findings.

EXPERIMENTAL DESIGN

The data for the study of frequency distribution of words by the number of meanings was obtained by taking stratified samples of main entries from English and Spanish dictionaries. The sample of English words was selected from the *Webster's New International Dictionary of the English Language*, Second edition, unabridged, G. & C. Merriam Co., Springfield, Mass., 1958. It contained a total of 1876 dictionary (i.e. lexical) items. For each lexical item in the sample, the number of meanings listed in the dictionary under

Table 1

Distribution of English Words by the Number of
Meanings. (The Sample Includes Personal,
Geographic and Other Names, Phrases etc.)

Number of Meanings x	Number of Words with x Meanings G(x)	Fraction of Words with x Meanings P(x)
1	1456	0.7761
2	186	0.0991
3	76	0.0405
4	54	0.0288
5	28	0.0149
6	17	0.0091
7	16	0.0085
8	4	0.0021
9	7	0.0037
10	3	0.0016
11	2	0.0011
12	2	0.0011
13	4	0.0021
15	2	0.0011
16	2	0.0011
17	2	0.0011
18	2	0.0011
19	1	0.0005
20	1	0.0005
22	1	0.0005
23	1	0.0005
24	1	0.0005
28	1	0.0005
31	1	0.0005
33	1	0.0005
34	1	0.0005
35	1	0.0005
37	1	0.0005
39	1	0.0005
43	1	0.0005
Total	1876	1.0000

that item was determined. All distinct categories of word senses, independently of their listing in the dictionary as major or minor, were counted in determining the total number of meanings for that particular dictionary item. For example, the number of meanings of the word INJECTION was taken to be equal to 7, and that of the word INKBERRY equal to 4 (see Figure 1).

The distribution of these 1876 English words by the number of their dictionary meanings is given in Table 1. From that table it can be seen that 1456 words had only one meaning each; at the other end of the spectrum, one of the words in the sample had as many as 43 meanings. Note, however, that this sample contained, in addition to single common words, also all kinds of proper names, short phrases etc. Furthermore, homographs were considered distinct words. Thus, no distinct dictionary entry was excluded from this sample, which, henceforth, will be referred to as the *base sample*.

Frequency distributions of sampled English words by the number of their meanings were also determined for modified operational definitions of the term "word" and for subsets of the *base sample* set of 1876 words by major grammatical categories, viz.:

EFECTO m. Resultado de una causa: *no hay efecto sin causa.* (SINÓN. V. *Consecuencia.*) || Documento mercantil. || Impresión: *el efecto producido por sus palabras fue muy grande.* (SINÓN. *Motivo, objeto.*) || Potencia transmitida por una máquina. || Artículo de comercio. || Rotación que se da a una bola de billar, a un balón, para obtener un recorrido o botes anormales. || —— PL Bienes, muebles, enseres: *efectos de escritorio.* || *Efectos públioos.* documentos de crédito emitidos por una corporación pública. || *Con, o en, efecto,* efectivamente; en conclusión. || *Hacer o surtir efecto,* dar una cosa el resultado que se esperaba de ella.

EFECTO: 9 MEANINGS

EFÍMERA f. Cachipolla, insecto.

EFIMERA: 1 MEANING

Figure 2. Two Examples of Lexical Items from the Spanish
Source Dictionary and the Number of Their
Dictionary Meanings.

- Distribution of words of the *base sample* by the number of meanings, except that homographs are considered single word forms.

- Distribution of words of the *base sample* by the number of meanings with proper names an phrases omitted from the original sample and homographs considered distinct words.

- Distribution of words of the *base sample* by the number of meanings with proper names and phrases omitted and homographs considered single word forms.

- Distribution of English nouns from the *base sample* by the number of meanings.

- Distribution of English adjectives from the *base sample* by the number of meanings.

- Distribution of English verbs (transitive and intransitive) from the *base sample* by the number of meanings.

- Distribution of English transitive verbs from the *base sample* by the number of meanings.

- Distribution of English intransitive verbs from the *base sample* by the number of meanings.

- Distribution of English adverbs from the *base sample* by the number of meanings.

The sample of Spanish language words was selected from the Spanish dictionary *Pequeno Larousse Illustrada* by Ramon Garcia and Pelayo y Gross, Ediciones Larousse, Paris, 1964. The sample size was 1957 words. As for English words, all meanings listed in the dictionary, independent of their classification, were counted in determining the total number of dictionary meanings of a given word. For example, the Spanish word EFECTO was found to have 9 dictionary meanings, and the word EFIMERA - only 1 meaning (Figure 2). The distribution of these Spanish words by the number of their dictionary meanings is given in Table 2.

As in the case of English data, frequency distribution of certain grammatical subcategories of the above Spanish *base sample* were determined, namely:

- Distribution of Spanish nouns by the number of their meanings.

304

Table 2

Distribution of Spanish Words by the Number
of Meanings (The Sample Includes Personal,
Geographic and Other Names, Phrases etc.)

Number of Meanings x	Number of Words with x Meanings $G(x)$	Fraction of Words with x Meanings $P(x)$
1	1342	0.6857
2	330	0.1686
3	129	0.0659
4	58	0.0296
5	34	0.0174
6	12	0.0061
7	11	0.0056
8	12	0.0061
9	10	0.0051
10	4	0.0020
11	2	0.0010
12	2	0.0010
13	1	0.0005
14	3	0.0015
15	1	0.0005
17	1	0.0005
19	3	0.0015
24	1	0.0005
27	1	0.0005
Total	1957	1.0000

- Distribution of Spanish adjectives by the number of their dictionary meanings.

- Distribution of Spanish verbs by the number of their dictionary meanings.

- Distribution of Spanish transitive verbs by the number of their dictionary meanings.

- Distribution of Spanish intransitive verbs by the number of their dictionary meanings.

- Distribution of Spanish reflexive verbs by the number of their dictionary meanings.

We also used the following published data on the frequency distribution of words by the number of meanings.

- Distribution of all Russian verbs listed in Ozhegov (1960) dictionary by the number of meanings, reported by Krylov and Yakubovskaya (1977).

- Distribution of Russian verbs starting with the letters I, K, and S from the same Ozhegov dictionary by the number of meanings, reported by Krylov and Yakubovskaya (1977).

- Distribution of Russian verbs starting with the letters I, K, and S and listed in the *Dictionary of the Modern Russian Literary Language (DMRLL)*.

- Distribution of a sample of 60,000 Hungarian words in Orszag's (1962) dictionary and reported by Pap (1967).

The data for the lexical frequency distribution of English morphemes and for the subclasses of suffix morphemes, nominal suffix morphemes, adjectival suffix morphemes, and prefix morphemes was compiled

Table 3

Observed Lexical Frequency Distribution of English Morphemes

Lexical Frequency x	Number of Morphemes with Lexical Frequency x G(x)	Fraction of Morphemes with Lexical Frequency x P(x)	Lexical Frequency x	Number of Morphemes with Lexical Frequency x G(x)	Fraction of Morphemes with Lexical Frequency x P(x)
1	3644	0.6933	43	1	0.0002
2	860	0.1636	46	1	0.0002
3	324	0.0616	48	4	0.0008
4	132	0.0251	49	1	0.0002
5	76	0.0145	52	2	0.0004
6	47	0.0089	53	1	0.0002
7	20	0.0038	55	1	0.0002
8	12	0.0023	56	1	0.0002
9	14	0.0027	57	1	0.0002
10	8	0.0015	62	2	0.0004
11	12	0.0023	65	2	0.0004
12	6	0.0011	68	2	0.0004
13	10	0.0019	70	2	0.0004
14	6	0.0011	72	1	0.0002
15	5	0.0010	75	1	0.0002
16	2	0.0004	82	2	0.0004
17	3	0.0006	85	1	0.0002
18	3	0.0006	87	1	0.0002
19	1	0.0002	91	1	0.0002
20	1	0.0002	101	1	0.0002
21	2	0.0004	102	1	0.0002
22	2	0.0004	113	1	0.0002
23	1	0.0002	121	1	0.0002
27	4	0.0008	136	1	0.0002
28	1	0.0002	148	1	0.0002
29	1	0.0002	155	1	0.0002
30	3	0.0006	179	1	0.0002
31	2	0.0004	187	1	0.0002
32	2	0.0004	195	1	0.0002
33	2	0.0004	210	1	0.0002
34	1	0.0002	241	1	0.0002
37	1	0.0002	372	1	0.0002
38	3	0.0006			
39	1	0.0002	Total	5256	1.0000
40	1	0.0002			
42	2	0.0004			

from *A Frequency Dictionary of English Morphemes* by Magnus Ljung (1974). The corpus used in Ljung's study corresponds almost entirely to the eight thousand words in Thoren (1959), which in turn comprises, with certain exceptions, the eight thousand most frequent words in Thorndike-Lorge (1959). Thoren is a work intended as a vocabulary guide for students and teachers of English.

A morpheme is defined as the smallest unit on the lexical level of language which will be needed for one reason or another in an appropriate linguistic description of that language. For instance, the word FOREMAN can be subdivided into morphemes FORE and MAN, both of which carry meanings, but no smaller parts of them do. By the lexical frequency of a morpheme it is understood the frequency of that morpheme in the word list. For example, the morpheme RAT - occurs in four different words, i.e. *ratio, ration, rational, ratify*, and consequently it is assigned lexical frequency of 4 (one should note that this is not an exact analogue of the prior notion of the number of dictionary meanings of a word).

Lexical frequency distribution of all morphemes is presented in Table 3. For lexical frequency distributions of the above subclasses of morphemes see Zunde and Zhou (1988). The same source contained lexical frequency data also for the subclasses of morphemes, namely: prefix morphemes, suffix morphemes, nominal suffix morphemes, and adjectival suffix morphemes.

SELECTION OF CANDIDATE DISTRIBUTION LAWS

The following theoretical distribution laws were selected to fit the observed data: truncated negative binomial distribution, zeta distribution, Yule distribution, Borel distribution and truncated Waring

Table 4

Theoretical Distributions Selected to Fit Observed Data

1. Truncated Negative Binomial Distribution:

$$P_t(x) = (Q^N - 1)^{-1} \binom{N + x - 1}{N - 1} (P/Q)^x, \quad N > -1, \quad P > 0, \quad Q - P = 1$$

2. Yule Distribution:

$$P(x) = A_\rho \frac{\Gamma(x)\Gamma(\rho + 1)}{\Gamma(x + \rho + 1)}, \quad \rho > -1$$

where $A_\rho = [\sum_{r=1}^{\infty} B(r, \rho + 1)]^{-1}$ and $B(\alpha, \beta)$ is the beta function.

3. Zeta Distribution:

$$P(x) = \frac{x^{-(\rho+1)}}{\sum_{r=1}^{\infty} r^{-(\rho+1)}} = x^{-(\rho+1)} \cdot [\xi(\rho + 1)]^{-1}, \quad \rho > 0$$

where $\xi(\cdot)$ denotes the Riemann zeta function which is defined by the equation: $\xi(x) = \sum_{j=1}^{\infty} j^{-x}$

4. Borel Distribution:

$$P(x) = \frac{x^{x-2}}{(x - 1)!} e^{-\beta x} \beta^{x-1}, \quad \beta < 1$$

5. Truncated Waring Distribution:

$$P_t(x) = \frac{\lambda - a}{a} \cdot \frac{a_{[x]}}{(\lambda + 1)_{[x]}}, \quad \lambda > a > 0$$

where $a_{[n]} = a(a + 1)(a + 2) \cdots (a + n - 1)$ and $(\lambda + 1)_{[n]} = (\lambda + 1)(\lambda + 2) \cdots (\lambda + n)$.

$$x = 1, 2, 3, \ldots, \quad for \; all \; distributions.$$

distribution (Table 4). For natural languages, the first three of these distribution laws were proposed by previous researchers, who studied distributions of words by the number of meanings. Thus, Pap (1967) and Krylov and Yakubovskaya (1977) claimed that negative binomial distribution (actually the truncated geometric distribution, which is the special case of negative binomial distribution) is the appropriate theoretical model for the distribution of Hungarian and Russian words by the number of meanings, Simon (1955) proposed Yule distribution as the most appropriate model of the distribution of English words by their frequency of occurrence, and Guiraud (1971) proposed the zeta distribution for French words. None of the above authors reported having used some statistical hypothesis tests of goodness of fit of their empirical data to proposed theoretical distributions in support of their conclusions. The other two distribution laws, Borel and truncated Waring distributions, were selected by the authors of this paper on the grounds of their apparent similarity in shape to the distributions of some of the empirical data. As to the distribution of morphemes by the number of meanings, the authors of this paper were not aware of any previous studies on that subject matter. Since the empirical data of this kind of frequency distribution seemed to be similar in shape to empirical data of the distribution of natural language words by the number of meanings, the same five theoretical distributions were retained for testing the goodnes-of-fit of morpheme data.

METHODS OF PARAMETER ESTIMATION AND DATA POOLING

For each of the five distribution laws, three different methods were used to estimate the parameters; in addition, a fourth estimation method, called the Mixed Estimate, was used to estimate the parameters of the truncated negative binomial distribution. The estimation methods are briefly described below:

307

Table 5

Best Fitting Theoretical Distributions to Observed
Frequencies of English Words by the Number of Their
Dictionary Meanings (Corresponding Parameter Estimation Methods Shown in Parenthesis)

ENGLISH DATA

		BEST-FIT		2-ND BEST	
		χ^2	K-S	χ^2	K-S
(1)	ALL DICTIONARY WORDS	NEG. BIN. (Mixed)	NEG. BIN. (Mixed)	N.A.	ZETA (Tails)
(2)	HOMOGRAPHS CONSIDERED A SINGLE WORD FORM IN (1)	NEG. BIN. (Mixed)	NEG. BIN. (Mixed)	N.A.	N.A.
(3)	PROPER NOUNS AND NAMES OMITTED IN (1)	NEG. BIN. (Mixed)	NEG. BIN. (Mixed)	N.A.	ZETA (Heads)
(4)	HOMOGRAPHS CONSIDERED A SINGLE WORD FORM IN (3)	NEG. BIN. (Mixed)	NEG. BIN. (Mixed)	N.A.	ZETA (Moments)
(5)	NOUNS	NEG. BIN. (Mixed)	NEG. BIN. (Mixed)	ZETA (Tails)	ZETA (Moments)
(6)	ADJECTIVES	ZETA (Heads)	ZETA (Heads)	NEG. BIN. (Mixed)	NEG. BIN. (Heads)
(7)	VERBS	N.A.	NEG. BIN. (Tails)	N.A.	BOREL (Moments)
(8)	TRANSITIVE VERBS	N.A.	BOREL (Moments)	N.A.	NEG. BIN. (Mixed)
(9)	INTRANSITIVE VERBS	BOREL (Heads)	YULE (Heads)	YULE (Heads)	NEG. BIN. (Moments)

Note: Critical value for the null (no-difference) hypothesis was $\alpha = 0.05$.
N.A. means that the null hypothesis was rejected.

- *The Moments Estimate.* For single parameter distribution laws, the unknown parameter was estimated from the sample mean. For two parameter distribution laws, the parameters were estimated from sample mean and sample variance.

- *The Heads Estimate.* For single parameter distributions, that parameter was estimated by equating the top head frequency of the sample data (i.e., the frequency corresponding to $x = 1$) with the corresponding theoretical frequency; for two parameter distributions, the parameters were estimated by equating the first two head frequencies of the empirical data with the corresponding theoretical frequencies.

- *The Tails Estimate.* For single paramter case, that parameter was estimated by equating (pooled) tail frequencies of the sample and corresponding theoretical distributions; for two parameter cases, the corresponding last two (pooled) tail frequencies were equated.

- *The Mixed Estimate.* Parameters were estimated using sample mean (or single parameter case) or sample mean and variance (for the two parameter case) and the top head or tail frequency.

Also, two different methods were used for pooling small classes at the tails of the distributions.

Table 6

Best Fitting Theoretical Distributions to Observed
Frequencies of Spanish Words by the Number of Dictionary
Meanings (Corresponding Parameter Estimation Methods
Shown in Parenthesis)

ENGLISH DATA

		BEST-FIT		2-ND BEST	
		χ^2	K-S	χ^2	K-S
(1)	ALL DICTIONARY WORDS	NEG. BIN. (Mixed)	NEG. BIN. (Mixed)	N.A.	ZETA (Tails)
(2)	HOMOGRAPHS CONSIDERED A SINGLE WORD FORM IN (1)	NEG. BIN. (Mixed)	NEG. BIN. (Mixed)	N.A.	N.A.
(3)	PROPER NOUNS AND NAMES OMITTED IN (1)	NEG. BIN. (Mixed)	NEG. BIN. (Mixed)	N.A.	ZETA (Heads)
(4)	HOMOGRAPHS CONSIDERED A SINGLE WORD FORM IN (3)	NEG. BIN. (Mixed)	NEG. BIN. (Mixed)	N.A.	ZETA (Moments)
(5)	NOUNS	NEG. BIN. (Mixed)	NEG. BIN. (Mixed)	ZETA (Tails)	ZETA (Moments)
(6)	ADJECTIVES	ZETA (Heads)	ZETA (Heads)	NEG. BIN. (Mixed)	NEG. BIN. (Heads)
(7)	VERBS	N.A.	NEG. BIN. (Tails)	N.A.	BOREL (Moments)
(8)	TRANSITIVE VERBS	N.A.	BOREL (Moments)	N.A.	NEG. BIN. (Mixed)
(9)	INTRANSITIVE VERBS	BOREL (Heads)	YULE (Heads)	YULE (Heads)	NEG. BIN. (Moments)

Note: Critical value for the null (no-difference) hypothesis was $\alpha = 0.05$.
N.A. means that the null hypothesis was rejected.

- *The Uniform Pooling Method.* According to this method of pooling small classes, the expected number of cases in every class at the tail of the distribution was set to about 5.

- *The Threshold Pooling Method.* According to this method of pooling, a threshold value, which depends on the observed frequencies, was chosen and all the entries at the tail below that threshold value were pooled into one class.

GOODNESS OF FIT TESTS

The goodness of fit of observed data to the above mentioned theoretical distribution laws was evaluated using (a) the chi- square test and (b) the Kolmogorov-Smirnov test. The latter is considered a strong competitor of the chi-square goodness of fit test whenever the hypothesized form of the distribution is completely specified (including the values of all parameters). In fact, it has been shown that in this situation it is a more powerful test. The critical value α was selected for both tests equal to 5%, i.e. the hypothesis that observed frequency data comes from a population distributed according to a particular theoretical distribution law (f.e., negative binomial law) is rejected if the probability of the test score taking the calculated value is greater than 0.05.

Table 7

Best Fitting Theoretical Distributions to Observed
Frequencies of Russian and Hungarian Words by the
Number of Their Dictionary Meanings   (Corresponding
Parameter Estimation Methods Shown in Parenthesis)

RUSSIAN DATA
(from secondary source)

		BEST-FIT		2-ND BEST	
		χ^2	K-S	χ^2	K-S
(1)	OZHEGOV DATA (entire)	N.A.	N.A.	N.A.	N.A.
(2)	OZHEGOV IKS	N.A.	NEG. BIN. (Heads)	N.A.	WARING (Moments)
(3)	DMRLL	N.A.	WARING (Mixed)	N.A.	N.A.

HUNGARIAN DATA
(from secondary source)

		BEST-FIT		2-ND BEST	
		χ^2	K-S	χ^2	K-S
(1)	PAP DATA	NEG. BIN. (Heads)	NEG. BIN. (Heads)	WARING (Moments)	WARING (Moments)

Note: Critical value for the null (no-difference) hypothesis was $\alpha = 0.05$.
N.A. means that the null hypothesis was rejected.

DISCUSSION OF THE RESULTS OF THE STUDY

Results for English Word Data

For the distribution of English words by the number of dictionary meanings, by far the best fit was obtained to the truncated negative binomial distribution. For the basic sample and its three variations (homographs considered a single word form, proper nouns and names omitted, homographs considered a single word form and proper nouns and names omitted), as well as for the nouns, the negative binomial distribution, using the mixed parameter estimation method, produced the best fit both in terms of the chi square and Kolmogorov-Smirnov statistic far above the 5% critical value. The Zeta distribution was a distant second. In fact, the null hypothesis for Zeta distribution was rejected for the *base sample* set of English words and for its variations when chi square method was used, and ranked second best in four out of the first five cases for Kolmogorov-Smirnov test (see Table 5).

For English adjectives, the Zeta distribution, using the heads method of parameter estimation, fitted the observed data best. Negative binomial was second best. For the remaining categories of English verbs in general and for transitive and intransitive verbs, none of the theoretical distributions qualified as a single best choice and for verbs and transitive verbs none of these distributions even qualified as acceptable in terms of the chi square test, although some did in terms of the Kolmogorov-Smirnov test. However, the empirical data for adjectives and verbs in general, as well as for the subcategories of transitive and intransitive verbs in particular, may not have been large enough to give sufficient confidence in the test results.

Table 8

Best Fitting Theoretical Distributions of Lexical Frequencies of
Morphemes (With Parameter Estimation Methods in Parenthesis)

		BEST-FIT		2-ND BEST	
		χ^2	K-S	χ^2	K-S
(1)	ALL MORPHEMES	N.A.	YULE (Heads)	N.A.	N.A.
(2)	SUFFIXES	NEG. BIN. (Mixed)	NEG. BIN. (Heads)	ZETA (Tails)	WARING (Tails)
(3)	NOMINAL SUFFIXES	NEG. BIN. (Mixed)	NEG. BIN. (Mixed)	WARING (Tails)	WARING (Tails)
(4)	ADJECTIVAL SUFFIXES	BOREL (Heads)	ZETA (Heads)	ZETA (Heads)	NEG. BIN. (Mixed)
(5)	PREFIXES	YULE (Tails)	YULE (Tails)	WARING (Tails)	ZETA (Tails)

Note: Critical value for the null (no-difference) hypothesis was $\alpha = 0.05$.
N.A. means that the null hypothesis was rejected.

Results for Spanish Word Data

The results for Spanish data are somewhat less conclusive than those for the English language words (see Table 6).

Nevertheless, truncated Waring distribution law with parameters estimated by the moments method appears to be uncontested choice out of the five selected theoretical distributions when the Kolmogorov-Smirnov test method is used. In any case, it certainly is a good candidate to eventually become an accepted empirical regularity.

Results for Russian and Hungarian Word Data

None of the three sets of the Russian language data passed the chi square goodness of fit test to the theoretical distributions at the 5% critical level. However, the Ozhegov's data on the distribution of Russian verbs starting with letters I, K, and S and similar data compiled from the DMRLL did pass the Kolmogorov-Smirnov test. For that data, the best fitting theoretical distributions were the truncated negative binomial and Waring. Data on frequency distribution by the number of meanings for Hungarian words was taken from an article by Pap (1967). This data was compiled by Pap for the whole corpus of 60,000 words of the Hungarian dictionary *A magyar nyelv ertelmezo szotara* (1962). None of the theoretical distributions qualified as good approximations by either one of the two testing methods. In his article, Pap claimed an excellent fit of the data to the geometric distribution (which is a special case of the negative binomial distribution) with the mean m = 0.5. However, no formal test was mentioned in his article, and the results of our goodness of fit test to that particular geometric distribution were negative, i.e. the hypothesis, that the Hungarian words are distributed by the number of meanings according to the geometric distribution was rejected at the critical level of 5%. The test results for Russian and Hungarian data are summarized in Table 7.

Results for English Morpheme Data

For the set of all morphemes, the only theoretical distribution which passed the Kolmogorov-Smirnov goodness of fit test (but not the chi square test) at the critical level of 5% was the Yule distribution. However, for the two largest subcategories of morphemes, the suffix morphemes and the nominal suffix morphemes, the truncated negative binomial distribution approximated the empirical data best relative to both methods of testing, with Waring and Zeta distributions ending the second best (see Table 8). For the two other subcategories of the morphemes the results are less uniform.[1]

Table 9

Best Fitting Theoretical Distributions with the Parameter
Estimation Methods Used for All Categories of Data

χ^2 Test (K-S Test)

	Neg. Bin. (Mixed)	Zeta (Heads)	Neg. Bin. (Tails)	Neg. Bin. (Heads)	Borel (Moments)	Borel (Heads)	Yule (Heads)	Yule (Moments)	Yule (Tails)	Waring (Mixed)
English										
(1)	⊕ (⊕)	- (+)	- (-)	+ (+)	- (-)	- (-)	- (-)	- (-)	- (-)	- (-)
(2)	⊕ (⊕)	- (-)	- (-)	+ (+)	- (-)	- (-)	- (-)	- (-)	- (-)	- (-)
(3)	⊕ (⊕)	- (+)	- (-)	- (+)	- (-)	- (-)	- (-)	- (-)	- (-)	- (-)
(4)	⊕ (⊕)	- (-)	- (-)	- (+)	- (-)	- (-)	- (-)	- (-)	- (-)	- (-)
(5)	⊕ (⊕)	- (+)	+ (+)	- (+)	- (-)	- (-)	- (-)	- (-)	- (-)	- (-)
(6)	+ (+)	⊕ (⊕)	+ (+)	+ (+)	- (+)	- (+)	+ (+)	+ (+)	+ (+)	- (-)
(7)	- (+)	- (+)	- (⊕)	- (+)	- (+)	- (+)	- (+)	- (+)	- (+)	- (+)
(8)	- (+)	- (+)	- (-)	- (-)	- (⊕)	- (-)	- (+)	- (+)	- (+)	- (-)
(9)	+ (+)	- (+)	+ (+)	- (+)	+ (+)	⊕ (+)	+ (⊕)	+ (+)	- (+)	+ (+)
Spanish										
(1)	- (+)	- (-)	- (-)	- (+)	- (-)	- (+)	⊕ (+)	+ (+)	+ (+)	+ (⊕)
(2)	+ (+)	- (+)	- (-)	- (+)	- (+)	- (+)	+ (+)	+ (+)	+ (+)	⊕ (⊕)
(3)	+ (+)	- (+)	- (-)	+ (+)	+ (+)	⊕ (+)	+ (+)	+ (+)	+ (+)	+ (⊕)
(4)	+ (+)	- (+)	- (-)	+ (+)	⊕ (+)	+ (+)	+ (+)	+ (+)	+ (+)	+ (⊕)
(5)	+ (+)	- (+)	+ (+)	+ (+)	⊕ (+)	+ (+)	+ (+)	+ (+)	+ (+)	+ (⊕)
(6)	- (+)	+ (+)	- (+)	- (+)	+ (+)	+ (+)	⊕ (+)	+ (⊕)	+ (+)	- (+)
(7)	- (+)	⊕ (+)	- (⊕)	- (+)	+ (+)	+ (+)	+ (+)	- (+)	+ (+)	- (+)
Russian										
(1)	- (-)	- (-)	- (-)	- (-)	- (-)	- (-)	- (-)	- (-)	- (-)	- (-)
(2)	- (+)	- (-)	- (-)	- (⊕)	- (-)	- (-)	- (-)	- (-)	- (-)	- (+)
(3)	- (-)	- (-)	- (-)	- (-)	- (-)	- (-)	- (-)	- (-)	- (-)	- (⊕)
Hungarian										
(1)	- (-)	- (-)	- (-)	- (-)	- (-)	- (-)	- (-)	- (-)	- (-)	- (-)
Morphemes										
(1)	- (-)	- (-)	- (-)	- (-)	- (-)	- (-)	- (⊕)	- (-)	- (-)	- (-)
(2)	⊖ (+)	÷ (+)	+ (-)	+ (⊕)	- (-)	- (-)	+ (-)	- (-)	± (+)	- (-)
(3)	⊕ (⊖)	+ (+)	+ (+)	+ (+)	- (-)	- (-)	+ (-)	- (-)	+ (+)	- (-)
(4)	+ (+)	+ (⊕)	+ (-)	+ (+)	- (-)	⊕ (-)	+ (+)	- (-)	+ (-)	- (-)
(5)	+ (+)	+ (+)	+ (+)	- (-)	+ (+)	- (-)	- (+)	- (-)	⊕ (⊕)	+ (+)

Note: Symbol " ⊕ " in an intersection of a row and a column means that the theoretical distribution corresponding to the column is the best fit to the category data indicated by the row at the 5% level of confidence.
Symbol " + " means that there was no reason to reject , at the 5% level of confidence, the hypothesis that the parent population is distributed as indicated by the column label.
Symbol " - " means that there is no evidence, at the 5% level of confidence, that the sample fits the theoretical distribution indicated by the corresponding column label.
Symbols in parenthesis are the ones for K-S test.

CONCLUSIONS

To facilitate an overall comparison and evaluation of the results of the study within and across languages, the best fitting theoretical distributions and the associated parameter estimation methods are assembled in Table 9.

By comparing the results across languages one has to conclude that there is no evidence that the frequency distribution of words by the number of meanings follows one particular distribution law for all languages. In particular, that seems not to be the case for English, Spanish, Russian, and Hungarian

---

[1]For complete data on fitting the observed distributions to theoretical distributions for all the above discussed categories see Zunde and Zhou (1988).

languages, although for the latter two the available data may not be sufficiently reliable for the purpose of a rigorous comparative analysis.

Within individual languages, there is strong evidence that the distribution of English words by the number of meanings is truncated negative binomial, and for Spanish - the truncated Waring, which in both cases hold not only for words in general, but also for grammatical categories (nouns, verbs, etc.).

For the Russian language data, the second sample passed the test for negative binomial distribution when Kolmogorov-Smirnov method of testing was used, the third sample could be fitted to the Waring distribution, but the first sample could not be fitted to any of the five theoretical distributions. The latter was the case for the Hungarian data, too.

On the other hand, we note that in quite a few cases several theoretical distributions approximate the empirical data well enough to pass the goodness of fit test at the critical level of 5%. Instead of giving simply priority to the one from among the theoretical distributions with the smallest value of the chi square or Kolmogorov-Smirnov statistic, a better approach might be to select that distribution law which has the most plausible interpretation in terms of some stochastic model.

With that in mind, let us consider the following scenario. At the point in time t, there are E distinct objects (concepts, events, entities) which have been labeled using N distinct labels (signs, words). The number of labels (words) i smaller than the number of objects to be labelled, i.e. N < E, so that, in general, one and the same label is assigned to several objects, in which case the labels (words) are said to have "multiple meanings". Let us group the labels (words) into classes by the number of meanings and let P(n,t) be the probability that at the time t an arbitrarily selected word belongs to the class of words with exactly n meanings. Assume that at the time t+1 a new object appears which is to be assigned a label.

Further assume that the selection of the label for the new object is done by stratified sampling from the strata of labels (words) with i = 1,2, 3,... referents (meanings) and that the probability of the new object being assigned a label (word) which already has n referents (meanings) is proportional to nP(n,t+1). There is also a constant probability α that a new label (word) is created for labeling the new object, i.e. α is the probability that a new label (word) will be produced to refer to or signify that object.

A stochastic model satisfying the above assumptions has been proposed by Simon (1955). The process is given by the following equations:

$$P(n, t+1) - P(n, t) = \lambda(t) [(n-1)P(n-1,t) - nP(n,t)]$$

$$P(1, t+1) - P(1, t) = \alpha - \lambda(t)P(1, t)$$

It can be shown that the steady state distribution of this stochastic process, with some simplifying assumptions for λ, is the Yule distribution, i.e.

$$P(n) = A_\rho \frac{\Gamma(n)\Gamma(\rho+1)}{\Gamma(n-\rho+1)} ,$$

$$\rho > -1, n=1, 2, \ldots$$

On the other hand, the negative binomial (truncated) distribution is obtained as the steady state solution of a stochastic process based on the following assumptions. Consider the family of classes of words $\{C_1, C_2, ..., C_j, ..., C_n\}$, where C_j is the set of words (dictionary items) such that each word in that set has j lexicographical meanings. We shall say that a word is in the j-th state if that word is an element of the class C_j. We shall say that a word is in the n-th state if that word belongs to the class of words which have n dictionary meanings. Furthermore we assume that during a fixed interval of time a word can acquire an additional meaning, but that no word can lose a meaning which it has acquired at some point in time. In other words, once a word becomes a lexicographical entry in a dictionary, it never disappears. Assume that during a short interval of time h each word has probability (λh + o(h)) to acquire a new meaning, where the constant λ represents the rate of increase in the number of lexicographical meanings of a word. The transition of a word from the j-th state to the (j+1)-st state is interpreted as the acquisition of one additional new meaning by that word. We shall assume that direct transitions from a j-th state are possible only to the (j+1)-st state. If at time t the number of classes is n, then the probability of such a transition at some time between t and t+h equals $n\lambda h$ + o(h). The probability P(n,t) that a word has exactly n meanings at time t is then given by the solution of the set of differential equations

$$dP(n, t)/dt = -n\lambda P(n, t) + (n-1)\lambda P(n-1, t)$$
$$dP(0, t)/dt = 0$$

where i is the initial number of classes, $P(i,0) = 1, P(n,0) = 0$ for $n \neq i$, and $P(n,t) = 0$ for all $n < i$ and all t. The solution then is:

$$P(n,t) = \binom{n-1}{n-i} e^{-i\lambda t} (1 - e^{-\lambda t})^{n-i}$$

This is a negative binomial distribution with parameters i and $e^{-\lambda t}$.

If in the above expression we let $n-i = x$, $i = N$, and $e^{\lambda t} = Q$, then we get the density function of the (untruncated) negative binomial distribution in the form

$$P_t(x) = \binom{N+x-1}{x} (P/Q)^x (1-P/Q)^N$$

in which it was presented in Table 4.

Further research is needed to determine which assumptions and initial condition are better supported by empirical evidence.

ACKNOWLEDGEMENT

Partial support of this research by the National Science Foundation under Grant Number IST-8219217 is hereby gratefully acknowledged.

REFERENCES

Altmann, G., Best, K.H., and Kind, B., (1987), A Generalization of the La of Semantic Diversification, *Quantitative Linguistics*, Vol. 32, pp. 130-139 (In German).

Andrukovich, P. F., and Korolev, E. I., 1977, The Statistical and Lexicogrammatical Properties of Words, *Autom. Doc. Math. Linguist.*, Vol. 11, No. 2, pp. 1-11.

Baker, S. J., 1950, The Pattern of Language, *Journal of General Psychology*, Vol. 42, No. 1, pp. 25-66.

Becker, C. A., and Killion, T. H., 1977, Interaction of Visual and Cognitive Effects in Word Recognition, *J. Exp. Psychol., Human Perceptions and Performance*, Vol. 3, No. 3, pp. 389-401.

Edmundson, H. P., 1977, Statistical Inference in Mathematical and Computational Linguistics, *International Journal of Computer and Information Science*, Vol. 6, No. 2, pp. 95-129.

Fuller, W., 1968, *An Introduction to Probability Theory and Its Applications*, Vol. I, John Wiley & Sons, New York.

Guiraud, P., 1954, Language and Communication, Informational Substance of Semantization, *Bulletin de la Societe de Linguistique de Paris*, Vol. 49, pp. 119-133. (In French.)

Guiraud, P., 1965, Diacritical and Statistical Models for Languages in Relation to the Computer, *The Use of Computers in Anthropology*, Hymes, D., ed., Mouton and Co., London, pp. 235-254.

Guiraud, P., 1971, The Semic Matrices of Meaning, *Essays in Semiotics*, Kristeva, J., Rey-Debove, J., and Umiker, D. J., eds., Mouton, Paris, pp.150-159.

Harris, Z., 1954, Distributional Structure, *Word*, No. 10, pp. 146-162.

Johnson, P. E., 1969, On the Communication of Concepts in Science, *Journal of Educational Psychology*, Vol. 60, No. 1, pp. 32-40.

Korolev, E. I., 1977, The Use of the Distributive Statistical Method in the Language Apparatus of Automated Information Systems, *Autom. Doc. Math. Linguist*, Vol. 11, No. 1, pp. 31-37.

Krylov, Yu. K., and Yakubovskaya, M. D., 1977, Statistical Analysis of Polysemy as a Language Universal and the Problem of the Semantic Identity of the Word, *Nauchno-Tekhnicheskaya Informatsiya*, Series 2, Vol. 11, No. 3, pp. 1-6.

Lewis, P. A., Baxendale, P. B., and Bennet, J. L., 1967, Statistical Discrimination of the Synonymy/ Antonymy Relationship Between Words, *Journal of the ACM*, Vol. 14, No. 1, pp. 20-44.

Ljung, M., 1974, *A Frequency Dictionary of English Morphemes*, AWE/Gebers, Stockholm, Sweden.

Meyer, D. E., and Schvaneveldt, R. W., 1976, Meaning, Memory Structure, and Mental Processes, *Science*, 192, (4234), pp. 27-33.

Orszag, L., 1962, *A magyar nyelv ertelmezo szotara*, Vol. 1-7, Budapest, Hungary (In Hungarian).

Ozhegov, S.I., 1960, *Lexicographic Collection*, Moscow (In Russian).

Pap, F., 1967, On Some Quantitative Characteristics of a Language Vocabulary, *Annales Institutti Philologiae Slavicae Universitatis Debreceniensis*, Vol 7, pp. 51-58 (In Russian).

Rubenstein, H., and Goodenough, J. B., 1965, Contextual Correlates of Synonymy, *Communications of the ACM*, Vol. 8, No. 10, pp. 627-633.

Simon, H. A., 1955, On a Class of Skew Distribution Functions, *Biometrika*, 42, pp. 425-440.

Terwilliger, R. F., 1968, *Meaning and Mind*, Oxford Univ. Press, New York.

Thoren, B., 1959, *8000 ord for 8 ars angelska*, Malmo, Gleerups

Thorndike, E. L., and Lorge, I., 1959, *The Teacher's Workbook of 30,000 Words*, 3rd ed. New York, Columbia University Press.

Zipf, G. K., 1949, *Human Behavior and the Principle of Least Effort*, Addison-Wesley Press, Cambridge, Mass.

Zunde, P., 1981, *On Empirical Laws and Theories of Information Science*, Research Report, Georgia Institute of Technology, Atlanta, GA, NTIS Access No. PB82-125998.

Zunde, P., 1987, Information Science Laws and Regularities: A Survey, Rasmussen, J., and Zunde, P., eds., *Empirical Foundations of Information and Software Sciences III*, Plenum Press, New York, NY, p. 243-270.

Zunde, P., and Zhou, H., 1988, *On Semantic Regularities of Language Use*, Research Report GIT-ICS-89/03, Georgia Institute of Technology, Atlanta, Georgia.

VII. DATABASE MODELS

DATABASE MANAGEMENT MODELS FOR REUSABILITY IN INTEGRATED

SOFTWARE ENGINEERING ENVIRONMENTS

Arthur M. Jones, Robert E. Bozeman,
and William J. McIver, Jr.

Morehouse College
Atlanta, Georgia

Abstract: One of the central problems in the area of reusability concerns the classification, evaluation, and retrieval of software components. This problem has grown in magnitude because of the growing interest in life cycle reuse. Previously, much of the interest in reuse had been confined primarily to the reuse of code. Currently, however, there is a great deal of interest in reuse of software at any point in the life cycle. This includes the requirements and design phases as well as having the capability of tracing the origin and revision histories of software components. In order to effectively manage such a large amount of information on reusable components, efficient database management systems must be employed.

In this paper, we evaluate the relational, object-oriented, and the non-first-normal-form data models for effectiveness, practicality, and serviceability when used in a reusable library. We also examine the appropriateness of these models for use with reusability tools in an integrated software engineering environment.

INTRODUCTION

The relational database model has become the most widely accepted approach to the management of data. However, the relational model is believed to be inadequate for modelling certain types of data structures such as hierarchical or lattice structures, and data with repeating values - characteristics which are present in Ada software components. The non-first-normal form relation model and the object-oriented data model have been developed for applications which are not well suited to the relational model.

Because of the life cycle approach to reusability, some attention must be given to integrated software engineering environments. Integrated environments should evolve to the point of being viewed as unified tools. Thus, models for reusability tools must also address the problems involved in interfacing with other components of such an environment. Some components which are likely to be integral parts of future software engineering environments are: formal software specification tools, CASE tools, debuggers, and syntax-directed editors.

In this paper we evaluate the appropriateness of the relational, non-first-normal form, and object oriented data models for use with reusability tools in an integrated software engineering environment.

REUSABILITY

The idea of building software systems from existing components is very old, perhaps old enough to have been recognized by Babbage. As a result of recent research, however, the concept of reusability has evolved in scope to include the knowledge gained during a software development life cycle as well as the software components themselves. That is, current opinion emphasizes that reuse archives should capture "process" along with "product".

Empirical Foundations of Information and Software Science V
Edited by P. Zunde and D. Hocking, Plenum Press, New York, 1990

Some researchers have predicted that the potential dividends from the investment in development and know-how is much greater than that from the software components. This, in spite of enormous technical barriers to the implementation of a practical reuse repository, was the compelling motivation for this research.

This study of data models, library strategies, and engineering environments was principally influenced by the desire to accommodate information pertinent to software parts and the process by which they were developed.

INTEGRATED SOFTWARE ENGINEERING ENVIRONMENTS

The motivations behind the use of integrated software engineering environments are well known. An environment consisting of a set of tightly coupled tools which presents a consistent user interface can stimulate system conception at a high-level of abstraction and can be configured to support a particular design methodology (e.g., object-oriented, top-down, etc.) (O'Brien, Halbert, and Kilian, 1987; Teitelbaum and Reps, 1981). The tools cooperate to support the development effort. A consistent user interface eliminates the need for the developer to perform mental context switches, which can reduce productivity (Delisle, Menicosy, and Schwartz, 1984).

In addition to having a common user interface among tools, a tightly coupled environment is one in which the tools share intermediate representations of software being developed in the environment (Delisle, Menicosy, and Schwartz, 1984). One approach that has been taken is to have the tools share a common database which manages all the forms and versions a software system may have during its life cycle (Hudson and King, 1987; Hudson and King, 1988; O'Brien, Halbert, and Kilian, 1987). The desirable characteristics of an integrated software engineering environment are:

1.   That it be extensible, that is, it supports the easy addition of tools to the environment; and

2.   That it supports interoperability, that is, all tools share the underlying database representations, and they properly interpret the representations.

Extensibility can be achieved in a large part through the use of a common database (O'Brien, Halbert, and Kilian, 1987). Interoperability can be achieved through the selection of an underlying database model which has flexible and robust modelling capabilities (Hudson and King, 1987; Hudson and King, 1988; O'Brien, Halbert, and Kilian, 1987). In this paper the relational, non-first-normal form, and the object oriented database models are examined for their ability to support these two characteristics.

THE PART SCHEMA

We define a part to be the fundamental, catalogued unit of a library. A part contains some or all of the products created during the software development life cycle phases of a software component. In addition, a part may have attributes stored with it along with its relationships to other parts. (section 7.3 Reusability Guidebook). Burton and Broida (1986) suggested that in a conservative count, there were in excess of sixty items in seven categories for which one may want information on a library entry. The broad categories were: Identification - 3 items; Description - 16 items; Component parts - 20 items; Environment/usage - 9 items; Ordering Information - 7 items; and Revision history - 11 items. In developing a prototype Ada Package Library, Burton and Broida narrowed the above list down to the following items:

1. Unit name
2. Author
3. Unit size
4. Source language
5. Date created
6. Date last updated
7. Category code
8. Overview
9. Algorithm description
10. Error/Exceptions generated
11. Up to 5 keywords (for retrieval)

12. Machine dependencies, if any
13. Program dependencies, if any
14. Notes

Part Extensibility

Initially, it is likely that only a minimum set of information categories can be agreed upon. However, a part is a "snapshot" of a continuing software development process as well as its products at different phases in the life cycle of a software component. The data items within a part will have to be updated when modifications to a software component, such as bug fixes, are made. Future software development tools and processes may necessitate the addition of new information categories to the library schema, as well as modifications to the existing schema. The library architecture therefore, provides for the addition and modification of information categories and their associated data elements.

Bulk Information

Bulk information such as source code and documentation maybe referenced by pointers; or if storage permits, bulk information may be stored in a library along with the other information contained on a part.

It has been recognized that higher degrees of reuse of information contained in monolithic items, such as specification documentation, could be promoted by expressing the information in small, reusable groups. For instance, specification documents could be manipulated as sets of smaller specifications (Burton and Broida, 1986).

It is highly desirable, therefore, for the library management system to provide services for manipulating bulk information items in the appropriate logical parts. This could be accomplished by storing logical and behavioral qualities, such as a parsing mechanism and the appropriate syntax, of a bulk information item in the library.

THE RELATIONAL MODEL

The relational model is the most studied and best understood of all the database models. Commercially, Relational Databases are the most widely available of all the database models. The relational model consists of three components:

1. relations
2. relational integrity rules
3. manipulative features

Relations

A relational database is a collection of data that is viewed by the user as a set of normalized relations whose contents may vary over time. In the relational model, all relations adhere to Codd's first normal form assumption - all attribute values are atomic. Thus, an attribute value may not be hierarchical or repeating structures. The key properties of relations are:

1. There are no duplicate tuples
2. Tuples are unordered (Top to Bottom)
3. Attributes are unordered (left to Right)
4. All attribute values are atomic.

Relational Integrity Rules. In order to maintain the integrity of a relational database, Codd imposed two constraints on the relations contained in the database. They are:

1. Entity Integrity: No attribute in the primary key of a relation is allowed to have a null value.
2. Referential Integrity: If some tuple t2 determines sometuple t1, then t1 MUST exist.

Manipulative Features. The relational model provides a set of operators and an assignment statement to allow the user to manipulate and extract information from a database. The operators are those from the Relational Algebra (i.e., select, project, cartesian product, join, union, intersection, set difference, and divide).

MODELLING WITH THE RELATIONAL MODEL

Schema Modification

The database design process for the relational model is well known. In designing a database of reusable parts, a part schema must ultimately be agreed upon along with the functional dependencies (FD's) which are desired to hold on them. This initial part schema will be in the form of a first-normal-form relation (i.e., one relation containing all of the part attributes). This relation must be then decomposed into smaller relations such that the FD's still hold. Decomposition is performed to eliminate the undesirable update properties of normalized (i.e., redundancy and update, insert, and deletion anomalies). This decomposition process must be repeated for any modification to the part schema. This aspect of the relational does not allow practical part extensibility - a database feature desired to support extensible integrated software engineering environments.

Integrity

No relational database product to date is fully relational. They lack support for primary or foreign keys and, therefore, do not support the two integrity rules (Date, 1986). Assuming a standard part schema were employed across a number of reuse libraries, the relational model can not be readily used to represent parts in a library that are missing values for one or more of their attributes. For example, a number of libraries may only contain primary search information - not source code. While other libraries may have parts of varying completeness.

Manipulative Features

One of Codd's motivations for developing the relational model, was to provide physical data independence, that is, the order of the tuples or attributes in a relation database is unimportant in using a database. However, it is Codd's first-normal-form assumption of relational databases and the unordered of relations that imposes a major limitation on the relational model. That is, tuples are accessed by atomic key values, only, and not by other relationships such as the order of the tuple or some other complex structures (Date, 1986).

There are several other major disadvantages of the manipulative component of the relational model. First, there is no ability to define abstract data types and the operations permitted them (only the relational operators are permitted). Therefore, there is no way to encapsulate and hide information from the user and behavioral semantics cannot be supported.

Secondly, certain domain and rage concepts are not supported, such as the prevention of inter-domain comparison or the ability to combine two values from different domains (e.g., velocity x time = distance). Also, the ability to make range specifications is not supported.

Finally, all relational database products to date lack fine-precision update and delete operations. Union and set difference could theoretically serve as fine-precision INSERT and DELETE functions, however, they do not handle error conditions (Date, 1986).

Hierarchies and Sets

As a result of the first-normal-form assumption of Codd's model, we are not able to easily represent hierarchies and sets (i.e., an attribute may not have a hierarchy or a set as a value). In general, unique identifiers must be used to associate parent attribute in one relation with the set values of its children in another relation. An attribute associated with a variable length list must also be represented this way (Smith and Zdonik, 1987).

Furthermore, most relational database systems do not have the capability of generating unique identifiers, provisions must be made for storing lists of identifiers and maintaining unassigned ones (Smith and Zdonik, 1987).

Distributed Relational Databases

In general, libraries must offer shared access to part sin an environment of networked, multi-user computer systems. However, are only a limited number of distributed relational database systems available.

NON-FIRST-NORMAL FORM RELATIONS

The Relational database model is based on Codd's first normal form assumption which states, in essence, that attribute values of all relations must be "atomic"; equivalently, at every row-and-column position within a relation table, there always exists exactly one value - never a set of values. The Non-First-Normal Form model, often referred to as the Unnormalized Model, is a variation of the Relational database where the first normal form assumption has been dropped. In these models, column entries are not restricted to atomic values, but are allowed to be sets or even other tables. An Unnormalized Relational model allows one to deal with structures as hierarchies and repeating values within the context of the relational model.

A number of authors have proposed ways of extending the relational database management systems to support hierarchical structures and complex objects (Haskin and Lorie, 1982; Jaeschke and Schek, 1982; Fischer and Thomas, 1983). In an effort to determine the feasibility of using an Extended Relational Database in an Ada reuse library, the features the model of Fischer and Thomas were investigated. A brief description of this model taken from the work of D. Gucht (1985) is given below.

The Unnormalized Relational Data Base model of Fischer and Thomas essentially consists of three components (see Gucht (1985)):

1. The set of data objects
2. The extended relational algebra
3. The extended data dependencies

The data objects consist of unnormalized relational structures. These are replacements for the flat relations used in the classical model. The extended relational algebra consists of (Gucht, 1985):

A.   The classical relational operators (union, difference, selection, projection and cartesian product) extended to unnormalized structures.

B.   The restructuring operators "NEST" and "UNNEST".

The two restructuring operators "NEST" and "UNNEST" appear to be the features that enable the model to handle more complex structures. The NEST operator takes a structure and groups over equal data values on some subset of the scheme of the structure. The UNNEST operator is the inverse of the NEST operator that it takes a structure that has been nested on some set of attributes and disaggregates the structure to make it into a flat relation. Using the NEST operator, complex structures be composed from flat or first normal form tables. Conversely, if one starts with a complex structure, it is possible create equivalent flat tables by employing the UNNEST operator. These features seem to be extremely useful in presenting the user with more realistic views of the database.

MODELLING WITH NON-FIRST-NORMAL FORM MODELS

In order to use Unnormalized structures an appropriate query language has to be designed. A possible candidate has been proposed by P. Dadam (Dadam, et al., 1986) in the prototype they developed. Consider the following example of portions of Reusable Software Components that must be managed in a library:

Schema	Attributes		
part	identification	classification	source_code
source_code	procedures	functions	
procedures	procedure_name	formal_part	
functions	function_name	formal_part	

If one wanted to store information of the type listed above using the procedures and techniques developed by P. Dadam et al, all of the complex objects would have a separate "Mini Directory" (for a detailed discussion of the Mini directories as well as the storage process, see P. Dadam et al (1986). In the Dadam prototype the Mini directory layout corresponds to the hierarchical structure of the complex object and is composed of subtuples which are linked by pointers. Each complex object gets its own local address space. This address space is represented by a page list that is stored in some appropriate Mini directory. Now using a generalized query language and the NEST and UNNEST operators it is possible to retrieve, delete, display, add new information to the above schema. Using the UNNEST operator, it is also possible to decompose the information above into a number of flat tables.

An Unnormalized model with a structure similar to the one described above seems to have some features that are appropriate for our library management model. However, because a large number of mini directories would have to be maintained, it appears that there might arise problems with access paths in retrieval operations. It is not clear whether the addressing systems proposed would be adequate especially for large complex objects.

OBJECT ORIENTED DATABASE MODELS

Objects

An object is an instance of a class. A class is a "template" defining the behavior of its instances (i.e., objects of the class). All conceptual entities in an object-oriented system (O-O system) are modelled as objects. These entities may be primitive types or complex part assemblies composed of other objects.

An object has private memory that is used for maintaining its state. The private memory consists of memory locations for *instance variables*. *Instance variables* are private memory locations in which an object maintains its individual state. The value of an *instance variable* is itself an object with no instance variables. Each object usually has a unique identifier that the system can keep track of.

Methods and Messages

Objects communicate with each other using messages. Each legal message that may be sent to an object is associated with a method. An object reacts to a message by executing a method. A method is a procedure contained in an object that is invoked when a certain message is sent to the object (methods actually reside in the objects class in order to save space). A message selector is an operator which invokes a method in an object. Each message is associated with a particular method and may have arguments. Methods describe the behavior of an object. They manipulate or return the state of an object.

Classes

Classes are used to group similar objects in order to conserve space used for storing methods and other shared memory. All objects in the same class contain the same instance variables and methods. However, the objects differ in their individual states (the values of their instance variables). In most object-systems, classes are objects themselves. With the class being treated as an object, one is able to create objects of a class by sending the appropriate "create" message to the class. Otherwise, an object that doesn't exist cannot send a message to itself.

Inheritance

In modelling, sometimes it may be found that a class or several different classes are specializations of one general class. While each of these classes contain unique features (methods instance variables) which make them special, they may share significant features with a more general class. It would be redundant to define the shared methods and instance variables each of these specialized classes. To solve this problem, object-oriented systems provide a feature called inheritance. With inheritance, class hierarchies may be built. A general class may have specialized classes of itself. All the instance variables and methods of a superclass are inherited its subclasses. Additional properties may then be added to the subclass to make it special.

Example: A Class Lattice

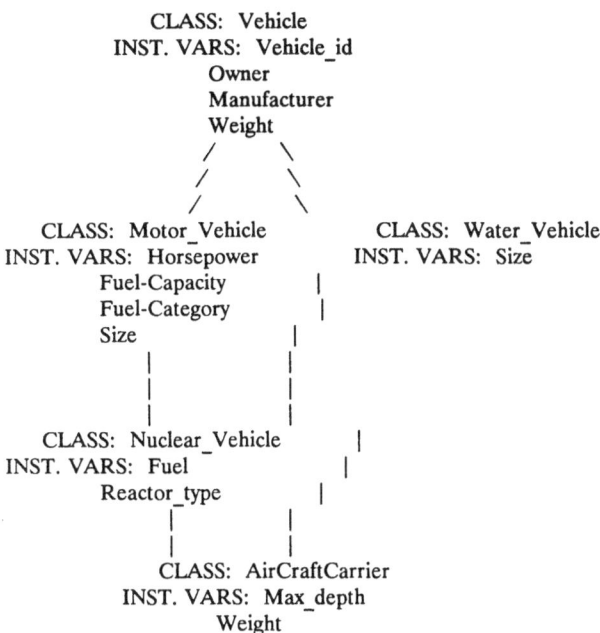

```
                CLASS:  Vehicle
            INST. VARS:  Vehicle_id
                  Owner
                  Manufacturer
                  Weight
                /      \
               /        \
              /          \
   CLASS:  Motor_Vehicle        CLASS:  Water_Vehicle
 INST. VARS:  Horsepower       INST. VARS:  Size
       Fuel-Capacity      |
       Fuel-Category      |
       Size               |
         |                |
         |                |
         |                |
   CLASS:  Nuclear_Vehicle     |
 INST. VARS:  Fuel             |
       Reactor_type            |
         |           |
         |           |
            CLASS:  AirCraftCarrier
        INST. VARS:  Max_depth
                  Weight
```

Multiple Inheritance and Conflict Resolution

In many object-oriented systems it is possible for a class to have several superclasses. From the example above, we can see that there is a potential conflict in the inheritance of the instance variable Size by the class Submarine. Does it inherit Size from the class Motor_Vehicles or from the class Water_Vehicle?

Conflict resolution among superclasses is usually handled by giving precedence to the closest superclass or by the ordering of the superclasses declared in the class. If the conflict is between a class and its superclass(s), precedence is given to the class. For example, if methods with the same name are declared in both a class, C, and its superclass, SC, the definition the method in the class, C, is selected in resolving the conflict.

MODELLING WITH THE OBJECT-ORIENTED DATABASE MODEL

Object-oriented database models provided several key advantages in modelling. All Modeling is performed with one concept, the object. The class hierarchy and inheritance facilitates design of databases. Objects are autonomous entities allows for flexible, robust designs.

Extensibility and interoperability are greatly supported by the encapsulation of structure and behavior within objects. An underlying database schema can be modified with no effect on applications which use it, if the interface specifications to the objects remain the same. Behavior can be defined for objects, on the context with which they interact with the outside world. This allows for interoperability. For example, an editor and a compiler would interact with a source code object much different ways.

Hierarchies and Sets

The predefined class lattice of a typical object-oriented programming system (SmallTalk, Loops, etc.) is as follows:

325

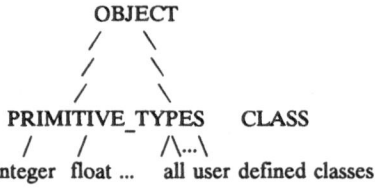

```
                    OBJECT
                    /    \
                   /      \
                  /        \
          PRIMITIVE_TYPES    CLASS
          /  /      /\...\
      integer float ...  all user defined classes
```

An extension to the class hierarchy was made in order to facilitate associative queries. The extended lattice is as follows.

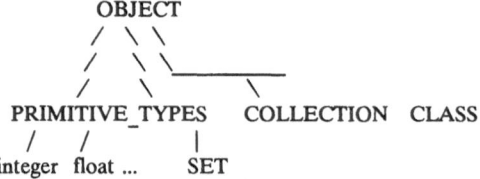

```
                    OBJECT
                    / \ \
                   /   \ _____
                  /     \       \
          PRIMITIVE_TYPES   COLLECTION  CLASS
          /  /              |
      integer float ...     SET
```

The class COLLECTION contains objects that are collections of other objects. This class provides methods for iterating over elements in a collection object. Instances of class SET are collections of objects with no duplicates (sets). The class SET provides methods for searching elements of a set, adding and deleting, etc.

Associative query capability is provided by implicitly creating instances of the class SETOF whenever a user defined class is created (Banerjee et al, 1987). An instance of the SETOF class contains all the instances of a particular class.

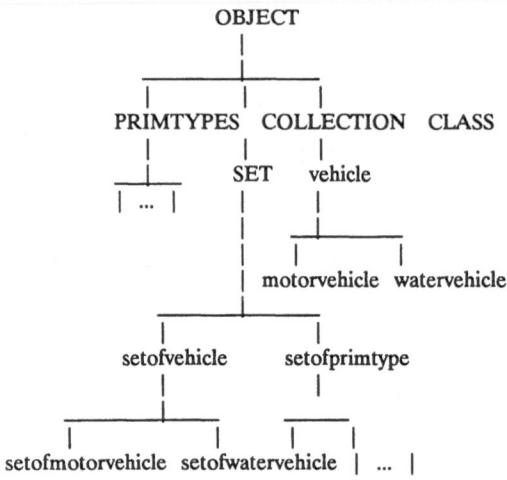

Semantics

Behavioral semantics are supported via methods and the message passing mechanism. The class hierarchy captures the structural semantic IS-A between classes and their superclasses. Several object-oriented databases implementations allow the IS-PART-OF relationship between objects, by allowing the definition of composite (or aggregate) objects. A composite is an object which contains other complex objects (i.e., objects which are not atomic such as instance variables) whose existences are dependent on the composite object. Such a composite object is known as a parent object, while the objects it contains are known as child objects. Additionally, some systems allow the establishment of other special relationships between children of different parent objects (Kim et al, 1987) and relationships with attributes and type constraints associated those relationships (Hudson and King, 1987; Hudson and King, 1988).

326

Performance

Most object-oriented systems to date are programming language - not database systems. Thus, query capabilities are not readily available through their use. Also, schema evolution update problems are not considered in these programming systems. There are, however, a number of experimental commercial object-oriented database systems which have been developed to address the problems of managing persistent objects and providing query capabilities for objects (Banerjee et al, 1987; Fishman et al, 1987; Hudson and King, 1987; Hudson and King, 1988; Purdy, Schuchardt, and Maier, 1987).

Object-oriented systems require a great amount of run-time support for the dynamic creation of objects. In addition, message in object-oriented programming language systems take more time than normal procedure calls.

CONCLUSION

The Object-oriented model offers far greater modelling capability of complex structures than the relational and the non-first-normal form models. Extensibility and interoperability are greatly supported by the encapsulation of structure behavior within objects. However, greater flexibility over the traditional object-oriented programming language models is necessary to provide greater semantic modelling capabilities and to support associative queries of objects.

REFERENCES

Banerjee, J., Chou, Hong-Tai, Garza, J. F., Kim, W., Woelk, D,. Ballou, N., and Kim, Hyoung-Joo, 1987, Data Model Issues for Object-Oriented Applications, *ACM Transactions on Office Information Systems*, No. 5, January 1987, pp. 3-26.

Burton, B., and Broida, M., 1986, Development of an Ada Package Library, *Proceedings of the Fourth Annual Conference on Ada Technology*, March 1986, pp. 42-50

Dadam, P., Kuespert, K., Andersen, F., Blanken, H., Erbe, R., Guenauer, J., Lum, V., Pistor, P., and Walch, G., 1986, A DBMS Prototype Support Extended NF2 Relations: An Integrated View on Flat Tables and Hierarchies, *ACM*, pp. 356-366.

Date, C. J., 1986, *An Introduction to Database Systems*, Volume 1, Addison-Wesley Publishing Co.

Delisle, N., Menicosy, D. Schwartz, M., 1984, Viewing a Programming as a Single Tool, *ACM*, August 1984, pp. 49-45.

Fischer, P. C., and Thomas, S. J., 1983, Operators for Non-First-Normal Form Relations, *Proceedings of IEEE Computer Software and Applications Conference*, pp. 464-475.

Fishman, D. H., Beech, D., Cate, H. P., Chow, E. C., Connors, T., Davis, J. W., Derrett, N., Hoch, C. G., Kent, W., Lyngbaek, P., Mahbod, B., Neimat, M. A., Ryan, T. A., and Shan, M. C., 1987, Iris: An Object Oriented Database Management System, *ACM Trans. on Office Information System*, Vol. 5, January 1987, pp. 48-69.

Gucht, Dirk Van, 1985, *Theory of Unnormalized Relational Structures*, Ph.D. Dissertation, Vanderbilt University, December 1985.

Haskin, R. L., and Lorie, R. A., 1982, On Extending the Functions a Relational Database System, *Proc. SIGMOD 82*, June 1982, pp. 207-212.

Hudson, S. E., and King, R., 1987, Object-oriented Database Support for Software Environments, *Proc. of ACM SIGMOD Intl. Conference of Management of Data*, May 1987.

Hudson, S. E., and King, R., 1988, The Cactis Project: Database for Software Engineering, *IEEE Trans. on Software Engineering*, June 1988.

Jaeschke, G., and Schek, H. J., 1982, Remarks on the Algebra of Non First Normal Form Relationships, *Proceedings of the SIGACT-SIGMOD on Principles of Database Systems*, March 1982, pp. 124-138.

Kim, W., Banerjee, J., Chou, Jong-Tai, Garza, J. F., and Woelk, D., 1987, Composite Object Support in an Object-Oriented Database System, *OOPSLA 1987 Proceedings*, October 1987, pp. 118-125.

O'Brien, Patrick, Halbert, D. C., and Kilian, M. F., 1987, The Trellis Programming Environment, *OOPSLA 1987 Proceedings October 1987*, pp. 91-102.

Purdy, Alan, Schuchardt, B., and Maier, D., 1987, Integrating an Object Server with Other Worlds, *ACM Trans. on Office Info. Systems*, January 1987, pp. 27-47.

Smith, Karen, and Zdonik, Stanley B., 1987, Intermedia: A Case Study of the Differences Between Relational and Object-Oriented Database Systems, *OOPSLA 1987 Proceedings*, October 1987, pp. 452-465.

Teitelbaum, Tim, and Reps, Thomas, 1981, The Cornell Program Synthesizer: A Syntax-Directed Programming Environment, *ACM*, September 1981, pp. 563-573.

AN ADAPTIVE DATA DISTRIBUTION MODEL FOR DISTRIBUTED DATABASES BASED ON

EMPIRICAL MEASUREMENT OF LOCAL AND GLOBAL DATABASE TRANSACTIONS

D. Motzkin

Computer Science Department
Western Michigan University
Kalamazoo, Michigan 49008

Abstract: This paper presents an adaptive distribution model which is used to periodically revise data distribution to ensure efficient transaction processing. The model is based on database statistics of transaction workload and network through-put which are obtained by empirical means.

The objective of the model is to produce a data distribution scheme for distributed databases which achieves minimum costs while maintaining a desired level of performance. A second objective of this model is to produce modifications to the data allocation that meet the changing needs, as transaction patterns vary over time.

It is shown that the adaptive model is easy to implement, efficient, provides reasonably accurate results and near optimal data distribution, which is responsive to changing user needs. The advantage of this model over previous work is discussed.

INTRODUCTION

The problem of data distribution of a relational database over a network has been studied extensively. However, some shortcomings of earlier work were addressed by Motzkin and Ivey (1987(a), 1987(b)). They have pointed out that some of the leading earlier methods such as the ones developed by Ceri et al. (1980), Ceri Martella, and Pellagatti (1982(a)), Ceri, Negri, and Pellagatti (1982(b)), Ceri and Navathe (1983(a)), Ceri, Navathe, and Wiederhold (1983(b)), Ceri and Pellagatti (1984); Chang and Cheng (1980), Change and Liu (1981, 1982); Dutta (1985); Irani and Khabbaz (1979, 1981); Jain (1987); Lin and Liu (1981); Kim and Moon (1987); Mazzarol, Tomasin, and Stoer (1977); Rakes, Franz and Se (1984); Ram (1987); Reddy (1981); Yu et al. (1981); and others were either too complex or required too many input parameters, or concentrated only on some subset of the data allocation problem.

Motzkin and Ivey (1987(a), 1987(b)) developed a new method for the computation of cost/benefit which, while practical in terms of computational complexity and amount of required input parameters, achieved optimal or near optimal data allocation schemes. The schemes achieved using this method integrated a variety of design aspects that were previously treated individually.

This paper is an extension of the work by Motzkin and Ivey (1987(a), 1987(b)). An adaptive design module is incorporated into the previous model. It provides continuous improvement of the data distribution based on empirical measurement of changing parameters and performance of the DDBMS (Distributed Database Management System) over time.

AN OVERVIEW OF THE MODEL

The design model is composed of two major components. The first component is a one time operation of creating an initial distribution. During this phase the system produces a near optimal data distribution scheme for a given network, global database, workload, and costs. The second component consists of an on-going reorganization process based on empirical measurement of changing DDBMS

Empirical Foundations of Information and Software Science V
Edited by P. Zunde and D. Hocking, Plenum Press, New York, 1990

329

parameters and performance. During this phase the system adapts itself to the changed environment and user needs.

The Initial Design

The initial design is the same as in Motzkin and Ivey (1987(b)), and is briefly summarized below.

The input for the initial design includes site and network parameters (cost, space availability, system reliability); database parameters (relations, tuples, attributes, etc.), transaction requirements (required data, reliability, etc.), and workload parameters (frequency of retrievals, updates, etc.).

The system first partitions the global relational database into disjoint horizontal fragments. These fragments are determined by transaction requirements and have the property that for each (transaction, fragment) pair the fragment is either completely required by the transaction or not at all. Next the fragments are to be assigned to sites. The objective of the design model is to achieve optimal design (least local and global cost). At this time the values $B(Fm,Si)$ are computed where $B(Fm,Si)$ denotes the benefit of fragment Fm to site Si.

$B(Fm,Si) = CN(Fm,Si)-CA(Fm,Si)$. In other words the benefit of allocating a fragment to a site is equal to differences between the cost, CN, of not allocating a fragment to a site, and the cost, CA, of allocating a fragment to a site. It was shown in Motzkin and Ivey (1987(a)) that when each fragment is allocated to all sites with positive benefit values, i.e. $B(Fm,Si)>0$, then optimal allocation is achieved. But, as was shown this optimal allocation cannot always be achieved. For example, a site may not have enough space for all fragments with positive benefit value. Near optimal allocation algorithms which efficiently handle such situations were described in Motzkin and Ivey (1987(a)). Improvements and refinements are described in Motzkin and Ivey (1987(b)).

Adaptation and Restructuring

In the course of time, the values of the parameters that affected the initial design of the DDBMS may change. Thus the costs of processing, storage, or communication may change; the transactions workload and requirements may change; and, even the size of the fragments may change (due to insertions and deletions). These changes may affect the magnitude and sign of some of the benefit values. Thus an allocation scheme that was initially optimal or near optimal may become average or even poor.

Numerous methods of update have been described. Some recent results include: Bassioni and Khave (1987); Bhargava (1987); Biswas and Brown (1987); Demus et al. (1988); Elmagarmid et al. (1988); Kahler and Risnes (1987); Mohan, Lindsay, and Obermare, (1986); O'Neil (1986); Sarih and Lynch (1987); Singhal (1987); Weihl (1987) and others.

However, the major objective of these works was to achieve concurrent updates and retrievals which maintain the data integrity and consistency. We have not found algorithms which utilize the experience with the data distribution, and the changed parameter values to revise and improve the data distribution.

In this paper we describe an adaptive module which provides continuous adaptation of the DDBMS to changing parameter values and user needs as well as to new information about the performance of the DDBMS that is obtained through experience.

The adaptive module consists of an on-going reorganization that continues throughout the life of the DDBMS. Each database transaction is expected to collect statistics regarding its workload, while each site is expected to contain up-to-date data regarding site parameters. The collected data is used periodically to determine the operational cost at each site, and the global cost of the DDBMS. The operational cost is compared with an expected cost of the revised, more optimal assignment. The expected cost of reorganization is also computed. If revision to the data allocation appears to be cost effective, then a recommended revision to the current data distribution is output.

An outline of the adaptive algorithm is provided in the 'The Adaptive Algorithm' section.

Cost and Benefit Calculations

The cost and benefit calculations use the same equations during the initial and adaptive phases. Of course, different data is used at each stage. The methods of computation have been refined and are a modification of the equations in Motzkin and Ivey (1987(b)). The revised cost and benefit equations are listed below. Detailed explanations can be found in Motzkin (1988).
THE FOLLOWING PARAMETERS ARE USED IN THE MODEL:

$FREQR(T_j,F,Si)$ = frequency of retrieval issued by transaction T_j to fragment F at site S_i

$FREQU(T_j,F,S_i)$ = frequency of updates issued by transaction T_j to fragment F at site S_i

$SEG(T_j)$ = the segment associated with transaction T_j

$SIZE(SEG(T_j))$ = the size in bytes of the segment associated with transaction T_j

$FREQR(T_j)$ = the number of unit retrievals required by T_j during a unit of time

$FREQU(T_j)$ = the number of unit updates required by T_j during a unit of time

UC = unit communication in bytes

UR = unit retrieval

UU = unit update

$CSP(F)$ = cost of space of F

CR = average cost of unit retrieval

CU = average cost of unit update

CC = average cost of unit communication between pairs of sites

$SIZE(F)$ = size of fragment F in bytes

$SIZE(W)$ = size of segment W

$CA(F,S_i)$ = cost of allocating fragment F to site S_i

$CN(F,S_i)$ = cost of not allocating fragment F to site S_i

$B(F,S_i)$ = benefit of allocating fragment F to site S_i

$P(F)$ = probability of failure of F

$P(S_i)$ = probability of failure at site S_i

FORMULATION

$$CA(F,S_i) = \sum_{j,\ T_j\ at\ S_i} CR * FREQR(T_j,F,S_i) + \sum CU *$$

$$\underset{j,\ T_j\ at\ S_i}{FREQU(T_j,F,S_i)}$$

$$+ \sum_{k}\sum_{j,\ T_j\ at\ S_k\ k\ \neq\ i} CU * FREQU(T_j,F,S_k) + CSP(F)$$

$$+ \sum_{k}\sum_{j,\ T_j\ at\ S_k\ k\ \neq\ i} FREQU(T_j,F,S_k) * (UU\ /\ UC) * CC$$

$$CN(F,S_i) = \sum_{j,\ T_j\ at\ S_i} CR * FREQR(T_j,F,S_i) +$$

$$\sum_{j,\ T_j\ at\ S_i} FREQR(T_j,F,S_i) * (UR\ /\ UC) * CC$$

$$B(F,S_i) = CN(F,S_i) - CA(F,S_i)$$

$$SIZE(F) \quad = \quad \sum_{i=i}^{n} REC\ SIZE(REL(F))$$

$$FREQR(T_j, F, S_i) = SIZE(F) * FREQR(T_j) / SIZE(SEG(T_j))$$

$$FREQU(T_j, F, S_i) = SIZE(F) * FREQU(T_j) / SIZE(SEG(T_j))$$

THE ADAPTIVE ALGORITHM

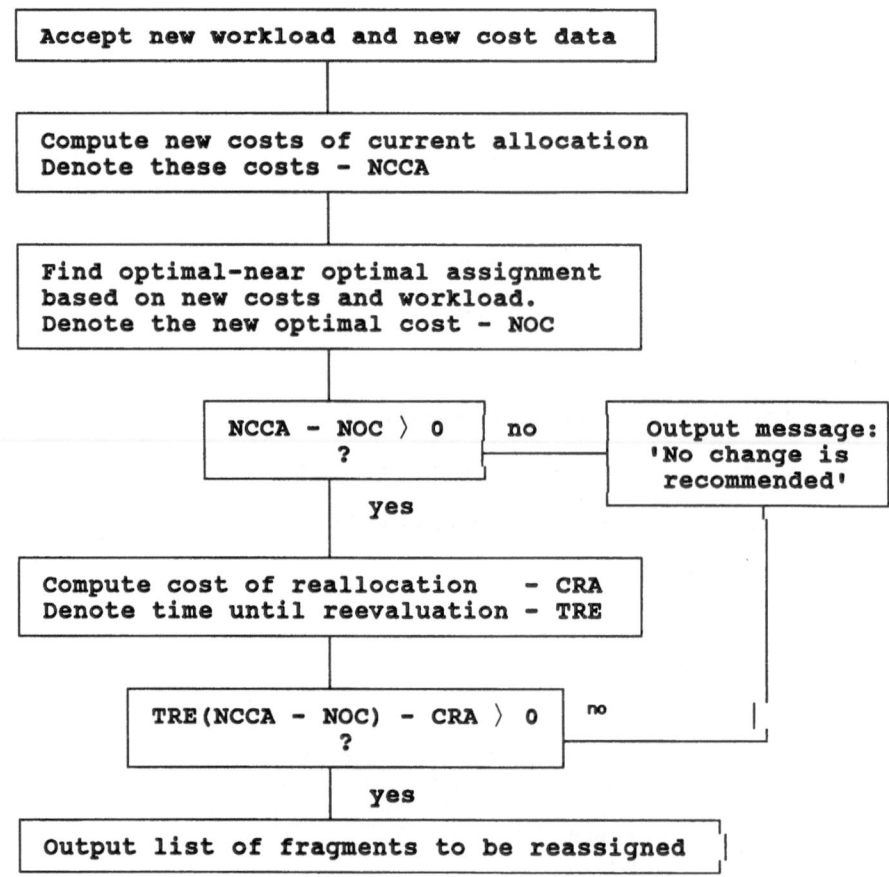

SAMPLE DATA AND EMPIRICAL RESULTS

In this section we demonstrate two of the experiments with the system on a small database and a network of three sites. The first example is detailed, and the second example consists of a summary of the system's work in a different situation.

Example 1: Reallocation of some fragments is beneficial during the adaptation phase.

The original database is composed of three global relations (See Table 1, Table 2, and Table 3.)

Table 1

EMPLOYEE RELATION

E#	SKILL	SALARY	PR#
E1	SK1	18000	PR1
E2	SK2	20000	PR1
E3	SK3	20000	PR2
E4	SK1	19000	PR2
E5	SK1	25000	PR2
E6	SK2	22000	PR3
E7	SK2	22000	PR3
E8	SK3	25000	PR3
E9	SK3	21000	PR3
E10	SK1	20000	PR4

Table 2

PROJECT RELATION

PR#	SKIL
PR1	SK1
PR2	SK1
PR2	SK3
PR3	SK3
PR4	SK1

Table 3

PLANT RELATION

PL#	PR#
PL1	PR1
PL1	PR2
PL2	PR3
PL3	PR4

There are twelve transactions. The data requirements of some of the transactions are listed below:

Transaction	Site	Data Requirement
1	1	SELECT PLANT.DAT WHERE PL# = PL1 TO TEMP
		SEMIJOIN EMPLOYEE.DAT WITH TEMP WHERE PR# = PR#.
2	1	SEMIJOIN PROJECT.DAT WITH TEMP WHERE PR# = PR# TO TEMP1
		SEMIJOIN EMPLOYEE.DAT WITH TEMP1 WHERE SKILL = SKILL

The workload and site parameters that were known during the initial design were:

NUMBER OF SITES	COST OF SPACE UNIT	COST OF UNIT RETRIEVAL	COST OF UPDATE	COST OF COMMUNICATION
3	0.001	0.40	0.80	2.00

Site	Failure Rate	Available Space
1	.10	40
2	.20	80
3	.10	40

Transaction Number	Site	Number of Retrievals	Number of Updates	Allowed Failure Rate
1	1	30	3	0.10
2	1	20	2	0.05
3	1	30	3	0.10
4	1	30	4	0.10
5	2	60	2	0.05
6	2	60	1	0.10

Transaction Number	Site	Number of Retrievals	Number of Updates	Allowed Failure Rate
7	2	50	5	0.10
8	2	30	2	0.10
9	3	15	3	0.10
10	3	40	4	0.10
11	3	20	2	0.10
12	3	45	3	0.10

During the initial phase the fragments were defined:

THE FRAGMENTS

Relations			Records			Fragments
EMPLOYEE	E#	Skill	Salary	PR#		
	E6	SK2	22000	PR3		F1
	E7	SK2	22000	PR3		
	E3	SK3	20000	PR2		F2
	E8	SK3	25000	PR3		F3
	E9	SK3	21000	PR3		
	E1	SK1	18000	PR1		F4
	E2	SK1	20000	PR1		
	E4	SK1	19000	PR2		
	E5	SK1	25000	PR2		
	E10	SK1	20000	PR4		F5

PROJECT	PR#	Skill	
	PR1	SK1	F6
	PR2	SK1	
	PR2	SK3	
	PR3	SK2	F7
	PR3	SK3	
	PR4	SK1	F8

PLANT	PL#	PR#	
	PL1	PR1	F9
	PL1	PR2	
	PL2	PR3	
	PL3	PR4	

The benefits of assigning fragments to sites were:

BENEFITS

FRAGMENT	SITE 1	SITE 2	SITE 3
1	-2.53	34.87	-2.53
2	4.62	6.31	-1.89
3	0.41	33.97	-3.43
4	14.17	-11.89	12.64
5	5.38	-7.29	11.84
6	17.59	-5.41	-5.41
7	-9.00	29.33	-9.00
8	-3.60	-3.60	11.73
9	7.79	5.79	16.79

The initial assignment of fragments to sites was produced:

SITE	FRAGMENT	COST	BENEFIT
S1	2 3 4 6 9	72.74	44.59
S2	1 2 3 7 9	103.06	110.28
S3	4 5 8 9	74.99	53.01

TOTAL COST   250.79   TOTAL BENEFIT   207.88

During the adaptation a modified workload exists:

Transaction Number	Site	Number of Retrievals	Number of Updates	Allowed Failure Rate
1		30	3	0.10
2		20	2	0.05
3		30	3	0.10
4		30	4	0.10
5		60	2	0.05

Transaction Number	Site	Number of Retrievals	Number of Updates	Allowed Failure Rate
6		60	1	0.10
7		50	5	0.10
8		30	2	0.10
9		15	6	0.10
10		40	10	0.10
11		20	8	0.10
12		45	7	0.10

The benefits of assigning fragments to sites become:

	BENEFITS		
FRAGMENT	SITE 1	SITE 2	SITE 3
1	-1.97	20.47	-1.97
2	2.44	3.45	-1.47
3	-0.37	19.77	-2.67
4	-0.33	-15.97	1.63
5	-10.40	-11.55	2.45
6	9.59	-4.21	-4.21
7	-7.00	16.00	-7.00
8	-11.20	-11.20	1.60
9	-3.81	-5.01	3.99

The costs of the initial allocation with the new workload are:

SITE	FRAGMENT	COST	BENEFIT
S1	2 3 4 6 9	80.47	7.53
S2	1 2 3 7 9	105.32	54.68
S3	4 5 8 9	86.33	9.67
	TOTAL COST 272.12	TOTAL BENEFIT	71.88

The costs of new optimal/near optimal allocation are:

SITE	FRAGMENT	COST	BENEFIT
S1	2 6	75.97	12.03
S2	1 2 3 7	100.31	59.69
S3	4 5 3 7	86.33	9.67
TOTAL COST/TOTAL BENEFIT		262.61	81.39

The cost of reallocation is: 5.31

The system recommendation is:

Time (6) · (current cost (272.13) - new optimal cost (262.61)) - cost of reallocation (5.31) > 0

FRAGMENT	NEW ALLOCATION	OLD ALLOCATION	ADD TO	CANCEL FROM
3	2	1 2		1
4	3	1 3		1
9	3	1 2 3		1 2

Example 2: No reallocation is recommended.

The initial allocation was:

SITE	FRAGMENT	COST	BENEFIT
S1	2 3 4 6 7 9	81.75	35.59
S2	1	178.46	34.87
S3	4 5 8 9	74.99	53.01
TOTAL COST/TOTAL BENEFIT		335.20	123.47

The costs of original allocation with the new workload are:

SITE	FRAGMENT	COST	BENEFIT
S1	2 3 4 6 7 9	113.68	110.32
S2	1	227.13	52.87
S3	4 5 8 9	87.37	80.63
TOTAL COST/TOTAL BENEFIT		428.18	243.82

The costs of new optimal/near optimal allocation are:

SITE	FRAGMENT	COST	BENEFIT
S1	2 3 4 5 6 9	104.52	119.48
S2	1	227.13	52.87
S3	4 5 7 8 9	96.37	71.63
TOTAL COST/TOTAL BENEFIT		428.02	243.98

The cost of reallocation is: 4.17

The system recommendation is: No reallocation is recommended

PERFORMANCE EVALUATION

It has been shown (Motzkin et al. 1987(b)) that the time required for the allocation algorithm is

$$0(S{\cdot}F{\cdot}\log(F) + F{\cdot}S{\cdot}\log(S)),$$

where

F = the number of fragments in the DDBMS
S = the number of sites in the DDBMS

If M = MAX(F,S) then the time requirement is bounded by

$$0(M{\cdot}\log(m)).$$

It is obvious that the periodic evaluation of reallocation using the up-to-date data requires the same time as the initial one. The evaluation of the cost of the actual reallocation is 0(NR) where NR is the number of records that must be moved to different sites. Therefore, the overall time requirement of the adaptive algorithm is of the same polynomial complexity as the initial allocation algorithm.

CONCLUDING REMARKS

A model for initial design and continuous revision and adaptation of distributed relational databases has been described. It was shown that an optimal design cannot always be achieved in reasonable time. The model incorporates heuristic methods to achieve near optimal initial design, and empirical methods to achieve continued optimal/near optimal allocation.

The following performance factors are considered: systems throughput, transaction workloads, response time and reliability requirements, and space availability. The cost components include local processing costs, transmission costs, reallocation costs, and space costs.

It is shown that any algorithm that generates an optimal solution will run in exponential time, thus, this model uses empirical results to verify and modify heuristic procedures.

The algorithms that have been developed are efficient and have polynomial time complexity. The data distribution is nearly optimal and is responsive to changing user needs and the system environment.

ACKNOWLEDGEMENT

The author wishes to thank Dr. Fred Boals for very valuable comments and suggestions.

REFERENCES

Bassioni, M. A., aud Khave, U., 1987, Algorithms for Reducing Rollbacks in Concurrency Control by Certification, *BIT*, Vol. 27, No. 4, pp. 442-457.

Bhargava, B., 1987, Transaction Processing and Consistency Control of Replicated Copies During Failures in Distributed Databases, *J. Manage Inf. Syst.*, Vol. 4, No. 2, pp. 93-112.

Biswas, J., and Brown, J. C., 1987, Simultaneous Update of Priority Structures, *Proceedings of the 1987 International Conference on Parallel Processing*.

Ceri, S., Martella, G., Deen, S. M., and Hammersley, P., 1980, Optimal File Allocation for a Distributed Data Base on a Network of Microcomputers, *Proceedings of the International Conference on Data Bases*, Aberdeen, Scotland, pp. 216-237.

Ceri, S., Martella, G., and Pellagatti, G., 1982, Optimal File Allocation in a Computer Network: A Solution Method Based on Knapsack Problem, *Computer Networks*, Vol. 6, No. 5, pp. 345357.

Ceri, S., Negri, M., and Pellagatti, G., 1982, Horizontal Partitioning in Database Design, *ACM-SIGMOD*.

Ceri, S., and Navathe, S. B., 1983, A Methodology for the Distribution Design of Databases, *Proceedings of COMPCON 83*, San Francisco, California.

Ceri, S., Navathe, S. B., and Wiederhold, G., 1983, Distribution Design of Logical Database Schemes, *IEEE-TSE*.

Ceri, S., and Pellagatti, G., 1984, *Distributed Database Principles and Systems*, McGraw-Hill.

Chang, S. K., and Cheng, W. H., 1980, A Methodology for Structured Database Decomposition, *IEEE-TSE*.

Chang, S. K., and Liu, A. C., 1981, A Database File Allocation Problem, *Proceedings of COMPSAC 81*, IEEE Computer Society.

Chang, S. K., and Liu, A. C., 1982, File Allocation in a Distributed Database, *Intern. J of Computer and Info. Science*, Vol. 2, No. 5, pp. 325-340.

Demus, A., Green, D., Hauser, C., Irish, W., Larson, J., Sheker, S., Sturgis, H., Swinehart, D., and Terry, D., 1988, Epidemic Algorithms for Replicated Database Maintenance, *Oper. Syst. Rev.*, Vol. 22, No. 1, pp. 8-32.

Dutta, A., 1985, Modelling of Multiple Copy Updates for File Allocation in Distributed Database, *Intern. J of Computer and Info. Science*, Vol. 14, No. 1, pp. 29-34.

Irani, K. B., and Khabbaz, N. G., 1979, A Model for Combined Communication Network Design and File Allocation for Distributed Database, *Proceedings of the First International Conference on Distributed Computer Systems*, Huntsville, AL, pp. 15-21.

Irani, K. B., and Khabbaz, N. G., 1981, A Combined Communication Network Design and File Allocation for Distributed Databases, *Proceedings of the Second International Conference on Distributed Computing*, Paris, France, pp. 197-210.

Jain, H. K., 1987, A Comprehensive Model for the Design of Distributed Computer Systems, *IEEE Trans. Softw. Eng.*, Vol. 13, No. 10, pp. 1092-1104.

Lin, J., and Liu, M. T., 1981, A Distributed Double-Loop Data Network for Very Large On Line Distributed Databases, *Proceedings of a Symposium on Reliability in Distributed Software and Database Systems*, IEEE, pp. 83-88.

Kahler, B., and Risnes, 0., 1987, Extending Logging for Database Snapshot Refresh, *Proceedings of the Thirteenth International Conference on Very Large Databases*.

Kim, S., and Moon, S. C., 1987, Non Redundant Allocation of Files in Distributed Database Systems, *Proceedings of TENCON 87: 1987 IEEE Region 10 Conference on Computers and Communications Technology*.

Mazzarol, G., Tomasin, E., and Stoer, J., 1977, Optimal File Allocation Problem and Relational Distributed Databases, *Proceedings of the Eighth IFIP Conference on Optimization Techniques*, Wurzburg, Germany, pp. 484-494.

Mohan, C., Lindsay, B., and Obermare, L. R., 1986, Transaction Management in R* Distributed Database Management System, *ACM Trans. Database Syst.*, Vol. 11, No. 4, pp. 378-396.

Motzkin, D., and Ivey, E., 1987, The Design of Distributed Databases with Cost Optimization and Integration of Space Constraint, *Proceedings of NCC 87*, pp. 563-572.

Motzkin, D., and Ivey, E., 1987(b), An Automated Tool for the Logical Design of Distributed Relational Databases, *Proceedings of the Twelfth Structured Methods Conference*, pp. 274-289.

Motzkin, D., 1988, *A Methodology for an Adaptive Distributed Database Design*, Technical Report TR 88-01, Computer Science Department, Western Michigan University.

O'Neil, P. E., 1986, The Escrow Transaction Method, *ACM Trans. Database Syst.*, Vol. 11, No. 4, pp. 405-430.

Rakes, T. C., Franz, L. S., and Se, A., 1984, A Heuristic Approximation for Reducing Problem Size in Network File Allocation Models, *Computers and Operations Research*, Vol. 11, No. 4, 387-395.

Ram, S., 1987, The File Allocation Problem: An Expanded Perspective, *Proceedings of the Twentieth Hawaii International Conference on System Sciences*.

Reddy, C. N., 1981, Distributed Data Base Systems, *Electro-Technol*, Vol. 25, No. 1, pp. 15-22.

Sarih, S. X., and Lynch, N. A., 1987, Discarding Obsolete Information in a Replicated Database System, *IEEE Trans. Software Eng.*, Vol. 13, No. 1, pp. 39-47.

Singhal, M., 1987, An Optimistic Concurrency Control Algorithm With Conflict Resolution in Replicated Database Systems, *Proceedings of the Twentieth Hawaii International Conference on System Sciences*.

Weihl, W. E., 1987, Distributed Version Management for Read-Only Actions, *IEEE Trans. Software Eng.*, Vol. 13, No. 1, pp. 55-64.

Yu, C. T., Siu, M. K., and Tai, F., 1981, Adaptive Clustering Schemes: General Framework, *Proceedings of COMPSAC 81*, IEEE Computer Society, pp. 16-20.

IMPLEMENTING RECURSIVE DATA STRUCTURES IN ADA

Ryan Stansifer and Weimin Du

Department of Computer Sciences
Purdue University
West Lafayette, IN 47907

Abstract: As clearly evidenced by Grady Booch in his book *Software Components with Ada* (Booch, 1987), data structures are an important part of reusable software components. The need for some of these software components arises, because of limitations in programming language design. In particular, the lack of recursive data structures in many languages requires contortions on the part of programmers that hampers the creation, the reuse, the portability, and the reliability of software components. We describe a preprocessor that translates definitions of recursive data structures to Ada.

INTRODUCTION

Programming and maintaining reliable software is a difficult task. There are many ways to attack the problem. There are syntax-directed editors to avoid syntax errors, verifiers to increase confidence in the reliability of the program, environments for program development and reuse, and many more. Programming language design can have an impact as well. Programming language constructs that model the programmers ideas naturally make it easier to program, easier to maintain the program, and facilitate reuse.

Several researchers have proposed very high level languages to facilitate reuse, see Cheathan (1984) for example. We remain in the context of the ADA programming language, and focus on a single language feature, recursive data structures. These data structures provide a convenient way to dispense with a large number of software components that might otherwise clutter up a library of reusable components. In this paper we suggest an ADA-like syntax for recursive data types, and describe a preprocessor that converts these type definitions into Ada. Specifically, each recursive definition is translated into an Ada generic package that implements the type.

Recursive Types

There is a feature present in conventional programming languages which has often been compared to the goto statement because it, too, is low-level. This feature is the pointer. Even the recently designed programming language Ada includes the pointer, despite the evidence that the pointer is just as detrimental to software reliability as the goto statement. In the words of C. A. R. Hoare (1975): "There are many reasons to believe that the introduction of references into a high-level language is a seriously retrograde step.". Some languages, like Smalltalk, have avoided pointers. An observation from the Smalltalk project team (Ingalls, 1978) succinctly states the reasons:

> Requiring the programmer to manage the allocation and deallocation of objects is out of the question in a true high-level language. It is a sure source of errors and it clutters the code with irrelevant pragmatics.

One solution is to replace pointers with more disciplined ways of constructing data types, just as the goto statement was replaced with more disciplined ways of indicating control of execution. The key observation is that pointers are often used to create recursive data structures. The following is an example of recursive data structure for binary trees using pointers taken from pages 309-310 of *Software Components with Ada* (Booch, 1987).

```
type Node;
Null_Tree : constant Tree := null;
type Tree is access Node;
type Node is
  record
    The_Item    : INTEGER;
    Left_Subtree  : Tree;
    Right_Subtree : Tree;
end record;
```

But other means for expressing recursive data structures have been known for a long time (Hoare, 1975; Kieburtz, 1976). The syntax for defining a binary tree in the ML programming language (Milner, 1984; Milner, 1985) is as follows:

```
datatype Tree = Leaf | Node of Tree * int * Tree;
```

The identifiers *Leaf* and *Node* are constructors. They are used to manipulate objects of type Tree without requiring pointers. The constructor *Leaf* corresponds roughly to the constant *Null_Tree* in the Ada definition. The two constructors are the only means by which a *Tree* can be created.

We wish to note from the outset that the price of this elegance is that storage management is removed from the programmers explicit control.

Universal Polymorphism

Writing subprocedures over and over again to implement essentially the same algorithm with only minor variations is a problem common to all conventional programming languages. The Ada programming language addressed the problem by incorporating generics. Ada generics have been touted as the solution to the problem of reuse, but generics only solve a small portion of the problem (Tracz, 1988). And, furthermore, in light of improvements in languages over the last ten years, the solution is ad hoc (Demers, 1982).

The best solution appears to be to incorporate this reuse into the type system of the language using universal polymorphism. Polymorphic type structures permit the flexibility of writing programs dependent on just the data structures directly involved without the additional complexity of new constructs in the language and without eliminating the possibility of compile time type-checking. For example, the type definition of a binary tree need not concern itself with the type of the information held at the nodes. Thus, in a language with universal polymorphism we may use the following definition of a tree.

```
datatype 'a Tree = Leaf | Node of Tree * 'a * Tree
```

The type variable *'a* can be replaced by any type.

Our preprocessor automatically generates Ada generics for polymorphic type definitions, thus increasing the extent of reusability.

THE TRANSLATION SCHEME

The preprocessor searches for input of the following form:

```
type rec <rec_type_name> (<type_param_1>, ..., <type_param_m>) is
  alternative
    <con_name_1> => <alternative_definition> ;
    <con_name_2> => <alternative_definition> ;

    ...
    <con_name_n> => <alternative_definition> ;
  end alternative;
```

This is the Ada-like syntax we use for recursive type definitions. The recursive type being defined has the name provided by the user in the place in the template labeled *<rec_type_name>*. This name must be a legal identifier in Ada. After this definition it can be used like any other type in ADA (declared in a generic package). Enclosed in parentheses is an optional list of type names. These types parameterize the type definition. The list can be omitted if the definition is not polymorphic. Each alternative represents a way in which a member of the recursive type can be constructed, and must be labeled uniquely. The recursive type, as well as the type parameters, can be used in the alternative. This is the source of the "recursiveness".

The syntactic category <*alternative_definition*> can take one of the following three forms:

1. <*identifier*> is <*type_definition*>
2. <*type_mark*>
3. *null*

where the syntactic categories <*type_definition*> and <*type_mark*> are from the Ada reference manual (United States DoD, 1983).

This input is translated into a generic package. The generic package generated by the preprocessor has a generic type parameter for each type listed in parentheses. The package provides an Ada type and three sets of functions: the constructors, the selectors, and the predicates. The constructors allocate new storage to create objects of the recursive data type. The selectors transform elements of the recursive type back into their constituent components. And the predicates are boolean functions which identify which of the various alternatives comprises an object. These are all the basic functions needed to perform any operation whatsoever on elements of the recursive type.

The translation of the recursive type definition into the generic package is easy to comprehend. The YACC program that implements the translation is given in the appendix. But the essence of the preprocessor can be understood by examining the translation of the following example:

```
generic
   type P is private;    -- generic formal type parameter
package T_Package is
   type T is private;    -- recursive type name
   type T1 is <type_definition>;
   type T2 is <type_definition>;

   function Con_Con1 (X: in T1) return T;
   function Con_Con2 (X: in T2) return T;

   function Sel_Con1 (X: in T) return T1;
   function Sel_Con2 (X: in T) return T2;

   function Is_Con1 (X: in T) return BOOLEAN;
   function Is_Con2 (X: in T) return BOOLEAN;

   Select_Error: exception;
   Uninit_Error: exception;

private
   type Tag_Type is (Tag1, Tag2);
   type Representation_Of_T (Tag: Tag_Type) is
     record
       case Tag is
         when Tag1 => Con1 : T1;
         when Tag2 => Con2 : T2;
       end case;
     end record;
   type T is access Representation_Of_T;
end T_Package;
```

Figure 1. Package Specification of Recursive Type T.

```
type rec T (P) is
   alternative
     Con1 => T1 is <type_definition> ;
   Con2 => T2 is <type_definition> ;
   end alternative;
```

The package specification is found in Figure 1. (We omit the package implementation which is obvious for the most part.) The recursive type *T* is represented by an access type to a variant record with two cases. This representation is private to the package and is not available to the user of the package except through the routines explicitly provided to manipulate the elements of type *T*. The function *Con_Con1* takes an argument of type *T1* and constructs an element of type *T*. The function *Con_Con2* does the same for an argument of type *T2*. The boolean functions *Is_Con1* and *Is_Con2* both take an argument of type *T*. They distinguish between the two methods of constructing objects of type *T*. The function *Sel_Con1* takes an argument of type *T* and returns the element of type *T1* that was used to construct the argument. Similarly for the function *Sel_Con2*.

The translation scheme illustrated in Figure 1 assumed that each alternative definition was of the form

   <identifier> is <type_definition>

In other cases, no type definition is made for the alternative. When the alternative definition is just a type mark, then the type of the data structure that represent the alternative has a name already, and it is used directly in the implementation of the recursive type. When the alternative definition is *null*, the corresponding case in the record definition of the recursive type is also *null*. In this case, there is no need for a selector for the alternative.

The package also provides for two exceptions: the *Select_Error* exception and the *Uninit_Error* exception. The first exception is raised if a selector function is applied to an element constructed by some other constructor. This exception will never be raised unless the meaning of the recursive type is misunderstood. The n constructors of a recursive type are mutually exclusive and exhaust the entire range of possibilities. Thus, the user will guard uses of the selectors by the appropriate predicate, usually in a construct similar to this:

```
if Is_Con1 (X)
   then ... Sel_Con1 (X) ... -- X is constructed by constructor1
elseif Is_Con2 (X)
   then ... Sel_Con2 (X) ... -- X is constructed by constructor2
elseif Is_Con3 (X)
...
else ... Sel_Con (X) ...   -- X is constructed by constructor n
```

The second exception, *Uninit_Error*, is raised, if the input value to the selectors or predicates has ont been given a value previously. A second possible cause for raising this exception concerns assignment. We discuss this later.

Binary Tree Example

We now consider the example of a binary tree, again. Here is its definition using the syntax for recursive types:

```
type rec Tree (Item) is
   alternative
     Leaf => null;
     Node => Node_Type is
       record
         The_Item    : Item;
         Left_Subtree : Tree;
         Right_Subtree : Tree;
       end record
   end alternative;
```

In the case of a binary tree we have one constructor, *Leaf* that has no arguments, i.e., it is a null_ary constructor. In the type definition, the keyword *null* appears indicating this fact. The other constructor, *Node*, has a record for an argument. The record is composed of three parts. The information part has type *Item*. The type *Item* is not defined here; it is a parameter of the definition of *Tree*. Different instances of *Tree* may substitute different types for Item. The other two parts have type *Tree*, the very type being defined.

Figure 2 shows the package specification created by the preprocessor. There is no selector for *Leaf*. And the constructor is not a function, but a constant.

The implementation of the functions specified in the package specification is not difficult. They are so simple that they should be compiled in-line for greater efficiency. We give the functions for the constructor *Node* below:

```
function Con_Node (X: in Node_Type) return Tree is
   T: Tree := new Representation_of_Tree (Tag2);
begin
   T. Node := X;
   return T;
end Con_Node;
```

The function *Sel_Node* raises the exception *Select_Error* if the argument is a *Tree* constructed by *Con_Leaf* instead of *Con_Node*.

```
function Sel_Node (X: in Tree) return Node_Type is
begin
   if (X.Tag = Tag2) then
```

```
generic
   type Item is private;
package Tree_Package is
   type Tree is private;
   type Node_Type is
      record
         The_Item      : Item;
         Left_Subtree  : Tree;
         Right_Subtree : Tree;
      end record;
   Con_Leaf : constant Tree;  -- deferred constant
   function Con_Node (X: in Node_Type) return Tree;
   -- No selector for 0-ary constructor
   function Sel_Node (X: in Tree) return Node_Type;
   function Is_Leaf  (X: in Tree) return BOOLEAN;
   function Is_Node  (X: in Tree) return BOOLEAN;
   Select_Error: exception;
   Uninit_Error: exception;
private
   type Tag_Type is (Tag1, Tag2);
   type Representation_Of_Tree (Tag: Tag_Type) is
      record
         case Tag is
            when Tag1 => null;
            when Tag2 => Node : Node_Type;
         end case;
      end record;
   type Tree is access Representation_Of_Tree;
   Con_Leaf: constant Tree := new Representation_Of_Tree (Tag1);
end Tree_Package
```

Figure 2. Package Specification of Binary Tree.

```
    return X.Node;
  else
    raiseSelect_Error;
  end if;
exception
  when CONSTRAINT_ERROR => raise Uninit_Error;
end Sel_Node;
```

If the parameter X is the null pointer, accessing X will cause a *CONSTRAINT_ERROR*. This indicates X is not a valid tree. The next and final function for the constructor *Node* is the predicate for *Node*.

```
function Is_Node (X: in Tree) return BOOLEAN is
begin
  return (X.Tag = Tag2);
exception
  when CONSTRAINT_ERROR => raise Uninit_Error;
end Sel_Node;
```

The user of the recursive type *Tree* considers *Tree* to be a type defined in the generic package *Tree_Package*. This requires that the package be instantiated and the desired naming accessibility be established. We show a typical instantiation of the generic package for binary trees.

```
package Int_Tree_Package is new Tree_Package (INTEGER);
subtype Int_Tree is Int_Tree_Package.Tree;
```

In the context of the generic instantiation above, the following block illustrates the exceptions:

```
declare
  X, Y:  Int_Tree;
  R: Node_Type;
  B:  BOOLEAN;
begin
  X := Con_Leaf;
  R := Sel_Node (X);   -- raises Select_Error, X is leaf
  B := Is_Leaf (Y);  -- raises Uninit_Error, Y undefined
end
```

Assignment and Equality

Some attention must be paid to the question of permitting assignment and equality on the recursive types constructed by the preprocessor. By making the type *T* limited private we could forbid assignment and equality. Although it is possible to program without these two operations, it may occasionally be useful to permit them. Examining the representation of the type *T*, we see it is an access type. Thus, assignment and equality, will be assignment of pointers and testing for pointer equality. As long as the user recognizes the "pointer semantics" of the recursive types this should cause no problem. Permitting assignment appears to have the disadvantage of allowing the user to assign *null* to a variable of type *T*. Since the same effect can be caused by uninitialized variables, the unwitting user could sabotage the recursive type abstraction. There is no meaningful interpretation to be given to the *null* pointer. This kind of abuse is detected and the exception *Uninit_Error* is raised. Notice that simple pointer representation of binary trees in Ada given at the beginning cannot distinguish between uninitialized variables and *Null* trees. This could possibly cause a subtle bug in a program using trees.

More useful than the pointer operations, may be the routines for copying a recursive data structure and testing structural equality. These functions can easily be written by the user. For instance, in the case of binary trees the following two subprograms perform the copying and testing:

```
procedure Copy (From: in Tree, To: out Tree) is
  Node : Node_Type;
begin
  if Is_Leaf (From) then
    To := Con_Leaf;
  else
```

```
   Node.The_Item := Sel_Node(From).The_Item;
   Copy (From= >Sel_Node(From).Right_Subtree, To= >Node.Right      Subtree);
   Copy (From= >Sel_Node(From).Left_Subtree, To= >Node.Left_Sub     tree);
   To := Con_Node (Node);
  end if;
end Copy;
```

The function *Copy* copies the entire data structure. The calls to *Con_Leaf* and *Con_Node* allocate new storage for the structure.

```
function Equal (X, Y: in Tree) return BOOLEAN is
  M, N: Node_Type;
begin
  if (Is_Leaf (X) and then Is_Leaf (Y)) then
  return (true);
  elseif (Is_Node (X) and then Is_Node (Y)) then
   M := (Sel_Node (X); N := Sel_Node (Y);
   return ((M.The_Item = N.Then_Item) and then
            Equal (M.Right_Subtree, N.Right_Subtree) and then
            Equal (M.Left_Subtree,  N.Left_Subtree));
  else return (false);
  end if;
end Equal;
```

Equality testing requires that equality be available on all the components. In the case of binary trees we need equality on the type *Item*. This is insured by making the generic formal type parameters all *limited private*.

The functions *Copy* and *Equal* could easily be provided automatically by the preprocessor, but we did not choose to do so.

DISCUSSION

One of the advantages of this scheme is that the representation of the recursive data type is not important for programming. The fact that *Int_Tree* is actually an access type to some hidden record is not relevant in programming, say, a tree traversal algorithm. The interface is very natural, and without pointers the associated errors are avoided.

The interface is very readable. A short recursive type definition is much easier to comprehend than a whole package. This only encourages reuse. In the words of Gargaro and Pappas (1987):

> Readability is an important issue in reusability because a part that is difficult to read will probably not be used.

Furthermore, the polymorphic nature of the tree definition is manifest in the definition of *Tree*. The package can be easily reused. For example, the information stored in the nodes of a binary tree may well be more complex than some integer value. We may wish to store a record of some sort at the nodes. Here is the form that an instantiation of the binary tree has for a type *RecordType*:

```
type RecordType = record ... end record;
package Record_Tree_Package is new Tree-Package (RecordType);
subtype Record_Tree is Record_Tree_Package.Tree;
```

This modification is conceptually quite easy, and it is pleasing that this new package is just as easy to understand as the package for integer binary trees. It is not necessary to digest an entire generic package to comprehend the polymorphic nature of the abstraction - it is evident in the type definition for *Tree*.

Reuse is not merely finding the appropriate generic and instantiating it with the appropriate parameters, rather reuse is also cloning new software from existing software which is similar, but not necessarily identical, to the requirements. This facility in the SmallTalk environment has led to much interest in object-oriented design for reuse. Recursive data definitions, because they are a succinct description of substantial data abstraction, are easy to modify. A limitless collection of recursive definitions are possible. Hence, a large library of software components can be eliminated allowing a library of reusable components to concentrate on other programming problems. Most of top-level data structures mentioned in *Software Components with Ada* (Booch, 1987) could be eliminated, but not all. Graphs, for example, are not a recursive data structure, so they might be best implemented using pointers directly.

We have indicated that the set of functions provided with a recursive type is complete. This is both good and bad. It is good, because we guarantee no gap in functionality. It is bad, because some application may wish to restrict the operations on some recursive data type. But a restriction to some set of operations is easily accomplished using the Ada package mechanism. Thus, a recursive and abstract type can be created.

It should be pointed out that many useless recursive type definitions can be built. For example, consider the following definition:

```
type rec Useless is
  alternative
    Con1 => Useless;
    Con2 => Con2_Type is
      record
        Field1 : INTEGER;
        Field2 : BOOLEAN;
        Field3 : Useless;
      end record;
  end alternative;
```

There are two ways to construct an object of type *Useless*. Either way requires that an object of type *Useless* already exist. Hence, there is no way to construct any object of type *Useless*. This is akin to programming a recursive function with out a base case.

When applications demand strict control over storage management, recursive data structures must be hand tailored to the specific application. Thus, we expect that the greatest advantage of the preprocessor will be realized in early stages of development of software. Much of the expense in searching for the right package for a particular data structure can be postponed until the software is working and efficiency concerns become a factor.

ACKNOWLEDGEMENT

The authors wish to acknowledge the support of Contract Number 540-1398-0593 from AIRMICS and Martin Marietta Energy Systems.

REFERENCES

Booch, Grady, 1987, *Software Components with Ada: Structures, Tools and Subsystems*, Benjamin/
    Cummings, Menlo Park, CA, 1987.
Cheathan, Thomas E., Jr., 1984, Reusability Through Program Transformation, *IEEE Transactions on
    Software Engineering*, Vol. SE-10, No. 5, September 1984, pp. 589-594.
Demers, Alan J., 1982, A Simplified Type Structure for Ada, *Jornadas En Computacion*, June 1982, pp.
    86-104.
Gargaro, Antony, and Pappas, T. L., 1987, Reusability Issues and Ada, *IEEE Software*, July 1987, pp. 43-51.
Hoare, Charles Antony Richard, 1975, Recursive Data Structures, *International Journal of Computer and
    Information Sciences*, Vol. 4, No. 2, June 1975, pp. 105-132.
Ingalls, Daniel H. H., 1978, The Smalltalk-76 Programming System Design and Implementation, *Conference
    Record of the Fifth Annual ACM Symposium on Principles of Programming Languages*, January
    1978, pp. 9-16.
Kieburtz, Richard B., 1976, Programming Without Pointer Variables, *Proceedings of Conference on Data:
    Abstraction, Definition and Structure*, pp. 95-107.
Milner, Robin, 1984, Proposal for Standard ML, *Conference Record of the 1984 ACM Symposium on LISP
    and Functional Programming*, pp. 184-197.

Milner, Robin, 1985, The Standard ML Core Language (Revised), *Polymorphism: The ML/LCF/Hope Newsletter*, Vol. 2, No. 2, October 1985.

Tracz, Will, 1988, Software Reuse Myths, *Software Engineering Notes*, Vol. 13, No. 1, January 1988, pp. 17-21.

United States Department of Defense, 1983, *Reference Manual for the Ada Programming Language*, United States Government Printing Office, 1983.

APPENDIX: THE PREPROCESSOR

In this appendix we list the YACC program that implements the preprocessor. We emphasize the productions of the grammar and omit some of the output routines.

```
%token  TYPE REC IDENT ALTERNATIVE END WHEN IS
%token  RECORD NULLCMD

%{
char identifier;[20]
#include <stdio.h>
#include "lex.yy.c"
int altCount;
char recTypeName[20], altNameTable[20][20],   altTypeTable[20][20];
%}

%start recursive_type_declaration

%%
recursive_type_declaration  :
    TYPE REC recursive_type_name polymorphic_part IS recursive_  type_definition ';'
            {
                    GeneratePackage();
            }
    ;

recursive_type_definition : ALTERNATIVE type_alternative_list END ALTERNATIVE
    ;

type_alternative_list        : type_alternative type_alter- native_list
        | / * empty */
    ;

type_alternative : WHEN alternative_name '=' '>' alternative_ definition ';'
     ;

alternative_definition : alternative_type_name IS type_defi-
nition
        | alternative_type_mark
    ;

polymorphic_part : '(' type_parameter_list ')'
            {
                    printf("package %s is\n", recTypeName);
                    printf("  type %s is private;\n", rec- TypeName);
            }
    | /* empty */
            {
                    printf("package %s is\n", recTypeName);
                    printf("  type %sis private;\n", rec- TypeName);
            }
    ;
```

```
type_parameter_list : type_parameter_mark ',' type_parameter_list
        | type_parameter_mark
        ;

type_definition : record_type_definition
        ;
record_type_definition : RECORD component_list END RECORD
            {
                    printf("      end record;/n");
            }
        ;

component_list : component_declaration_list
        ;

component_declaration_list : component_declaration compo- nent_declaration_list
        | component_declaration
        ;

component_declaration : field_name':' component_subtype_mark ';'
        ;

recursive_type_name : IDENT
            {
                    strcpy(recTypeName, identifier);
                    printf("generic\n");
            }
        ;

type_parameter_mark : IDENT
            {
                    printf("  type %s is private;\n", identifier);
            }
        ;

alternative_name : IDENT
            {
                    InsertAltName(identifier);
            }
        ;

alternative_type_name : IDENT
            {
                    printf("  type %s is\n", identifier);
                    printf("      record\n")
                    InsertAltType(identifier);
            }
        ;

alternative_type_mark : IDENT
            {
                    InsertAltType(identifier);
            }
        ;

field_name : IDENT
            {
                    printf("      %s: ", identifier);
            }
        ;
```

```
component_subtype_mark : IDENT
            {
                    printf("%s;[n", identifier);
            }
      ;

%%
```

VIII. SOFTWARE MEASUREMENT AND METRICS

ADA REUSABILITY ANALYSIS AND MEASUREMENT

Victor R. Basili, H. Dieter Rombach, John Bailey,
and Alex Delis

Department of Computer Science
University of Maryland
College Park, Maryland 20742

Abstract: The demand for software has exceeded the industry's capacity to supply it. Projects are frequently scaled down, delayed or even cancelled because of the time and effort required to develop the software for them. Further, the demand for software will continue to increase in the foreseeable future. Software reuse provides an answer to this dilemma. Although process and tool reuse is common practice, lifecycle product reuse is still in its infancy. Ultimately, reuse of early lifecycle products might provide the largest payoff, however for the near term, gains can be realized and further work can be guided by understanding how software can be developed with a minimum of newly-generated source lines of code.

This paper describes several parallel studies being conducted at the University of Maryland Department of Computer Science which address various related software reuse topics.

One important result of these efforts has been the identification of a set of guidelines which can be used to assist developers to create more inherently reusable software, to select reusable parts from existing software, and to modify existing software to improve its generality and reusability while preserving its functionality. Although the guidelines are written with respect to the development and reuse of systems written in the Ada language, since Ada is the medium for these studies, they apply generally to software engineering.

RELATED REUSE PROJECTS

The studies introduced above are part of a set of reuse-related projects being conducted at the University of Maryland Department of Computer Science. One of the studies forms a foundation for the rest of the projects by providing a scheme to describe and classify reuse research according to several possible dimensions. The following introduces two of the dimensions of that classification scheme. These are then used to show how the other projects can be given both context and scope in terms of their contribution to issues of reuse.

Beginning with the distinction between software processes and software products as an organizational dimension, the study of reuse can be described as the study of the creation and the use (processes) of reusable software products. Although attempting to study just the processes or the product alone necessarily involves at least some knowledge and assumptions about the other, it is important to define at least the central focus for a given research effort. For example, the data binding and transformation measuring projects, the principal studies in this paper, emphasize an understanding of what constitutes a viable reusable product. They do not emphasize reuse processes, such as that of retrieving a reusable product when one is needed.

Another dimension which is useful for scoping a reuse research effort is whether the work is more concerned with product syntax or semantics. For example, the two principal projects in this paper do not address the practical issues of whether a reusable product is actually useful, but rather are limited to an examination of the structure of a product in order to assess whether it is theoretically usable in different contexts. As with the process-product division, there are interactions between syntactic and semantic research. For example, a reusable product which is very general and flexible, a syntactic aspect, may not encapsulate a sufficient amount of functionality to make its use worthwhile, a semantic issue. Nevertheless, it is necessary to develop our knowledge in one direction at a time to avoid being overwhelmed by the total number of directions that are available. For further details, this categorization of the dimensions of software reusability has been outlined by Basili and Rombach (in preparation).

In addition to this conceptual work to develop a reuse classification scheme, there are five other reuse-oriented projects at the Department. The second project is a model of the flows of reusable information in the form of both processes and products which occur in a software development organization (Basili and Rombach, 1988). The third and fourth projects are general tool developments, including an Ada Static Source Code Analyzer which accepts syntactically correct Ada and performs various counts pertaining to the usage of Ada language constructs, facilities, and capabilities of that code (Doubleday, 1987), and an Ada Test Coverage Analyzer which instruments syntactically correct Ada so that test coverage can be computed at run time. These two are not strictly reuse-related studies, however, they contribute to needs that arise during the selection, evaluation, and reuse of existing products and processes. The final two projects, the Ada data binding analyzer and the transformation-for-reusability technique, are partly conceptual, but are currently revealing guidelines to enhance reuse. These guidelines, along with the need to automate the analyses, will evolve into specifications for specific reuse-oriented tools. It is these two projects that are covered in the remainder of this paper.

ADA DATA BINDING ANALYSIS

The first of the two projects which are covered in detail in this paper is a data binding analysis technique for Ada. This research seeks to evaluate the reusability of Ada software systems by analyzing the interconnectivity among their components. An Ada Data Binding Analyzer has been designed whose function is to accept syntactically correct Ada source code as input and compute various data binding measures. Data binding measures are used for characterizing the inter-module structure (interfaces) of Ada programs, where any active program unit (non-package, non-generic) can be considered a module. In addition, cluster analysis is performed to group modules of a system on the basis of the strength of their coupling. The research involves developing a technique to compute and weight coupling strengths, where coupling is based on references to variables and parameters (data binding). It also involves the interpretation and validation of those results.

The definition of a data binding given by Basili and Turner (1975) is:

Let x be a global variable and p and q program components. If p assigns x and q references it, then the triple (p, x, q) is a data binding between the two program segments.

The existence of the data binding triple may mean that q is dependent on the performance of p because of the global x . Clearly, the order of the three elements is important since binding (q, x, p) is not identical to (p, x, q) though it can be the case that both bindings are present. The triple identifies a unidirectional communication path between the two modules. The total number of bindings among the system modules represents the degree of connectivity among the component pairs within a system structure.

The above definition describes a particular form of binding, known as an Actual Data Binding according to the classification of four progressively stronger bindings which are given by Hutchens and Basili (1985) and paraphrased here:

1. A Potential Data Binding (PDB) is defined as a triple (mod1, x, mod2) where mod1 and mod2 are modules which are both in the static scope of the variable x. A PDB reflects the potential of a data interaction between the two components based only upon the locations of mod1, mod2, and x.

2. A Used Data Binding (UDB) is defined as a PDB where both mod1 and mod2 make use of x for either reference or assignment. It reflects an active relationship between mod1 and mod2. Generally speaking, UDB is harder to calculate than PDB since the implementation of components must be analyzed to discover the references or assignments to x.

3. An Actual Data Binding (ADB) is defined as a UDB where mod1 assigns a value to x and mod2 references it. The ADB relation is not commutative like the previous two since it distinguishes between reading the value of x and updating it. Because of this distinction,

the calculation of ADB is more complex than that of UDB. An ADB indicates that there could be a flow of information from mod1 to mod2 via the variable x. The relative order of the execution of usages of x in the different modules is ignored, however.

4.   A Control Flow Data Binding (CFDB) is defined as an ADB where control can pass to mod2 after mod1 has had control. To distinguish between an ADB and a CFDB, the possible control flows through the program must be analyzed to decide that the value provided by mod1 could be referenced by mod2 at some time before the program terminates. Because of the added control analysis, recognizing CFDB's is substantially more difficult than only recognizing ADB's.

Actual Data Bindings were first applied in the SIMPL family of languages and described in Basili and Turner (1975), to examine issues of visibility. In Hutchens and Basili (1985), Actual Data Bindings were utilized to determine the modularity of FORTRAN programs. However, these definitions need to be extended for an Ada environment where the role of global variables can be minimized through the use of local scoping and persistent, but, hidden variables.

By extending the definition to include parameters as well as variables, a more reasonable representation of data bindings in Ada code is possible. Such a view of Ada software can provide useful information about the viability of reusing various substructures within that code. In theory, there should be some way of characterizing the production and consumption of data values in a program which can provide guidance about where reusable code in that program might be found. For example, in a well--structured Ada program that lends itself well to the reuse of its components, we might expect to find that references to any given variable are localized (as would occur with state variables or data structures in a package body) while references to a parameter of a subprogram or entry are more widely distributed (as in the case of an abstract data type).

Note that the analyses does not deal with problems of aliasing. Currently, only one level of data bindings is examined. Resolving aliasing would complicate the analysis task significantly, requiring data flow analysis techniques, and has not been attempted at this time.

In addition to the inclusion of parameters along with global variables, the definition of a global variable needs to be extended for Ada to mean not only variables with library-level scopes but also any variable whose scope includes both of the modules under consideration. This could be a variable which is local to one module but global to another (where the second module is nested within the first) or a variable which is external to both modules but is not necessarily at the library level.

Moreover, the definition of a module must be determined when analyzing Ada code for data bindings. For this, the Myers definition of a module was used as a point of departure. In Myers (1978), a module is a set of executable program statements that meet three criteria:

a.   It is a closed subroutine; it implements a distinct piece of computation
b.   It can be called from any other module in the program
c.   It can be compiled separately

Based on Myers' characteristics, subprograms (procedures and functions) qualify as modules. Ada subprograms are constructs of a "closed subroutine" nature, and with minor restrictions can be separately compiled. Further, library unit subprograms as well as subprograms declared in the visible part of a library unit package can be called from any other module in the system, assuming the use of an appropriate context clause. By extending the definition to enclosed scopes, any subprogram, library level or nested, qualifies as a module. No differentiation is made between the declaration and the body of a subprogram, even if they are in different compilation units. Both are considered to be part of the same module.

Tasks are also considered modules for the same reasons. Although the calls to a task are actually calls to entries, similar to calls to the visible operations of a package, the task itself is active, unlike a package. Again, a task declaration and body are together considered a single module. Unlike subprograms and tasks, packages are not active and cannot be called, so they are not considered modules. Rather, they constitute a (possibly empty) set of modules.

When performing data binding analyses for the purpose of examining reusability, generics are not considered separately, but follow the same classification as their non-generic counterparts. Therefore, only generic subprograms are considered, and the generic (generic formal parameter lists) are disregarded in the analysis. It would also be possible to examine the bindings between generic instantiations and other modules, however, the instantiations of a generic are not particularly interesting when the goal is to discover reusable portions of the analyzed software. Other possible candidates for modules which were rejected include block statements, package body initializations, and accept statements. It would be theoretically possible to include these structures as modules, however, they did not fit easily into the chosen definition by Myers.

The following are two definitions which are specific to Ada and which arise from the preceding discussion.

> **Definition I:** Let mod1 and mod2 be two subprograms or tasks where mod1 calls mod2, and let the object x be a part of the mod2 interface (formal parameter list), then if mod1 assigns x and mod2 references it the binding (mod1, x, mod2) exists, and if mod2 assigns x and mod1 references it the binding (mod2, x, mod1) exists.

Note that in Ada the mode of the formal parameter x limits the availability of the possible bindings. The binding (mod1, x, mod2) can only exist if x is an in or in out parameter and the binding mod2, x, mod1; can only exist if x is an in out or out parameter. The mode does not guarantee a binding, however, since both an assignment and a reference must also be made.

> **Definition II:** Let mod1 and mod2 be two subprograms or tasks and let the scope of object x extend to both modI and mod2. If mod1 assigns x and mod2 references it, then the binding exists.

Except for the removal of the stipulation that x be a global variable, this second definition parallels the original definition in Basili and Turner (1975). Note that these definitions can be applied whether or not the modules in question are visible at the library level or nested, or even if they are nested inside one another. Note also that the defined bindings are those that occur through execution and not through elaboration (such as through initializations or default value assignments).

Cluster Analysis

After the set of data bindings in a program has been identified, a cluster analysis is performed to identify which modules are strongly coupled with other modules and therefore may not be good candidates for reuse, and which modules are found to be independent of others and therefore potentially useful on their own. A cluster analysis results in a hierarchical system decomposition based on the strength of the data bindings among the modules.

To perform a cluster analysis on a set of modules (typically a complete program), first a matrix, B, is constructed that is of N X N dimensions, where N is the number of components. Each matrix element $B(k,1)$ contains the total number of bindings between component k and component 1. (The direction of the binding is no longer important, so the matrix is symmetric with a zero diagonal.)

The algorithm used to identify clusters is then applied iteratively in a bottom up fashion. The first clusters are identified as those components that are bound with the highest strength, according to the matrix. A cluster is then redefined as a single module, and a new (smaller) matrix is computed. The process is repeated, each time collapsing modules into single modules for the next iteration, building a tree-gram of the system modules. Eventually, all the elements coalesce in a single group that is the complete system cluster.

The iteration process is documented in the form of a treegram that expresses the differences and similarities (with respect to data bindings) of the components involved in the analysis. The specific cluster analysis technique used in this project is more completely described in Hutchens and Basili (1985).

Reuse Guidelines Based on Data Bindings

The data binding metrics and cluster analysis techniques introduced above have been manually applied to a limited set of small Ada programs. Based upon this experience a set of guidelines has been derived for developers to keep in mind when designing and building reusable Ada components:

- Avoid multiple level nesting in any of the language constructs.

Multiple level nesting of components results in a deeply clustered tree-gram from which it is difficult to extract reuse candidates. The use of a single level of components results in very flat tree-grams and, therefore, reusable components can be extracted much more easily.

- The use of the "use" clause is not recommended.

358

Data binding analysis becomes more complicated in the presence of "use" clauses since naming and visibility mechanisms must be employed in order to decide upon the correct binding of names. Further, the readability of programs is increased when expanded names are used.

- The interfaces of the subprograms should use the appropriate abstraction for the parameters passed in and out.

The abstraction of the interface components should be at the appropriate level. In this way a large number of parameters in the formal parameter list which could make the analysis complicated can be avoided.

- Components should not interact with their outer environment.

The software should not deal with globals, should be free of side-effects and should reference objects at a local level.

- Appropriate use of packaging could greatly accommodate reusability.

Packaging is a logical way to group homogeneous collections of objects, subprograms and tasks. Even though subprograms from the same package sometimes do not cluster together due to the nature of the implemented concept (abstract data types often exhibit this tendency since they often share one or more type definitions but not variables) it is still true that reasonable packaging can assist enormously in the effort to reuse software.

REUSE THROUGH GENERALIZATION: MEASUREMENT AND TRANSFORMATION

This project seeks to define transformation techniques which can be applied to existing Ada software in order to extract reusable functionality from it. By measuring the amount of transformation which must be performed to convert an existing program into one composed of maximally reusable components, an indication of the reusability of that program can be obtained. After applying all of the transformations which are reasonable or practical, if there remain desired transformations that cannot be performed cost effectively, then those unapplied transformations constitute a measure of the latent non-reusability of the software.

The advantages of transforming existing software into reusable components, rather than creating reusable components as an independent activity, include: 1) software development organizations are likely to have a large supply of previous projects which could yield reusable components; 2) developers of ongoing projects do not need to adjust to new and possibly unproven methods in an attempt to develop reusable components, so no risk or development overhead is introduced; 3) transformation work can be accomplished in parallel with line developments, but be separately funded (this is particularly applicable when software is being developed for an outside customer who may not be willing to sustain the additional costs and risks of developing reusable code), 4) the resulting components are guaranteed to be relevant to the application area and recognizable to the developers, and 5) the cost is low and controllable.

As discussed in the first section, this project only attempts to identify theoretically reusable software. Thus, it is concerned only with the syntax of reusable software. It does not address issues of practical reusability, such as whether a reusable component is useful enough to encourage other developers to reuse it instead of redeveloping its function. The goal of the transformations is to identify and extract components from a program which are not dependent on external declarations, information, or other knowledge. Transformations are needed to derive such components from existing software systems since inter-component dependencies arise naturally from the customary design decomposition and implementation integration processes used for software development.

To guide the transformations which will result in increased independence among the components of a program, a model is used which distinguishes between software function and the declarations on which that function is performed. The functions become the independently reusable parts and the declarations become the application-specific parts of the software. However, this is not to say that only strict functions are extracted for reuse since the model is recursive. A declaration (also known as an object) can be seen as being constructed from lower level declarations onto which some functionality has been grafted. Similarly, this new declaration can be combined with other declarations and functionality to yield yet another declaration which solves an even larger portion of the overall problem being solved. This model is somewhat analogous to the one used in Smalltalk programs where objects are assembled from other objects plus programmer-supplied specifics. However, it is meant to apply more generally to Ada and other languages that do not have support for dynamic binding and full inheritance, features that are in general unavailable when strong static type checking is required.

Applying this model to existing software means that any lines of code which represent reusable functionality must be encapsulated and parameterized in order to make them independent from their surrounding declaration space (if they are not already independent). The language construct in Ada which enables this transformation is, of course, the generic. Generics that are derived by generalizing existing program units, through the removal of their dependence on external declarations, can then be offered as independently reusable components for other applications.

Unfortunately, declarative independence is just one way that a program unit can rely on its external environment. Removing the compiler-detectable declarative dependencies and producing a new generic unit is no guarantee that the new unit will actually be independent. There can be dependencies on data values that are related to values in neighboring software, or even dependencies on protocols of operation that are followed at the point where a resource was originally used, but which might not be followed at a point of later reuse. (An example of these kinds of dependencies is given later in this section.) To be completely useful, the transformation process would need to identify and remove this other dependence as well as declarative dependence. For now, however, this work only acknowledges these additional dependencies while concentrating on mechanisms to measure and remove declarative dependence.

Declarative Dependence

In a language with strong static type checking, such as Ada, any information exchanged between communicating program units must be of some type which is available in both units. Since Ada enforces name equivalence of types, where a type name and not just the underlying structure of a type introduces a new and distinct type, the declaration of the type used to pass information between units must be global to both of those units. The user of a resource, therefore, is constrained to be in the scope of all type declarations used in the interface of that resource. In a language with a fixed set of types this is not a problem since all possible types will be globally available to both the resource and its users. However, in a language which allows user-declared types, any inter-module communication with such types must be performed in the scope of those programmer-defined declarations. This means that the coupling between two communicating units increases from data coupling to external coupling (or from level two to level five on the traditional seven-point scale of Myers, where level one is the lowest level of coupling) (Myers, 1978).

Static type checking, therefore, is a mixed blessing. It prevents many errors from entering a software system which might not otherwise be detected until run time. However, it limits the possible reuse of a module if a specific declaration environment must also be reused. Not only must the reused module be in the scope of those declarations, but so must its users. Further, those users are forced to communicate with that module using those external types rather than its own, making the resource master over its users instead of the other way around. It is common to use a set of global types to facilitate communication among the components of a program, however this practice prevents most, if not all, of the developed software from being used in any other program. The following is an abstraction of such a situation:

```
-- context:
package Global_Types is
   type Typ1 is ...
end Global_Types;

-- resource:
with Global_Types;
package Useful_Functions is
   procedure Proc (P1 : out Global_Types.Typ1);
end Useful_Functions;

-- user:
with Global_Types;
with Useful_Functions;
procedure User is
   Obj1 : Global_Types.Typ1;
begin
   Useful_Functions.Proc (Obj1);

end User;
```

The above illustrates the general case of a context-resource-user relationship. The dependencies among these three units can be illustrated with a directed graph. This form of dependency is related to the data binding dependencies discussed earlier. However, it is a dependence on type declarations and not on object declarations that is important here. Nevertheless, the theory of data binding and cluster analysis could be extended to cover any relationship defined between modules, whether object dependence, type dependence, or any other. A graph of the dependency in the example above can be seen in Figure 1.

A resource does not always need full type information about the data it must access in order to accomplish its task. A common example would be a simple data base which stores and retrieves data but which does not take advantage of the information contained within that data. In cases such as this, it is possible to write or transform the resource so that any context or dependencies it requires are supplied by its users. Then, only the essential work of the module needs to remain. This "essence only" principle is the key to the transformations sought. Only the design of a module remains, with any details needed to produce the executing code, such as actual type declarations or specific operations on those types, being provided later by the end users of the resource. In languages such as Smalltalk which allow dynamic binding, this information is bound at run time. In Ada, where the compiler is obligated to perform all type checking and thereby eliminate many of the problems that can occur with dynamic binding, generics that are bound at compilation time can be used to free the text of a resource from depending directly on external type definitions.

Using the following package declaration and body, which is an abstraction of a hypothetical but structurally typical Ada package, one transformation is illustrated:

```
-- resource:
with Decls;
package Store is
  procedure Put (Obj  : in Decls.Typ);
  procedure Get_Last (Obj  : out Decls.Typ);
end Store;

package body Store is
  Local : Decls.Typ;
  procedure Put (Obj  : in Decls.Typ) is
  begin
    Local := Obj;
  end Put;
  procedure Get_Last (Obj  : out Decls.Typ) is
  begin
    Obj := Local;
  end Get_Last;
end Store;
```

The above component can be transformed into the following one which has no dependencies on external declarations:

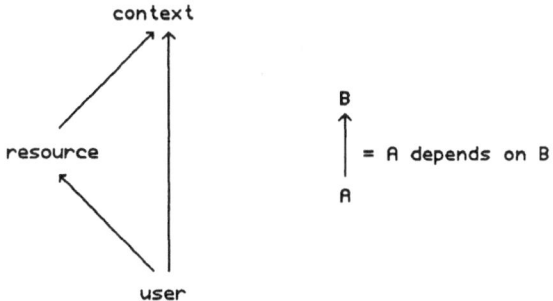

Figure 1. General Case of a Context-Resource-User Relationship.

```
-- generalized resource:
generic
  type Typ is private;
package General_Store is
  procedure Put (Obj  : in Typ);
  procedure Get_Last (Obj  : out Typ);
end General_Store;

package body General_Store is
  Local  : Typ;
  procedure Put (Obj  : in Typ) is
  begin
    Local  := Obj;
  end Put
  procedure Get_Last (Obj  : out Typ) is
  begin
    Obj  := Local;
  end Get_Last;
end General_Store;
```

Note that, by naming the generic formal parameter appropriately, none of the identifiers in the code needed to change, and the expanded names were merely shortened to their simple names. This minimizes the handling required to perform the transformation (although automating the process would make this an unimportant issue). This transformation required the removal of the context clause, the addition of two lines (the generic part) and the shortening of the expanded names. The modification required to convert the procedure to a theoretically independent one constitutes a reusability measure. Formal rules for counting program changes have already been proposed and validated (Dunsmore and Gannon, 1977), and adaptations of these counting rules (such as using a lower handling value for shortening expanded names and a higher one for adding generic formals) are being considered as part of this work.

Although the above illustration shows the context, the resource, and the user as library level units, declaration dependence can occur, and transformations can be applied, in situations where the three components are nested. For example, the resource and user can be co-resident in a declarative area, or the user can contain the resource or vice versa. For clarity, the examples in this paper will always show the components at the library level.

In addition to measuring the reusability of a unit by the amount of transformation required to optimize its independence, reusability can also be gauged by the amount of residual dependency on other units which cannot be eliminated, or which is unreasonably difficult to eliminate, by any of the proposed transformations. For any given unit, therefore, two values can be obtained. The first reveals the number of program changes which would be required to perform any applicable transformations. The second indicates the amount of dependence which would remain in the unit even after it was transformed. The original unit in the example above would score high on the first scale since the handling required for its conversion was negligible, implying that its reusability was already good (i.e., it was already independent or was easy to make independent of external declarations). After the transformation, there remain no latent dependencies, so the transformed generic would receive a perfect reusability score.

Note that the object of any reusability measurement, and therefore, of any transformations, need not be a single Ada unit. If a set of library units were intended to be reused together then the metrics as well as the transformations could be applied to the entire set. Whereas there might be substantial interdependence among the units within the set, it still might be possible to eliminate all dependencies on external declarations.

In the above example, one reason that the transformation was trivial was that the only operation performed on objects of the external type was assignment. Therefore, it was possible to replace direct visibility to the external type definition with a generic formal private type. A second example illustrates a slightly more difficult transformation which includes more assumptions about the externally declared type. In the following example, indexing and component assignment are used by the resource.

Before transformation:

```
-- context
package A is
  type Item_Array is array (Integer range < >) of Natural;
end A;
```

```
-- resource
with A;
procedure B (Item : out A.Item_Array) is
begin
  for I in 1..10 loop
    Item (I) := 0;
  end loop;
end B;

-- user
with A, B;
procedure C is
  X : A.Item_Array (1..10);
begin
  B (X);
end C;
```

After transformation:

```
-- context
package A is
  type Item_Array is array (Integer range < >) of Natural;
end A;

-- generalized resource
generic
  type Component is range < >;
  type Index is range < >;
  type Gen_Array is array (Index range < >) of Component;
procedure Gen B (Item : out Gen Array);
procedure Gen B (Item : out Gen Array) is
begin
  for I in 1..10 loop
    Item (I) := 0;
  end loop;
end Gen B;

-- user
with A, Gen B;
procedure C is
  X : A.Item Array (1..10);
procedure B is new Gen B (Natural, Integer, A.Item Array);
begin
  B (X);
end C;
```

The above transformation removes compilation dependencies, and allows the generic procedure to describe its essential function without the visibility of external declarations. However, it also illustrates an important additional kind of dependence which can exist between a resource and its users, namely information dependence.

Information Dependence

In the previous example, the literal value 10 is a clue to the presence of information that is not general. In fact, even the appearance of the literal value 0 (the value assigned to the components) is not even necessarily general. Therefore, either of the following would be an improvement over the transformation shown above:

```
generic
  type Component is range < >;
  type Index is range < >;
  type Gen_Array is array (Index range < >) of Component;
```

```
procedure Gen_B (Item : out Gen_Array);
procedure Gen_B (Item : out Gen_Array) is
begin
  for I in Item'Range loop
    Item (I) := Component'First;
  end loop;
end Gen_B;
```

- or -

```
generic
    type Component is range < >;
    type Index is range < >;
    type Gen_Array is array (Index range < >) of Component;    Init_Val : Component := Component'First;
procedure Gen_B (Item : out Gen_Array);
procedure Gen_B (Item : out Gen_Array) is
begin
  for I in Item'Range loop
    Item (I) := Init_Val;
  end loop;
end Gen_B;
```

Note that the last transformation allows the user to supply an initial value, but also provides the lowest value of the component type as a default. An additional refinement would be to make the component type private which would mean that Init_Val could not have a default value. Information dependencies such as the one illustrated here are harder to detect than compilation dependencies. The appearance of literal values in a resource is often an indication of an information dependence.

Protocol Dependence

A third form of dependence has been identified, known as protocol dependence, where the user of a resource must obey certain rules to ensure that the resource behaves properly. For example, a stack which is used to buffer information between other users could be implemented in a not-so-abstract fashion by exposing the stack array and top pointer directly. In the following illustration, all users of the stack must follow the same protocol of decrementing the pointer before popping and incrementing after pushing, and not the other way around:

```
-- resource:
package Bad_Stack is
    Data : array (1..100) of Character;
    Pointer : Integer range 1..101 := 1;
end Bad_Stack;

-- Push user example:
with Bad_Stack;
use Bad_Stack;
procedure Push is
begin
  if Pointer <= 100 then
    Data (Pointer) := '@';
    Pointer := Pointer + 1;
  end if;
end Push;

-- Pop user example:
with Bad_Stack;
use Bad_Stack;
procedure Pop is
    X : Character;
begin
  if Pointer > 1 then
```

```
    Pointer := Pointer - 1;
    X := Data (Pointer);
  end if;
end Pop;
```

Notice that in addition to the protocol dependence, an information dependence is indicated by the appearance of the literal values 1, 100, and 101 (but not the '@' since that is only data in the user code). Notice, also, that one could argue that the dependence on type Character from package standard might be considered a declaration dependence which ought to be removed. Although the mention of Standard in a context clause is unnecessary, meaning the resource and its users are already compilation-independent, the identification and removal of the use of Character in the resource (by replacing it with a generic formal private type) would improve the generality of the resource.

Formalizing the Technique

The following is a formalization of the objectives of transformations which are needed to remove declaration dependence.

1. Let P represent a program unit.

2. Let D represent the set of n object declarations, d(1)..d(n), directly referenced by P such that d(i) is of a type declared externally to P, but not in package Standard (for library units, this visibility must be obtained through a "with" clause).

3. Let 0(1)..0(n) be sets of operations where 0(i) is the set of operations applied to d(i) inside P.

4. P is completely transformable if each 0(i)(j) can be replaced with a predefined or generic formal operation.

The earlier example transformation is reviewed in the context of these definitions:

1. Let P represent a program unit.

    P = *procedure* B (Item : *out* A.Item_Array) *is* ...

2. Let D represent the set of n declarations, d(1)..d(n), directly referenced by P such that d(i) is of a type declared externally to P, but not in package Standard.

    D = { A.Item_Array }

3. Let 0(1) .. 0(n) be sets of operations where 0(i) is the set of operations applied to d(i) inside P.

    0(1) = { indexing by integer types, integer assignment to components }

4. P is transformable if each 0(i)(j) can be replaced with a predefined or generic formal operation.

Indexing can be obtained through a generic formal array type. Although no constraining operation was used, the formal type could be either constrained or unconstrained since the only declared object is a formal subprogram parameter. Since component assignment is required, the component type must not be limited.

```
type Component is range < >;
type Index is range < >;
```

followed by either:

```
type Gen_Array is array (Index) of Component;
```

365

or:

type Gen_Array *is array* (Index *range* < >) *of* Component;

Notice that some operations can be replaced with generic formal operations more easily than others. For example, direct access of array structures (illustrated earlier) can generally be replaced by making the array type a generic formal type. However, direct access into record structures (using "dot" notation) complicates transformations since this operation must be replaced with a user-defined access function.

Experience with Transformations

To test the feasibility of the transformations proposed, a 6,000-line Ada program written by seven professional programmers was examined for reuse transformation possibilities. The program consisted of six library units, ranging in size from 20 to 2,400 lines. Of the 30 theoretically possible dependencies that could exist among these units, ten were required. Four transformations of the sort described above were made to three of the units. These required an additional 44 lines of code (less than a 1% increase) and reduced the number of dependencies from ten to five, which is the minimum possible with six units. Using one possible program change definition, each transformation required between two and six changes.

A fifth modification was made to detach a nested unit from its parent. This required the addition of 15 lines and resulted in a total of seven units with the minimum six dependencies. Next, two other functions were made independent of the other units. Unlike the previous transformations which were targeted for later reuse, however, these transformations resulted in a net reduction in code since the resulting components were reused at multiple points within this program. Substantial information dependency was identified but remained among the units, however.

Reuse Guidelines Based on Dependencies

As with the data binding analysis, manual application of the principles and techniques of generic transformation and extraction has revealed several interesting and intuitively reasonable guidelines relative to the creation and reuse of Ada software.

- Avoid direct access into record components except in the same declarative region as the record type declaration.

Since there is no generic formal record type in Ada (without dynamic binding such a feature would be impractical) there is no straightforward way to replace record component access with a generic operation. Instead, user-supplied access functions are needed to access the components and the type must be passed as a private type. This is unlike array types for which there are two generic formal types (constrained and unconstrained). This supports the findings of others which assert that direct referencing of non-local record components adversely affects maintainability (Gannon, Katz, and Basili, 1983).

- Minimize non-local access to array components.

Although not as difficult in general as removing dependence on a record type, removing dependence on an array type can be cumbersome.

- Keep direct access to data structures local to their declarations.

This is a stronger conclusion than the previous two, and reinforces the philosophy of using abstract data types in all situations where a data type is available outside its local declarative region. Encapsulated types are far easier to separate as resources than globally declared types.

- Avoid the use of literal values except as constant value assignments.

Information dependence is almost always associated with the use of a literal value in one unit of software that has some hidden relationship to a literal value in a different unit. If a unit is generalized and extracted for reuse but contains a literal value which indicates a dependence on some assumption about its original context, that unit can fail in unpredictable ways when reused. Conventional wisdom applies here, also, and it might be reasonable to relax the restriction to allow the use of 0 and 1. However, experience with a considerable amount of software which makes the erroneous assumption that the first index of any string is 1 has shown that even this can lead to problems.

- Avoid mingling resources with application specific contexts.

Although the purpose of the transformations is to separate resources from application specific software regardless of the program structure, certain styles of programming result in programs which can be transformed more easily and completely. By staying conscious of the ultimate goal of separating reusable function from application declarations, whether or not the functionality is initially programmed to be generic, programmers can simplify the eventual transformation of the code.

- Keep interfaces abstract.

Protocol dependencies arise from the exportation of implementation details that should not be present in the interface to a resource. Such an interface is vulnerable because it assumes a usage protocol which does not have to be followed by its users. The bad stack example illustrates what can happen when a resource interface requires the use of implementation details, however even resources with an appropriately abstract interface can export unwanted additional detail which can lead to protocol dependence.

CONCLUSIONS AND FUTURE DIRECTIONS

Two ongoing research projects seeking to characterize and measure aspects of reusability in Ada software have been described. The first project applies for the first time the results of earlier data binding work to the Ada language (Basili and Turner, 1975). The second project motivates the transformation of Ada software to yield reusable components and describes a technique to accomplish that transformation. Both projects yield measures that provide visibility into Ada software for the purpose of identifying and evaluating portions of it for reuse.

By applying the principles described by each of the studies, several guidelines concerning the structure of reusable Ada code were revealed. All of the guidelines discovered so far are intuitively satisfying in that they complement rather than contradict conventional software engineering wisdom. Not all have been previously associated with promoting reusability, however. Instead, most have been previously recommended with respect to promoting readability and maintainability.

Several tools have been identified and described as a result of these studies. A tool to calculate data binding metrics could be used to highlight regions of reusability in existing software. Then, a tool to assist in the identification of inter-unit dependence as well as one to perform the necessary modifications to a unit in order to extract it as a reusable component could be used. Similar tools could also be used to characterize the software in order to provide feedback to the developers on the reusability of their code. Such tools would serve a purely measurement function. For example, the two methods of measuring reusability relating to the transformability of software (measuring both initial dependence and latent unremovable dependence) could be automated in order to guide a developer to write resources that are properly encapsulated and interfaces that are sufficiently abstract. Although this research does not propose to develop these tools, it is currently specifying their operation as a way of more clearly defining the techniques and principles involved in the study.

REFERENCES

Basili, V. R., and Rombach, H. D., 1988, The TAME Project: Towards Improvement-Oriented Software Environments, *IEEE Transactions on Software Engineering*, Vol. SE-14, June 1988.

Basili, V. R., and Rombach, H. D., in preparation, Software Reuse: A Framework.

Basili, V. and Turner, A., 1975, Iterative Enhancement: A Practical Technique for Software Development, *IEEE Transactions on Software Engineering*, Vol. SE-1, December 1975, pp. 390-396.

Doubleday, D. L., 1987, *ASAP: An Ada Static Source Code Analyzer Program*, TR1895, University of Maryland Department of Computer Science, College Park, Md., August 1987.

Dunsmore, H. E., and Gannon, J. D., 1977, Experimental Investigation of Programming Complexity, *Proceedings ACM/NBS 16th Annual Tech. Symposium: Systems and Software*, Washington D.C., June 1977.

Gannon, J. D., Katz, E., and Basili, V. R., 1983, Characterizing Ada Programs: Packages, *Proceedings*

Workshop on Software Performance, Alamos National Laboratory, Los Alamos, New Mexico, August 1983.

Hutchens, D., and Basili, V. R.,1985, System Structure Analysis: Clustering with Data Bindings, *IEEE Transactions on Software Engineering*, Vol. 11, No. 8, August 1985, pp. 749-757.

Myers, G., 1978, *Composite/Structured Design*, Van Nostrand Reinhold, New York.

OBJECT-BASED MEASUREMENT IN THE REQUIREMENTS SPECIFICATION PHASE

D. L. Carver, D. W. Cordes, and Nancy Gautier

Department of Computer Science
Louisiana State University
Baton Rouge, LA

Abstract: Effective software measurement enhances the software development environment. One aspect of software measurement that merits additional exploration is the pre-design phase. Research during the past two decades has shown the importance of the requirements engineering phase of the software development process. As a complement to the increased emphasis on the requirements engineering environment, we to investigate properties of the requirements phase that can provide information on the difficulty of the problem to be solved by the proposed software system. In this paper, we develop measurements that provide a characterization of the difficulty of the proposed system at the early stage of requirements definition. The characterization measurements are from an object-oriented perspective. They are based on solution objects, actions, and the level of interaction among the objects. We describe an automated tool that generates the information needed to evaluate the measurements. These characterizations provide objective measures that can be used as input to the early evaluation of problem difficulty that is required when cost and time estimates must be formulated.

INTRODUCTION

The requirements specification phase is a critical phase of the software development process. In this phase, the definition and analysis of the user's needs are identified and analyzed. The result of the analysis is a precise description of the intended behavior of the system. This description is a definition of the functions the system will perform but it is not a description of how the system will perform them. The requirements specification phase is typically initiated with a natural language document, prepared by the user, in which the proposed system is described. The quality of the delivered system is directly related to the effectiveness of the specification team in gathering complete, correct information about the system.

Many problems that are uncovered at the time of system delivery can be traced to the requirements phase. Functions that are expected by the user but are not identified during requirements definition are often not exposed until acceptance testing or some period of time after system installation. As software development proceeds through requirements definition, specification, design, coding, testing, implementation, and maintenance, the cost to fix errors increases dramatically. If an error is introduced during requirements definition, but not discovered until a later phase, it is typically necessary to cycle back to the requirements definition state to correct the error. For example, a design error takes potentially 1.5 to 3 times the effort of an implementation error to correct (Yeh et al., 1984). In addition, it is estimated that approximately 64% of the errors in a typical system are introduced during requirements specification and design phases (Charette, 1986). Thus, the requirements specification phase has a vital impact on the success of the system.

In addition to the technical reasons that make the requirements phase a critical phase, other pragmatic and non-technical reasons are very important. System predictions are computed at the beginning of the software development process. One type of prediction is required when the feasibility study is performed. Given the system information acquired during the requirements phase, the specification team, or in some cases, a managerial group, must determine whether the system is a feasible candidate for

Empirical Foundations of Information and Software Science V
Edited by P. Zunde and D. Hocking, Plenum Press, New York, 1990

369

computerization. The feasibility includes not only the technical aspects, but also cost estimates. These cost estimates are computed by numerous methods, ranging from ad hoc approaches to formula based approaches. In order to make reasonable cost estimates, some type of analysis of the system based on the requirements document must be performed. Thus, accurate estimations are critically important for both the user and the developer.

METRIC USE THROUGHOUT THE SOFTWARE DEVELOPMENT LIFE CYCLE

Software metric use has become an integral part of software related predictions. There is a general need for metrics that apply to early phases of software development. Specific metrics, applied to all phases of software development, can be useful for providing assistance regarding proper development approaches to apply to the next phase, for predicting required resources, and for exposing possible areas of complexity reduction. Most of the work in metrics for software prediction has revolved around product metrics, metrics that measure the software product itself. Common product metrics include lines of code, cyclomatic complexity (McCabe, 1976), and software science (Halstead, 1977). There has been an increasing awareness that application of metrics to phases preceding the coding phase of software development is beneficial. This awareness of the need for metrics in the early phases has accompanied the increased awareness of the importance of the early phases of software development. Design metrics have been developed to investigate the relationship of factors such as coupling, cohesion, number of modules, modularity, and module size to various aspects of software (Conte, Dunsmore, and Shen, 1986). In addition to the pursuit of metrics for design, it is appropriate to investigate properties of the requirements phase that have relevance to the evaluation of the difficulty of the problem to be solved. A need for metrics for prediction at the requirements level is expressed in Ramamoorthy, Garg, and Prakash (1986). In this paper, we describe a framework for measurement in the requirements phase from an object-oriented perspective.

OBJECT-ORIENTED SOFTWARE DEVELOPMENT

Object oriented software development is primarily a result of the work of Booch (1986). Earlier work by Abbott (1983), was an influence on the definition of the object-oriented approach. It is an approach which is driven by objects and their associated attributes. An object is defined by Booch (1986):

> an *object* is an entity whose behavior is characterized by the actions it suffers and that it requires of other objects.

Objects from the real-world domain are identified and used to produce the structure of the system. The object-oriented software development process is based on a five-step procedure. The first step is the identification of the objects and their attributes. This identification is typically done in an informal manner by first identifying the nouns, pronouns, and noun clauses and then subjectively selecting those objects that are of primary interest. Once these objects have been identified, their attributes are identified by an informal evaluation of the adjective and the adjectival phrases. The second step is the identification of the operations of interest. This identification is done informally by identifying the verbs, verb phrases, and the predicates. Once the operations are identified, attributes of the operations are determined for the adverbs and the adverbial phrases. The operations are then related to the appropriate object. The third step is the identification of the visibility of the objects. The visibility is based on both functional and hierarchical relationships. Step four is the definition of the formal interfaces among the objects based on the visibility factors. Finally, step five is the implementation of the solution to the system.

The object-oriented software paradigm is typically initiated at the design phase. A suitable requirements analysis technique is required to precede the object-oriented design and development process. Jackson Structured Development Methodology (Jackson, 1983), and Systems Requirements Methodology (Alford, 1977), have been suggested as viable requirements analysis approaches (Booch, 1986). As the benefits of object-oriented software development are widely recognized, they are not delineated in this paper. However, a discussion of the benefits is provided in Booch (1986).

OBJECT CHARACTERISTICS AS A BASIS FOR REQUIREMENTS-BASED MEASUREMENT

One of the shortcomings of most existing measurement techniques is that they generally cannot be computed until the coding or possibly the design phase. While these measures can provide support for the coding, testing, and implementation phases, they do not provide assistance for the earlier phases of software development. In particular, during the requirements specification phase, the developer is required to provide the user with estimates of time and cost. Yet, few measurable techniques are available to help with the estimation process. We are investigating factors that will provide support for the analysis of project difficulty at the earliest stage of software development, the requirements phase.

Measurement at the requirements level should provide indication of the difficulty of the problem to be solved by the software system, information relative to the appropriate approach for the ensuing steps of the software development process, and indication of complex portions of the problem. In this work, we are using an automated object-based requirements model to provide measurable factors that constitute a framework for an early characterization of the difficulty of the software problem. This framework is necessarily based on the level of abstraction that exists at the requirements definition level. This characterization is intended as a descriptive tool as opposed to an evaluation tool. Kearney (Kearney et al., 1986) differentiates a descriptive tool from an evaluation tool. A descriptive tool is applied to a process based function such as manpower allocation and an evaluation tool is used to evaluate a product based function such as quality level. Kearney suggests that different characteristics are meritorious for the two types of tools. For example, a descriptive tool may be useful for determining difficulty of problem or program understanding but it does not have to inherently suggest ways of reducing the understanding difficulty, as an evaluation tool should.

Among the factors that are relevant to this descriptive framework from an object-oriented viewpoint are number of objects that must be considered, number of operations on the objects in the solution of the system, and the degree of interaction among the objects. An initial comprehension of the difficulty level required to develop a software system to solve a given problem is typically formulated from the reading of the initial requirements document. This high-level formulation is affected by the quantity of objects as well as the actions surrounding the objects. The initial comprehension difficulty is typically formulated without a formalized analysis. An identification of the total number of objects in the document provides some level of non-subjective information about the difficulty of the problem. Thus, T is defined as:

$$T = \{objects\ in\ the\ requirements\ document\}.$$

However, only a subset of the set of the objects in T is actually an integral part of the requirements. Therefore, the quantification of the number of objects that actually participate in the solution provides a more detailed level of information about the difficulty of the problem. Thus, we proposed a characterization based on a semantic evaluation of the level of impact each object has on the actual problem. An object that serves as an actor or a recipient of other objects but is not an object property is classified as a solution object. This first level of characterization is defined as the cardinality of the set of solution objects:

$$C_1 = |S|$$

where S = {solution objects}.

This basis of this characterization is that an identification of the objects that are central to the functions of the system provides descriptive information about the complexity of the system.

Yet another level of comprehension can be derived by examining the types of activity surrounding the solution objects. There are objects that actually instigate actions and objects that only suffer actions of other objects. The objects that instigate actions are termed abstract state machine objects and the objects that only suffer actions are referred to as abstract data type objects. We use the following terminology to indicate these sets of objects.

$$SM = \{solution\ objects\ classified\ as\ abstract\ state\ machines\}$$

$$DT = \{solution\ objects\ classified\ as\ abstract\ data\ types\}$$

We propose a second level of characterization

$$C_2 = |SM| + a$$

where $a = \#$ actions $\forall\ o \in SM$.

This characterization is based on the assumption that active objects and their associated actions introduce a higher level of difficulty than passive objects.

Clearly, the following relationships hold among these sets:

$S \subseteq T$, $SM \subseteq S$, $DT \subseteq S$, $SM \cap DT = 0$, and $SM \cup DT = S$.

We can distinguish yet another level of information by investigating the level of interaction of the objects in SM with other objects in SM and the interaction of the objects in SM with objects in DT. If o1, o2 $\in$ SM, then an interaction of o1 $\in$ SM with an o2 $\in$ SM is inherently more complicated than an interaction of an o1 $\in$ SM with o2 $\in$ DT, due to the passive state of the DT objects. The interactions of SM objects with other SM objects should be weighted more heavily than interactions of SM objects with DT objects. Thus, we propose a third level of characterization as a tuple

$C_3 = (ISM, IDT)$

where ISM = interactions of SM objects with SM objects.

IDT = interactions of SM objects with DT objects.

The tuple supplies separate information for the SM and DT visibility. The interactions are computed separately in order to make possible the flexibility of assigning a weight factor to the different types of interactions. Thus, this characterization is based on the type of visibility present within the abstract state machine objects.

These three characterization measures provide objective evaluation information about the difficulty of the problem as it is presented early in the requirements phase. These measures are based on solution objects, objects that instigate actions, number of actions instigated, and types of interactions with other objects. The validation of these measures relative to an evaluation of problem difficulty can be approached from different perspectives. First, we note that we have presented measures that are intended to characterize the initial requirements document from the perspective of the objects and their associated actions. We have not developed a model or formula that produces a difficulty factor or a definitively specified relationship. In MacClennon (1982), three approaches to metrics evaluation are discussed. The first approach suggests that a formal metric evaluation should generally produce agreement with an informal evaluation. The second approach suggests that properties of a formal measure should agree with properties of the informal measure. Thirdly, a formal evaluation should be the initial step in the development of a theory that has strong predictive and explanatory powers.

These three validation approaches relate to these characterizations in the following manner. First, this characterization is intended to supersede the informal subjective analysis by providing a formalized evaluation methodology. Thus, we contend that while a certain level of agreement should hold, much of the value of the characteristics come from identification of object information that is not immediately available through an informal, subjective analysis.

The second approach of reasonable properties is applicable. An informal evaluation suggests that a document with ten solution objects presents a more difficult problem than a document with five solution objects. In addition, an informal evaluation suggests that a document that describes five objects that instigate actions involving other active objects presents a more difficult problem than a document with five objects that instigate actions involving only passive objects. Thus, these characterizations do not violate properties that are expected in an informal appraisal.

The third approach to validation relates to the use of the measures in a broader model relating to specific prediction characteristics. The development of this type of model, based on these object characteristics, is desirable. Validation for such a model should include a tracing of the software system through specification, design, coding, testing, and implementation. This traceable information can then be used to compare the model with the actual difficulty of system implementation.

METHODOLOGY FOR QUANTIFICATION OF OBJECT CHARACTERISTICS

We have developed a system designed to model the initial user requirements from an object-oriented perspective. The system KAPS, Knowledge-based Assistance for Program Specifications, develops a specification environment which supports an object-based requirements analysis modeling process. From the model, we can compute, in a straightforward manner, the characterizations cited in the previous section. The KAPS methodology is a combination of an automated analysis supported by interactive user input at the early stages. The input to the system is the user's document, represented in a natural language format. The document is transformed by a parse module into an internal parsed structure. The parsing process performs a syntactic parse in a sentence-by-sentence fashion. From the LISP parsed structures, the information is converted to a set of knowledge base facts that follow a predefined, standardized representation scheme. Representation formats for system events, object properties, and object hierarchies are utilized. Following the establishment of the facts, analysis is performed that is intended to enhance the reliability, testability, and traceability of the information in the initial user's document.

Based on the information in the knowledge base, KAPS provides an automated process that generates an object-oriented specification. Initially, all objects in the requirements document are identified. An object is classified as a live object if it functions as an actor or a recipient within a system event. In addition, system attributes that function as event objects are included in the live object set if they require separate modeling. Separate modeling is required if the event object is visible to more than one object in the live object set, if it has properties that function as actors or recipients, or if its visibility is increased due to a property defined for another object. Objects that do not require separate modeling are considered as internal objects.

From the live object set, the solution objects are selected. The criteria for inclusion in the solution object set is that the object is not a property of another live object. Once the solution objects are established, further analysis is done to determine whether each object initiates action. Objects that initiate action are classified as abstract state machines and objects that only suffer actions are classified as abstract data types. Additional analysis is performed by KAPS to identify properties, action definition, and definition of objects contained within a solution object. A comprehensive treatment of KAPS is provided in Cordes (1988).

KAPS produces a model in a predefined template format that describes the results of the analysis of the objects, operations, and visibilities. From this model, the three characterizations introduced in the previous section can be computed.

OBJECT ORIENTED REQUIREMENTS MODEL - AN EXAMPLE

An example of the model produced by KAPS is provided for the following portion of a requirements specification. This specification is a modification of a specification found in EVB Software Engineering's *Object-Oriented Design Handbook* (1985).

"Senders may create letters and send letters. The system deposits letters in the appropriate mailbox. Receivers may check their mailbox for mail. Receivers may remove letters from the mailbox, read letters and discard old letters. Receivers may also replace letters in their mailbox."

Solution Objects

letter
receiver
sender
system

Object-Oriented Model

package letter

        model   Abstract Data Type
        requires   < >
        contains   < >
        end   letter

package receiver

        model   Abstract State Machine
        requires   letter
        contains   < >
        procedure   check [mailbox:*internal*]
      -- receiver check mailbox for mail
        procedure remove [letter:*external*]
      -- receiver remove letter from mailbox

Table 1

Mail Object Characteristics

System	T	S	SM	DT	Actions	SM Interactions	DT Interactions
Mail	5	4	3	1	8	0	7

```
procedure read [letter:external]
   -- receiver read letter
procedure discard [letter:external]
   -- receiver discard old [letters that have not
         been read and are no longer needed] letter
procedure replace [letter:external]
   -- receiver replace letter also in mailbox
internal   mailbox
```
end receiver

package sender
```
model       Abstract State Machine
requires    letter
contains    < >
procedure create [letter:external]
   -- sender create letter
procedure send [letter:external]
   -- sender send letter
```
end sender

package system
```
model       Abstract State Machine
requires    letter
contains    < >
procedure   deposit [letter:external]
   -- system deposit letter in appropriate [the
         mailbox that matches address on letter]
               mailbox
```
end system

In this example, five objects were identified from the initial document, T = {letter, mailbox, receiver, sender, system}. Four solution objects were identified, S = {letter, receiver, sender, system}. The first object *letter* was classified as an abstract data type and the remaining three objects were classified as abstract state machines because they initiated actions. Thus, SM = {receiver, sender, system} and DT

Table II

Mail SM Object Information

Object	Actions	Interactions with SM	Interactions with DT
receiver	5	0	4
sender	2	0	2
system	1	0	1

Table III

Package Object Characteristics

System	T	S	SM	DT	Actions	SM Interactions	DT Interactions
Package	9	7	6	1	8	2	4

= {letter}. Each of the three objects in SM requires the DT object *letter*. For the SM object *receiver*, five procedures (actions) are identified. Four of the procedures have the same DT object, *letter*, as the recipient of the action. The fifth procedure utilizes the object *mailbox* which is modeled internally. The SM object *sender* instigates two actions with the DT object *letter* as the recipient of both actions. The object *system* instigates one action with the DT object *letter* as its recipient. The DT object *letter* is thus visible to each object in SM. This visibility is through four unique actions within *receiver*, two unique actions within *sender*, and one action within *system*. These enumerations are summarized in Tables I and II. Evaluation of the three characterization measures provides:

$$C_1 = 4$$
$$C_2 = 11$$
$$C_3 = (0,7)$$

This mail system can be described as a system that contains four primary objects, three objects that instigate a total of eleven actions, and no interactions among active objects. Information supplied in Table II is useful for determining complexity levels of individual objects and their associated actions. Clearly, the object *receiver* is responsible for the highest number of actions, but it does not interact with other active objects.

ADDITIONAL SYSTEM CHARACTERIZATIONS

The characterization of an additional system is given below. The characterization is based on results of the application of KAPS to the initial requirements document. This document is a modified version of a requirements document cited in Swartout and Balzer (1986).

Initial Requirements Document

"The package router is a system that distributes packages into destination bins. The packages arrive at the source station which routes the packages to the destination bin. The station is connected by pipes to the destination bins. The pipes are connected by two-position switches. The switches route the package down the pipes. An optical reader scans the packages at the source station. The optical reader determines the destination bin. The package waits briefly in the exit pipe as the package router sets the switch positions. After the switches are checked, the package is released down the pipe."

Object Information

T = {destination bin, package, package router, pipe, reader, source station, switch, switch position, system}

S = {package, package router, pipe, reader, source station, switch, system}

SM = {package router, pipe, reader source station, switch, system}

DT = {package}

Table IV

Package SM Object Information

Object	Actions	Interactions with SM	Interactions with DT
package router	1	0	0
pipe	1	1	0
reader	2	0	1
source station	1	0	1
switch	2	1	1
system	1	0	1

The object information is summarized in Tables III and IV. The characterizations are

$C_1 = 7$
$C_2 = 14$
$C_3 = (2,4)$

The system can be characterized as a system that contains seven solution objects, six objects that instigate fourteen actions, and two objects that each interact with another active object. Clearly, the objects *reader* and *switch* are more complex than the other objects due to their activity levels.

These characterizations measures applied to the two example documents in this paper have identified the number of objects that play an integral role in the problem. This type of information is useful for an analysis to determine the difficulty of the problem. The measures have also identified the role the objects perform in the problem and have classified the actions based on the state of the recipient objects. The object classification information provides an added dimension to the description of the objects, their visibility, and the relationship among the objects. Thus, these measure provide a descriptive framework that supports the early activities of the requirements definition process.

SUMMARY

In this paper, we have defined three characterizations techniques for application to the initial requirements document. These characterizations are for the purpose of providing objective information for use with the estimation and predictive processes that are required at the requirements level. Thus, they are presented as descriptive tools. The first characterization is based on objects that function as actors or recipients of other objects, but are not properties of other objects. This measure provides a method to identify the solution objects that are central to the functions of the system.

The second characterization is based on the role each of the solution objects has in the system. It identifies those objects that actually instigate actions and quantifies the number of actions that are instigated. This information provides a method to identify objects that are participating in the system's actions and to what degree they are active.

The third characterization is based on a visibility analysis of the objects. It quantifies the visibility of each object and also quantifies visibility in terms of other action producing objects and other passive objects. This information provides a method to identify those objects that have a complex level of interaction with other active objects.

The primary goal of these characterization measures is to reduce the level of subjectivity in the evaluation of the difficulty of the problem, early in the requirements process. These characterizations are of increased value when compared with characterizations of previous projects in similar environments. In addition to the subjectivity reduction, these characterizations provide support for the determination of the suitability of an object-oriented approach to the development of the system. Finally, these characterizations indicate potentially complex portions of the problem. An object having a high number of interactions with other active objects constitutes a potentially complex factor in the system.

We have presented measurable characteristics of the initial requirements document from an object-oriented viewpoint. We have also described an automated system that supports the computation of these characteristics. Further work in this area includes validation of a specific relationship of these individual characteristics to problem difficulty and the development of a difficulty model based on a combination of these characterizations.

REFERENCES

Abbott, R. J., 1983, Program Design by Informal English Descriptions, *Communications of the ACM*, Vol. 26, No. 11, pp. 882-984.

Alford, M., 1977, A Requirements Engineering Methodology for Real Time Processing Requirements, *IEEE Trans on Soft Eng*, Vol. SE-3, No. 1.

Booch, G., 1986, Object-Oriented Development, *IEEE Trans Soft Eng*, Vol. SE-12,No. 2, pp. 211-221.

Charette, Robert N., 1986, *Software Engineering Environment Concepts and Technology*, McGraw Hill, New York.

Conte, S. D., Dunsmore, H. E., and Shen, V. Y., 1986, *Software Engineering Metrics and Models*, Benjamin/Cummings, Menlo Park, CA.

Cordes, David W., 1988, *An Object-Oriented Paradigm for Requirements Specification*, Ph.D. Thesis, Louisiana State University.

EVB Software Engineering, 1985, *Object-Oriented Design Handbook*, EVB Software Engineering, Inc.

Halstead, M. H., 1977, *Elements of Software Science*, Elsevier North-Holland, New York.

Jackson, M. A., 1983, *System Development*, Prentice-Hall.

Kearney, Joseph K., Sedlmeyer, Robert L., Thompson, William B., Gray, Michael A., and Adler, Michael A., 1986, Software Complexity Measurement, *Communications of the ACM*, Vol. 29, No. 11, pp. 1044-1050.

MacClennon, Bruce J., 1982, Simple Metrics for Programming Languages, *Symposium on Empirical Foundations of Information and Software Science*, November 1982.

McCabe, Thomas J., 1976, A Complexity Measure, *IEEE Trans Soft Eng*, Vol. SE-2, No. 4, pp. 308-320.

Ramamoorthy, C. V., Garg, Vijay, and Prakash, Aterl, 1986, Programming in the Large, *IEEE Trans Soft Eng*, Vol. SE-12, No. 7, pp. 769-783.

Swartout, William, and Balzer, Robert, 1986, On the Inevitable Intertwining of Specification and Implementation, *Software Specification Technology*, Gehani, N., and McGettrick, A. D., eds., Addison-Wesley, Workingham, Eng.

Yeh, Raymond T., Zave, Pamela, Conn, Alex Paul, and Cole, George E., Jr., 1984, Software Requirements: New Directions and Perspectives, *Handbook of Software Engineering*, Vick, C. R., and Ramamoorthy, C. V., eds., Van Nostrand, New York.

COMPARISON OF SUBJECTIVE ENTROPY AND

USER ESTIMATES OF SOFTWARE COMPLEXITY

John Stephen Davis, Melody J. Davis, and
Monique M. Law

Department of Management
Clemson University
Clemson, SC

Abstract: We investigated subjective entropy, a new information-theoretic measure of program comprehensibility which accounts for semantics and pragmatics involved in programmer-program interaction. Student subjects were administered subjective entropy tests on program samples in dBase III and Lotus 1-2-3 Macro Languages. Since the test employed an automated tool and required an average of only 20 minutes, we found it practical to administer. Subjective entropy scores indicated that the program in Lotus 1-2-3 macro language was more difficult to understand. The scores were consistent with expert opinion and with the subjective ratings of the subjects.

INTRODUCTION

Most of the current approaches to measuring software complexity are linked to syntactic properties of program code. One of the main problems is that such measures are based on assumption that the syntactic properties of a program influence programmer understanding (and hence programmer tasks) regardless of the skill and experience of the programmer (Kearney, et. al., 1986). Intuitively, measures which account for the programmer-program relationship should be more useful than those which consider only the program code.

Thus we were motivated to investigate a new measure, Subjective Entropy, which accounts for not only the syntactics, but also for semantics and pragmatics involved in programmer-program interaction. We planned to evaluate the Subjective Entropy measure by comparing Subjective Entropy scores with subjects' ratings of program complexity. We also hoped to learn more about the practicality of the Subjective Entropy procedure and the suitability of the interactive software tool we employed to administer tests.

THE SUBJECTIVE ENTROPY MEASURE

Subjective Entropy was adapted by Zunde (1985) from a technique used by Shannon (1951) to measure natural language comprehension. In Shannon's procedure, a subject guesses a missing letter of a randomly selected portion of a text. The tester says "correct" or "wrong". If the guess is wrong, the test continues until the correct letter has been chosen. This guessing process is repeated for a certain number of missing letters. Shannon's measure of the subject's comprehension of the text is derived from the number of wrong guesses for each letter.

Adapting Shannon's approach to the measurement of computer program comprehension required making it less labor-intensive for both the experimenter and the subject. To allow the administrator to handle more than one subject at a time, Zunde (1985) developed an automated tool to apply the Subjective Entropy measure. After several experiments were conducted with this minicomputer-based tool, we redesigned the tool to run on the IBM Personal Computer to facilitate administering tests and to increase portability. The tool includes a "guessing aid" to expedite the process of choosing each missing character in the program sample. The screen displays a portion of the program sample, with one character deleted. The characters of the programming language are divided into two groups, which are displayed at the bottom of the screen. The subject may either guess a specific character or, if unsure of the correct letter, choose the group that he believes is most likely to contain the correct character. After each selection of one of the groups, whether or not it contains the right letter, and also after any wrong guess of a specific character, the display at the bottom of the screen is modified such that the previous correct group is split to form new left-hand and right-hand groups. A subject is free at any time to either select a specific character or choose one of the groups. The subject continues to guess until he has selected the right letter, or until it is the only remaining possibility. The goal of the subject is to make as few wrong choices as possible.

The Subjective Entropy score is derived from the number of wrong guesses in the following way (Zunde's (1985) report provides a more detailed discussion). Let p be the number of wrong guesses divided by the maximum number of possible guesses. Then Subjective Entropy (H) is calculated as follows:

$$H = 5p - (5/2)[p \log(p) + (1 - p)\log(1 - p)].$$

Since this value is based on the information-theoretic notion of uncertainty, called entropy, a lower score indicates less uncertainty (and thus greater comprehension).

PROGRAM SAMPLES USED IN THE EVALUATION

Our experiment was oriented on the available subjects, 19 undergraduate students enrolled in a course in business software. We chose program samples in Lotus 1-2-3 macro and dBase III, because students gained hands-on experience with these software packages during the course. We adopted the Lotus program from a popular textbook (Duffy and Duffy, 1987, pages 60- 62). The dBase program was written by the authors to perform the same function as the Lotus program (see Appendix A).

In accordance with Zunde's (1985) procedure for administering tests, we randomly deleted 78 characters in each program sample. Appendix B shows the deletions for the dBase program.

EXPERIMENTAL PROCEDURE

We wished to test the null hypothesis that subjects' intuitive ratings of program complexity would be uncorrelated with their Subjective Entropy scores. Of secondary interest was to determine whether subjects performed differently with the two program samples, and whether their performance was associated with indicators of their academic achievement.

Table 1

Subjective Entropy Scores at
Beginning (End) of Semester

Lotus	3.46	(3.03)
dBase	1.30	(1.47)

Table 2

Correlations of Student Grade Point
Averages (BPA) with Subjective Entropy
Scores at Beginning (End) of Semester

	Overall GPA	Computer-Related Course GPA	No. of Computer-Related Courses
Lotus	.01 (.43)	-.42 (-.41)	-.10 (.23)
dBase	.04 (.17)	-.08 (.19)	-.26 (.27)

We conducted tests in the second week and during the last week of the semester, using our interactive tool running on an IBM PC. Each subject took both a Lotus and a dBase test, one immediately after the other. Half the subjects, selected at random, took the Lotus test first, and half took the dBase test first.

We repeated the tests during the last week of the semester. The program samples were the same as those in the first tests. Since we again randomly deleted characters in the samples, the deleted characters were not the same as in the first tests. At the conclusion of these tests, subjects completed a questionnaire about the tests.

RESULTS

We calculated relative performance by subtracting the Subjective Entropy value for the dBase test from the value for the Lotus test. We found that the correlation of subjects' intuitive ratings with performance at the end of the semester was .59 ($p < .01$).

The intuitive ratings were based on responses to the questionnaire. Subjects indicated which program was easier to understand, using a "semantic differential" scale (Osgood, 1967), where -3.5 represented "Lotus much easier" and +3.5 represented "dBase much easier."

The average response to the aforementioned question was 1.8. Of the 19 subjects, 18 rated dBase easier to understand. In both test sessions, performance was better for the dBase than for the Lotus program (Table 1).

None of the indicators of academic achievement was significantly correlated with performance on any of the tests (Table 2).

DISCUSSION

The better performance with dBase and the general preference of dBase are consistent with the intuition of the authors. The Lotus macro language has been criticized by others for its lack of clarity (Xenakis, 1987). Subjective Entropy seems to have accounted for the easier comprehensibility of the program in the dBase language.

Table 3

Time to Complete Test in Minutes
at Beginning (End) of Semester

Lotus	16.8	(12.6)
dBase	8.9	(8.6)

The insignificant correlations of indicators of academic achievement with Subjective Entropy suggest that this measure accounts for something other than general ability of the subject.

Administration of the tests was straightforward. None of the subjects expressed any confusion about the testing procedure. Tests averaged less than 20 minutes in duration (Table 3) not counting verbal instructions and a practice exercise. The maximum overall time (for the slowest subject to complete a Lotus test at the beginning of the semester) was 39 minutes.

CONCLUSION

This experiment provided strong evidence that the Subjective Entropy test is practical to administer. Strong claims concerning the validity of the measure must await further investigation. We cannot be sure without further evidence that this measure would work in the same manner for larger programs or programs in other languages. Since our subjects were novices, we cannot assume that any of our findings pertain to professional programmers.

ACKNOWLEDGMENT

This work was partially supported by the National Science Foundation under Grants No. CCR-8712816 and CCR-8804393.

REFERENCES

Duffy, T. and Duffy, W., 1987, *A Casebook: Four Software Tools*, Wadsworth Pub. Co., Belmont, CA.

Kearney, J. K., Sedlmeyer, R. L., Thompson, W. B., Gray, M. A., and Adler, M. A., 1986, Software Complexity Measurement, *Comm. of the ACM*, Vol. 29 No. 11, pp. 1044-1050.

Shannon, C.E., 1951, Prediction and Entropy of Printed English, *Bell System Technical Journal 30*, pp. 50-64.

Zunde, P., 1985, *An Information-Theoretical Metric for Testing Program Comprehension*, AIRMICS Tech. Rep. RARI-85-1, Atlanta, Georgia.

Xenakis, J.J., 1987, 1-2-3: A Dangerous Language, *Computerworld*, June, pp. 31-34.

APPENDIX A -- Part of the dBase III Sample Program Used in Experiments (see Appendix B for deleted characters in this part)

```
SET TALK OFF
USE dept_sales
APPEND BLANK
REPLACE dept WITH "Deli"
REPLACE last_year WITH 700
REPLACE this_year WITH 575
REPLACE change WITH this_year - last_year
REPLACE pct_change WITH change / last_year * 100

APPEND BLANK
REPLACE dept WITH "Bakery"
REPLACE last_year WITH 1000
REPLACE this_year WITH 1100
REPLACE change WITH this year - last_year
REPLACE pct_change WITH change / last_year' * 100
```

```
SET TALK OFF
USE dept_sales
APPEND BLANK
REPLACE dept WITH "Deli"
REPLACE last_year WITH 700
REPLACE this_year WITH 575
REPLACE change WITH this_year - last_year
REPLACE pct_chang      change / last_year * 100

APPEND BLANK
REPLACE dept WITH "Bakery"
REPLACE last_year WITH 1000
REPLACE this_year WITH 1100
R      change WITH this_year - last_year
REPLACE pct_change WIT ge / last_year * 100
```

A METRICS-DRIVEN APPROACH TO THE AUTOMATIC ACQUISITION OF

SOFTWARE ENGINEERING KNOWLEDGE

Robert G. Reynolds

Dept. of Computer Science
Wayne State University
Detroit, Michigan 48202

Abstract: The goal of the Partial Metrics Project is to develop a quantitative basis within which to describe the development of software modules using the stepwise refinement of pseudocode.

Metrics-based acquisition of the knowledge structures needed by a model of module design process is outlined. Partial metrics are used to guide the acquisition process to constrain the complexity of the resultant knowledge structures. This should support the efficient reuse of these structures by the programming model. The current prototype which is under development on a TI Explorer Lisp workstation is discussed.

INTRODUCTION

Herbert Simon (1986) suggested that one of the bottlenecks in the automation of software design was the lack of quantitative information about the design process. It is the goal of the Partial Metrics project to develop quantitative models of decision-making activities performed at different phases of the software life-cycle. These models are then to be used as a basis for the acquisition of software engineering knowledge about the relevant phases.

Currently, the focus of the project is on the implementation phase of the life-cycle. The specific decisions of interest are those that underlie the implementation of code in an arbitrary target language in terms of successive stepwise refinements of a pseudocode description. The examples used as a basis for generating the associated models come primarily from the software engineering literature. The resultant models reflect the external results of a programmer's reasoning process as opposed to the internal mechanisms whereby these decisions are achieved. The latter topic has been the focus of research by Soloway and others (Johnson and Soloway, 1987).

METRICS TO DESCRIBE THE EXTERNAL EFFECTS OF REFINEMENT DECISIONS

The external effects of a refinement decision can be manifest in two basic ways:

1.   A change in the syntactic structure of the pseudocode program.

2.   A change in the implementation subgoals associated with pseudocode program.

In order to measure the effect of a refinement decision it was necessary to produce measures to quantitatively assess the changes in each. Partial metrics were developed as a means to describe changes in a pseudocode program's structural complexity (Reynolds, 1984). A partial metric is computed relative to a specific model of a pseudocode or partial program. In terms of this model, each program consists of

Empirical Foundations of Information and Software Science V
Edited by P. Zunde and D. Hocking, Plenum Press, New York, 1990

385

a projected part and a prescribed part. The prescribed part corresponds to reserved words and symbols in the target language.

The projected part corresponds to implementation tasks that remain to be carried out by the programmer. These tasks are represented in the code by the presence of stubs. The position of each stub in the code implicitly determines the syntactic class associated with that stub. The implied syntactic class is a characterization of the implementation task in syntactic terms.

A variety of metrics had been developed by software engineers to assess the structural complexity of completed code programs that have only a prescribed component. A partial metric is one that is able to compute the contribution of both the prescribed and the projected part in order to produce an overall estimate of structural complexity. It was demonstrated that a number of standard metrics, such as McCabe's, McClure's, and Halstead's, can be extended to measure the complexity of pseudocode programs. These extended metrics are especially good predictors of complexity when the code is less than 75% prescribed.

A second class of metrics was developed to measure the change in subgoal complexity as the result of a refinement. These metrics are termed refinement metrics and measure language support for refinement decisions (Reynolds, 1988). In particular, they are used to estimate the decision-making effort associated with the implementation of a program stub into completed code.

Two contributions to effort are measured explicitly by these metrics. First, the distance to the goal of complete implementation is measured in terms of grammatical production. This measurement is called elaboration depth. Second, the number of choices to be made in each step is measured by elaboration breadth. The two contributions are combined to produce an overall index of effort termed refinement volume. Further discussion of these metrics can be found in (Reynolds, 1987).

Partial metrics and refinement metrics have been used to characterize heuristics associated with particular decisions that underlie the refinement process (Reynolds, 1987). One such heuristic is a rule to resolve conflicts in the refinement process. That is, if there exists more than one projected term or stub in the current pseudocode, which one should be refined next. The specific rule was capable if predicting the designers choice in over 95% of those refinements where choices existed.

THE CURRENT PROTOTYPE

The current prototype of the Partial Metrics System has 3 components, each of which is implemented in LISP on an Explorer LX workstation. The components are a refinement engine, a knowledge compiler, and a knowledge base. The refinement engine, like that of Barstow (1979), is rule-based. It takes appropriate refinement plans from the knowledge base and uses them to generate implemented code for some specified language. The rules that make up the system are language independent. They require both a description of a grammar for the target language and a refinement plan in order to produce implemented code.

The refinement plans are expressed as semantic networks using a syntax similar to that of Barstow (Barstow, 1979). A refinement plan is generated from an existing code module by the knowledge compiler. The knowledge compiler works by applying the rules from the refinement engine in reverse order on the target module. The result is the generation of a hierarchy of successively more abstract descriptions of the module by removing selected code segments (or chunks) from the program and replacing them with stubs. Each of these chunks is then described as a semantic network, expressed using concepts in the selected grammar. Next, the individual refinements are combined to form a semantic network that represents a tree of refinements required to instantiate a version of the target module. The final step will involve the generation of a set of conditions for the triggering of this plan during this refinement process. This latter step has yet to be implemented.

Both the knowledge compiler and refinement engine are language independent, and, therefore, require a specification of the BNF grammar for the target language. At this time grammars for Ada, C, OPS5, Pascal, and Prolog are available. Presently, the system has been used to generate plans for small (10-25 lines) structured programs in Pascal. Future work will include use of the existing system with larger programs and the automatic generation of triggering conditions for plans.

ACKNOWLEDGEMENTS

This research has been supported in part by the Institute for Manufacturing Research, and in part by the Institute for Information and Technology.

REFERENCES

Barstow, David, 1979, *Knowledge Based Program Construction*, Elsevier-Holland, New York, NY.

Johnson and Soloway, 1987, PROUST: An Automatic Debugger for Pascal Programs, *Artificial Intelligence and Instruction*, Kearsley, G., ed., pp. 49-67. Addison-Wesley, Reading, MA.

Reynolds, Robert G., 1984, Metrics to Measure the Complexity of Partial Programs, *J. Syst. Software*, Vol. 4, (1), pp. 75-91, April 1984.

Reynolds, Robert G., 1987, Metric Based Reasoning About Pseudocode Design in the Partial Metrics System, *Information and Software Technology*, Vol. 29, No. 9, pp. 497-502, November, 1987.

Reynolds, Robert G., and Maletic, J., 1988, *Refinement Metrics: Measures of Decision-Making Effort in the Stepwise Refinement Process*, Department of Computer Science Research Report, Wayne State University, September, 1988.

Simon, Herbert, 1986, Whether Software Engineering Needs to be Artificially Intelligent?, *IEEE Transactions on Software Engineering*, Vol. SE-12, No. 12, pp. 762-732, July, 1986.

IX. SOFTWARE ENGINEERING

OBSERVING ADA SOFTWARE COMPONENTS

Byoungju Choi, Rich DeMillo, Weimin Du,
and Ryan Stansifer

Purdue University
West Lafayette, IN 47907

Abstract: The constant need to judge the reliability of software components does not end after the component is operational. Obtaining a history of a component's performance requires the capability to observe and record the execution of a component. We examine various ways in which this can be done in the context of the Ada programming language. We discuss how the observation can be integrated with the software development environment.

1.   INTRODUCTION

In his introduction to the special issue of *IEEE Software* on reuse (Tracz, 1987), Will Tracz likens used programs to used cars. He identifies several key issues in their reuse: standard features, mileage, maintenance records, reputation, appearance, standards, and warranty. We are interested in providing the prospective customer honest information about the mileage and maintenance record of used programs.

In reuse environments, software components are designed, tested, used, and sometimes checked in and out of libraries of reusable components. By the same token, building systems in reuse environments involves building portions of the system following a "normal" software development process and reusing some components that are available in the reuse library. There is current interest in adapting or exploiting features of Ada and other modern programming languages to enable and facilitate reuse on the assumption overall system development costs will decrease as a result (Biggerstaff and Richter, 1987; Freeman, 1983; Tracz, 1988).

It would, of course, be very helpful if component reuse could also be used to enhance system quality. This is an especially attractive concept in reuse environments since components that have been used previously have an operational history that may be a good indicator of overall quality. For example, a library component that is supposed to be very reliable may, in fact, have undergone major and catastrophic failures when it was used in previous designs. Another component may have performed with flawless robustness over such a length of time and in so many different settings that its reliability in a specified new design is highly likely.

Since such historical information persists beyond syntactically or semantically meaningful activations of a component, new mechanisms, protocols and design guidelines are probably required to enable reuse engineers to also reuse operational histories. This paper investigates some possible approaches to providing such capabilities. The principle concept developed is the *observation* of Ada packages.

Observations are defined and recorded by triggering certain events. The nature of the events which trigger the observation varies depending on the kind of application being considered. We have identified four types of observations:

1.   Security Observations - these observations are defined by access events.

2.   Usage Profile Observations - these observations are defined by frequency and context of activation or invocation.

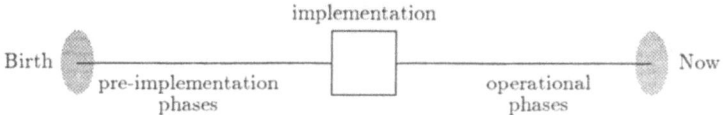

Figure 1. The Lifecycle Diagram.

3.   Reliability Observations - these observations are used to record reliability events such as failure or fault invocation.

4.   Performance Observations - these observations are used to record operational values of non-functional engineering parameters such as execution efficiency, memory utilization, or performance relative to a fixed set of criteria.

An observation package is an Ada package that is bound to a reused component at the moment the component is checked out of the reuse library. The observation package records observations made during the operational use of the component. A check-in procedure is then used to detach the reused component and the record of check-in procedure is then used to detach the reused component and the record of observations from the library, which are used to update a log file in the reuse library.

2.   SOFTWARE LIFECYCLE AND REUSE

It is widely recognized that reuse can be applied to more than just code. In fact, reuse of design and specification may yield greater returns than reuse of code. It is our thesis that reuse can be extended to operational phases as well. Figure 1 shows a time line representing the life of a software component from conception to the present. In pre-implementation phases, designs and specifications can be reused. During implementation code can be reused. After implementation it is the operational experience that is reused.

It is our goal to design a software management environment which encourages and facilitates reuse that is appropriate at all stages of the lifecycle. We are particularly interested in generating and maintaining operational history. We give some examples of what this environment is like.

Example 1. Supposed that a fielded software component raises and handles some exception when some anomalous event happens. We wish to know how often this actually occurs. We check the component out of the library again, this time specifying that we want to observe exceptions, and put the component back into operation. Later we query how often the exception was raised and what routines handled it.

Example 2. We wish to know how many times some routines are called to know which ones are worth the trouble to optimize. We indicate which routines to monitor. After the execution we obtain a histogram.

Not all events worthy of observing take place after the software is fielded. It is possible to view debugging and testing as a special form of observation that takes place earlier in the software lifecycle. A unified view of software management as observation may prove useful in designing a consistent software development environment.

3.   METHODOLOGY

There are several ways to maintain the operational history of a software component. The most simple is to rely on a programming discipline. It could be a matter of policy that all programs be written with code to make the observations possible. Obviously, enforcement would be a problem. It would be better to have an environment that automatically inserts the observation mechanisms.

However, we envision a software management environment where observation is an integral part of all aspects of software development. At each point in the software lifecycle the developers have information relevant to the observation process. A software management environment will allow these insights to be recorded. For example, during the design of a software component it is obvious that certain segments of the component are used to recover from particular faults, say, the failure of some external sensor. The development environment should make use of this information to monitor that segment and log all failures of the sensor.

Clearly, the observation process must be in contact with the compiler to generate the extra steps needed to record the observations. A cooperative compiler can provide much useful analysis-syntax trees, basic block determination, etc. We envision an interaction with the compiler much like that of debugging. Consider the example of a C compiler with a debugging option. This option causes the compiler to generate certain instructions that the debugging program can effect, even after the program is compiled. An Ada compiler which optionally adds special observation code would be the most efficient approach.

We can approximate the modifications to a compiler for the Ada programming language, by giving a preprocessor which transforms an Ada source program to a semantically equivalent Ada program. This is the approach that we take here.

Figure 2 depicts how the observation process works. The first step is retrieval. The exact nature of this mechanism is not important for the present, with one exception. The mechanism must be able to select a software component based on its operational history. The second step is the linking. In this step the software component is modified to perform the observations required. This will require access to predefined observation packages. We are currently investigating the nature of these packages. The next step is the actual execution of the component. During the execution a log is written of the appropriate

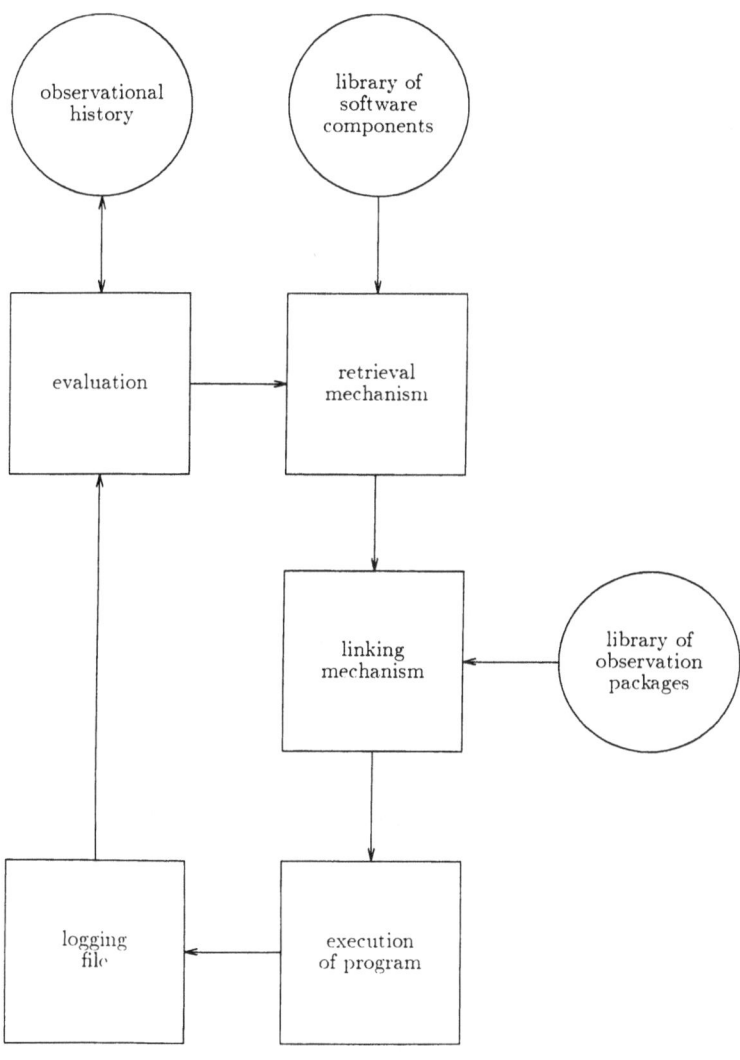

Figure 2. The Observation Process.

```
pragma    ::=  pragma observe (type, level);
type      ::=  exception | usage | pre_condition (condition) |
               post_condition (condition)
level     ::=  subprogram | basic_block | statement
```

Figure 3. Syntax for Pragma *Observe*.

events. The fourth step is the evaluation of the log and the merging of the log with any previous operational history.

Thus, we must address the following problems. How do we specify the kind of observation? How do we couple the operational history with a software component? How do we evaluate an observation log? We discuss each of these issues in the next sections.

4.   SPECIFICATION OF OBSERVATION

We assume that we have a library of Ada software components. By some retrieval mechanism (Owen, Gagliano, and Honkanen, 1988) an Ada component is removed from the library. According to the requirements of the observation, the Ada source is transformed. The transformed source is compiled and then run. The new observational results are then merged with the observational history of the component.

In this section, we focus on how to specify the observation process and the transformation process. The language is shown in Figure 3.

The pragma *observe* applies to all relevant program segments after the pragma is encountered in the course of compiling the program. The pragma command *pragma observe off* ends the extent of the library unit text relevant to the previous *pragma*. The "scope" of the text which will perform any observations is intervening text or the rest of the file. That is similar to the *pragma list* (United States Department of Defense, 1983).

There are several varieties of observations. The first argument to the *observe* pragma specifies the kind of observation to be performed. The following is a list of those that we have studied.

1. *usage*: Counts the number of times the program unit is executed.

2. *exception*: Logs which program unit raises an exception and which exception handlers handle it.

3. *pre_condition*: Verifies that the condition is true before the execution of every program unit.

4. *post_condition*: Verifies that the condition is true after the execution of every program unit.

Other kinds of observations will certainly be desired.

The second argument to the *observe* pragma specifies the level at which the observation is to take place. The level is the granularity or the frequency that the observation occurs. There are three levels:

1. *subprogram*
2. *basic_block*
3. *statement*

For purposes of explanation, we consider the *usage* observation at each of the three levels. At the *subprogram* level the number of times each subroutine is called is recorded. At the *basic_block* level the number of times each basic block is executed is recorded. At the *statement* level the number of times each statement is executed is recorded. Naturally, the finer the granularity the more events are observed, so the extra data comes at a cost.

5.   COUPLING THE HISTORY TO THE COMPONENT

The operational history of a software component must persist beyond the interval of time in which the component is actually executing. We take the usual solution in such cases and appeal to the outside

```
with OBSERVE, TRIANGLE_UTILS;

package EXAMPLE is
  type TRIANGLE is record
    EDGE1, EDGE2, EDGE3: real;
  end record;
  T: TRIANGLE;
  procedure SAMPLE_TRIANGLE;
  procedure TRANSFORM_TRIANGLE(X: TRIANGLE);
end EXAMPLE;

package body EXAMPLE is
use OBSERVE, TRIANGLE_UTILS;

pragma observe(type=>post_condition(T.EDGE1+T.EDGE2>T.EDGE3),
               level=>subprogram);

pragma observe(type=>usage,
               level=>subprogram);

procedure SAMPLE_TRIANGLE is
begin
  T.EDGE1 := SAMPLE_EDGE1;       -- in package TRIANGLE_UTILS;
  T.EDGE2 := SAMPLE_EDGE2;
  T.EDGE3 := SAMPLE_EDGE3;
end SAMPLE_TRIANGLE;

procedure TRANSFORM_TRIANGLE(X: TRIANGLE) is
begin
  T.EDGE1 := TRANSFORM_EDGE1(X); -- in package TRIANGLE_UTILS;
  T.EDGE2 := TRANSFORM_EDGE2(X);
  T.EDGE3 := TRANSFORM_EDGE3(X);
end TRANSFORM_TRIANGLE;

end EXAMPLE;
```

Figure 4. An Ada Program With the Pragma *Observe*.

environment, the operating system, to maintain the data in files. The observation packages maintain a number of files which are only indirectly accessible to the user. One file is kept for each kind of observation. When an observation is added to the file, the library unit being observed is written to the file. In this way the results of observations are linked to the programs being observed.

Eventually, a library data base will be used to maintain the observations and to provide access to the information stored. Queries about the performance of the software can be answered. This will be used both in the selection of software and by the maintainers of the library.

If Ada had some other mechanism for persistence, like some other languages (Atkinson and Buneman, 1987), then the observational history could be maintained entirely in Ada.

6.   EVALUATION OF OBSERVATIONS

Evaluation of the operational history of a software component appears to be difficult. The types of events that can be observed automatically are often too general to directly indicate the kinds of problems one would like to detect. Insofar as evaluation is possible there is no problem with integrating evaluation software. This software takes the observational results of some component as input and draws conclusions that may be useful to the retrieval mechanism or to the maintenance of the software library itself.

```
              with OBSERVE, TRIANGLE_UTILS;

              package EXAMPLE is
                type TRIANGLE is record
                  EDGE1, EDGE2, EDGE3: real;
                end record;
                T: TRIANGLE;
                procedure SAMPLE_TRIANGLE;
                procedure TRANSFORM_TRIANGLE(X: TRIANGLE);
              end EXAMPLE;

              package body EXAMPLE is
              use OBSERVE, TRIANGLE_UTILS;

              procedure SAMPLE_TRIANGLE is
              begin
                TRACE_IN((SUB_PROGRAM, "EXAMPLE    ", "SAMPLE_TRI"));
                USAGE;
                T.EDGE1 := SAMPLE_EDGE1;        -- in package TRIANGLE_UTILS;
                T.EDGE2 := SAMPLE_EDGE2;
                T.EDGE3 := SAMPLE_EDGE3;
                if not (T.EDGE1+T.EDGE2>T.EDGE3)
                  then POST_CONDITION("T.EDGE1+T.EDGE2>T.EDGE3");
                end if;
                TRACE_OUT;
              end SAMPLE_TRIANGLE;

              procedure TRANSFORM_TRIANGLE(X: TRIANGLE) is
              begin
                TRACE_IN((SUB_PROGRAM, "EXAMPLE    ", "TRANSFORM_"));
                USAGE;
                T.EDGE1 := TRANSFORM_EDGE1(X); -- in package TRIANGLE_UTILS;
                T.EDGE2 := TRANSFORM_EDGE2(X);
                T.EDGE3 := TRANSFORM_EDGE3(X);
                if not (T.EDGE1+T.EDGE2>T.EDGE3)
                  then POST_CONDITION("T.EDGE1+T.EDGE2>T.EDGE3");
                end if;
                TRACE_OUT;
              end TRANSFORM_TRIANGLE;

              end EXAMPLE;
```

Figure 5. After the Transformation.

7.   AN EXAMPLE

        In this section we consider an example demonstrating what effects the observation pragma has on
the execution of an Ada program and how the logging of observations actually takes place.
        In Figure 4 we show the source code of a simple component that might reside in the library of
reusable software components. The source code includes two observation pragmas. The first pragma is
to observe when a condition fails to hold. The condition is given as part of the arguments to the pragma.
The second pragma requests an execution count. Both pragmas have set the level to be *subprogram*. This
means that the events to be observed will be triggered by the entry and exit of subprograms.
        In this example, the scope of the pragmas includes two subprograms: the procedure *SAMPLE_*
TRIANGLE and the procedure *TRANSFORM_TRIANGLE*. These routines in the package *EXAMPLE*
provide the means to get the sides of a triangle and to transform the sides. *EDGE1, EDGE2,* and *EDGE3*
are the lengths of the tree sides. The first pragma has type *post_condition*. This type of pragma tests a
global assertion on exit of relevant program units. In this case the assertion is:

        T.EDGE1 + T.EDGE2 > T.EDGE3

```
TIME_STAMP: AUG. 1, 1988. 11:49:23
ACTIVATED: subprogram SAMPLE_TRI of package EXAMPLE

TIME_STAMP: AUG. 1, 1988. 11:51:02
ACTIVATED: subprogram TRANSFORM_ of package EXAMPLE

TIME_STAMP: AUG. 1, 1988. 11:59:31
ACTIVATED: subprogram TRANSFORM_ of package EXAMPLE

TIME_STAMP: AUG. 1, 1988. 11:59:50
ACTIVATED: subprogram SAMPLE_TRI of package EXAMPLE

TIME_STAMP: AUG. 1, 1988. 12:30:10
ACTIVATED: subprogram TRANSFORM_ of package EXAMPLE

TIME_STAMP: Aug. 1, 1988. 12:30:10
POST_CONDITION: T.EDGE1+T.EDGE2>T.EDGE3
FAILED_AT: subprogram TRANSFORM_ of package EXAMPLE

TIME_STAMP: AUG. 1, 1988. 12:49:16
ACTIVATED: subprogram SAMPLE_TRI of package EXAMPLE

TIME_STAMP: AUG. 1, 1988. 12:53:44
ACTIVATED: subprogram TRANSFORM_ of package EXAMPLE
```

Figure 6. The Log File.

and the assertion will be tested at the end of the two subprograms. This assertion, the triangular inequality, is a rough check on the validity of the data. The assertion must be a boolean valued expression. If its value is false, the event is recorded in the log file. If its value is true, then no action takes place. Notice that if the assertion was checked after every statement it would not hold as the values of *EDGE1*, *EDGE2*, and *EDGE3* are changed one at a time in the two subprograms.

The second pragma:

pragma observe (type = > usage, level = > subprogram);

requests that execution of the two procedures be noted.

The semantics of the observations enabled by the two pragmas can be seen in the next figure, Figure 5. This figure depicts an Ada program that explicitly records the events requested by the pragmas. As far as the user of the package is concerned there is no change in behavior. However, behind the scenes the requested observations are taking place, and are being logged.

A sample log is shown in Figure 6. The log indicates that the two procedures being observed were run seven times and that once the post condition failed. We anticipate that evaluation tools will be written to digest the observational history and aid in the judging of the software components.

The package specification of the observation package used in this example is shown in Figure 7. The observation package holds the bookkeeping routines necessary to perform the logging. A stack, called the tracing stack, is used to record when the execution of a program unit is begun. The procedure *TRACE_IN* pushes the stack. When the execution of the unit is complete the name of the unit is popped off the tracing stack. The procedure *TRACE_OUT* pops the stack. In this way the current unit being executed is maintained for logging purposes. The observation of exceptions poses a special problem in this regard. The elaboration of the declarative part of the subprogram raise an exception. Since it is most natural to associate this event with the subprogram (although the exception cannot be handled in the subprogram), it may be desirable to define the beginning of execution for a subprogram to be before elaboration. This can be achieved by putting the whole body of a program including its declarative part in a *begin-end* block.

8.   CONCLUSION

The methods we have used thus far assume that the software component resides in the library of components as Ada source code.   In practice one would   prefer the object code in order to avoid

```
package OBSERVE is

    type UNIT_NAME is (SUB_PROGRAM, BASIC_BLOCK, STATEMENT);

    -- location of program unit is identified by package
    -- name and procedure name
    type WHERE(OBS_LEVEL: UNIT_NAME) is
            record
              PACKAGE_ID, PROCEDURE_ID: string(1..10);
              case OBS_LEVEL is
                when SUB_PROGRAM => null;
                when BASIC_BLOCK => BLOCK_ID: positive;
                when STATEMENT   => STMT_ID: positive;
              end case;
            end record;

    procedure TRACE_IN(CURRENT: in WHERE);
      -- push the unit name CURRENT on the tracing stack

    procedure TRACE_OUT;
      -- pop the tracing stack

    procedure EXCEPTION_RECORDING(EXCE: in string; HANDLER: in WHERE);
      -- log the exception EXCE as handled in unit HANDLER
      -- the exception was raised in unit on top of tracing stack

    procedure PRE_CONDITION(PRE_COND: in string);
      -- log the condition PRE_COND as having failed at the beginning
      -- of the unit on top of the tracing stack

    procedure POST_CONDITION(POST_COND: in string);
      -- log the condition POST_COND as having failed at the end
      -- of the unit on top of the tracing stack

    procedure PROFILING;
      -- log the usage of the unit on top of tracing stack

  end OBSERVING
```

Figure 7. The Specification of the Observation Package.

recompiling the code every time it is checked out. This is possible with the compilers help. The observation code could be enabled by directly modifying the object code produced by the compiler. This is similar to what happens with a debugger.

Compiler assistance is critical in making the observation process efficient. The overhead of keeping track of the beginning and ending of program units is quite high. But cooperation with the compiler can make this overhead lower, especially in the case of monitoring exception handling.

ACKNOWLEDGEMENT

The authors wish to acknowledge the support of Contract Number 540-1398-0593 from AIRMICS and Martin Marietta Energy Systems.

REFERENCES

Atkinson, Malcolm P., and Buneman, O. Peter, 1987, Types and Persistence in Database Programming Languages, *ACM Computing Surveys*, Vol. 19, No. 2, June 1987, pp. 105-190.
Biggerstaff, R., and Richter, C., 1987, Reusability Framework, Assessment and Directions, *Proceedings of the Hawaii Conference on System Sciences*, January 7-10, 1987, pp. 530-535.

Freeman, P., 1983, Reusable Software Engineering: Concepts and Research Directions, *Proceedings of ITT Workshop on Reusability in Programming*, September 7, 1983.

Owen, G. S., Gagliano, R., and Honkanen, P., 1988, Tools for the Storage and Retrieval of Reusable MIS Software in Ada, *ACM 88 Computer Science Conference*, pp. 535-539.

Tracz, Will, 1987, Reusability Comes of Age, *IEEE Software*, July 1987, pp. 6-8.

Tracz, Will, 1988, Software Reuse Myths, *Software Engineering Notes*, Vol. 13, 1, January 1988, pp. 17-21.

United States Department of Defense, 1983, *Reference Manual for the ADA Programming Language*, United States Government Printing Office.

KEESEE: A BEHAVIORAL OBJECT-ORIENTED DATABASE FRAMEWORK FOR

SOFTWARE ENGINEERING

Jonathan Bein*[1], Bernard Bernstein*, Roger King*,
Jay Lightfoot**, Cathleen Wharton*,
and Emilie Young*

*Computer Science Department
University of Colorado
Boulder, Colorado 80309

**College of Business Administration
University of Colorado
Boulder, Colorado 80309

Abstract: In this paper, we discuss a research project, KeeSee (KEE[TM2] Software Engineering Environment), which is concerned with the support of software engineering environments (SEE's) by database systems. The general topic of database support for software engineering has recently received significant attention from the database community. In these projects it has been frequently noted that software engineering (and engineering in general) places a new set of constraints on a DBMS. A common theme in database research is that existing data models do not suffice to support the following characteristics of SEE's: long transactions, hierarchically structured objects, complex derived data, and version management. Current efforts to address the bottleneck in existing data models can be classified into two categories: object oriented systems and relational extensions.

The prototype KeeSee software is implemented in KEE, an object-oriented environment for constructing expert systems. KEE provides facilities for inheritance, hypothetical databases, rules, demons, queries, message passing, and truth maintenance. The KeeSee project makes particular use of the multiple inheritance in KEE and message passing in defining database functionality to support a SEE. Essentially, one defines the necessary database functionality through the multiple inheritance capabilities in KeeSee. Then, software tools are integrated by defining additional methods for object types. In this manner, the advantages of object-oriented programming are used to both define the database functionality and also to incorporate software tools. As a result, the KeeSee system has turned out to be easy to use and modular for implementers and users of the SEE.

There are two main results from this study. First, the breadth of functionality in KEE is an essential component for supporting future SEE's. Second, method inheritance and object specialization provide a powerful mechanism for defining the SEE as well as integrating tools. Combining these results with current trends in database support for software engineering suggests that an efficient implementation of a system like KEE, combined with database technology is an important component of the ultimate platform for software engineering.

---

[1]Also Bolder Heuristics, 1877 Broadway, Suite 405, Boulder, CO 80302.

[2]KEE[TM] is a trademark of Intellicorp Inc.

Empirical Foundations of Information and Software Science V
Edited by P. Zunde and D. Hocking, Plenum Press, New York, 1990

401

INTRODUCTION

In this paper, we discuss KeeSee, (KEE Software Engineering Environment), a prototype implementation of a toolkit aimed at providing database support for Software Engineering Environments (SEEs). The primary objective of the KeeSee research effort is to investigate behaviorally object-oriented implementations of database support for a SEE. A secondary objective is to study software reusability in a SEE through information retrieval. These objectives are further elaborated below.

Our pursuit of the primary objective is motivated by work within the object-oriented database community, which has focused on structurally object-oriented systems (SOOS) to support SEEs, e.g. DAMOKLES (Dittrich, Gottard, and Lockemann, 1986). As defined in Hull (Hull and King, 1987), structurally object- oriented systems use relationships as the main mechanism for modeling, whereas behaviorally objectoriented systems use message passing via methods. In contrast, KeeSee is used to investigate the use of behaviorally object-oriented systems (BOOS) as a framework for a SEE.

Related to our primary objective is the fact that many BOOS have a wide variety of associated software tools. Thus, the typical BOOS provides a great deal more than just an elegant programming paradigm - it is tool rich. However, at the onset of the KeeSee prototype, BOOS that were sufficiently tool rich for our purposes lacked transaction management, security, journaling, and recovery, etc. These database amenities (as defined in Maier, Stein, Otis, and Purdy (1986) are an integral part of a database management system (DBMS). As part of our primary objective, we intentionally sacrifice the performance gained from systems with database amenities in order to study the importance of various primitives from a BOOS[3]. This contrasts with the majority of work from the database community which has focused on fixing or designing efficient implementations of data models to address the demands of a SEE. The BOOS that we chose for our study is KEE (Knowledge Engineering Environment) because it is one system which provides an object-oriented representation with inheritance, as well as tools for user interface development, rule based programming constructs, and view maintenance. An introduction to KEE is provided in the Appendix.

Another aspect of our primary objective is to consider the use of a BOOS to support a variety of SEEs. For example, we want to support the database administrator who needs to maintain tight control over security privileges, as well as developers who operate in a loose research environment where the distinction between user and administrator is blurred. Achieving this objective is hard because it is difficult to assemble an appropriate collection of primitives for such a broad spectrum of functionality. If primitives are too application specific, then SEEs of one type may be more easily supported than another. If the primitives are too general, users spend too much time creating their own tools. As emphasized in Carey, DeWitt, Richardson and Shekita (1986), one should be able to assemble a DBMS to support different types of environments.

Our secondary objective concerns a mechanism for increasing software reuse. Information retrieval systems provide a means for accessing *documents* based on the (re)formulation of keyword queries. Data retrieval systems provide a means for accessing *records* via a query language. This aspect of the research effort emphasizes the importance of information retrieval (see Salton and McGill (1983) rather than data retrieval as a means for increasing software reusability. This emphasis is based on the intuition that software objects are more akin to documents in a document database, than records in a record database. Consequently, for KeeSee users, the central activity is the iterative reformulation of queries to retrieve software objects, not the generation of queries as in a conventional database query language such as SQL.

A preliminary conclusion of this research is that the functionality in a BOOS like KEE is extremely valuable for constructing an environment to support software engineering. However, for great advancement, this environment also requires database amenities and additional data modeling primitives. The remainder of this paper describes results gathered from the implementation of KeeSee. The next section of this paper covers the implementation approach that was used to augment KEE with database amenities and software engineering tools. The third section provides details about the design decisions and lessons learned in the implementation of the KeeSee toolkit. The fourth part demonstrates the progress made in the issue of information retrieval.

KEESEE ARCHITECTURE

As stated previously, the main goal of the KeeSee research effort was to investigate the use of a BOOS as a basis for SEEs. This approach contrasts with the database community's work to support SEEs through a SOOS. Both approaches seek to support the tough requirements imposed on a DBMS by

---

[3]As we will see, KeeSee provides database amenities using a BOOS.

standard engineering paradigms, i.e. interactive, long, and nested transactions, derived and hierarchically structured data, and version control. The selection of the software primitives that compose a framework which satisfies those requirements is a difficult one. In KeeSee, we attempted to minimize the tradeoff between general and specific primitives by providing a hierarchy of types of varying granularities. The granular approach allows a developer to locate the appropriate tool in the hierarchy, either by direct access or through the addition (as opposed to the modification) of primitive specifications.

KeeSee exploits the principles behind multiple inheritance and mixins as described in (Stefik and Bobrow, 1986). A *mixin* defines a class of objects that cannot be instantiated unless combined with other non-mixin classes. For example, one may define a *sweet and sour* mixin that is not instantiable unless it is combined with other independent classes like *chicken* or *shrimp*. The novel aspect of the KeeSee approach, is that *all* functionality, including database amenities, are mixins based on KEE objects.

As shown in Figure 1, KeeSee (at level three) is implemented on top of KEE which (in our system) runs on a Symbolics Lisp Machine. KEE, at level two, is built on top of Common LISP (at level one). KeeSee provides a set of mixins (at level three) that allow a database administrator to create a DBMS/SEE (at level four), within which an end developer can create user application programs (at level five). This set of mixins was chosen to allow database functionality and to provide for some basic software engineering utilities. As shown, KeeSee provides mixins for concurrency, security, project management, journaling and recovery, derivability, relationships, versioning, and graphability.

The main activity of a KeeSee DBA is to carefully choose the right combination of mixins for the desired DBMS/SEE. Figure 2 shows a small example of the use of these mixins. Here the *generic-software-object* class inherits from the *concurrency-mixin*, *security-mixin*, and *journaling-mixin*. The *generic-version-software-object* inherits from *generic-software-object* class and the *version-mixin*. The hexagonal objects in the figure typify the content at level four of the KeeSee architecture. Once this DBMS/SEE is established, a set of generic access methods associated with all KeeSee objects allows the user to create,

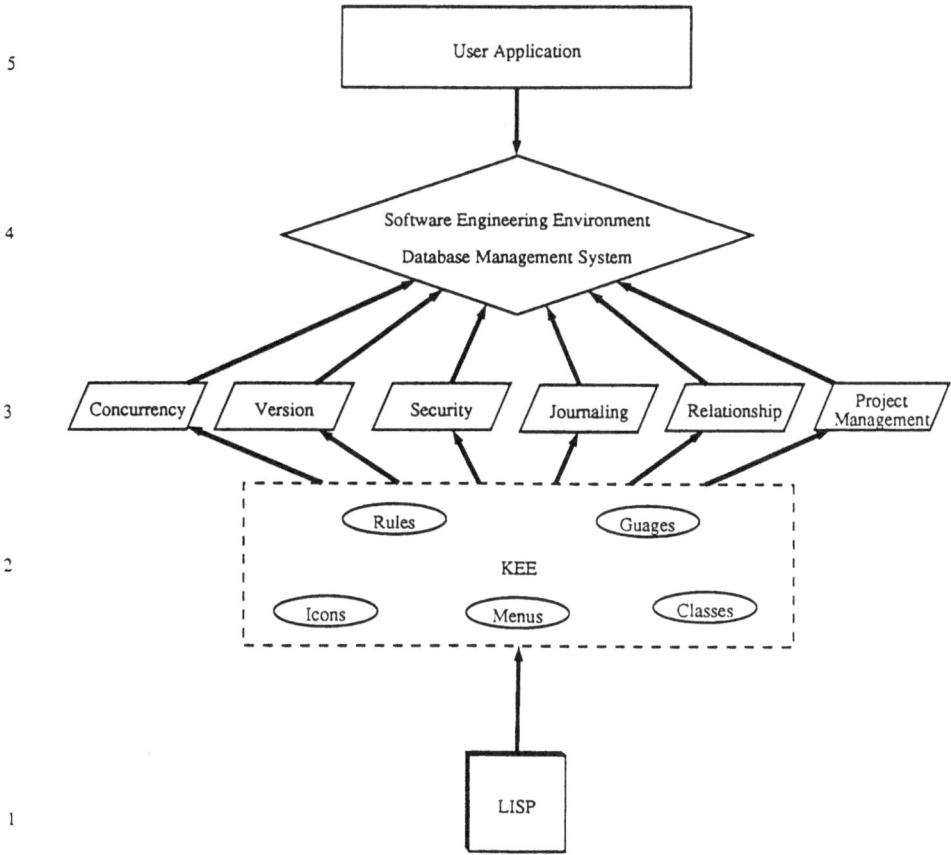

Figure 1. The KeeSee Architecture.

access, and modify software objects when developing application software at level five.

The generic access methods of a DBMS usually include *read, write, modify, append, edit, create*, and *delete*. In a standard DBMS, database amenities are combined into one procedure that implements each access method. Using the normal object-oriented implementation of access methods will not work in a multiple inheritance network. For instance, suppose that a given class inherits from the *concurrency-mixin* and from the *security-mixin*. If each mixin class has a read method, there will be a conflict during inheritance. How should this be resolved? Most systems either disallow such cases or settle upon a conflict resolution scheme (see Stefik and Bobrow, 1986) to decide from which parent the conflicting slot should really derive. Neither approach is sufficient for KeeSee because we need the functionality of both access methods, so instead, we selected a solution involving *aggregate access* methods.

For KeeSee, we selected a basic set of aggregate access methods (read, write, modify, append, edit, create, and delete). Using these methods, the mixin developers incorporate *primitive access methods* such as *read-concurrent-object* or *write-concurrent-object* into each mixin. Each primitive method has a type that corresponds to one of the aggregate methods. For example, *read-concurrent-object* is of type *read*, whereas *write- concurrent-object* is of type *write*. Then, when a class is defined, each aggregate access method is composed of the primitive access methods inherited by that class. The resulting aggregate access method consists of a compiled sequence of calls to the primitive access methods. Priorities for the primitive access methods in the calling sequence within the aggregate access method are developer specified. In theory, one should be able to write primitive access methods without considering other existing methods, in practice, however, some coordination is required.

MIXINS: THE KEESEE TOOLKIT FOUNDATION

In this section, the mixins that were investigated in the context of KeeSee are described. We studied two main classes of mixins:

1.   There are mixins related to software engineering functionality which include versioning, scheduling, and graphability.

2.   There are mixins related to database management functionality which include concurrency, journaling and recovery, relationships, security, and graphability. The implementation of the relationships mixin represents an extension to the KEE data model, whereas the other mixins implement database amenities.

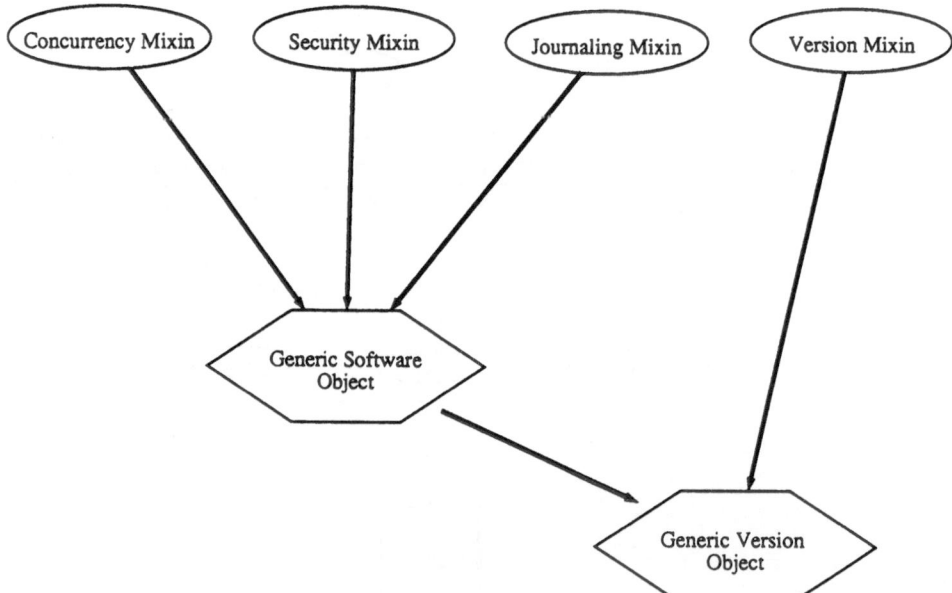

Figure 2. A Mixin Example: A La Carte Concurrency Hierarchy.

The functionality associated with each mixin is taken from standard textbook definitions. For example, one of the definitions of locking is found in (Ullman, 1982). The main goal is to determine whether the aggregate access methods approach is feasible to implement an important subset of database and software engineering functions. Each mixin is implemented as a KEE unit. In turn, aggregate and primitive methods were implemented as KEE methods. In the subsections below, the functionality, implementation, and evaluation of each mixin is discussed. Broader discussion of results regarding mixins is given in the last two sections.

Graphability

One of our objectives in KeeSee is to provide a database administrator with tools that allow the creation of a SEE that shields the user from KEE. The graphability mixin provides a means for making KeeSee objects and relationships graphically visible on a terminal. In turn, users can browse the schema and data (see Bryce and Hull, 1986; Goldman, Goldman, Kanellakis, and Zdonik, 1985) that are part of a SEE. In addition to the aggregate methods, graphability objects have methods for drawing, moving, and centering within an interactive window. This functionality was routinely implemented in KEEPictures (see Appendix) which provides object-oriented graphics. Because this approach of using object-oriented programming to support graphics has been extensively investigated (in *Programming the User Interface*, Symbolics, Inc., 1987, and Ingalls, 1981), we will not cover it here. Figure 3 shows the user's interface with objects that contain the graphability mixin.

Relationships

One of the objectives of modern data models is to make semantic information explicit in a database schema (Hull and King, 1987). Relationships defined between classes of objects are one of the principle means to meet this objective. Because KEE is primarily a BOOS, explicit support for relationships is not provided in the representation language. The KeeSee project used mixins as a basis to provide a primitive facility to define relationships. As shown in Figure 4, there is a single root relationship, *basic-relationship*. This root relationship cannot be used as a mixin since it has no behavior, and only serves as a placeholder for the *binary-mixin* branch of the hierarchy. Although it is not apparent from the hierarchy, the subclasses of *quantity-mixin* are mutually exclusive.

A particularly salient use of relationships in KeeSee appears in the *derives* relationship, which is a many-to-one relationship. There is a method associated with the derived object that traverses each input in a derivation of the object. For example, in Figure 5, there is a derivation graph of an executable object, *ES1* which is derived from binary objects *OS1* and *OS2*. *OS1* is derived from source module *MS1* and *OS2* is derived from source module *MS2*. Notice that the objects are of different types: source, binary, and executable. Associated with each object type is a *derivation type*, which may have either primitive, eager, or lazy as a value. The derivation type determines how and when to update obsolete software objects. In this example, source objects are primitive, binary objects are eager, and executable objects are lazy. Darkened objects are out of date. In KeeSee, when *MS1* is updated, then so is *OS1*. But, *ES1* remains out of date, since its derivation type is lazy. However, a request for *ES1* will cause a rederivation.

Implementing relationships as objects is consonant with the BOOS spirit of KEE. The benefit of this approach is that one can easily associate additional functionality with a relationship by adding more methods as shown above. This is in contrast to the standard implementation of relationships where it is difficult for an application programmer to access them.

Versioning

Software configuration management (SCM) is a necessary component of any software engineering environment. It is the task of SCM to provide access to all versions of the software system that have ever existed during the course of the software development process. This must be done in a timely and efficient manner through a smooth user interface. The process of providing this access often involves generating new software objects from existing ones. This requires that the system maintain a traceable trail of the *revisions* and *variants* created during the lifetime of the system. At other times the process involves using *derivers* to transform object(s) into their new form. Regardless of the specific methods involved, SCM is important because it adds an historical dimension to the software project.

In contrast to other DBMS-oriented attempts to handle versioning (Habermann and Notkin, 1986), KeeSee implements version control with behavioral objects. Within KeeSee, SCM activities are provided by the *versions-mixin*. The advantage to implementing versions as a mixin is that certain objects may not need versioning. In those cases, the version mixin is excluded and the overhead of versioning is avoided.

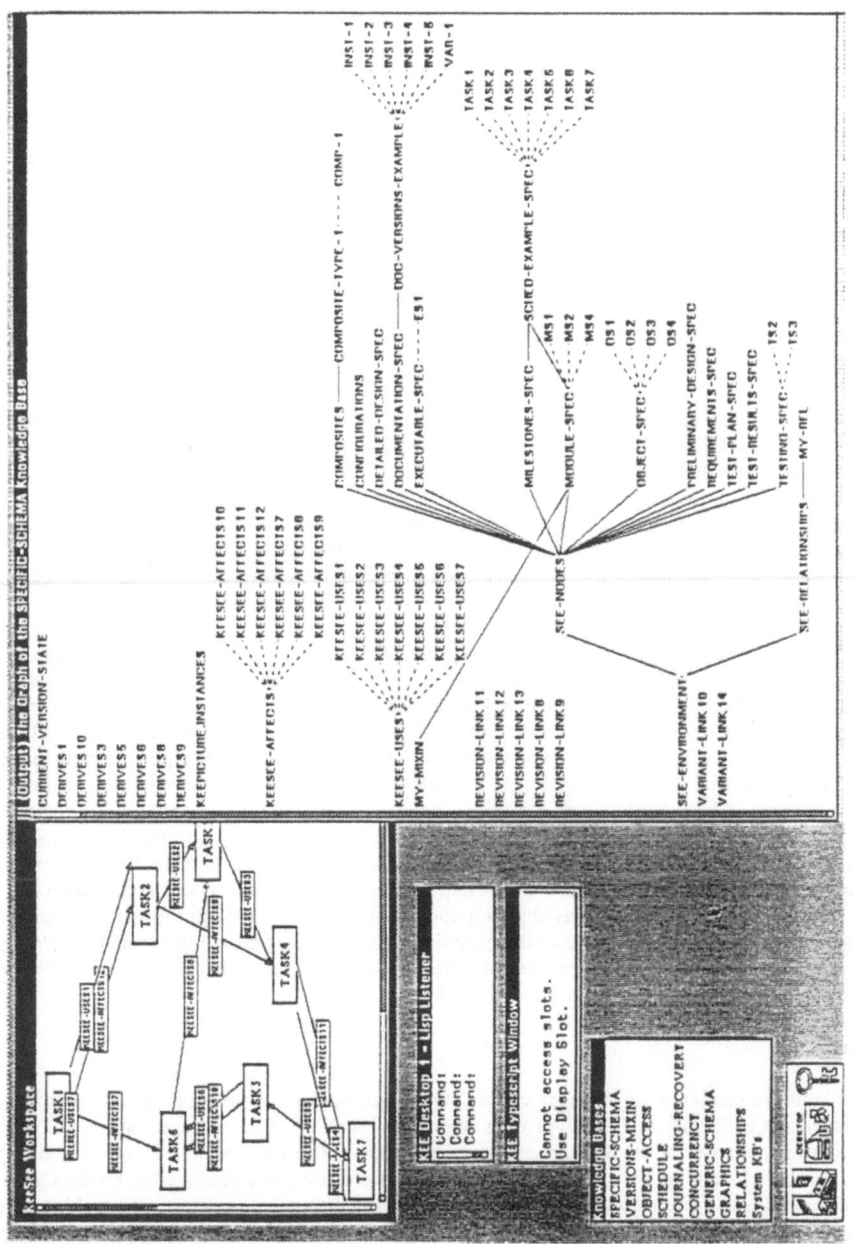

Figure 3. KeeSee's User Interface and Example SEE Schema.

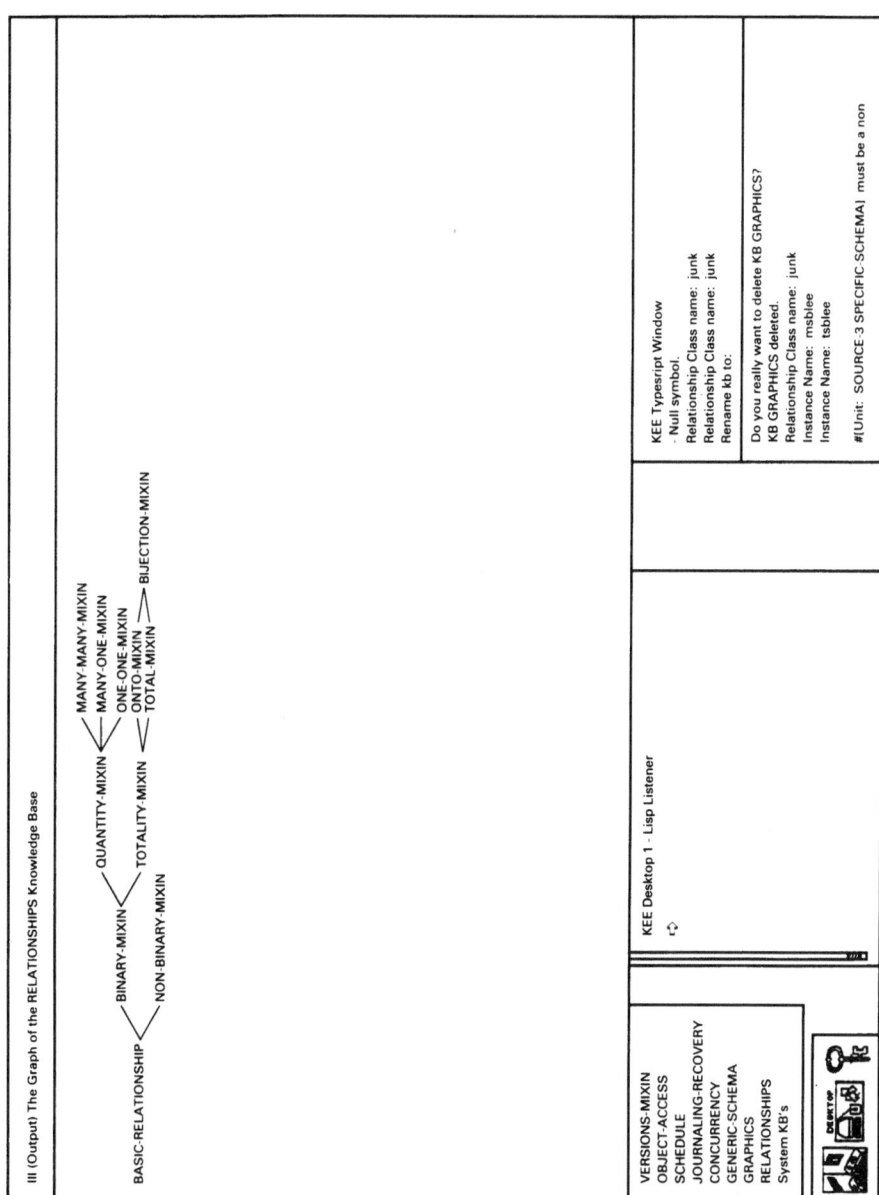

Figure 4. Relationship Hierarchy.

407

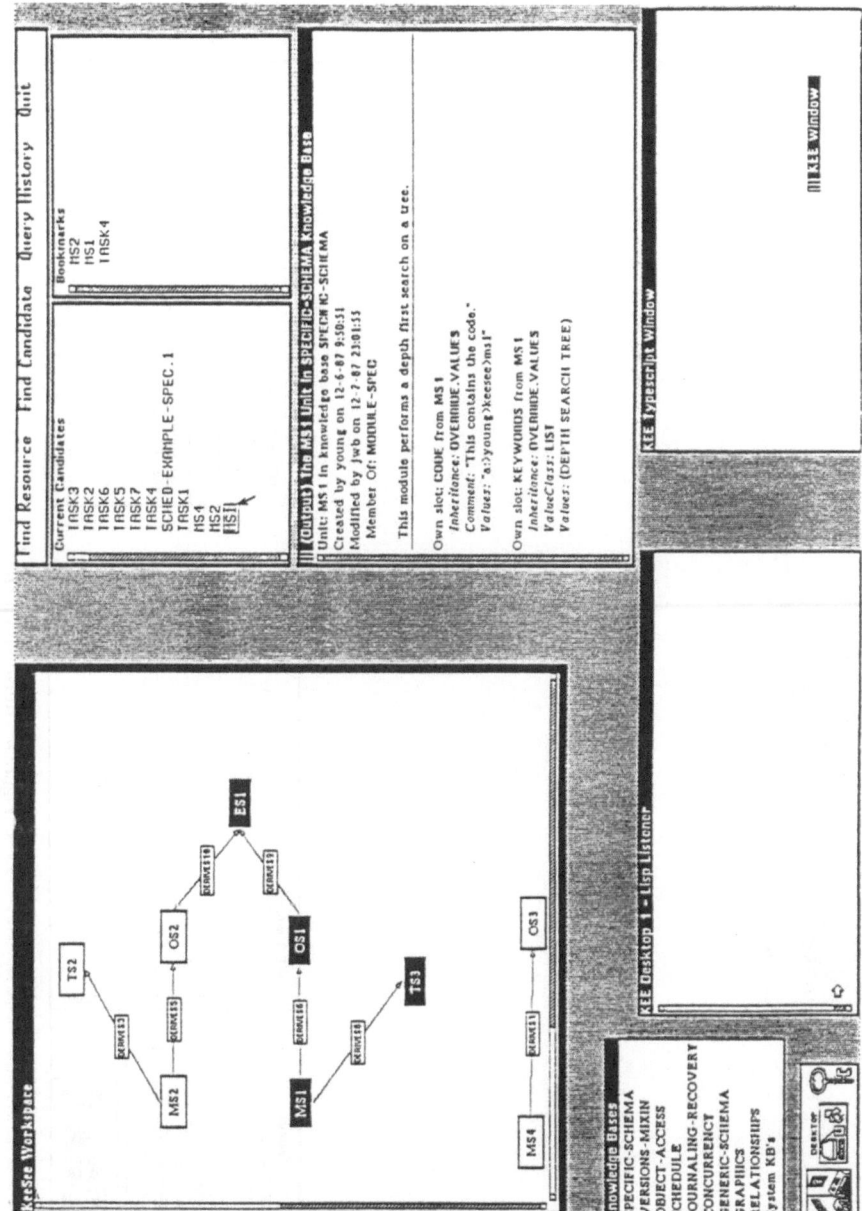

Figure 5. Derivation Graph and Resource Retrieval Interface.

408

The three distinct types of mixins for versioning defined within KeeSee are atomic units, configuration units, and composite units. These types closely conform to the objects described in Tichy (1985), Tichy (1987), and Bersoff, Henderson, and Siegel (1979). In particular, atomic units may include objects for source code, executable images, documentation text files, graphics images, and any other non-structural objects defined by the user. Configuration units are structural elements that keep a list of the units that made up a particular system state. In this way, an entire system state can be reconstructed at will. Composite units are the derivers in KeeSee.

Four types of relationship links for connecting the various software objects are supported in KeeSee. These are *revision links*, *variant links*, *configuration links*, and *composite links* (Tichy, 1985; Tichy, 1987). *Revision links* connect objects to those that precede and supercede. *Variant links* connect an object to its parallel development paths. *Configuration links* connect an object to the configurations of which it is a member. Finally, *composite links* connect objects to the composite object which contains its derivers.

Security

A mechanism for providing secure access to objects in a software engineering environment requires a great deal of flexibility. Different organizations may have widely differing security philosophies. Even within an organization users may belong to more than one development group and group members may change at any time. The *security mixin* achieves this level of flexibility with access control lists, capabilities and permissions.

Permissions are the set of operations possible for an object, for example, execute, read and write; while capabilities define the users associated with a group or project. For instance, Jones is a member of the Speech Project and is also on the Quality Assurance Review Board. The database administrator defines the set of capabilities and then decides the set of permissions that are allowed for each capability.

An access control list is simply a list of the defined capabilities and permissions for those capabilities. Every KeeSee object that inherits the security mixin has its own access control list stored as an attribute. When a user creates an object, he defines the values of permissions. When a user wants to perform an operation on an object, for example read a subroutine, there is a system check to find out which capabilities the user is a member of and checks the object's permissions for those capabilities.

There are two important characteristics of an object-oriented implementation of security. First, the DBA has a mechanism to implement a variety of security policies. Second, in situations where security (as in the versions mixin) is not necessary, one can exclude the security mixin and thereby reduce function call overhead.

Concurrency, Journaling, and Recovery

The *concurrency mixin* in the KeeSee environment was designed to take into account differing levels and types of concurrency, and also to examine issues of compatibility with related mixins such as the *journaling* and *recovery mixin*. These database amenities were investigated, with the treatment of each object in the KeeSee environment as an item to be locked and monitored.

To allow for concurrent access to software components, the method of access and protocol followed is handled by the concurrency mixin. While it seems that timestamps can be implemented in the KeeSee environment, it appears that locking methods are more easily implemented and offer an easier, more flexible solution. This intuition is based on the underlying "tree" structure of KeeSee, where various levels of item locking (i.e. a tree protocol) can be used. For instance, it seems likely that at some time, the entire database (i.e. SEE), a mixin, a package, a particular test plan component, or a group of module specifications, may need to be locked. Since the mixin architecture implies that each of these items are distinct objects in a tree hierarchy, locking appears to be the most viable formulation. Locks can be implemented in KeeSee using methods to control object access.

To assure that all transactions executing within SEE do not leave the DBMS/SEE in an inconsistent state, techniques of journaling and recovery must be used in KeeSee. Specifically, each alteration of an object must be monitored and recorded. If a REDO paradigm is used then any time that recovery is needed, the mixin can interact with the relationships and derivability mixin, in order to bring the DBMS/SEE into consistent form. Whatever techniques are used to handle the recovery of long or nested transactions, must also be implemented as part of the journaling and recovery mixin. Though not completely implemented, it seems that both of these mixins are quite suitable to the object-oriented KeeSee management system.

409

Project Management

The *scheduling mixin* was investigated to see how a common software engineering paradigm (resource scheduling and project management) can be integrated into a BOOS. Specifically, it handles the scheduling of resources (i.e. people, software, and hardware) using the simple technique of critical path analysis (Wagner,1975). End users can use the mixin to establish, update, examine, and determine the milestones associated with end user defined software components, and those people working on them. The software and hardware resources fall into one of two classes, *Composite-Task-Mixin* and *Atomic-Task-Mixin*, which handle large software projects and their individual modules respectfully. A *People-Mixin* handles information regarding application project employees. In addition to scheduling resources, this mixin performs an analysis of project stages, using existing database relationships and the Critical Path Method (Archibald and Villoria, 1967).

The scheduling mixin was rapidly constructed and integrated into KeeSee. It relies upon the derivability and graphability mixins. This demonstrates that at least one common software engineering application can work in a KeeSee paradigm. In the future, other functionality in KEE, e.g. rules, may be incorporated into this mixin.

SOFTWARE REUSABILITY THROUGH INFORMATION RETRIEVAL

Part of the KeeSee research effort has focused on a mechanism for increasing software reuse through database support. Software reuse is a necessity in today's SEEs. Not only does software reusability improve code reliability and quality, but it ensures greater developer productivity and higher software standards and portability. Unfortunately, despite the need and benefits, it is posited that only 5 percent of the code is reused in an average SEE (Frakes and Nejmeh, 1987).

The major reason for this low percentage is that software resources are difficult to locate. To justify the software reuse it must be easier to find and incorporate a software module than it would be to build it from scratch. Tools that aid in software reusability must be capable of retrieving all and only the relevant software objects useful to the developer. Hence, a tool must have both high *recall* and *precision* (Salton and McGill, 1983).

KeeSee includes a component to address these issues in recall and precision, for both the creator and reuser. The component is based on the principles behind information retrieval systems (i.e. *document* access systems), since software modules are more similar to documents than records as used in data retrieval systems. In KeeSee, objects such as software modules are accessed through keyword specification in an interactive environment. Two tools are provided for the user in KeeSee's top level interface for information retrieval. One is for resource retrieval and the other is for resource creation.

Resource Retrieval

The resource retrieval component of the KeeSee environment allows users to search for an object based on its attributes. For example, a user can search for all subprograms created by user Smith, that were modified sometime between December 12 and January 5.

The top, right of Figure 4 shows KeeSee's resource retrieval tools. The top menu contains the resource retrieval commands, while the *Current Candidates* window displays the objects matched to the query. The *Bookmarks* window displays a history of object titles retrieved (or specific object titles selected by the user through other means), and the objects selected by the user from the *Current Candidates* window are displayed in the *KEE Output* window.

In KeeSee, software modules are treated as objects of some resource class. After selecting a resource class to search (i.e. "Hardware Object", "Software Object", "Person", or any database administrator defined class such as "Documentation Object"), search keys for class attributes are specified. Example attributes include "author" and "creation date" for software objects and "telephone number" or "email address" for objects of type person. The top-level object classes are automatically differentiated by the searchable attributes as- sociated with each class.

Resource Creation

One key to successful reuse of software lies with the resource creator. Resource objects must be modular and well documented to be useful to other developers. For instance, a reuser must be able to immediately examine the module's maintenance record and warranty. Additionally, the module's appearance and options are of immeasurable importance (Tracz, 1987).

To facilitate these qualities in a module, KeeSee helps authors to include descriptive information in the resource object. To create a software object the user must specify a name for the object and which subclass best describes the object, e.g. "documentation", "test plan", "function", or "subroutine". Subclass types are determined by the database administrator. KeeSee automatically records the author, date of creation, and date of last modification, while the user must supply all other attributes. Currently, the only additional attributes supplied by the KeeSee environment are *Description* and *Keywords*. The database administrator could add other useful attributes such as *Environmental Requirements*, *Input*, *Global Variables*, and *Output*.

Even though KeeSee maintains a limited keyword index, it could be extended. For instance, the keyword index can be treated as a thesaurus, in order to provide for higher recall. A recent study has shown that the probability of two people choosing the same term to describe an object is < 0.20 (Furnas, Landauer, and Gomez, 1987), therefore, by encouraging a constrained keyword index with many synonyms, queries can be generalized or refined by choosing more or specific classes. Unfortunately, the space overhead required to maintain a thesaurus in the dynamic collections found in a SEE may be prohibitive.

SYSTEM EVALUATION

In this section we present an evaluation of KeeSee from the perspective of performance, ease-of-use, and modularity. An evaluation of KEE as the basis for KeeSee is also given.

Performance

Although performance was not a primary focus in this study, now that KeeSee is implemented, it is interesting to informally evaluate whether the approach taken and algorithms used, would scale up if an underlying system like KEE used database management techniques instead of virtual memory. None of the algorithms used in KeeSee are exponential in time or space. Further, with the exception of those caveats and situations noted below, we have concluded that KeeSee will scale up to handle larger applications.

One issue that must be addressed in a larger system involves the resource retrieval subsystem. Even though we use an inverted index for the keywords attribute, indices were not used for the other search keys. This resulted in a linear search of objects to match keywords or other specifications to attribute values. With our test schema, search and retrieval has been instantaneous, however, for large quantities of software objects this technique is not sufficient and will not scale-up. Instead, an inverted index or other standard technique for information retrieval is necessary for other search keys.

A second part of the system that will not scale up is that of the versioning mechanism, which does not use any form of delta files. There are many forms of data compression techniques (Heckel, 1978; Bersoff, Henderson, and Siegel, 1979; Hunt and McIlroy, 1976) that can reduce the storage overhead inherent in multiple versions and configurations. We assert that incorporating such techniques into KeeSee is possible.

Finally, some of the approaches to user interface management need to be changed. For instance, it is not reasonable to display all of the objects on the screen for even small software engineering efforts. Further, screen clipping and scrolling can result in a navigational nightmare. At a minimum, sophisticated layout algorithms that are parsimonious in the choice of what objects display on the screen are necessary. However, it is computationally expensive to perform a high quality graphic layout. A similar problem exists for the DBA who interacts with a graphic depiction of the schema. Work discussed in King and Melville (1984), and Bryce and Hull (1986), provides some encouraging results on the problem we have just discussed, however, that work was carried out in the context of small databases also.

Ease of Use

Ease of use in KeeSee is evaluated from the developer and DBA perspectives. Although KEE was easy for us to learn, it was a design criterion to minimize both the developer's and DBA's awareness of KEE in two respects. First, users should not need to know the representation language of frames and objects in KEE. Second, users should not have to understand KEE's user interface. Since KeeSee provides a resource retrieval facility and a graphical display of object relationships, we were able to satisfy this criterion for developers.

For the DBA, however, there must be a substantial understanding of the KEE representation language and user interface. To create and tailor aggregate methods, the DBA must be aware of the classes of objects provided in KeeSee, and he must also be knowledgeable about writing KEE methods. In short, KeeSee succeeds in shielding the developer, but not the DBA, from KEE. As the use of aggregate access methods becomes articulated, we hope to develop an interface that requires less understanding of the underlying representation.

Modularity

The techniques of multiple inheritance and object-oriented programming promote a high degree of modularity. In fact, various parts of KeeSee were rapidly assembled and changed using this philosophy of mixin modularity. Aggregate methods allowed us to augment standard approaches to method combination and composition, in order to provide a uniform mechanism for module integration. However, the actual utility of this approach is application dependent.

In KeeSee we integrated two classes of software: database management facilities and software engineering utilities. Both were integrated smoothly. In theory, the aggregate method facility should permit the integration of any mixin. In practice, certain combinations do not work well together. Nonetheless, the aggregate method approach is suitable for combining small sets of software engineering primitives, as in KeeSee.

Using KEE to Support a DBMS/SEE

In our opinion, the behaviorally object-oriented aspects of KEE have provided a useful basis for constructing KeeSee. Object-oriented representation proved to be a real asset in providing database support for a SEE. The primary conclusion reached is that KEE needs its functionality extended, not changed. As shown in KeeSee, the necessary extensions include explicit support for relationships and database amenities.

The inheritance system of KEE was very beneficial to the KeeSee environment. KeeSee relied on the default means for value inheritance rather than more esoteric forms such as intersection. In addition, KEE provides a means for describing facets on attributes (see Appendix) which were critical for the implementation of primitive and aggregate access methods. They permitted us to declare that a primitive method was a certain type such as read, write, etc.

KEE provides useful windowing and object-oriented graphics tools, which allowed us to rapidly implement the graphability mixin as the basis for the developer's interface. In contrast, however, much of the resource retrieval subsystem relied on primitives from the underlying LISP machine for menus, and mouse sensitive text. This indicates one area where KEE's functionality must be extended.

Since it was an explicit goal of the research effort to emphasize resource retrieval through a graphic interface, users did not use the KEE query language at all. Moreover, the query language was not used in the implementation of KeeSee either. It is our belief that, in some ways, KEE's query language is a relational query language attached to an object-oriented system. For example, although function calls are naturally embedded in queries, there is no distinction between function calls to external Lisp programs and function calls which invoke methods or demons. We find this surprising since method invocation is a quintessential notion in KEE.

Finally, resource limitations prevented us from exploring KEE's AI primitives (rules, truth maintenance mechanisms, and worlds (see Appendix)) in our implementation. We believe that rules have a useful place in this environment as critics or consistency checkers in the schema and applications. Further, work described in Balzer (1985), and Fischer(1987) has shown rules and demons to be extremely useful, in software engineering. During the early phases of KeeSee's design, it appeared that KEE Worlds were a panacea for everything from views to versions. In the end, their limited efficiency for large applications prevented them from being used.

CONCLUSIONS AND FUTURE DIRECTIONS

We still believe that the worlds and truth maintenance facilities in KEE have important implications for database applications. Future work must concentrate, both analytically and empirically, on the utility of worlds and truth maintenance as applied to SCM and user views. In doing so, more information may result as to how each of these AI paradigms can improve the quality of non-AI areas, such as database systems.

Another topic of further study is in the area of derived data. In KEE, there are several ways to derive data, including rules, active values, methods, and truth maintenance. Given that derived data is a central concern in SEEs, it is desirable to determine which among these alternatives can provide the most efficient, yet natural solution to the problem. Additionally, if one considers the interaction between the different types of derivation: eager, lazy, and opportunistic, we can determine which alternative provides the best solution under certain circumstances.

The utility of aggregate methods has been introduced and touched upon in the prototype implementation of KeeSee. An obvious extension to the current KeeSee implementation is to provide a sufficiently large set of mixins for a fully functional DBMS/SEE. At this point, we do not have a good feeling for how large this set should be. In the process, the adequacy of the aggregate mixin approach can be tested, and the complex interactions between mixins can be examined in more detail.

Our primary objective in KeeSee is to investigate a BOOS as a means for implementing a DBMS to support SEE. There are two aspects to this objective. First, we want to understand how the tool rich environments that are normally associated with a BOOS can be used in conjunction with the BOOS itself to meet our objective. Second, we want to see how a BOOS can be used to provide support for a variety of software engineering environments. Aggregate and primitive access methods that are used in KeeSee extend the traditional approaches to method combination. As yet, we see no reason that they cannot be used as a means for building a toolkit that will allow assembly of a multitude of SEEs. This toolkit relies heavily on the multiple inheritance and message passing facilities of a system like KEE.

REFERENCES

Archibald, R., and Villoria, R., 1967, *Network-Based Management Systems (Pert/CPM)*, John Wiley and Sons Inc., New York.

Balzer, R., 1985, Automated Enhancement of Knowledge Representations, *Proceedings of the Eighth International Conference on Artificial Intelligence*, Los Angeles, CA.

Bersoff, Edward H., Henderson, Vilas D., and Siegel, Stan G., 1979, Software Configuration Management: A Tutorial, *IEEE Computer*, Vol. 12, No. 1, January 1979, pp. 6-14.

Bryce, D. and Hull, R., 1986, SNAP: A Graphic-Based Schema Manager, *Proceedings of the Second IEEE Intl. Conf. on Data Engineering*, February 1986.

Carey, M., DeWitt, D., Richardson, J., and Shekita, E., 1986, Object and File Management in the EXODUS Extensible Database System, *Proceedings of the Twelfth International Conference on Very Large Databases*, August 1986.

Dittrich, K.R., Gotthard, W., and Lockemann, P.C., 1986, DAMOKLES - A Database System for Software Engineering Environments, Lecture Notes, *Computer Science: #224, Advanced Programming Environments, Proceedings of the International Workshop*, Goos and Hartmanis, eds., Springer Verlag, June 1986, pp. 353-371.

Fischer, G., 1987, A Critic for Lisp, *Proceedings of the 10th International Joint Conference on Artificial Intelligence*, Milan, Italy, August 1987.

Frakes, W. B. and Nejmeh, B. A., 1987, Software Reuse Through Information Retrieval, *SIGIR Forum*, Winter 1987, pp. 30-36.

Furnas, G. W., Landauer, T. K., and Gomez, L. M., 1987, The Vocabulary Problem in Human-System Communications, *Communications of the ACM*, Vol. 30, No. 11, pp. 964-972.

Goldman, K. J., Goldman, S. A., Kanellakis, P. C., and Zdonik, S. G., 1985, ISIS: Interface for a Semantic Information System, *Proceedings ACM SIG MOD, International Conference on the Management of Data*.

Habermann, A. Nico and Notkin, David, 1986, Gandalf: Software Development Environments, *IEEE Transactions on Software Engineering*, Vol. 12, No. 12, December, pp. 1117-1127.

Heckel, Paul, 1978, A Technique for Isolating Differences Between Files, *Communications of the ACM*, Vol. 21, No. 4, April 1978, pp. 264-268.

Hudson, S., and King, R., 1986, CACTIS: A Database System for Specifying Functionally-Defined Data, *Proceedings of the Workshop on Object-Oriented Databases*, Pacific Grove, California, September 23-26, 1986.

Hull, A.R., and King, A.R., 1987, Semantic Database Modeling: Survey, Applications, and Research Issues, *ACM Computing Surveys*, September 1987.

Hunt, J.W., and McIlroy, M.D., 1976, An Algorithm for Differential File Comparison, *Computing Science Technical Report*, No 41, Bell Laboratories, June 1976.

Ingalls, Daniel H., 1981, The Smalltalk Graphics Kernel, *BYTE*, No. 6, August 1981, pp. 168-194.

King, R., and Melville, S., 1984, SKI: A Semantics Knowledgeable Interface, *Proceedings of the 10th International Conference on Very Large Databases*, Stockholm, Sweden.

Maier, A., Stein, D., Otis, A., and Purdy, A., 1986, Development of an Object-Oriented DBMS, *Proceedings of the Conference on Object-Oriented Programming Systems, Languages and Applications September 29-October 2, 1986*, pp. 472-482.

Salton, G., and McGill, M., 1983, *Introduction to Modern Information Retrieval*, McGraw-Hill.

Stefik, M., and Bobrow, D., 1986, Object-Oriented Programming: Themes and Variations, *AI Magazine*, Vol. 6.

Symbolics, 1986, *Reference Guide to Streams, Files and I/0*, Symbolics Inc., Cambridge, MA, pp. 170-180.

Symbolics, 1987, *Programming the User Interface*, Symbolics Inc., Cambridge, MA.

Tichy, W.F., 1985, RCS - A System for Version Control, *Software - Practice and Experience*, Vol. 15, No. 7, July 1985, pp. 637-654.

Tichy, W.F., 1987, Tools for Software Configuration Management, unpublished paper as of Fall 1987.

Tracz, W., 1987, Reusability Comes of Age, *IEEE Software*, July 1987, pp. 6-8.

Ullman, J., 1982, *Principles of Database Systems*, 2nd Ed., Computer Science Press, Rockville, MD.

Wagner, H., 1975, *Principles of Operations Research*, Prentice-Hall, Inc., Englewood Cliffs, N.J.

APPENDIX: KEE BACKGROUND INFORMATION

KEE is an object-oriented programming environment developed for AI research and application. Its ancestral roots stem from LOOPS and Smalltalk. Unlike Smalltalk, it is implemented on top of LISP rather than built from scratch, yet like its ancestors, the emphasis is on the use of objects in an interface.

Modules in KEE are called knowledge bases. A knowledge base consists of one or more units, where a unit is the main data structure in KEE and corresponds to objects from other object-oriented systems. Each unit has a unique name within a knowledge base and units are composed of slots. A slot is thus equivalent to an attribute or field in a tuple. Slots may be viewed as sets of objects or there may be order imposed upon the objects via a slot. The values of a slot may be non-atomic, thus objects can point to one another through slot values. Also, a slot may have data type restrictions and impose requirements for a minimum or maximum cardinality.

Users may add other attributes to slots through facets. Facets are essentially attributes on attributes. Everything in KEE is implemented using units, so classes and instances are units in KEE. Rules, knowledge bases, and graphic icons are also units. Since classes are implemented as units, their definition is dynamically extensible by sending messages. Consequently, certain types of optimizations are ruled out because there is not a semantic distinction between different types of objects: they are all units.

KEE has a wide spectrum of functionality and there are seven components of KEE that form somewhat novel primitives in a SEE. First, the inheritance mechanism in KEE is quite flexible. There are two completely different types of inheritance. One type is slot inheritance where the developer may decide whether or not a slot is inherited from one class to another class or instance. The other type of inheritance involves values. In this case, when the slot itself is inheritable, the values to the slot may be inherited in different ways. For instance, one might say that the color of an elephant is grey unless one is speaking of the much hackneyed Clyde. Otherwise, one can say that the color of Clyde is a union of the default color from all the classes from which Clyde inherits. Various other set operations can be used in slot inheritance.

Second, KEE has a contexts mechanism, which allows one to circumscribe sets of facts and perform operations on each set. These contexts allow one to impose different views on a given set of facts. Although contexts were originally motivated by the needs of various search regimes in AI problem solving tasks, they seem to have immediate implications for database issues in version and configuration management, as well as user views.

Third, KEE has a rule language. While it is true that some database systems now include a rule based component, it is usually a primitive facility added as an afterthought. The rule system of KEE is considered integral. Because the rule components also include backward chaining rules, the kinds of queries expressed in Datalog (a special subset of Prolog) can be expressed in KEE. The utility of deductive queries is starting to receive attention in the database community, however, it appears that this interest has not focused on SEEs. As with other parts of the system, each rule is an object itself.

Fourth, active values or demons exit in KEE, which allow for the execution of a function every time the value of a slot is read or modified. A simple use of this facility in a DBMS/SEE is updating derived data.

Fifth, KEE provides a message passing facility similar to that in Flavors, LOOPS, or Smalltalk. Procedures or functions are associated with slots. The value returned is based on what the procedure returns. The invocation of methods, in contrast to the active values previously described, is done by a user program. Thus, in a sense, active values and messages are complements.

Sixth, KEE provides a relational like query language called Tell-and-Ask. One can query the knowledge base to find units matching various conditions, however, the *Tell-and-Ask* query language is not relationally complete.

Finally, there is a strong emphasis on the user interface. The programmer interface to the system is highly interactive, and the primitives that are available for building user interfaces include a graphics language called KeePictures, instrumentation primitives such as gauges, and a set of menus and window primitives, of course all implemented as units.

ENVIRONMENTAL EFFECTS ON THE DETECTION OF ERRORS IN SOFTWARE SYSTEMS

Catherine L. Bullard and W. Michael McCracken

Software Engineering Research Center
Georgia Institute of Technology
Atlanta, Georgia 30332-0280

Abstract: It is very important for software developers to thoroughly test their software. Since programs are tested in a specific environment, however, some errors are difficult, if not impossible, to detect by traditional testing methods such as path analysis. A program may contain errors that are masked by the environment in which it was developed and tested. One such element in a program's environment is the value to which memory is initialized. Mistakes in initialization would not appear until the software is ported to an environment in which memory has a different initialization value, when the software would mysteriously stop working correctly.

To prevent "mystery errors" and increase software portability, a programmer should be aware of the types of errors that are undetectable for a particular machine and system. These errors must be looked for specifically, realizing that test data will never expose them. Systems programmers also should be aware of the masking affect of different memory initialization values and use values that hide the fewest types of errors. This paper examines errors that programmers tend to make with FORTRAN to determine what values in memory could mask each. A "best" initialization value is proposed for FORTRAN, and findings are extrapolated to other programming languages such as Ada.

INTRODUCTION

Program testing is an important part of software development. One of the goals of testing is to demonstrate a program works correctly on at least a subset of its input domain. Black box testing techniques, such as functional testing (Howden, 1980), compare the results of a program's execution to that predicted by its specification. A problem with these techniques, however, lies in the fact that the software is tested in a specific environment, that is, with a particular compiler and operating system on a particular piece of hardware.

Aspects of the environment can decrease the effectiveness of testing by masking errors in the software. For example, an environment may evaluate the left operand of a binary operator first, then evaluate the right operand. Suppose a FORTRAN program has been developed in that environment which contains the following fragment and function.

```
        |
num3 = num2 * Func (num2)
num2 = num3 / 2
        |

function Func (i)
  i = i + 1
  Func = i * 2
  return
  end
```

In this example, Func's side effect will cause problems if the operands are evaluated in a different order, such as in an environment that evaluates functions before scalar variables. However, in this environment, the error in re-assigning num2 in Func is masked by the order in which the operands are evaluated. In its development environment, it will behave as specified, even though the code obviously contains an error. This illustrates that errors masked during testing can be detected through techniques that require static examination of the code, such as walk-throughs (DeMillo et al., 1987).

Naturally, if a system is developed, tested, and used on the same machine with the same compiler and operating system for its entire operational life, the masked error will never manifest itself as a fault. However, if the system is ported to another environment, previously working software may mysteriously fail, even though no changes were made to the software itself.

Many things differ between environments, such as numerical representations, the order in which operands of an expression are evaluated, method of parameter passing, and the amount of memory available for dynamic allocation (Bullard et al., 1988; Spafford, 1987; Wallis, 1982). This paper analyzes the errors that can be masked by a class of memory initialization policies. First, it describes the problem and our approach. Next, it presents the types of errors that can be masked by the memory initialization policy. Then it shows the implication this has for program testing. Last, it draws conclusions about the value to which memory should be initialized by an environment.

PROBLEM DESCRIPTION

Most programmers agree that referencing variables before they are assigned is poor programming practice. Despite good intentions, however, variables can accidentally be left uninitialized. In FORTRAN, for example, a variable need not be declared; any misspelling becomes a new variable. Other languages require variable declarations, but the wrong variable could still be used. If a program has two variables with similar names, the name of one could accidentally be replaced with the other in the initialization statement. The intended variable remains uninitialized and retains the memory initialization value. As another case, the variable could be initialized properly, but replaced in a later statement with the similarly spelled but as yet uninitialized variable.

Moreover, despite the arguments against leaving variables uninitialized, some programmers still allow the operating system or compiler to initialize them. This is a temptation when initializing a number of variables in a program to zero on an operating system that is known to initialize memory to zero. Algorithms to detect the possibility that a variable has been used before it was initialized are available, such as that discussed in Fischer and LeBlanc (1988). However, many compilers do not make this check.

As stated earlier, when a program contains uninitialized variables, the portability is reduced. Even between machines which use the same operating system, variables are initialized differently. For example, on a Vax 11/780 running 4.3 BSD Unix and using the FORTRAN compiler F77, an uninitialized integer was assigned the value zero. On a Pyramid 90X running the same operating system and using the F77 compiler, the variable was assigned the value 50860. A program with uninitialized variables that works in one environment will probably not work when ported to an environment with a different memory initialization value.

Use of uninitialized variables is not just a problem for the developers of portable software. Most software that is developed will at some time be used in a different environment, even if the change is to another version of the same operating system or compiler, and as the example illustrated, the environment can mask program errors. The memory initialization value is another aspect in the environment that can mask errors. In this case, masking occurs when an error is undetectable due to the value of an uninitialized variable in the erroneous statement. Since masked errors cannot be detected with typical testing techniques, the value used can reduce the effectiveness of program testing.

HYPOTHESIS AND APPROACH

Memory can be initialized by an operating system or by a compiler in a number of different ways. This paper assumes an initialization policy in which every byte of memory is filled with the same value, dividing possible values into four types. The first fills every byte with zero, resulting in commonly used program values. For example, an integer taking on the memory initialization value would have the value zero. A boolean variable would have the value FALSE. Note that these and the following values were determined on a Vax 11/780 with 4.3 BSD Unix.

The second type fills every byte with negative one. This initialization also results in commonly used values. An integer variable would take on the value negative one; a boolean variable would have the value TRUE.

The third type fills every byte with some positive number, resulting in a common logical value (TRUE) but a very large (at least 2**24) positive integer value for a four-byte integer. The fourth does likewise with some negative number less than negative one. An integer value would be very small (at most -2**24), but a boolean variable would have a common logical value (TRUE).

In this work, we focused attention on the FORTRAN language for several reasons. This language is commonly used in the scientific community. A number of numerical software libraries exist in the public domain for use on a variety of machines. Software is continually being developed for addition to these libraries, and, therefore, attention must be paid to developing software that is as portable as possible. Additionally, error studies are available that define typical errors made by FORTRAN programmers such as that by Youngs (1971). These studies were used to determine errors that would be masked by the environment.

The FORTRAN error studies we reviewed describe mistakes that programmers typically make. A programmer might reference the wrong variable, for example. This mistake is more common in a language like FORTRAN, which does not support strong typing nor enforce variable declaration, than in a language like Ada or Pascal. However, programmers can make this mistake even in a typed language. A program may have two variables of the same type with similar, easily confused names. It may have two records with similar names, in which the right component of the wrong record may be referenced.

Another typical error is to use the wrong operator in an arithmetic operation or a comparison. The minus operator may be used instead of the plus, or a less than operator inadvertently substituted for a less than/equal to operator. A third error is caused by leaving off or using the wrong unary operator.

Much has been written about programmer errors. Moreover, software existing techniques, such as mutation analysis (DeMillo et al., 1978; DeMillo et al., 1979) and error seeding, have been developed to test programs suing the knowledge of these typical errors. Several testing tools, such as the Mothra software testing environment (Demillo et al., 1988), automate the mutation analysis methodology. Current research is investigating the application of this testing methodology to Ada (Appelbe et al., 1988; Bowser, 1988).

We have used knowledge of FORTRAN programmer errors to evaluate the effect of each of the four types of initialization values on the detection of those errors. The errors were grouped according to the statements in which they could occur. The value types were rated for the masking effect they could have on each error in a statement. The ratings were assigned according to the possibility that the presence of an uninitialized variable in a statement could mask the additional presence of the error in question in the same statement.

EFFECTS ON ERROR DETECTION

The effects of memory initialization values on the detection of errors is largely determined by the value that an uninitialized variable has. This depends on the variable's type. The value it takes on for that type then determines its behavior. As an example, consider the following code fragment.

```
program frag
integer j, k, m
k = 0
j = 0
m = 2
    |
```

Suppose that the following erroneous fragment was coded, instead of the correct fragment shown above.

```
program frag
integer j, k, m
j = 0   <- k is no longer initialized
j = 0
m = 2
    |
```

Since k was not initialized, it will have the memory initialization value. This error, in which one variable replaces another, will be undetected in an environment which initializes every byte to zero, as k will be assigned that value by default. In any other environment, k would be assigned an unexpected value and the error could be detected.

This example illustrates a key element of the masking problem. The referencing error was masked in the above fragment when the uninitialized variable was assigned the value that should have been used in that place (k was initialized properly). It was assigned a value that was commonly used in the program. If an uninitialized variable is given some bizarre value, most likely that value would not be the same as the value that should have been used in that place. Here, if the uninitialized variables were assigned some large positive number, the errors would be detectable. The main reason why the variables can mask errors in the program is that they are given common values, values that the variable they replace might have had.

White box testing techniques, in contrast, require more than that a program's behavior matches its specification. Instead, they access the program code that implements the specification explicitly. Some white box techniques measure qualities such as the extent to which all statements or branches have been exercised. Others provide a measure of confidence that certain errors are not present in the code. While they may not specifically reveal the use of uninitialized variables, they can indirectly guide the programmer in detecting such errors.

Mutation analysis, for example, can be used to detect uninitialized variables. Mutation analysis is a testing technique that guides the tester in selecting data that is able to distinguish the program under test from programs that differ from it slightly. These similar programs are called "mutant" programs, and are formed by introducing an error into the original program, one that programmers typically make. For example, some mutants are formed by replacing a variable with every other variable in the program. Others are formed by replacing an arithmetic operator with every other arithmetic operator. When a test case causes a mutant to produce output different from that produced by the original program, the error has been shown not to exist in the original, and the mutant is "killed". If an error of the type revealed by mutation analysis exists, some test case designed to kill a mutant will actually produce incorrect results when executed with the original program.

Some mutants, however, will always produce the same output as the original program. These are logically equivalent to the original, and, hence, are called "equivalent" mutants. Suppose that a program contains an incorrect variable reference that causes an uninitialized variable to be referenced, and that this error is masked by the memory initialization value. One of the mutants will reference the intended variable instead of the incorrect one, and will actually be correct. However, since the error is masked by the environment, the mutant will always produce the same output as the original in this environment. When the programmer examines the code to see if this mutant is equivalent, he may realize that an uninitialized variable was used and has the same value as the intended variable. In this indirect way, mutation analysis can help reveal errors masked by the environment (Bullard and Spafford, 1987; Spafford, 1987).

In analyzing the effects that a memory initialization value has on the detection of program errors, we weighed the possibility of any effect on how common the value given to an uninitialized variable was. To do this, we divided the analysis into three parts for each type of value that we examined. The first part determines the effect when the variable references numeric data; the second part, character data; and the third part, logical data.

Numerical Data

When every byte is initialized to some positive value, a four byte integer has a very large positive value, around or greater than $2**24$. Similarly, a very small negative value, around or less than $-2**24$ results when each byte is initialized to some negative value less than negative one. It's not likely that any initialized variables in a program would have the same value, and, therefore, the values are uncommon.

On the other hand, a four byte integer has the value -1 when memory is initialized to -1 and has the value 0 when memory is initialized to 0. Both of these are commonly used values. In fact, variables in a program are often initialized to zero. This makes it even more likely that another variable in the program will have the same value as an uninitialized variable, which leads to a greater probability that other errors will be undetectable.

Only FORTRAN statements with arithmetic, logical, or string expressions could contain uninitialized variables. Input statements accept values for variables. If the wrong variable is listed in an input statement that reads initial values, the intended variable would be uninitialized. The incorrect reference could be undetectable if the uninitialized variable has the same value as that read. This is possible for any of the initialization value types, though it is more likely for -1 or 0.

The assignment, output, RETURN, DO, and CALL statements all may contain arithmetic expressions. In each case, an error in which an uninitialized variable is referenced instead of an intended variable will be undetected if the uninitialized variable has the same value as the intended variable. As before, this is possible for any of the initialization value types, but more likely for -1 or 0. The assignment statement may also have an error in which the destination variable is incorrect. If this error occurs in an initialization section of a program, the intended variable is inadvertently left uninitialized. This error will not be detected if the intended variable is given the value it should have had. Again, this is possible for any type, but in an initialization section this will probably be zero.

The computed GO TO statement has an integer expression. If the result of that expression is an integer greater than the number of statement labels listed in the statement or less than 1, the action taken depends on the compiler. For some, execution continues with the statement directly following the computed GO TO. An incorrectly referenced variable could go undetected if the expected action was that control would go to the next statement. If the expected result of the expression was 1, for example, and the first statement label was that of the next statement, then any initialization value could easily cause the expected action and mask the incorrect reference error. Another error occurs if some value position sends control to the wrong statement. Suppose a program should contain the following fragment.

```
        |
    i = 4
    ...
    go to (3, 9, 12, 3), i
3   -some statement-
        |
```

However, it contains the following erroneous portion instead.

```
        |
    i = 4
    ...
    go to (3, 9, 12, 12), k  <- k is some uninitialized variable
                              and the wrong label is referenced
3   -some statement-
        |
```

When k is uninitialized and has some value other than 1, 2, 3, or 4, control will drop to the next statement. This action masks the statement label error that when i is 4, controls goes to the statement labelled 12 rather than the one labelled 3.

The arithmetic if statement also contains an arithmetic expression and could, therefore, have an incorrectly referenced variable. If the variable actually referenced is uninitialized, the error goes undetected when the result has the same sign as the intended result (negative, positive, or zero). A statement label error could occur and remain undetected in the same manner as the one discussed with the computed go to statement. Similarly, the logical if statement could contain a relational expression that has an incorrect variable reference. The error would go undetected if the result of the relation were the same as the intended result. This is true for any of the statements that might have a relational expression: output, call, return, or assignment.

Character Data

An uninitialized character variable in an environment that initializes memory to -1 or 0 will have some control character value on the Vax 11/780. If an expression with character variables has an incorrect variable reference and the variable actually referenced is uninitialized, the error should be detectable. In an environment that initializes to some positive or negative number, it is possible that an uninitialized variable could have the value of a printable character. Therefore, it is possible, though improbable, that an incorrect variable reference would be masked.

Logical Data

On the Vax 11/780, logical variables can have only one of two values, uninitialized variable in an environment that initializes to zero has the value .FALSE. Such a variable in an environment that initializes to anything else has the value .TRUE. Both of these are common values, being the only two values a logical variable can have. Therefore, any incorrect variable references would as likely be undetectable as detectable. Likewise, any inadvertent operator substitutions would have as much chance of yielding the intended result as an incorrect result. Uninitialized logical variables mask errors equally in any environment. No initialization value is better than the others.

CONCLUSIONS

This paper has shown that the value to which memory is initialized can have an effect on the detection of software errors. Initializing each byte to some value greater than zero or less than negative one is less likely to mask errors than initializing to -1 or 0, because the values that an uninitialized variable would have are uncommon values. Incorrect variable references in which an uninitialized variable is mistakenly referenced are undetectable when the value of the variable referenced is the same as that of the intended variable. This occurs more often when the uninitialized variable has a common value.

Of course, when the error occurs in a relational expression, any of the values could mask it when the result of the relation is the same as the expected result. We also showed how any initialization value could mask flow of control errors in the arithmetic if and computed go to statements, as well as referencing errors.

Uninitialized character data will probably not mask errors in any expressions, though positive or negative values less than -1 could result in printable ASCII characters. Conversely, any initialization value could mask errors when a logical variable is left uninitialized.

In comparison, the four types of initialization values are equally rated for character and logical data. For numerical data, however, initializing to -1 is more likely to mask errors because the values of uninitialized variables are more likely to appear in the program, masking reference errors. Initializing to 0 also gives uninitialized variables a value that is likely to appear in the program. Additionally, program variables are often explicitly initialized to zero. A referencing error could easily occur and remain undetected in the initialization section. Moreover, when programmers know that a system initializes to zero they may purposely leave variables uninitialized to allow the system to initialize them, rather than explicitly initializing them in the program. This encourages poor programming practice and reduces portability of those programs. If the program is moved into an environment that follows a different memory initialization policy, the program may no longer behave correctly.

For more effective testing, a programmer should notice what types of errors tend to be masked by the initialization value used in his development and test environment. He should realize these are undetectable and examine the code specifically for those errors, knowing they won't be detected by his test data.

In this study, we looked at the FORTRAN language. The results, however, can be applied to other languages. Other languages are not quite as flexible as FORTRAN; variables must be declared to be used. In FORTRAN, uninitialized variables can easily occur, just by misspelling a variable name. Languages such as Ada which require variable declaration avoid such mistakes. It is possible, however, to have variable names of the same type which are spelled similarly, making it relatively easy to mistake one for another. Even these languages generally do not flag uninitialized variables. They permit programmers to have the system initialize variables and do not alert programmers to inadvertent use of uninitialized variables.

The effects of the value used to initialize memory have implications for system designers, software developers, and testers. Support systems, such as compilers and operating systems, are intended to facilitate software development, and so designers should choose a value that masks the fewest errors. Developers want their software to be as close to correct as possible and should avoid the use of uninitialized variables. As well, much software is developed for reuse in a different environment, so reliance on a particular initialization value can decrease the software's reusability. Those testing software should look beyond current input-output behavior to the errors that can be masked in an environment. Awareness of the environmental effects on the detection of errors can facilitate the production of portable software, and thus to more cost effective development of software systems.

REFERENCES

Appelbe, W. F., DeMillo, R. A., Guindi, D. S., King, K. N., and McCracken, W. M., 1988, Using Mutation Analysis for Testing Ada Programs, *Proceedings of Ada-Europe '88*, Munich, W. Germany, June 1988.

Bowser, John H., 1988, *Reference Manual for Ada Mutant Operators*, GIT-SERC-88/02, Georgia Institute of Technology, Atlanta, GA.

Bullard, Catherine L., and Spafford, Eugene H., 1987, *Testing Experience with Mothra*, GIT-SERC-87/04, Georgia Institute of Technology, Atlanta, GA.

Bullard, Catherine L., Guindi, D., Ligon, W., McCracken, W. M., and Rugaber, S., 1988, Verification and Validation of Reusable Ada Components, *Proceedings of the EFISS*, Plenum Press, New York, NY.

DeMillo, R. A., Lipton, R. J., and Sayward, F. G., 1978, Hints on Test Data Selection: Help for the Practicing Programmer, *Computer*, Vol. 11, pp. 34-41, 4 April 1978.

DeMillo, R. A., Lipton, R. J., and Sayward, F. G., 1979, Program Mutation: A New Approach to Program

Testing, *Software Testing, Volume 2: Invited Papers*, Infotech International, pp. 107-126.

DeMillo, R. A., Martin, R. J., McCracken, W. M., and Passifume, J. F., 1987, *Software Test and Evaluation*, Benjamin/Cummings, Menlo Park, CA.

DeMillo, R. A., Guindi, D. S., McCracken, W. M., Offutt, A. J., and King, K. N., 1988, An Extended Overview of the Mothra Software Testing Environment, *Proceedings of the Second Workshop on Software Testing, Verification, and Analysis*, Computer Society Press, Banff, Canada, 19-21 July 1988.

Fischer, Charles N., and LeBlanc, Richard J., Jr., 1988, *Crafting a Compiler*, Benjamin/Cummings, Menlo Park, CA, pp. 651-669.

Howden, William E., 1980, Functional Testing and Design Abstractions, *Journal of Systems and Software*, No. 1, pp. 307-313.

Spafford, Eugene H., 1987, *Initializing Uninitialized Memory*, GIT-SERC-87/02, Georgia Institute of Technology, Atlanta, Georgia.

Wallis, Peter J., 1982, *Portable Programming*, John Wiley and Sons, New York, NY.

Youngs, E. A., 1971, *Error Proneness in Programming*, PhD Thesis, University of North Carolina.

X. SOFTWARE REUSABILITY

ISSUES IN REUSABLE ADA LIBRARY TOOLS

Ross A. Gagliano, Martin D. Fraser, G. Scott Owen
and Pentti A. Honkanen

Department of Mathematics and Computer Science
and Department of Computer Information Systems*
Georgia State University
Atlanta, GA 30303-3083

Abstract: This current research program on software reuse is investigating library tools for *describing, classifying, cataloging, organizing* and *managing* Ada reusable software components. The major research results are the development and prototyping of classification methods and the evaluation of library tools for software reuse generally, and Ada components for management information systems specifically. The prototype system integrates the Faceted Classification Scheme (FCS) and conceptual closeness maps. Future research areas include the development of tools for reusable components libraries and expert systems for software development with natural language interfaces.

BACKGROUND

Reuse is gaining in recognition as an acknowledged way to overcome rising software costs (Jones, 1984; Jones et al., 1985) While the idea is not new, reusability has become more practicable since the introduction of the Ada language system with its package concepts (Burton and Broido, 1986). Additionally, success has been achieved in Ada mass production techniques, specifically in the software factory projects (Scacchi, 1986). The greatest current need, however, is for standards and guidelines in both software tool development and application, particularly as they apply to reusable libraries (Gagliano, Fraser, and Owen, to appear; Standish, 1984).

Previous research in software reusability has been concerned with classification methods (Prieto-Diaz, 1985; St. Dennis et al., 1986), specification techniques (Liskov and Berzins, 1979; Litvintchouk and Matsumoto, 1984), and, to a lesser degree, system functional decomposition (Gagliano et al., 1988). The trend in research now appears to be in developing methods for describing, classifying, and cataloging software (Palmer and Nguyen, 1986). Specific interest is now being shown in research on library development for Ada objects (Booch, 1987(a); Booch, 1987(b)) and reusable components for large-scale information systems (Gagliano, Owen, and Honkanen, 1987).

STAMIS AND REUSABLE LIBRARIES

Whereas earlier research has focused on general classification and specification techniques (Owen, Gagliano, and Honkanen, 1988), only limited efforts have been directed towards library tool development for either particular Ada objects (Booch, 1987(a); Booch, 1987(b); Conn, 1986; Conn, 1987) or reusable components for standard systems. The technical monitor of this research, AIRMICS, is concentrating on software reuse for the military administrative and logistical information systems or STAMIS (Standard Army Management Information Systems).

The STAMIS span the entire spectrum of systems from some of the embedded variety through those of the routine day-to-day administrative operations (Kruskal, 1964(a)). To classify all of the STAMIS

Empirical Foundations of Information and Software Science V
Edited by P. Zunde and D. Hocking, Plenum Press, New York, 1990

427

operations is no small task and one which requires very careful planning. Furthermore, current STAMIS environments consist of a very large number of disjoint programs, particularly when viewed from both the programming and sharing of data. Such a spectrum of systems places serious constraints on reusability.

In the STAMIS, COBOL is the most common language and it is not very amenable to reusability. For all STAMIS operations to be converted immediately to Ada, with or without reusability, is not practicable. However, to require conversions to Ada for new applications and for reprogramming systems where drastic revisions are being made may be more reasonable goals.

As the emphasis on Ada usage continues and expands from embedded to command and control systems, the extent and nature of these tools and their libraries will become large and varied. Appropriate classification and data base methods are needed to make reusable libraries succeed: potential users find what software is available for their use. Any significant transition from COBOL to Ada will require a considerable greater effort toward tools associated with: code generation, testing, translation, certification and validation, such as CASE (Computer Aided Software Engineering) (Suydam, 1987).

REUSABLE SOFTWARE COMPONENTS

Two factors have been found to be important for control of modern software development and maintenance costs. The first is the use of Reusable Software Components (RSC's) whose main advantages are a decrease in system cost and an increase in software reliability (Lubars, 1986). Nonetheless, more reliable code is more expensive, dictating that the cost of RSC's be amortized over many reuses.

The second factor is the use of the Ada language which has several features that support RSC development (Booch, 1987(a); Booch, 1987(b)). These include: *encapsulation* (separate package compilation, and individual package components for specifications and bodies); *information hiding* (using constructs such as private types); *generics* (a form of component template with constituent details provided as needed); and *strong data typing* (checking across program units, within data contexts, etc.).

In general, a RSC must be: available to a broad class of users, some of whom may have no advance knowledge of its existence; readily retrievable; easily understood, once retrieved, as to its limitations and conditions for use; and completely self contained and documented. To achieve these conditions, an effective classification method must be implemented within an automated storage and retrieval system.

THE GSU FCS PROTOTYPE

The Faceted Classification Scheme (FCS) was selected for RSC classification in the Georgia State University (GSU) research project. The FCS was originally implemented at the University of California-Irvine (Prieto-Diaz, 1985) and is now being implemented at several other locations (Guerrieri, 1988; Prieto-Diaz and Freeman, 1987; SofTech, 1986). Rather than using hierarchical keyword descriptors, the FCS represents each software module by a descriptor which is a tuple of terms. Each component of a tuple is a term selected from a controlled vocabulary (thesaurus) to represent a facet.

The GSU FCS prototype system is being developed as a tool for RSC management (hence the name GSU RSC_MGT System). A variety of software modules have been classified in the RSC_MGT System. Exercising the system's search and retrieval functions automatically supplies information on similarities among terms in each facet. This information together with prior distances derived from applications of supertypes (Prieto-Diaz, 1985) are used to estimate conceptual (which are really perceptual) distances between terms in a facet. In turn, these distances are used by the system to make recommendations to users on likely expansions of queries during search and retrieval sessions.

Significant progress has been made in both developing and implementing conceptual closeness distance measures and installing a test data base which serves primarily to demonstrate the RSC_MGT System capabilities. This data base is comprised of "shell" RSC's each of which contains a descriptor and a catalog number. The facets correspond to Booch's hierarchical classification, and the descriptors represent several hundred items taken from published components (Booch, 1987(a)). In addition, comparisons have been made to some components from the SIMTEL Repository which is located at White Sands, NM (Conn, 1986; Conn, 1987).

We are continuing with identification and evaluation of other potential components that could be added to this demonstration data base. Equally importantly, we are obtaining access to other currently available descriptions of components for the purposes of further expanding the RSC_MGT System and testing scenarios for the FCS prototype.

The GSU design of a conceptual closeness mapping is based on the suggestion (Kruskal, 1977) that the "concept of 'similarity' is built into the human nervous system." This idea allows constructing a distance measure using perceived similarities. Specifically, we expect that future software library users will perceive similarities between components if:

a.   the RSC's are classified with the same term of a facet; or

b.   the semantics of the terms within a facet are perceived to be sufficiently synonymous; e.g., a term of a facet in an initial query is associated with RSC's which are accepted after searching but which have descriptors with some other terms in that facet.

The notions of similarity and dissimilarity can be operationalized (Chatfield and Collins; 1980) through the use of frequencies of "perceived similarity" between pairs of objects. Such frequencies are often obtained in similar experiments from groups of individuals or judges. Therefore, the higher the frequency, the greater the perceived similarity.

This method then measures dissimilarity by computing the relative frequencies (the original frequencies divided by the group size) and subtracting these proportions from 1 (zero is assigned to pairs whose objects are the same). The resulting complemented proportions satisfy the three conditions for a Dissimilarity Coefficient (DC) (Jardine and Sibson, 1971), namely, that DC between two objects is non-negative, 0 when the objects are the same, and symmetric.

Such dissimilarity values are essentially proximity data which can be interpreted (Kruskal, 1977) as rankings of similarity between various objects in a collection. In this project, frequencies of semantic similarities are obtainable from the second operation (see b) described above; i.e., the perceived likeness of two terms is implied by initiating a search for a RSC with term t of a facet and ultimately accepting one classified with t'.

The central problem becomes one of generating distances between terms in a facet which can be interpreted as their conceptual closeness. We solve the problem by considering only one facet at a time (Prieto-Diaz, 1985) and employing Multidimensional Scaling (MDS) (Kruskal, 1964(b); Kruskal, 1977). MDS appears to be appropriate (Seber, 1984) for mapping proximities to distances in such a way that the rankings are preserved in the distances. Thus, it is reasonable to expect that MDS can provide distances which are consistent with the semantics of the terms in a facet.

Design of MDS-Generated Distances

In implementing the conceptual closeness idea, we utilize the following design schema. Let the thesaurus consist of n facets, with the i th facet having m_i terms. A user initiates a search with an initial descriptor of the general form $<t_1,...,t_n>$, where t_i is a term in the thesaurus for facet i. This initial descriptor is then recorded. If the system produces no acceptable matches, the user changes the descriptor until a list of acceptable RSC's is obtained. The RSC's in this list satisfy some modified final descriptors, say $<t'_1,...,t'_n>$, which may differ in one or more terms from the initial descriptor. Assuming the case that these RSC's are acceptable to the user, the system will update a cumulative history, maintained by facet, of the frequencies of the perceived similarities between terms in the facet.

The abstract data type for this history is simply a two-way table of counts. Updates are then made as follows:

a.   If t /= t', then add 1 to the count in the tt'- and t't- cells. For example, if t = t_2 and t' = t_1 then add 1 to the count in row 2, column 1 and to the count in row 1, column 2.

b.   Define the diagonal cell values to be 0.

Then, each Frequency Table is mapped into a Dissimilarity Matrix whereby:

a.   N = total of cell values.

b.   If non-diagonal cell, then cell value <-- 1 - (cell value / N).

c.   If diagonal cell, then cell value <-- 0.

d. All dissimilarities lie between 0 and 1.

Results of Monte Carlo experiments (Graef and Spence, 1979) indicate that the data on larger dissimilarities is very influential in generating distances that are good fits to the dissimilarities. Thus, special attention is paid in this project to the non-structural 0 frequencies because cells with a non-structural value of 0 give dissimilarities of 1, the largest possible dissimilarity. Bayesian techniques (specifically, pseudo-Bayes, or empirical Bayes) have been developed for obtaining "smoothed" relative frequencies which can distinguish such non-structural zero proportions (Bishop, Fienburg, and Holland, 1975; Good, 1965).

Bayesian Smoothing

The Bayesian smoothing technique is based on "supertypes" (Prieto-Diaz, 1985), which are used to compute the prior probabilities in the smoothing process. The overall conceptual distance design resembles a posterior data analysis in which prior distances are modified based on the similarity data observed during library use.

Let f_{jk} be the frequency of perceived similarity of terms t_j and t_k in facet i. These frequencies are obtained from the frequency table maintained for each facet by the RSC_MGT system. Because the low frequency similarities are exactly those which give the large dissimilarities (for f_{jk} near 0, $1 - f_{jk}/N$ is near 1), it is important to estimate the f_{jk}'s that are near or at 0 with as much information as possible. The use of pseudo-Bayes techniques will allow prior assessments of similarity to be incorporated into the estimates of the similarity frequencies as follows.

First, the pseudo-Bayes estimate, $f_{jk}{}^*$ of the frequency of the similarity of t_j and t_k in facet i can be found in Bishop, Fienburg, and Holland (1975):

$$f_{jk}{}^* = N(f_{jk} + K\pi_{jk}) / (N + K),$$

where

$$N = \Sigma f_{jk},$$

$$K = (N^2 - \Sigma f_{jk}{}^2) / \Sigma (f_{jk} - N\pi_{jk})^2,$$

and π_{jk} is the prior probability that users perceive t_j and t_k similar.

The prior probabilities π_{jk} are determined as follows. The Prieto-Diaz notion of supertypes (Prieto-Diaz, 1985) creates groups of terms which express similarities at a semantically high level. That is, while two terms in a facet have relatively distinct meanings at the thesaurus level, grouping them under the same supertype expresses some perceived common or shared meanings. By specifying distances, one gauges the level or degree of aggregation needed for terms to have a shared meaning.

Let d_{jk} be the distance between terms t_j and t_k in, say, facet i, obtained using the Prieto-Diaz supertype technique. Then, for example, $d_{12} < d_{13}$ means that t_1 and t_2 are perceived to have similar meanings at a lower level of aggregation than are t_1 and t_3, so t_1 and t_2 are closer semantically to t_1 and t_3.

The similarity perceived to be shared by two terms is inversely proportional to the specified distance between them. Accordingly, π_{jk} should express great uncertainty about any similarity in t_j and t_k when d_{jk} is large. That is, π_{jk} should be inversely proportional to the a priori distances d_{jk}:

$$\pi_{jk} = c / d_{jk} \text{ for } j \neq k, \text{ and } \pi_{jj} = 0,$$

where c is the constant of proportionality. Since $\Sigma \pi_{jk}$ is required by the axioms of probability theory,

$$c = 1 / \Sigma (1 / d_{jk}).$$

Thus, the quantities

$$(1 / d_{jk}) / (1 / \Sigma (1 / d_{jk})), \ j \neq k,$$

are substituted for π_{jk} to complete formula (1) for $f_{jk}{}^*$.

In summary, the steps in computing the conceptual closeness distances within a facet are:

a. determine the a priori distances d_{jk};

b.   collect the raw similarity frequency data f_{jk} as the users operate the RSC_MGT system;

c.   replace f_{jk} with the pseudo-Bayes estimates of similarity, $f_{jk}*$, in the computation of dissimilarity; i.e., compute the "smoothed" dissimilarities:

$$1 - f_{jk}* \, / \, N;$$

d.   compute the conceptual closeness distances by multidimensional scaling of the "smoothed" dissimilarities.

Initialization

A second use for the prior distances derived from the supertypes is in the initialization of the library system. When the system is installed, $f_{jk} = 0$ for all j and k because no user data has been recorded. However, the prior distances can be used as the conceptual closeness distances until frequency data is available.

ADA IMPLEMENTATION OF THE RSC_MGT SYSTEM

The GSU RSC_MGT System consists of 13 Ada packages with approximately 5,000 lines of source code. The modes of operation are: the establishment of a data base; the normal execution of searching and retrieval; and the MDS updating of conceptual closeness based on usage. There is a Help facility and a built-in thesaurus. The query also allows the use of "wild cards". After retrieving an initial data item or RSC descriptor, the following actions can be taken: change a term in the query, modify the query using wild cards, or retrieve additional data items based on the distances. The system can assist the user in modifying a query by suggesting terms which are conceptually like a term in the current descriptor based on conceptual closeness distances.

The RSC_MGT library system saves both the initial and final descriptors, the final accepted list of RSC's, and updates the frequency tables which are maintained in a file. A second Ada program computes both the dissimilarity matrices from the frequency data and the conceptual closeness distances using Bayesian smoothing and Kruskal's MDS algorithm. (There does not appear to be a more efficient algorithm (Seber, 1984). This second program is run off-line.

Two issues remain under investigation: the perceptual interaction and the sparseness of the frequency table. The first issue, that of perceptual interaction or facet orthogonality, arises in the following way. Although the facets may be treated one at a time, it may happen that the acceptability of RSC's initially described with term t in facet i changes with different occurrences of terms in facet j. Such a situation can be described as a two-facet interaction in the perception of similarities.

This lack of orthogonality can be detected and analyzed with MDS by considering pairs $\{t_i, t_j\}$ of terms from the two facets as unit terms and comparing the distances determined between these pairs with those from facet i alone. This situation is intriguing; therefore, experiments are being planned to investigate its effects.

For the second issue, if the number of terms in a facet is very large, then the frequency table may consist of only zeros and ones, even after recording many searches. If this situation arises, although it is unlikely to occur, then the dissimilarities can be computed as Wilkinson metrics (Chatfield and Collins, 1980). A criterion for switching to this mode of determining dissimilarities could be useful, but due to its rarity, its development priority is low.

OTHER TOOLS AND THEIR IMPLEMENTATION

Three other tool implementations have been considered, beyond those associated with the FCS and conceptual closeness retrieval algorithms.

Functional Decomposition Tools

Recently, a method was proposed (Gagliano et al., 1988) based on Object Oriented Design (OOD) which reaffirms the role of functionality in software development; *vis a vis*, data flow diagrams. A prototype tool has been proposed for development which would assist a system designer in describing a system in a family of digraphs which indicate candidates for reusability. The implementation could require dedicated hardware, and, at a minimum, new software for feasibility and applicability testing.

Commercial CASE Tools

GSU has completed a survey of approximately 50 software development companies principally engaged in embedded systems. The size of the companies ranged from 5 to 200 employees, operating in several hundred to over 50,000 square feet of space, with 10 to 15 different CPU's and often supporting hundreds of engineers. Each company was asked to provide information on:

a.   the extent of the internal utilization of CASE tools;

b.   the library functions (classification, cataloging and retrieving) of reusable software components.

While individual responses are protected, consolidated results of the survey are being made available to the participating companies. A summary of the results is as follows.

With respect to CASE products, 60% of the companies report that they use commercially developed tools, 70% develop their own internal products, whereas 80% of the tools were earmarked for software development and life cycle support. These tools include: editors, analyzers, coders, debuggers, handlers, generators, and testers. The major uses are for configuration management, data base manipulation, graphics support, and PDL tools.

Ada use is already present in about two-thirds of the companies with 10-15% planning to install an Ada compiler in the near future. Of those that have implemented Ada, 10% have developed their own compilers. Of the other major languages in use: 40% of the companies reported some usage of COBOL, 50% FORTRAN, 10% BASIC, 70% C, 20% JOVIAL, 20% CMS-2, 10% Pascal and 10% PL-1.

Seventy percent of these companies reported some library use. However, library use and development was viewed mainly as project specific activities. Further, of these companies, strictly manual library operations were reported by 70%, while only 28% were automated.

Data Base Management Systems Interface

SQL is a standard relational Data Base Management Systems (DBMS) language for both data manipulation and data description which allows the creation, modification and deletion of relational schemes. However, SQL has two limitations. First, SQL supports only one data structure, the base table (a twodimensional array). Second, SQL does not support the concept of a primary key, as all SQL keys (or indexes) are secondary for processing efficiency.

Consistent with OOD, the interface between the RSC_MGT system and the DBMS is a package. The function and interaction of this package is that of a transformer which converts an input that describes a RSC with an n-tuple of terms into a set of SQL commands that retrieve the appropriate RSC. The transformer consists of two objects, RSC storer and RSC retriever, and is implemented by embedding SQL instructions in the host code of the RSC_MGT system.

The RSC_MGT system will export a RSC descriptor to the transformer which adds a system generated unique primary key to the facet vector and stores it in a base table, FACET-CLASS. The RSC is stored in a "source" base table, called RSC.

To retrieve a RSC, a user enters the RSC descriptor and type (code, document, etc.). Each of the n terms in a descriptor are required to be an exact value or a wild card. The transformer accepts this information, generates SQL commands, executes them, and returns the RSC to the user. If this RSC satisfies the user, the process terminates. Otherwise, control returns to the RSC_MGT system which allows the user to modify the descriptor. (Modifications are based upon user decisions or system recommendations generated from the conceptual closeness distances.) This process continues until user termination.

Data Structures. Consistent with the relational model, all data in the SQL language is represented in the form of base tables or views, user defined constructs derived from base tables. A primary key is a minimal set of attributes that uniquely defines a tuple in a table (no null values). The primary key concept is indirectly enforced using three tables ISN, FACET-CLASS and RSC.

The table ISN(k), initialized to zero, has a single attribute k which is a system controlled internal sequence identifier (ISN) to keep track of the RSC's in the database. The second table is

FACET-CLASS (t1, t2, ...,tn, k),

with terms t1, ..., tn from the thesaurus which are supplied by the originator of the RSC at initial storage time. Since the order of the RSC's in FACET-CLASS is immaterial, the corresponding data structure can be a heap, and only the order of entry into the database is tracked via ISN. The third table is RSC (k, type, d), where d is the stored RSC text, and type describes the RSC as code, document, etc.

Table Construction. The SQL syntax below creates the table and enforces the concept of a primary key for the attribute k. This is accomplished by not allowing null values and requiring that duplicate values be rejected by the system.

```
CREATE TABLE FACET-CLASS (
        T1, CHAR(20),
            ...
        TN, CHAR(20),
        K, INTEGER, NOT NULL)
IN DBSPACE PAH.RSC1

CREATE UNIQUE INDEX TX ON FACET-CLASS (K)
```

Note that the term length (20) is arbitrary, and can be changed to any desired length.

```
CREATE TABLE RSC (
        TYPE CHAR(10),
        DESC VARCHAR(254),
        K INTEGER NOT NULL)
IN DBSPACE PAH.RSC1

CREATE TABLE ISN ( K, INTEGER NOT NULL)
IN DBSPACE PAH.RSC1
```

RSC Storage. All storage is handled by the transformer. Let the RSC be stored in an string array named, for example in the case of Ada code, NEW-CODE, with the appropriate values for the terms (T1-IN, ..., TN-IN).

Input: NEW-CODE, T1-IN, ..., TN-IN,
       TYPE-IN (for this example set to the value CODE).

Output: A new entry in the tables FACET-CLASS and RSC.

```
Algorithm: UPDATE ISN SET K = K+1
        SELECT K INTO :KVAL FROM ISN
        INSERT INTO FACET-CLASS
            VALUES ( :F1-IN, :F2-IN, ..., :FN-IN, :KVAL)
        INSERT INTO RSC
            VALUES ( :TYPE-N, :NEW-CODE, :KVAL)
```

RSC Retrieval. The retrieval algorithm, part of the transformer, is invoked by the user through embedded code in the RSC_MGT system. The xterms in a descriptor are assumed to be typed as: WILD-CARD (value is "*"), or EXACT-TYPE (a string from the thesaurus).

FUTURE PLANS AND EXTENSIONS

With the implementation of the prototype GSU RSC_MGT System, several extensions to this research are now possible. Three additional tools are planned: a Reuse Effort Assessment (REA) tool; a Closeness Measure Update (CMU) tool and a Specification Development (SD) tool. The REA tool will advise the user on final selections of RSC's from the list retrieved by the RSC_MGT System by providing easily interpretable degrees of membership in the key RSC reusability attributes of size, structure and documentation weighted by user experience.

The current RSC_MGT System furnishes a feedback feature which is used to modify the perceptual closeness distances. The system collects the necessary data and will perform the distance calculations, but the users must decide when an update is needed. The CMU tool will automate this decision process and help the user decide when a conceptual closeness distance update is needed. The SD tool and the issue of software specification tools are dealt with elsewhere in these proceedings (Owen, Gagliano, and Fraser, 1988).

SUMMARY

Reusability of software offers the prospect of controlling the rising costs of software development and maintenance. In order to store and retrieve reusable components (Ada packages, specifications and associated information), software tools and other library components are needed to assist in their management. This paper has presented some of the results of research at Georgia State University that is being conducted towards these ends.

ACKNOWLEDGMENT

This research has been supported through the Martin Marietta Energy Systems, Inc., Oak Ridge, TN 37831 (under Project DE-AC05-840R21400), the Army Institute for Research in Management Information, Communications and Computer Sciences (AIRMICS), Atlanta, GA 30332-0800, and the STARS Program.

The authors acknowledge the contributions of Graduate Research Assistants Mr. Nilesh H. Mehta and Ms. Joan M. Peters who worked on the prototype RSC_MGT system.

REFERENCES

Bishop, Y. M. M., Fienburg, S. E.,, Holland, P. W., 1975, *Discrete Multivariate Analysis*, MIT Press.

Booch, G., 1987(a), Software Components with Ada, Menlo Park: Benjamin Cummins.

Booch, G., 1987(b), *Software Engineering with Ada*, Menlo Park: Benjamin Cummins (2nd ed.).

Burton, B., and Broido, M., 1986, Development of an Ada Package Library, *Proceedings of the Annual National Conference on Ada Technology*, pp. 42-50.

Chatfield, C., and Collins, A. J., 1980, *Introduction to Multivariate Analysis*, New York: Chapman and Hall.

Conn, R. 1987, *The Ada Software Repository and the Defense Data Network*, New York: Zoetrope.

Conn, R., 1986, *Ada Software Repository Master Index*, Los Altos, CA: Echelon, Inc., 1986.

Gagliano, R. A., Fraser, M. D., Schaefer, M. E., and Owen, G. S., 1988, Functionality in the Reusability of Software, *Proceedings of the ACM 88 Computer Science Conference*, pp. 540-545, February 1988.

Gagliano, R. A., Fraser, M. D., and Owen, G. S., Guidelines for Reusable Ada Library Tools, *Ada Reusability Guidebook*, Project DE-AC05-840R21400, Martin Marietta Energy Systems, Inc, to appear.

Gagliano, R. A., Owen, G. S., and Honkanen, P. A., 1987, *Functional Specifications of Reusable Software in Ada*, Final Technical Report (DAAL03-86-D-0001), AIRMICS, June 1987.

Good, I. J., 1965, *The Estimation of Probabilities*, MIT Research Monograph, No. 30.

Graef, J. and Spence, I., 1979, Using Distance Information in the Design of Large Multidimensional Scaling Experiments, *Psychology Bulletin*, Vol. 36, pp. 60-66.

Guerrieri, E. 1988, Searching for Reusable Software Components with the RAPID Center Library System, *Proceedings of the 6th National Conference on Ada Technology*, pp. 395-406, March 1988.

Jardine, N., and Sibson, R., 1971, *Mathematical Taxonomy*, New York: John Wiley & Sons Ltd.

Jones, T. C. 1984, Reusability in Programming: A Survey of the State of the Art, *IEEE Transactions on Software Engineering*, Vol. SE-10, No. 5, pp. 544-552, September, 1984.

Jones, B., Litvintchouk, S., Mungle, J., Krasner, H., Melby, J., and Willman, H., 1985, Issues in Software Reusability, *ACM SIGSOFT Software Engineering Notes*, Vol. 10, No. 2, pp. 108109, April, 1985.

Kruskal, J. B., 1964(a), Multidimensional Scaling by Optimizing Goodness of Fit to a Nonmetric Hypothesis, *Psychometrika*, Vol. 29, pp. 1-27.

Kruskal, J. B., 1964(b), Nonmetric Multidimensional Scaling: A Numerical Method, *Psychometrika*, Vol. 29, pp. 115-129.

Kruskal, J. B., 1977, The Relationship Between Multidimensional Scaling and Clustering, *Classification and Clustering*, J. Van Ryzin ed., New York: Academic Press, 17-44.

Liskov, B. H., and Berzins, V., 1979, An Appraisal of Program Specifications, *Research Directions in Software Technology*, P. Wegner (ed.), MIT Press, pp. 276-301.

Litvintchouk, S. D., and Matsumoto, A. S., 1984, Design of Ada Systems Yielding Reusable Components: An Approach Using Structured Algebraic Specification, *IEEE Transactions on Software Engineering*, Vol. SE-10, No. 5, pp. 544-552, September, 1984.

Lubars, M. D., 1986, Affording Higher Reliability Through Software Reusability, *ACM SIGSOFT Software*

Engineering Notes, Vol. 11, No. 5, pp. 39-42, October 1986.

Owen, G. S., Gagliano, R. A., and Fraser, M. D., Knowledge Based Tools for Reusable Ada Software, else where in these *Proceedings of the 6th Symposium on EFISS*.

Owen, G. S., Gagliano, R. S., and Honkanen, P. A., 1988, Tools for the Storage and Retrieval of Reusable MIS Software in Ada, *Proceedings of the ACM 88 Computer Science Conference*, pp. 535-539, February.

Palmer, J. D., and Nguyen, T., 1986, A Systems Approach to Reusable Software Products, *IEEE SMC Conference Proceedings*, pp. 1410-1414, October.

Prieto-Diaz, R., and Freeman, P., 1987, Classifying Software for Reusability, *IEEE Software*, pp. 6-16, January.

Prieto-Diaz, R., 1985, *A Software Classification Scheme*, Information and Computer Science Technical Report 85-19, University of California, Irvine.

St. Dennis, R., Stachour, P., Frankowski, E., and Onuegbe, E., Measurable Characteristics of Reusable Ada Software, *Ada Letters*, Vol. VI, No. 2, pp. 41-50, March-April.

Scacchi, W., 1986, Shaping Software Behemoths, *UNIX Review*, Vol. 4, pp. 47-55, 10 October 1986.

Seber, G. A. F., 1984, *Multivariate Observations*, New York: John Wiley & Sons.

SofTech ISEC RAPID Investigation Analysis of RAPID Potential: Interim Report, SofTech, Inc., September 2, 1986.

Standish, T. A., 1984, An Essay on Software Reuse, *IEEE Transactions on Software Engineering*, Vol. 10, No. 5, pp. 494-497, September.

Suydam, W., CASE Makes Strides Toward Automated Software Development, *Computer Design*, Vol. 26, No. 1, January 1, 1987, pp. 49-70.

VERIFICATION AND VALIDATION OF REUSABLE ADA[1] COMPONENTS

C. K. Bullard, D. S. Guindi, W. B. Ligon, W. M. McCracken,
and S. Rugaber

Software Engineering Research Center
Georgia Institute of Technology
Atlanta, Georgia 30332

Abstract: This paper discusses the verification and validation (V&V) of reusable software written in the Ada programming language. The research includes methodological and experimental studies of aspects of V&V that are affected when reusable components are considered.

There are two aspects of reuse of concern to V&V: portability and adaptability. In the former case, the reusable component must be moved from one hardware/operating system environment to another. Usually, the intended functional behavior remains the same, and the main V&V concern is to assure that assumptions made by the software about the computing environment are not violated.

The latter case is concerned with incorporating a component into a new application environment. The Ada generic facility supports this by allowing developers to "instantiate" a component in a variety of ways, depending on the requirements of a new application. The characteristics that may be altered are delineated in such a way that the developer need only look at the specification and not the body of a generic component in order to understand what it does.

We have taken two approaches to investigating the V&V of reusable software. The first is methodological. It looks at the total software development life cycle to understand how reuse perturbs traditional methodologies. Its purpose is to characterize reuse errors and propose techniques for limiting them.

The other approach is experimental. We have adapted an existing methodology (Mutation Analysis) to detect instances of reuse errors. This tells us whether reuse errors are easily detectable and how easy it is to modify existing methods and tools. In particular, it can detect instances of Ada code that are not portable to new environments or not adaptable to different applications.

THE PROBLEM

Introduction: Motivation for the Work

The purpose of this research is to investigate the verification and validation (V&V) of reusable software components written in the Ada programming language. Software *reuse* is the process of using a software component in a context other than the one for which it was originally developed. Reuse is attractive because it can reduce the amount of effort required to develop software as well as improve the quality of the resulting systems. Design and implementation costs can be reduced if pre-existing components can be utilized, and V&V costs can be reduced if the components have been adequately tested when they were built, instead of having to be completely reexamined every time they are used.

If a component is independent of environmental peculiarities, then V&V efforts taken during developing need not be redone when the component is reused. Unfortunately, such independence is

---

[1]Ada is a registered trademark of the U. S. Government - Ada Joint Program Office.

Empirical Foundations of Information and Software Science V
Edited by P. Zunde and D. Hocking, Plenum Press, New York, 1990

437

unlikely. Dependencies can arise from the hardware, the operating system, the compiler, or the application environment in which the component is used. A viable strategy for the V&V of reusable components must address these dependencies and try to move as much effort as possible to the development stage where it needs to be performed only once. The purpose of this paper is to explore these special requirements that reusable components place upon the V&V process and then to propose methods and techniques to satisfy them.

One objective of the research is to determine the applicability of techniques and methods from traditional V&V to the V&V of reusable components. The next subsection presents definitions of terms from traditional V&V that are used in the remainder of the paper, after which concepts related specifically to the V&V of reusable components are introduced. The next major section examines several V&V techniques and their applicability to detecting reuse problems. The two sections that follow this examine reuse issues in detail and present characterizations of those issues. The first is concerned with portability problems, and the second is concerned with adaptability. Reusable components can be used in environments quite different from those imagined by the original designers, implementors and testers. The final section discusses how this freedom overwhelms traditional V&V approaches, and what can be done to address the problem.

Traditional V&V

Verification and validation were originally thought of as activities that occur at the completion of the development phase of the software lifecycle, whereas contemporary methods emphasize that V&V activities be carried out throughout the lifecycle (DeMillo, McCracken, Martin, and Passafiume, 1987). Thus V&V encompasses activities beyond those referred to as testing. Testing may be thought of as a proper subset of V&V, in that it does not normally include static methods, nor does it typically occur until after implementation, at the unit, integration and system levels.

V&V is a sub-process that occurs as a part of the overall software development process. V&V has been formally defined by the Joint Logistics Commanders (Joint Logistics Commanders, 1983) as: "Verification is the iterative process of determining whether the product of each step of the computer software development process fulfills all requirements levied by the previous step. Validation is the evaluation, integration, and test activities carried out at the system level to ensure that the finally developed CSCIs (Computer Software Configuration Items) satisfy the user's and supporter's requirements set down as performance and design criteria in the system and software requirements specification." These definitions and common practice dictate that software be verified at every step of the software development process and that validation be conducted as well.

Many techniques are used to achieve the required levels of verification and validation. The remainder of this section defines the terminology typically used to describe these activities. The first four terms are used to describe methods of V&V by what they do and how they do it. That is, analysis methods are describing what types of V&V can be conducted (static or dynamic) and testing strategies describe how the V&V is conducted (white or black box). Following those terms is a description of unit and integration testing. The goal of any V&V method (strategy or technique) is to minimize the errors in the deliverable software and to do that at a minimal cost. These definitions ar taken from DeMillo (DeMillo, McCracken, Martin, and Passafiume, 1987).

Static Analysis. The verification of a software product by observing or analyzing the product without executing it. Static analysis includes, but is not limited to structured walkthroughs, design reviews, desk checking, and checking for adherence to standards, as well as the automatic analysis of program properties such as the occurrence of uninitialized variables.

Dynamic Analysis. The verification of a software product by executing the software and observing its behavior in reference to its specification. Some examples of dynamic analysis are coverage methods such as path analysis, domain testing, and mutation analysis.

White Box Testing. Includes testing techniques that determine correctness by observing the internal structure and logic of the program under test.

Black Box Testing. Includes testing techniques that determine correctness by observing the functional (i.e., input/output) behavior of the program under test.

Unit Testing. Testing of individually compilable units of software such as subprograms, procedures, routines, etc. These tests typically rely on the aforementioned analysis methods and testing strategies to achieve the required degree of confidence. This level of testing is concerned with whether or not the unit meets the specification of its intended behavior. This is sometimes referred to as testing for correctness.

Integration Testing. Integration testing is a broad category that usually includes sub-system as well as system testing. It is concerned with the correctness of interfaces between units as well as validation of a system's function.

To minimize the cost of V&V, it is desirable to reduce the amount of integration testing while possibly increasing the amount of unit testing. This is based on the observations that unit testing is less expensive to conduct and that the cost of correcting errors rises with the increasing level of integration of the software. In addition, testing techniques tend to be more effective at the unit level whether they be formal verification or mutation testing.

Formal Methods. In addition to testing and static analysis, formal methods are sometimes used to demonstrate the correctness of a program. Formal methods, sometimes called formal verification or program verification, are concerned with formally proving that a program is correct with respect to its specification, or in some cases proving the correctness of the design of a system. In addition to formal verification, formal techniques are sometimes used to specify a program without the use of rigorous proof techniques.

Specification. The description of the intended behavior of a program. Specifications range from formal, based on mathematical logic, to completely informal using natural language descriptions of the functions the program is to perform.

Adequacy. (Budd and Angluin, 1982) A term used to describe how well a set of test data exposes errors in a program based on a specific criterion. An example of this is how well a set of test data exposes mutation analysis error classes. An adequacy criterion can be used to indicate when a testing method may be terminated.

Requirements. The properties and constraints that a software system must satisfy. Included in the requirements are the non-functional and functional requirement of the system.

Functional Requirements. The services or features of the software system required by the user; its behavior.

Non-Functional Requirements. The constraints or restrictions placed on the software system, such as reliability, timing, and sizing limitations, and maintainability.

Mutation Analysis. (DeMillo, 1988) A test technique that measures the error exposing ability of test data on a program by creating slightly changed versions of the program and seeing how the test data detects those changes.

V&V for Reuse

Reuse Errors. Normally, in developing software, one of the major difficulties that arises is software errors. A software *error* is an anomaly that causes a component to behave differently from its specification. In software reuse, it may be the case that a component's behavior meets it specification in its intended environment, but fails to meet its specification in some other environment. For example, if a component depends on the order in which a compiler evaluates the sub-expressions of an expression, it may not behave as intended when compiled with a compiler employing a different policy. This type of anomaly is called a *reuse error.*

This definition of a reuse error raises an interesting question: if a component fails to meet its specification in some environment, is the component in error, or should the specification have required the component to operate properly in both the original and the new environments? Currently, issues of environmental compatibility are considered non-functional requirements, if they are mentioned at all: "The system will be targeted for an XYZ-2000 processor under OS with the X compiler." The advent of software reuse, however, demands that environment compatibility be considered as an explicit requirement, if the goal is to produce software that is independent of its environment, and, therefore, as reusable as possible. This question may well be answered by the method used to "repair" the error: if the code changed, it is a coding or design error, if the specification is modified, it is a specification error.

Portability and Adaptability. In attempting to classify and understand reuse errors, there are two different kinds of environments to consider: a machine environment and an application environment. The *machine environment* includes not just the physical hardware, but a virtual machine that incorporates the operating system and any run-time environment and conventions set up by the compiler. In a sense, the machine environment includes all that the reusable software component regards as "the system" and is unchangeable (system modifications notwithstanding). The *application environment*, on the other hand, is composed of other application-programmer written components with which the reusable software component is to be used. The application environment is essentially the "user" of the reusable component, and that use is generally changeable, since it is programmer code as opposed to system code.

Software reuse can, therefore, be divided into two activities: porting and adapting. To *port* a component is to change its machine environment, and to *adapt* a component is to change its application environment. Reuse errors are, therefore, divided into portability errors and adaptability errors. A *portability error* is one that occurs when a reusable component is moved from one machine environment to another, and an *adaptability error* is one that occurs when a reusable component is used in an application environment different than that for which it was originally designed. Effectively, portability and adaptability define two interfaces a reusable software component must consider: an interface with the machine, or *machine interface*; and an interface with the application, or *application interface*. It is with respect to these two interfaces that reuse errors occur.

Characterization. The distinction between portability and adaptability is central to the understanding of reuse errors and affects the V&V methods used in the development of reusable software components. The major distinctions are as follows:

1) Portability errors are contained entirely within the reusable component. Problems such as this can be detected during unit testing, as opposed to system testing.

   Adaptability errors span the application interface and, in fact, represent only potential errors in the component itself. It is meaningless to say that an actual error exists until some sort of environment is present. The major difficulty is that it is impossible to anticipate all of the potential application environments in which the reusable component will be used. These problems must be considered at system integration time, although the potential for an adaptability error may be detectable by considering the isolated component.

2) According to the Ada language definition, components that have portability errors are considered "erroneous". The Ada Language Reference Manual (Department of Defense, 1980) points out the places in the language where behavior is undefined or some latitude is given to the compiler writer or system. While such a component may behave correctly in one machine environment, its correctness is nonetheless incomplete. Such problems can often be detected with static analysis, as the occurrence of language constructs is easily recognizable.

   A component with an adaptability error, on the other hand, may be perfectly correct in and of itself, but its correctness depends on the way in which it is used. Obviously, such a problem does not lend itself well to formal verification techniques since the "error" may not exist at all until the component is placed in a new application environment.

3) Portability has been studied for some time, and is relatively well understood. In addition, a considerable amount of research has been performed developing tools to detect portability errors. The bibliography lists several references to specific portability problems with Ada (Digital Equipment, 1985; Barnes, 1984; Nilssen and Wallis, 1984), as well as several for other languages such as C (Johnson, 1979) and FORTRAN (Ryder, 1974). This does not imply that these portability issues have been solved, but Ada has managed to isolate many of them in such a way as to improve their manageability.

   Adaptability, on the other hand, has traditionally been the bane of software testing and evaluation. Combining separately tested components into a system yields a combinatoric explosion of interactions that can yield errors. Most V&V techniques either become infeasible when used on an entire system or fail to address the interface problem and so suffer from a lack of effectiveness. The central problem in V&V for reusable software components is the integration/interface problem.

```
        :
        :
A : Integer;
        :
        :
FUNCTION foo (parm : in Integer) RETURN Integer IS
BEGIN
        A := parm;
        RETURN A;
END foo;
        :
        :
PROCEDURE bar (parm1, parm2 : IN OUT Integer) IS
BEGIN
        parm1 := A * foo(parm2);
END bar;
        :
        :
```

Figure 1. An Example.

An Example. As an example, consider the Ada code fragment in Figure 1. The function foo modifies the exported global variable A. Later, in procedure bar, a statement contains both A and a call to foo in the same expression. Since Ada does not define the order of evaluation of terms in an expression, this code contains a potential reuse error.

If the subprograms foo and bar and variable A are all part of the same reusable component, then this component has a portability error because the component will not behave correctly in a machine environment that uses an order of evaluation different from that expected by the programmer. A V&V method for reusable Ada components should detect this reuse error during unit testing.

If, on the other hand, function foo and variable A are in the same reusable component, but procedure bar is in the application environment, then this component has an adaptability error because the component is dependent on its use by the application environment. In this instance, the application environment's use has the potential for an order of evaluation error. This could not be detected by examining the component in isolation, but must be looked for during integration testing.

Many of the same issues and problems come up in both portability and adaptability. In many cases, adaptability errors are really portability errors that have been "split" such that part of the error is in the reusable component, and part is in the application environment. This comes from the rather interesting fact that many of these problems involve more than one point in the program. Note that in the example, it is difficult to say whether the implementation of function foo, or the statement in procedure bar is in error. This type of error is called a *two point error*.

Other Definitions. Other definitions of the term portability and adaptability exist. A typical definition of portability is "a qualitative judgement on how easy it is to change a given program such that it can be recompiled by a different compiler and then run with the required behavior, generally on a different target" (Nilssen and Wallis, 1984). Therefore, a completely portable program would not require any changes to compile and run in a new machine environment. This definition is consistent with the one above, except that in reuse V&V, a quantitative rather than qualitative analysis is desirable.

Popular definitions of adaptability are not so uniform. Wallis (1982) in *Portable Programming*, defines adaptable: "used to describe software that requires a significant amount of work to move to another machine ... simply by making changes that are regular enough to be made by computer". This definition describes adaptability as a special case of portability. Our definition of adaptability is similar to portability, but involves changing the application environment instead of the machine environment. Lecarme and Gart (1986), in *Software Portability*, define adaptability: "the ease with which (a program's) properties can be modified. Adaptation is made without changing the program environment, and remains adaptation only so long as the new properties are closely related to the old ones". These definitions differ significantly from the one above in that in both instances the adapted program is modified whereas the definition above is intended to deal only with cases where no component source code is actually modified, only the application environment. Under the definition above, pure software adaptation (with no porting involved) is accomplished by using a pre-compiled reusable component via the Ada WITH statement, and the only modification allowed is through changing the resources provided to the adapted component. If modified code is considered, all notions of pre-existing reliability are lost, because there is no way of knowing what changes have been made or how they affect the operation and functionality of the program.

DETECTION MECHANISMS

There are a variety of mechanisms for detecting errors in traditional V&V. One of the goals of this project is to study the exploitation of these techniques for detecting reuse errors. Reuse presents significant problems to overcome because analysis cannot always be performed at the component level, but must consider the interaction between components. At the same time, exhaustive testing of software component interfaces remains an intractable problem. Our approach is to understand the portability and adaptability issues at the component's machine and application interfaces. This understanding can guide the selection and combination of different V&V methods and techniques to comprise a solution that intelligently analyzes software component interfaces with minimal effort.

Towards this end, this section discusses some of the approaches that can be used to analyze or test for portability and adaptability errors. First, three traditional approaches are presented: simulation, static analysis, and mutation analysis. Finally, constraint-based analysis is introduced as a promising new technique for detecting reuse errors.

Simulation

The obvious first approach to testing for reuse errors is to simply test a reusable module in a variety of environments. This approach extends the traditional notion of testing to include input that describes the execution environment. The most noticeable disadvantage is that this requires a multitude of machines and compilers. The next problem is that it does not consider new machines and compilers that are yet to come to market. This problem can be somewhat lessened by constructing an interpretive system that is capable of simulating a wide variety of run-time systems with parameters to control machine properties such as word size, order of evaluation, memory initialization policy, and parameter passing conventions.

The same ideas apply to adaptability. A component can be tested via a testing harness that simulates a wide variety of applications environments. Again, the same problems are present as with the portability case, only they are more profound because the potential application environments in which a component might be used cannot be easily characterized by a set of well understood parameters.

The real problem with this approach is that there is no guarantee that simply running a component in each environment will, in fact, cause potential errors to occur. Also, this kind of testing produces no measure of adequacy, no way to gauge the correctness of the component, and no way of understanding what has and has not been considered in the event the component is actually moved to a new environment.

On the other hand, simulation may be the only approach available to deal with portability problems that involve component interaction and timing issues such as those that arise with Ada tasks. In order to make this approach feasible, a testing method should include adequacy criteria that reduce the amount of testing needed and provide a measure of a test suite's effectiveness. As such, simulation is useful as a foundation for mutation analysis and constraint-based testing.

Static Analysis

The next approach is to look at static measures of a component's portability and adaptability. Techniques exist to statically analyze code and recognize program and language structures that are non-portable or non-adaptable. Such a approach has the advantage that it does not require a complex environment modeling system or a roomful of machines. Also, static analysis requires less overhead because the code is never actually executed. Moreover, it provides a definite measure of reusability. This is an appealing approach for detecting some portability errors because many machine dependencies occur as language constructs, are localized, and are well understood. An example of such a tool is the ADAMAT static analysis tool (ADAMAT, 1988).

Adaptability errors, on the other hand, pose a problem because dependencies are often in two parts. In a reusable component, there may be a potential reuse error, and the application environment may use the component in such a way as to realize the error. When a reuse error crosses the application interface in this manner, it is impossible to detect by analyzing the component in isolation. At best, a static analysis tool could detect those areas that create the potential for the error. In many of these situations, however, this potential cannot be easily removed. Therefore, since all of the target application environments are unknown, a static analysis tool has to be run on the entire application each time a reusable component is used.

For example, if the function foo and the variable A in Figure 1 are part of a reusable component, a static analysis tool could detect that the function modifies an exported variable and is, therefore, not as adaptable as possible. It is not likely, however, that foo can be re-written in such a way as to remove this potential adaptability error. Using only static means, it is impossible to say whether foo will work properly with bar unless the combined application is analyzed.

The main disadvantage of static analysis is that in many cases it cannot do more than detect the possibility of reuse errors. Many reuse errors involve component interaction and timing issues, which are not exercised by static methods.

Mutation Analysis

Another approach is to use mutation analysis techniques to measure the adequacy of a set of test data with respect to a defined set of errors and reuse errors. Mutation analysis starts with a description of reuse errors and develops a set of mutation operators that create variant programs. A test data set's ability to distinguish the original program from the variants provides a measure of that test data set's adequacy in detecting the errors.

Previous research (DeMillo, Lipton, and Sayward, 1978; Budd, DeMillo, Lipton, and Sayward, 1978; Budd, Hess, and Sayward, 1980; Budd, 1980; DeMillo and Spafford, 1986) has developed a set of mutation operators for traditional errors based on error studies (Goodenough and Gerhart, 1975). More recently, mutation operators have been developed for Ada (Bowser, 1988; Appelbe et al., 1988). Errors that involve component interfaces are handled in these systems by mutating the entire application. The question arises whether these operators are sufficient to detect reuse errors if the test data set is simulated in the various target environments. In other words, if test data set T is adequate to detect all standard mutants of program P in environment E1, and if P is executed on T in a new environment E2, then any of some class of reuse errors that exist in environment E2 will be detected.

Experimental evidence has shown, unfortunately, that this does not hold because it is possible to have more than one specific interface point between components (for example, by calling a function more than once), and it is possible to distinguish all of the generated mutants without exercising the path that contains the reuse error. To remedy this, the method could be altered to require that all of these paths be exercised, but then the number of mutants created, and their subsequent overhead, increases greatly. The number of paths that must be exercised needs to be limited to those that hold a potential for error.

An alternate approach is to extend mutation analysis by developing new mutation operators for reuse errors. This approach generalizes the notion of program input and output beyond simple values to include variables, types, subprograms, and run-time environment parameters such as order of evaluation policy, word size, and memory initialization policy. The tester would manipulate these inputs in order to detect the reuse errors introduced by a set of mutation operators. Obviously, this requires a machine simulation system such as that described above in order to work with portability errors.

Using this kind of extension, components can be tested individually for traditional errors and the application environment can be tested in conjunction with the component specifically for reuse errors. In this case, all paths need not be tested directly, only enough to test the critical elements of the component interface and its environment. Since the new operators focus on potential reuse errors that exist at the component interface, the number of mutants would be reduced.

The advantage of this approach is that there is a definite measure of the adequacy of the tests and the method is not dependent on running tests in all possible environments. In essence, by focusing on reuse errors, the various environmental parameters are considered independently and combination effects only need to be considered when they are necessary to detect a specific error. This approach also provides the possibility of working with timing-dependent problems, such as the Ada rendezvous, that cannot be achieved with static methods.

To investigate this approach, a prototype Ada mutation system was constructed and some experiments were run. One of the experiments involved adaptability testing for Ada generics that take a function as a parameter. A generic was written that depended on it formal functional parameter being commutative and associative. It was demonstrated that the current set of mutation operators could not detect this dependency. A new operator was defined that was capable of detecting this problem.

Unfortunately, the efforts so far have not been able to construct such an operator for many of the reuse errors. Instead, most of the proposed mutation operators result in mutants that are distinguished only if an error exists and input is provided that causes the erroneous behavior in the original. If the original program is correct, the behavior of the mutant is always the same as the original. If the test data can distinguish between the mutant, then there is an error, but if it cannot, there are two possibilities: either the program is correct or the test data is inadequate.

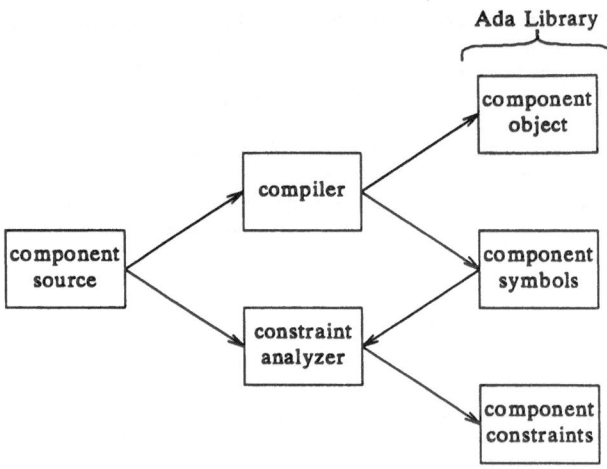

Figure 2. Constraint Analysis Component Development.

Constraint Based Analysis

Finally, there is the possibility of combining static analysis with mutation analysis and a relatively new technique - constraint-based analysis (Weyuker and Ostrand, 1980; Offutt, 1988). In this approach a static analysis tool is used to detect and record potential reuse errors with a component's library information (Figure 2). This record defines a constraint on the component's use that, if violated, could cause a reuse error. When the component is used in an application, the constraints are used to generate mutants that test the application environment to see if they, in fact, cause the error to occur (Figure 3). For example, static analysis can detect that one of a reusable component's functions fails if one of its parameters is out of range. This information can be stored with the component's library module. The information can be used to generate a mutated program that raises an exception at each point the function is called if that parameter is out of range.

As components are combined, the constraints can be propagated - creating new constraints that detect when the higher level components violate the lower level constraints or any of their own constraints. Once the constraints propagate to the top level, they can be used as a measure of the system's correctness against the specifications.

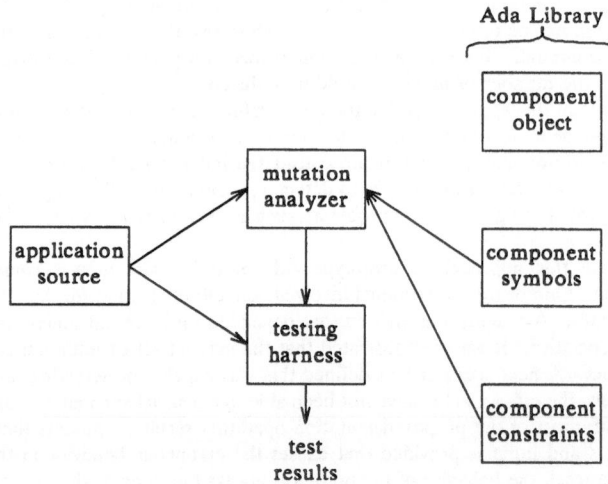

Figure 3. Constraint Analysis Application Development.

It is not necessary that the constraints be determined by static analysis or that mutation testing is used to test the constraints. In some cases, static analysis may be more effective at determining a constraint violation (for example, order of evaluation errors), or the programmer may have to assert constraints for more complex adaptability errors (for example, protocol dependencies) via a PRAGMA or by some other means. In any case, this approach is promising because it limits the amount of testing needed for the reusable component to those areas where a known potential for a reuse error exists.

This approach is an improvement over the strictly static approach in that it deals with the two point error issue by recording the potential errors at module implementation time and because it detects actual reuse errors at component integration time - without completely re-analyzing the components. It is also an improvement over mutation analysis because the execution overhead is reduced. A component would be mutation analyzed for standard errors but the problems with inter-procedural errors (reuse errors) is resolved by limiting the scope of the testing to those areas where known potential for errors exists. Constraint propagation helps not only in guiding a hierarchical testing method, but can also be used for automatic generation of test data that exercises the constrained paths.

CLASSIFICATION OF PORTABILITY ERRORS

Porting software between machines is a type of software reuse that is well-understood and has been much described (Wallis, 1982; Nilssen and Wallis, 1984; Barnes, 1984). Less well understood are methods of preventing these dependencies and of correcting them when they are detected. Presented in this section are several ways in which portability issues can be characterized to help software developers prevent or detect them.

Portability problems vary depending on the application domain or development method in use. When a multi-tasking application is developed, timing and synchronization considerations become an important concern. Numerical applications may require that special attention be given to the precision and correctness of the environment's arithmetic functions. Issues characterized in this manner can be used to program defensively, to detect occurrence, or to document what cannot be avoided.

Another way to look at portability issues is the manner in which they can be detected. Issues associated with a particular statement or a particular program fragment can be detected with static methods. The presence of an UNCHECKED CONVERSION PRAGMA can be detected in such a manner and indicates a non-portable statement. A function that modifies a global variable has a potential dependency on the form of the expression used to call it. However, this situation can be detected statically. Other issues require execution of the program to detect the problems caused by an active process interacting with and changing the state of its environment.

A third way to look at portability issues is based on the Ada constructs used. The language designer or someone learning a language studies it feature by feature. Manuals or development tools point out undefined or implementation-dependent features. The Ada Language Reference Manual (Department of Defense, 1980) tells which properties are undefined and includes an appendix describing an implementation's machine dependencies. The remainder of this section looks at portability problems from these three viewpoints.

Types of Application

This categorization is based on the assumption that it is better to avoid constructing non-portable code than to correct or remove a non-portable construct after it has been written. The person who best knows a piece of software, and, thus, who can best prevent or document non-portable sections of code, is the one writing the software. As software is developed, decisions are made that affect its portability. A decision may introduce new concerns, or alleviate others. For example, a programmer decides some numerical computations are necessary for an application. Now he must worry about such things as word size, how the machine handles overflows, and the accuracy with which the machine and run-time system implements arithmetic operations. If he then decides that the data will never exceed some small value, his decision eliminates concerns about word size and overflow.

Some portability issues are a concern no matter what the type of application. For example, the way a compiler compiles the source, the optimizations used, the algorithms chosen, all affect the space the object code occupies and its execution time. A program that executes on one machine may not be able to fit on another machine that has the same amount of space, when compiled with a different compiler. Any program that inadvertently accesses a variable before it has been assigned may become dependent on the memory initialization policy. Most issues, however, are related to the application and method of development. This characterization indicates when a programmer developing a piece of software must worry about a particular portability issue.

Numerical. When an application is primarily concerned with numerical computations, issues such as convergence and error propagation arise. For example, when numbers become larger than the machine can represent, some machines signal overflow while others continue silently with an incorrect result. Other concerns include whether the format of numbers is one's complement or two's complement, whether floating point numbers that cannot be represented are rounded or truncated, what is the precision available for floating point numbers, and how bytes are aligned (Spafford, 1988).

Multitasking. A programmer coordinating the execution of several Ada processes has a difficult task in writing portable code. Two compilers may produce differing object programs for the same source, even if they reside on the same hardware and operating system. The timing of these object programs will differ, and so coordinated processes may not interact in the same manner when compiled differently. Unsynchronized use of shared variables is a portability issue when a programmer develops coordinated processes. Other problems arise when an implementation permits the use of machine priorities, as priority levels may differ between machines.

Dynamic Memory Allocation. Some applications make heavy use of dynamic memory allocation. Structures that grow and shrink dynamically can outgrow the space available to a program. Machines differ in the amount of space they allow for dynamic allocation. The method of allocating pointers also differs between machines. A program that depends on a particular allocation strategy must indicate this, as its portability will be affected (Spafford, 1988).

Systems Programming. A programmer may decide to specify the way an object of a particular type is represented, the maximum space to be used to store the object or its storage location. This may be done to tailor the code for a particular machine and obviously will not work on other machines. However, it may be an attempt to parameterize the code so that it will behave properly regardless of the underlying machine. For example, if a construct may be represented differently on other machines, it may be represented in terms of machine-specific symbolic constants. Even though this can make software more portable, another compiler may not be able to represent the construct as specified, thus making the software non-portable. Unchecked conversions also depend on a machine's representation and may not be portable.

Detection

A characterization based on prevention can help in the development of portable software. However, it doesn't say anything about detecting potentially non-portable sections of existing code. This subsection discusses how the various detection mechanisms apply to different types of portability problems.

Static Analysis. Certain features of a language are potentially non-portable and can be detected simply by searching for them in the code. These include specifications for the representation of complex types, unchecked conversions, unchecked deallocation, machine code insertions, and use of machine constants. The presence of any of these doesn't necessarily mean that a portability problem exists, just that the potential for a problem exists. The potential for other portability issues, such as a dependency on a particular order of evaluation or on a particular memory initialization policy, can also be detected through static analysis.

Simulation. Portability issues that stem from a dependence on the way the environment and the executing program interact cannot be detected by statically examining the code. These portability issues depend on the way the environment does such things as allocating and laying out storage, passing parameters, and elaborating library units. The synchronization of multiple processes is highly dependent on the manner in which the processes interact with the environment. The interaction must be observed to detect such dependencies. Problems associated with these issues can be detected through executing the software on simulations of different environments.

Mutation Analysis. Other portability issues lead to problems that can be detected through manipulation of input. Still others vary from machine to machine with a small number of options, such as whether the machine raises an exception on overflow or continues silently with an incorrect value. These issues include whether a machine rounds or truncates values that have no representations and how it handles operations on singular values (e.g., negative zero on a one's complement machine). Mutation analysis detection mechanisms that can simulate specific environments can be used to detect problems associated with such issues.

446

Constraint Analysis. Despite a developer's best attempts at making a piece of software portable, a program may still have minimal requirements that an environment must fulfill for the program to execute properly. For example, numerical software may require at least a certain precision for floating point calculations. A program may need an unusual amount of memory available for dynamic allocation. Constraint analysis can be used to develop a set of constraints that must be satisfied by an environment to execute the program.

Language

A third way to characterize portability issues is based on the language used. Portability issues are categorized by the language constructs in which they arise. The portability of a piece of software can then be described in terms of the constructs used and the problems associated with those specific constructs. Naturally, a programmer who is trying to develop portable software can utilize such a characterization when deciding what constructs to use.

Some of the books written about software portability talk about portability in terms of the various language elements. In particular, Nilssen and Wallis (1984) describe portability issues for Ada by pointing out potential problems in each section of the Ada Language Reference Manual (Department of Defense, 1980). The manual itself mentions when the implementation of a feature or an algorithm is undefined and, therefore, varies between different machines.

Summary

The language-based and the application-based characterizations can be used to alert developers of portability problems inherent in the decisions they make about the use of a particular language constructs and in the type of application being built. Developers can be guided in documenting issues that have not been resolved so that non-portable sections of code can be easily located and modified when necessary. The characterization based on detection can guide measurements of software portability. It also defines the limitations of the detection mechanisms.

CLASSIFICATION OF ADAPTABILITY ERRORS

Software adaptation is the process of moving a reusable software component from one application environment to another. Adaptability errors are anomalies that cause a reusable component to fail to behave correctly when used in an application environment for which it was not designed.

The software adaptation process involves the selection and retrieval of components from a library of software parts. Such a process presumably would be based on the Ada compilation unit structure and would utilize packages and generics to group components and allow for their customization. Furthermore, some sort of database would be available for selecting an appropriate component based on its specification. It is up to the application developer and this system to determine the suitability of a reusable component for a given application. To realize a cost savings in reusing a component, it must be possible to make such a determination from a component's specification because the cost of understanding source code is high.

Ada goes beyond most other languages in its separation of specification from implementation. Moreover, it provides encapsulation mechanisms that encourage the production of modules with strictly limited interactions with their invoking environments. In an ideal world, the Ada specification mechanism would provide a complete description of all dependencies between a module and its environment. In such a world, all reuse errors would be detectable as violations of the specification, and traditional V&V mechanisms could be used to detect them.

There are several areas in which Ada's specification mechanisms are insufficient to describe important interactions between a reusable component and its application environment. In the first area, responsibility for providing certain auxiliary capabilities, such as concurrence control, is difficult to describe in an Ada module specification. In the second area, the language gives too much freedom to the user, and abuses can lead to subtle reuse errors, such as when two arguments to a procedure are aliases for the same variable in the calling environment. The next two subsections describe these two areas.

Architectural Concerns

When a software system is designed, there are typically areas of concern that go beyond the strictly functional specification of the module. For example, if dynamic memory allocation is being used in a software system, whose responsibility is it to manage/free allocated objects? It may be the local responsibility of the module that provides the objects, or it may be the responsibility of a general-purpose memory manage component. In either case, it is important that the responsibility be explicitly specified.

This section gives examples of four types of architectural decisions regarding the responsibility for managing certain capabilities. Grady Booch (1986) presents these issues in the following classification. E. V. Berard (GRACE Notes, 1987) has presented a similar list of general issues that involves greater detail and issues that relate to the time and space performance of a component. Both Booch and Berard sell collections of components organized around these decisions.

Concurrence. Components are designed as one of sequential, guarded, concurrent, or multiple. Each of these categories describe a different level of client application concurrency control. *Sequential* allows only one thread of control; *guarded* requires the client to enforce mutual exclusion; *concurrent* provides mutual exclusion; and *multiple* allows multiple simultaneous readers.

Space Utilization. Components are rated as either bounded or unbounded, which describe an object's space allocation scheme. *Unbounded* objects can grow dynamically as long as memory is available, while *bounded* objects have some programmer-imposed maximum size.

Space Reclamation. Components are classified as unmanaged, managed, or controlled, each of which describes a different level of garbage collection control. *Unmanaged* components rely on the machine environment to do garbage collection; *managed* components perform their own garbage collection; and *controlled* components perform garbage collection even for multiple client tasks.

Iterator Availability. Components are rated as one of iterator or noniterator, each of which indicates the availability, or lack of availability of an iterator. An iterator is an operation associated with an abstract data type that yields the elements of an object of that type, one at a time upon request. *Noniterator* components have no iterator, and *iterator* components do have an iterator. Iterators are generally used with looping constructs to perform an action on each element of a data structure without exposing the implementation of that structure.

According to Booch, reusable components should be classified along each of these dimensions, and this classification should be made part of the component specification. Thus, it is an adaptability error for an application to use a component, assuming one classification, when in fact the component does not meet that requirement.

For example, assume there is a component that implements a priority queue that is to be used by an application. This component may have been constructed with the assumption that only a single program or Ada task will be executing the code at any given time, but the application may require the component to allow multiple threads of control and manages the concurrency with an appropriate set of controls. In such a situation, it is highly likely that an adaptability error will occur. Here the application environment places a demand on the component that is unrelated to the functional properties of the component. How a component is designed with respect to these issues must become part of all reusable component specifications in order to deal with this type of adaptability error. A V&V method for reusable components should include methods for verifying that a component meets this part of its specification. Some reasonable classification similar to Booch's makes an appropriate addition to standard functional specifications.

Implementation Concerns

The issues presented by Booch and Berard are fairly general in nature and involve features that often must be designed into a component. Dealing with these problems is a matter of recording this classification in the component specification and considering this information when the component is selected. Even though a component may be properly characterized along each of these dimensions, there may be the potential for improper use of the component that will lead to an adaptability error. Taking the example above, the priority queue component may be properly specified as allowing multiple threads of execution, but may require the application environment to use a provided set of routines in a protocol that assures mutual exclusion, such as a graph-based locking protocol. If the application environment fails to use the protocol properly, the component may fail.

This type of error is very similar to those mentioned above except that it is much more component-specific and represents an error in the application's environment, as opposed to an error or omission in the component's specification. Besides being more local, these problems relate more closely to the program's implementation than to its design. Moreover, they reflect instances where the semantics of Ada offer the programmer subtle opportunities to get into trouble. For example, aliasing problems arise because it is possible to give two or more names to the same element of a program's state.

These errors can also be taken as a measure of a component's robustness, its ability to deal with improper or unexpected input. For example, a functional formal parameter to a generic unit must have its type as well as the types of its arguments specified. However, other important properties, such as whether it is commutative are not explicitly mentioned. The following is a list of some of the areas where this kind of adaptability error can be found:

Order of Evaluation Errors. A component may export an object and a function that modifies the object. If the application environment uses the object and the function in the same expression, on opposite side of the same assignment, in argument expressions for the same procedure call, in two index expressions for the same ARRAY object, in components of the same aggregate, within the same range expression, or as guards in the same SELECT statement, then the potential exists for a dependency on the order of evaluation.

Aliasing Errors. A component may export an object and a procedure that takes an IN OUT or ACCESS argument of the same type. If the application environment calls the procedure with the object as the argument, then the potential exists for the object to be referred to via two name within the component. Similarly, the problem may arise if the component exports a procedure that takes two IN OUT or ACCESS arguments of the same type, and the application environment calls the procedure with the same object for both arguments.

Domain Errors. A subprogram's behavior may only be defined if an argument or object's value is within some range or bears some relationship ($>$, $<$, $=$, etc.) to some other argument or object's value, and the application environment invokes the subprogram when the condition is not met. In many cases Ada provides mechanisms such as subranges for dealing with this class of problem. There will always be instances, however, where a component requires more of its parameters than the language permits it to specify. The case of the formal generic functional parameter described above is an example.

Protocol Errors. The specification of an Ada component places requirements on the parameters of the component when it is used. The specifications, however, are restricted to describing a single invocation or access to the component. If the component retains some internal state between, then there may be some limitations on the legal sequences by which the component may be invoked. For example, a stack component should never have more POP calls than PUSH calls. Although these situations can be checked for explicitly at run time, there is no static specification mechanism for dealing with them in Ada. If the component relies on the application environment to maintain such constraints, then the potential for a reuse error exists when the component is moved to a new application environment. These problems are called protocol errors. Another example occurs if a component exports two subprograms and the number of times one is called may not exceed the number of times the other is called by more than N times (as would be the case in a bounded implementation of a queue). There are numerous examples of protocol errors such as the use of semaphores and initialization of sub-systems. Any component that has some notion of state may be susceptible to protocol errors.

The common thread among these categories of implementation concerns is that the component in question is designed in such a way as to allow a client application to misuse the component. There exists the potential for an error. The realization of the error exists somewhere across the application interface in the application environment itself, otherwise the error is either a portability error (as in the case of aliasing, order of evaluation, etc.) or a traditional error (as in the case of a domain error). For this reason, traditional V&V techniques are of little use, since there is not enough context to determine the existence of an error, regardless of the computational power available. A possible solution is to utilize constraint-based analysis to develop usage constraints that can be stored with a component's specification and utilized by an integration testing tool to test a client application for compliance with the constraints. Such a system could use a variety of techniques (e.g., static analysis, mutation testing) to both determine the constraints and test for their compliance. Complex constraints, such as usage protocols might be specified by the programmer as assertions included in the specification.

ISSUES

Objective

Traditionally, the goal of V&V is to reach a point in the software development lifecycle where it can be stated that a component is free from errors. In practice, the best that can be achieved is to determine that a component is free from a restricted class of errors. This often involves assuming the component, after design and coding, is relatively close to being correct, as discussed in DeMillo (1978).

In a similar fashion, it would be desirable to determine that a component is free from reuse errors. Due to the wide range of portability and adaptability reuse errors, however, this goal must be limited to a restricted class of reuse errors. The objective then is to develop a notion of adequacy for a restricted class of reuse errors that aids developers in the V&V process in developing and utilizing reusable components effectively. Such a notion should help to limit the combinatoric explosion involved in testing a system built from reusable components.

Adequacy and Reuse Errors

In attempting to develop a testing method to determine the correctness of a component, it is desirable to have some sort of adequacy criterion. An *adequacy criterion* for a class of errors is a condition such that if a test data set satisfies the criterion, then the test data set is capable of detecting all of the class of errors that might exist in a component (Weyuker, 1983). In essence, an adequacy criterion is a mechanism for determining when component testing can be stopped. An example of an adequacy criterion is "the test data will cause each and every statement in the component to be executed at least once". There is, however, no guarantee that a test data set that satisfies an adequacy criterion will be effective in detecting other classes of errors (Weyuker, 1988). The well known *statement coverage* criterion mentioned above is deficient at discovering any detectable traditional errors (Walsh, 1985), but may be used in combination with more powerful criteria such as those developed through mutation analysis (DeMillo et al., 1988) to produce effective adequacy criteria.

In dealing with reuse errors, the first problem is to understand what it means to be free of reuse errors. Previous sections of this paper have discussed what reuse errors are, but it is not clear that it is even possible to develop components that do not have reuse errors. For example, almost any component has at least a few arithmetic operations. Since arithmetic can be highly machine dependent, it may be impossible to write a completely machine-independent component. Similarly, it can be difficult to develop programs without introducing adaptability errors such as aliasing errors.

Therefore, the goal should be to develop adequacy criteria such that if a test data set satisfies the criteria for a component, then when the test data set is executed against the component in some environment, the test data set will detect any errors that exist in the new environment, rather than criteria that simply determine the existence of reuse errors in the isolated component. In contrast to traditional adequacy, that was relative to a set of errors, reuse adequacy is relative to both a set of errors and a target environment. This is achieved by describing the test data set in terms of the environment, and should be reflected in the component specification.

The bulk of this research has been concentrated on understanding the class of reuse errors. Reuse errors are more complicated than traditional errors because software reuse implicitly involves a wide variation in environments. Portability issues are complicated because the semantics of even the most basic machine operations such as arithmetic are not uniformly defined. Adaptability is similarly complicated by the total freedom an application environment has in using a component or supplying dependent module to the component that may or may not perform as the component expects it to.

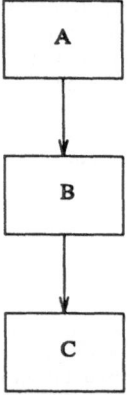

Figure 4. A Typical System with Reuseable Component B.

Conclusions

Figure 4 depicts a typical software reuse situation, where B is a reusable component, A is that part of the environment that depends upon (or calls) B, and C is that part of the environment that B depends upon (or calls). As an example, A could be a database application; B, an Ada generic implementation of a binary search tree (BST); and C, the Ada run-time system, operating system, and hardware, and the function '>' that B uses to create a total order of the elements in its data structure. This function is supplied as a functional argument in the instantiation of B.

B has two interfaces to its environment: its interface to the system, the *machine interface*, and its interface to the application, the *application interface*. These two interfaces can be separated by redrawing the diagram as in Figure 5, with the A to B interface representing *adaptability* and the B to C interface representing *portability*. Figure 5 notes that a portion of A, the *application environment*, should really be positioned as depended on by B (as the function '>' would be in the example), and a portion of C, the *machine environment*, should really be positioned as dependent on B (as would be the case if B was responsible for management of dynamic memory). These additional dependencies are indicated by the use of braces.

Portability Issues. Consider the effects of portability errors in testing B. Because B calls C and reacts according to the results of C, B's correctness depends on the semantics of C. In particular, all of the portability errors discussed above arise when B assumes the semantics of C to be different than they are. The obvious solution to this problem would be to design B such that it does not depend on C at all, but this is entirely infeasible, as even the most fundamental machine characteristics, such as arithmetic, vary considerably from machine to machine. As new machines are designed, the possibility for new portability problems are compounded.

The dilemma can be stated as follows. Traditional black box testing measures correctness by looking at the behavior of a component, such as B above, and everything that it relies upon. But these dependencies are beyond the control of the designer of the reusable component. Consider the example of the generic Binary Search Tree: if B (the generic) is provided a function '>' that implements a less-than function (instead of a greater-than function expected), then the behavior of B may not match its specification. Nevertheless, there is nothing wrong with B; B's correctness depends on the validity of its functional argument.

The problem with portability errors is that components are specified in absolute terms, regardless of the machine environment. In order to deal with portability issues in correctness, specifications must be at least partially dependent on the machine environment. The dependent part of the specification can be parameterized: the behavior of component B expressed relative to a part of the machine environment C. With a parameterized specification, it becomes possible to create a well-defined virtual machine so that all specifications and subsequent testing can be performed in terms of that machine. A testing environment then would provide the capability to test a component's dependence on this environment at the places defined by the portability error characterization.

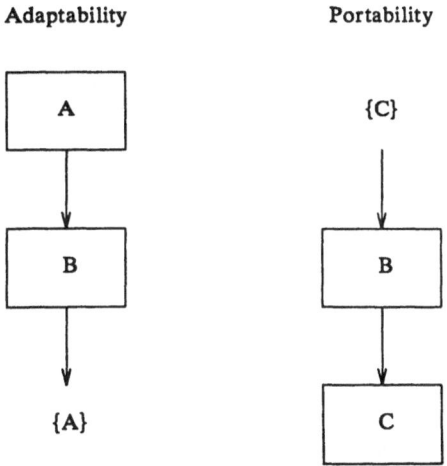

Figure 5. A Typical System Showing Adaptability and Portability.

Finally, it is worth noting that Ada, does not provide adequate support for specifying components in this fashion. Support is provided for coding ada parameterized components via machine attributes such as 'Machine_EMax and 'Machine_Overflows, 'Storage_Size and subrange attributes such as 'First and 'Last. Ada specifications, however, do not constrain the implementation of components to use these parameters beyond the use of subranges and types. Currently, such specification would be included as Ada comments, and would, therefore, be unenforceable.

Adaptability Issues. Now consider the effects of adaptability errors in testing the system A B C with an adequate set of test data, T. Weyuker (1988) states in her *anti-decomposition* property of adequacy criteria that if "there exists a program P and a component Q such that T is adequate for P, T' is the set of vectors of values that variables can assume on entrance to Q for some t in T and T' is not adequate for Q". This means even if A B is adequately tested, B has not necessarily been adequately tested. Weyuker also states in her *anti-composition* property that "there exists programs P and Q, and test set T such that T is adequate for P, and the set of vectors of values that variables can assume on entrance to Q for inputs in T is adequate for Q, but T is not adequate for P;Q". This means isolated unit testing of B is insufficient to detect errors that arise from the combination of A and B - which are exactly the adaptability errors described above.

Therefore, reusable components cannot be adequately tested for reuse errors within some existing application environment, nor can they be tested without any application environment at all. Instead, some sort of virtual application environment must exist to test the component that can be systematically altered to effect the simulated adaptation of the component, thereby exercising the potential reuse errors of the component. This result bears a comfortable resemblance to the well-defined virtual machine for testing portability issues, but may not seem as obvious.

Testing under such a virtual environment amounts to the development of explicit constraints on the use of the component B, defining those application implementations that would result in the incorrect use of B. These constraints are then used as a kind of negative specification against any target application environment A, thereby limiting the testing of A to exactly those areas that are known to create problems when A is used with B.

Further Work

The research conducted to date has been concerned with understanding the nature of the problems involved in V&V for reusable Ada components. Specifically, it has concentrated on looking at the principle reuse concerns, adaptability and portability, how they are manifested in the Ada language, and at developing an understanding of adequacy for reuse errors.

Two areas of further work look particularly promising for making the results of this investigation useful in a practical sense. The first is the development of tools. A prototype analyzer for Ada programs has been constructed as a means to detect certain reuse problems. This tool should be extended via simple source code analysis techniques to detect a wider class of problems. Furthermore, this tool can become the basis for a V&V extension to an Ada development environment for determining adaptability constraints. These constraints would be stored in the Ada component library, and utilized for generating specific tests when the component is used in an application (Figures 2 and 3).

The second area concerns the relation between white box and black box testing. Problems with adapting a component to a new environment involve the functional (black box) behavior of the component. Most of our tools (Ada compiler, Mothra, the prototype Ada analyzer) use white box techniques. We would like to use the black box specification of the component's behavior to drive a white box analysis. Specifically, we would like to improve the detection of reuse errors and facilitate the generation of test data by making direct use of the program's functional specifications.

ACKNOWLEDGEMENT

This work is supported under Contract 19K-CN982C under Prime Contract DEAC05-840R21400 through Martin Marietta Energy Systems.

REFERENCES

Appelbe, W. F., DeMillo, R. A., Guindi, D. S., King, K. N., and McCracken, W. M., 1988, Using Mutation Analysis for Testing Ada Programs, *Proceedings of Ada Europe*, Munich.

Barnes, J. G. P., 1984, *Programming in Ada*, Addison-Wesley Publishers, Reading, MA.

Booch, G., 1986, *Software Components with Ada*, 2nd Ed., Benjamin/Cummings Publishing Company, Menlo Park, CA.

Bowser, J., 1988, *Reference Manual for Ada Mutant Operators*, Technical Report GIT-SERC-88/02, Software Engineering Center, Georgia Institute of Technology, Atlanta, GA.

Budd, T. A., DeMillo, R. A., Lipton, R. J., and Sayward, F. G., 1978, The Design of a Prototype Mutation System for Program Testing, *Proceedings NCC, AFIPS Conference Record*, pp. 623-627.

Budd, T. A., 1980, *Mutation Analysis of Program Test Data*, PhD Dissertation, Yale University, New Haven, Connecticutt.

Budd, T. A., Hess, R., and Sayward, F. G., 1980, *EXPER Implementor's Guide*, Department of Computer Science, Yale University.

Budd, T. A.,and Angluin, D., 1982, Two Notions of Correctness and Their Relation to Testing, *Acta Informatica*, Vol. 18, No. 1, Springer-Verlag, pp. 31-45.

DeMillo, R. A., Lipton, R. J., and Sayward, F. G., 1978, Hints on Test Data Selection: Help for the Practicing Programmer, *Computer*, Vol. 11, No. 4.

DeMillo, R. A., and Spafford, E. H., 1986, The Mothra Software Testing Environment, *Proceedings of the 11th Nasa Software Engineering Laboratory Workshop*, Goddard Space Center.

DeMillo, R. A., McCracken, W. M., Martin, R. J., and Passafiume, J. F., 1987, *Software Testing and Evaluation*, Benjamin/Cummings, Menlo Park, CA.

DeMillo, R. A., Guindi, D. S., King, K. N., McCracken, W. M., and Offutt, A. J., 1988, An Extended Overview of the MOTHRA Mutation System, *Proceedings of the Second Workshop on Software Testing, Verification, and Analysis*, Banff Alberta.

Department of Defense, 1980, *Ada Programming Language, MIL-STD-1815*, Superintendent of Documents, U. S. Government Printing Office, Washington, D.C.

Digital Equipment Corporation, 1985, Portability and the Portability Summary, *Developing Ada Programs on VAX/VMS*, Maynard, MA.

Dynamics Research Corporation, 1988, *ADAMAT. An Introduction to the Concepts and Principles of Dynamics Research Corporation's Ada Measurement and Analysis Tool*, Andover, MA, 1988.

EVB Software Engineering, 1987, *GRACE Notes*, Frederick, MD.

Goodenough, J. B., and Gerhart, S. L., 1975, Toward a Theory of Test Data Selection, *Proceedings of the International Conference on Reliable Software*, Vol. 10, No. 6, ACM SIGPLAN, pp. 493-510.

Johnson, S. C., 1979, Lint, a C Program Checker, *UNIX Programmer's Supplementary Documents*, Vol. 1, Berkeley, CA.

Joint Logistics Commanders, 1983, *Workshop on Post Deployment Software Support*, Orlando, FL.

Lecarme, O., and Gart, Mireille Pellissier, 1986, *Software Portability*, McGraw-Hill, New York, NY.

Nilssen, J., and Wallis, P. J., ed., 1984, *Portability and Style in Ada*, Cambridge University Press, Cambridge.

Offutt, A. J., 1988, *Automatic Test Data Generation*, GIT-ICS 88/28, PhD Dissertation, Georgia Institute of Technology, Atlanta, GA.

Ryder, B. G., 1974, The PFORT Verifier, *Software -- Practice and Experience*, Vol. 4, pp. 359-377.

Spafford, E. H., 1988, *Extending Mutation Testing to Find Environmental Bugs*, Technical Report SERC-TR 21-P, Software Engineering Research Center, Purdue University, W. Lafayette, IN.

Wallis, P. J., 1982, *Portable Programming*, John Wiley and Sons, New York, NY.

Walsh, P. J., 1985, *A Measure of Test Case Completeness*, PhD Dissertation, State University of New York.

Weyuker, E. J., and Ostrand, T. J., 1980, Theories of Program Testing and the Application of Revealing Subdomains, *IEEE Transactions of Software Engineering*, Vol. 6, No. 3, pp. 236-246.

Weyuker, E. J., 1983, Assessing Test Data Adequacy Through Program Inference, *TOPLAS*, Vol. 5, No. 4, pp. 641-655.

Weyuker, E. J., 1988, The Evaluation of Program-Based Software Test Data Adequacy Criteria, *Communications of the ACM*, Vol. 31, No. 6, pp. 676-686.

THE RAPID CENTER: A MODEL FOR SOFTWARE REUSE POLICY

Ted Ruegsegger

SofTech, Inc.
460 Totten Pond Road
Waltham, MA 02154-1960

Abstract: This paper discusses the RAPID[1] Center, a support center for software reuse. Developed by the U.S. Army and SofTech, the RAPID Center provides expert assistance and sophisticated tools to ISEC engineers. The project is funded by the STARS[2] program.

After defining the goals of the RAPID Center and the approaches used to attain them, the author presents a functional model of the RAPID Center, describing activities, inputs, outputs and controls. These abstract functional requirements suggest an organizational model with specific categories of staff, whose duties are described in detail.

The RAPID Center defines a software reuse policy for the supported organization, and continually revises the policy to ensure that it helps foster an environment favorable to successful software reuse. The policy should address development, maintenance, and employment of reusable software; library operations; reuse advocacy; and the transition of the RAPID Center to a larger scope of operation.

BACKGROUND

The U.S. Army Information Systems Engineering Command (ISEC) develops and maintains Standard Army Multicommand Information Systems (STAMIS). These large programs, traditionally written in COBOL, are costly to build and even more costly to maintain. Not surprisingly, the notion of software reusability is tremendously appealing to an organization like ISEC, especially with today's emphasis on Ada. Several years ago, ISEC asked SofTech to examine a sample of typical ISEC applications and determine whether software reuse would be feasible. This investigation revealed a tremendous potential for software reuse in that software components of significant size could be reused in many ISEC applications (Ruegsegger, 1987; *ISEC RAPID Investigation Final Report*, 1986).

SofTech recommended that ISEC establish a pilot program to define and coordinate software reuse policy and support effective software reuse in existing projects. ISEC concurred, and contracted with SofTech to develop the RAPID Center (Fornaro, 1987) as a focus for the RAPID program. Funded by the STARS program, the project is intended to:

- Establish a support center for software reuse to provide ISEC software engineers with a significant, meaningful aid to developing Ada programs;

- Enhance ISEC's reputation as a leader in Ada and software reuse;

---

[1]RAPID is an acronym for *Reusable Ada Packages for Information System Development*. The RAPID Center supports the RAPID program at the U.S. Army Information Systems Engineering Command (ISEC), Washington, D>C> Software Development Center (SDC-W).

[2]STARS is a DoD initiative in *Software Technology for Adaptable, Reliable Systems*.

- Capitalize on the results of the RAPID Investigation and demonstrate the value of a coherent RAPID program;

- Prepare for the growth of the RAPID program from the single-project level to the SDC and ISEC levels; and

- Document practical experience of great value to ISEC and to government software engineering programs such as STARS.

GOALS OF THE ISEC RAPID PROGRAM

Software reuse *per se* is not enough; ISEC expects tangible benefits from a successful RAPID program.

Lower Costs

Reuse of software should require less labor, or labor at lower skill levels, than original design and development. The greatest impact should be in maintenance, the most costly part of the software life cycle; heavy reuse means less software to maintain, and greater productivity from what remains.

Interoperability

Reuse favors the emergence of standard software architectures, standard interfaces among software components, and standard protocols for data interchange. This makes software easier for users to understand and facilitates system integration.

Quality

Reused software is less likely to have problems than newly developed software, since it is more mature and probably better tested. While this extra quality assurance effort increases the development cost of the component, it pays for itself because it is not repeated with each use.

Technology Transfer

A successful reuse program exposes ISEC's engineers to a broad range of software engineering issues and promotes sharing of knowledge and experiences among different projects. In addition, ISEC's work in RAPID has been widely acclaimed in the Ada community, in which ISEC is a prominent participant.

PROGRAM APPROACH

There are three aspects to the problem, each of which must be addressed for such a program to succeed.

Motive

The greatest obstacles to software reuse are not the technical challenges, but human attitudes and organizational barriers. Distrust of software from strangers and of guidance from "experts" who are "here to help you", pride in established ways, resentment of outside interference, and reluctance to "be the first" are natural feelings that make people skeptical of such a program. They may even have the perception that software reuse threatens their jobs.[3]

Organizations, too, have policies and practices that militate against software reuse, mainly because these evolved in an environment where it was never a significant issue. Performance measures reflect this; so do planning, scheduling, and budgeting procedures, many of which are tied to accounting practices which bring immediate, unfavorable attention to any deviations.

---

[3]In fact, in ISEC and most of DoD, the backlog of software work in general and software maintenance in particular is steadily increasing. Even a wildly successful reuse program could only slow this increase and make it more controllable; reversing the trend will require advances in the state of the art.

A successful program wins people over by showing them real benefits. This means we need ways to measure success, and an energetic campaign of publicity. We need a policy that supports, rather than contradicts or circumvents, existing policy and practice.

Means

To be effective, promises of benefits must be founded on methodology and technology that can deliver them. Users need fast, low-cost, "friendly" access to reusable software. Special arrangements need to be made for maintenance of reusable software components--delays in getting "bugs" fixed make enemies the program can ill afford. The program should teach and foster the principles of modern software engineering, on which effective software reuse depends. Furthermore, it should emphasize software architectures that make maximum use of existing components: in many cases these architectures are directly reusable themselves.

Opportunity

To make the most of existing software, resources must be directed toward identifying which software has the most potential for reuse. Cost savings have two aspects: the amount of code reused; and the number of times it can be reused. Some large complex software systems may be reusable in only one or two other applications, but be enormously productive owing to their size, i.e., the avoidance of the cost of developing them "from scratch". Other components, though small, are profitable because they are widely usable.

At the same time, applications should be compared to see which can make the most use of existing components. These "lucrative targets" may employ reusable architectures, or may be unusually adaptable as a result of firstrate, modular design.

FUNCTIONAL MODEL OF THE RAPID CENTER

To help define the requirements for the RAPID Center, the development team used SofTech's Structured Analysis and Design Technique (SADT)(*An Introduction to SADT Structured Analysis and Design Technique*, 1976; Dickover, McGowan, and Ross, 1977) to develop a functional model. Figure 1 is a context diagram showing all the data ("objects" in current parlance) that interact through the RAPID Center's activities. The data are represented by arrows on the diagram.

Arrows pointing away from the box, on the right, indicate outputs. Given the approach described above, the output corresponding to "Motive" is *RAPID policy and publicity*, which includes policy recommendations, reuse "advocacy", and solicitations for user feedback. The RAPID Center also provides

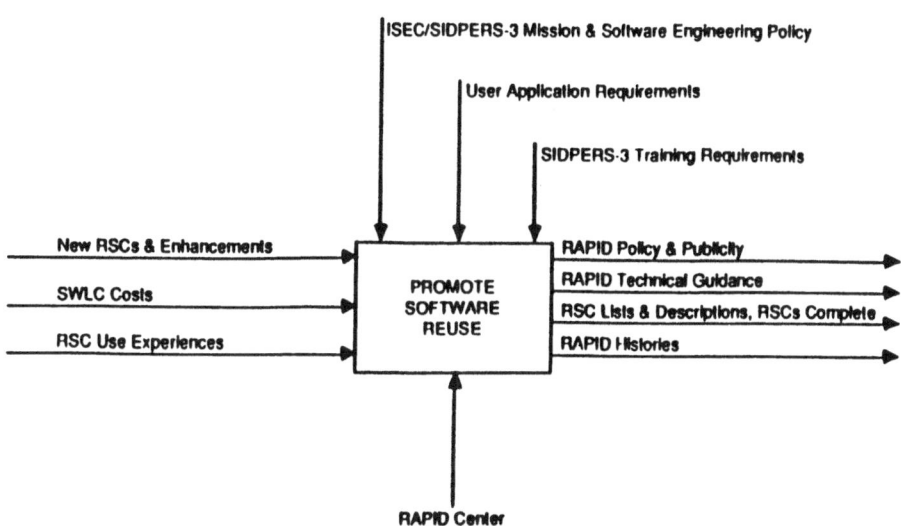

Figure 1. RAPID Center Context Diagram.

technical guidance to ISEC software engineers on a wide range of subjects related to reuse; this addresses "Means" and "Opportunity". Also under "Means", the Center includes an automated library which helps users find reusable software components (RSCs) that meet their needs. After perusing *RSC lists and descriptions*, they obtain the actual software, *RSCs complete*. The RAPID Center also tracks the progress of the RAPID program, providing *RAPID histories* for review by management.

Significant inputs, shown by arrows entering the left side of the box, are *new RSCs and enhancements* (raw material for the RSCs in the library), *software life cycle costs*, and *RSC use experiences* (collected by the RAPID Center to assess program effectiveness and forming a basis for decision support and new policies).

Controls on the RAPID Center's activities, indicated by arrows on the top of the box, are the *ISEC/SIDPERS-3[4] mission and software engineering policy* (affecting all outputs), *user application requirements* (determining which RSCs the library recommends), and *SIDPERS-3 training requirements* (as a demand for *technical guidance*).

Taking into account the inputs, outputs, and controls, a good description summarizing all the activities of the RAPID Center is the single activity PROMOTE SOFTWARE REUSE, shown here as the label of the box. The RAPID Center, as the mechanism, or object performing the function, is represented by an arrow on the bottom of the activity box.

At the other ends of the arrows are the activities of the Center's environment--its users, the SIDPERS-3 community, ISEC, and the software engineering world at large. The scope of the model is bounded by this interface.

Figure 2 is a detail diagram, showing the individual activities which together make up the function *PROMOTE SOFTWARE REUSE*. Note that the "boundary arrows" extending to the borders of the diagram correspond to the arrows in the "parent" diagram, Figure 1.

In the first box, *DEVELOP & MAINTAIN RSCs*, the *RAPID Center staff*, guided by *RAPID policy*, ensure that the software components submitted to the library are of acceptable quality, complete, and properly documented. Some *new RSCs and enhancements* are submitted from outside the center; the staff complete them as needed and test them. Other components are developed by the staff in response to *recommendations for new RSCs and enhancements*. *Bug reports* are analyzed and problems corrected; *change notices* are distributed to users (as recorded in the *RSC use log*). The primary output of this activity is *library RSC packages*. Such a package includes the complete component as the user will receive it, along with test results and suitability assessments used by the library to aid the user.

The second box, *CATALOG & RETRIEVE RSCs*, depicts the activity of the *RAPID Center Library*, a software system which identifies reusable software components corresponding to   *user application*

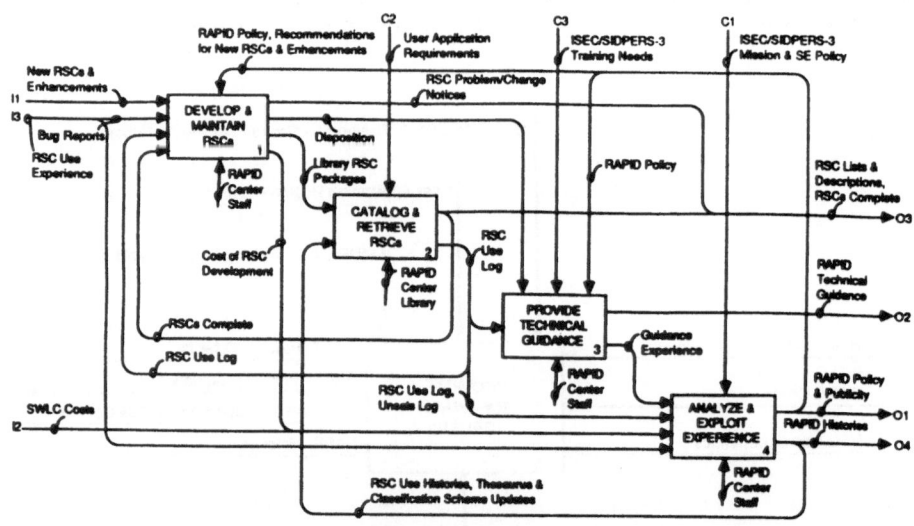

Figure 2. RAPID Center Detail Diagram.

---

[4]SIDPERS-3 is the third and latest version of the Army's Standard Installation/Division Personnel System, initially selected as the host project for the RAPID Center.

requirements (Guerrieri, 1988). *Descriptions of RSCs*, including RSC use histories and suitability assessments (in library RSC packages) help the user make the list of candidate RSCs grow steadily smaller. When the user makes a choice, the library provides everything the user needs to know to obtain the component source code and all documentation. The source code for most components is obtained from the library directly, though the library may well identify components in other libraries or available commercially. The library compiles an *RSC use log* and a log of unsatisfied user requirements.

In the third box, *PROVIDE TECHNICAL GUIDANCE*, the RAPID Center staff help software engineers identify and develop RSCs from ongoing work, use the RAPID library, and integrate RSCs into new work.

In the fourth box, *ANALYZE & EXPLOIT EXPERIENCE*, the emphasis is on "Motive". To support the primary mission of promoting software reuse (via the primary output *RAPID policy & publicity*), the staff track the Center's experience in running the library (*RSCs used, unsatisfied requirements*) and guiding users, and track users' experiences with RSCs they have drawn from the library. The staff also collect costs from inside and outside the Center to compare software reuse with conventional development. Much of this data, analyzed and condensed, is provided to managers as *RAPID histories* for decision support. Those histories pertaining to the use of individual RSCs are fed back into the library as descriptive information to help users evaluate RSCs. *Unsatisfied user requirements* result in *recommendations for new or enhanced RSCs*, or in updates to the thesaurus or classification scheme, depending on why they were unsatisfied.

ORGANIZATIONAL MODEL OF THE RAPID CENTER

As Figure 3 shows, the RAPID Center organization includes six skill categories.

The RAPID Center Manager

The RAPID Center manager is responsible for the RAPID Center's role in attaining the goals identified above, and fills the role of the "standard bearer" of software reuse for supported projects. Specific duties are:

Define and Maintain RAPID Policy and Standards. As experience with reuse accumulates, new methodologies and technologies are developed, the application domain expands, and the ISEC community becomes more sophisticated in developing and employing reusable software, the RAPID policy must

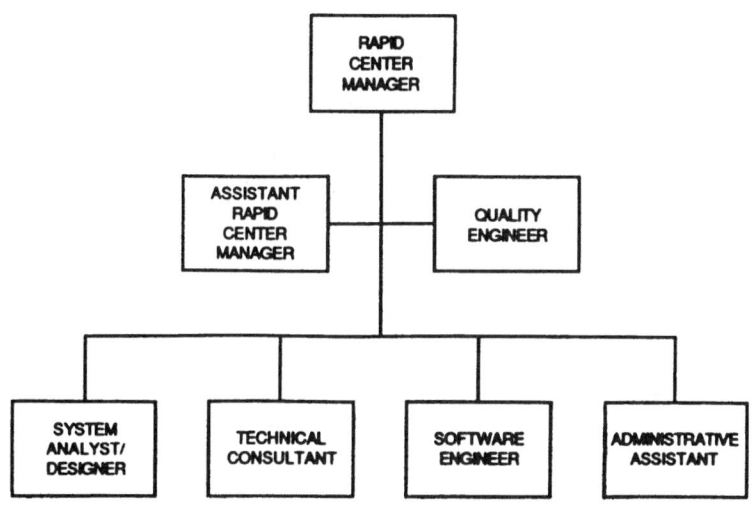

Figure 3. RAPID Center Organization.

likewise evolve. The RAPID Center manager must maintain a proper balance between efficacy and flexibility--too rigid a policy fosters an oppressive procedural burden and stifles participation, while too general a policy provides inadequate or ambiguous guidance.

Analyze RAPID Experience. Throughout its lifetime, the RAPID Center collects experiences related to library use, the usefulness of the software collection, cost impacts, project participation, user and management attitudes and perceptions, and a myriad other interrelated issues. The RAPID Center manager must coordinate the collection of this data and the continuous process of evaluation and inference that yields solutions to real needs.

Publicize RAPID Experience. The success of the RAPID program depends in large measure on the perceptions of ISEC project staff. Accomplishments of individual designers and programmers in realizing reuse-related improvements, as well as the progress of the program as a whole, should be made known to ISEC and the software engineering community. The RAPID program is unique in many ways, and the technical and organizational knowledge gained is of interest and value to a large audience.

Stay Abreast of Developments Elsewhere. The RAPID Center manager must be an active participant in conferences and symposia pertinent to software engineering, in general, and software reuse, in particular.

Manage the RAPID CENTER. Like any manager, the RAPID Center manager must exercise management responsibilities such as budgets, schedules, staff career development, and coordination of all the activities of an organization of highly skilled individuals. In this the RAPID Center manager is aided by the Assistant RAPID Center manager. An important duty of the manager is training the assistant to fill the lead role, not only in the absence of the manager, but to support future expansion as the scope of the RAPID program enlarges.

The RAPID Center is characterized by personnel with strong technical skills in software engineering. To fill the dual roles of technical lead and organizational head, the RAPID Center manager must be an experienced system analyst as well as a manager, and requires skills in cost analysis, technical writing, and public speaking.

The Assistant RAPID Center Manager

The responsibilities of the RAPID Center manager encompass too many tasks for a single person to discharge. Moreover, continuity of the RAPID Center and the RAPID program is threatened by concentrating so much experience in a single person. For both these reasons, the organization includes an assistant to the manager. While junior to the manager in experience, the assistant RAPID Center manager requires all the same skills and carries out the same duties.

The Quality Engineer

Reusable software components must meet stringent quality standards, not only because they will be widely distributed, but because they are the tangible product of the RAPID program as seen by most project personnel. The users' perceptions of their quality is a direct measure of user satisfaction with the program.

To assure the quality of RAPID RSCs, a dedicated Quality Engineer is assigned to the staff. This individual performs all those activities generally associated with software quality assurance, and coordinates these activities with those of other QA personnel assigned to particular projects.

The System Analyst/Designers

Successful software reuse depends on a global understanding of the domain. The primary mission of the system analyst/designers is to understand the entire domain of applications within the supported project or organization, and find common functions that could be reused as standard software components. They attend project reviews and maintain contact with project managers, advising project staff on architectural issues affecting reusability and on existing components which could be reused.

Identify Opportunities

The system analyst/designers constantly seek opportunities to reuse existing components from the growing library. They also identify opportunities to "reuse" components that do not yet exist, in the form of functions known to be needed in more than one application. Categories of applications containing such functions are "lucrative targets", where the benefits of reuse are ample and highly visible.

Identify Potential RSCs

Much software that exists, or is under development, has potential for reuse. The RAPID system analyst/designers look for functional components that would make profitable RSCs--those aimed at lucrative targets and others providing a high return on investment, either by a large number of reuses or by large savings per reuse. Where lucrative targets are identified, but no components exist, it will often be worthwhile to initiate development directly, using RAPID Center resources.

Stay Abreast of Commercial Software

In accordance with DoD policy, Commercial Off-the-Shelf (COTS) software should be used whenever it can meet user needs at less cost to the Government. Since the volume of COTS software in the area of Ada components is growing rapidly, system analyst/designers must be aware of COTS components suitable for use in the application domain. All aspects of suitability must be considered; in particular, COTS RSCs should be selected with attention to the degree of support available.

System analyst/designers require strong skills in Ada and system engineering, and a familiarity with the applications supported.

The Technical Consultants

A comprehensive policy and clear written guidance cannot by themselves ensure an effective program of software reuse. There is no substitute for personal, "hands-on" assistance at the programmer level. The RAPID Center technical consultants provide these services and support training in the methodology and technology of reusable software. Their duties include:

Assist Library Users. Although the RAPID Center library is designed to be used by the novice, personal assistance helps overcome the natural human distrust of new environments. The best leadership is by example, and a guided "walk-through" applies this principle at the level of the individual programmer, whose understanding and acceptance is critical to success. In addition, the availability of human staff to answer questions and solve problems emphasizes the organizational commitment to RAPID.

Assist RSC Users. With the best "reuser's manuals" in the world, programmers will still have questions and problems with RSCs freshly obtained from the RAPID Center library. The technical consultants provide guidance and support to programmers integrating RSCs and their documentation into ISEC applications.

Follow-up On Library Users. When users extract RSCs from the library, they must specify a date when they expect to be able to provide "feedback" about their success or problems with the RSCs. On these dates, the technical consultants contact users to solicit their experiences, which are analyzed and passed on to other staff members, as appropriate, for further action.

Assist RSC Developers. It is likely that most development of reusable components will be done by RAPID Center software engineers. However, many components will be derived directly from application software and, as experience grows, ISEC project engineers will play an increasing role in RSC development. In each case, the RAPID Center technical consultants provide valuable guidance.

Train. The principles of software reusability are, by and large, those of good modern software engineering practice. Nonetheless, the development and employment of reusable software raises certain issues that the practitioner needs to understand. The technical consultants advise the RAPID Center manager on training needs and resources, design and prepare training materials, and conduct training.

Technical consultants need strong skills in Ada and software engineering, and teaching skills are highly desirable.

The Software Engineers

The RAPID Center software engineers are responsible for the growing collection of reusable software in the library, and for the smooth operation of the library itself. Their duties include:

Develop RSCs. At least initially, most development of reusable components will be done by RAPID Center software engineers. In this they are guided by the system analyst/design- ers, who identify lucrative target applications and functions likely to yield the most profitable RSCs.

Maintain RSCs. Although RSCs are subjected to stringent testing and evaluation, problems will undoubtedly occur. Fast response to problem reports is extremely important for two reasons:

1. Problems in reused software affect multiple applications, with correspondingly greater effect.

2. Users' natural distrust of software written by strangers is reinforced by "bugs". Unresponsive support only makes matters worse, especially since bugs are likely to occur when time is short. On the other hand, fast, effective maintenance will not only allay distress, but earn the respect of users when they learn they can rely on the RAPID Center.

Classify RSCs. The ability of the RAPID Center library software to locate RSCs that match the users' needs depends directly on how well the RSCs are classified within the framework of the standard scheme (*Rapid Center Library Procedures (Draft)*, 1988). The software engineers ensure that RSCs are classified correctly, and review classifications as the library evolves.

Evaluate RSCs. As experience grows, application engineers will play an increasing role in RSC development. Software will also be obtained from other agencies, as well as the commercial market (COTS). The software engineers review all components submitted to the library to ensure that they meet RAPID standards (*Reusability Standards for the SIDPERS-3 RAPID Center (Final Draft)*, 1988).

Document RSCs. Since reusable software requires certain documentation beyond the standards of conventional software, the software engineers must prepare any that is lacking. In particular, every library RSC must have an implementer's guide, or "reuser's manual" (*Reusability Standards for the SIDPERS-3 RAPID Center (Final Draft)*, 1988), containing specific guidance for its employment as a reusable item.

Operate the Library. The RAPID Center library is a complex software system. The software engineers ensure that it operates reliably.

Maintain the Library Software. Besides the normal maintenance demands of any complex software system, the RAPID Center library places additional burdens on the software engineers, since it is constantly evolving as new search methods ar implemented and new capabilities are added. While other RAPID Center staff members analyze requirements and design new features, the software engineers are those who implement and test the enhancements.
    The position of software engineer requires strong skills in Ada, software engineering, and technical writing; a thorough knowledge of the library classification scheme; and familiarity with the host hardware and operating system.

The Administrative Assistant

An organization with as many responsibilities as the RAPID Center has a substantial clerical and administrative burden. Naturally, the administrative assistant has the normal duties associated with running an office, but there are additional responsibilities related to the RAPID Center's mission:

Process Performance Reports. Many reports are available from the RAPID Center library software. The administrative assistant generates these as required and distributes them. In addition, the RAPID Center staff are responsible to ISEC for numerous status and advisory reports, which the administrative assistant prepares and distributes.

Process Problem Reports. The administrative assistant is the users' point of contact for problems with RSCs from the library, ensuring that all requisite information is obtained and submitted in a standard format, and forwarding this to the software engineers. The administrative assistant also distributes resulting updates and change notices.

Enter Updates. The administrative assistant enters revisions to RSC documentation, histories, and other text to the RAPID Center library, as well as updates to the user accounts.

The administrative assistant requires not only standard clerical and administrative skills, but a familiarity with the software engineering environment. In a RAPID Center of any significant size, the administrative assistant heads a staff of clerical personnel.

CONCLUSIONS

Effective reuse of existing software is not primarily a technical problem -- the technology and methodology are available now, and advancing almost daily. In any but the smallest groups, human and organizational perceptions and behavior patterns conflict with the objectives of software reuse.

A program like ISEC's RAPID needs a clear definition of the specific benefits expected, altogether with a clear strategy for obtaining those benefits. The strategy must address all three aspects of the problem:

Motive

Foster attitudes and an environment favorable to reuse.

Means

Make the technology accessible to the entire group.

Opportunity

Match means to needs to maximize success.

The organization outlined herein defines specific duties and responsibilities which implement such a strategy. The actual size of the RAPID Center staff will vary according to the size of the supported organization, its geographical dispersion, and the scope of the application domain. Each of the positions described may well be filled by an entire staff.

Establishing and operating a RAPID Center requires a commitment to provide resources and leadership. Until software reuse is a "way of life", the RAPID Center must lead the way. With a sound policy and attention to the needs and perceptions of the supported engineering staff, the RAPID program should more than pay for itself.

REFERENCES

An Introduction to SADT Structured Analysis and Design Technique, SofTech Technical Report 9022-78R, 1976, SofTech, Inc., Waltham, MA 02154-1960, November 1976.

Dickover, M., McGowan, C., and D. Ross, 1977, Software Design Using SADT, *Proceedings of the Association for Computing Machinery (ACM) National Conference*, Seattle, WA, October 1977. Also available as *SofTech Technical Report TP-061*, SofTech, Inc., Waltham, MA 02154-1960.

Fornaro, M., 1987, RAPID Centers: Software Libraries of the Future, *Interface (US Army Information Systems Engineering Command)*, Vol. X, No. 3, Ft. Belvoir, VA 22060-5456, October 1987.

Guerrieri, E., 1988, Searching for Reusable Components with the RAPID Center Library System, *Proceedings of Sixth National Conference on Ada Technology*, Alexandria, VA, March 1988, pp. 395-406. Also available as *SofTech Technical Report TP-259*, SofTech, Inc., Waltham, MA 02154-1960.

ISEC RAPID Investigation Final Report, 1986, SofTech, Inc., Contract No. 3285-4-247/13, SofTech, Inc., Waltham, MA 02154-1960, November 1986.

RAPID Center Library Procedures (Draft), 1988, SofTech, Inc., Contract No., 3451-4-112/11, SofTech, Inc., Waltham, MA 02154-1960, June 1988.

Reusability Standards for the SIDPERS-3 Rapid Center (Final Draft), 1988, SofTech, Inc. Contract No. 3451-4-012/6.1, SofTech, Inc., Waltham, MA 02154-1960, February 1988.

Ruegsegger, T., 1987, RAPID: Reusable Ada Packages for Information System Development, *Proceedings of ISEC Technology Strategies '87*, Alexandria, VA, February 1987. Also available as *Softech Technical Report TP-239*, SofTech, Inc., Waltham, MA 02154-1960.

KNOWLEDGE BASED TOOLS FOR REUSABLE ADA SOFTWARE

G. Scott Owen, Martin D. Fraser, and Ross A. Gagliano

Department of Mathematics and Computer Science
Georgia State University
Atlanta, GA 30303

Abstract: Based on a research program at Georgia State University on software reusability and metrics, an investigation is being made into library tools for managing Ada Reusable Software Components (RSC's). The effort is directed towards the development and evaluation of library tools that will be useful in managing libraries of Ada RSC's. A major focus of the work, and the primary subject for this paper, is the development of a Knowledge Based Software Assistant (KBSA) to ease the transition from informal to formal requirements and specifications. This system will interact with the user in a domain specific limited natural language to generate a set of formal specifications or requirements in one of the currently used formalisms. We plan to interface this system with our RSC storage and retrieval system, which was presented in the companion paper.

INTRODUCTION

If one views the software life cycle as proceeding from left (requirements and specifications) to right (detailed design, coding and testing), then advances in Software Engineering have usually started at the right and moved to the left. An example of this was structured programming which became structured design, and then structured analysis.

A similar situation is occurring in the development of methods for RSC's. Initial efforts have focused primarily on classifying, storing, and retrieving reusable code. While this problem is not yet solved and is still in the research stage, we must start the effort to "move left" in the life cycle. Our ultimate goal in reusability is to be able to reuse requirements, specifications, and design, as well as code. A major obstacle is that requirements and specifications are usually expressed in informal natural language rather than by some formal method. Formal requirements or specification methods are advantageous in that they lend themselves to automated analysis but are difficult to generate and understand.

There are many research issues involved in such a project. This paper focuses attention on two fundamental problem areas. The first is the natural language interface. Unrestricted natural language understanding is very difficult and not yet attainable by machine (Charniak and McDermott, 1986). However, a limited domain interface is possible, although still difficult.

The second issue is the type of formal specification to be generated. There are several types of formal specifications which depend upon the specific application. Formal specification techniques can be classified into two classes (Fairley, 1985), relational notations and state-oriented notations.

Relational notations are based on the concepts of entities (named elements in a system) and attributes (which are specified by applying functions and relations to the named entities). There are several types of relational notations. One is a formal specification language based on algebraic axioms or predicate calculus. This type is best for specifying Abstract Data Types (ADT's). A second relational notation is regular expressions which are useful in specifying the correct syntax for symbol strings.

The second class of formal specification techniques consists of state-oriented notations, such as decision tables, event tables, transition tables, and finite-state mechanisms. Decision tables are useful for specifying complex logic and much previous work has been done on their use in software specification,

Empirical Foundations of Information and Software Science V
Edited by P. Zunde and D. Hocking, Plenum Press, New York, 1990

465

particularly in MIS applications. However, it is difficult to construct a complex decision table that is both complete and unambiguous.

In the following sections we will discuss several possible formal specification methodologies.

FORMAL SPECIFICATION METHODOLOGIES

SmallTalk to Ada

Object-Oriented Design or Development (OOD) is a new design and development methodology for the production of Ada software systems. This methodology emphasizes the creation and manipulation of objects which may be instances of ADT's. OOD has been claimed to be especially appropriate for Ada because one of the strengths of the Ada package concept is the ability to develop objects.

The development and use of objects has also been strongly recommended as the most effective method for the development of reusable Ada packages or reusable code in general (Meyer, 1987). Some investigators have suggested that the best way to develop reusable modules is in the form of generic Ada packages. One problem in the development of these reusable objects is determining the precise required functionality of the object. A second problem is in testing the developed packages and assuring that they indeed possess the required functionality, which requires that test programs be written and used. This process can be resource consuming if the required behavior and attributes of the objects are not rigidly determined before they are developed.

In software development, there are two general approaches. The first is to use a set of rigid specifications, either formal or informal, and the second is to develop prototype systems and then modify these systems. A more optimal approach is a combination of the two methods; i.e., to develop and follow a set of specifications but to use these specifications first to develop a prototype system. This prototype system can be modified until it satisfies the customer and then a final production system can be developed which has the same functionality as the prototype system.

For the prototyping method to be feasible, it must be possible to rapidly develop and modify the prototype. This is not possible directly in Ada since modifications require the recompilation of the affected packages. A separate rapid prototyping tool is needed, preferably one in which the developed prototype can be easily converted to an Ada system. For the development of reusable Ada packages the prototyping tool should be object oriented and should be able to simulate the generic capabilities of Ada.

An excellent candidate for a rapid prototyping tool for the development of reusable Ada Packages is Smalltalk-80 (Diederich and Milton, 1987). Smalltalk-80 is the quintessential object oriented system and is the basis for much of the OOD methodology. In Smalltalk-80 system development consists of the creation of different objects or classes of objects and the description of their behavior. It is a well established and fully integrated software development environment and ideal for the rapid prototyping of systems.

A system developed in Smalltalk consists of a set of classes or objects which interact by the sending and receiving of messages. The behavior of the objects is easily modified until a satisfactory system has been built. In the final system the behavior of the objects has been completely defined. These objects, and their behavior, would then serve as the set of specifications for the implementation of the Ada Packages which would emulate them in the production system. Because Smalltalk uses dynamic typing, the generic capability of Ada can be easily emulated in Smalltalk.

To illustrate the feasibility of this approach in a demonstration project, we would create a prototype system in Smalltalk and then convert this prototype to an Ada production system. This project would test the practicality of using this approach to develop Ada systems and reusable Ada Packages.

State-Oriented Notations

A second type of formal specifications is the use of state-oriented notations, such as decision tables, transition tables, or event tables. These methods provide an excellent way of capturing complex decision logic or conditionally required actions. These state-oriented notations have been available for several years and numerous articles and books have been written concerning their use. Despite their attractive properties, they have not been used extensively because of the problems in correctly constructing them. It has proven to be difficult to construct a complex decision table which is unambiguous, complete, and not overspecified.

This is an area where a KBSA could be useful. A KBSA could be constructed which would interactively assist the user in producing a correct table. The system could carry on a limited domain natural language dialogue with the user which allowed the user to enter the decisions or conditions. The system could then check the resultant table and query the user if problems were found. This process would continue until a complete, unambiguous and not over specified Table was created. The system could also

466

use mathematical techniques, such as the Quine-McCluskey method (Pfleeger and Straight, 1985), for minimalizing the resultant Table.

Predicate Logic Formalisms

There are two specification formalisms, based on predicate logic which we will consider. The first is the language PROLOG and the second is the Vienna Development Method (VDM).

PROLOG. PROLOG (which is short for PROgramming in LOGic) is a declarative programming language based on predicate logic. A PROLOG program is essentially a set of facts and rules. Thus, PROLOG can be considered as an executable specification language for systems whose specifications can be expressed by a set of facts and rules. PROLOG is a good choice for rapid prototyping because PROLOG systems are usually interpreted. One possible software development method would be to develop the formal specification as a PROLOG program, modified until the specification is completely determined, and then implement the specification in Ada.

A way to ease the transition between PROLOG and Ada would be to use a PROLOG interpreter written in Ada. Then as the system is transitioned to Ada, the corresponding PROLOG predicates could be hard coded into Ada. This would allow for a system which could be continuously evolved from one that is primarily a PROLOG interpreter into a complete Ada implementation. A similar method has been suggested for software development in Modula-2 (Muller, 1986).

We have obtained a partial PROLOG interpreter, written in Ada, and are in the process of expanding it to handle more predicates. When we have developed a sufficiently powerful and robust PROLOG system then we will test the above software development scenario.

Vienna Development Method. The Vienna Development Method (VDM) is a predicate calculus based formalism (Jones, 1986), which has been applied to different areas of software specification; e.g. computer graphics (Duce, Fielding, and Marshall, 1988). This approach to software development uses implicit specification of functions and, more generally, operations and a model-oriented approach to specifying data types.

An implicit specification of a function or operation defines what is to be computed, but does not say how to carry out the computation. The aim is to use mathematical abstractions to represent the essential activities of a program while excluding considerations such as efficient ways to use space or time which often account for much of the implementation detail. By hiding algorithmic detail at the specification stage, it is hoped that a broader range of implementations is likely to be suggested.

Operations on states are an extension of the familiar mathematical notion of a function of an argument. A "state" is the set of external variables which can be accessed and changed by the operation. An operation is the generic name for a fragment of text which behaves as a program to the extent that it is affected by states and parameters, and, in turn, affects states and resulting values.

Similarly, the model-oriented approach to specifying data types avoids implementation dependencies by describing the behavior of the data type, namely, the relationship between the results of the operators of the data type. If the behavior of a data type is understood, it can be used regardless of how it is implemented. State-based data types are constructed using functional data types which have operators that are functions, whose results are determined by the parameters. Programs, however, access and change state variables external to their parameters. Thus, the model-oriented approach to specifying state-based data types consists of defining a set of states, invariants (restrictions on state- field values), and initial states and of specifying implementable operations whose external variables are parts of the state.

Functions and operations are formally introduced by an implicit specification which consists of three parts: the signature, or declaration; the pre-condition; and the post-condition. The pre-condition is the set of assumptions about the function parameters or operation states and parameters. The post-conditions give properties that function parameters and their results or operation states and their results must satisfy after execution.

All pre- and post-conditions of an implicit specification are expressed rigorously in predicate calculus. (The notations and conventions of VDM are reasonable choices advocated because it has reached a level of maturity and acceptance.) Proof obligations arise when a direct definition of a formally specified function or operation is asserted to satisfy the implicit specification.

The motivation for this formalism stems from the belief and experience that such specifications can give greater understanding than is normally achievable with informal, natural language specifications. Formal specifications can prompt questions whose answers often lead to better architecture. Thus, work put into formal specifications can pay off even if informal development methods are used.

Program proofs are important not just for establishing correctness but because proof steps lead to a process of operation decomposition which provides a framework for developing implementations in terms of primitives available in the implementation language. Thus a design process can be based on formal specifications:

1. Record a design step with assumptions about its subcomponents.
2. Prove the design step correct under the assumptions.
3. Proceed to specifications of the subcomponents.

Each step of development is isolated by its specifications. This gives protection in testing: each stage of the development relies only on the result of the preceding stage.

Implementing Data Types. Specifications are built around abstract states with operations specified by pre- and post-conditions. Both the data types and the operations must be eventually implemented. The first step toward implementation is to develop techniques for reifying data abstractions onto data types in the implementation language. Data reification does not automate the design process (creativity and invention are not replaced), but it does provide a way for recording designs and the proof obligations needed to show correctness. Formal structures may aid designers by helping them to clarify their choices.

The overall style of specification uses models of data types and accomplishes implicit specification by pre- and post-conditions. High level design decisions usually involve representations of data. Implementation bias increases with such transitions. At the end of the transformations are the data types of the implementation language.

The key to relating an abstract data type and its representation is a retrieve function. This function maps the representation onto the abstract value, thus giving an interpretation of the representation. These functions regain or retrieve abstractions from among implementation details. A retrieve function is adequate if there is at least one representation for any abstract value. Often, discharging an adequacy proof obligation has the practical effect of revealing bias in the specification state, the abstract value.

Thus, the first step toward implementation is data reification. The second step requires that operations be re-specified on the chosen representations. The proof obligations for operations are handled by viewing the operations on representations using the retrieve function. At the completion of this re-specification, however, operations are still implicitly specified.

Implementing Operations. The process of operation decomposition is the final step in implementation. This process develops implementations in terms of primitives in the implementation language and the support environment. The process is iterative. A design is presented as a combination, through control constructs, of specified subproblems. A compositional development method permits the verification of a design in terms of the specification of its subprograms. This method keeps the correctness of one step from becoming dependent on the subsequent development of the subprograms.

The process of operation decomposition gives rise to proof obligations. In turn, proof ideas lead to program development by providing a framework for the designer's commitments which makes verification easier.

Given a specification, the task is to prove that a program fragment satisfies the specification. Thus the program fragment becomes an argument from the assumptions (pre-conditions) to the conclusion (post-conditions). The proof proceeds by rules given in VDM notation and convention and similar to the ordinary logic deduction rules. There is one proof rule for each implementation construct. A simple example is combining two operations by executing them in sequence.

Proof obligations prompt program design. For example, if two fragments are combined using sequential execution, the precondition of the second may be made considered for generalization to conform to the post-condition of the first. This generalization prompts reuse considerations for the second operation elsewhere in the program. Thus, decomposition has prompted reuse considerations in the program design.

DEVELOPMENT OF A KBSA FOR FORMAL SPECIFICATIONS

The KBSA (or the VDM Assistant) will be used by the software engineer in system development. This KBSA will carry on a limited domain natural language dialogue with the software engineer and develop both a formal specification in the VDM formalism and a high level design in the OOD formalism. The system will be interfaced to the GSU RSC_MGT library management system (Gagliano et al , 1988) and will be able to identify and locate RSC's which can be used in the system development.

Design

The VDM Assistant will consist of the following components:

Natural Language Interfacer (NLI). This component carries on a natural language dialogue with the software engineer. The NLI accepts the description of the software system and converts it into an internal knowledge representation. If the description is incomplete or ambiguous, the NLI then queries the user to clarify the description.

Object Builder (OB). This component analyzes the software system description (the knowledge representation output of the NLI) and, using the OOD methodology, creates a high level system design. This design will include both a textual and a graphical depiction of the set of objects and their dependencies.

Specification Builder (SB). This component converts the knowledge representation output of the NLI into the VDM formalism.

RSC MGT Interfacer (RMI). This component converts the knowledge representation output of the NLI into a set of terms for the RSC_MGT system.

Development

The development of these tools will be as follows:

1. Develop the NLI with a grammar and vocabulary to handle a particular domain. We are initially working with a PROLOG Natural Language system which analyzes sentences using a definite clause grammar. The system converts the sentences into facts and rules which are then dynamically asserted into the knowledge base. Since the V is based on predicate calculus, this is a good candidate for the internal knowledge representation.

2. Develop a formal VDM description of several of the relevant software components and analyze just how this is done. This is necessary both to have test cases and to determine how the system will accomplish this task.

3. Develop the Object Builder.

4. Develop the Specification Builder.

5. Develop the RSC_MGT Interface.

SUMMARY

The software life cycle proceeds from left (requirements and specifications) to right (detailed design, coding and testing). Advances in Software Engineering have usually started at the right and moved to the left. A similar situation is occurring in the development of methods for RSC management. Our initial efforts have focused primarily on classifying, storing, and retrieving the code portion of a RSC. While this problem is not yet solved and is still in the research stage, efforts to "move left" in the life cycle should be started. Our ultimate goal in reusability is to be able to reuse requirements and specifications and not just code.

Two important research issues, relevant to the construction of a KBSA, have been identified in this project. The first is the natural language interface. The second is the type of formal specification to be generated. Our major research effort will be to develop a KBSA which will convert a limited domain natural language specification into a high level OOD design and a VDM formal specification. There are two secondary research efforts. The first is to investigate the use of Smalltalk-80 as a rapid prototyping tool for defining Ada objects. The second is to investigate the use of PROLOG as a rapid prototyping tool to specify a system which could then be easily evolved into an Ada implementation.

REFERENCES

Charniak, E., and McDermott, D., 1986, *Introduction to Artificial Intelligence*, Addison-Wesley, 1986. See also Rich, E. 1983, *Artificial Intelligence*, McGraw-Hill; and Winston, P. H., 1984, *Artificial Intelligence*, Addison-Wesley.

Clancey, W. J., 1987, Methodology for Building an Intelligent Tutoring System, *Artificial Intelligence and*

Instruction: Applications and Methods, Kearsley, G., (ed.), Addison-Wesley, pp. 193-227.

Diederich, J., and Milton, J., 1987, Experimental Prototyping in Smalltalk, *IEEE Software*, Vol. 4, No. 3, pp. 50-64, May, 1987.

Duce, D. A., Fielding, E. V. C., and Marshall, L.S., 1988, Formal Specification of a Small Example Based on GKS, *ACM Transactions on Graphics*, Vol. 7, No. 3, pp. 180-197, July 1988.

Fairley, R., 1985, *Software Engineering Concept*, McGraw-Hill.

Gagliano, R. A., Fraser, M. D., Owen, G. S. and Honkanen, P. A., 1988, Issues in Reusable Ada Library Tools, appears elsewhere in these *Proceedings of the 6th Symposium on Empirical Foundations of Information and Software Sciences (EFISS)*.

Jones, C. B, 1986, *Systematic Software Development Using VDM*, Prentice/Hall International (UK) Ltd.

Meyer, B., 1987, Reusability: The Case for Object-Oriented Design, *IEEE Software*, Vol. 4, No. 2, pp. 50, pp. 50-64, March 1987, Artificial Intelligence and Formal Specifications.

Meyer, B., 1985, On Formalism in Specifications, *IEEE Software*, Vol. 2, No. 1, pp. 6-26, January 1985.

Muller, C., 1986, Modula-2 Prolog: A Software Development Tool, *IEEE Software*, Vol. 3, No. 6, pp. 39-45, November 1986.

Owen, G. S., Gagliano, R. A., and Honkanen, P. A., 1987, Functional Specifications of Reusable MIS Software in Ada, *Proceedings of the Joint Ada Conference Fifth National Conference on Ada Technology and Washington Ada Symposium*, pp. 19-26, March 1987.

Park, O., Perez, R. S., and Seidel, R. J., 1987, Intelligent CAI: Old Wine in New Bottles, or a New Vintage, pp. 11 - 45, *Artificial Intelligence and Instruction: Applications and Methods*, Kearsley, G. (ed.), Addison-Wesley, 1987.

Pfleeger, S. L., and Straight, D. W., 1985, *Introduction to Discrete Structures*, John Wiley & Sons.

A MODEL FOR LIFE CYCLE REUSABILITY IN INFORMATION

AND SOFTWARE ENGINEERING

Dr. Charles W. McKay

Software Engineering Research Center
High Technologies Laboratory
University of Houston Clear Lake

Abstract: A four level conceptual model is used to address life cycle reusability of processes and products which are traceable across three environments: host, integration, and target. Major components of the model are separated and structured by virtual interfaces. An object-oriented, semantic modeling approach integrates the perspectives of the four levels from the top view perceived by the client to the bottom view of the object representations in the project object base.

INTRODUCTION

A previous paper (McKay, 1987) described the top level of the conceptual model (i.e., the client's view of the host environment where software is developed and sustained). This same paper also described objects and structuring of virtual interfaces. Therefore, only a brief summary of these points will be provided. This paper will build on this foundation to describe three successively lower levels of the model.

The second level depicts the software engineering processes and products that are potentially a part of any software application's life cycle as viewed by both the technical and the management personnel in the host environment. The third level depicts a multi-view library and component management support needed within the host environment to support reusability across multiple projects and across all three environments. The fourth level addresses the object representation support needed in the life cycle project object base.

FIRST LEVEL ABSTRACTIONS

Figure 1 depicts the top level of a conceptual model of the life cycle to be addressed by a systems and software support environment (McKay, 1987). This level of detail reflects the perspective of the client for the automated system. The rectangles labeled P1 through P6 represent phases of the life cycle. The elongated S shaped figure to the right of the ellipse is marked P7, maintenance and operation. This icon represents successive iterations through the first six phases. For the purposes of this model, a phase may be defined as a discrete period of time and activities delineated by a beginning and an ending event for each iteration in the incremental evolution of the life cycle.

The first phase (P1) represents system requirements analysis. All subsequent phases may involve three sets of staggered activities in time. For example, P2 begins with the translation of a section of the system requirements into software requirements. In turn, these two will contribute to P2 activity referred to as hardware requirements analysis. Finally, a third P2 activity will use these three sets of results for operational requirements analysis. Similarly, the resolution into software, hardware, and operational concerns are mapped in staggered time to P3, preliminary design, and the subsequent phases. The forth phase is detailed design. This precedes P5, coding and unit test, which exists in a staggered time relationship to ongoing activities of P6, computer software component integration.

Empirical Foundations of Information and Software Science V
Edited by P. Zunde and D. Hocking, Plenum Press, New York, 1990

471

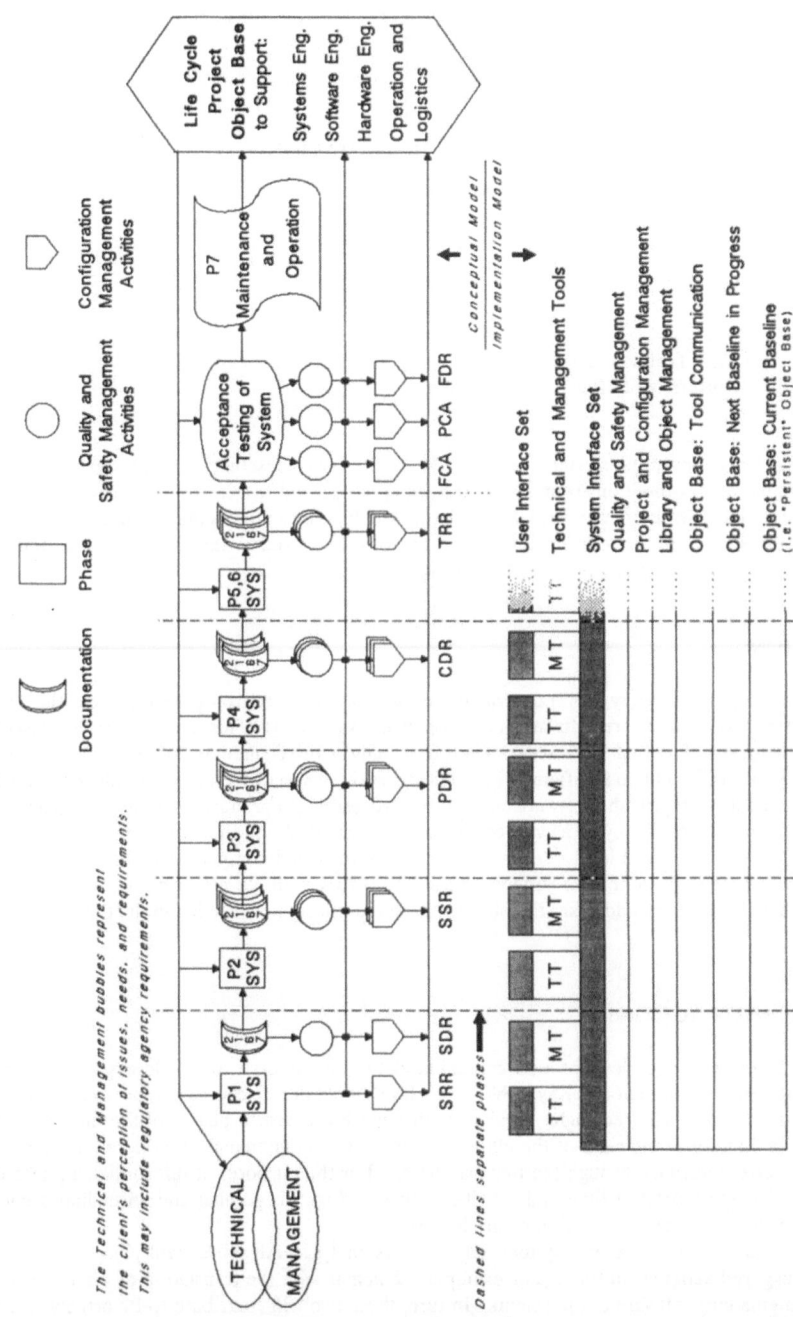

Figure 1. First Level Abstractions: Conceptual Model of a Life Cycle Support Environment.
Implementation Model of this Life Cycle Support Environment.

The closed pairs of double parallel arcs represent documentation requirements tailored from DOD Standard 2167A such as the SMAP of NASA. For example, the closed pair of parallel arcs separating the rectangles for P1 and P2 represent the systems requirements analysis documentation. This documentation set creates a vertical stable interface set separating each iteration of systems requirements analysis on the left from the beginning of a transformation into software requirements on the right. For example, the first iteration of systems requirements analysis on the left from the beginning of a transformation into software requirements on the right. For example, the first iteration of systems requirements analysis, Pl, might satisfy a minimum threshold of requirements for a small, identifiable segment of the systems requirements documentation. When this threshold is reached, automatically a signal is triggered to freeze the attributes of that segment of the document and to signal the quality management team they can begin verification and validation (shown in the small circles). Upon the recommendation of the quality management team to project management, a configuration management decision (shown in the tab as "SDR", system design review) determines whether this portion of the document should be placed under configuration management. The decision is forwarded to the project object base which also triggers both a report to the team doing systems requirements analysis and a signal to initiate activities of the team who will take this portion of the systems requirements and begin transforming them into software requirements. Later, the software requirements analysis will create a corresponding segment of the software requirement analysis document shown as the closed pair of parallel arcs separating P2 and P3. When a threshold for this segment of the document is reached, automatically the system is triggered to freeze the attributes of this part of the work so that the results may be evaluated by the quality management team. Other documents identified in the figure include: software design specification document; software design documentation; and software development documentation. As stated earlier, the circles represent verification and validation activities by members of the quality management team. These activities are in accord with a version of DOD Standard 2168 tailored to meet the needs of the application.

The tabs represent configuration management decision points. The first one shown on the left is the "SRR", system requirements review. This represents the decision of the client to award the contract for a particular portion of the automated system to a contractor. At this point, an instantiation of the tools and rules plus the environmental framework is established for the contractor and the contract becomes one of the first items in the life cycle project object base to enter configuration control. Subsequent configuration management decisions are identified from left to right as system design review, software specification review, preliminary design review, critical design review, test readiness review, functional configuration audit, physical configuration audit, and formal qualification review.

The ellipse which is to the left of the P7 icon represents acceptance testing. This is a transition milestone from the acceptance of a developed baseline for the target environment to the maintenance and operation that sustains the baseline in the future. The life cycle project object base shown at the right hand side of the figure supports: systems engineering, software engineering, hardware engineering, operational engineering, and the management of people and logistics. (Please note: the icons and general organization of the conceptual model were adapted from McDermid and Ripken (1984).)

In contrast to phases, activities have been defined as the process of performing a series of actions or tasks. Thus, some activities take place within phases. Others, such as quality management, integration and configuration management, information and object management, document generation, and other forms of communication, are pervasive throughout the life cycle. Together, the concepts of phases, activities, a life cycle project object base, and required documentation as stable interface sets help to explain the mapping of the conceptual model to the implementation model at the bottom of the figure. (The mapping is explained in the 1987 paper by this author.)

SECOND LEVEL ABSTRACTIONS

Figure 2 preserves the structure and the icons of the first level abstractions, but the details have been expanded to reflect the needs of the technical and management personnel who work with the life cycle support environment to develop and sustain automated systems. Two new icons have been added at this second level. The diamond shapes represent relationships between entities on either side. The closed pairs of single parallel arcs represent information products needed within the environment. This is in contrast to the closed pairs of double parallel arcs which represent information that is both needed within the environment and is contractually required documentation. Together these two information related icons are the only representatives of "products" depicted in this second level abstraction of the conceptual model. Each instance of a "process" icon (i.e., rectangles, circles, and tabs) is always separated from any other process icon by one or more information product icons. For example, the left side of Figure 1 shows a message flow from the technical representatives of the client into the Pl phase (Systems Requirements Analysis). In turn, messages flow from this phase to build the Systems Requirements Analysis Document.

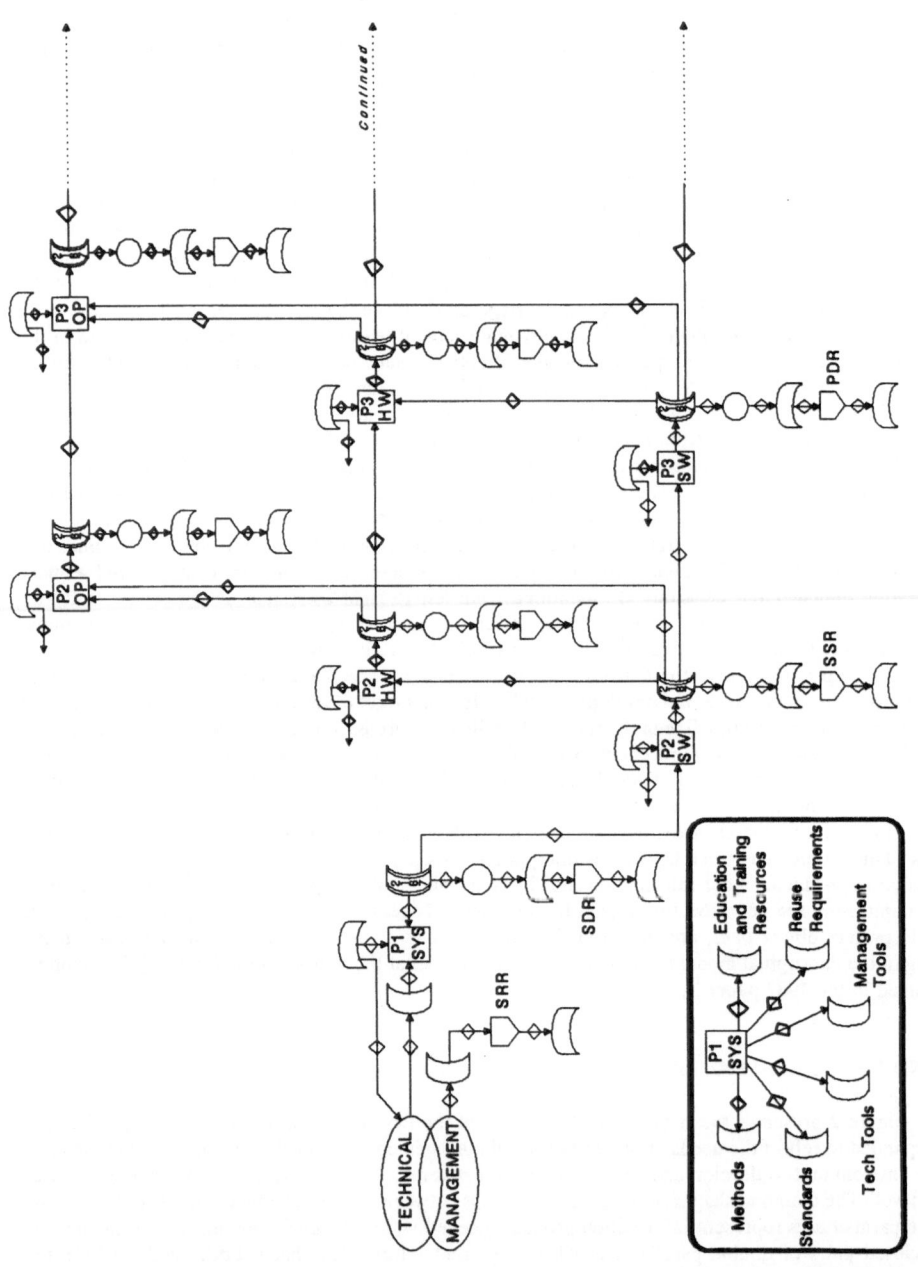

Figure 2. Second Level Abstractions: A Taxonomy of Taxonomies. The Life Cycle Support Environment has attributed relationships to all interfaces, phases, quality and safety activities, and project configuration management activities.

Figure 2 reveals additional details about what is formally or informally taking place. As shown, a relationship is defined between the technical representatives of the client and a set of information products. In turn this set of information products represented by the icon has a defined relationship to the Pl process. Note that the relationships, the product entity and the process entity, all have defined properties (i.e., attributes) which are not shown, but are an important part of this level of the model. For example, the information icon might represent completed check lists, questionnaires, or interview transcripts where each of these entities has its own attributes and provides important information which should be preserved by the environment and its users. Similarly the relationships have attributes describing, for instance, what part of the total information a particular client representative is responsible for providing and in what context.

Attributes may also reflect spatial and temporal properties. As one example, if the information to be obtained is classified, then attributes on the information will reflect this. However, attributes on the relationship with the appropriate client representative may restrict the representative from providing the information in any manner other than from a secure processing site. Another example of the use of such attributes is associated with three input message relationships provided to the P2 icon representing the human factors process of determining operational interface requirements. When the message is generated that some component of proposed hardware requirements is ready for human factors review, two earlier messages relative to this same component should have already been received. First, the related systems requirements were prepared by the Pl process. Then the software first approach of the P2 process produced a set of software requirements resulting from the proposed solution approach. This posted a message to the hardware requirements analysis part of P2. After examining the related part of the systems requirements and the resulting software requirements, the hardware specialists produced the associated hardware requirements, which in turn posted the message to the human factors team. This again points out that every process icon can only be related to information product icons. If nothing else, these information icons represent persistent, audit-trail snapshots of the messages that are exchanged between process entities (e.g., the information icon representing the memos and reports forwarded by the quality and safety management icons to the project and configuration management icons).

Note that the conceptual model does not dictate a choice of methodologies for any of the processes. Instead, it merely reflects an organization of the major processes and products that shows their relationships and provides an opportunity to characterize the important properties of the processes, products, and relationships. Thus, this is a semantic model represented in entity-attribute/relationship-attribute (EA/RA) form. Furthermore the model is object-oriented in that all process and product icons represent objects and all relationship icons represent messages conveying: context (e.g., normal vs exception); services (e.g., control flow); and resources (e.g., data flow) with spatial and temporal properties as well as others. Therefore, the conceptual model reflects an organization of both software engineering behaviors as well as information. For this reason, the level two abstractions are sometimes referred to as a "taxonomy of taxonomies" for life cycle support environments. As shown by the example in the lower left hand corner of Figure 2, each object icon may be further decomposed into subtaxonomies (e.g., a given life cycle support environment may have a number of methods, standards, etc. which are supported for Systems Requirements Analysis).

THIRD LEVEL ABSTRACTIONS

Figure 3 depicts a multi-view snapshot of how the information products of Figure 2 can be organized for library and component management. The figure is also useful for explaining how such processes as configuration management and subsystem generation interact with the information products under library management. The upper right corner of the figure shows a collection of actual information objects. Depending upon which information icon in Figure 2 that the actual object icon, such as A111, is associated with, A111 could be any persistent information object such as a component of a requirements document, a schedule, a budget memo, or an Ada generic package. Each actual object is associated with its own primary entity at birth. The primary entity contains three principal parts: the symbolic identification of the actual object (e.g., the name assigned by the human creator); the life cycle unique identifier (assigned at birth by the life cycle support environment); and the type of the actual object. This container of metainformation can be replicated in multiple views of a library and may be assigned different attributes as needed in each of the views. For example, suppose that A111 is an Ada generic package that has been certified by quality and safety management as being approved for use in this environment. Suppose further that A111 has been classified and placed under configuration management in two different classification schemes (i.e., views) available to users in this environment (i.e., a hierarchial taxonomy and a conceptual closeness taxonomy for reusable Ada software components). The upper left corner of Figure 3 shows a portion of the hierarchial taxonomy. Classification rules have been applied to categorize A111 as one of the leaf nodes in this semantic model of all reusable components listed in this taxonomy.

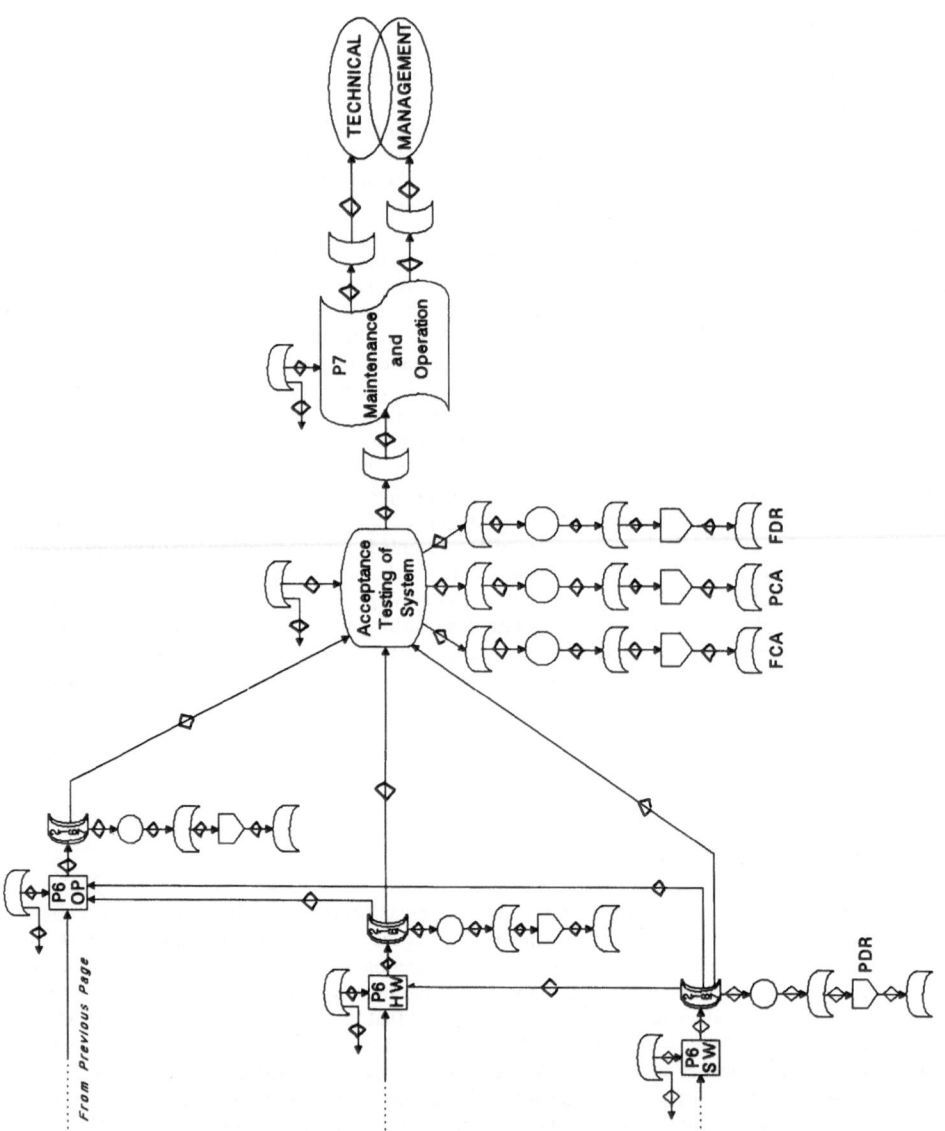

Figure 3. Third Level Abstractions: Library and Component Management.

However the leaf node is not a copy of the actual Ada generic, but of its primary entity. Furthermore, all attributes relative to this classification are attached to the primary entity copy in this taxonomy. Since the current taxonomy is under configuration management as a table framework (McKay, 1987), it too has a primary entity and an actual object has been formed as a persistent representation of exactly which reusable components are under baseline control as viewed by this taxonomy at this time. Although it is not shown in this figure, one can envision another stable framework based upon a conceptual closeness classification. Another relationship would be shown emanating from the primary entity to the left of A111 and connecting to another copy of the primary entity in the semantic model of the components organized in this second taxonomy. This semantic model shows the relationships among the classified entities and contains attributes as appropriate for the classification. Since the view captured in this taxonomy is also under baseline control as a stable framework, the entire semantic model has also been assigned its own primary entity and persistent copy of this configuration control item has been created as an actual object

The lower half of this figure also illustrates how the model supports subsystem generation and audit trails. For example, suppose a stable framework has been created for each of the following components of the Open Systems Interconnection Model for network communications: virtual file store services; virtual terminal services; MAP (Manufacturers Automation protocol); etc. The figure shows that two instantiations of A111 are used in the virtual file store subsystem, two more are used in the virtual terminal software and one in the MAP. Relationship attributes capture the instantiation parameters in each case. Since each stable framework is under baseline control, each has its own primary entity and actual object copy. This is what a user needs to obtain classes one and two of virtual file store, class one of virtual terminal, and all of MAP, a primary entity can be created on behalf of the user and associated with a work space. Only the necessary subsets of the first two plus all of MAP will be copied to the workspace. This is now a semantic model of all software components needed to generate the user's communications subsystem. This stable framework is copied as an actual object to persistent storage (for configuration control audit support) and then used to select and instantiate the actual software for the user. Note that if a fault is ever reported in a particular instantiation of A111, information is available on every copy that has been exported from this environment. Furthermore, if the fault can only affect one particular set of instantiation conditions, the environment has sufficient knowledge of the history of utilization of this component that only the endangered subsystems need receive attention.

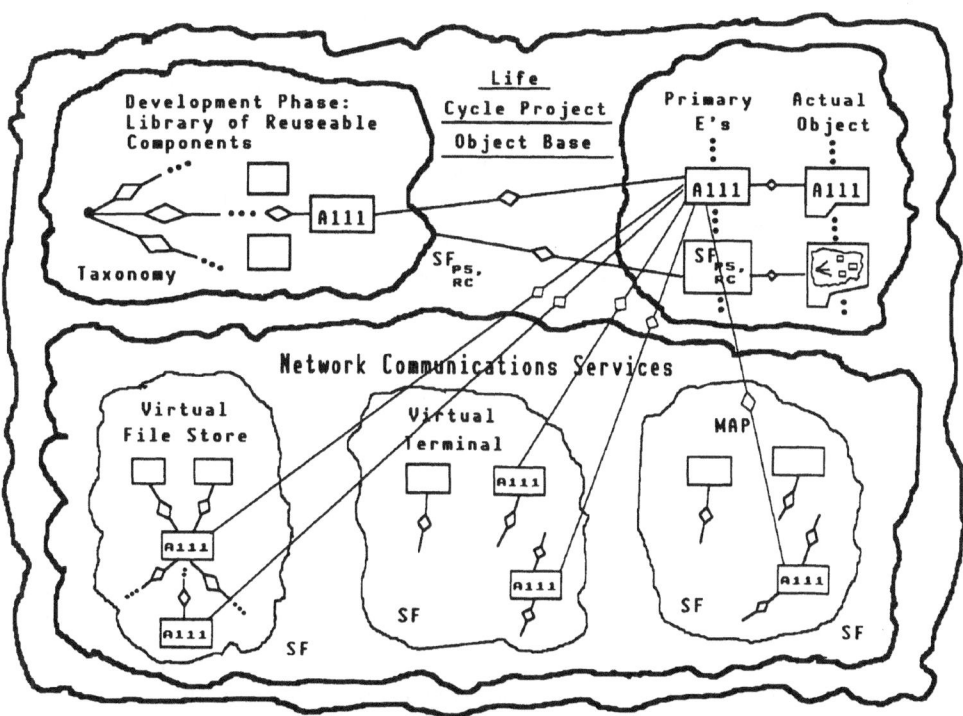

Figure 4. Third Level Abstractions: Library and Component Management.

FOURTH LEVEL ABSTRACTIONS

While Figure 3 introduces the concept of primary entities and their role in library and component management, the figure clearly does not provide sufficient detail to understand the underlying complexities of managing component variations, revisions, releases, associated test sets, design rationale, etc. Figure 4 is intended to provide these representation level insights for the conceptual model.

As shown, there is another representation of objects of a given type beneath the primary entity. For example, an Ada source code component might with two other packages make them visible and useful to the public portion of its Abstract Interface Specification (AIS). This context information is depicted by the two relationships to their primary entities. Note that to support intelligent, incremental recompilation, the relationship attributes should indicate what services and resources of these two packages are actually accessed by this package (as opposed to simply indicating visibility). Thus, if a subsequent change to one of the two packages impacted a part that was not accessed by this component, then this component should not have to be recompiled.

This representation also facilitates a meaningful approach to developing and sustaining rational information. This is because for a given context, the AIS of an object expresses what services and resources are provided, affected, or consumed by the object. For each of these services and resources the AIS specifies how well it is to be supported, and under what circumstances. (McKay, 1987). Therefore, the rationale shown related to the AIS (public specification) should be built by the criteria of: "Would the reason for this particular context, service, or resource be unambiguously obvious to a future peer?" If the answer is yes, then no further comment is desirable. If the answer is not a definite yes, then an explanation is in order. By path name navigation (i.e., primary_ _entity_id.AIS.rationale), document generator tools can access such information. Also, note that the information in the AIS is precisely what is needed by the black box test team. Thus, the specification of black box tests associated with the object is shown to be related to the AIS as well as to the actual tests, the test results, and rationale for any commission or omission in the test specifications that would not be unambiguously obvious to a future peer of the test team.

All Ada objects have a logically private AIS whether it is explicitly declared by the designer or implicitly provided by the implementation of the compiler and package SYSTEM. In essence, the private AIS answers the same questions as the public AIS but from a very different perspective. Whereas the public AIS represents the object to external users, the private AIS represents the object to the run time environment. Logically, it binds the AIS part and the implementation part of the object to the run time resources. Thus the private AIS of variation 1 in the figure may represent a default binding to the processor and bus structure of the host environment. The private AIS of variations 2 and 3 may represent a binding to a particular target processor and bus which are very different from the host processor and bus. The implementation part of variation 2 may represent a fast and coarse algorithm and data structure. The implementation part of the third variation may represent a slower, but, more precise combination. In any of these, there can be revisions which in turn can be controlled for external release.

The principal point in understanding the relationship of Figure 4 to Figure 3 is to realize that it isn't just the primary entity that is recorded in the views of the various stable frameworks of Figure 3. Instead the primary entity serves as the root of a path name that identifies the configuration item for a particular view. Thus, the latest revision and release of the implementation part of variation 3 may be under today's baseline control in a particular taxonomy of reusable components (i.e., Al11,AIS_Public. AIS_Private_2.Variation_3) whereas the same primary entity, but, with a different path name suffix might have been under baseline control in this taxonomy yesterday.

CONCLUSION

This paper presented four abstraction levels of a conceptual model which integrates a combined behavioral and information perspective of the processes and products of a life cycle support environment. The model was designed to support reusability of both products and processes because reusability itself is an important part of good engineering products and good engineering processes. As an example of how both can be promoted, consider the following scenario. Many years from now, a systems requirements engineer is working in a mature life cycle support environment implemented as a mapping from this conceptual model. After capturing a subset of the systems requirements for the desired system enhancement, the workstation screen suddenly flashes a message from a demon in the environment to the engineer. The demon has found a good conceptual closeness match to a set of very similar requirements captured in the project object base years earlier. The engineer works with the demon to trace the evolution of this early subset to respective software, hardware, and operational interface requirements. The engineer is interested both in the resulting AIS's showing what was done and in the associated rationale showing

478

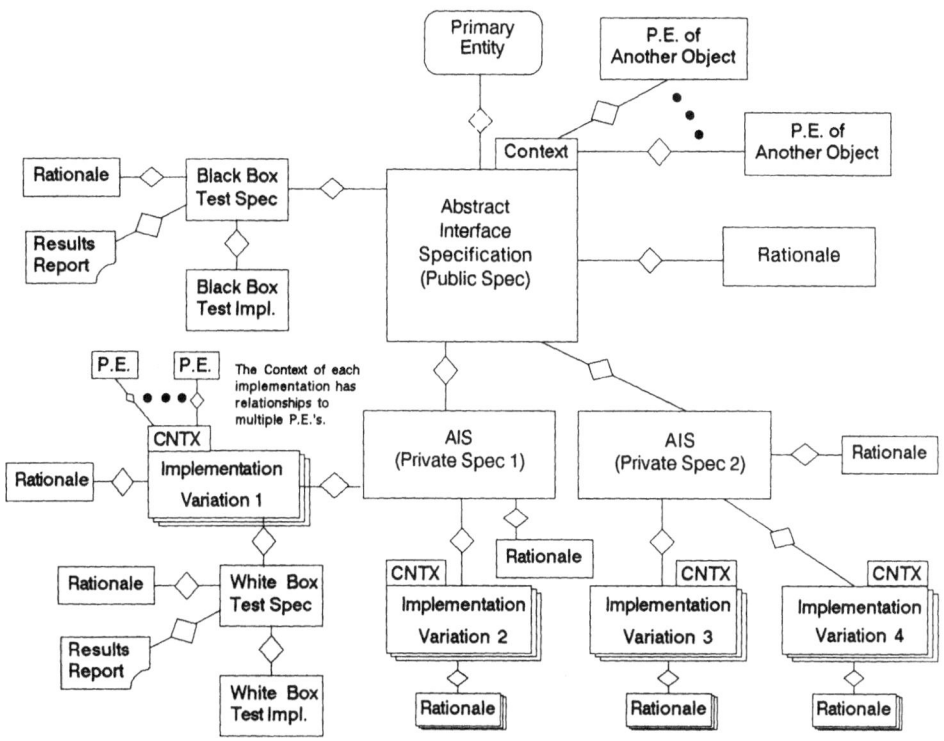

Figure 5. Fourth Level Abstractions.

why. If the results of this query are promising, the engineer will pursue the traceable results to the persistent information objects in the next phase. Eventually, if the whats and whys are acceptable (within reasonable limits of modification) all the way through the implementation, and a successful deployment and operation history is evident, a new subsystem can be generated. Not only have products been reused, but of equal or greater importance, the processes that successfully evolved these products have also been reused.

ACKNOWLEDGEMENTS

The author wishes to thank Mr. Gary O'Neal and Mr. Erik Geisler of the SERC/HTL@UHCL for their help in evolving the model. The work was partially funded by Grant 2-5-51537 with support from: STARS, AIRMICS, and DOE and participation of Martin Marietta Energy Systems and six other universities. The views of the author do not necessarily reflect those of the sponsors or other participants.

REFERENCES

CAIS (DOD STD 1838)/CAIS A (Proposed as DOD STD 1838A), 1986/1988, *Common Ada Programming Support Environment (APSE) Interface Set (CAIS)*, Department of Defense.
DOD STD 2167A, 1988, *Military Standard: Defense Software Development*, Department of Defense.
IRDS, 1985, *(draft proposed) American National Standard: Information Resource Dictionary System*, American National Standards Institute.
McDermid, J. and Ripken, K., 1984, *Life Cycle Support in the Ada Environment*, Cambridge University Press.
McKay, C., 1987, A Proposed Framework for the Tools and Rules to Support the Life Cycle of the Space Station Program, *IEEE Compass 1987*, TH0196-6/87/0000-0033.
SMAP Series, 1986, *NASA Software Management and Assurance Plan Guidebooks and Data Item Descriptions*, NASA.

INDEX

Abstraction level, 471
Actions interpreter, 249
Activity model, 11
Ada software, 341, 355, 391, 427, 437, 465
Adaptability, 209, 329, 437
Adequacy, 437
Agent, 169
Allocation, 329
Ampliative reasoning, 29
Analysis, 25, 231, 269, 355, 369, 391, 437
Application
  software dimension, 177
  model, 209
Architecture, 177, 437
Architectural requirements, 177
Assessment, 177
Automation, 3, 131

Behaviorally object oriented system, 401
Benefit, 329
Black box testing, 25, 437
Blackboard architecture, 99
Brown Corpus, 269

CAST, 39
COBOL, 427
Cognitive user skills, 231
Cognitive model, 83
Cognitive process, 99
Communication, 21, 51, 281
Complexity, 29
  measure, 385
Computer based system, 83
Computer integrated system, 51
Conceptual distance, 427
Conceptual model, 109
Conceptual similarity, 427
Conceptualization
  principle, 109
  of uncertainty, 29
Constraint analysis, 177, 437
Control, 249
Cooperative agent, 169
Cooperative work, 281
Cost, 329

Data
  base, 319, 401
    design, 131
  binding analysis, 355
  dimension, 177
  distribution model, 329
  flow oriented model, 11
  model, 109, 131
  sharing, 177
  structures, 341
Decision making, 259
Declarative dependence, 355
Design, 231
  tools, 131
Designer behavior, 99
Discourse analysis, 281
Distributed system, 329
Distribution of words by the number of
    meanings, 301
Diversity of meaning, 301
Dynamic analysis, 437
Dynamic modeling, 169
Dynamic system, 249

Entity-relationship approach, 145
Entity-relationship model, 109
Entropy, 29, 269
Ergonomics, 231
Error, 437
  detection, 25
Evaluation, 145
  procedure, 221
Evidence theory, 29

FORTRAN, 417
Faceted classification scheme, 427
Fault diagnosis, 237
First normal form, 319
Formal methods, 437
Fuzzified evidence theory, 29
Fuzzy sets, 29, 259

Generalized information system (GIS), 201

Homomorphism, 29
Human behavior, 249

Empirical Foundations of Information and Software Science V
Edited by P. Zunde and D. Hocking, Plenum Press, New York, 1990

481